THE OXFORD INDIA
GANDHI

The Oxford India Collection is a series which brings together
writings of enduring value published by OUP.

Other titles include

The Oxford India Ghalib
The Oxford India Ramanujan
The Oxford India Premchand
The Oxford India Illustrated Corbett
The Second Oxford India Illustrated Corbett
The Oxford India Illustrated Children's Tagore
The Illustrated Premchand: Selected Short Stories
The Illustrated Sálim Ali: The Fall of a Sparrow
The Illustrated Tigers of India
The Illustrated Cultural History of India

Forthcoming

The Oxford India Tagore
The Oxford India Elwin

*I never really wrote an autobiography. What I did write
was a series of articles narrating my experiments with truth
which were later published in book form. More than twenty
years have elapsed since then. What I have done or pondered
during this interval has not been recorded in chronological
order. I would love to do so but have I the leisure?*

Mohandas Karamchand Gandhi, 25 February 1946

THE OXFORD INDIA
GANDHI

Essential Writings

Compiled and edited by
GOPALKRISHNA GANDHI

OXFORD
UNIVERSITY PRESS

OXFORD
UNIVERSITY PRESS

YMCA Library Building, Jai Singh Road, New Delhi 110 001

Oxford University Press is a department of the University of Oxford.
It furthers the University's objective of excellence in research, scholarship,
and education by publishing worldwide in

Oxford   New York
Auckland   Cape Town   Dar es Salaam   Hong Kong   Karachi
Kuala Lumpur   Madrid   Melbourne   Mexico City   Nairobi
New Delhi   Shanghai   Taipei   Toronto

With offices in
Argentina   Austria   Brazil   Chile   Czech Republic   France   Greece
Guatemala   Hungary   Italy   Japan   Poland   Portugal   Singapore
South Korea   Switzerland   Thailand   Turkey   Ukraine   Vietnam

Oxford is a registered trade mark of Oxford University Press
in the UK and in certain other countries.

Published in India
by Oxford University Press, New Delhi

© Navajivan Trust 2008

The moral rights of the authors have been asserted
Database right Oxford University Press (maker)

First published 2008

Photographs: Gandhi in Noakhali hat, Delhi, November 1947 (p. i);
Gandhi in London, 1909 (p. ii)

ISBN-13: 978-0-19-569047-7
ISBN-10: 0-19-569047-8

Typeset in LegacySerif-Book 10.5/12.8
by Eleven Arts, Keshav Puram, Delhi 110 035
Printed in India at Roopak Printer, Delhi 110 032
Published by Oxford University Press
YMCA Library Building, Jai Singh Road, New Delhi 110 001

To all those who have sought to demean or iconize him, hurt or
worship him, reject or make a rule-book of him; and to those
who have invoked him to serve their self-interest but have
abandoned him in his continuing battles, for it is they
who make the 'essential' Gandhi come searingly alive

And to the memory of Ramchandra Gandhi (1937–2007)

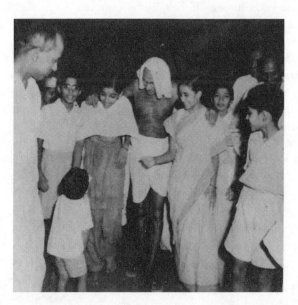

Gandhi, Delhi, 1947—his grand-daughter Tara is to his right,
grandson Rajmohan (in spectacles) further to her right,
grandson Ramchandra front right, and with his back to
the camera, the editor of this volume, Gopalkrishna

TIME MAGAZINE
Monday 5 April 1948

Unmystical Metaphor

Sir:

I ... read with great interest the very able article on my father, Mahatma Gandhi [*TIME*, Feb. 9]. It was of the high standard you have led people to expect. ... I profoundly agree with the thesis of the writer that there was something more human and greater than 'mysticism' in Gandhi. But the 'notably unmystical metaphor' which you attribute to him—'If we Indians could only spit in unison, we would form a puddle big enough to drown 300,000 Englishmen'— was never uttered by him. I know that the metaphor was used by some other public speaker during the great agitation led by my father round about 1920. His only connection with the metaphor was to deplore the use of such language even to express a truth. On a pure point of fact it is necessary to emphasize that Gandhi was one of the most refined persons in the world, refined in his scanty dress, in his speech, in his manners. There are many small and fine points about Gandhi on which I would always have something or other to say, if only by way of information, even if I lived for ages.

Devadas Gandhi
New Delhi, India

CONTENTS

Acknowledgements

These selections have been drawn principally from *The Collected Works of Mahatma Gandhi* and from works published in his lifetime or written shortly thereafter by his associates. The Editor gratefully acknowledges permissions, advice, and assistance rendered to him by the individuals and institutions named below. Without them this work would have been impossible. Needless to say, the compilation's weaknesses are the Editor's, its strengths are of those to whom this acknowledgement is gratefully made. To Tuhin Kumar Mukherjee and to Tapas Kumar Das, my special thanks for invaluable help with the proofs.

Individuals

Shri Sailesh Bandyopadhyay, Professor Himadri Banerjee, Shri Dhruba Basu, Shri Jyoti Basu, Ms Kinnari Bhatt, Smt Tara Gandhi Bhattacharjee, Shri Nitin Bhimani, Shri Sadhin Kumar Chatterjee, Professor Supriya Chaudhuri, Shri Tapas Kumar Das, Smt Varsha Das, Dr Uma Das Gupta, Professor Amalendu De, Professor Barun De, Shri Jitendra Desai, Shri Narayan Desai, Shri Keshav Desiraju, Professor Uma Dhupelia-Mesthrie, Shri Rajmohan Gandhi, the late Professor Ramchandra Gandhi, Professor Suparna Gooptu, Dr Ramachandra Guha, Shri Ravindra Kumar, Smt Uma Mazumder, Smt Kirti Menon, Shri Bhaskar Mitter, Shri Amrutbhai Modi, Shri Shunil Kumar Mukerjei, Shri Tuhin Kumar Mukherjee, Professor Supriya Munshi, Shri Anil Nauriya, Mr Sakari Nuottimaki, Ms Dina Patel, Smt Shobhana Ranade, Shri Enuga S. Reddy, Shri Saktidas Roy, and Shri Tridip Suhrud.

Institutions

Navajivan Prakashan Mandir, Ahmedabad, Sabarmati Ashram, Ahmedabad, *The Statesman,* Kolkata, *Ananda Bazar Patrika* Group, Kolkata, *The Hindustan Times*, Nehru Memorial Museum & Library, New Delhi, Gandhi Sangrahalaya, Barrackpore.

Gopalkrishna Gandhi

Guide to Readers

Most entries in this compilation are drawn from *The Collected Works of Mahatma Gandhi*. The excerpts used are, more often than not, partial reproductions. Ideally, when excerpts are partial, the elisions should be indicated by dots, e.g., 'He never wore stockings or boots ... then called "whole boots".' It has been the Editor's endeavour to place dots wherever they ought to be. But the occasional slippage from this procedure is likely to have occurred in one excerpt or another. So the reader is requested to regard a *CWMG* entry in this compilation as a partial reflection of the original, for a full corroboration of which there can be no alternative but a reference to the relevant volume of the *CWMG*. In case a reader wishes to reproduce the excerpt she or he is advised to refer to the *CWMG* or the source concerned for corroboration prior to the reproduction. Readers are requested to regard the entries in the *CWMG* (original edition) as inviolable.

For the very early and the concluding portions of the compilation, the Editor has drawn from the epic works of Pyarelal—the *Early Phase* and *Last Phase* volumes—published by Navajivan in 1965 and 1958 respectively. Each entry from those volumes is ascribed, as are those from other sources.

When the *CWMG* itself has drawn the entry from another source, this compilation does not invariably refer to the earlier source. At some places, where the Editor has come across a reference directly from the earlier source, he has not acknowledged the *CWMG*, though the *CWMG* has also reproduced it.

Spelling variations of the same name are very often conditioned by the fact that I have followed the spelling of the original and the *CWMG* although the same person's spelling can differ from other references to that person.

The spellings of place names in the main body of the text conform to those used in the original texts without bringing them in line with the current mode, e.g., 'Shantiniketan' as distinct from 'Santiniketan'. Even in the footnotes pre-1947 spellings have been used, e.g., Poona, as different from Pune and Calcutta as distinct from Kolkata.

The footnotes in the *CWMG* have often been varied or added to by the Editor, to bring in new information or to sharpen the context. The 'ji' used in the *CWMG* after 'Gandhi' has not been employed in this compilation, for reasons of consistency with the Introduction and prefatorial entries.

The headings for different entries are also the Editor's, not necessarily those used in the *CWMG*. The datelines are also the Editor's, giving [where possible] the venue of the communication's origin, with the date, month, and year in that order.

At the end of the ascription, *G*, *H*, or *E* indicate the language in which the entry was originally written—Gujarati, Hindi, or English.

Gopalkrishna Gandhi

ABBREVIATIONS

LD	*London Diary* (1888), quoted in *CWMG*, vol. 1
SiSA	*Satyagraha in South Africa* by M.K. Gandhi, translated from the original in Gujarati by Valji Govindji Desai (Ahmedabad: Navajivan, 1928)
A	*An Autobiography—The Story of My Experiments with Truth* by M.K. Gandhi, translated from the original in Gujarati by Mahadev Desai (Ahmedabad: Navajivan, 1930)
P, *MG:LP*	*Mahatma Gandhi: Last Phase* (Ahmedabad: Navajivan, 1956)
P, *MG:EP*	*Mahatma Gandhi: Early Phase* (Ahmedabad: Navajivan, 1965)
JJD—*AIPSA*	*An Indian Patriot in South Africa,* Joseph J. Doke (1909)
HK	*Hermann Kallenbach—Mahatma Gandhi's Friend in South Africa* by Isa Sarid and Christian Bartolf, Gandhi-Information-Zentrum, Selbstverlag; 1997
RP	Robert Payne, *The Life and Death of Mahatma Gandhi,* (Smithmark, 1969)
Tendulkar	D.G. Tendulkar, *Mahatma—Life of Mohandas Karamchand Gandhi,* 8 vols. (The Publications Division, Government of India, 1960)

INTRODUCTION

'Not another book of Gandhi sayings, please!' I can hear a bookstore browser say. '*Enough for everyone's need, not for anyone's greed— An eye for an eye will end up making the whole world blind—Western civilization is a good idea—the Seven Deadly Sins.* We know them all and don't want any more of those.'

And the reaction would be right.

Repetition has made one of the world's most compelling, challenging, transformational, and passionate persons the one thing he never was—boring. It has made that most original person clichéd. One of my aims in selecting passages from his works has been to redeem the living Gandhi from the plaster-cast image of the Mahatma. And also—the reader may be disappointed to learn this—to de-ascribe some of these 'well-known' quotes such as those given above which are not Gandhi's. These quotes (including the one about Cripps' offer being 'a post-dated cheque on a crashing bank') are embroidered versions of his thinking. They are not untrue to his spirit, but they are not in words spoken or written by him.

When it comes to Gandhi, I believe, it is better to be accurate than to be under an illusion, even an eloquent one that seeks to do well by him. I have, therefore, relied on sources that are beyond doubting, mainly the monumental *Collected Works of Mahatma Gandhi* (in its original edition) edited for the major part by Professor K. Swaminathan, books with 'Gandhi quotes' written in his life-time and the works such as those of Millie Graham Polak[1], Mahadev Desai[2], and Prabhudas Gandhi[3], which also appeared during his lifetime, as well as those of and his immediate associates like Pyarelal[4], Manu

Gandhi[5], and Nirmal Kumar Bose[6], which were published after Gandhi was no more.

'Gandhi Readers' and 'Selected Works of Gandhi' have appeared regularly. They are excellently produced and accompanied, as in the ones compiled by Raghavan Iyer (OUP 1993) and Rudrangshu Mukherjee (Penguin 1993) with incisive introductions. Such works will continue to be put together, for the Gandhi 'mine' is so large and deep that it will keep revealing nuggets not known to have existed.

But frequency has made the 'Gandhi Book of Quotations' a somewhat tedious *genre*, even as veneration has made that searingly self-critical man another thing he never wanted to be—an icon. Cement statues of him abound, toothless grin below lenseless spectacles on a face that is in the very pink of health. They caricature a man whose *presence*, as different from his physical appearance, was uncommonly powerful and challenging. Anthologies can also become the same: devoid of his grip over individuals' attention and his grasp over subjects.

I do not know what OUP India's thinking was when it asked me to attempt yet another compilation of Mahatma Gandhi's essential writings. Was not Raghavan Iyer's volume in the same OUP series still very much in circulation? In the course of a long walk in the bracing autumnal air of Oslo in 2002 Ramachandra Guha said to me, 'There is always room for another Gandhi anthology and if you follow an approach to the selection that is new, you will be assisting the student of modern history.' I sent my 'yes' to OUP shortly thereafter.

What (I asked myself) should my approach to a new selection from Gandhi be? There are many more qualified to do a thematic compilation of his great and transformational ideas, his powerful statements in Court, his editorials. If it is to give me satisfaction, I realized, mine will have to be a story—in *his* words. The story of his life as Gandhi might himself have narrated it, to a restless grandson. Narrated in time snatched between visitors, meetings, marches, mud packs, bursts of temper, explosions of love. A story as expressed in speeches and articles, but also in diary entries, letters and, most importantly, in conversations.

While I thought upon all this (as is my wont) I hallucinated. 'Relate to me please, Bapu, the life within your Life. The actual thing about you, not just your discourses.'

'What makes you think I should do something special for you?'

'If you could bare your most intimate thoughts to Kallenbach[7] and to Millie Polak, if you could speak of your body's involuntary behaviour to Prema Kantak[8], if you could distil your innermost thoughts into epigrams for the benefit of Anand Hingorani[9], surely you can tell me something about my great grandfather, my great grandmother, my grandmother, my uncles, and about your fantastic friends—the people who were essential to your becoming what you are.'

After a pause, came this reply: 'Very well, then, but on one clear understanding. You will honestly and sincerely try to read as much as you possibly can of what I have said or written, heavy and dull though it may seem. And as you do that, I, on my part, will place in your hands a little pencil that will mark out for you the "story", as you call it.'

The dream ended with that. And work began—in a very white Norwegian winter. It suffered interruptions as I got back to India, to the summers and monsoons of Kolkata and to the demands of a daily 'Engagements List' which confronted me each morning.

But the mines of the *Collected Works*, the megalithic sites of his assorted words elsewhere, and the little dolmens of others' records *were* entered and with 'his' pencil as the instrument, marked. M. Radhakrishnan painstakingly copy-typed hundreds of pages for me in his spare time in Oslo. Later, in Kolkata, Tuhin Kumar Mukherjee worked beyond his official duties indefatigably and with insight on that material. Radhakrishnan, Tuhin, and I were on something like a dig, bringing a 'lost script' to light. The text was neither familiar nor fantastic. It was just fresh. The pages had the dust of neglect on them. Sometimes, overwhelmed, I touched my head with it. Not because I regarded it as holy but because it sounded like honesty's own voice. Sometimes, shaken, I broke down. Often, I raced through the words as if towards him, saying 'Bapu! You never told me *that* before!'

'But you never asked.'

With millions the world over, I had read Gandhi on his father, Karamchand Gandhi, the *karmayogi*. I had carried a mental image of the brave and principled Diwan who ran the Durbar at Porbandar for twenty-seven years, at Rajkot for eight, and at Vankaner for one. But this time, the Gandhi 'pencil' marked out something I had missed in his description of 'Kaba' Gandhi's human side: *Our household was turned upside down when my father had to attend the Durbar during a Governor's visit. He never wore stockings or boots...then called 'whole boots'. His general footwear was soft leather slippers. If I was a painter, I could paint my father's disgust and the torture on his face as he put his legs into stockings and his feet into ill-fitting and uncomfortable boots. He had to do this.* I could now better understand MKG's distaste for heavy footwear and passion for making, with his hands, simple sandals.

I had also missed young Mohan's comment on the ways of his father's workplace, the Durbar: *I knew then, and know better now, that much of my father's time was taken up by mere intrigue... Everyone talked in whispers.* I could now see the origins of his utter openness whether in the spoken or written word, as well as in action.

The Kathiawari turban acquires a new meaning in Gandhi's wry comment: *There is a saying that Kathiawaris have as many twists in their hearts as they have in their puggrees.* As also in the assessment which seems to carry a sigh in it: *I know how turbid Kathiawari politics is.* These lines were not in the *Autobiography*. They occurred in different documents. But the 'pencil' Gandhi had given me was marking and connecting them for the retelling of the life within the Life, the 'essential' story.

His mother's image, firmly etched in the lampblack of a widow's piety, is that of an ascetic. I was, therefore, delighted to learn[10] in Pyarelal's work of Gandhi's remark on being shown a 3000 years' old pair of silver anklets by the museum curator at Taxila: *Just like what my mother used to wear!* I had not associated Putlibai with silver anklets. Of course she would have worn them as she, the Diwan's wife, went in and out of the Rajkot palace. How good it felt to know of Putlibai's ornaments! Putlibai combined[11] a religiose nature with a restless particularism in household matters. Despite the fact that domestic help abounded in the house and there were three daughters-in-law about, Putlibai supervised the running of the house from dawn to midnight, sitting down to her own meal after all others had eaten. There can be no doubt that something of the restless 'manager' in Gandhi came to him from his mother.

That Karamchand Gandhi had been married thrice before taking Putlibai as his fourth wife, was known. But I had not fully grasped the social context of this serial matrimony, until I reread Gandhi. Illness and early mortality had taken its toll on the female half of the Gandhi family, the first three wives of the Diwan dying at ages twenty, eighteen, and twenty-six. Three very young women had preceded Putlibai of whom the first two had presented Karamchand Gandhi with a daughter each. The third wife was alive yet when Putlibai entered the Gandhi household. Pyarelal records that Kaba asked the childless invalid if she would mind his remarrying. 'You may,' she said astringently, 'if you can find someone to offer his daughter's hand[12].' Quite a character, that third wife must have been.

Putlibai and Karamchand Gandhi had, in that order, a son— Lakshmidas, then a daughter, Raliyat (who, contrary to the then prevailing average for female longevity, lived to ninety), then another son, Karsandas and, born on 2 October 1869, Mohandas. Karamchand was 47 and Putlibai 25 when Mohandas was born.

Like all those who have read biographies of MKG, I knew that he was an average student[13] known better for his good nature than for brightness of mind or speech. But there was more to learn about the Diwan's youngest son from his own writings. I did not really know he had *roamed about the villages in a bullock cart* and been treated by villagers to *jawar roti, curds, and eight anna pieces.* This, for me, was news. Did the future village-roamer's collecting of donations for public causes begin here? Likewise, did his preoccupation, verging on an obsession, with hygiene begin in Porbandar as well? *I have seen in my childhood in Porbandar cows freely eating human faeces. The practice appeared to me to be revolting and the feeling has persisted to this day.*

The roaming and the observing from atop bullock carts was joined by furtive smoking, self-doubt, depression including the contemplation, not uncommon in pre-teenage adolescents, of suicide. But these sallies in independence were soon to be curtailed at age thirteen by the institution of marriage. Mohandas had been betrothed twice before Kasturba appeared on the horizon—an unassimilated detail. And both the brides-to-be had died as little girls. We have read Gandhi's description of the marriage ceremony, but have missed the role of Mohandas' sister-in-law Nandkunvar, wife of his elder brother Lakshmidas Gandhi. The equation of a woman with her husband's young brother is of the stuff of jesting in north Indian literature. Nandkunvar, but eight years older than Mohandas, occurs fleetingly, like a side wavelet, in his recounting of the nuptial's surge ... *My brother's wife had thoroughly coached me about my behaviour on the first night. I do not know who had coached my wife ... But no coaching is really necessary in such matters. The impressions of the former birth are potent enough* ... Leaving something to the imagination about two thirteen-year olds 'hurled into the ocean of life' after 'coaching' can be stronger than explicitness. The source for this? Gandhi himself, of course, and nowhere else than in the *Autobiography*. How easily one can miss the essential while in search of the great!

Marriage and Kasturba occasion much retrospection in Gandhi's writings. That is known. Wanting to go beyond Nandkunvar's instructions, Mohan, at the age of sixteen, had acquired a booklet on the subject. (This acquiring of 'primers' and 'self-instructors' was to be a lifelong trait). But the ready-reckoner obviously spared no thought for the readiness, physical or mental, of the partner. Mohandas' graphic account of his making love to his pregnant wife at the moment of his father's dying belongs to the highest *genre* of confessional autobiography. That scene has been cited repeatedly—and imaginatively embellished—by biographers. But that episode is best explored through the narrator's own words. Gandhi, in retrospective remorse, talks of the *poor mite*[14] that was born soon after, and its predictable end. He warns succeeding generations not to repeat his mistake. So keen is Gandhi to draw the general from the particular that he does not linger on that short-lived trauma. Reversing the process to seek the particular lost in the general is not easy. But is infinitely rewarding. At age seventeen he procured yet another self-instructor in conjugal relations for the princely sum of Rs 10.

Harilal, the eldest son was born when Kasturba and Mohandas were going on nineteen. Gandhi has described that parentage in terms that bear his unique stamp. Ramchandra Gandhi in his unusual Foreword to Tridip Suhrud's translation (Orient Longman 2007) of C.B. Dalal's Gujarati classic *Harilal Gandhi: A Life* says:

On one point (Harilal's being born to the teenage couple) Bapu seems to me to be theologically wrong. He thought that his own carnal nature as a youth was punished by God in the form of a bad son. Surely God must have more things to do than punish fathers with recalcitrant sons!

Mohandas left for England when Harilal was not quite one year old. The three years between 1885 (when Kaba Gandhi died) and 1888 (when Mohandas sailed for England) occur in the autobiography sketchily. But the essential story of that intervening period can be pieced together from his comments that lie scattered elsewhere than his *Autobiography*. Dominating that story is Sheikh Mehtab[15] a classmate of Mohandas' elder brother Karsandas, later to become his own friend and an influential one at that. Gandhi says *Sheikh Mehtab...kept me under his thumb for more than ten years ...* Of those ten the three years—1885 to 1888—saw that influence at its most intense. Not only did Mehtab introduce Mohandas to the eating of meat in order to become 'as strong as the Englishman' but took Mohandas, a married teenager, to a brothel. That 'nothing happened' in that expedition is not the point; Mehtab in that period also brought Mohandas and Kasturba close to a rupture. *I broke her bangles, refused to have anything to do with her, and sent her away to her parents.* 'Suspicion' was at the root of this behaviour. It was, really, Kasturba who should have been suspicious but, no, it was Mohandas who was fed on suspicion which, because it was unfounded, hurt. Kasturba left for her parental home. How and in what circumstances she returned, is not recorded. There must, most certainly, have been tears of anger and of reconciliation.

Mohandas' threefold 'promise' to his mother on the eve of his departure for London in 1888 is, again, well-known. Not so Mohandas' description of the parting from Kasturba: *I kissed her and she said 'Don't go'. What followed I need not describe.* Our plaster-saint image of Mahatma Gandhi is the poorer without the Mohandas who could be reckless, tender, and passionate. It misses, too, the amazing transformation of that passion from its strong physical roots to its stronger emotional bole and, in time, to the even stronger canopy of spiritual energy.

I have found Mohandas the son, the young husband, the crusader for the rights of Indians in South Africa, the leader of India's freedom struggle to be, most consistently, a man of intense passions.

There is an essentiality to Gandhi's use of 'potent' vocabulary, his elisions being of a voltage higher than that of his words. Mehtab travelled with Mohandas to Bombay to see him off at the pier. Mohandas resisted being propositioned by a pimp at Malta—an experience he describes without coyness. But he nearly 'fell' in England. He describes his 1890 experience, as a law student, of a rubber of bridge in Portsmouth—*Every player indulges in innocent jokes as a matter of course ... and I also joined in. Just as I was about to go beyond the limit, leaving the cards and the game to themselves* ... His train of thought and words to match are interrupted. But it is clear that the 'limit' of this bridge player (*that* skill in him, of playing bridge, being in itself, a discovery for me) was to be reached after a rough passage. He says, quite simply, he had been moved by the Portsmouth landlady to 'lust' but stopped just in time, *quaking, trembling, and with beating heart.* There is a disarming frankness to his saying elsewhere *While he* (a would-be barrister) *is in England, he is alone, no wife ... no parents ... no children ... He is the master of his time ...*

There is no trace of any letter written by Mohandas from London to Kasturba (which would have had to be read out to her, as she had not yet learnt to read) nor any mention of her in the circumstances of his return under the cloud of his mother's death. 'I could even check the tears,' he writes while describing his reaction to the news of Putlibai's dying, 'and took to life as if nothing had happened.' The couples' second son Manilal arrived within a year of Mohandas' return from England.

If passion was at work in Mohandas, a rarer draw of another, contrary passion, also began to make itself felt very early. Gandhi describes his making the acquaintance in Bombay, at age twenty-three, of Raychandbhai. The Jaina jeweller-cum-ascetic had a *passion to see God face to face.* Gandhi says *no one else has ever made on me the impression that Raychandbhai did.* If Mehtab had dominated the baser instincts in Mohandas at age seventeen , Raychandbhai was impacting on him with the same force, six years on.

The essential passion in Mohandas changed and alternated but never lost its intensity. Passions, both temporal and spiritual, were at work in the young Mohandas. The former yielded quickly and decisively to the latter. Raychandbhai is but a cameo in Gandhi's life, but one that is central to the story.

An essentiality about Gandhi's narrative style is its leanness. Gandhi's understatements are far stronger than dramatization can be. The famous refusal to remove his *pugree* in Durban, so effectively portrayed in celluloid and in print, is described by Gandhi in but two short sentences:

The magistrate kept staring at me and finally asked me to take off my turban. This I refused to do and left the court.

The two words 'refused' and 'left' say it all.

The even more celebrated Pietermaritzburg episode has been the very soul of Gandhi theatre, screen, and legend. But how has the protagonist related it? The actual moment of eviction is captured in just three sentences:

The constable came. He took me by the hand and pushed me out. My luggage was also taken out.

After the verbal resistance offered by Gandhi to the constable at Pietermaritzburg, he had been outdone physically although his spirit had remained unbowed. The next day, when at Pardekoph he was again manhandled in the stagecoach by the white man in charge of the vehicle, he refused to be physically defeated.

I clung to the brass rails of the coachbox and was determined to keep my hold even at the risk of breaking my bones ... He let go my arm.

Unlike at Pietermaritzburg Gandhi won at Pardekoph both spiritually and physically. He has said, *My active non-violence began from that date.* This 'activeness' was also to include something else he describes doing—for the first time in his life—between Pietermaritzburg and Pardekoph. Which was to employ a civic amenity, the telegraph office, for sending out wires by way of public complaint and private communication against the abuse of power by authorities.

Gandhi's 'essential writing' in the public domain can also be taken to have begun with this act. That style of writing matures, very quickly, from an articulation of complaints over a personal hurt to issues affecting the public. When, barely a year after Pietermaritzburg and Pardekoph, he is pushed off President Street in Pretoria by a guard, Gandhi refuses to proceed against the man saying: *I have made it a rule not to go to court in respect of any personal grievance.*

He is already a rule-maker and, by the law of opposites, becoming a rule-breaker. And a rule-amender as well. Describing the brutal attack on him by a group of white youths on a Durban street on 13 January 1897, Gandhi once again holds on to a railing as he is battered. *If I had lost hold of the bar, I would have struggled on, would perhaps have slapped or bitten the man and would have resisted till death.*

Gandhi 'slapping and biting'! An amendment, a codicil, to his non-violence. Hard to believe, but there it is and—in his own words. Sonja Schlesin (1887–1956) had joined Gandhi's Johannesburg office as a stenotypist in 1903 and served him and the cause of Indian South Africans with rare zeal. But she was her own person. Gandhi writes: *Miss Schlesin in her folly started smoking a cigarette in my presence. I slapped her and threw away the cigarette ...* (Johannesburg, 1903)

Strange as it seems (and very irritating as it must have been to Kasturba) two years after he arrived in South Africa, Gandhi invited his Rajkot friend Mehtab to join him in his establishment there. The opportunity was readily seized by Mehtab until one day ...

Durban, 1895

I saw it all. I knocked at the door. No reply! I knocked heavily so as to make the very walls shake. The door was opened. I saw a prostitute inside. I asked her to leave the house, never to return.

Gandhi *(turning to Mehtab): Is this how you requit my trust in you? From this moment I cease to have anything to do with you. I have been thoroughly deceived and have made a fool of myself. You cannot stay here any more ...*

Barrister Gandhi[16] was a casque of very contrary acids. An opponent of public wrongs and a defender of individual rights in

Durban, he was quite a wielder of authority at home. Throwing his childhood friend Mehtab out of his Durban home with excellent reason, he very nearly did the same to Kasturba—with no real provocation. She had said to him, 'Keep your house to yourself and let me go.' *I forgot myself. I caught her by the hand, dragged the helpless woman to the gate, which was just opposite the ladder, and proceeded to open it with the intention of pushing her out. The tears were running down her cheeks in torrents, and she cried: Have you no sense of shame? Must you forget yourself? Where am I to go? I have no parents or relatives here to harbour me ... I put on a brave face, but was really ashamed and shut the gate. If my wife could not leave me, neither could I leave her.*

How do we know of this unacceptable behaviour of Gandhi towards his wife? Not from her, not from witnesses. From him. From the 'essential' Gandhi. In all these episodes we see Gandhi employing force, the personal force of his mind-actuated body. We see a Gandhi who is putting his hands to a use we do not quite associate with him. He is no different here from the rest of us who have used or do use force in one form or the other when outraged, disdained, or insubordinated by those over who we feel we have some authority. But it is significant that it is not Schlesin, Mehtab, or Kasturba who have complained to the world about their experience. It is Gandhi himself who has recorded the incidents as being part of those experiments which made up the sum total of his evolving personality.

And lest it be thought that Gandhi stood for the use of physical force in those or similar circumstances, it is important to see that he was constantly making new tools for his satyagrahic intervention, tools which used his sense of outrage but sublimated it into something other than rage, into a greater and more potent energy, a capacity to turn the arrow of hurt into himself, to bear the resultant pain and use that pain to transform people and circumstances.

Bearers of the 'Gandhian' tag would be uncomfortable reading Gandhi's description of his Boer War days: *I myself served wine to the stone-breakers in my corps and served bidis to others. Discretion is very necessary in doing all such things. Generosity to others is as necessary as strictness with oneself.* But bearers of the spirituous tray dare not see a sanction in that quote either!

I have given these illustrative sepia-images from the early album of his life to explain my approach to the selections in this compilation and to reiterate that this volume is not about the Gandhi who writes but the Gandhi who 'works'. He does so, in the pages of this anthology through the pencil placed in my hands by the Gandhi storyline. The reader may not expect in this volume illuminated glimpses into Gandhian thought or his 'philosophy'. There are exceptionally good studies of those which can be turned to. Nor need the reader look in this volume for Gandhi epigrams, those ready one-liners that are looked for, at short notice, for a speech or for the deadlined article that has to be written for an anniversary.

Hopefully, this anthology will be regarded neither as shelf-fodder, nor as a pocket-thumber but as something that can be read chronologically as Gandhi's posthumous autobiography. I hope it will help complete his story in his own words from where he had left it in *The Story Of My Experiments With Truth*. Or, if Gandhi's 'themes' are being sought, as a compilation that can be read in the reverse, with the 'General Index' as an entrepot.

The appearance in December 2006 of Rajmohan Gandhi's *Mohandas* (Penguin/Viking) has placed in the reading world the best possible recounting of Gandhi's life within the covers of a single book. This storyline anthology has, in a sense, been rendered redundant by *Mohandas*. But although a researched biography is more complete than a self-abnegating autobiography can ever be, it cannot quite substitute the protagonist's own word. This is not a summary of his *Collected Works*, nor is it a selection of his catchwords. It is his—just his—essential story.

Notes

1. Betrothed to H.S.L. Polak, Millie Graham arrived in Johannesburg on 30 December 1905. Gandhi and Henry Polak received her at the station. Millie and Henry were married the same day. The excerpts used in this compilation are from Millie's memoir 'Mr Gandhi: The Man', Allen & Unwin, 1931.
2. Mahadev Haribhai Desai (1892–1942), lawyer and man of letters joined Gandhi in September 1917 and remained with him as secretary, diarist and *alter ego* until his sudden death on 15 August 1942 in the Aga Khan Palace prison, Poona.
3. Prabhudas Chhaganlal Gandhi (1901–95), a grand-nephew of Gandhi's and an outstanding writer in Gujarati.

4. Pyarelal (1899-1982). Participant in all movements led by Gandhi from 1920 onwards, secretary to Gandhi after Mahadev Desai's demise in 1942, among the seventy-nine Dandi Satyagrahis in 1931, principal biographer of Gandhi in 'The Last Phase' and 'The Early Phase' volumes.

5. Manu Gandhi (1927-69), a grand-niece of the Mahatma who wrote a daily diary in Gujarati, part of which was translated into English and published under the title The Miracle of Calcutta by Navajivan, Ahmedabad, in 1959.

6. Professor N.K. Bose (1901-72) anthropologist, teacher, freedom-fighter, and analyst of Gandhi whose 'My Days with Gandhiji' is regarded as a major study.

7. Hermann Kallenbach (1871-1945) a prosperous Jewish architect of German descent, settled in Johannesburg.

8. Premabehn Kantak (1904-85) teacher of the Satyagraha Ashram school, she joined Sabarmati on 26 May 1929.

9. Anand Hingorani (b. 1907) was one of the Dandi marchers, worked for the weekly Harijan and collected Gandhiji's scattered writings and received, for some time, 'A Thought For A Day' specially written for him by Gandhi.

10. Pyarelal in MG: EP I, p. 192.

11. Prabhudas Gandhi in Jivan-nun Parodh (Navajivan, 1948).

12. Pyarelal in MG: EP I, p. 186.

13. Talking to the students of the Gujarat Mahavidyalaya (National College, Ahmedabad) at the Sabarmati Ashram on 13 January 1921, Gandhi said: 'When I was a student, Geometry was at first simply over my head. Till I came to the thirteenth theorem, everything was blank. But the moment the teacher explained that theorem on the blackboard, there was a sudden flash of light in my mind and since then I felt interested in Geometry.' Gandhi said in a speech at the Law College in Travancore in March 1925 (Mahadev Desai's Diary, Vol. 6, pp. 103-4): 'I never had a brilliant career. I was all my life a plodder. When I went to England ... I couldn't put together two sentences correctly. On the steamer I was a drone ... I finished my three years in England as a drone.'

14. The original Gujarati has 'balak' which can be applied to a male or female child but is perhaps tilted towards the likelihood that this was a male offspring.

15. Sheikh Mehtab (1866-1937) Gandhi's best known classmate from Standard II A of Alfred (or Kattyawar) High School, Rajkot; a strong and persuasive character, swashbuckling athlete, and daredevil, later with Gandhi in South Africa where having abused Gandhi's hospitality

was expelled by Gandhi from the house; talented poet and propagandist in Urdu for the Indian cause in South Africa.

16. Burnett Britton, in *Gandhi Arrives in South Africa* (Greenleaf Books, Canton, Maine; 1999) writes: As a junior reporter for the *Natal Mercury* in 1900 and then as a solicitor, Major Cecil Cowley had frequent occasions to observe Gandhi representing Indians 'quickly, well, and effectively' in the Durban courts. He told the author that Gandhi's 'manner was not aggressive but pleading. He was no orator. When addressing the court he was not eloquent, but rather otherwise; and in his submissions he did not actually stammer, but prefaced his speeches and comments by repeated sibilants, for instance: Ess-ess-ess your worship, ess-ess-ess this poor woman was attending an invalid sister and was on her way home after the curfew bell had gone when she was arrested by the police. I ask ess-ess-ess that she should not be sent to gaol, but cautioned ess-ess-ess. ess-ess-ess.'

Part One

1869–85

Father: Karamchand Uttamchand Gandhi

Home Life

At his feet, his son, Mohandas.

Autograph, dated 29-10-1934, at the lower edge of a
formal photograph of Karamchand Gandhi, seated

*So, father, your son is now, in your eyes, no better
than a common thief*

Quoted in Pyarelal's MG: EP, *p. 212*

Grocers' premises assail the olfactories. The Sanskrit-based word
for 'odour' used in Hindi, Gujarati, and many a language in north
India is *gandh*. Mohandas, son of Karamchand Uttamchand
Gandhi begins his autobiography with the matter-of-fact and un-
etymological observation that the Gandhis were 'originally grocers'.
Whence, that family name. I have often recalled, in the context of
that name, the concluding line in George Orwell's essay[1] on Gandhi:
'... regarded simply as a politician, and compared with the other
leading political figures of our time, how clean a smell he has
managed to leave behind!'

Orwell, who also refers to Gandhi having 'disinfected the political
air' says incisively that Gandhi 'could, if he had chosen, have been a
brilliant success as a lawyer, an administrator, or perhaps even a
businessman'. He did indeed become all of these, but on his own
terms, turning legal practice towards conciliation, administration
towards public service, and business acumen into massive fund-
raisings for public causes and the management of such funds with
auditorial rectitude.

After the 'grocer' reference Gandhi quickly adds, with characteristic word-thriftiness, that for three generations his family had been 'Prime Ministers (*Diwans*) in several Kathiawar States' meaning, thereby, that administering and politics, not grocering, had become the Gandhis' calling for several decades preceding his birth in the Karamchand Gandhi household.

Five generations of Gandhis had lived in the house at Porbandar, after Mohandas' great grandfather Harjivan Gandhi bought it, as Pyarelal tells us, for Rs 165. It is in this three-storeyed house built around the three sides of a courtyard that our 'story-teller' was born. The 'lying-in' room was dark, stuffy, and was where Karamchand Gandhi's mother Lakshmi generally spent her days.

Mahadev Desai wrote in *Navajivan*, after seeing this dingy room: 'It is as if Bapu took birth in this dark room to rid the world of darkness.'

Part One of this compilation is concerned with the Gandhi *haveli* (the large joint-family house) into which he was born and the daily rhythms of its life. Karamchand, clearly an iconic figure for Mohandas, does not escape the son's criticism for 'carnality'—a strong phrase to use for one who was married four times and only once 'concurrently' in an age when polygamy, especially following a wife's death, was not uncommon.

If the record of Karamchand's consulting his third wife on his fourth venture in matrimony is any indication, the women in the Gandhi household were not exactly voiceless. Putlibai herself emerges in Gandhi's narration as a strong personality, both as wife and widowed mother of four—perhaps an indication of her comparative seniority in age.

This Part describes Putlibai's homebound austerities as well as her place under the princely sun. The senior women of the Court seem to have not just held her in high esteem but sought her counsel. This image of the woman albeit 'private' and unlettered being committed to a larger world, held great appeal for the son. And to an extent can be said to have played a role in his trying to mould his child-wife Kastur to a 'design'. It is regrettable that Gandhi has been silent on the chemistry between his mother and his sisters-in-law on the one hand and Kastur on the other. We only have tangential records of the trying experience of Kastur's raising little Harilal as 'a single parent' over the three years when Mohandas was away in England (1888–91), and then raising Harilal and Manilal, likewise, for another three years when he was in South Africa (1893–6) before the family set up home in Durban.

In the entries contained in the earlier sections of this Part, it is the son that speaks although he is already a husband and a father.

Gandhi's descriptions, in passing, of his two child-betrothals before his marriage at thirteen, give us glimpses of the prevalent customs pertaining to betrothal, nuptials, and maternity. They also say something of the importance of weddings as distinct from marriage, the latter being almost a corollary to the former. Weddings were lavish affairs, in which the 'clan' came into fullness, with feasting being an important feature.

Kastur herself, born in Porbandar in the same year as Mohandas, in a house that can be seen from the Gandhis' haveli in Porbandar, from the very start of her life with Mohandas emerges as very much her own person. She does not yield easily to her teenage husband's tantrums, whimsicality, and truancy without an argument.

* * *

This Part tells us something of Karamchand Gandhi the man, the householder, Diwan, and father. 'Kaba' Gandhi, as he was known among his friends and family, was Prime Minister of three princely States for nearly four decades. During this period, the 'Raj' saw as many as nine Governors General enter office in distant Calcutta: We can catch vignettes of Hardinge I (1844–8), Dalhousie (1848–56), Canning (1856–62), Elgin (1862–4), Lawrence (1864–9), Mayo (1869–72), Northbrook (1872–6), Lytton I (1876–80), and Ripon (1800–4). If Hardinge's inauguration of the First Sikh War may not have had any direct effect over Kathiawar, the threat to princely autonomy by the British power would not have been lost on the Porbandar, Rajkot, and Vankaner courts, where Karamchand Gandhi was Diwan. Dalhousie's taking over of the Punjab and the Oudh would have caused an imperial tremor to be felt more sharply in Porbandar and, certainly, the Doctrine of Lapse would have created tension in the palace where the ability to generate heirs would now become an attribute of statehood rather than an index of manhood.

Karamchand Gandhi's prime ministership was at the penultimacy of its zenith when the 'Mutiny' broke out and brought the flutter of revolt to Kathiawar's immediate vicinity in north-western and central India. And famine raged over the region in the year—1869— as Lawrence, Canning's trusted lieutenant handed over the viceroyalty to Mayo. Unbeknownst to any of the 'players' at the time, a step taken by Mayo was to reappear in the life of the just-born Mohandas—and that of the Raj—some six decades later. This was the raising by Mayo across India of a tax on salt. Lytton I was, likewise, to do something which the then ten-year-old school student in Rajkot was to challenge irreversibly—the abolition of the Cotton Duty on imports of textiles from Lancashire.

But by the time the lamp of Karamchand's life was flickering to a close, the Raj had begun to see the value of associating Indians of maturity and integrity with local government. Ripon's role in the passing of the Local Governments' Act came just as Karamchand was demitting office and—life.

The son, however, was to see un-Riponian hauteur in British officers of smaller stature as he sought a passage to England in order to strengthen his own claims to his father's mantle or, indeed, to any future of worth in a Kathiawar where intrigue and political manoeuvring were gaining leverage.

Gandhi's view of temporal authority as high-mindedness exerting itself for the common weal was clearly influenced by his father's example. He describes Karamchand's manner of functioning in public office (which, in turn, was influenced by that of *his* father, Uttamchand) in terms of admiration and reverence. That his father wielded power but not wealth, he reflects upon and shares with his reader as something that was both natural and remarkable. The absence in his father of the common political vices of suspicion, intrigue, and flattery are described by him matter-of-factly but also prescriptively. His descriptions of his father show Karamchand Gandhi as being wise, even shrewd, and yet trusting of the human potential for good.

I have cited Orwell earlier. Another Orwell quote comes to mind: '[Gandhi] seems to have been quite free from that maniacal suspiciousness which, as E.M. Forster rightly says in *A Passage to India*, is the besetting Indian vice, as hypocrisy is the British vice.

Although no doubt he was shrewd enough in detecting dishonesty, he seems whenever possible to have believed that other people were acting in good faith and had a better nature through which they could be approached.'

Of himself, Gandhi 'gives it away' almost absent-mindedly. If 'I was a good boy, but not a bright boy' is both a self-description which holds being good above being bright, it does not regard the two as being mutually exclusive. In the main, young Mohandas emerges, in his words, as a lad who was all too eager to absorb the little message as well as the larger one, the 'primer' as well as Gospel. There is a touching vulnerability in his description of the impact made on his mind by the book and the play on Shravana, the 'good seed' of *Ramanama* planted in his mind by the housemaid Rambha, even as there is candour to his telling us of his reading up, a little later, in sheer knowledge-hunger, self-instructors on the conjugal life. Animal instinct has not been hinted at under such high aeges very often.

To the desire to 'learn' to be good and to be bright is joined the desire to be strong. And here, into the portal of this desire, enters Sheikh Mehtab. Three years his senior, Mehtab is the stuff of which Hindi film villains were made some years ago but not any longer; we are more understanding of the nuances of life. Mehtab is a foil to Gandhi, without the presence of which our subject's life would have been like a Concordance to Scripture, a book of virtuous synonyms. Sheikh Mehtab is Gandhi's Book of Antonyms. And absolutely irreplaceable as a result. He is the temptation which makes its resistance so appealing, the precipice which gives Gandhi's will its climactic edge, the tong which, trying to give the ingot a certain shape, itself melts in the furnace.

This Preface will close with the observation that Part One of this compilation is about births, childhood, adolescence, procreation, and death—a cycle complete in itself. But a cycle which is in the form of a foretaste of the life ahead where all these crucial transactions were to recur sublimated and sometimes distorted on a steadily widening canvas. A half-sentence in the *Autobiography* had escaped me; the 'pencil' now marked it out for me '... the passion for truth was innate in me ...' And the 'me' Gandhi is writing about is around 15 years of age.

The Gandhis

THE GANDHIS seem to have been originally grocers.[2] But for three generations, from my grandfather, they were Prime Ministers[3] in several Kathiawar States.

A, p. 1, written in November 1927; G

My Father

KABA[4] GANDHI married four times in succession, having lost his wife each time by death.[5] He had two daughters[6] by his first and second marriages. His last wife, Putlibai,[7] bore him a daughter and three sons, I being the youngest. My father was a lover of the clan, truthful, brave and generous, but short-tempered. To a certain extent he might have been given to carnal pleasures. For he married for the fourth time when he was over forty. But he was incorruptible and had earned a name for strict impartiality in his family as well as outside.

A, p. 1; G

THOUGH MY father was the Prime Minister of more than one native state, he never hoarded money. He spent all that he earned in charity and the education and marriages of his children, so we were practically left without much cash. He left some property, and that was all. When asked why he did not collect money and set it aside for his children, he used to say that his children represented his wealth, ...

Interview to The Vegetarian, *London, 13 June 1891;*
CWMG, Vol. 1, p. 43; E

OUR HOUSEHOLD was turned upside down when my father had to attend the Durbar during a Governor's visit. He never wore stockings or boots...then called 'whole boots'. His general footwear was soft leather slippers. If I was a painter, I could paint my father's disgust and the torture on his face as he was putting his legs into his stockings and his feet into ill-fitting and uncomfortable boots.[8] He *had* to do this.

Harijan, 3 February 1940, p. 436; G

... (HENCE), I knew then, and know better now, that much of my father's time was taken up in mere intrigues. Discussions started early in the morning and went on till it was time to leave for the office. Everyone talked in whispers. ...

CWMG Vol. 24, p. 170 E

I KNOW how turbid Kathiawari politics is.

CWMG Vol. 50, p. 422

THERE IS a saying that Kathiawaris have as many twists in their hearts as they have in their puggrees.

CWMG Vol. 87, pp. 242-3; G

... MY HOROSCOPE was always kept perfect and up to date but that practice died away with my father. He used to take interest in it and got the yearly forecast from it. ...

CWMG Vol. 81, p. 314 E

My Mother

JUST LIKE what my mother used to wear.[9]

P, MG: EP, p. 192

SHE WAS deeply religious ... She would take the hardest vows and keep them without flinching. Illness[10] was no excuse for relaxing them. I can recall her once falling ill when she was observing the Chandrayana[11] vow, but the illness was not allowed to interrupt the observance.

My mother had a strong commonsense. She was well informed about all matters of State, and the ladies of the Court thought highly of her intelligence. Often I would accompany her, exercising the privilege of childhood and I still remember many lively discussions she had with the widowed mother of the Thakor Saheb.[12]

A, p. 2; G

MOTHER WOULD not allow us to see an eclipse at all, as she was afraid that evil would befall us if we did.

The Diary of Mahadev Desai, *Vol. 1 (1932), p. 22*

I TOLD my mother that she was entirely wrong in considering physical contact with Uka[13] as sinful.

Young India, *27 April 1921, p. 135 (Presidential address at the Suppressed Classes Conference, Ahmedabad)*
P, MG: EP, *p. 127; E*

Mohandas: Are you telling me I can hit Elder Brother?
Putlibai: When brothers and sisters quarrel with each other, they square it out among themselves. If your brother hits you, you can return the blow.
Mohandas: Well, let him hit me then. I won't hit back ...
Putlibai: Moniya, wherefrom has this come to you?

Reconstructed from P, MG: EP, *p. 195*

MAHADEV DESAI while examining the proofs of the school edition of the autobiography (in the Yeravda Jail in 1932, on 31 March): In connection with the austerities of your mother, you have used the word 'saintliness'. Don't you think 'austerity' here would be more appropriate?

MKG: No. I have used the word saintliness deliberately. Austerity implies external renunciation, endurance, and sometimes even hypocrisy. But saintliness is an inner quality of the soul. My mother's austerity was only an echo of her inner life. If you notice any purity in me, I have inherited it from my mother, and not from my father. Mother died at the early age of forty. I have been a witness of her behaviour in the flower of youth, but never did I see in her any frivolity, any recourse to beauty aids or interest in the pleasures of life. The only impression she ever left on my mind is that of saintliness.

The Diary of Mahadev Desai, *Vol. 1 (1932), p. 51*

MKG: I remember that we used coir-string cots in our house when I was a child. My mother used to rub fresh ginger on it.

MD: What is that? I do not understand what she did.

MKG: When she had to prepare ginger pickle, the ginger skin was not removed with a knife, but by rubbing it against the coir string.

The Diary of Mahadev Desai Vol. 1 (1932), p. 307

Mary Chesley[14]: From what sources do you get your conception of God?

MKG: From my childhood, remembering my mother's constant visits to the temple. Sometimes these were as many as four or five a day, and never less than two. Also my nurse[15] used to tell me I must repeat the name of God if I felt afraid.

CWMG Vol. 59, p. 460 E

The Diwan's Son

1879

I ROAMED about the villages in a bullock cart. As I was the son of a Diwan, people fed me on the way with juwar roti and curds and gave me eight anna pieces.

Chandrashanker Shukla, Reminiscences of Gandhiji, *Vora, 1951, p. 110*

I HAVE seen in my childhood in Porbandar cows[16] freely eating human faeces. The practice appeared to me to be revolting and the feeling has persisted to this day.

CWMG Vol. 61, p. 191 E

AT SCHOOL the teachers did not consider me a very bright boy. They knew I was a good boy, but not a bright boy.

CWMG Vol. 65, p. 100 E

AS A rule I had a distaste for any reading beyond my school books ... But somehow my eyes fell on a book purchased by my father. It was *Shravana Pitribhakti Nataka* (a play about Shravana's devotion to his parents). I read it with intense interest. There came to our place about the same time itinerant showmen. One of the pictures I was shown was of Shravana carrying, by means of slings fitted from his shoulders, his blind parents on a pilgrimage. The book and the picture left an indelible impression on my mind. 'Here is an example for you to copy,' I said to myself. The agonized lament of the parents over Shravana's death is still fresh in my memory. The melting tune moved me deeply, and I played[17] it on a concertina which my father had purchased for me.

A, pp. 3–4; G

MY HEAD used to reel as the teacher was struggling to make his exposition on geometry understood by us ... I know now that what I took four years to learn of arithmetic, geometry, algebra, chemistry, and astronomy I should have learnt easily in one year if I had not to learn them through English but Gujarati. My grasp of the subjects would have been easier and clearer. My Gujarati vocabulary would have been richer. I would have made use of such knowledge in my own home. This English medium created an impassable barrier between me and the members of my family, who had not gone through English schools. My father knew nothing of what I was doing. I could not, even if I had wished it, interest my father in what I was learning. For though he had ample intelligence, he knew not a word of English. I was fast becoming a stranger in my own home. I certainly became a superior person.

CWMG Vol. 67, p. 160 E

Rambha[18], Rama, And Rama Raksha

... (BECAUSE) I learned to rely consciously upon God before I was 15 years old.

CWMG Vol. 69, p. 9 E

THERE WAS in me a fear of ghosts and spirits. Rambha, for that was her name, suggested, as a remedy for this fear, the repetition of Ramanama. I had more faith in her than in her remedy, and so at a tender age I began repeating Ramanama to cure my fear of ghosts and spirits. This was of course short-lived, but the good seed sown in childhood was not sown in vain. I think it is due to the seed sown by that good woman Rambha that today Ramanama is an infallible remedy for me.

Just about this time, a cousin of mine who was a devotee of the *Ramayana* arranged for my second brother and me to learn *Rama*

Raksha. We got it by heart, and made it a rule to recite it every morning after the bath.

A, *pp. 19–20; G*

My Marriage

1882

IT IS my painful duty to have to record here my marriage at the age of thirteen ... The elders decided to have my second brother, [19] who was two or three years my senior, a cousin possibly a year older, and me, married all at the same time. In doing so there was no thought of our welfare, much less our wishes ... I do not think it meant to me anything more than the prospect of good clothes to wear, drum beating, marriage processions, rich dinners, and—a strange girl to play with. The carnal desire came later. I can describe how it came but let not the reader be curious about it ...

My brother's wife[20] had thoroughly coached me about my behaviour on the first night. I do not know who had coached my wife. I have never asked her about it, nor am I inclined to do so now. The reader may be sure we were too nervous to face each other. We were certainly too shy. How was I to talk to her, and what was I to say? The coaching could not carry me far.

But no coaching is really necessary in such matters. The impressions of the former birth are potent enough. ...

A, *p. 6; G*

Kasturbai

I MUST say I was passionately fond of her.[21] Even at school I used to think of her and the thought of nightfall and our consequent meeting was ever haunting me. Separation was unbearable.

A, *p. 7; G*

1883

ABOUT THE time of my marriage, little pamphlets costing a pice, or a pie (I now forget how much), used to be issued, in which conjugal love, thrift, child marriages, and other such subjects were discussed. Whenever I came across any of these, I used to go through them cover to cover, and it was a habit with me to forget what I did not like, and to carry out in practice whatever I liked. Lifelong faithfulness to the wife, inculcated in these booklets as the duty of the husband, remained permanently imprinted on my heart. Furthermore, the passion for truth was innate in me, and to be false to her was therefore out of the question. And then there was very little chance of my being faithless at that tender age. But the lesson of faithfulness had also untoward effect. 'If I should be pledged to be faithful to my wife, she also should be pledged to be faithful to me,' I said to myself. The thought made me a jealous husband. Her duty was easily converted into my right to exact faithfulness from her, and if it had to be exacted, I should be watchfully tenacious of the right. I had absolutely no reason to suspect my wife's fidelity, but jealousy does not wait for reasons. I must needs be forever on the lookout regarding her movements and therefore she could not go anywhere without my permission. This sowed the seeds of a bitter quarrel between us. The restraint was virtually a sort of imprisonment. And Kasturbai was not the girl to brook any such thing. She made it a point to go out whenever and wherever she liked. More restraint on my part resulted in more liberty being taken by her, and in my getting more and more cross.

A, pp. 6–7; G

A 'Friend'

1883–4

AMONGST MY few friends at the high school I had, at different times, two who might be called intimate. One of these was originally my elder brother's friend.[22] They were classmates. I knew his weaknesses but I regarded him as a faithful friend. My mother, my eldest brother, and my wife warned me that I was in bad company. I was too proud to heed my wife's warning ... He informed me that many of our teachers were secretly taking meat and wine ...'We are a weak people because we do not eat meat. The English are able to rule over us because they are meat-eaters. You know how hardy I am and how great a runner too. It is because I am a meat eater. ...'

My elder brother[23] had already fallen. He therefore supported my friend's argument. I certainly looked feeble-bodied by the side of my brother and this friend. They were both hardier, physically stronger, and more daring. This friend's exploits cast a spell over me. He could run long distances and extraordinarily fast. He was an adept in high and long jumping. He could put up with any amount of corporal punishment. He would often display his exploits to me and, as one is always dazzled when one sees in others the qualities one lacks oneself, I was dazzled by this friends' exploits ...

A day was thereupon fixed for beginning the experiment. It had to be conducted in secret ... We went in search of a lonely spot by the river and there I saw for the first time in my life, meat. There was baker's bread also. I relished neither. The goat's meat was as tough as leather. I simply could not eat it. I was sick ...

I GOT over my dislike for bread, forswore my compassion for the goats, and became a relisher of meat-dishes, if not of meat itself. This went on for about a year ... there was the obvious difficulty about frequently preparing expensive savoury meat-dishes. I had no money to pay for this 'reform'. My friend had therefore always to find the wherewithal. I had no knowledge where he found it. But find it he did, because he was bent on turning me into a meat-eater.

THE SAME company would have led me into faithlessness to my wife. But I was saved by the skin of my teeth. My friend once took me to a brothel ... I sat near the woman on her bed but I was tongue-tied. She naturally lost patience with me and showed me the door with abuses and insults. I then felt as though my manhood had been injured and wished to sink into the ground for shame. But I have ever since given thanks to God for having saved me. I can recall four more similar incidents in my life ... From a strictly ethical point of view, all these occasions must be regarded as moral lapses; for the carnal desire was there and it was as good as the act.

A, pp. 11–14; G

SHEIKH MEHTAB was behind this[24]. He kept me under his thumb for more than ten years ... I broke her bangles, refused to have anything to do with her and sent her away to her parents. ...

CWMG Vol. 72, p. 127 E

A Confession

1884

I DID not dare to speak. Not that I was afraid of my father beating me. No. I do not recall his having ever beaten any of us. I was afraid lest he should be pained and strike his forehead in anguish. ... I decided to write out the confession, to submit it to my father and ask for his forgiveness.

I wrote it[25] on a slip of paper and handed it to him myself ... I was trembling ... He was then suffering from a fistula and was confined to bed ... He read it through, and pearl drops trickled down his cheeks, wetting the paper. For a moment he closed his eyes in thought and then tore up the note. He had got up to read it. He again lay down. I also cried ... Those pearl-drops cleansed my heart, and washed my sin away.

A, p. 17; G

My Father's Illness And Death

1884-5

DURING PART of his illness my father was in Porbandar. There every evening he used to listen to the Ramayana. The reader was a great devotee of Rama—Ladha Maharaj of Bileshvar ... He would sing the *Dohas* (couplets) and *Chopais* (quatrains), and explain them, losing himself in the discourse and carrying his listeners along with him. I must have been thirteen at that time, but I quite remember being enraptured by his reading. That laid the foundation of my deep devotion to the Ramayana. Today I regard the Ramayana of Tulasidas as the greatest book in all devotional literature.

JAINA MONKS also would pay frequent visits to my father, and would even go out of their way to accept food from us—non-Jainas. They would have talks with my father on subjects religious and mundane.

He had, besides, Musalman and Parsi friends, who would talk to him about their own faiths, and he would listen to them always with respect, and often with interest. Being his nurse, I often had a chance to be present at these talks. These many things combined to inculcate in me a toleration for all faiths.

Only Christianity was at the time an exception. I developed a sort of dislike for it. And for a reason. In those days Christian missionaries used to stand in a corner near the high school and hold forth, pouring abuse on Hindus and their gods. I could not endure this.

A, pp. 20–1; G

16 November 1885

THE TIME of which I am now speaking is my sixteenth year. My father, as we have seen, was bed-ridden[26] ... I had the duties of a nurse. This was also the time when my wife was expecting a baby—a circumstance which as I can see today meant a double shame for me. For one thing I did not restrain myself, as I should have done at a time when religion, medical science, and commonsense alike forbade sexual intercourse. I was always glad to be relieved from my duty and went straight to the bedroom after doing obeisance to my father ...

IT WAS 10.30 or 11 p.m. ... My uncle[27] offered to relieve me. I was glad and went straight to the bedroom. My wife, poor thing, was fast asleep. But how could she sleep when I was there? I woke her up. In five or six minutes, however, the servant knocked at the door...'Father is no more ...' I had but to wring my hands. I felt deeply ashamed and miserable. I ran to my father's room ... My father ... had made a sign for pen and paper and written: 'Prepare for the last rites'. He had then snapped the amulet off his arm and also his gold necklace and flung them aside. A moment after this he was no more. ...

Before I close this chapter of my double shame, I may mention that the poor mite[28] that was born to my wife scarcely breathed for more than three or four days. Nothing else could be expected.

A, pp. 16–19; G

An Obeisance

'AT HIS feet, his son, Mohandas'.

Autograph,[29] dated 29-10-1934, at the lower edge of a formal photograph of Karamchand Gandhi, seated.

Part Two

1887-91

As a student in London

In London

My name is Gandhi. You have of course never heard of it.

This Part opens with Mohandas leaving school in 1887, the year in which Lord Dufferin was giving 'cautious countenance' to the Indian National Congress formed two years earlier and a liberal breeze had begun to blow over urban India. Pollen of a new fragrance was also in the village air, with Dufferin announcing tenancy legislation benefiting peasants. Dadabhai Naoroji had handed over the Congress baton to Badruddin Tyabji at a session of the party in Madras and the Indian Council Act of 1892 was getting readied, which would pave the way for an Indian to be elected, for the first time, to the Legislative Council.

It was in this transitional India that Mavji Dave, a Brahmin friend of the Gandhi family asked Mohandas (who had just written an examination essay in English 'On the Advantages Of A Cheerful Disposition') whether he would not rather go to England than continue studying in India. Mohandas' answer was ready in minutes; his bags were to become so as well, within a few months. It is remarkable that in a shaky address at a farewell party given to him in his school, Gandhi said audaciously, '*I hope that some of you will follow in my footsteps and after your return from England you will work wholeheartedly for big reforms in India.*'

What reforms did he have in mind? Was he already beginning to think politically?

Gandhi was to write, not soon thereafter, in his still unformed English, '*I am not a man who would, after having formed any intention, leave it easily.*'

Mohandas at 19 was a warm-blooded young man. And because he was wanting to be 'a bright boy', Orwell could say, 'There was a time, it is interesting to learn, when he wore a top hat, took dancing lessons, studied French and Latin, went up the Eiffel Tower, and even tried to learn the violin—all this was the idea of assimilating European civilization as thoroughly as possible. He was not one of those saints who are marked out by their phenomenal piety from childhood onwards, nor one of the other kind who forsake the world after sensational debaucheries. He makes full confession of the misdeeds of his youth, but in fact there is not much to confess. As a frontispiece to the book[1] there is a photograph of Gandhi's possessions at the time of his death. The whole outfit could be purchased for about 5 pounds and Gandhi's sins, at least his fleshly sins, would make the same sort of appearance if placed all in one heap.'

Gandhi's grand-nephew Prabhudas Gandhi, in his *Jivan-nun Parodh* says Kastur's jewellery was sold to finance, in part, Mohandas's travel expenses.

Gandhi's account of his three years' stay in London at the personal level is best summarized in the statement 'I know every nook and corner of London'. Until not long ago critics of Gandhi used to say that his time in London, coming within five years of the death of Karl Marx (1818–83) could have elicited some comment on that shaper of world thought. Similarly, his writings betray no interest in the discoveries of Charles Darwin who died just six years before Gandhi's arrival in London. Perhaps Gandhi *was* unaware of Darwin and Marx until much later—a reflection on Gandhi's intellectual curiosity at the time. But it ought to be noted that he was not unfamiliar with the work of certain contemporaries of a school of thought different from his, like Charles Bradlaugh. Gandhi attended the atheist's funeral.

Outside of his legal studies, Gandhi's principal preoccupation was, undoubtedly, quaint—the seeking and propagating of vegetarian food. One does not get from him as many graphic descriptions of London's social scene as one would have liked to. A 'regular' reader of *The Daily News, The Daily Telegraph*, and *The Pall Mall Gazette* could have told us something about Jack the Ripper who was prowling about London's streets around the time Gandhi was walking down Bond Street getting his evening suit, craning his neck around Farrington

Street looking for a vegetarian restaurant, and watching public houses in London 'where people went in sober and came out ... dead drunk'.

In terms of mental growth, however, no three years in Gandhi's life witnessed change in the fast-track as those between 1888 and 1891. This is clear as an 'essentiality' in his writings during the period. His English became firm, his thinking steadied itself, and he became aware of a larger world outside Porbandar. The reader might well say 'no big deal in that; it could not be otherwise'. But that change reflected an inner steeling of resolve to be himself, no matter how strong the ambient influence. His steadfast adherence to certain forms of diet was only the outer and most visible form of this resolve. The process was by no means easy. Nor was it without some slippages. The London years saw the making of one who could, given a 'jolt', become someone who could turn things around.

There is something of a swot in a man who is called to the bar on the 10 June 1891, is enrolled on 11th, and gets on board a ship back for home on 12th. But that was and is Gandhi. Never losing a moment, nor a cent. He has said, after all, that he came from a family of grocers.

London Beckons

I PASSED the matriculation[2] examination in 1887 ...

'On The Advantages Of A Cheerful Disposition'
    (Subject of the essay in English written by Gandhi in the Matriculation Examination[3]).

WE HAD in Mavji Dave, who was a shrewd and learned Brahman, an old friend and adviser of the family. He kept up his connection with the family even after my father's death ... Joshiji—that is how we used to call old Mavji Dave—turned to me with complete assurance, and asked 'Would you not rather go to England than study here?' Nothing could have been more welcome to me ... My mother, however, was unwilling. She had begun making minute enquiries ... I said: 'Will you not trust me? I shall not lie to you. I swear to you that I shall not touch any of those things ...'[4]

A, Part I; G

(BUT) I am not a man who would, after having formed any intention leave it easily.[5]

LD, CWMG Vol. 1, p. 4; E and G

... IT WAS Friday night. I was given an address by my school fellows. I was quite uneasy when I rose up to answer the address. When I spoke half of what I had to speak I began to shake. ...

CWMG Vol. 1, p. 8; E

'I HOPE that some of you will follow in my footsteps and after your return from England you will work wholeheartedly for big reforms in India.'

Report in The Kathiawar Times (12.7.1888) of 18/19-year old
Gandhi's 'speech' at a farewell function organized at his school, the
Alfred High School, Rajkot, on 4-7-1888; CWMG Vol. 1, p. 2; G

... (WHEN THE day for departure came) my mother was hiding her eyes, full of tears, in her hands but the sobbing was clearly heard. I did not weep, even though my heart was breaking. Last but not least came the leave-taking with my wife. It would be contrary to custom for me to see or talk to her in the presence of friends. So I had to see her in a separate room. She, of course, had begun sobbing long before. I went to her and stood like a dumb statue for a moment. I kissed her, and she said, 'Don't go'. What followed I need not describe. ...

CWMG Vol. 1, p. 45; E

Modh Bania Community Leader: In the opinion of the caste, your proposal to go to England is not proper. Our religion forbids voyages abroad ... One is obliged there to eat and drink with Europeans!
MKG: I am helpless. I cannot alter my resolve.
Leader: Will you disregard the orders of the caste?
MKG: I am really helpless. I think the caste should not interfere.

Adapted from A, pp. 36–7

SOME OF the clothes I liked and some I did not like at all. The necktie which I delighted in wearing later, I then abhorred. The short jacket I looked upon as immodest.

A, Part I; G

Setting Sail

September 1888
... IT WAS for the first time in my life that I sailed in a steamship. I enjoyed the voyage[6] very much ... For some days I did not speak a word to the fellow-passengers. I always got up at 8 a.m. in the morning and washed my teeth, then went to the w.c. and took my bath. The arrangement of the English water closets astonished a native passenger. We do not get there water and are obliged to use pieces of paper.

LD, CWMG Vol. 1, pp. 9–10; E

...THE CONSTRUCTION of the Suez Canal[7] I am not able to understand. It is indeed marvellous. I cannot think of the genius of a man who invented it ... It is as broad as the Aji[8] at Ramnath. ...

LD, CWMG Vol. 1 pp. 11–12; E

18/19 September 1888

A MAN at Brindisi: Sir, there is a beautiful girl of fourteen, follow me, sir, and I will take you there, the charge is not high, sir. ...

MKG: Go Away.

Adapted from LD, CWMG Vol. 1, p. 13

London, At Last

29 September 1888

MR MAZMUDAR, [9] Mr Abdul Majid[10] and I reached the Victoria Hotel. Mr Abdul Majid told in a dignified air to the porter of the Victoria Hotel to give our cabman the proper fare. Mr Abdul Majid thought very highly of himself, but let me write here that the dress which he had put on was perhaps worse than that of the porter. ...

LD, CWMG Vol. 1, pp. 15–16; E

... I WAS quite dazzled by the splendour of the hotel. I had never in my life seen such a pomp. My business was simply to follow the two friends in silence ... Then we were to go to the second floor by a lift. I did not know what it was. He at once touched something which I thought was lock of the door. But as I afterwards came to know it was the bell and he rang in order to tell the waiter to bring the lift. The doors were opened and I thought that was a room in which we were to sit for some time. But to my great surprise we were brought to the second floor.

LD, CWMG Vol. 1, p. 16; E

DR MEHTA[11] gave me a hearty greeting. He smiled at my being in flannels. As we were talking I casually picked up his top-hat, and trying to see how smooth it was, passed my hand over it the wrong way and disturbed the fur. Dr Mehta looked somewhat angrily at what I was doing and stopped me. But the mischief had been done. The incident was a warning for the future. This was my first lesson in European etiquette.

A, p. 27; G

I WASTED ten pounds on an evening suit made in Bond Street, the centre of fashionable life in London; and got my good and noble-hearted brother to send me a double watch-chain of gold. It was not correct to wear a ready-made tie and I learnt the art of tying one for myself. While in India, the mirror had been a luxury permitted on the days when the family barber gave me a shave. Here I wasted ten minutes every day before a huge mirror, watching myself arranging my tie and parting my hair in the correct fashion. My hair was by no means soft, and every day it meant a regular struggle with the brush to keep it in position. Each time the hat was put on and off, the hand would automatically move towards the head to adjust the hair, not to mention the other civilized habit of the hand every now and then operating for the same purpose when sitting in polished society.

A, p. 31; G

I HAD the privilege to see Dadabhai Naoroji[12] in 1888 for the first time. A friend of my father's had given me a letter of introduction to him, and it is worth noting that this friend was not at all acquainted with Dadabhai. He, however, took it for granted that anyone from the public could write to such a saintly person. In England, I found that Dadabhai came in contact with all students. He was their leader and attended their gatherings ... My first acquaintance with the extent of Indian poverty was through Dadabhai's book.[13]

Navajivan, 7 September 1924; G

Applying To The Inner Temple

6 November 1888

I, *MOHANDASS Karamchand Gandhi*,[14] aged *19* of Baron's Court the *youngest* son of *Karamchand Uttamchand Gandhi* of *Porbander India deceased* in the Country of _____ add father's profession (if any) _____ and the condition in life and occupation (if any), of the Applicant DO HEREBY DECLARE, that I am desirous of being admitted a Member of the HONOURABLE SOCIETY of the INNER TEMPLE, for the purpose of keeping terms for the Bar; and that I will not, either directly or indirectly, apply for or take out any Certificate to practise, directly or indirectly, as a Special

Pleader or Conveyancer, or Draftsman in Equity, without the special permission of the Masters of the Bench of the said Society....

Dated this 6th day of *November 1888.*

I, Mohandas Karamchand Gandhi of 10, Barons Court Rd West Kensington, aged 19 the youngest son of Karamchand Uttamchand Gandhi of Porbandar India deceased in the County of _____ (if any) _____ and the condition in life and occupation (if any), of the Applicant said father's profession

DO HEREBY DECLARE, that I am desirous of being admitted a Member of the *HONOURABLE SOCIETY* of the *INNER TEMPLE,* for the purpose of keeping terms for the Bar; and that I will not, either directly or indirectly, apply for or take out any Certificate to practise, directly or indirectly, as a Special Pleader or Conveyancer, or Draftsman in Equity, without the special permission of the Masters of the Bench of the said Society.

AND I DO HEREBY FURTHER DECLARE, that I am not an Attorney-at-Law, Solicitor, a Writer to the Signet, a Writer of the Scotch Courts, a Proctor, a Notary Public, a Clerk in Chancery, a Parliamentary Agent, an Agent in any Court, original or appellate, a Clerk to any Justice of the Peace; nor do I act, directly or indirectly, in any such capacity, or in the capacity of Clerk of or to any of the persons above described, or as Clerk of or to any officer in any Court of Law or Equity.

Dated this 6th day of November 1888.

(Signature) *M. K. Gandhi*

WE, the undersigned, do hereby certify that we believe the above-named Mohandas Karamchand Gandhi to be a gentleman of respectability, and a proper person to be admitted a Member of the said Society.

a Barrister of the Inner Temple and Lincoln's Inn
a Barrister of Lincoln's Inn

By an Order of the Bench Table dated the 2nd of June, 1865, it is Ordered that Notice of the two under-mentioned Rules be given, and it is hereby given, to every person who applies to be admitted to this Inn, or to be called to the Bar:

"1.—That no person in Holy Orders be admitted as a Student or called to the Bar by this Society, without first undertaking and signing a Declaration that he has not for the last 12 months held any Clerical preferment or office, or performed any Clerical functions; and that he will not, while a Member of the Society, hold such preferment or office, or perform such functions.

"2.—That any person who is afterwards found to have either made such Declaration untruly, or not to have declared the fact of his being in Holy Orders, shall be liable to have his name removed from the books of the Society, and, if at the Bar, to have his Call vacated."

Expense of Admission .£10 5 2
Stamp Duty . . 25 1 3
£35 6 5
Fee for attendance at Lectures . 5 5 0
£40 11 5

Mr. LAWRENCE, Treasurer.

Admit *M. K. Gandhi*

(facsimile)
(Signature) *M. K. Gandhi*

Living In London

1888–91

I USED to walk about 8 miles every day and in all I had three walks daily...Even the coldest weather or densest fog did not prevent me from having my usual walks.

SEND ME some *mashaala* and fine-ground *saalam*[15] in tinplated light-weight containers.

Letter in Gujarati to the family in Rajkot, November 1888;
Gandhiji Ni Dinavari *(1976),* Navajivan, *compiled by C.B. Dalal*

IN INDIA I had never read a newspaper. But here I succeeded in cultivating a liking for them by regular reading. I always glanced over *The Daily News, The Daily Telegraph,* and *The Pall Mall Gazette.* This took me hardly an hour. I therefore began to wander about. I launched out in search of a vegetarian restaurant...

A, p. 29–30; G

'MY NAME is Gandhi. You have, of course, never heard of it.'

To the humanitarian Henry S. Salt (1851–1939) at
The Central, a vegetarian restaurant, 16 Saint Bride Street off
Farrington Street, London, in October or November 1888
quoted by Pyarelal in MG: EP, *p. 246*

... OIL AND butter play an important part in the preparation of vegetables (in India). Often gram flour is mixed with them. Simply boiled vegetables are never eaten. I never saw a boiled potato in India.

From a talk entitled 'Foods of India', given at The Waverly Restaurant,
London, on 21 April 1891 and published in The Vegetarian Messenger,
London, 1 June 1891, CWMG Vol. 1, p. 40; E

I CAME in contact with those who were regarded as pillars of vegetarianism and began my own experiments in dietetics. I stopped taking the sweets and condiments I had got from home. The mind having taken a different turn, the fondness for condiments wore away, and I now relished the boiled spinach cooked without condiments. Many such experiments taught me that the real seat of taste was not the tongue but the mind.

A, *p. 35; G*

(I STOOD in front of) those great palaces called public houses in London, where people went in as sober men and came out ... dead drunk.

CWMG *Vol. 26, p. 390; E*

MY COWARDICE was on a par with my reserve. ...

My landlady's[16] daughter took me one day to the lovely hills around Ventnor ... chattering away all the while. I responded to her chatter sometimes with a whispered 'yes' or 'no' or at the most, 'yes, how beautiful'. She was flying like a bird whilst I was wondering when I should get back home ... In spite of her high-heeled boots, this sprightly young lady of twenty five dashed down the hill like an arrow. I was shamefacedly struggling to get down. She stood at the foot smiling and cheering me and offering to come and drag me. How could I be so chicken-hearted? With the greatest difficulty, and crawling at intervals, I somehow managed to scramble to the bottom. She loudly laughed 'bravo' and shamed me all the more. ...

A, *p. 39; G*

MY LANDLADY in London always used to say 'whenever I am down there is nothing like a glass of stout to pick me up'.

(*from* 'Louis Fischer Papers' *deposited in the New York Public Library.*)

I KNOW every nook and corner of London where I lived for three years and somewhat of Oxford and Cambridge and Manchester too ... I used to read in the Inner Temple Library, and would often attend Dr Parker's[17] sermons in the Temple Church. ...

CWMG *Vol. 76, p. 287; E*

THERE WAS a great exhibition at Paris in 1890. I had read about its elaborate preparations and I also had a keen desire to see Paris. So I thought I had better combine two things in one and go there at this juncture. A particular attraction of the Exhibition was the Eiffel Tower, constructed entirely of iron, and nearly 1000 feet high ... There was a restaurant on the first platform and just for the satisfaction of being able to say that I had had my lunch at a great height, I threw away seven shillings on it ... There is no art about the Eiffel Tower. In no way can it be said to have contributed to the real beauty of the Exhibition. Men flocked to see it and ascended it as it was a novelty and of unique dimensions. It was the toy of the Exhibition. We are attracted by toys and the Tower was a good demonstration of the fact that we are all children attracted by trinkets.

A, p. 47; G

Dr Josiah Oldfield:[18] Why not accept Christianity?
MKG: I would not care to study Christianity without having studied my own religion first.

Quoted in JJD–AIPSA *1909; p. 30*

ABOUT THE same time I met a good Christian from Manchester in a vegetarian boarding house. He talked to me about Christianity. I narrated to him my Rajkot recollections. He was pained to hear them. He said, 'I am a vegetarian. I do not drink. Many Christians are meat-eaters and drink, no doubt; but neither meat-eating nor drinking is enjoined by Scripture. Do please read the Bible.' I accepted his advice, and he got me a copy. I have a faint recollection that he himself used to sell copies of the Bible, and I purchased from him an edition containing maps, concordance, and other aids. I began reading it, but I could not possibly read through the Old Testament. I read the Book of Genesis, and the chapters that followed invariably sent me to sleep. But just for the sake of being able to say that I had read it, I plodded through the other books with much difficulty and without the least interest or understanding. I disliked reading the Book of Numbers.

But the New Testament produced a different impression, especially the Sermon On The Mount which went straight to my heart. I compared it with the Gita.

A, p. 42; G

AND HOW could I help knowing something of atheism too? Every Indian knew Bradlaugh's[19] name and his so-called atheism. ...

It was about this time that Bradlaugh died. He was buried in the Woking Cemetery. I attended the funeral, as I believe every Indian residing in London did. A few clergymen also were present to do him the last honours. On our way back from the funeral we had to wait at the station for our train. A champion atheist from the crowd heckled one of these clergymen. 'Well, sir, you believe in the existence of God?'

'I do', said the good man in a low tone.

'You also agree that the circumference of the Earth is 28, 000 miles, don't you?' said the atheist with a smile of self-assurance.

'Indeed.'

'Pray tell me then the size of your God and where he may be?'

'Well, if we but knew, He resides in the hearts of us both.'

'Now, now, don't take me to be a child', said the champion with a triumphant look at us.

The clergyman assumed a humble silence.

This talk still further increased my prejudice against atheism.

A, p. 43; G

IN ENGLAND, when I had to study hard, I used to spend not more than half an hour all told for preparing my morning and evening meals. In the morning I used to make some porridge which took exactly 20 minutes. If I prepared something in the evening, it would be a soup, which required only a little watching and no stirring. So the only time I spent after the soup would be for mixing the ingredients. I would then put the mixture on the stove and, while sitting by its side to watch it, read some book.

The Diary of Mahadev Desai Vol. 1, p. 249; CWMG Vol. 15, p. 47; G

DURING THE last year, as far as I can remember, of my stay in England, that is in 1890, there was a Vegetarian Conference at Portsmouth to which an Indian friend[20] and I were invited ...

We returned from the Conference in the evening. After dinner we sat down to play a rubber of bridge, in which our landlady joined, as is customary in England even in respectable households. Every player indulges in innocent jokes as a matter of course, but here my companion and our host began to make indecent ones as well. I did not know that my friend was an adept in the art. It captured me and I also joined in. Just when I was about to go beyond the limit, leaving the cards and the game to themselves, God through the good companion uttered the blessed warning: 'Whence this devil in you, my boy? Be off, quick!'

I was ashamed. I took the warning, and expressed within myself gratefulness to my friend. Remembering the vow I had taken before my mother, I fled from the scene. To my room I went quaking, trembling, and with beating heart, like a quarry escaped from its pursuer.

I recall this as the first occasion on which a woman, other than my wife, moved me to lust.

A, p. 44; G

I PASSED my examination, [21] was called to the bar on the 10 of June 1891 and enrolled in the High Court on the 11th. On the 12th I sailed[22] for home.

A, p. 50; G

WHO SHOULD go to England?[23] ... all who can afford should go to England ... While in England, he is alone, no wife ... no parents ... no children ... He is the master of his time.

CWMG Vol. 1, pp. 68–71; E

Doke:[24] What idea did you form of English life? Did it impress you favourably?

MKG (emphatically): Yes, even now, next to India, I would rather live in London than in any other place in the world.

To Joseph J. Doke in 1908, AIPSA, p. 32; E

Part Three

1891–3

Gandhi and Kasturba, Johannesburg,
July 1914

BACK IN INDIA

The sahib said 'you must go now' ... He called his peon
and ordered him to show me the door. I was still
hesitating when the peon came in, placed his hands
on my shoulders, and put me out of the room ...
This shock changed the course of my life.

This Part is brief and proportionate to the period in Gandhi's life to which its entries pertain: the three years that he spent in India on his return from London as a barrister until his departure for South Africa. That he wrote home regularly from London is well established and documented.

His elder brother Lakshmidas kept Mohandas in modest means. The thrifty student did not fail to cut his own needs in order to live simply and also, on occasion, as Pyarelal tells us, to send some of the money he received from his brothers back to India—to Sheikh Mehtab, a rather remarkable phenomenon. Of his letters, if any, to Kasturba no trace remains. Perhaps the 'culture' of 19th century Kathiawari domesticity did not permit that interaction. There is also no reference in his autobiography to his eagerness to rejoin his wife, the arrival in Bombay being overcast by the news of Putlibai's death.

That the reunion with Kasturba was decreed by nature to be as passionate as it was private needs no greater documentation than provided by the birth of their second son Manilal, within a year of Gandhi's return home. Sheikh Mehtab does not feature prominently in records of this three-year interregnum in India (Rajkot and Bombay). In fact Mehtab is replaced in the position of 'exclusive friend' by another very contrary spirit.

The major friendship formed in London, with Dr Pranjivan Mehta, led to Gandhi's getting to meet the person who came nearest to becoming his spiritual 'guru'. Rajachandra, [1] or Raychandbhai as he was addressed by friends, was eight years Mohandas' senior. He was the son-in-law of Dr Mehta's brother. He was a jaina by choice and though a householder, and a businessman, something of a reclusive meditationist.

It may be fair to say that it is from Rajchandra that Gandhi acquired his sense of the 'inner voice', which he was later to describe in the following words:

REASON AND THE INNER VOICE

What do you mean by asserting that there is no guiding force in the universe? How can we make such an assertion? My statement seems to have been somewhat twisted in this context. I have only said that Truth is identical with God and you may take it to be the Moving Spirit. In this context *karta*[2] does not have the meaning we usually attribute to it. Therefore Truth is *karta* as well as *akarta*.[3] But this is only an intellectual explanation. There is nothing wrong in this matter in believing whatever one's heart accepts, as no man has perfect knowledge of God nor can he express whatever little knowledge he has. It is true that I do not depend upon my intellect to decide upon any action. For me the reasoned course of action is held in check subject to the sanction of the inner voice. I do not know if others would call it the mysterious power or whatsoever. I have never deliberated upon this nor analysed it, I have felt no need of doing so either. I have faith, and knowledge, too, that a Power exists beyond reasoning. This suffices for me. I am unable to clarify this any further as I know nothing more in the matter.

Letter, dated 25 May 1932, to Bhuskute[4] *(H) Mahadevbhaini Diary*
Vol. 1, pp. 173–4

* * *

The brief sojourn in India was notable for a major experience for Gandhi. It was his first direct encounter of Raj hauteur and of what, in strictly legal terms, would tantamount to being manhandled. He describes the episode with Sir Charles Ollivant[5] in vivid detail but with maximum fairness to the protagonist of the rudeness. The experience taught Gandhi the criticality of contexts. A cordiality in England can become alchemized into arrogance in India; an acquaintance can become a different being when occupying a position of authority. It is one of the ironies of history that, some years later, it was given to another barrister of Kathiawari origin, Muhammad Ali Jinnah,[6] who is regarded in history as an adversary of Gandhi, to have put this particular English official firmly in his place—again, in a different context.

* * *

Work did not come Gandhi's way; humiliation did. And if it was a Brahmin who had encouraged the nineteen-year-old Gandhi to go to London to join the Inns of Court, a Muslim now opened a door for the twenty-five-year-old barrister to go to a new country, a new continent to earn and save some money. What was waiting to be earned was a monumental reputation and what was waiting to be saved was a community's honour.

I Return Home

MY DEAR brother[7] had come to meet me at the dock ... I was pining to see my mother.[8] I did not know that she was no more in the flesh to receive me back into her bosom. The sad news was now given me, and I underwent the usual ablution. My brother had kept me ignorant of her death, which took place whilst I was still in England. I did not give myself up to any wild expression of grief. I could even check the tears, and took to life just as though nothing had happened.

A, p. 73; G

Raychandbhai

Bombay
July 1891

DR MEHTA[9] ... introduced me to Raychand or Raychandra, the son-in-law of an elder brother of Dr Mehta ...

Raychandbhai's commercial transactions covered hundreds of thousands. He was a connoisseur of pearls and diamonds. No knotty business problem was too difficult for him. But all these things were not the centre round which his life revolved. That centre was the passion to see God face to face.

Though I was then groping and could not be said to have any serious interest in religious discussion, still I found his talk of absorbing interest. I have since met many a religious leader or teacher. I have tried to meet the heads of various faiths, and I must say that no one else has ever made on me the impression that Raychandbhai did.

And yet in spite of this regard for him I could not enthrone him in my heart as my Guru. The throne has remained vacant and my search still continues.

A, p. 52–3; G

I SEEK a guru. That a guru is needed I accept. But, as long as I have not come upon a worthy guru, I shall continue to be my own guru.

CWMG Vol. 14, p. 75; H

I HAVE always been one who would not miss a chance for a jest.[10]

CWMG Vol. 21, p. 430; G

A Shock

Rajkot
Between 1891 and April 1892

MY BROTHER[11] had been secretary and adviser to the late Ranasaheb of Porbandar before he was installed on his *gadi*, and hanging over his head at this time was the charge of having given wrong advice when in that office. The matter had gone to the Political Agent[12] who was prejudiced against my brother. Now I had known this officer when in England, and he may be said to have been fairly friendly to me. My brother thought that I should avail myself of the friendship and, putting in a good word on his behalf, try to disabuse the Political Agent of his prejudice.

I could not refuse him, so I went to the officer much against my will. I knew I had no right to approach him and was fully conscious that I was compromising my self-respect. But I sought an appointment[13] and got it. I reminded him of the old acquaintance, but I immediately saw that Kathiawar was different from England; that an officer on leave was not the same as an officer on duty. The *sahib* was impatient. 'Your brother is an intriguer. I want to hear nothing more from you. I have no time. If your brother has anything to say, let him apply through the proper channel.'

The answer was enough, was perhaps deserved. But selfishness is blind. I went on with my story. The sahib got up and said: 'You must go now.'

'But please hear me out', said I. That made him more angry. He called his peon and ordered him to show me the door. I was still hesitating when the peon came in, placed his hands on my shoulders and put me out of the room.

The sahib went away as also the peon, and I departed, fretting and fuming. I at once wrote out and sent over a note to this effect: 'You have insulted me. You have assaulted me through your peon. If you make no amends, I shall have to proceed against you.'

Quick came the answer through his *sowar*.[14]

'You were rude to me. I asked you to go and you would not. I had no option but to order my peon to show you the door. Even after he asked you to leave the office, you did not do so. He therefore had to use just enough force to send you out. You are at liberty to proceed as you wish.'

Sir Pherozeshah Mehta[15] happened to be in Rajkot at this time, having come down from Bombay for some case. But how could a junior barrister like me dare to see him? So I sent him the papers of my case, through the vakil who had engaged him, and begged for his advice. 'Tell Gandhi,' he said, 'such things are the common experience of many vakils and barristers. He is still fresh from England, and hot-blooded. He does not know British officers. If he would earn something and have an easy time here, let him tear up the note and pocket the insult. He will gain nothing by proceeding against the sahib, and on the contrary will very likely ruin himself. Tell him he has yet to know life.'

The advice was as bitter as poison to me, but I had to swallow it. I pocketed the insult, but also profited by it. 'Never again shall I place myself in such a false position, never again shall I try to exploit friendship in this way, ' said I to myself, and since then I have never been guilty of a breach of that determination. This shock changed the course of my life.

A, *Part II; G*

My Search For A Job

Bombay
16 November 1891

To
The Prothonotary and Registrar
of the High Court of Judicature
Bombay

Sir,
I am desirous of being admitted as an Advocate of the High Court. I was called to the Bar in England on the 10th June last. I have kept twelve terms in the Inner Temple and I intend to practice in the Bombay Presidency.

CWMG Vol. 1, p. 50; E

Bombay
Between April and August 1892

School Principal: Are you a graduate?
MKG: No. But I have matriculated from London University.
Principal: Right enough, but we want a graduate.
MKG: I had Latin as my second subject.
Principal: Thank you, this will do. Now you can go.

Adapted from A, p. 57, G and P, MG: EP, p. 254

To South Africa

Rajkot
Early 1893

IN THE meantime a Meman firm from Porbandar wrote to my brother making the following offer: 'We have business in South Africa. Ours is a big firm, and we have a big case there in the Court, our claim being £40, 000. It has been going on for a long time. We have engaged the services of the best vakils and barristers. If you sent your brother there, he would be useful to us and also to himself ...'

This was hardly going there as a barrister. It was going as a servant of the firm. But I wanted somehow to leave India. There was also the tempting opportunity of seeing a new country, and of having new experience. Also I could send £105 to my brother and help in the expenses of the household. I closed with the offer without any haggling, and got ready to go to South Africa.

A, *p. 61; G*

April 1893

WHEN STARTING[16] for South Africa I did not feel the wrench of separation which I had experienced when leaving for England. My mother was now no more. I had gained some knowledge of the world and of travel abroad ... This time I only felt the pang of parting from my wife. Another baby[17] had been born to us since my return from England. Our love could not yet be called free from lust, but it was getting gradually purer. Since my return from Europe, we had lived very little together; and as I had now become her teacher, however indifferent, and helped her to make certain reforms, we both felt the necessity of being more together, if only to continue the reforms.

But the attraction of South Africa rendered the separation bearable. 'We are bound to meet again in a year,' I said to her, by way of consolation and left ...

A, *p. 62; G*

Part Four

1893-7

Founders of the Natal Indian Congress, 1895;
Gandhi standing fourth from the left

In South Africa—The Initial Years

*I am yet inexperienced and young and, therefore, quite liable
to make mistakes. The responsibility undertaken is quite
out of proportion to my ability ... [Yet] I am the only
available person who can handle the question.*

This Part is about Gandhi's first three years in South Africa, 1893–6.
This was a phase when the underutilized barrister found, for the
first time in his life, a cause beyond himself and became a public
figure recognized for his integrity, intelligence, and an apparently
inexhaustible fund of energy. *Satyagraha In South Africa* (1928) and
The Story Of My Experiments With Truth (1930) are the books
where Gandhi describes this major transition in his life. Later in
life, in letters and conversation, he was to recount these as defining
experiences. Drawing from that body of essential expression, Part
Four of this volume re-enacts that dramatic phase.

This was also the period when an outstanding Indian, Bal
Gangadhar Tilak was rising to prominence in Indian politics and
another Indian of epic stature, Swami Vivekananda was preparing
to sail to Chicago for the World Parliament of Religions where an
unanticipated and unprecedented recognition awaited his charismatic
articulation of Vedanta.

Gandhi's 'launching' was, however, of an altogether different order.
It is not difficult to draw a connection between Gandhi's delayed
reaction to the insult offered to him in Charles Ollivant's office room
which he says 'changed the course' of his life and the reflexive
responses to the episode of the puggaree in the Durban Court and
to the one, now famous, at the Pietermaritzburg railway station.

Four years short of a century after that episode, on 25 April 1997, President Nelson Mandela conferred the freedom of the city of Pietermaritzburg posthumously on Gandhi. Mandela said on that compelling occasion:

> Your Worship the Mayor of Pietermaritzburg;
> Your Excellency the High Commissioner for India,
> Ladies and gentlemen;
> Citizens of Maritzburg,
> Today we are righting a century-old wrong. This station, once one of the world's most notorious symbols of discrimination, intolerance, and oppression, today proclaims a message of dignity restored. ...
> Just as the incident we are commemorating fired Gandhi's resistance to oppression, may today's award inspire us all to join hands to realize our shared vision of a better life for all.
> Mr Mayor,
> ... Your Council's decision to confer the Freedom on the platform of this station—and to transport us along the route that Gandhi travelled in 1893—is a fine example of how communities across the land are helping to recover and celebrate our history. ...
> It is a token of our appreciation of Mahatma Gandhi's enormous contribution to the birth of a New Pietermaritzburg and the New South Africa. It is a token of our gratitude to the people of India who stood by us during the darkest moments in our history.

Within hours of that experience of 31 May 1893, Gandhi began turning into a skilful drafter of memorials. The cause? The protection of the dignity of British Indians in South Africa. Simultaneously and typically of his public role in later life, he asked the Indian community in South Africa to do some introspection as well about their lifestyles, their petty divisions, their lack of self-discipline. Disfranchisement was staring the Indian South African in the face. Gandhi set up the Natal Indian Congress, styled after the Indian National Congress. The political organizing involved in the fighting for the political rights of the Indian community was as new to him as it was to the community. And though increasingly supportive of his initiatives, the community left him in this initial period to shoulder the brunt of the struggle by himself.

While Indians in South Africa were in the process of losing the chance to exercise basic political rights, back home in India, around this time, Governor General Lansdowne was introducing the Indian Council Act under which Gopal Krishna Gokhale was to enter the legislature and, incidentally, begin to play a decisive role in shaping the young Gandhi's public career. This was also the time when in London, another Kathiawari, Muhammad Ali Jinnah, was fine-tuning his legal studies and, under Naoroji's guidance, acquiring political spurs.

Gandhi's increasing public and political involvement and a busy calendar of legal work left him virtually no time to miss his little family that had stayed back in Rajkot. Curiously, he asked his friend Sheikh Mehtab to come over and 'run' the home for him. Eighteen ninety five brought that decade-old friendship to an abrupt end. An entry in this Part describes how that snapping came about.

In 1896, Gandhi decided to make a visit home and bring Kastur and the two boys to South Africa where, he saw, work was going to detain him for a long time. Jinnah returned to India the same year from London, and joined the Indian National Congress. Disembarking in Calcutta (now Kolkata), Gandhi travelled extensively within the country, giving speeches and press interviews on the plight of Indians in South Africa. He prepared, while in Rajkot, 6000 copies of a tract which came to be known as *The Green Pamphlet*, highlighting in detail the disabilities suffered by Indians in South Africa.

Reports of the campaigning done by Gandhi in India reached South Africa before his return with the family on 13 January 1897.[1] That day brought Gandhi to death's door but stayed the action there.

This Part deals with two major evolutions in and within Gandhi. The first is the movement of the private Mohandas, son of Karamchand, to the public 'M.K. Gandhi'. The second is of one whose instinctive preference for not hurting fellow beings was beginning to evolve slowly through inner 'pulls' and outer 'pushings', into a system of interconnected ideas on non-violence, both as a philosophy as well as a method.

It also gives a representative excerpt from a statement of accounts that Gandhi prepared for rendering to the Natal Indian Congress which had advanced him money to cover his expenses over the six months' visit to India in 1896, when he met his future political mentor Gokhale for the first time. I have found that 'grocer's list' fascinating for what it tells us not just of Gandhi's frugality and careful handling of scarce cash, but of the range of his interests and activities. These included—effortlessly—petitionings to the Viceroy, tipping a magician and going to the theatre. Entertainment was part of the twenty-seven-year-old barrister's Indian itinerary and he did not stint on hiring porters and punkah-pullers in Madras for fourteen days.

The *Puggaree*

May 1893

THE PORT of Natal is Durban, also known as Port Natal. Abdulla Sheikh[2] was there to receive me ... Abdulla Sheikh was practically unlettered, but he had a rich fund of experience ... My dress marked me out from other Indians. I had a frock-coat and a turban, an imitation of the Bengal *pugree*. ...[3]

On the second or third day of my arrival, he took me to see the Durban court. There he introduced me to several people and seated me next to his Attorney.[4] The magistrate kept staring at me and finally asked me to take off my turban. This I refused to do and left the court. So here too there was fighting in store for me.

A, *Part II; G*

'My Ignorance'[5]

... WHEN I first went to South Africa, I had absolutely no idea as to what 'p. note' meant. For a few days I hid my ignorance, but at the cost of increasing uneasiness. I realized that it was impossible for me even to understand Dada Abdulla's case, so long as I did not know what the abbreviation 'p. note' stood for. I, therefore, declared my ignorance forthwith. When I came to know that this formidable 'p. note' meant only 'promissory note', I burst into a loud laugh, not at my ignorance but at my false shame, because no dictionary could have revealed this mystery of 'p. note' to me. So the straight thing is to immediately ask a knowing person whatever we are ignorant about. It matters little if we are dubbed fools, but it would be really harmful if, out of our ignorance, we commit a blunder.

The Diary of Mahadev Desai *Vol. 2, p. 54*

'I Refuse To Get Out'

31 May 1893

THE TRAIN[6] reached Maritzburg, the capital of Natal, at about 9 p.m. Beddings used to be provided at this station. A railway servant came and asked me if I wanted one. 'No,' said I, 'I have one with me.' He went away. But a passenger came next, and looked me up and down. He saw that I was a 'coloured' man. This disturbed him. Out he went and came in again with one or two officials. They all kept quiet, when another official came to me and said, 'Come along, you must go to the van compartment.'

'But I have a first class ticket', said I.

'That doesn't matter', rejoined the other. 'I tell you, you must go to the van compartment.'

'I tell you, I was permitted to travel in this compartment at Durban, and I insist on going on in it.'

'No, you won't', said the official. 'You must leave this compartment, or else I shall have to call a police constable to push you out.'

'Yes, you may. I refuse to get out voluntarily.'

The constable came. He took me by the hand and pushed me out. My luggage was also taken out. I refused to go to the other compartment and the train steamed away. I went and sat in the waiting room, keeping my hand-bag with me, and leaving the other luggage where it was. The railway authorities had taken charge of it.

It was winter, and winter in the higher regions of South Africa is severely cold. Maritzburg being at a high altitude, the cold was extremely bitter. My overcoat was in my luggage, but I did not dare to ask for it lest I should be insulted again, so I sat and shivered. There was no light in the room. A passenger came in at about mid-night and possibly wanted to talk to me. But I was in no mood to talk.

I began to think of my duty. Should I fight for my rights or go back to India, or should I go on to Pretoria without minding the insults, and return to India after finishing the case? It would be cowardice to run back to India without fulfilling my obligation. The hardship to which I was subjected was superficial—only a symptom of the deep disease of colour prejudice. I should try, if possible, to root out the disease and suffer hardships in the process. Redress for wrongs I should seek only to the extent that would be necessary for the removal of the colour prejudice.

So I decided to take the next available train to Pretoria.

A, p. 67; G

'He Was Strong And I Was Weak'

1 June 1893

THE TRAIN reached Charlestown in the morning. There was no railway, in those days, between Charlestown and Johannesburg, but only a stage-coach, which halted at Standerton for the night *en route* ... Passengers had to be accommodated inside the coach but as I was regarded as a 'coolie' and looked a stranger, it would be proper thought the 'leader', as the white man in charge of the coach was called, not to seat me with the white passengers. There were seats on either side of the coaches. The leader sat on one of these as a rule. Today he sat inside and gave me his seat ...

At about three o'clock the coach reached Pardekoph. Now the leader desired to sit where I was seated, as he wanted to smoke and possibly to have some fresh air. So he took a piece of dirty sack-cloth from the driver, spread it on the footboard and, addressing me, said, 'Sami,⁷ you sit on this, I want to sit near the driver.' The insult was more than I could bear. In fear and trembling I said to him, 'It was you who seated me here, though I should have been accommodated inside. I put up with the insult. Now that you want to sit outside and smoke, you would have me sit at your feet. I will not do so, but I am prepared to sit inside.'

As I was struggling through these sentences, the man came down upon me and began heavily to box my ears. He seized me by the arm and tried to drag me down. I clung to the brass rails of the coachbox and was determined to keep my hold even at the risk of breaking my wrist bones. The passengers were witnessing the scene—the man swearing at me, dragging and belabouring me, and I remaining still. He was strong and I was weak. Some of the passengers were moved to pity and exclaimed: 'Man, let him alone. Don't beat him. He is not to blame. He is right. If he can't stay there, let him come and sit with us.' 'No fear', cried the man, but he seemed somewhat crestfallen and stopped beating me. He let go my arm, swore at me a little more, and asking the Hottentot servant who was sitting on the other side of the coachbox to sit on the footboard, took the seat so vacated.

A, p. 68; G

MY ACTIVE non-violence began from that date.

In an interview to Dr John Mott, an American missionary,
Harijan December 1938

Sacred Or Superstitious?

June 1894

MR COATES[8] had great affection for me. He saw, around my neck, the Vaishnava[9] necklace of tulasi[10] beads. He thought it to be superstition, and was pained by it. 'This superstition does not become you. Come, let me break the necklace.'

'No, you will not. It is a sacred gift from my mother.'

'But do you believe in it?'

'I do not know its mysterious significance. I do not think I should come to harm if I did not wear it. But I cannot, without sufficient reason, give up a necklace that she put round my neck out of love and in the conviction that it would be conducive to my welfare. When, with the passage of time, it wears away and breaks of its own accord, I shall have no desire to get a new one. But this necklace cannot be broken.'

A, p. 75; G

I DID not discard the tulsi-kanthi, but, after I had worn it for some years in South Africa, it left me, that is, it snapped.

I don't regard the practice as an essential requirement of sanatana dharma[11] and so, when the kanthi snapped, I did not replace it.

CWMG Vol. 53, p. 16 E

A Patrol's Kick

Pretoria
1894

I ALWAYS went out for a walk through President Street[12] to an open plain. President Kruger's[13] house was in this street—a very modest, unostentatious building ... Only the presence of a police patrol before the house indicated that it belonged to some official ... Once, one of these men without giving me the slightest warning, without even asking me to leave the footpath, pushed and kicked me into the street. I was dismayed. Before I could question him as to his behaviour, Mr Coates, who happened to be passing the spot on horseback, hailed me and said: 'Gandhi, I have seen everything. I shall gladly be your witness in court if you proceed against the man. I am very sorry you have been so rudely assaulted.'[14]

'You need not be sorry', I said. 'What does the poor man know? All coloured people are the same to him. He no doubt treats Negroes just as he has treated me. I have made it a rule not to go to court in respect of any personal grievance. So I do not intend to proceed against him.'

But I never again went through this street.

A, *p. 79; G
P*, MG: EP, *p. 493*

Letter To Dadabhai Naoroji

Durban
5 July 1894

THE FIRST Parliament of Natal under Responsible Government has ... for the most part occupied itself with legislation affecting Indians, by no means favourably ... The reasons given for the sweeping measure to disfranchise Indians were that they had never exercised the Franchise before, and that they were not fit for it ... I earnestly request your undivided attention to the cause ...

I am yet inexperienced and young and, therefore, quite liable to make mistakes. The responsibility undertaken is quite out of proportion to my ability ... I am the only available person who can handle the question. You will, therefore, oblige me very greatly if you will kindly direct and guide me and make necessary suggestions which shall be received as from a father to his child.

CWMG *Vol. 1, pp. 139–40; E*

An Open Letter[15]

Durban
Before 19 December 1894

... EVERYONE I have met with in the Colony has dwelt upon the untruthfulness of the Indians. To a limited extent I admit the charge. It will be very small satisfaction for me to show, in reply to the objection, that other classes do not fare much better in this respect, especially if and when they are placed in the position of the unfortunate Indians ... They cannot dare tell the truth, even for their wantonly ill-treated brother, for fear of receiving ill-treatment from their master. They are not philosophic enough to look with equanimity on the threatened reduction in their miserable rations and serve corporal punishment, did they dare to give evidence against their master. Are these men, then, more to be despised than pitied? Are they to be treated as scoundrels, deserving no mercy, or are they to be treated as helpless creatures, badly in need of sympathy? Is there any class of people who would not do as they are doing under similar circumstances?

CWMG *Vol. 1 pp. 157–9*

August 1895[16]

AN INDIAN named Balasundaram was, in 1894, so ill-treated by his master that two of his teeth were nearly knocked out; they came out through his upper lip causing an issue of blood sufficient to soak his long turban in it. His master admitted the fact but pleaded grave provocation, denied by the man. On receiving the punishment, he seems to have gone to the Protector's house which was close by his master's. The Protector sent word that he must go to his office the next day. The man went, then, to the Magistrate who was much moved at the sight. The turban was kept in court and he was at once sent to the hospital for treatment. The man after having been kept in the hospital for a few days was discharged. He had heard about me and came to my office. He had not recovered sufficiently to be able to speak. I asked him, therefore, to write out his complaint in Tamil which he knew. He wanted to prosecute the master so that his contract of indenture might be cancelled. I asked him if he would be satisfied if his indenture was transferred ... wrote a letter to his master imploring him to consent to the transfer. The master would do nothing of the kind. The magistrate treated us quite differently. He had seen the man while the blood was yet dripping from his lips. The deposition was duly made. On the day of hearing, I explained the whole circumstances and again appealed to the master in open court and offered to withdraw the complaint if he consented to the transfer. The Magistrate then gave the master to understand that, unless he considered my offer more favourably than he seemed to do at the time, consequences might be serious for him. He went on to say that he thought the man was brutally treated. The master said he gave provocation. The Magistrate retorted: 'You had no business to take the law in your own hands and beat the man as if he were a beast.' He adjourned the case for one day in order to enable the master to consider the offer made by me. The master, of course, came down and consented. The Protector then wrote to me that he would not agree to transfer unless I submitted a European name he could approve of. Happily, the Colony is not quite devoid of benevolent men. A Wesleyan local preacher and solicitor, out of charity, undertook to take over the man's services, and thus ended the last act of this painful drama ... This is only a typical instance showing how hard it is for the indentured men to get justice.

> *Burnett Britton, in* Gandhi Arrives in South Africa
> *(Greenleaf Books, Canton, Maine; 1999); CWMG Vol. 2, pp. 20–2*

The 'Friend' Again

1895

[Pyarelal writes: *Gandhiji's multifarious activities left him hardly a moment to attend to his domestic affairs ... To free himself from such cares he, therefore, invited his boyhood friend Sheikh Mehtab who came from Rajkot and was installed in the house*[17] *... Believing that he had reformed, Gandhiji trusted him implicitly. But Mehtab had not changed.]*

MKG's cook (reaching Gandhi in his office[18]): Please come home
   at once. There is a surprise for you.
MKG: Now what is this? How can I leave the office at this hour to
   go and see it? You must tell me what it is.
Cook: You will regret it, if you don't come. That is all I can say.

[*I felt an appeal in his persistence. I went home accompanied by a
clerk[19] and the cook who walked ahead of us. He took me straight
to the upper floor ...' (A. p. 99)*]

Cook (pointing to Sheikh Mehtab's room bolted from inside): Open
   the door and see for yourself.

[*I saw it all. I knocked at the door. No reply! I knocked heavily so as
to make the very walls shake. The door was opened. I saw a prostitute
inside. I asked her to leave the house, never to return'. (A. p. 99)*]

MKG (turning to Mehtab): From this moment I cease to have
   anything to do with you. I have been thoroughly deceived and
   have made a fool of myself. Is this how you requit my trust in you?
SM: I will expose you.
MKG: I have nothing to conceal. Expose whatever I may have done.
   But leave me this moment.

[On Mehtab's refusing to leave, MKG to Lawrence, 'Please go and
inform the Superintendent of Police, with my compliments that a
person living with me has misbehaved himself and I do not want to
keep him in my house, but he refuses to leave. I shall be much obliged
if police help can be sent to me.' (A. p. 100)]

SM(unnerved): Please do not inform the police. I am sorry, I have
   misbehaved. I will go.

[*SM then left*][20]

Cook to MKG: I too am going! I cannot stay in your house; you are
   too easily misled. This is no place for me.

                    Reconstructed from A, Part II and P, MG: EP, pp. 492–3

ONLY RARELY and only between like natures, can friendship be altogether worthy and enduring ... In friendship there is very little scope for reform ... All exclusive intimacies are to be avoided. He who would be friends with God must remain alone, or make the whole world his friend.

A, p. 16

In Bombay[21]

1896

WHILST BUSY in Rajkot with the pamphlet on South Africa, I had an occasion to pay a flying visit to Bombay. It was my intention to educate public opinion in cities on this question by organizing meetings, and Bombay was the first city I chose. First of all I met Justice Ranade, [22] who listened to me with attention, and advised me to meet Sir Pherozeshah Mehta.

... Sir Pherozeshah carefully listened to me. I told him that I had seen Justice Ranade and Tyabji.[23] 'Gandhi,' said he, 'I see that I must help you. I must call a public meeting here.'

A, p. 106; G

IN ACCORDANCE with Sir Pherozeshah's instructions I reported myself at his office at 5 p.m. on the eve of the meeting.

'Is your speech ready, Gandhi?' he asked.

'No, sir,' said I, trembling with fear, 'I think of speaking *extempore*'.

'That will not do in Bombay. Reporting here is bad, and if we would benefit by this meeting, you should write out your speech, and it should be printed before daybreak tomorrow. I hope you can manage this?'

I felt rather nervous, but I said I would try.

'Then, tell me, what time should Mr Munshi come to you for the manuscript?'

'Eleven o'clock tonight', said I.

... This was the first meeting of the kind in my experience. I saw that my voice could reach only a few. I was trembling as I began to read my speech. Sir Pherozeshah cheered me up continually by asking me to speak louder and still louder. I have a feeling that, far from encouraging me, it made my voice sink lower and lower.

A, *pp. 107–8; G*

1896[24]

Accounts[25]

17th September
Printing 6000 copies pamphlet 110-0-0
September
Times of India Directory 10-15-0

21st September
Telegram to Sir W. W. Hunter 113-2-0
Bhimbhai for copying, assisting, etc. 20-0-0
Fruit 2-6-0
Pens 0-4-0
Stamps 0-8-0
Porter for taking books to Institute 0-1-3

27th September
Telegram to Durban 99-6-0

October
Sending Rs 100 by money order 2-1-0
Telegrams—Madras 2-0-0

14th October
Railway station, Madras 0-4-0
Guide 0-4-0
Porter 0-2-0
Carriage (whole day) 4-2-3
Trickman 0-0-6
Papers and envelopes 2-10-0
Carriage for station 1-8-0

15th October
Carriage 4-6-0
Letter carrier 0-10-0

Paper 0-4-0
Tram 0-1-0

16th October
Stamps 1-0-0
Carriage 2-3-0
Paper 0-8-0
Dhobi 1-0-0

17th October
Papers 0-14-0
Carriage (whole day) 4-3-0

18th October
Carriage (half day) 2-3-0
Andrews donation 7-0-0
Sulphur ointment 0-2-0

19th October
Tram fare 0-9-0
Telegram to Wacha 1-6-0
Papers 1-0-0

20th October
Dhobi 0-4-0
Papers 0-12-0
Punkah coolie 0-2-0

21st October
Note paper 0-14-0
Ink and pins 0-3-0
Tape 0-1-0
Magician 0-8-0
Papers 0-10-0
Lace 0-1-0

22nd October
Carriage 2-4-0
Sweets 0-5-3

Photograph 0-6-0
Papers 0-12-0
Tram 0-13-0

23rd October
Carriage 5-0-0
Tram 0-10-0
Stamps 0-8-0

27th October
Carriage 3-4-0
Inland telegrams 18-12-0
Madras Standard a/c. telegrams
& address 30-0-0
Butler's gratuity 9-0-0
Waiter 1-0-0
Bhangi 0-8-0
Cook 1-0-0
Gardener 0-2-0
Keeper 0-2-0
Luggage to Calcutta 3-0-0
Andrews 5-0-0
Hotel bill 74-4-0
Papers 0-10-0
Dhobi 0-12-0
Punkah coolies (14 days) 3-4-0
Fare to Calcutta 122-7-0

31st October
Tea and bread on way to Calcutta 0-9-0
Breakfast 1-15-0
Tiffin 0-7-0
Paper 0-2-0
Porter at station 0-6-0
Porter at Asansol 0-2-0
Porter at hotel 0-4-0
Carriage to hotel 1-0-0
Carriage & theatre 4-12-0

6th November
Carriage 5-4-0

7th November
Theatre 4-0-0
Carriage 1-4-6

8th November
Dhobi 0-4-0

9th November
Hindi & Urdu books 0-12-6
Urdu & Bengali books 4-8-0
Blue books 2-8-0
Carriage 1-2-0
Stamps 0-8-0
Telegram [to] P.N. Mukerjee 2-6-0
Dhobi 0-4-0

10th November
Blue books Bengal Sectt. 11-12-0
Carriage 1-13-6
Telegram *Standard*, Abdulla Coy. 4-14-0
Dhobi 0-3-0
Letter carrier 0-4-0
Paper 0-1-0
Carriage 1-0-0

30th November
Telegram to Secy. of Viceroy 5-4-0

                    P, MG: EP, *p. 730*; CWMG, *Vol. 2, pp. 105–15; E*

The Green Pamphlet

Rajkot
September 1896

THIS UNEXPECTED[26] interview with the editor[27] of *The Pioneer* laid
the foundation of the series of incidents which ultimately led to my

being lynched in Natal. I went straight to Rajkot without halting at Bombay and began to make preparations for writing a pamphlet on the situation in South Africa. The writing and publication of the pamphlet took about a month. It had a green cover and came to be known afterwards as the 'Green Pamphlet'. In it I drew a purposely subdued picture of the condition of Indians in South Africa. The language I used was more moderate than that of the two pamphlets which I have referred to before, [28] as I knew that things heard of from a distance appear bigger than they are. Ten thousand copies were printed and sent to all the papers and leaders of every party in India. *The Pioneer* was the first to notice it editorially. A summary of the article was cabled by Reuter to England, and a summary of that summary was cabled to Natal by Reuter's London office. This cable was not longer than three lines in print. It was a miniature, but exaggerated, edition of the picture I had drawn of the treatment accorded to the Indians in Natal, and it was not in my words. We shall see later on the effect this had in Natal. In the meanwhile every paper of note commented at length on the question. To get these pamphlets ready for posting was no small matter. It would have been expensive too, if I had employed paid help for preparing wrappers etc. But I hit upon a much simpler plan. I gathered together all the children in my locality and asked them to volunteer two or three hours' labour of a morning, when they had no school.[29] This they willingly agreed to do. I promised to bless them and give them, as a reward, used postage stamps which I had collected. They got through the work in no time. That was my first experiment of having little children as volunteers.

A, *pp. 103–4*

'Coolie' And 'Sammy'

Madras[30]
26 October 1896

... EVERY INDIAN without distinction is contemptuously called a 'coolie'. He is also called 'Sammy', 'Ramasammy', anything but 'Indian'. Indian schoolmasters are called 'coolie schoolmasters'. Indian storekeepers are 'coolie storekeepers'. Two Indian gentlemen from

Bombay, Messrs Dada Abdulla and Moosa Hajee Cassim, own steamers. Their steamers are 'coolie ships'.

There is a very respectable firm of Madras traders by name, A. Colandaveloo Pillay & Co. They have built a large block of buildings in Durban; these buildings are called 'coolie stores', and the owners are 'coolie owners'. ...

We are the 'Asian dirt' to be 'heartily cursed', we are 'chock-full of vice' and we 'live upon rice', we are the 'stinking coolie' living on 'the smell of an oiled rag', we are 'the black vermin', we are described in the Statute books as 'semi-barbarous Asiatics, or persons belonging to the uncivilized races of Asia'. We 'breed like rabbits' and a gentleman at a meeting lately held in Durban said he was sorry we could not be shot like them. ...

CWMG Vol. 2, pp. 71–2; E

A Tempestuous Return

Durban
13 January 1897

... As soon as we landed[31] some youngsters recognized me and shouted, 'Gandhi, Gandhi' ... Then they pelted[32] me with stones, brickbats, and rotten eggs. Someone snatched away my turban, whilst others began to batter and kick me.

A burly fellow came up to me, slapped me in the face and then kicked me. I was about to fall down unconscious when I held on to the railings of a house nearby. I took breath for a while and when the fainting was over, proceeded on my way. But I remember well that even then my heart did not arraign my assailants.

A, p. 117 and SiSA, p. 54; G

When I held on to that bar,[33] I was mentally prepared for death. I could not have inflicted any serious injury on my assailant. If, however, I had lost hold of the bar, I would have struggled on, would perhaps have slapped or bitten the man and would have resisted till death.

CWMG Vol. 51, pp. 24–5; G

Part Five

1898–1901

With the Indian Ambulance Corps during the Boer War of 1899–1900;
Gandhi sitting (second row) fourth from the left

Settling in South Africa

Kastur: '*... What right have you to my necklace?*'
Mohandas: '*... Is the necklace given to you for your service or my service?*'
Kastur: '*I have toiled and moiled for you day and night. Is that no service?*'

From Pietermaritzburg onwards, the 'personal' in Gandhi began yielding almost with each passing day to the 'public'. This Part contains writings essential to an understanding of that irreversible transition. Kastur, transported from the quietude of domesticity across a stormy sea to a life of hectic public interventions in her own space as Gandhi's wife, is at the heart of this section of the compilation.

Encouraged by her husband, prior to their departure for South Africa, to adopt the Parsi way of wearing her sari and to attire the children in a manner they were unused to, Kastur was being the very epitome of adjustment. Thrown overnight into a world of strangers albeit many of them Gujarati speaking, living in a house and surroundings that were totally unfamiliar in architecture, fitments, furniture, plumbing, and 'kitchen-ing', she was also seeing for the first time large numbers of people of a different ethnic origin— Caucasian, African, and Chinese. And even from among those of Indian origin she was coming to know and live amongst those belonging to religious denominations other than her own, speaking languages her ears were unused to, eating kinds of food, though vegetarian, she had not known of.

Gandhi's love of her was demanding; his demands on her were loving. But they were not conventional! Nor were they consistent. They changed as he grew. And they could change rapidly as well as radically. She had now given Mohandas their third son, Ramdas. No reader can miss the fact that the young Mohandas did not give Kastur's maternity much respite. The first 'mite' (to use Gandhi's phrase) was born when both were barely sixteen, Harilal when they had just turned eighteen. Manilal was born within a year of Gandhi's return from London and Ramdas, born in Durban, had been conceived even before Mohandas and Kasturba left for South Africa after his brief sojourn in India in 1896. The birth in 1900 of Devadas, the fourth and last son, came three years after Ramdas' arrival. This Part describes that event and shows, once again, Gandhi's penchant for self-instructors or primers—this time in midwifery and child-rearing.

And then, change again! The heat of passion was to turn to the ice of abstinence. Train journeys and books have turned chapters in few lives as they have in Gandhi's. There is a reference to another 'book' read in a train journey that might have triggered the decision to abjure sex *if only I willed it.* There are no details available of Kastur's being an equal party to the decision, although she does not seem to have raised any objection.

In the larger domain outside the house, Gandhi was being more than consensual, addressed increasingly by Indian South Africans as 'Bhai' rather than 'saheb', Gandhi appreciating the 'sweet flavour' of that expression. He says ex-indentured Indians (mostly Tamil) used the expression as well, which means there was a cross-lingual bonding taking place within the diverse Indian community in South Africa, something Gandhi was to value and propagate later.

Gandhi's self-image in South Africa was that of a British Indian, his three years in London having sharpened that image to include a sense of complete racial equality. He had experienced no colour prejudice in Victorian England, whence his shock at Ollivant's behaviour in Rajkot and his inability to accept without protest the colour-based discriminations he was a daily witness to in South Africa. Every British Indian was, he felt, as entitled to political rights as a Briton was. Since, in his view, rights brought with them responsibilities, he lost not a moment in seizing the opportunity of the Boer War (1899–1902) to demonstrate that the Indian in South Africa was second to no Briton in fighting on the British side of the ballistic divide. Organizing 1000 volunteers to enter a zone of war, albeit as non-combatants, was no ordinary matter. 'Gandhibhai' did precisely that. His letter to the *The Times of India* in Bombay dated 18 May 1900 shows how Gandhi had now become not just a leader of the Indians as a propagandist and tractarian, but a field-level organizer of great skill.

In 1901, Gandhi felt that the end—successful for the British—of the Boer War marked a watershed in his engagement with South Africa. He decided to return home.

The fact that he was earning good money as a lawyer, which should normally have been an incentive to continue in South Africa, was working contrarily in the very contrary mind of M.K. Gandhi. As the date for leaving drew close, farewell gifts poured in. So did a mother of all arguments with Kasturba which was won in typically Indian fashion by the father of all male determinations—the husband's 'extorting' of consent.

'Bhai'

ABDULLA SHETH refused to address me as 'Gandhi'. None, fortunately, ever insulted me by calling or regarding me as 'saheb'. Abdulla Sheth hit upon a fine appellation—'bhai', i.e., brother. Others followed him and continued to address me as 'bhai' until the moment I left South Africa. There was a sweet flavour about the name when it was used by the ex-indentured Indians.

A, Part III; G

Ashamed

Durban, 1898

THE HOUSE[1] was built after the Western model and the rooms rightly had no outlets for dirty water. Each room had therefore chamber-pots. Rather than have these cleaned by a servant or a sweeper, my wife or I attended to them. The clerks who made themselves completely at home would naturally clean their own pots, but the Christian clerk[2] was a newcomer, and it was our duty to attend to his bedroom. My wife managed the pots of the others, but to clean those used by one who had been a *panchama*[3] seemed to her to be the limit, and we fell out. She could not bear the pots being cleaned by me, neither did she like doing it herself. Even today I can recall the picture of her chiding me, her eyes red with anger, and pearl drops streaming down her cheeks, as she descended the ladder, pot in hand ...

I was far from being satisfied by her merely carrying the pot. I would have her do it cheerfully. So I said, raising my voice: 'I will not stand this nonsense in my house.'

The words pierced her like an arrow.

She shouted back: 'Keep your house to yourself and let me go.' I forgot myself, and the spring of compassion dried up in me. I caught her by the hand, dragged the helpless woman to the gate, which was just opposite the ladder, and proceeded to open it with the intention of pushing her out. The tears were running down her cheeks in torrents, and she cried: 'Have you no sense of shame? Must you forget yourself? Where am I to go? I have no parents or relatives here to harbour me. Being your wife, you think I must put up with your cuffs and kicks? For Heaven's sake behave yourself, and shut the gate. Let us not be found making scenes like this!'

　I put on a brave face, but was really ashamed and shut the gate. If my wife could not leave me, neither could I leave her.

A, pp. 168–9; G

A Religious Preacher

Durban
23 February 1898

Dear Mr Bhajekar,[4]

　I have your very interesting and important letter. Let there be no haste in sending out a religious preacher.[5] A religious preacher working on the European lines will not succeed here or for that matter anywhere amongst the orthodox Indians.

　... Could not Swami[6] himself be induced to pay us a visit? I shall do everything I can to make his mission a success. He can work both among Indians and Europeans. I take it he moves freely among the Indians the highest as well as the lowest. He is sure to do one thing if he comes. He will electrify the Europeans by his eloquence and possibly hypnotize them into linking the 'Coolies' in spite of themselves. Though the Europeans here are very obstinate they are not so as never to listen to reason.

　I very rarely write unreservedly but I thought this was one of those occasions when it is allowed to and even obligatory on a man to throw off his reserve.

　You may place this letter before the Swami if you so wish it.

I am yours truly
M.K. Gandhi

Childbirth

Durban
1900

I HAD two sons born in South Africa, and my service in the hospital was useful in solving the question of their upbringing. My independent spirit was a constant source of trial. My wife and I had decided to have the best medical aid at the time of her delivery, but if the doctor and the nurse were to leave us in the lurch at the right moment, what was I to do? Then the nurse had to be an Indian. And the difficulty of getting a trained Indian nurse in South Africa can be easily imagined from the similar difficulty in India. So I studied the things necessary for safe labour. I read Dr Tribhuvandas' book, *Ma-ne Shikhaman*—Advice To A Mother—and I nursed both my children according to the instructions given in the book, tempered here and there by such experience as I had gained elsewhere. The services of a nurse were utilized—not for more than two months each time—chiefly for helping my wife, and not for taking care of the babies, which I did myself.

The birth of the last child[7] put me to the severest test. The travail came on suddenly. The doctor was not immediately available, and some time was lost in fetching the midwife. Even if she had been on the spot, she could not have helped delivery. I had to see through the safe delivery of the baby.

A, pp. 124–5; G

Domestic Chores

Mahadev Desai: Did you always have a cook in your house before you removed to Phoenix?

MKG: No. The last cook we had left because I would not let him use chillies. After that we managed without a cook. Cooking, washing clothes, cleaning the lavatories, grinding grain—everything was done by members of the family. We had a hand-mill made of steel which cost £6. It could be worked not by one but by two persons. Working at it was the first thing I did in the morning and I would take any one who was available as my fellow-worker.

We had to stand as we worked, and in a quarter of an hour we had sufficient flour for the day, fine or coarse just as we pleased.
The Diary of Mahadev Desai Vol. 1, (1932) pp. 53–4

The Wounds Of War

18 April 1900

PERHAPS, IN reading the accounts published from day to day of the Boer War[8], you[9] have followed the movements of the Indian community in connexion with it in so far as they have been chronicled by the newspapers. But, I am also aware that the Press has not been able to give anything like a full account of the doings of the Indians in South Africa ...

The (Indians') offer was ultimately accepted in connection with the Indian Ambulance Corps which, at the instance of the military authorities, was formed in Natal. The bearers for the Corps consisted mostly of indentured Indians supplied by the estates in Natal, ...

... Thus, about 1000 Indian bearers, and thirty leaders (no more of the latter being really necessary), carried the wounded after the battle of Colenso, and by their arduous work commanded the admiration of all concerned and more than satisfied the patients themselves ...

The nature of the work this time was, if possible, more exacting and, undoubtedly, more risky. The Indians, contrary to the announcement that they were to work without the range of fire, had to fetch the wounded from within the range, at times shells falling within hardly 100 yards of them, all this, of course, being unavoidably due to the unexpected reverse at Spion Kop and retirement from Vaalkranz. The bearers and the leaders had to march with their charge to a distance of 25 miles, from Spearman's Camp to Frere, over the Natal roads which, as you are aware, are very rough and hilly, at one time doing a distance of over 125 miles in a week. ...

CWMG, Vol. 3, pp. 174–5; E

... IN THE Boer War I myself served wine to the stone-breakers in my corps and served *bidis* to others. Discretion is very necessary in doing all such things. Generosity to others is as necessary as strictness with oneself.

CWMG *Vol. 63, p. 379; E*

A Wound At Home

October 1901

ON MY relief from war-duty I felt that my work was no longer in South Africa but in India. Not that there was nothing to be done in South Africa, but I was afraid that my main business might become merely money-making.

So I requested my co-workers to relieve me. After very great difficulty my request was conditionally accepted, the condition being that I should be ready to go back to South Africa if, within a year, the community should need me.

Gifts[10] had been bestowed on me before when I returned to India in 1896, but this time the farewell was overwhelming. The gifts of course included things in gold and silver, but there were articles of costly diamond as well.

One of the gifts was a gold necklace worth fifty guineas, meant for my wife. But even that gift was given because of my public work, and so it could not be separated from the rest.

'You may not need them', said my wife. 'Your children may not need them. Cajoled, they will dance to your tune. I can understand your not permitting me to wear them. But what about my daughters-in-law? They will be sure to need them. And who knows what will happen tomorrow? I would be the last person to part with gifts so lovingly given ...

And pray what right have you to my necklace?'

'But,' I rejoined, 'is the necklace given to you for your service or for my service?'

'I agree. But service rendered by you is as good as rendered by me. I have toiled and moiled for you day and night. Is that no service?'

These were pointed thrusts, and some of them went home. But I was determined to return the ornaments. I somehow succeeded in extorting a consent from her.

A, *pp. 134–5; G*

Part Six

1901-2

During the early years of legal practice,
Johannesburg, 1900

VISITING HOME

*I went to the Kashi Vishvanath temple for darshan ... I had no
mind to give any dakshina. So I offered a pie. The panda in
charge got angry and threw away the pie. He swore at me
and said, 'This insult will take you straight to hell.'*

*This did not perturb me. 'Maharaj,' said I, 'whatever fate
has in store for me, it does not behove one of your class to
indulge in such language. You may take this pie if you like,
or you will lose that too.'*

*'Go away,' he replied, 'I don't care for your pie.' And then
followed a further volley of abuse.*

*I took up the pie and went my way, flattering myself that
the Brahman had lost a pie and I had saved one. ...*

The family deposited in Porbandar/Rajkot, Gandhi made his way
to Calcutta to attend the annual session of the Congress. While Lord
Curzon, the Viceroy, did not oblige Gandhi with the appointment
Gandhi had sought, the Congress platformed this espouser of the
cause of Indian South Africans.

Calcutta fascinated and shook Gandhi. He could not 'bear' the
sight of sheep being sacrificed to Kali, was 'taken aback by the
splendour that surrounded' Sister Nivedita, but found Bengali
music greatly appealing.

Likewise, the filth at Kashi pained him, as did the avarice of
priests. Violence and opulence repelled Gandhi equally.

Politics was stirring in his veins and though the Congress had been hospitable to him, it was not yet 'his' scene or company; nor was he kin to the party's temperament.

Family chores closed-in on his attention, leading to a decision to set up home in Bombay and start legal work there. Strange man, to have given up a lucrative practice in Durban, a large villa, and high public standing, for an unpredictable legal practice in Bombay! And an uncertain political future in a country with social conditions that disgusted him.

But, for a brief while, the angel of domesticity shone on the Gandhi household as it moved to 'a fine bungalow in Santa Cruz'. One can imagine the relief with which Kasturba must have set up her new house in surroundings that were her own and near (but not too near!) the in-laws' in Kathiawar with her husband—for once, exclusively 'her own'.

Gandhi took out a season's ticket for his daily rail journey from Santa Cruz to Churchgate to reach his chambers. He loved being the only first class passenger on that train, he says candidly, and began to earn money.

Here was a man who had mobilized a thousand men for service in a major war, had become the undisputed leader of the Indian community in South Africa, withdrawing into domesticity and enjoying the change of role. If by a re-conjunction of his destiny, Gandhi had not been recalled to South Africa and his resumed work there had not plunged him further into the vortex of mass politics, this head of the Durban-returned family in Santa Cruz would have become a prosperous Gujarati lawyer with, perhaps, sporadic forays into political discussions.

But the Santa Cruz–Churchgate commuter's future had been settled, unbeknownst to him.

In Calcutta

December 1901–January 1902
THERE WERE yet two days for the Congress[1] session to begin. I had made up my mind to offer my services to the Congress office in order to gain some experience.

Babu Bhupendranath Basu[2] and Sjt. Ghosal[3] were the secretaries. I went to Bhupenbabu and offered my services. He looked at me, and said: 'I have no work, but possibly Ghosalbabu might have something to give you. Please go to him.'

So I went to him. He scanned me and said with a smile: 'I can give you only clerical work. Will you do it?'

'Certainly', said I. 'I am here to do anything that is not beyond my capacity.'

... Sjt. Ghosal used to get his shirt buttoned by his bearer. I volunteered to do the bearer's duty, and I loved to do it, as my regard for elders was always great. When he came to know this, he did not mind my doing little acts of personal service for him. In fact he was delighted. Asking me to button his shirt, he would say, 'You see, now, the Congress secretary has no time even to button his shirt. He has always some work to do.' Sjt. Ghosal's naivete amused me, but did not create any dislike in me for service of that nature.

A, pp. 138–9; G

IN THE Congress at last. The immense pavilion and the volunteers in stately array, as also the elders seated on the dais, overwhelmed me. I wondered where I should be in that vast assemblage.

Sir Pherozeshah had of course agreed to admit my resolutions, but I was wondering who would put it before the Subjects Committee, and when.

'So have we done?' said Sir Pherozeshah Mehta.

'No, no there is still the resolution on South Africa. Mr Gandhi
has been has been waiting long', cried out Gokhale ...[4]

A, pp. 139–40; G

LORD CURZON held his *darbar*[5] about this time. Some Rajas and
Maharajas who had been invited to the darbar were members of the
club.[6] In the club I always found them wearing the fine Bengali
dhotis and shirts and scarves. On the darbar day they put on trousers
befitting *khansamas*[7] and shining boots. I was pained and inquired
of one of them the reason for the change.

'We alone know our unfortunate condition. We alone know the
insults we have to put up with, in order that we may possess our
wealth and titles, ' he replied.

'But what about these khansama turbans and these shining
boots?' I asked.

'Do you see any difference between khansamas and us?' he
replied, and added, 'they are our khansamas, we are Lord Curzon's
khansamas.' I was distressed to see the Maharajas bedecked like
women—silk pyjamas and silk achkans, pearl necklaces round their
neck, bracelets on their wrists ...

A, p. 141; G

KALICHARAN BANERJI[8] had spoken to me about the Kali temple, which
I was eager to see, especially as I had read about it in books. So I
went there one day ...

On the way I saw a stream of sheep going to be sacrificed to Kali.
We were greeted by rivers of blood. I could not bear to stand there. I
was exasperated and restless. I have never forgotten that sight.

That very evening I had an invitation to dinner at a party of
Bengali friends. There I spoke to a friend about this cruel form of
worship. He said: 'The sheep don't feel anything. The noise and the
drum-beating there deaden all sensation of pain.'

I could not swallow this. I told him that, if the sheep had speech,
they would tell a different tale. I felt that the cruel custom ought to
be stopped ... but I also saw that the task was beyond my capacity.

I hold today the same opinion as I held then. To my mind the
life of a lamb is no less precious than that of a human being. I should

be unwilling to take the life of a lamb for the sake of the human body. I hold that, the more helpless a creature, the more entitled it is to protection by man from the cruelty of man. But he who has not qualified himself for such service is unable to afford to it any protection. I must go through more self-purification and sacrifice, before I can hope to save these lambs from this unholy sacrifice. It is my constant prayer that there may be born on earth some great spirit, man or woman, fired with divine pity, who will deliver us from this heinous sin, save the lives of the innocent creatures, and purify the temple. How is it that Bengal with all its knowledge, intelligence, sacrifice, and emotion tolerates this slaughter?

A, pp. 144–5; G

Sister Nivedita

January 1902

... IT WAS impossible to be satisfied without seeing Swami Vivekananda. So with great enthusiasm I went[9] to Belur Math, mostly, or may be all the way, on foot. I loved the sequestered site of the Math. I was disappointed and sorry to be told that the Swami was at his Calcutta house, lying ill, and could not be seen.

I then ascertained the place of residence of Sister Nivedita[10], and met her in a Chowringhee mansion. I was taken aback by the splendour that surrounded her, and even in our conversation there was not much meeting ground ...

I met her again at Mr Pestonji Padshah's[11] place. I happened to come in just as she was talking to his old mother, and so I became an interpreter between the two. In spite of my failure to find any agreement with her, I could not but notice and admire her overflowing love for Hinduism. I came to know of her books later.[12]

A, p. 145; The Diary of Mahadev Desai Vol. 1 (1932); G

Kashi

22 February 1902

I WENT to the Kashi Vishvanath temple for darshan. I was deeply pained by what I saw there.

The approach was through a narrow and slippery lane. Quiet there was none. The swarming flies and the noise made by the shopkeepers and pilgrims were perfectly insufferable.

When I reached the temple, I was greeted at the entrance by a stinking mass of rotten flowers. The floor was paved with fine marble, which was however broken by some devotee innocent of aesthetic taste, who had set it with rupees serving as an excellent receptacle for dirt.

I went near the *jnana-vapi* (Well of Knowledge). I searched here for God but failed to find Him. I was not therefore in a particularly good mood. The surroundings of the jnana-vapi too I found to be dirty. I had no mind to give any *dakshina*.[13] So I offered a pie. The *panda*[14] in charge got angry and threw away the pie. He swore at me and said, 'This insult will take you straight to hell.'

This did not perturb me. 'Maharaj, ' said I, 'whatever fate has in store for me, it does not behove one of your class to indulge in such language. You may take this pie if you like, or you will lose that too.'

'Go away, ' he replied, 'I don't care for your pie.' And then followed a further volley of abuse.

I took up the pie and went my way, flattering myself that the Brahman had lost a pie and I had saved one. But the Maharaj was hardly the man to let the pie go. He called me back and said, 'All right, leave the pie here, I would rather not be as you are. If I refuse your pie, it will be bad for you.'

I silently gave him the pie and, with a sigh, went away.

A, pp. 148–9; G

Manilal

Bombay
November 1902

SCARCELY HAD I moved into my new house[15] when my second son Manilal, who had already been through an acute attack of small-pox some years back, had a severe attack of typhoid, combined with pneumonia and signs of delirium at night.

'Your son's life is in danger, ' said the good doctor[16]. 'We could give him milk diluted with water, but that will not give him enough nourishment. As you know, I am called in by many Hindu families, and they do not object to anything I prescribe. I think you will be well advised not to be so hard on your son.'

Though Manilal could not have made his choice, I told him what had passed between the doctor and myself and asked him his opinion.

'Do try your hydropathic treatment', he said. 'I will not have eggs or chicken broth.'

But the temperature persisted, going up to 104 degrees. At night he would be delirious. I began to get anxious. What would people say of me? What would my elder brother think of me?

My mind was torn between these conflicting thoughts. It was night. I was in Manilal's bed lying by his side. I decided to give him a wet sheet pack. I got up, wetted a sheet, wrung the water out of it and wrapped it about Manilal, keeping only his head out, and then covered him with two blankets. To the head I applied a wet towel. The whole body was burning like hot iron, and quite parched. There was absolutely no perspiration.

I was sorely tired. I left Manilal in the charge of his mother, and went out for a walk on Chaupati to refresh myself. It was about ten o'clock. Very few pedestrians were out. Plunged in deep thought, I scarcely looked at them. 'My honour is in Thy keeping, Oh Lord, in this hour of trial,' I repeated to myself. Ramanama was on my lips. After a short time I returned, my heart beating within my breast.

No sooner had I entered the room than Manilal said, 'You have returned, Bapu?'

'Yes, darling.'

'Do please pull me out. I am burning.'

'Are you perspiring, my boy?'

'I am simply soaked. Do please take me out.'

I felt his forehead. It was covered with beads of perspiration. The temperature was going down. I thanked God. ...

Manilal was restored to health, but I saw that the Girgaum house was not habitable ... At last we hit upon a fine bungalow in Santa Cruz ... I took a first class season ticket from Santa Cruz to Churchgate, and remember having frequently felt a certain pride in being the only first class passenger in my compartment ... I prospered in my profession better than I expected. ...

A, pp. 151–3; G

Part Seven

1902-5

Gandhi with associates (H.S.L. Polak
to his right and Sonja Schlesin to
his left) in Johannesburg,
South Africa, 1905

RETURNING TO SOUTH AFRICA

*... if one's heart is pure, calamity brings in its train men
and measures to fight it.*

This Part begins appropriately with a 'But ...'.

South Africa, smitten by its Bhai, was not going to let him rest. He was summoned back as the Secretary of State for the Colonies was coming to South Africa and the community needed him to memorialize the visitor. With an alacrity that was now standard with Gandhi, he broke up the 'settled establishment' in Santa Cruz, Bombay, and left. 'It is wrong' he was to record while describing this unanticipated departure from the even tenor of life, 'to expect certainties in this world'. Kasturba and his own four children were left behind but, architect of the unpredictable that he was, even in that rushed departure, Gandhi took with him two nephews in order to set them up in business there. Nepotism is generally executed by the strong at the expense of the deserving 'others'. Here it was being exercised at the cost of his immediate family. Of Kasturba's feelings on the developments no record exists. But a certain rankling commenced its work in the mind of seven-year-old Harilal.

Gandhi reached Durban on Christmas Day, 1902 and before two days had elapsed, he had drafted a petition addressed to Joseph Chamberlain which shows a mastery of the art of terse drafting, tough fact-portraying, and gentle unctioning.

This was the high noon of the Empire. Curzon ruled India with élan, having created the North West Frontier Province (1900) and having taken upon himself the task of organizing with éclat the Delhi Durbar (1903). The partitioning of Bengal was two years away when Gandhi was memorializing Chamberlain but it should have been clear to any political observer that London was not, at that point of time, going to give the cause of Indian South Africans any priority. It was, after all, capital of an Empire that was on the march.

The elegant Surendranath Banerjea presided over the Congress held in Ahmedabad in 1902 which did not significantly revisit the issues Gandhi had raised in Calcutta the previous year. The Congress meeting under the Presidentship of Lal Mohan Ghose in Madras in 1903 did not take up South Africa either, nor that which met in Bombay in 1904 with Henry Cotton in the presidential Chair.

But in 1905 when Gokhale, who had played a leading role in the setting-up of The Servants of India Society on 12 June 1905 took the chair at the Benares Congress, things began to change for the Indian cause in South Africa. This bespoke Gokhale's receptivity and Gandhi's unremitting lobbying.

Meanwhile, our protagonist in South Africa was deepening his 'self'. If the 'private' was becoming political and public, this latter entity was discovering that politics had horizons beyond pamphleteering and propagandizing.

Gandhi met and made the acquaintance, around this time, of Hermann Kallenbach, which was to open a new chapter in his South African odyssey. This new preoccupation was to give his South African experience a binary character—he was to maintain his Durban base but also start one in Johannesburg with the opening of an office that was to do less with the practice of law than with a wider politics, leading to the commencement of *Indian Opinion* as a multilingual journal reflecting the substance of its effective name. In Johannesburg Gandhi's preferred mode of transportation was a bicycle, when it was not his two legs.

Gandhi had, by this time, to his spiritual satisfaction controlled the libido. But not his temper. We see some writings of his testifying to sudden outbursts of anger in him. Distance from family and the unrelieved stress of public activity, despite the relieving company of Kallenbach, could not but exact a price.

The Kallenbach connection was to be joined by one with another white friend of Jewish origin, H.S.L. Polak. These two new 'energies' in his life, saw the first experiment by Gandhi in what can be called the Ashram mode of life—Phoenix Settlement, near Durban. The mass field organizer in Gandhi had been inaugurated in the Boer

War and the tractarian in him fulfilled in *Indian Opinion*. And now the communitarian organizer was discovered in this settlement run on the lines prescribed by Ruskin in *Unto This Last*.

The Mahatma was now clearly in the making, with Kallenbach and Polak playing key roles.

But what of the family in India? It was rather neglected. Gandhi did not take long to send for Kasturba and the sons in 1905. The sons, that is, minus Harilal.

Back In South Africa

December 1902

BUT IT may be said that God has never allowed any of my own plans to stand. He has disposed them in his own way. Just when I seemed to be settling down as I had intended, I received an unexpected cable from South Africa: 'Chamberlain[1] expected here. Please return immediately' ... I remembered my promise ... gave up the chamber and started for South Africa. I had an idea that the work there would keep me engaged for at least a year, so I kept the bungalow and left my wife and children there.

The separation from wife and children, the breaking up of a settled establishment[2], and the going from the certain to the uncertain—all this was for a moment painful, but I had inured myself to an uncertain life. I think it is wrong to expect certainties in this world ...

I reached[3] Durban not a day too soon. There was work waiting for me. The date for the deputation to wait on Mr Chamberlain had been fixed. I had to draft the memorial to be submitted to him and accompany the deputation.

A, pp. 153–4; G

Durban
27 December 1902

To
The Right Honourable Joseph Chamberlain
His Majesty's Principal Secretary of State for The Colonies
Durban

Right Honourable Sir,

... That the indentured Indians, upon whom depends the prosperity of this Colony, after the completion of their indentures, have to pay a poll-tax of three pounds sterling every year, if they decide to remain in the Colony, is, in our humble opinion and as has been admitted by His Excellency Lord Elgin[4], bad enough. But now a Bill has passed through the Natal Parliament imposing the tax on their children above the age of thirteen years in the case of girls and sixteen years in the case of boys. That Bill is now before you for consideration ...

We need hardly add more. We know we have your sympathy, and we pray that you will be graciously pleased to exercise your great influence in our behalf.

We have the honour to remain,
Your most obedient and humble servants,
M.K. Gandhi
And fifteen others
Colonial Office Records: Petitions and Memorials, *1902,*
C.O. 529/1; CWMG *Vol. 3, pp. 320–2; E*

Hermann Kallenbach[5]

1903

WE MET by accident.

A, *p. 200; G*

HE IS a man of strong feelings, wide sympathies, and childlike simplicity. He is an architect by profession, but there is no work, however lowly, which he would consider to be beneath his dignity.

HK, *p. 16; E*

Stenographers

1903–4

IN JOHANNESBURG[6] I had at one time as many as four Indian clerks, who were perhaps more like my sons than clerks. But even these were not enough for my work. It was impossible to do without typewriting, which, among us, if at all, only I knew. I taught it to two of the clerks, but they never came up to the mark because of their poor English ...

But a permanent stenotypist was now needed ... She was Miss

Schlesin[7], introduced to me by Mr Kallenbach. ... She was about seventeen when she came to me. Some of her idiosyncrasies were at times too much for Mr Kallenbach and me. She had come less to work as a stenotypist than to gain experience. Colour prejudice was foreign to her temperament. She seemed to mind neither age nor experience. She would not hesitate even to the point of insulting a man and telling him to his face what she thought of him. Her impetuosity often landed me in difficulties, but her open and guileless temperament removed them as soon as they were created. I have often signed without revision letters typed by her, as I considered her English to be better than mine, and had the fullest confidence in her loyalty.

A, pp. 171–2; G

MISS SCHLESIN in her folly started smoking a cigarette in my presence. I slapped her and threw away the cigarette. For the first time she cried before me and apologized and wrote to me afterwards saying that she would never do such a thing again and that she had recognized my love.

CWMG Vol. 84, p. 295; G

'Indian Opinion'

June 1903

ABOUT THIS time Sjt. Madanjit[8] approached me with a proposal to start *Indian Opinion* and sought my advice. He had already been conducting a press, and I approved of his proposal. The journal was launched in 1903[9], and Sjt. Mansukhlal Naazar[10] became the first editor. But I had to bear the brunt of the work, having for most of the time to be practically in charge of the journal ...

During ten years, that is, until 1914, excepting the intervals of my enforced rest in prison, there was hardly an issue of *Indian Opinion* without an article from me. I cannot recall a word in those articles set down without thought or deliberation, or a word of conscious exaggeration, or anything merely to please. Indeed the journal became for me a training in self-restraint ...

A, pp. 173–4; G

Plight Of Indentured Labour

1903–8

... THE INDENTURED Indian is practically helpless. He comes from India in order to avoid starvation. He breaks asunder all the ties, and becomes domiciled in Natal in a manner that the free Indian never does. To a starving man, there is practically no home. His home is where he can keep body and soul together. The Association he forms in Natal among his own class are to him the first real friends and acquaintances, and to expect him to break that is nothing short of cruelty.

Indian Opinion *17.9.1903*

[ON AN average, 42 Chinese were flogged in a Johannesburg mine every day, including Sundays, towards the beginning of this year (1905). Gandhi's report described how an offender]

... is made to take off his trousers and lie face down on the ground, while one policeman holds down his legs, another his head, and the third flogs him. If the man makes the slightest movement a fourth presses him down with his foot. Strikes are at times so severe that they cause the flesh to cut and swell the skin.

[Gandhi was probably the first person to identify indentured labour as another form of slavery]

Slavery was at first a substitute for cattle, and indentured labour was a substitute for slavery. Indenture must be prohibited by law and the main duty of Natal Indians in this matter is to start an agitation on a big scale, to adopt satyagraha if necessary and bring the system of indenture to an end.

Indian Opinion *3.10.1908*
The South African Gandhi—An Abstract of the Speeches and Writings of M.K. Gandhi *(Madiba Publishers, Institute for Black Research, University of Natal, Durban; 1996), pp. 963–4*

The Plague

February 1904

THERE WERE a few Indians also working in the mine[11], twenty-three of whom suddenly caught the infection, and returned one evening to their quarters in the location with an acute attack of the plague.

Sjt. Madanjit bravely broke open the lock of a vacant house, and put all the patients there. I cycled to the location, and wrote to the Town Clerk to inform him of the circumstances in which we had taken possession of the house.

Dr William Godfrey[12], who was practicing in Johannesburg, ran to the rescue as soon as he got the news, and became both nurse and doctor to the patients. But twenty-three patients were more than three of us could cope with.

It is my faith, based on experience, that if one's heart is pure, calamity brings in its train men and measures to fight it. I had at that time four Indians in my office ... So I decided to sacrifice all four—call them clerks, co-workers or sons.

It was a terrible night—that night of vigil and nursing. I had nursed a number of patients before, but never any attacked by the black plague. Dr Godfrey's pluck proved infectious. There was not much nursing required. To give them their doses of medicine, to attend to their wants, to keep them and their beds clean and tidy, and to cheer them up was all that we had to do.

The indefatigable zeal and fearlessness with which the youths worked rejoiced me beyond measure. One could understand the bravery of Dr Godfrey and of an experienced man like Sjt. Madanjit. But the spirit of these callow youths!

So far as I can recollect, we pulled all the patients through that night.

A, pp. 177–9; G

The Magic Spell Of A Book

June 1904

POLAK[13] CAME to see me off at the station, and left with me a book to read during the journey, which he said I was sure to like. It was Ruskin's *Unto This Last.*

The book was impossible to lay aside, once I had begun it. It gripped me. Johannesburg to Durban was a twenty-four hours' journey[14]. The train reached there in the evening. I could not get any sleep that night. I determined to change my life in accordance with the ideals of the book.

The teachings of *Unto This last* I understood to be:

1. That the good of the individual is contained in the good of all.
2. That a lawyer's work has the same value as the barber's, in as much as all have the same right of earning their livelihood from their work.
3. That a life of labour, i.e., the life of the tiller of the soil and the handicraftsman, is the life worth living.

... Thereafter I at once advertised for a piece of land situated near a railway station in the vicinity of Durban. An offer came in respect of Phoenix. Mr West[15] and I went to inspect the estate. Within a week we purchased twenty acres of land. It had a nice little spring and a few orange and mango trees. Adjoining it was a piece of 80 acres which had many more fruit trees and a dilapidated cottage. We purchased this too, the total cost being a thousand pounds[16].

A, pp. 181–2; G

Ramdas

Johannesburg
Autumn 1905

I HAD promised my wife that I would return home within a year[17]. The year was gone without any prospect of my return, so I decided to send for her and the children.

On the boat bringing them to South Africa, Ramdas[18], my third son, broke his arm while playing with the ship's captain. The captain looked after him well and had him attended to by the ship's doctor. Ramdas landed with his hand in a sling. The doctor had advised that, as soon as we reached home, the wound should be dressed by a qualified doctor. But this was the time when I was full of faith in my experiments in earth treatment. I had even succeeded in persuading some of my clients who had faith in my quackery to try the earth and water treatment.

What then was I to do for Ramdas? He was just eight years old. I asked him if he would mind my dressing his wound. With a smile he said he did not mind at all. It was not possible for him at that age to decide what was the best thing for him, but he knew very well the distinction between quackery and proper medical treatment. And he knew my habit of home treatment and had faith enough to trust himself to me. In fear and trembling I undid the bandage, washed the wound, applied a clean earth poultice, and tied the arm up again. This sort of dressing went on daily for about a month until the wound was completely healed. There was no hitch, and the wound took no more time to heal than the ship's doctor had said it would under the usual treatment.

A, p. 187; G

Part Eight

1906-9

Gokhale with Gandhi, Kallenbach, and members of the
Reception Committee, Durban

THE STRUGGLE IN SOUTH AFRICA

... my mind is now quite clear, my aspirations are higher, and I have no desire for worldly enjoyments of any type whatever.

With the family, save for Harilal, with him Gandhi came to 'run' two establishments—one in the Phoenix Settlement near Durban and another in Johannesburg. The bachelor Hermann Kallenbach and Henry S.L. Polak and his wife Millie Graham Polak based in Johannesburg became close friends of the Gandhis, in the personal as well as public-political domains.

The Gandhis' lifestyle continued to change in the direction of simplification. Income thinned, savings shrank, and remittances to the larger ancestral family in Gujarat became untenable. His eldest brother Lakshmidas and he suffered a strain in relations, giving Gandhi an opportunity to state in black and white what had, of course, been obvious to those who observed him: 'I am now a stranger to fear.' Gandhi's distancing from Harilal began in the phase covered in this Part of the compilation which shows the father disapproving of his son's plans to marry but not being able to prevent the nuptials. As also an acknowledgement of his distancing from his brother Lakshmidas who had meant so much to him as to have been a point of reference. ('What would my elder brother think of me?', Gandhi had asked himself when trying hydrotherapy on Manilal barely four years earlier.) His letter of 'renunciation' to Lakshmidas shows the influence of Raychandbhai and Ruskin working on his own self-alchemizing mind.

This phase saw Gandhi as a foot-soldier in the field in a new opportunity to demonstrate his prowess in mass organization, during the 'Zulu Rebellion'. This event brought him, albeit from the 'opposite side', in close physical proximity to the Zulu. Gandhi disliked the government's action and viewed it as 'manhunt'. He regarded the opportunity he had of nursing wounded Zulus as a 'privilege' and was to say much later that this experience gave him an insight into 'what war by white men against coloured races meant'. In the midst of another war, World War II, he was to expand on his incipient thoughts of this phase when in a conversation with an African visitor from Johannesburg he said, 'You must become Africans once more'.

As the Zulu 'Rebellion' drew to a close, Gandhi turned inward. He decided to entrench himself in *brahmacharya* on the ground 'I should not have been able to throw myself into the fray had my wife been expecting a baby. ... The very first change I made in my mode of life was to stop sharing the same bed with my wife ...'

Shortly thereafter, came an Ordinance that shook Indian self-respect. It asked all Indians in the Transvaal to register their names with finger and thumb impressions and take out a certificate of registration. 'Better die,' the barrister said, 'than submit to such a law' and satyagraha took birth. But it was decided that measures for resisting the 'Black Act' would include and in fact start with memorials to the local government and to Whitehall.

On the home front, Harilal arrived in South Africa in September 1906, with his wife Gulab, to Kasturba's great delight.

This Part deals with the strengthening of the family's size though not of family 'time' and with Gandhi's first visit to England from South Africa. The triumphs and betrayals of that initiative, its human and political facets, have an essentiality to them. The six weeks' stay seemed initially to have worked, with Lord Elgin, the Secretary of State for the Colonies giving Gandhi to understand that he would not advise His Majesty to bring the Transvaal Ordinance into operation. But Transvaal was becoming free of Britain's supervisory control and the same Lord Elgin left it to Pretoria to pass the very law he had recommended the vetoing of.

Gandhi's response by way of disciplined mass action was swift and was grounded unwaveringly in non-violence. The significance of this has not always been appreciated. Gandhi's earlier 'mass' mobilizations were in the nature of non-combatant participation in an armed theatre—the Boer War and the Zulu 'Rebellion'. Now for the first time Gandhi was *launching* a mass movement and keeping it uncompromisingly 'non-violent'.

It is also noteworthy that satyagraha was born as a method to be adopted after the route of negotiation had not only been tried but saturated. In other words 'satya' was to be seen and shared civilly. And only when negotiation was spurned or betrayed was 'agraha' to be invoked. In January 1908, Gandhi had his first experience of jail, and of working with brave compatriots like Thambi Naidoo. He also had his first taste of the art of negotiation without compromising on basics, and of parleying with the mighty who can be very stubborn but also very human—in this case, Jan Christian Smuts.

If confrontation with the authorities led to his first imprisonment, a close-door negotiation with Smuts led to misunderstanding and his first experience of physical assault at the hands of a fellow Indian.

Satyagraha, as he was beginning to define it to himself, meant trusting the opponent's word. Gandhi had understood Smuts to say he would repeal the Act if most Indians registered voluntarily. Gandhi took it upon himself to recommend voluntary registration on the ground that the removal of the element of compulsion changed the nature of the enactment—a debatable point. Smuts repudiated the understanding and refused to repeal the Act. Satyagraha was resumed and among the jail goers now was Harilal who showed traits associated with the father and came to be called 'chhota Gandhi'. 'I want every Indian to do what Harilal has done', a proud Mohandas Karamchand Gandhi wrote to the editor of *Indian Opinion* on 20 August 1903.

Gandhi used the journal to offer views that were civilizational no less than political, universal no less than local:

ACCIDENT?

The catastrophe at Paris[1] must have filled all the portions of the globe where the news reached with gloom. We can well imagine the feelings of the victims and the survivors. To us, these untoward happenings are not merely accidents but we look upon them as divine visitations from which we, if we choose, may learn rich lessons. To us, they show a grim tragedy behind all the tinsel splendour of the modern civilization. The ceaseless rush in which we are living does not leave any time for contemplating the full results of events such as have placed Paris in mourning for the time being. The dead will be soon forgotten, and in a very short time, Paris will again resume its usual gaiety as if nothing whatsoever had happened. Those, however, who will give the accident, if so it may be called, more than a passing thought, cannot fail to realize that behind all the splendour and behind all the glittering appearances there is something very real which is missed altogether. To us, the meaning is quite clear, namely, that all of us have to live the present life merely as a preparation for a future, far more certain and far more real. Nothing that the modern civilization can offer in the way of stability can ever make any more certain that which is inherently uncertain; that, when we come to think of it, the boast about the wonderful discoveries and the marvellous inventions of science, good as they undoubtedly are in themselves, is, after all, an empty boast. They offer nothing substantial to the struggling humanity, and the only consolation that one can derive from such visitations has to come from a firm faith not in the theory, but in the fact, of the existence of a future life and real Godhead. And that alone is worth having or worth cultivating which would enable us to realize our Maker and to feel that, after all, on this earth we are merely sojourners.

Gandhi and fire went together in South Africa. He burnt the offending certificates. Another jail experience followed, containing a close encounter with custodial violence—at the hands of a fellow prisoner.

The Zulu And Their Historic Rebellion

1905-6

A FAIR complexion and a pointed nose represent our ideal of beauty. If we discard this superstition for a moment, we feel that the Creator did not spare Himself in fashioning the Zulu to perfection. And, if we believe that there must be beauty in everything fashioned by nature, we would not only steer clear of all narrow and one-sided conceptions of beauty, but we in India would be free from the improper sense of shame and dislike we feel for our own complexion if it is anything but fair.

SiSA, pp. 7–8; G

IMPORTANT EVENTS, the effects of which will not be forgotten for many years, took place in Natal last week...The Kaffirs[2] in Natal rose against the poll-tax. Sergeants Hunt and Armstrong were killed in the revolt. Martial law was declared in Natal ... Some Kaffirs were prosecuted under the martial law, and twelve of them were condemned to death ... The Kaffirs from neighbouring areas and their chiefs were invited to witness the execution...Twelve lives have been taken for two. The twelve Kaffirs were blown to death at the mouth of a cannon on Monday.

IO, April 1905; TGB, p. 11; E

THOUGH THE 12 Kaffirs were put to death, the rebellion instead of being quelled has gathered strength ... The dead (in a clash with Chief Bambata[3], who had been deposed and was leading the rebellion) included those who had shot the 12 Kaffirs. Such is the law of God... Bambata is still at large. There is no knowing how all this will end.

IO, April 1905; TGB, p. 12; E

THE ZULU 'rebellion' broke out in Natal just while attempts were thus being made to impose further disabilities upon Indians in the Transvaal. I doubted then and doubt even now if the outbreak could be described as a rebellion, but it has always been thus described in Natal.

I made an offer to the Government to raise a Stretcher-Bearer Corps for service with the troops. The offer was accepted[4].

We found that the wounded Zulus would have been left uncared for, unless we had attended to them. No European would help to dress their wounds ... We had to cleanse the wounds of several Zulus which had not been attended to for as many as five or six days and were therefore stinking horribly. We liked the work. The Zulus could not talk to us, but from their gestures and the expression of their eyes they seemed to feel as if God had sent us to their succour.

SiSA, pp. 89–91; G

BECAUSE ONE man, Bambata, their chief, had refused to pay his tax, the whole race[5] was made to suffer. ... I shall never forget the lacerated backs of Zulus who had received stripes and were brought to us for nursing because no white nurse was prepared to look after them. And yet those who perpetrated all those cruelties called themselves Christians. They were 'educated', better dressed than the Zulus, but not their moral superiors.

THIS WAS no war but a manhunt. ... To hear every morning the reports of the soldiers rifles exploding like crackers in innocent hamlets, and to live in the midst of them was a trial. But I swallowed the bitter draught, especially since the work of my corps consisting only in nursing the wounded Zulus.

A, p. 192; G

... I AND my companions were privileged to nurse the wounded Zulus back to life. It is reasonable to suggest that but for our services some of them would have died. I cite this experience not to justify my participation however indirect it was. I cite it to show that I came through that experience with greater non-violence and with richer love for the great Zulu race. And I had an insight into what war by white men against coloured races meant.

CWMG Vol. 68, p. 269; E

Jesus Christ

Johannesburg

January 1906

[MILLIE GRAHAM Polak recounts: *I recalled the beautiful head of Christ that adorned the wall over his desk. When I noticed it the first time, I had said to him: 'How beautiful that is!'*]

'YES I love to have it there. I see it each time I raise my eyes from my desk. It is, indeed, beautiful'[6].

'Respected Brother'[7]

Johannesburg

27 May 1906

I HAVE your letter of the 17 April. I do not know what to say. You are prejudiced against me. There is no remedy against prejudice. I am helpless. I can only reply to your letter in full.

1. I have no idea of distancing myself from you.
2. I claim nothing there.
3. I do not claim anything as mine.
4. All that I have is being utilized for public purposes.
5. It is available to relations who devote themselves to public work.
6. I could have satisfied your desire for money if I had not dedicated my all for public use.

I have never said that I have done much for my brothers or other relations. I have given them all that I could save. If I have mentioned this, it is not out of pride, and then only to friends.

Rest assured that I will cheerfully assume the burden of supporting the family in case you pass on before me. You need have no fear on that score.

I am not now in a position to send you money as you desire.

It is well if Harilal[8] is married; it is also well if he is not. For the present at any rate I have ceased to think of him as a son ...

You may repudiate me, but still I will be to you what I have always been.

I do not remember that I expressed a desire to separate from you when I was there. But even if I did, my mind is now quite clear, my aspirations are higher and I have no desire for worldly enjoyments of any type whatever.

I am engaged in my present activities as I look upon them as essential to life. If I have to face death while thus engaged, I shall face it with equanimity. I am now a stranger to fear.

I like those who are pure in heart. Young Kalyandas[9], Jagmohandas' son, is like Prahlad in spirit. He is therefore dearer to me than one who is a son because so born.

Adapted from translation in CWMG Vol. 5, pp. 334–5; G

Working For The Wounded, Walking With God

July 1906

I HAD been wedded to a monogamous ideal ever since my marriage, faithfulness to my wife being part of the love of truth. But it was in South Africa that I came to realize the importance of observing brahmacharya even with respect to my wife. I cannot definitely say what circumstance or what book it was, that set my thoughts in that direction, but I have a recollection that the predominant factor was the influence of Raychandbhai, of whom I have already written.

... What then, I asked myself, should be my relation with my wife? Did my faithfulness consist in making my wife the instrument of my lust? So long as I was the slave of lust, my faithfulness was worth nothing. To be fair to my wife, I must say that she was never the temptress. It was therefore the easiest thing for me to take the vow of brahmacharya, if only I willed it. It was my weak will or lustful attachment that was the obstacle.

Even after my conscience had been roused in the matter, I failed twice. I failed because the motive that actuated the effort was none the highest. My main object was to escape having more children.

A, p. 125; G

MARCHING, WITH or without the wounded, through these solemn solitudes, I often fell into deep thought. I pondered over brahmacharya[10] and its implications and my convictions took deep root ... I could not live both after the flesh and the spirit. On the present occasion, for instance, I should not have been able to throw myself into the fray had my wife been expecting a baby ... The very first change I made in my mode of life was to stop sharing the same bed with my wife or seeking privacy with her.

A, pp. 193–4; G

A Venal Ordinance And The Birth Of Satyagraha

Johannesburg
1906–7

ON RETURN from the war, I read the draft Ordinance ...

Every Indian, man, woman, or child of eight years or upwards, entitled to reside in the Transvaal, must register his or her name with the Registrar of Asiatics and take out a certificate of registration.

The Registrar was to note down important marks of identification upon the applicant's person, and take his finger and thumb impressions.

SiSA, pp. 91–2; G

BETTER DIE than submit to such a law ...

With a view to seeing some literature on the subject, I read a volume on finger impressions by Mr Henry, a police officer, from which I gathered that finger prints are required by law only from criminals.

SiSA, p. 93; G

THE PRINCIPLE called satyagraha[11] came into being before that name was invented. Indeed when it was born, I myself could not say what it was. In Gujarati also we used the English phrase 'passive resistance' to describe it. When in a meeting of Europeans I found that the term 'passive resistance' was too narrowly construed, that it was supposed to be a weapon of the weak, that it could be characterized by hatred, and that it could finally manifest itself as violence, I had to demur to all these statements and explain the real nature of the Indian movement. It was clear that a new word must be coined by the Indians to designate their struggle.

But I could not for the life of me find out a new name, and therefore offered a nominal prize through *Indian Opinion* to the reader who made the best suggestion on the subject. As a result Maganlal Gandhi[12] coined the word 'Satagraha' (Sat = truth, Agraha = firmness) and won the prize. But in order to make it clearer I changed the word to 'Satyagraha' which has since become current in Gujarati as a designation for the struggle.

A, *p. 194; G*

WE RESOLVED to call a mass meeting[13] of the Indians at Pretoria.

Mr Kachhalia[14] was one of the speakers at the meeting. He made a very short speech ... His face reddened, the veins on his neck and on the head were swollen with the blood coursing rapidly through them, his body was shaking, and moving the fingers of his right hand upon his throat, he thundered forth: 'I swear in the name of God that I will be hanged but I will not submit to this law, and I hope that every one present will do likewise.' ... I was rather doubtful whether Kachhalia Sheth would be able fully to translate his brave words into action. I am ashamed of this doubt now, and every time I think of it.

... Others then knew him very much better than I did, as many of them were personally familiar with this obscure hero. They knew that Kachhalia only says what he means and means what he says.

SiSA, *pp. 123–4*

IN THE Transvaal itself we took all necessary measures for resisting the Black Act such as approaching the Local Government with memorials etc.

I submitted to the community that if a deputation[15] was to go to England, it was as well that they realized their responsibility in the matter still more fully. ... Some proposed to cut the Gordian knot by asking me to go alone, but I flatly declined. ... My advice was that there must be a Musalman gentleman going with me, and that the personnel should be limited to two.

SiSA, *pp. 108–9*

Mr H.O. Ali and myself ... set to work as soon as we reached England. We got printed the memorial to be submitted to the Secretary of State which we had drafted in the steamer on our way to England. Lord Elgin was Secretary of State for the Colonies and Lord (then Mr) Morley Secretary of State for India. We met Dadabhai and through him the British Committee of the Indian National Congress. We placed our case before it and signified our intention to seek the cooperation of all the parties, as advised by Dadabhai.

SiSA, p. 110

In ENGLAND and other Western countries there is one, in my view, barbarous custom of inaugurating movements at dinners. The British Premier delivers in the Mansion House on the 9th of November an important speech in which he adumbrates his programme for the year and publishes his own forecast of the future, and which therefore attracts universal notice. Cabinet ministers, among others, are invited to dinner by the Lord Mayor of London, and when the dinner is over, bottles of wine are uncorked, all present drink to the health of the host and the guest, and speeches too are made while this merry business is in progress. The toast for the British Cabinet is proposed, and the Premier makes the important speech referred to in reply to it. And as in public, so in private, the person with whom some important conversations are to be held is, as a matter of custom, invited to dinner, and the topic of the day is broached either at or after dinner. We too had to observe this custom not once but quite a number of times, although of course we never touched meat or liquor. We thus invited our principal supporters to lunch. About a hundred covers were laid.

SiSA, pp. 111–12

AFTER A stay in England of about six weeks we returned to South Africa. When we reached Madeira, we received a cablegram from Mr Ritch[16] to the effect that Lord Elgin had declared that he was unable without further consideration to advise His Majesty the King that the Transvaal Asiatic Ordinance should be brought into operation. Our joy knew no bounds.

But the ways of Providence are inscrutable ... the castles we had laboriously built toppled down and passed into nothingness.

SiSA, p. 112

As soon as we landed at Cape Town, and more so when we reached Johannesburg, we saw that we had overrated the Madeira cablegram.

Lord Elgin (had) made an outward show of friendliness to the Indians, while at the same time he really and secretly supported the Transvaal Government and encouraged it to pass once more the very law which he had vetoed himself. This is not the only or the first case of such tortuous policy followed by the British Empire. Even an indifferent student of its history will easily recall similar incidents.

SiSA, pp. 115–16

The first of July 1907 arrived, and saw the opening of permit offices. The community had decided openly to picket each office, that is to say, to post volunteers on the roads leading thereto, and these volunteers were to warn weak-kneed Indians against the trap laid for them there ... If the police abused or thrashed them, they must suffer peacefully; if the ill-treatment by the police was insufferable they should leave the place. If the police arrested them, they should gladly surrender themselves. If some such incident occurred in Johannesburg, it should be brought to my notice. At other places the local secretaries were to be informed, and asked for further instructions. Each party of pickets had a captain whose orders must be obeyed by the rest.

This was the community's first experience of that kind. All who were above the age of twelve were taken as pickets, so that there were many young men from 12 to 18 years of age enrolled as such.

SiSA, p. 125

I would like to introduce to the reader one out of the several leading Indians who constituted the first batch of prisoners. Shri Thambi Naidoo was a Tamilian born in Mauritius where his parents had migrated from Madras State. He was an ordinary trader. He had practically received no scholastic education whatever. But a wide experience had been his schoolmaster...He had never seen India. Yet his love for the homeland knew no bounds. Patriotism ran through his very veins. His firmness was pictured on his face. He was very strongly built and he possessed tireless energy. He shone equally whether he had to take the chair at meetings and lead them, or whether he had to do porter's work. He would not be ashamed of carrying a load on the public roads. Night and day were the same to him when he set to work. And none was more ready than he to sacrifice his all for the sake of the community. If Thambi Naidoo had not been rash and if he had been free from anger, this brave man could easily have assumed the leadership of the community in the Transvaal in the absence of Kachhalia ...

SiSA, pp. 136–7

'Hip, Hip, Hooray'

Phoenix
1908

[IN A Phoenix grove, six-year-old Prabhudas, calling for Gandhi's third son, nine-year-old Ramdas, had said 'Laamdaash'.]

MKG: Prabhudas, shout 'hip, hip, hooray' as often and as loudly as you can.

[Prabhudas, raising his voice, tries.]

MKG: Now say 'Hooray Ramdas'.

[Prabhudas manages to repeat the sounds correctly.]

Prabhudas Gandhi Jeevan-Prabhat, *1952*

The First Experience Of Jail

January 1908

IN JAIL[17] I was asked to put off my own private clothing. I knew that convicts were made naked in jail. We had all decided as satyagrahis voluntarily to obey all jail regulations so long as they were not inconsistent with our self-respect or with our religious convictions. The clothes which were given to me to wear were very dirty. I did not like putting them on at all. It was not without pain that I reconciled myself to them from an idea that I must put up with some dirt. After the officers had recorded my name and address, I was taken to a large cell, and in a short time was joined by my compatriots who came laughing and told me how they had received the same sentence as myself, and what took place after I had been removed. I understood from them that when my case was over, the Indians, some of whom were excited, took out a procession with black flags in their hands. The police disturbed the procession and flogged some of its members. We were all happy at the thought that we were kept in the same jail and in the same cell.

The cell door was locked at 6 o'clock. The door was not made of bars but was quite solid, there being high up in the wall a small aperture for ventilation, so that we felt as if we had been locked up in a safe.

SiSA, pp. 138–9; G

... I HAD no idea of what jail life was like when I launched on satyagraha in South Africa. But once inside the prison it became to me like a palace, a sanctuary, a place of pilgrimage, where I learnt things which probably I would not have outside.

CWMG Vol. 69, p. 256; E

The First Settlement With Smuts

January 1908

WE HAD thus been in jail for a fortnight, when fresh arrivals brought the news that there were going on some negotiations about a compromise with the Government. After two or three days Mr Albert Cartwright, editor of *The Transvaal Leader,* a Johannesburg daily, came to see me ... and brought with him terms of a settlement[18] drafted or approved of by General Smuts[19]. I did not like the vague language of the document, but was all the same prepared myself to put my signature to it with one alteration.

SiSA, pp. 142–3; G

Cartwright: Will not this letter do?
MKG: No, Mr Cartwright, not until this alteration is made.
Cartwright: But everything is achieved by compromise.
MKG: There can be no compromise on principles.

CWMG Vol. 12, p. 525; E

ON 30 January 1908, Mr Vernon, the Superintendent of Police, Johannesburg, took me to Pretoria to meet General Smuts. He told me...I accept the alteration you have suggested in the draft. I have consulted General Botha also, and I assure you that I will repeal the

Asiatic Act as soon as most of you have undergone voluntary registration. When the bill legalizing such registration is drafted, I will send you a copy for your criticism. I do not wish there should be any recurrence of the trouble, and I wish to respect the feelings of your people.'

So saying General Smuts rose. I asked him, 'Where am I to go? And what about the other prisoners?'

The General laughed and said, 'You are free this very moment. I am phoning to the prison officials to release the other prisoners tomorrow morning. But I must advise you not to go in for many meetings or demonstrations, as in that case Government will find itself in an awkward position.'

I replied, 'You may rest assured, that there will not be a single meeting simply for the sake of it. But I will certainly have to hold meetings in order to explain to the community how the settlement was effected, what is its nature and scope, and how it has added to our responsibilities.'

'Of such meetings,' said General Smuts, 'you may have as many as you please. It is sufficient that you have understood what I desire in the matter.'

SiSA, pp. 144-5; G

Mir Alam[20]: What will you do yourself?

MKG: I have decided to give ten finger-prints.

MA: It was you who told us that ten finger-prints were only required from criminals.

MKG: Yes I did, and rightly. But ... an indignity yesterday is today the hallmark of a gentleman. If you require me to salute you by force and I submit to you, I will have demeaned myself ... But if of my own accord I salute you as a brother or fellow man, that will be counted in my favour before the Great White Throne.

MA: We hear you have sold the community to General Smuts for 15,000 pounds. I swear with Allah as my witness that I will kill the man who takes the lead in applying for registration.

MKG: One may not swear to kill another in the name of the Most High. However that may be, it is my clear duty to take the lead in giving finger-prints ... To die by the hand of a brother, rather than by disease ... cannot be for me a matter for sorrow.

A Man In The Shadow

Johannesburg
2 February 1908

[Millie Graham Polak recounts: *One evening a big meeting of Indians and sympathizers was held in the Masonic Hall, Johannesburg. The large gathering overflowed the confines of the hall, and crowded up the doorway and porch. Mr Gandhi was the chief speaker and always drew a big crowd to him wherever he went. At the close of the meeting Mr Gandhi came down from the platform and talked with a few people; then he and I walked out together. As we reached the outer door I noticed a man standing in the shadow of it. Mr Gandhi also specially noticed him, it was evident, for he went directly to him and linked his arm in the man's, saying something in a quiet, earnest voice to him. The man hesitated for one moment, then turned and walked away with Mr Gandhi, I meantime keeping my place on the other side of him. We walked the length of the street. I did not understand what the others were talking about, even could I have heard it. But I could not hear, for both men were speaking in a very low voice. At the end of the street the man handed something over to Mr Gandhi and walked away. I was somewhat puzzled by the whole proceeding and, as soon as the man had gone, I asked Mr Gandhi ...*]

MGP: What did the man want—anything special?.

MKG: Yes, he wanted to kill me.

MGP: To kill you? To kill you? How horrible! Is he mad?

MKG: No, he thinks that I am acting traitorously towards our people; that I am intriguing with the Government against them, and yet pretending to be their friend and leader.

MGP: But that is all wicked and dreadful. Such a man is not safe; he ought to be arrested. Why did you let him go like that? He must be mad!

MKG: No, he is not mad, only mistaken; and you saw, after I had talked to him, he handed over to me the knife he had intended to use on me.

MGP: He would have stabbed you in the dark. I ...

MKG: Do not disturb yourself so much about it. He thought he wanted to kill me; but he really had not the courage to do so. If I were as bad as he thought I was, I should deserve to die. Now we will not worry any more about it. It is finished. I do not think that man will attempt to injure me again. Had I had him arrested I should have made an enemy of him. As it is, he will now be my friend.

Millie Graham Polak, in Mr Gandhi: The Man, *Allen & Unwin, 1931*

My Reward

Johannesburg
10 February 1908

... WHEN AT a quarter to ten on Monday morning I set out towards the Registration Office in the company of Mr Essop Mia, Mr Naidoo, and a few other Indians, I did feel that there might be an attack on me. In fact, I had spotted two of the assailants near the office. They walked alongside of us. I then became surer. But I decided that I should not, as I had declared earlier, mind being assaulted by my own brethren.

Some way ahead, one of the men asked, 'Where are you all going?'. Mr Essop Mia was about to answer, when I interrupted saying, 'I am going [to the Registration Office] to give my finger-impressions. The others, too, will do the same. If you want to give your thumb-impressions [only], you can do that.' My only recollection of what followed is that I received very severe blows.

I took severe blows on my left ribs. Even now I find breathing difficult. My upper lip has a cut on one side. I have a bruise above the left eye and a wound on the forehead. In addition, there are minor injuries on my right hand and left knee. I do not remember the manner of the assault, but people say that I fell down unconscious with the first blow which was delivered with a stick. Then my assailants struck me with an iron pipe and a stick, and they also kicked me. Thinking me dead, they stopped. I only remember having been beaten up. I have an impression that, as the blows started, I uttered the words *He Rama!* Mr Thambi Naidoo and Mr Essop Mia intervened. Mr Naidoo was hit as a result and injured on the ear. Mr Essop Mia received a slight injury on a finger. As I came to, I got up with a smile. In my mind there was not the slightest anger or hatred for the assailants.

On reflection, I feel that we fear death needlessly. ...

Indian Opinion, *22.2.1908;* CWMG *Vol. 8, pp. 93–4; E*

WHEN I regained consciousness, I saw Mr Doke bending over me. 'How do you feel?' he asked me.

'I am all right,' I replied, 'but there is pain in the teeth and the ribs. Where is Mir Alam?'

'He has been arrested along with the rest.'

'They should be released.'

SiSA, pp. 153–4; G

The Tyranny Of Affection

Johannesburg
May 1908

[Hermann Kallenbach relates: *On the morning on which he had to go to meet General Smuts at Pretoria for a very important interview I found him (be)rating me generally for something that I had omitted to do ... That was the tyranny of his affection but that affection is my proudest possession.*]

HK: It is no use your wasting your time over domestic trifles when you must be thinking of the interview you are going to have with General Smuts.

MKG (flaring up): No, these little things are to me of as much importance as the big ones. They touch the very core of our life and truth is one whole, it has no compartments.

Cited in Harijan, *29.5.1937 from* Mahadev Desai's weekly '*Letter*'; E

Smuts Plays Foul

May–June 1908

I SAID last week that General Smuts might play foul. It has now been proved that there has been foul play. It is known for certain that he has no intention of repealing the obnoxious Act. The government has not yet made the news public, but it has spread in the Indian community, and everyone's blood is up ...

Indian Opinion, *30.5.1908*; CWMG *Vol. 8, p. 266*; E

... I BELIEVE that, in seeing General Smuts as I saw him, I acted correctly and in accordance with my conscience, but time has shown that they were right. Time has shown also that I need not have gone to General Smuts as I did ...

General Smuts says that he never made any promise of repeal, but there are documents, which the world will see, which will show, at least, that there was a talk and a conversation with reference to the repeal of the Act. ...

Speech at mass meeting on 24 June 1908, Johannesburg.
Indian Opinion, *4.7.1908*; CWMG *Vol. 8, pp. 319–20; E*

Harilal

8 August 1908[21]

The Editor
Indian Opinion

Sir,

I have received inquiries from many quarters as to why I sent Harilal, my son, to gaol. I give some reasons below:

1. I have advised every Indian to take up hawking. I am afraid I cannot join myself since I am enrolled as an attorney. I therefore thought it right to advise my son to make his rounds as a hawker. I hesitate to ask others to do things which I cannot do myself. I think whatever my son does at my instance can be taken to have been done by me ...

I want every Indian to do what Harilal has done ...

I remain,
Satyagrahi
Mohandas Karamchand Gandhi
CWMG *Vol. 8, pp., 432–3; E*

'I Ask You To Burn These Certificates'

Johannesburg
16 August 1908

... I DID not come out of the gaol before my time was up in order that I might leave the hardships that I was suffering there—personally, I was not undergoing any hardships whatever ... No, gentlemen, the servant who stands before you this afternoon is not made of that stuff, and it is because I ask you to suffer everything that may be necessary ... that I ask you this afternoon to burn all these certificates. (Cries of 'we are ready to burn them'.)

> Speech at mass meeting on 16 August 1908, Johannesburg;
> Indian Opinion, 22.8.1908; CWMG Vol. 8, p. 458; E

... WHILE RETURNING from Durban, I was arrested at Volksrust Station on 7 October (1908) for being without my certificate of voluntary registration and refusing to give my finger-impressions.

> CWMG Vol. 9, p. 120; E

... I WAS then sentenced to a fine of Rs 25 or to two months' hard labour. This made me very happy, and I congratulated myself on what I considered to be my good fortune in being allowed to join the others in gaol.

After the sentence was passed, we were issued gaol uniforms. We were supplied each with a pair of short breeches, a shirt of coarse cloth, a jumper, a cap, a towel, and a pair of socks and sandals. I think this is a very convenient dress for work. It is simple, and wears well. We should have nothing to complain about such a dress ...

> CWMG Vol. 9, p. 124; E

... BUT I did not spend two full months in that gaol. I was suddenly sent away to Johannesburg for a few days ...

... I was in gaol uniform throughout the journey. I had some luggage with me, which I was made to carry myself. The distance from the gaol to the station had to be covered on foot. After arriving at Johannesburg, I had (again) to reach the gaol on foot, carrying the luggage myself. The incident provoked strong comments in newspapers ...

It was evening when we reached[22] Johannesburg, so that I was not taken where I could be among other Indians. I was given a bed in a cell of the prison where there were mostly Kaffir prisoners who had been lying ill. I spent the night in this cell in great misery and fear ...

The reason why I felt so uneasy was that the Kaffir and Chinese prisoners appeared to be wild, murderous, and given to immoral ways. I did not know their language. A Kaffir started putting questions to me. I felt a hint of mockery even in this. I did not understand what it was. I returned no reply. He asked me in broken English why I had been brought there in that fashion. I gave a brief reply, and then I lapsed into silence. Then came a Chinese. He appeared to be worse. He came near the bed and looked closely at me. I kept still. Then he went to a Kaffir lying in bed. The two exchanged obscene jokes, uncovering each other's genitals. Both these prisoners had charges of murder and larceny against them. Knowing this, how could I possibly sleep? ...

CWMG Vol. 9, pp. 147–9; G

I HAD one further unpleasant experience in the Johannesburg Gaol. In this gaol, there are two different kinds of wards. One ward is for Kaffir and Indian prisoners sentenced to hard labour. The other is for prisoners who are called as witnesses and those who have been sentenced to imprisonment in civil proceedings. Prisoners sentenced to hard labour have no right to go into this second ward.... I was told by the warder that there would be no harm in my using a lavatory in the second ward. I therefore went to one of the lavatories in this ward. At these lavatories, too, there is usually a crowd. Moreover, the lavatories have open access. There are no doors. As soon as I had occupied one of them, there came along a strong, heavily-built, fearful-looking Kaffir. He asked me to get out and started abusing me. I said I would leave very soon. Instantly he lifted me up in his arms and threw me out. Fortunately, I caught hold of the door-frame, and saved myself from a fall. I was not in the least frightened by this. I smiled and walked away; but one or two Indian prisoners who saw what had happened started weeping. Since they could not offer any help in gaol, they felt helpless and miserable. ...

CWMG Vol. 9, p. 161; G

To 'Lower House'

14 October 1908
King Edward's Hotel[23]
Wednesday

My dear Lower House,

I have just received your charming letter. I purposely refrained from writing to you as really there was nothing to write about. Not a day has passed on which I have not thought of you. We know each other so well that we talk to each other without talking and see without seeing.

I know too that the Lower House thinks more of the Upper House in its absence and can therefore quite understand its doing nothing which ought not to be done.

I fear that the punishment I shall receive today will be trivial. No serious charge seems to be pending. I must be content with even little. I feel quite happy. Rustomji[24], Dawad[25], and others are likewise happy. Dawad is everybody's pick me up.

With love

Yours sincerely
M.K.Gandhi
Gillian Berning (ed.), Gandhi Letters: From Upper House To Lower House (1906–14), *Local History Museum, Durban, 1994, p. 11.*

'Dear Daughter In Law'[26]

Volksrust
Saturday, 16 January 1909[27]

Chiranjivi Chanchal,

I was arrested, deported, again arrested, and am now released on bail. I shall now proceed to Johannesburg ...

... I think Harilal will have to stay at Johannesburg (gaol) till the struggle is over...

... None can say when Ba[28] will completely recover. Even when she is fully restored, your role will not be affected. You have to behave as mistress of the house. Do not forget that we are very poor.

Blessings from
Mohandas
CWMG *Vol. 9, p. 150; G*

'You Are Unhappy'

Wednesday; 27 January 1909

Chiranjivi Harilal,

Your letter to hand. I can see that you are unhappy. I have got to accept your opinion as to whether you would be happy or not on account of separation[29]. However, I see that you will have to undergo imprisonment for a long period. I would like to know what you think about it. Please write to me in detail. The struggle is likely to be a prolonged one. Let me know what arrangement should be made in regard to Chanchal during your absence. More when I have time.

> Blessings from
> Mohandas
> CWMG *Vol. 9, p. 173; E*

Two-Fold Struggle

29 January 1909

My ENTHUSIASM is such that I may have to meet death in South Africa at the hands of my own countrymen ... In this struggle, a two-fold inner struggle is going on. One of them is to bring the Hindus and Muslims together.

> *Letter to Maganlal Gandhi*, CWMG *Vol. 9, p. 175; G*

To 'Lower House'

Phoenix
5 February 1909

My dear Lower House,

That Saturday morning I woke with a dream that the house I was sleeping in was on fire. I woke up in time to leave the house but not to shut it. I therefore concluded that Mrs G died at the time. What folly? That was the time when she rallied under Dr Nanji's[30] skilful treatment & on Sunday I greeted her in comparatively good condition. I do not know whether she will survive the present illness.

Dr Nanji, contrary to our compact gave her beef extract & in informing me of the breach told me that as occasion required he would repeat the performance. After my return & during my absence from his house, he gave the extract again. From his own standpoint he was right. But intrinsically he was wrong. At very great risk and amid rainy weather I removed her to Phoenix yesterday. Dr & Mrs Nanji were grieved. They do not believe in water treatment. They consider me to be a brutal husband & Dr Nanji certainly considers me to be either mad or over conceited. I have risked friendships for the sake of a principle. And for the sake of it I had no difficulty in incurring their displeasure, much as I should like to have avoided doing so in respect of those whom I owe so much.

I do not think she suffered in transit, she had a cold hipbath and one sitzbath today. I gave her some fruit also. She appears to be none the worse for it. She is probably better. But she has lost heart. She cannot bear the idea of my leaving her bedside for a single minute. Like a baby she clings to me & hugs me. I fear that my departure next week will send her to her grave. It is a great conflict of duty for me. Yet there is no doubt in my mind that I must leave her next week and accept the King's hospitality.[31]...

I have filled this letter simply with Mrs G's illness, showing that she absorbs my attention to the exclusion of everything else.

With kind regards

Yours sin(cere)ly
Upper House

[PS]

As luck wd have it, I had to go to her immediately on finishing above. I have now returned to the table 10.30pm.

MG

Gillian Berning (ed.), Gandhi Letters: From Upper House To Lower House (1906–14), *Local History Museum, Durban, 1994, pp. 12–13*

'We Are Happier Here'

Volksrust Prison[32]
Transvaal
26 February 1909

Chiranjivi Chanchal,

I am sorry not to have any letter from you. I see that Ba is getting better. Please read good writings and poems to her. Always write to me after consulting her ...

The change that I made in your diet is to be adhered to as an order from me. Take sago and milk regularly. Feed Rami[33] at the breast for a few days more. Take sufficient food after feeding her also. Your health will not improve so long as you do not get open air. I need not write more.

Blessings from
Mohandas

[PS] Harilal and I are quite well. Be sure that we are happier here than you. Please read out this letter to Ba.

CWMG *Vol. 9, p. 200; G*

Solitary Confinement[34]

Pretoria Prison
March–May 1909

...ONLY A pitch-black wall separated one of the greatest murderers in South Africa and me. We were both in isolation cells by design, for we were both considered dangerous to society. I had to suffer in that cell for nearly two months. ...

CWMG *Vol. 22, p. 245; E*

'My Dear Son'[35]

Pretoria Prison
Transvaal
25 March 1909

I HAVE a right to write one letter per month and receive also one letter per month. It became a question with me as to whom I should write to. I thought of Mr Ritch, Mr Polak, and you. I chose you, as you have been nearest my thoughts in all my reading.

As for myself I must not, I am not allowed to, say much. I am quite at peace and none need worry about me. I hope mother is now quite well ...

And how is Chanchi[36]? Tell her I think of her everyday. I hope she has got rid of all the sores she had and that she and Rami are quite well. I was much struck by one passage in Nathuramji's[37] introduction to the *Upanishads*. He says that the brahmacharya stage, i.e., the first stage—is like the last, i.e., the *Sanyasin* stage. This is true. Amusement only continues during the age of innocence, i.e., up to twelve years only ... Of amusement after I was twelve, I had little or none. If you practice the three virtues, if they become part of your life, so far as I am concerned, you will have completed your education—your training ...

Remember please that henceforth our lot is poverty. The more I think of it, the more I feel that it is more blessed to be poor than to be rich. The uses of poverty are far sweeter than those of riches ...

And now I close with love to all and kisses to Ramdas, Devadas and Rami.

CWMG Vol. 9, pp. 205–9; E

'The Nearest Are Always There'

Johannesburg
1909

[Millie Graham Polak recounts: *We were talking of the value of courtesy in friendship one day. I had said that I did not like the idea that, because I was near to the heart of a person, I need not have the same courtesy shown to me as would be shown to a stranger.*]

MKG: But, it is the privilege of affection and friendship that it has not to show formality.

MGP: I am not making a plea for formality, but why should it be considered more right for a man, for example, to open a door for a stranger when the same man would not attempt to open it for his wife?

MKG: But a man does not need to be always thinking about his own. His own are a part of himself.

MGP: That argument may make an appeal to my heart but it does not to my brain.

MKG: Then your brain is wrong. I have often told you so; you should not trust it.

MGP: I am serious. I want to know what you really think about it.

MKG: Does a man think about his arm, then, or pay special attention to it? Of course not; it is a part of him, and is cared for with the rest of him. Our nearest are like that, a part of our very selves, and, as such, can seem to be forgotten, but they are always there.

MGP: I think I sometimes prefer to be thought of, then, as someone perhaps a little farther away. I don't want to be put on one side as an unconscious bit of the body by those I love!

MKG: Then what do you want?

MGP: Well, I do not want the price I pay for love to be that I am ignored.

MKG: But if you know you are the heart of another, do you need to be told it, and shown it?

MGP: Yes. I do; most certainly I do.

MKG: That is not identification, as all true love should be!

MGP: I am afraid we are getting too involved. To return to the beginning, I say again, I think it wrong to omit the acts of thoughtful courtesy and self-control to those who have the first claim upon our consideration, and to reserve our smiling best for the stranger. I see it happen and it vexes me, for I cannot justify it.

MKG: Then do not worry yourself by thinking about it!

from Millie Graham Polak's Mr Gandhi: The Man

Part Nine

1909-14

Gandhi and C.F. Andrews,
South Africa, 1914

TRIALS AND TRIUMPH IN SOUTH AFRICA

I have a strain of cruelty in me.

In 1909, out of jail, Gandhi was asked by the Indians in South Africa to go once again to London to ask for relief.

Lord Minto II was Viceroy of India. Calcutta—then the imperial capital of India—was in a different mood from that of the Curzon era. Naoroji, with his great reputation in London, had presided over the Congress in Calcutta in 1906, the opposition to the Partition of Bengal had occasioned a level of opposition not known in India earlier, Jinnah in the Viceroy's Council was raising the issue of Indians in South Africa trenchantly, the Muslim League had come into being (1906) and if the Moderate section of the divided Congress after 1907 was becoming difficult to ignore, the Extremist section was becoming impossible to curb. And, most disturbing for Whitehall and for Gandhi, the politics of assassination was in the air.

Gandhi spent nearly four months in London. The very day Gandhi landed on his deputation in London, Madan Lal Dhingra shot dead Sir Curzon Wyllie, a political aide to the Secretary of State for India. And on the day Gandhi left London, a bomb was hurled by extremists in Ahmedabad in the wake of Lord and Lady Mayo. While in London, he: (i) shifted from Hotel Cecil to the less expensive Westminster Palace Hotel; (ii) met Secretary of State for India Lord Morley; (iii) met Suffragette leader Emeline Pankhurst; (iv) met Secretary of State for Colonies, Lord Crewe; (v) wrote to Leo Tolstoy about the Indians' struggle in South Africa; (vi) addressed a gathering of thirty Hindu, Muslim, and Parsi speakers of Gujarati on 'Matrubhasha' (the mother tongue); (vii) addressed the Emerson Club, Hampstead Peace and Arbitrative Society on 'East and West';

(viii) addressed a gathering to mark Dussehra (24 October) at the Nazimuddin Restaurant, Bayswater, as President of the meeting with the other speaker being none other than Vinayak Damodar Savarkar; and (ix) visited the Indian Union Society and the Indian Majlis, Cambridge.

During this stay in London, Gandhi's London-based friend Dr Pranjivan Mehta expressed a desire to finance the legal study in England for any one of Gandhi's sons, with Harilal or Manilal on his mind, but Gandhi said his nephew Chhaganlal would avail the offer. This was to gall on Harilal.

If the need for amelioration in South Africa and for Swaraj in India were occupying Gandhi's thoughts, so was the question of ends and means and, going further, questions pertaining to modern civilization. The philosopher and the politician alternated in the thirty-nine-year-old barrister's mind and he unburdened himself in several pages that he penned in Gujarati during his return journey aboard the S.S. *Kildonan Castle*. These were to appear as a seminal book, *Hind Swaraj*.

That work of importance has been cited and quoted from so frequently that I have chosen to encourage the reader to go to the original *in extenso* rather than provide excerpts. But one of the sentences from that work I have included is about his imaginative anticipation of future mechanical devices which stunned me as a forecasting of the computer, the internet, and 'on-line' technology.

Satyagraha was to continue in South Africa, with more and more volunteers being needed. These were, necessarily, 'family' men and women. Their dependents needed to be taken care of. Where was the money for that? Where was the space? At Kallenbach's initiative Gandhi set up a second ashram, Tolstoy Farm, near Johannesburg for the families of the Satyagrahis, including his own.

During this period Gandhi did not write as 'essentially' as he was to, later. His essential thinking of this period was to emerge in written form only some fifteen years later when in Yeravda Prison he began to write the serialization of *Satyagraha in South Africa*. This Part draws from that later recapitulation of the unfolding events and evolving thought-processes. Hindsight did not rob that text of any vividness. It, of course, added the maturity of experience to the retelling.

The fluctuating relations with Kasturba and his sons, especially Harilal and Manilal, the use of disciplinary intervention on Ashram inmates and the preferment of a valued colleague like Sorabji Shapurji Adajania over his son are of the stuff of character-portrayals in a novel. Gopal Krishna Gokhale's visit to South Africa is as a poultice over a painful injury. Equally, that visit, with its negotiations in Pretoria, marks the beginning of the end of Gandhi's South African phase.

But the end of this phase comes only after a major climacteric, provided by the judgement of Justice Searle of the Cape Supreme Court which had the effect of declaring all marriages not performed in accordance with Christian rites and registered with the Registrar of Marriages, as illegal.

Gandhi orchestrated, in response to this judgement, a protest the like of which had not been known in South Africa. This Part contains cameos of that epic transaction and the 'Great March' of April 1913. Another interview with Smuts ensued, with Gandhi being clearly in the stronger bargaining seat. And an Agreement was arrived at, releasing Gandhi for the battles that awaited him in India. But the route to Bombay lay via London where Gandhi wanted to confer with Gokhale who was in that city at the time.

If Gandhi's preferring Chhaganlal and, later, Adajania to Harilal for sponsorship to London caused strains within the family, we can see that the arrival from India of C. F. Andrews, whose rapport with Gandhi was instantaneous and intense, created a tension within Kallenbach. Gandhi had to becalm his loyal friend who had altered his lifestyle and career-path to merge with Gandhi, and whom Gandhi had come to regard as his 'nearest' and 'dearest' friend—with what effect on Polak, we do not know.

Was there an inconsistency here? Or just an outgrowing?

Towards the beginning of 1914 Kasturba just about recovered from a near fatal illness, Manilal's 'episode' with 'Jeki' Doctor led Gandhi to fast, breaking his spirit and weakening his body. Harilal had already left to chart his own rebellious course. Gandhi sent the 'Phoenix' party to India directly, under Maganlal's charge and in very Indianized attire to look for the beginnings of the thread of a new life in India—no easy task for a group that was Indian in every respect but raised in distant South Africa according to the nostrums of a man whose 'love' was 'tyrannical' and who in his own words had 'a strain of cruelty' in him.

Gandhi and Smuts had reconciled but the Gandhi 'family' was in a state of upheaval. Accompanied by Kasturba and perhaps, as an act of mollification by Kallenbach, who had felt 'threatened' by Andrews, Gandhi left South Africa's shore for the last time on 18 July 1914.

Kallenbach needed further mollifying. Not just because of the Andrews factor but because the outbreak of World War I made the German-born Kallenbach, in London, an internee who could not accompany Gandhi, as had been planned, to India.

To 'Lower House'

London
11 July 1909

My dear Lower House,

Overworked! The atmosphere of London now no longer appeals to me as it did years ago[1]. The whole of the bustle seems to be meaningless. I am sure if you were here, you will feel much the same if you brought your tranquil mind & were not intoxicated with love of pleasure which is killing. This does not mean that we are not coming here when we can. Only we are going to live out of the way in a distant place far from the madding & ignoble strife.

I shall not forget the promise to the Buffer House[2].

Yours sin(cere)ly
Upper House

Gillian Berning (ed.), Gandhi Letters: From Upper House To Lower House (1906–14), *Local History Museum, Durban, 1994, p. 13*

A Promise To Kallenbach

Westminster Palace Hotel[3]
London, 30 August 1909

YOU REMIND me of friendships of bygone ages of which one reads in histories & novels: I promise this—that I shall ever pray that I may ever retain the seat I have found in your heart and that I may do nothing to forfeit that love which is almost superhuman.

'Henceforth, The Struggle Will Be Sharp'

London[4]
2 September 1909

Chiranjivi Harilal,

... Henceforth the struggle will be very sharp. I see father and son spending a lifetime in jail. On my part, I am prepared for it but I would like to know your state of mind about this. I pray to God that you be afforded all the energy required ... I keep feeling it is good that you and I be together in jail. ...

Blessings from
Bapu

Gandhijinu Khovayelu Dhan: Harilal Gandhi by Nilam Parikh,
published by Navajivan, 1998; translated to the Editor.

'Our Worst Enemy Is Our Weakness'

1 October 1909[5]

IT IS my firm belief that if you are weak, no matter whether you show your weakness in words or not, if you leave unconsciously an impression of it on your opponent ... our worst enemy is our weakness.

from Hermann Kallenbach—Mahatma Gandhi's Friend in South Africa
by Isa Sarid and Christian Bartolf, Gandhi-Information-Zentrum,
Selbstverlag; 1997

To 'Lower House'

London
9 October 1909
Saturday

My dear Lower House,

Only a line today. The book I wanted to send you I have not got yet. I must reserve it for next week.

I spoke to a good audience yesterday on the ethics of Passive Resistance[6]. I saw that I failed to find a response. Could I when I said that if a robber robbed me I should not offer violence—or physical resistance even if I was capable of using it! However it has set the friends thinking. I am writing this amid great disturbance so I will finish.

Yours sin(cere)ly
Upper House

Gillian Berning (ed.), Gandhi Letters: From Upper House To Lower House (1906–14), *Local History Museum, Durban, 1994, p. 14.*

To 'Lower House'

London
12 October 1909

My dear Lower House,

Your letter as usual. I envy you your walk in sandals. I wish I could join you. My feet are rotten through having to have the boots on from 8 a.m. or 9 a.m. to 12 or 2 midnight ...

I am glad of the presentation of the address to you by the white city Bazaar. In your opinion the work you put in may not be very much. But those who are never fond of honest work thought much of it. That is the tribute vice pays to virtue. And yet we often fail to realise the grandeur of a strictly moral life and the satisfaction it gives.

Yours sin(cere)ly
Upper House

Gillian Berning (ed.), Gandhi Letters: From Upper House To Lower House (1906–14), *Local History Museum, Durban, 1994, p. 14*

London, 5 November 1909

... I am itching to join him[7].

CMWG *Vol. 9, p. 513; E*

LORD AMPTHILL rendered us invaluable help. He used to meet Mr Merriman, General Botha, and others and at last he brought a message from the General. Said he: 'General Botha appreciates your feelings in the matter, and is willing to grant you minor demands. But he is not ready to repeal the Asiatic Act or to amend the Immigrants Restriction Act. He also refuses to remove the colour bar....'

And after delivering the message Lord Ampthill said, 'You see that General Botha concedes all your practical demands, and in this work-a-day world we must always give and take ...'

I said: 'We are both highly obliged to you for the trouble you have taken...The Indians for whom I speak are comparatively poor and inferior in numbers, but they are resolute unto death ...'

SiSA, pp. 209-10

DURING MY stay in England I had occasion to talk with many Indian anarchists. My booklet *Indian Home Rule* written during my return voyage to South Africa on board S.S. *Kildonan Castle* (November 1909) and published soon afterwards in *Indian Opinion* had its birth from the necessity of having to meet their arguments as well as to solve the difficulties of Indians in South Africa who held similar views.

SiSA, p. 211

Hind Swaraj[8]

CIVILIZATION

Reader: ... Now will you tell me something of what you have read and thought of this civilization?

Editor: Let us first consider what state of things is described by the word 'civilization'. Its true test lies in the fact that people living in it make bodily welfare the object of life. We will take some examples. The people of Europe today live in better-built houses than they did a hundred years ago. This is considered an emblem of civilization, and this is also a matter to promote bodily happiness. Formerly, they wore skins, and used spears as their weapons. Now, they wear long trousers, and, for embellishing their bodies, they wear a variety of clothing, and, instead of spears, they carry with them revolvers containing five or more chambers. If people of a certain country, who have hitherto not been in the habit of wearing much clothing, boots, etc., adopt European clothing, they are supposed to have become civilized out of savagery. Formerly, in Europe, people ploughed their lands mainly by manual labour. Now, one man can plough a vast tract by means of steam engines and can thus amass great wealth. This is called a sign of civilization. Formerly, only a few men wrote valuable books. Now, anybody writes and prints anything he likes and poisons people's minds. Formerly, men travelled in waggons. Now, they fly through the air in trains at the rate of 400 and more miles per day. This is considered the height of civilization. It has been stated that, as men progress, they shall be able to travel in airships and reach any part of the world in a few hours. Men will not need the use of their hands and feet. They will press a button, and they will have their clothing by their side. They will press another button, and they will have their newspaper ... This civilization is such that one has only to be patient and it will be self-destroyed.

CWMG *Vol. 10, pp. 19–21*

Freeing India By Assassination

Reader: ... At first we shall assassinate a few Englishmen and strike terror; then, a few men who will have been armed will fight openly. We may have to lose 2,000,000 or 2,500,000 men, more or less but we shall regain our land. We shall undertake guerrilla warfare, and defeat the English.

Editor: That is to say, you want to make the holy land of India unholy. Do you not tremble to think of freeing India by assassination? What we need to do is to sacrifice ourselves. It is a cowardly thought, that of killing others. Whom do you suppose to free by assassination? The millions of India do not desire it. Those who are intoxicated by the wretched modern civilization think these things. Those who will rise to power by murder will certainly not make the nation happy. Those who believe that India has gained by Dhingra's[9] act and other similar acts in India make a serious mistake. Dhingra was a patriot, but his love was blind. He gave his body in a wrong way; its ultimate result can only be mischievous.

CWMG *Vol. 10, p. 42; E*

IT IS being said in defence of Sir Curzon Wyllie's assassination that...just as the British would kill every German if Germany invaded

Britain, so too it is the right of any Indian to kill any Englishman ... The analogy ... is fallacious. If the Germans were to invade Britain, the British would kill only the invaders. They would not kill every German whom they met ... They would not kill an unsuspecting German, or Germans who are guests.

14 August issue of Indian Opinion

A Command

Durban Pier
end-1909

He shan't move an inch.[10]

Prabhudas Gandhi, Jeevan Prabhat, *pp. 197–8*

Tolstoy Farm

1910

THE DEPUTATION which now returned from England did not bring good news. But I did not mind what conclusions the community would draw from our conversations with Lord Ampthill. I knew who would stand by us till the end. My ideas about satyagraha had now matured and I had realized its universality as well as its excellence. I was therefore perfectly at ease. *Hind Swaraj* was written in order to demonstrate the sublimity of satyagraha and that book is a true measure of my faith in its efficacy. I was perfectly indifferent to the numerical strength of the fighters on our side. But I was not free from anxiety on the score of finance.

But I had faith in God who did not even then desert me but raised me from the slough of despondency. If on the one hand I had to tell the Indians on our landing in South Africa that our mission had failed, on the other hand God relieved me from financial difficulty. As I set my foot in Cape Town I received a cable from England that Mr (afterwards Sir) Ratanji Jamshedji Tata had given Rs 25,000 to the Satyagraha funds. This sum amply sufficed for our immediate needs and we forged ahead.

SiSA, p. 212; G

TILL NOW the families of jail-going Satyagrahis were maintained by a system of monthly allowances in cash according to their need ...

SiSA, p. 213; G

There was only one solution for this difficulty, namely, that all the families should be kept at one place and should become members of a sort of co-operative commonwealth. Thus there would be no scope for fraud, nor would there be injustice to any.

SiSA, pp. 213–14

BUT WHERE was the place suitable for a settlement of this nature? To live in a city would have been like straining at a gnat and swallowing a camel. ...

The place required then must be in the Transvaal and near Johannesburg. Mr Kallenbach, whose acquaintance the reader has already made, bought a farm of about 1,100 acres and gave the use of it to Satyagrahis free of any rent or charge (30 May 1910). Upon the farm there were nearly 1000 fruit-bearing trees and a small house at the foot of a hill with accommodation for half-a-dozen persons. Water was supplied from two wells as well as from a spring. The nearest railway station, Lawley, was about a mile from the farm and Johannesburg was 21 miles distant. We decided to build houses upon this Farm and to invite the families of Satyagrahis to settle there.

SiSA, p. 214; G

HERE WE insisted that we should not have any servants either for the household work or as far as might be even for the farming and building operations. Everything therefore from cooking to scavenging was done with our own hands. As regards accommodation for families, we resolved from the first that the men and women should be housed separately. The houses therefore were to be built in two separate blocks, each at some distance from the other. For the time it was considered sufficient to provide accommodation for ten women and sixty men. Then again we had to erect a house for Mr Kallenbach and by its side a school house, as well as a workshop for carpentry, shoemaking, etc.

SiSA, p. 215; G

THE WEAK became strong on Tolstoy Farm and labour proved to be a tonic for all.

SiSA, p. 217; G

THE WORK before us was to make the Farm a busy hive of industry, thus to save money and in the end to make the families self-supporting. If we achieved this goal, we could battle with the Transvaal government for an indefinite period. We had to spend some money on shoes. The use of shoes in a hot climate is harmful, as all the perspiration is absorbed by the feet which thus grow tender. As in India, no socks were needed in the Transvaal but we thought that the feet must be protected against thorns, stones, and the like. We therefore determined to learn to make sandals. There is at Marianhill near Pinetown a monastery of German Catholic monks called the Trappists, where industries of this nature are carried on. Mr Kallenbach went there and acquired the art of making sandals. After he returned, he taught it to me and I in my turn to other workers.

SiSA, p. 219; G

A SCHOOL was indispensable for the youngsters and the children. This was the most difficult of our tasks and we never achieved complete success in this matter till the very last. The burden of teaching work was largely borne by Mr Kallenbach and myself. The school could be held only in the afternoon, when both of us were thoroughly exhausted by our morning labour, and so were our pupils. The teachers therefore would often be dozing as well as the taught.

SiSA, pp. 220–1; G

IN SOUTH Africa[11] we slept in the open not only when it was extremely cold but even when it was raining. In the cold weather we used any number of blankets, and during the rainy season we kept a mackintosh on the top. We had even thought out some method of covering the face. We were fanatical experimenters, determined to carry everything to its legitimate conclusion. For instance we consumed a large number of onions when we found that they were nutritious. And at one time I took a lot of tamarind with *gud* (treacle) and water as it is anti-scorbutic as well as much cheaper than lemons.

Mahadev Desai's Diary Vol. 1, 1932, p. 85

THE BOYS and girls met freely. My experiment of co-education on Tolstoy Farm was the most fearless of its type. I dare not today allow, or train children to enjoy, the liberty which I had granted the Tolstoy Farm class. I have often felt that my mind then used to be more innocent than it is now, and that was due perhaps to my ignorance. Since then I have had bitter experiences, and have sometimes burnt my fingers badly. Persons whom I took to be thoroughly innocent have turned out corrupt. I have observed the roots of evil deep down in my own nature; and timidity has claimed me for its own.

SiSA, *p. 222; G*

ALL OF us slept in an open verandah. The boys and the girls would spread themselves around me. There was hardly a distance of three feet between any two beds. Some care was exercised in arranging the order of the beds, but any amount of such care would have been futile in the case of a wicked mind. I now see that God alone safeguarded the honour of these boys and girls. I made the experiment from a belief that boys and girls could thus live together without harm, and the parents with their boundless faith in me allowed me to make it.

One day one of the young men made fun of two girls, and the girls themselves or some child brought me the information. The news made me tremble. I made inquiries and found that the report was true. I remonstrated with the young men, but that was not enough. I wished the two girls to have some sign on their person as a warning to every young man that no evil eye might be cast upon them, and as a lesson to every girl that no one dare assail their purity. The passionate Ravana could not so much as touch Sita with evil intent while Rama was thousands of miles away. What mark should the girls bear so as to give them a sense of security and at the same time to sterilize the sinner's eye? This question kept me awake for the night. In the morning I gently suggested to the girls that they might let me cut off their fine long hair. On the Farm we shaved and cut the hair of one another, and we therefore kept scissors and clipping machines. At first the girls would not listen to me. I had already explained the situation to the elderly women who could not bear to think of my suggestion but yet quite understood my motive, and they had finally accorded their support to me. They were both of them noble girls. One of them is alas! now no more. She was very bright and intelligent. The other is living and the mistress of a household of her own. They came round after all and the very hand that is narrating this incident set to cut off their hair.

SiSA, *pp. 222–4*

I used to make the Ashram boys start at 4 a.m. and walk 21 miles[12]. Then they would take some refreshment. Then again in the evening they would walk 21 miles to get back, making 42 miles in all.

WHILE TEACHING the boys and girls of Tolstoy Farm in South Africa, I happened to read to them Wordsworth's 'Character of the Happy Warrior'.[13]

To 'Lower House'

Durban
February 1910
Sunday

My dear Lower House,
    I am nearing Durban. The train will reach late ...
    Have you written to Miss Prellenburg?
Prescription
<u>no worry</u>
Fruit & bread
bread & fruit
no cocoa
milk if necessary

Yours sin(cere)ly
Upper House

Gillian Berning (ed.), Gandhi Letters: From Upper House To Lower House (1906–14), *Local History Museum, Durban, 1994, p. 15.*

'No Beauty In Jewellery'

Tolstoy Farm
Sunday, 8 January 1911[14]

Chiranjivi Chanchal,
    I was very glad to read your long and interesting letter. Ba also read it with interest. Harilal will read it on his release tomorrow.

I hasten to write this today as I have no time at the office. I am at the Farm just now. It is 9 p.m. You must be getting *Indian Opinion* regularly.

Do you ever go out for a walk? It is good that you have kept up the habit of reading.

I wish you not to wear jewellery for fear of being criticized if you don't. There is no beauty in jewellery ... there is no beauty in perforating the nose and the ears and inserting something there or in wearing ornaments round the neck or the arms. However, I say nothing about putting on bangles round the wrists, as their absence would suggest something inauspicious.

It would be enough if we put on these things to prevent talk.

These are my views. Think over them and do as you deem proper. ...

CWMG, *Vol. 10, pp. 397–8; G*

Tolstoy Farm
19 March 1911

Chiranjivi Maganlal,[15]

... The more defects you discover in Harilal, the more love you should have for him. One requires a great deal of water to put out a big fire. To overcome the baser element in Harilal's nature, you have to develop in yourself and pit against it a more powerful force of goodness. Give him the coat too when he asks for a shirt ...

Letter to Maganlal Gandhi, CWMG *Vol. 10, p. 476; G*

To 'Lower House'

Tolstoy Farm
Lawley Station
Transvaal
21 February 1911

My dear Lower House,

You will be glad to learn that it has been raining steadily the whole day and even as I write this at 9 p.m., the heavenly music of the gently dropping water pleases the ear. Naturally there has been little outdoor work done today. Naidoo[16] has been making cases and wooden pillows. You were right as to the latter. The form you saw did not answer. He had made yesterday a pillow after the style suggested by you. It answered the purpose admirably and I certainly preferred it to the ordinary coil or feather pillow ...

T. Raju finished sewing his father's sandals so that we have now produced a handsewn pair on the farm. Harilal completed John's sandals today practically without any guidance from me. I propose now to devote more time to the schooling of the children. I gave them some physical drill also. They were or seemed to be quite delighted. I wish you could give them about $^1/_2$ hour every Sunday. Mine is so uncouth and ignorant.

Please remember you are to try to make cheese without rennet.

So far as possible I propose now to go to Town only once a week. Constant presence on the farm is necessary in order to avoid squabbles.

With love

Yours sin(cere)ly
Upper House
Gillian Berning (ed.), Gandhi Letters: From Upper House To Lower House (1906–14), *Local History Museum, Durban, 1994, p. 17*

'Harilal—Unsettled In Mind'

Johannesburg
18 May 1911

Chiranjivi Maganlal,

... It is just as well that Harilal[17] has left. He was much unsettled in mind. He has assured me that he does not in the least resent the arrangement I had made regarding Phoenix. He bears no ill will towards any of you. He was angry with me, really ... He seemed to me to have calmed down after this outburst. I pointed out his error in believing what he did. He saw it partly. ...

Letter to Maganlal Gandhi, CWMG *Vol. 11, pp. 77–8*; G

Johannesburg
18 May 1911

Chiranjivi Chhaganlal,

He[18] gave vent to all his pent-up feelings on Monday evening. He feels that I have kept all the four boys very much suppressed, that I did not respect their wishes at any time, that I have treated them as of no account, and that I have often been hard-hearted. He made this charge against me with the utmost courtesy and seemed very hesitant as he did so. In this, he had no thought of money at all in his mind. It was all about my general behaviour. Unlike other fathers, I have not admired my sons or done anything specially for them, but always put them and Ba last; such was the charge.

Letter to Chhaganlal Gandhi; The South African Gandhi *(1996) edited by Fatima Meer, pp. 1088–9; G*

Sorabji Shapurji Adajania

Now AS satyagraha was made to embrace the Immigration Act as well, satyagrahis had to test the right of educated Indians to enter the Transvaal. The committee decided that the test should not be made through any ordinary Indian ...

... I therefore recommended to the Committee that they should take Sorabji at his word, and eventually Sorabji proved himself to be a first class satyagrahi. He not only was one of the satyagrahis who suffered the longest terms of imprisonment, but also made such deep study of the struggle that his views commanded respectful hearing from all. His advice always betrayed firmness, wisdom, charity, and deliberation. He was slow to form an opinion as well as to change an opinion once formed. He was as much of an Indian as of a Parsi, and was quite free from the bane of narrow communalism. After the struggle was over Doctor Mehta[19] offered a scholarship in order to enable some good satyagrahi to proceed to England for the Bar. I was charged with the selection. There were two or three deserving candidates, but all the friends felt that there was none who could approach Sorabji in maturity of judgment and ripeness of wisdom, and he was selected accordingly. The idea was, that on his return to South Africa he should take my place and serve the community.

SiSA, pp. 192–4; G

Durban
17 June 1911

My dear Lower House,
I have been here for Sorabji since yesterday. He had an address and a dressing case. Sorabji is a gem. The more I see him the more I

love him. It is now 10 p.m. We have just returned from the Point[20]
after seeing him off ...
　　With love

Yours

Upper House

Gillian Berning (ed.), Gandhi Letters: From Upper House To Lower
House (1906–14), *Local History Museum, Durban, 1994, p. 19*

To 'Lower House'

Phoenix

23 June 1911

Friday

My dear Lower House,

　　My fi(n)gers are aching with too much writing. I therefore try
the left hand while I am waiting for the folding to commence. We
shall be very late today. There is much to print today. The number
will be extra heavy. The Durban Indians[21] surpassed themselves
yesterday. 3000 men acted as one man. I know that there is still
much of the theatre behind this action. Still what they did was
certainly most creditable. I hope you will make time to read the
whole number of I.O.[22] most carefully. I want you to criticize the
Coronation leading article[23].

　　This will be my last letter before my return.

　　With love

Yours

Upper House

Gillian Berning (ed.), Gandhi Letters: From Upper House To Lower
House (1906–14), *Local History Museum, Durban, 1994, p. 19*

Phoenix

23 July 1911

LOWER HOUSE is hereby informed that Upper House has just heard
that the circulation of I.O. has been prohibited in India. If the news
be true, welcome Andamans[24].

Gillian Berning (ed.), Gandhi Letters: From Upper House To Lower
House (1906–14), *Local History Museum, Durban, 1994, p. 20*

Tolstoy Farm
Lawley Station
Transvaal
On the train
1911

My dear Lower House,

'God give me love and care and strength to help my ailing brother!' That brother is Kennedy for the time being. Will you ask for love and care and strength to help him? Contemplate the good in him and you will transform him. It will bring you peace and joy.

With love
Upper House

Gillian Berning (ed.), Gandhi Letters: From Upper House To Lower House (1906–14), *Local History Museum, Durban, 1994, p. 20.*

29 October 1911[25]

I HAVE I think often told you that no man may be called good before his death. Departure by a hair's breadth from the straight + narrow path may undo the whole of his past.

Hermann Kallenbach—Mahatma Gandhi's Friend in South Africa *by Isa Sarid and Christian Bartolf, Selbstverlag; 1997*

Phoenix
3 September 1912

Dear Lower House,

We had an undisturbed journey this time. Devadas much enjoyed himself as he had his companions. He is working very well. If he continues it would certainly be a great gain. Polak comes tomorrow. I walked to town yesterday with Desai[26]. We lost our way and lost nearly an hour so we took the train at Umgeni[27].

Albert has benefited immensely. He is no trouble to anybody. He eats too very moderately and fearlessly slept at night under the trees. He showed me with pride his pearl white teeth. He keeps himself in a very clean condition and passes the whole day in the garden reading ...

Yours sin(cere)ly
M.K. Gandhi

Gillian Berning (ed.), Gandhi Letters: From Upper House To Lower House (1906–14), *Local History Museum, Durban, 1994, p. 22.*

'Sorabji Should Become A Barrister And You Should Strengthen Your Character'

Lawley
16 October 1912

Chiranjivi Harilal,

I have your letter after so many months ... You have not understood the step I have taken regarding Sorabji. The chief thing is that he is a Parsi, and it befits a Hindu to encourage him. If Sorabji succeeds in becoming a barrister, his responsibilities will increase ... now you should only attend to the strengthening of your character in your own way—that is all I want. I am sure you will change your ideas in future.

You have again succumbed to passion in regard to Chanchal[28]. I can well understand it. ...

CWMG *Vol. 11, p. 333; G*

Gokhale And Cold Soup

November 1912

GOKHALE ARRIVED[29] in South Africa while we were still living on the Farm.

There was no cot on the Farm, but we borrowed one for Gokhale. There was no room where he could enjoy full privacy. For sitting accommodation we had nothing beyond the benches in our school. ... He had been put up in Mr Kallenbach's room. His dinner would get cold while we brought it from the kitchen to his room. I prepared special soup, and Kotval special bread for him, but these could not be taken to him hot. We managed as best we could. Gokhale uttered not a syllable, but I understood from his face what a folly I had committed. When Gokhale came to know that all of us slept on the floor, he removed the cot which had been brought for him and had his own bed too spread on the floor. This whole night was a night of repentance for me. Gokhale had a rule in life which seemed to me a bad rule. He would not permit any one except a servant to wait upon him. He had no servant with him during this tour. Mr Kallenbach and I entreated him to let us massage his feet. But he would not let us even touch him.

SiSA, *pp. 226–7; G*

'Gandhi, You Will Always Have Your Own Way'

I HAVE always insisted on speaking either in the mother tongue or else in Hindustani, the *lingua franca* of India, and thanks to this insistence I have had much facility in establishing close relations with the Indians in South Africa ... I told Gokhale that these friends would be highly pleased if he spoke in Marathi and I would translate his Marathi into Hindustani. Gokhale burst into laughter and said, 'I have quite fathomed your knowledge of Hindustani, upon which you cannot exactly be congratulated. But now you propose to translate Marathi into Hindustani. May I know where you acquired such profound knowledge of Marathi?' I replied, 'What is true of my Hindustani is equally true of my Marathi. I cannot speak a single word of Marathi, but I am confident of gathering the purport of your Marathi speech on a subject with which I am familiar ...' 'You will always have your own way, ' said Gokhale. 'And there is no help for me as I am here at your mercy.'

SiSA, pp. 242–3; G

GOKHALE'S INTERVIEW with the ministers lasted for about two hours, and when he returned, he said, 'You must return to India in a year. Everything has been settled. The Black Act will be repealed. The racial bar will be removed from the emigration law. The £3 tax will be abolished.' 'I doubt it very much, ' I replied, 'you do not know the ministers as I do. Being an optimist myself, I love your optimism, but having suffered frequent disappointments, I am not as hopeful in the matter as you are. But I have no fears either. It is enough for me that you have obtained this undertaking from the ministers.'

SiSA, pp. 244–5; G

'I Want To Be Your Pupil'

Dar-Es-Salam
4 December 1912

Dear Mr Gokhale,
    ... Will you forgive me for all my imperfections? I want to be a worthy pupil of yours. This is not mock humility but Indian

seriousness. I want to realize in myself the conception I have of an Eastern pupil. We may have many differences of opinion, but you shall still be my pattern in political life.

One word from the quack physician. Ample fasting, strict adherence to two meals, absence of condiments of all kinds from your food, omission of pulses, tea, coffee, etc., regular taking of Kuhne baths, regular and brisk walking in the country (not the pacing up and down for stimulating thought), ample allowance of olive oil and acid fruit and gradual elimination of cooked food—and you will get rid of your diabetes and add a few more years than you think to your life of service in your present body. ...

CWMG *Vol. 11, pp. 351–2; E*

To 'Lower House'

Phoenix
17 January 1913

My dear Lower House,

You will pardon my not writing to you often. Not a minute to spare. It is wonderful what the human system is capable of doing when it is put to it. My work at the farm is nothing compared to what I am going through here. Boys have altered accordingly. More when we meet if you are coming shortly or when I have a little more leisure for writing.

With love

Yours sin(cere)ly
Upper House

Gillian Berning (ed.), Gandhi Letters: From Upper House To Lower House (1906–14), *Local History Museum, Durban, 1994, p. 23.*

February 1913
Saturday

My dear Lower House,

A week has gone by without a line from you! This is unpardonable.

Yours
Upper House

Gillian Berning (ed.), Gandhi Letters: From Upper House To Lower House (1906–14), *Local History Museum, Durban, 1994, p. 23.*

Phoenix
5 March 1913[30]

REFUSE TO believe that you are weak (and) you will be strong. Believe continuously that you are wicked (and) you will sink.

Hermann Kallenbach—Mahatma Gandhi's Friend in South Africa
by Isa Sarid and Christian Bartolf, Selbstverlag; 1997

Phoenix
31 March 1913

My dear Lower House,

You w(oul)d like to read this. You may destroy it after perusal. There is a likelihood of passive resistance reviving[31]. But I have not the time to write to you at length at present.

Manilal, Ramdas, and the two new arrivals and two more with Jeki walked to the falls[32] today. They carried Jeki part of the way in the hammock.

Upper House
Gillian Berning (ed.), Gandhi Letters: From Upper House To Lower House (1906–14), *Local History Museum, Durban, 1994, p. 25*

When Marriage Is Not A Marriage

March 1913

AT THIS time there was a case in which Mr Justice Searle of the Cape Supreme Court gave judgement on 14 March 1913 to the effect that all marriages were outside the pale of legal marriages in South Africa with the exception of such as were celebrated according to Christian rites and registered by the Registrar of Marriages.

SiSA, p. 251; G

April 1913

PATIENCE WAS impossible in the face of this insult offered to our womanhood. We decided to offer stubborn Satyagraha irrespective of the number of fighters. Not only could the women now be not prevented from joining the struggle, but we decided even to invite them to come into line along with the men. We first invited the sisters who had lived on Tolstoy Farm. I found that they were only too glad to enter the struggle.

SiSA, p. 252; G

The Great March

April 1913

I KNEW that the step of sending women to jail was fraught with serious risk. Most of the sisters[33] in Phoenix spoke Gujarati. They had not had the training or experience of the Transvaal sisters. Moreover, most of them were related to me, and might think of going to jail only on account of my influence with them ...

SiSA, pp. 254–5; G

April 1913

Kasturba: I am sorry that you are not telling me about this. What defect is there in me which disqualifies me for jail? I also wish to take the path to which you are inviting the others.

MKG: There is no question of distrust in you. I would be only too glad if you went to jail but it should not appear at all as if you went at my instance ...

Kasturba: You may have nothing to do with me if being unable to stand jail I secure my release by an apology. If you can endure hardships and so can my boys, why cannot I? I am bound to join the struggle.

MKG: Then I am bound to admit you to it. Even now reconsider the matter if you like and if after mature thought ...

Kasturba: I have nothing to think about, I am fully determined.

Adapted from SiSA, p. 255

Stolen Lemons[34]

Phoenix
May 1913

DEVADAS ATE stolen lemons at Inanda Falls although he had promised not to do such a thing again. When he was faced with the fact, he was inclined to be naughty and sharp. This grieved me much. And his last defence broke me entirely. He said he did not immediately confess his guilt as he was afraid of being hit by me, as if I am in the habit of hitting boys. And so I felt that by way of a lesson to him I would deposit a few slaps on my cheeks which I did and then felt the grief so much that I wept bitterly.

HK, *p. 96; E*

Phoenix
20 May 1913

My dear Lower House,
    Your letters of (sic) late, few by far as they have been, have been more remarkable for what they do not say than for what they do say. But I must take what you give me—not what I would have ...

With love
Upper House

[PS]
    I walked to town yesterday to see Hoosen whose days on earth seem to be numbered. He was pleased to receive your letter. He cherished these as treasures. I walked on Sunday morning with the boys to the Falls. I returned immediately—being back at 10-25, i.e., the return journey in 1-25 minutes. I see that my capacity for walking remains as it was before. But I w(oul)d like to test myself still more, if I had the time.

Upper House
Gillian Berning (ed.), Gandhi Letters: From Upper House To Lower House (1906–14), *Local History Museum, Durban, 1994, pp. 26–7*

'A Thunderbolt'

July 1913

IN THOSE days I had to move between Johannesburg and Phoenix. Once[35] when I was in Johannesburg I received tidings of the moral fall of two of the inmates[36] of the Ashram. News of an apparent failure or reverse in the satyagraha struggle would not have shocked me, but this news came upon me like a thunderbolt. The same day I took the train for Phoenix. Mr Kallenbach insisted on accompanying me. He had noticed the state I was in. He would not brook the thought of my going alone, for he happened to be the bearer of the tidings which had so upset me.

During the journey my duty seemed clear to me. I felt that the guardian or teacher was responsible, to some extent at least, for the lapse of his ward or pupil. So my responsibility regarding the incident in question became clear to me as daylight. My wife had already warned me in the matter, but being of a trusting nature, I had ignored her caution. I felt that the only way the guilty parties could be made to realize my distress and the depth of their own fall would be for me to do some penance. So I imposed[37] upon myself a fast for seven days and a vow to have only one meal a day for a period of four months a half.

A, pp. 208-9; G

[Millie Polak writes: ... *On seeing Mr Gandhi, I was shocked at his appearance. He looked so depressed and ill. He greeted me, but without his usual warmth and smiling welcome. I had never seen him look so sad and troubled before. Even when affairs in the community had looked their darkest, his faith in the right working out of a Divine plan upheld him and gave him serenity and hope. But this day he looked as though the light had been quenched within him; he sat slack, with all the fight out of him.*]

MGP: What is the matter? Are you not well or has something happened?

MKG: The worst has happened!

MGP: The worst? What do you mean?

MKG: A dreadful thing has happened among ourselves.

MGP: But what is it? Please tell me what has happened!

MKG: —has been guilty of destroying her chastity. She has had physical relationship with—!

MGP: That is indeed terrible! Are you sure it is true?

MKG: Only too true! She has confessed all to me.

MGP: Still, I don't quite understand. How could it happen? When did it happen? I thought you knew how she spent all her time, and where she went to. How, then, could this have taken place?

MKG: I thought I knew—myself and knew her movements, but it seems I did not. When I thought she was simply taking a walk with her book, she was meeting—, with the result I have told you.

MGP: Has it been going on for long?

MKG: Yes, sometime. I seem to be almost the only one quite ignorant of what was going on around me. And now what am I to say to her family? For I am responsible to them for her!

MGP: But surely you are not blaming yourself for this, are you? How could you possibly have suspected that such a shocking thing could happen?

MKG: Whom else should I blame, if not myself? I must have neglected something. The responsibility must fall on me.

MGP: I do not think so. Of course, you cannot be held blameworthy. —was not ignorant. She knew what she was doing. She has behaved disgracefully! It is dreadful for you, I know; but no one can hold you responsible for it. What are you going to do next?

MKG: I must tell her family at once, and must accept their rebuke.— is full of remorse. She realizes how wicked she has been, and has done nothing but cry for the last 24 hours, and is starving herself.

MGP: Well, a fast will do her good. I have no sympathy at all with her. But I am sorry for—. What could he know of sex-passion before this? He has just been trapped. However, what are you going to do about him?

MKG: I do not know what to do about either of them yet. They must both punish themselves. Of course, I cannot trust them to meet each other again, unless someone else is present, and I cannot send either away from my care.

MGP: Is there to be a baby?

MKG: No, thank God! At least that much is spared me.

MGP: Well, that is something to be thankful for! It is, indeed, dreadful enough for you without that to complete it.

MKG: I have told—that I must share the burden of her guilt, and I hope by fasting to expiate it.

> *Millie Graham Polak in* Mr Gandhi: The Man, *pp. 142–6.*
> *The author withheld the names which have subsequently*
> *been mentioned in published records and in Uma*
> *Dhupelia-Mesthrie's biography of Manilal Gandhi.*

NEVER BEFORE have I spent such days of agony as I am doing now. I talk and I smile, I walk and eat and work, all mechanically these days.

I can do no writing whatever. The heart seems to have gone dry. The agony I am going through is unspeakable. I have (during this period) often wanted to take out the knife from my pocket and put it through the stomach. Sometimes I have felt like striking my head against the wall opposite, and at other times I have thought of running away from the world.

> *Fragment of letter,* 22 April 1914, *Gandhiji in Sadhana;*
> CWMG *Vol. 12, p. 410; G*

The Supreme

> Phoenix[38]
> 9 September 1913

I FIND that if we have trust in the supreme every difficulty we face, shows its own way out of it. 'One step enough for me' was not spoken by an inexperienced man.

> Hermann Kallenbach–Mahatma Gandhi's Friend in South Africa
> *by Isa Sarid and Christian Bartolf, Selbstverlag; 1997)*

'It Hurts Me'

> Durban
> 17 October 1913

Chiranjivi Harilal,

It hurts me to have no letters from you. Your lethargy in this matter makes you doubly guilty. The first guilt is that you neglect the duty which you owe to your father, and the second that you break your promise to me that you would write regularly. ...

> Bapu
> CWMG *Vol. 12, p. 242; G*

The Marching Great

> October 191R

IT WAS now only left for us to march. The labourers were informed one evening that they were to commence the march early next morning (28 October 1913), and the rules to be observed on the march were read to them. It was no joke to control a multitude of 5000 or 6000 men ... My experience of the Boer War and the Zulu 'rebellion' stood me in good stead on the present occasion.

SiSA, p. 267; G

ONE OF them was pregnant while six of them had young babies in arms. But one and all were eager to join and I simply could not come in their way. These sisters were with one exception all Tamilians.

SiSA, p. 253; G

THE WOMEN's bravery was beyond words. They were all kept in Maritzburg jail, where they were considerably harassed. Their food was of the worst quality and they were given laundry work as their task.

THE RATION consisted of rice and *dal*. We had a large stock of vegetable, which could not be cooked separately for want of time and cooking pots and was therefore mixed with dal. The kitchen was active all the 24 hours, as hungry men would arrive at any time of the day or night.

I was the leader among the cooks. Sometimes there was too much water in the dal, at other times it was insufficiently cooked. The vegetable and even the rice was sometimes ill-cooked. I have not seen many people in the world who would cheerfully gulp down such food.

Thus far I have dealt with the pleasant memories. As for the unpleasant, I found that when the men had a little leisure, they occupied it with internal squabbles. What was worse, there were cases of adultery. There was terrible overcrowding and men and women had to be kept together. Animal passion knows no shame. As soon as the cases occurred, I arrived on the scene. The guilty parties were abashed and they were segregated. But who can say how many such cases occurred which never came to my knowledge?

SiSA, pp. 269–70; G

... WHEN THE Phoenix batch went to prison, Johannesburg could not remain behind. The women there became restive. They were fired with the desire to be in gaol ...

The plan was that in Newcastle the women should meet the

indentured labourers and their wives, give them a true idea of their conditions and persuade them to go on strike on the issue of the £3 tax. ...

CWMG *Vol. 12, pp. 511–12; G*

... IN NEWCASTLE, the agents of the mine-owners were trying to lure away the workers. Not a single person had yielded; even so, it was the duty of the Council of Action to keep them away from all temptation. It seemed desirable, therefore, that they should march from Newcastle to Charlestown. The distance is about 35 miles. To provide railway fares for thousands was out of the question. It was therefore arranged that all able-bodied men and women should do the journey on foot. The women who could not walk were to be taken by train ... The following conditions were read out to them:

1. It was probable that I would be arrested. Even if this happened, they were to march on until arrested themselves. Though every effort would be made to provide them with meals, etc., on the way, they should not mind, if by chance, food was not available on some day.
2. For the duration of the struggle, they should abstain from drinks.
3. They must not retreat even in the face of death.
4. They should expect no shelter for night halts during the march, but should sleep on the grass.
5. No trees or plants on the way should be harmed in the least nor should any article belonging to others be touched.
6. If the Government's police came to arrest anyone, the latter should willingly surrender.
7. No resistance should be offered to the police or any others; on the contrary, beating should be patiently borne and no attempt should be made to protect oneself by offering violence in return.
8. They should cheerfully bear the hardships in gaol and live there as if the gaol were a palace ...

And so, the first batch started on its march. On the very first night, we had the experience of sleeping out on the grass. On the way, warrants were received for the arrest of about 150 persons and they surrendered themselves readily ...

CWMG *Vol. 12, pp. 514–15; E*

... IT HAPPENED so with General Smuts. At the last moment I telephoned to him. He put the receiver down in anger, but I thrust myself on him. As a result he relented and I was in a stronger position. Today we are friends. The basis of my fight is love for the opponent. I could not have fought the Dutch and the English without love in my heart for them, and without a readiness for compromise. But my compromise will never be at the cost of the cause or of the country.

CWMG Vol. 71, p. 353; E

Valliamma[39]

HOW CAN I forget her? Valliamma R. Munuswami Mudaliar was a young girl of Johannesburg only sixteen years of age. She was confined to bed when I saw her. As she was a tall girl, her emaciated body was a terrible thing to behold.

'Valliamma, you do not repent of your having gone to jail?' I asked.

'Repent? I am even now ready to go to jail again if I am arrested', said Valliamma.

'But what if it results in your death?' I pursued.

'I do not mind it. Who would not love to die for one's motherland?' was the reply.

Within a few days after this conversation Valliamma was no more with us in the flesh, but she left us the heritage of an immortal name.

SiSA, pp. 257–9; G

Enter Andrews[40]

Durban
2 January 1914

Servindia
Poona City

Andrews[41] Pearson[42] duly honoured[43]. Feeling well. They send love. Rough passage.

Gandhi
CWMG Vol. 12, p. 314; E

CFA: Isn't it simply a question of Indians' honour?

MKG: Yes! That is it, that is it. That is the real point at issue.

CFA: Then, I am sure you are right to stand out. There must be no sacrifice of honour.

Quoted in Sykes & Chaturvedi's Life of C.F. Andrews,
Allen and Unwin, London, 1950

Durban[44]
3 January 1914

Servindia
Poona City

... Andrews wants me pass one week with him Phoenix. Have agreed. Subject your sanction feel Harilal should come. He vowed see struggle through as resister. Should be permitted fulfil obligation. My opinion gaol other experiences substantial education.

Gandhi
CWMG *Vol. 12, p. 316; E*

'Devadas Has Proved A Hero'

110, Field Street
Durban
4 January 1914

My dear boy[45],

I was delighted to receive your letter ... Ramdas is looking well and has done well. Devadas has proved a hero. He has developed a sense of responsibility which was unexpected. Purbhoodas did almost equally well, but he is not so quick as Devadas ... You will be pleased to hear that I had become a most industrious student at Bloemfontein and I was sincerely sorry to have my studies interrupted. I gave about eight hours a day to solid reading and writing, principally Tamil. The authorities kindly gave me every facility ... With love from us all.

Yours sincerely,
Bapu
CWMG *Vol. 12, pp. 317–18; E*

Hurbat Singh

Durban
After 5 January 1914

To
The Editor
Indian Opinion

... Is there an Indian who will not shed tears of joy at the glorious death of such an Indian? When Hurbatsingh's[46] body is carried to the cremation ground, I do hope that every Indian will follow it on foot right up to the ground[47]. By paying this homage, we shall not only honour the memory of the departed one but shall also honour India and ourselves.

I am
India's bond-slave
Mohandas Karamchand Gandhi
CWMG *Vol. 12, pp. 319–20;* G

Interview With Smuts

Pretoria
16 January 1914

MKG: I seek definite assurances on four points. First, the £3 tax.

Smuts: Will you be satisfied if the payment of the licence money is abolished but the licence retained and no further alteration made in the provision of Natal Act 17 of 1895?

MKG: I think this solution meets my requirements but I would urge that if the license is to be retained, it be made a standing licence not subject to annual renewal. Then there is the marriage question.

Smuts: Your expectations in this regard are not unreasonable and I imagine they will be satisfied if statutory recognition of *de facto* monogamous wives were accorded.

MKG: On the admission of South Africa-born Indians into the Cape Province, I seek an assurance that the law would be so addressed that the education test would not be applied to such Indians.

I do not press for legislation on this point. On the Orange Free State law a slight verbal amendment of its terms would meet the difficulty.

Smuts: The Government has already signified their willingness to accept your suggestion on this point.

MKG: If you can give me a clear assurance in writing on these four points, I would regard it as disposing of the whole general question of Indian grievances.

Adapted from CWMG *Vol. 12, pp. 324–5*

Manilal—'Serve Mr Andrews'

Phoenix
Tuesday, 3 February 1914

Chiranjivi Manilal,

... I was very much hurt that you ate chillies. It is possible that you will not feel the effects just now. But never forget that *tamasic food*[48] cannot but have an evil effect. I am sure it will do you good in future if you discipline your senses. For all that I can see, there has been no spiritual gain to you through your experience of gaol. You have great need to cultivate thoughtfulness. It is a rare gain to have come into contact with Mr Andrews[49]. I should like you to take the fullest advantage of the occasion by preserving the utmost purity[50]. So far, Mr Andrews has expressed himself perfectly satisfied about you.

Keep an account of every pice you spend. Have no shame about doing any work for Mr Andrews. You may even massage his calves. Having done so once myself, I know that he probably finds it agreeable. Polish his shoes and tie up the laces. You must not forget to write to me every day. Maintain a diary of meetings with all persons and the developments from day to day.

Blessings from
Bapu

(PS) It is impossible to say anything about Ba's health[51].

CWMG *Vol. 12, pp. 340–1; translation revised; G*

A Delusion

In the train
On the way between
Johannesburg and Cape Town
14 February 1914[52]

WHAT A snare, a delusion this wretched civilisation in the midst of which you and I are still living ... the bitter fruit of which we are still tasting.

'I Want The Discipline Of Obeying Someone I Love'

Cape Town
27 February 1914

Dear Mr Gokhale,

For the time being I am at Cape Town watching the course of events. I do not want to inflict on you any news about the struggle. I shall be as brief as I possibly can.

Mr Andrews and Mr Pearson are truly good men, we all like them very much ...

If there is a settlement in March, I propose to leave for India in April ...

My present ambition you know. It is to be by your side as your nurse and attendant. I want to have the real discipline of obeying someone whom I love and look up to. I know I made a bad secretary in South Africa. I hope to do better in the Motherland if I am accepted ...

I remain
Yours sincerely
M.K. Gandhi
CWMG *Vol. 12, pp. 360–1; E*

'Dearest And Nearest'

27 February 1914[53]

THOUGH I love and almost adore Andrews so, I would not change you[54] for him. You still remain the dearest and nearest to me and so far as my non-selfish nature is concerned I know that in my lonely journey through the world you will be the last (if even that) to say goodbye to me ... What right had I to expect so much from you.

Ba

Cape Town
About 1 March 1914

... NOTHING CAN be said about Ba's health. One does not know when she will leave the bed, if at all. Just now, she wants support even when she want to sit up in the bed. She lives for the most part on *neem* juice, taking grapes or orange juice occasionally. She is at peace, however. ...

CWMG *Vol. 12, p. 367; G*

'Be My Right Hand, Harilal'

Cape Town
2 March 1914

Chiranjivi Harilal,

I have your letter. You apologize in every letter of yours and put up a defence as well. It all seems to me sheer hypocrisy now. For years, you have been slack in writing letters, and then coming forward with apologies. Will this go on till death, I forgiving every time? And what is the point of my forgiving? Forgiving has a meaning only to the extent that the person who has apologized does not err again ... I see that your ideas and mine differ very much. Your conception of your duty as a son differs from mine, but I have no right to enquire what your duty is. If you go on doing your duty as you in all sincerity conceive it to be, I shall be perfectly satisfied ...

If you wish to live as I want you to, stay with me and be my right hand ...

Bapu
CWMG *Vol. 12, pp. 367–9; G*

'Do Not Hide Your Mistakes'

Cape Town
4 March 1914

Chiranjivi Manilal,

I have your letter. You ought not to have hidden from me the fact that you lost the tin of water. Just think how much care I take even in regard to such things and take a lesson from it. But that lesson you will take only if you lay open your heart before me. You will not be able to learn anything so long as you try to hide your mistakes from me, even for a moment ...

Ba is somewhat better today; but still the crisis is not over. She is bed-ridden. Mrs Gool and her children are a great help.

Blessings from
Bapu
CWMG *Vol. 12, p. 372; G*

'Ba's Condition Has Grown Very Bad'

Cape Town
5 March 1914

Chiranjivi Devadas,

Improve your handwriting. Ba's condition has grown very bad of late. She and I both believe that medical treatment has had altogether an adverse effect on her. She herself had asked for such treatment. After she had had two or three doses, her condition became serious. She can eat no food at present. She took a few grapes yesterday, but it seems they did not agree with her. Even if the end is death, we have made up our minds to have no fear of it. ...

Blessings from
Bapu
CWMG *Vol. 12, p. 373; G*

'There Is A Cremation Ground Here ...'

7, Buitencingle, Cape Town
8 March 1914

Chiranjivi Maganlal,

... Perhaps the settlement may not come off; other things also might happen. Nevertheless, we want to leave as soon as a settlement is reached; it is therefore necessary to make all the preparations ...

I see good improvement today in Ba's health. If she survives, take it for certain that our (nature cure) remedies and faith in God have saved her. She has come to realize that the doctor's medicine was the cause of her breakdown. She was tempted by a desire to take the doctor's treatment and I did not interfere. The punishment she received was severe and so the lesson learnt was equally valuable. Ba showed infinite capacity for patience. She did not trouble me at all. The Gools[55] showed great love. The doctor is a generous man. He does not interfere much with what I do. We wanted very much to satisfy him, but Ba later showed great firmness. I always read the *Ramayana* to her and sing prayer songs. She appears to listen to these attentively. I repeat Ramanama also. The intention behind all this is not that she should survive; it is that, whether she lives or dies, her mind should be pure and tender. I have made all preparations and inquired about everything in case she dies. There is a cremation ground here equipped with the necessary facilities. It is four miles away.

Blessings from
Mohandas
CWMG *Vol. 12, pp. 378–80; G*

Fear of Death

Cape Town
10 March 1914[56]

It is because we fear death so much for ourselves that we shed tears over the deaths of others.

Hermann Kallenbach—Mahatma Gandhi's Friend in South Africa
by Isa Sarid and Christian Bartolf, Selbstverlag; 1997)

'In Case I Die Suddenly ...'

Cape Town
11 March 1914

Chiranjivi Chhaganlal,

... In case I die suddenly, be the reason this or any other, I want to set down here certain ideas which I have thought out and which I have not so far placed before you.

... At present, the family has fallen on evil days ... All of them are busy multiplying, arranging marriages, etc. The utmost limit of a grandmother's or a daughter-in-law's ambition is to get (the grandson or) the son married.

How may we save ourselves from this? If possible, we should take another road. We should become farmers, in the first instance. If, to our misfortune, that should bring unbearable hardships on us, we should labour as weavers, etc., and live in the same state as we do in Phoenix. We must reduce our wants to the minimum. ...

CWMG *Vol. 12, pp. 380–1; G*

'We Should Welcome Death ...'

Cape Town
14 March 1914

Chiranjivi Manilal,

... Ba is now getting better ...

You need not be disturbed by the intrigues that are being hatched there. No man can hasten or delay my death even by a minute. The best way of saving oneself from death is to go seeking it. It is no doubt our duty to take care of our life in a general way. More than this we need not do. We should rather welcome death whenever it comes ...

Blessings from
Bapu
CWMG *Vol. 12, p. 386; G*

'Nagappen, Narayanaswamy, And Hurbatsing Were As Much My Brothers ...'

The Editor
Indian Opinion

Sir,

I have been so overwhelmed with wires from different parts of the Union expressing sympathy with my wife and myself regarding the death of my brother[57] in India that it is impossible for me to thank severally the Associations and individual senders. Numerous messages have been received from Durban, Maritzburg, Johannesburg and other places. I thank all most heartily for their sympathy. Whilst doing so I would like to say just a word. To me as a passive resister and as a firm believer in the oneness of the Soul, my brother's loss should occasion no greater pain than the death of Nagappen, Narayanasamy, and Hurbatsing, who were just as much my brothers as my blood brother whose loss so many friends are mourning with me. Valliamah Moonsamy's untimely end is, if possible, a greater stab from the hand of Death than my brother's end ...

Finally, may I ask those friends who have overwhelmed me with their sympathy in my bereavement to help me, if the points of passive resistance are satisfactorily settled in the near future, in my desire to return to India to fall at the feet of my brother's widow and to take charge of the domestic cares of five widows in my father's family, in which the hand of death now leaves me the responsible head, according to the Hindu usage.

I am, etc.,

M.K. Gandhi

CWMG *Vol. 12, pp. 390–1; E*

17 April 1914

How curious! No matter how intimate I may be with Andrews or Gokhale or anyone else, you will always be you to me. I have told you, *you* will have to desert me and not I you.

To Kallenbach quoted by Martin Green in Gandhi,

Voice of a New Age Revolution *(1993), p. 180; E*

'I Have A Strain Of Cruelty In Me ...'

22 April 1914

... I HAVE a strain of cruelty in me, as others say, such that people force themselves to do things, even to attempt impossible things, in order to please me. Lacking the necessary strength, they put on a false show and deceive me. Even Gokhale used to tell me that I was so harsh that people felt terrified of me and allowed themselves to be dragged against their will out of sheer fear or in the attempt to please me, and that those who found themselves too weak assumed an artificial pose in the end. I put far too heavy burdens on people. ...

CWMG *Vol. 12, pp. 410–11; G*

Farewell Letter To Indians In South Africa

Johannesburg
Before 15 July 1914

Dear Brother or Sister,

On the eve of my departure from South Africa, I should like to leave a brief message in writing.

... We are very dirty and some of us behave so abjectly, because of greed, that the whites feel disgusted, as they well might. If the leaders exert themselves, they can end all the filthiness that we notice around us ... This state of affairs must change.

Gold-smuggling by members of the community is on the increase. Some Indians want to get rich quick. They will get into trouble and disgrace the name of the community as a whole. I wish they would rein themselves in.

... Though I am leaving for the motherland, I am not likely to forget South Africa. I should like friends who may have occasion to go to India to come and see me there. I do intend, of course, to work in India in regard to the disabilities here. And I shall be able to work better if the people in South Africa ask for my services. I think the expenses to be incurred in India on this work by way of stationery, postage, printing, etc., should be met from here. The money I have been given I propose to use only for this purpose.

Above all, I wish to say that it is up to the community to win its freedom and that its ultimate weapon, an irresistible one, is satyagraha.

If I have harmed any Indian, knowingly or unknowingly, if I have been the cause of pain to anyone, I crave God's forgiveness and theirs.

I am, of course, a satyagrahi and I hope always to remain one, but in December[58] last I fell more under the spell of indenture. Since then the term *girmitio* (indentured labourer) is already in use about me in Gujarati.

I am,
As ever,
The community's indentured labourer,
Mohandas Karamchand Gandhi
CWMG *Vol. 12, pp. 481–6; G*

A Great Wrench

July 1914

THUS THE great satyagraha struggle closed after eight years, and it appeared that the Indians in South Africa were now at peace. On 18 July 1914, I sailed for England, to meet Gokhale, on my way back to India, with mixed feelings of pleasure and regret—pleasure because I was returning home after many years and eagerly looked forward to serving the country under Gokhale's guidance, regret because it was a great wrench for me to leave South Africa, where I had passed twenty-one years of my life sharing to the full in the sweets and bitters of human experience, and where I had realized my vocation in life.

SiSA, p. 306

Part Ten

1914-25

Opening a khadi shop in Bombay, 1921

Returning to India—The First Decade

*I thought I could finish the wheel of rebirth in this incarnation.
I know now that I can't and that I shall have to return to it.*

When Gandhi, with his wife Kasturba, left South Africa for London
en route India on 18 July 1914, he was forty-five and already a celebrity.
'M. K. Gandhi, Attorney' to his clients and 'Gandhibhai' to the Indian
community of South Africa, he was already known in India and in
England as a man of restless zeal but also a calm self-assurance with
which he had run three disciplined, mass non-violent campaigns in
South Africa spread over eight years. And, more to the point, had run
them successfully. Gandhi's securing the 'Smuts–Gandhi Agreement'
of 1914, which settled the issue of the validity in South Africa of the
marriages which were held legal in India (with some qualifications
in regard to plural marriages), abolished the annual tax of £3 on ex-
indentured labourers and their wives and children, and obtained
the promise that existing laws will be administered in a just manner
and with due regard to vested rights, were no mean achievements.

Gokhale's 1912 visit to South Africa and his instrumentality in
sending C.F. Andrews and W.W. Pearson to South Africa in 1913
had played a role in the denouement. It had also formalized, in a
sense, Gokhale as Gandhi's clear political mentor. A mentor as much
for his ascetic way of life as for his high-minded politics and untiring
advocacy of Home Rule. In his catechistic *Hind Swaraj* Gandhi has
the impatient 'Reader' ask the 'Editor' (Gandhi):

Reader: We must look upon Mr Dadabhai with respect. Without
   him and men like him, we should probably not have the spirit
   that fires us. How can the same be said of Professor Gokhale?
   He has constituted himself a great friend of the English; he says

that we have to learn a great deal from them, that we have to learn their political wisdom, before we can talk of Home Rule. I am tired of reading his speeches.

Editor: If you are tired, it only betrays your impatience. We believe that those, who are discontented with the slowness of their parents and are angry because the parents would not run with their children, are considered disrespectful to their parents. Professor Gokhale occupies the place of a parent. What does it matter if he cannot run with us? A nation that is desirous of securing Home Rule cannot afford to despise its ancestors. We shall become useless, if we lack respect for our elders. Only men with mature thoughts are capable of ruling themselves and not the hasty-tempered. Moreover, how many Indians were there like Professor Gokhale, when he gave himself to Indian education? I verily believe that whatever Professor Gokhale does, he does with pure motives and with a view to serving India. His devotion to the Motherland is so great that he would give his life for it, if necessary. Whatever he says is said not to flatter anyone but because he believes it to be true. We are bound, therefore, to entertain the highest regard for him.

Reader: Are we, then, to follow him in every respect?

Editor: I never said any such thing. If we conscientiously differed from him, the learned Professor himself would advise us to follow the dictates of our conscience rather than him. Our chief purpose is not to decry his work, but to believe that he is infinitely greater than we are, and to feel assured that compared with his work for India, ours is infinitesimal. Several newspapers write disrespectfully of him. It is our duty to protest against such writings. We should consider men like Professor Gokhale to be the pillars of Home Rule. It is a bad habit to say that another man's thoughts are bad and ours only are good and that those holding different views from ours are the enemies of the country.

Reader: I now begin to understand somewhat your meaning. I shall have to think the matter over.

Gandhi's primary purpose in going to London from South Africa was to meet Gokhale (who was then in Britain) before resuming life and work in India and also, presumably, to acquaint the many people he had met in 1906 there with the positive development in South Africa.

Gandhi's arrival in London was overtaken by the outbreak of World War I. Weak though he was from his recent fast and exhausted, too, perhaps from the cathartic experiences of 1913–14, the man who had 'plunged' into the Boer War and the Zulu 'Rebellion' got to work no sooner than he disembarked. He offered his services for the war effort, evoking a surprised question on violence and non-violence sent long-distance by Polak. Gandhi's answer was frank. He was not winning marks for consistency in *ahimsa*. '... It is not always given to one to be equally clear about one's duty', he said. 'A votary of truth is often obliged to grope in the dark.' Proceeding on a line of thought at odds with *Hind Swaraj*, he felt 'man cannot be wholly free from *himsa*' and that 'so long as he continues to be a social being, he cannot but participate in the himsa that the very existence of society involves.'

A reception awaited 'Mr and Mrs Gandhi' organized by his English and Indian friends at the Hotel Cecil. The line-up of hosts and guests was extraordinary. Presided over by the Congress President of the day, Bhupendranath Bose, the meeting was attended by Muhammad Ali Jinnah, Lala Lajpat Rai, Satchidanand Sinha, and the grand poet Sarojini Naidu who garlanded the couple. None in the hall could have guessed that two of the persons present—Gandhi and Jinnah—would be hailed as 'Fathers' of two 'Nations', some three and a half decades later.

The volunteering for the war effort was bedevilled by technicalities and a further breakdown in Gandhi's health. He had to leave for India wrapped up in 'Mede's plaster' with strict medical instructions given by a young Indian doctor Jivraj Mehta, to be observed while on the journey home. Gandhi and Kasturba reached Bombay on 9 January 1915. Fully into the vow he had taken in 1906 of brahmacharya and wholly committed to working for Indian emancipation, Gandhi was a loyal subject of the British Crown as he stepped on Indian soil. Gokhale had preceded Gandhi and arranged a reception for the arriving couple.

Gandhi had, for several months in South Africa, been wearing clothes in the style of indentured labourers. While in England he had changed over to simple clothes in the western style but he chose to disembark in India in Kathiawari attire—dhoti, a long tailored shirt-coat, a shawl, and a turban. Formalities over, within 24 hours of disembarking at 7.30 a.m. Gandhi held separate meetings on the very same day with Gokhale, with Sir S. Srinivasa Sastri, and gave an interview to a representative of *The Times of India*.

The next day (10 January) he met Tilak and on 13 January, Dadabhai Naoroji and Pherozeshah Mehta. So, within four days of his 'final' return, Gandhi had already met the leading lights of the Indian political firmament.

Gokhale informed Gandhi that the Governor of Bombay was desirous of seeing him. That meeting, which took place on 14 January, was of no ordinary significance. Here was the representative of the Viceroy and vicariously of the King, taking the initiative in seeing a man whom the Raj had kept at a distance on his visit in 1901 and whose work in South Africa could not but have held grim forebodings. Lord Willingdon, the Governor, was later to become Viceroy (1931–6) and Gandhi's record of their Bombay meeting of 14 January 1915 which had appeared in print by the time Willingdon took that office in New Delhi, was never controverted by the representative of the King-Emperor.

Gandhi visited Santiniketan, within days of his arrival and conferred with Tagore. But death snatched Gokhale from him, leaving the 'pupil' shaken. Gandhi toured India, as he had promised Gokhale, without making too many public comments, and set up his first Ashram near Ahmedabad, replicating the pattern of the Phoenix Settlement. As with Phoenix, this ashram (later to move towards the river Sabarmati) was to become the base for his activities. These grew apace and extended to the tackling of wrongs, political and social, throughout the length and breadth of the country.

The Gokhale-enjoined 'silence' was broken by Gandhi in Benares, the occasion being the inauguration of the Benares Hindu University on 6 February 1916. He took on the British, he took on the Indians. He took on the Rajas, he took on the anarchists. He spared no one on the dais, nor most of those that comprised the audience.

Crises had chased Gandhi in South Africa. They did that in India as well. Gandhi used a self-devised methodology of his own in 1916 to study the 'indigo scene' in Motihari, Champaran (Bihar). How scale and accuracy of coverage can obtain official redress was shown by that initiative. He writes: 'The work of recording statements of the ryots' grievances (progressed) apace. Thousands of such statements were taken, and they could not but have their effect. The ever growing number of ryots coming to make their statements increased the planters' wrath, and they moved heaven and earth to counteract my inquiry. The *tinkathia* system which had been in existence for about a century was thus abolished, and with it the planters' *raj* came to an end.'

Kripalani writes in *Gandhi: His Life and Thought* (1970) 'The success in Champaran was an object-lesson to the whole country in the potency of satyagraha. The most helpless and timid sections of the Indian population had been roused as though by a miracle to cast off their fear and had become conscious of their self-respect as human beings. We have seen how Gandhiji, when he was working for the removal of injustice, also worked for reform in the social life of the people through self-help and mutual cooperation. It was in Champaran that Gandhiji came to be known as the "Mahatma", the Great Soul.'

Rajendra Prasad joined him during this campaign which began to change his basic position in the British Raj.

Gandhi had sent his sons, as we have seen, and some of his younger relatives a few months earlier to India. They visited the Gurukula *Kangri* run by Swami Shraddhananda and Santiniketan where they were received as 'the Phoenix Party' and housed by Tagore.

Rajmohan Gandhi writes in *Mohandas* (Penguin-Viking 2006): 'Through language and dress Gandhi was inviting a direct, personal link with non-elite Indians. On their part the embarrassed, shocked or amused elite leaders thought that the strange man they were welcoming would soon disappear into the Indian wilderness.'

Meeting Tagore for the first time in Santiniketan in 1915, as also two future lifelong associates, J.B. Kripalani and D.B. 'Kakasaheb' Kalelkar, Gandhi also met G.D. Birla for the first time in Calcutta, on this 1915 visit to Bengal.

Lokamanya Tilak's Home Rule League launched in Poona and Annie Besant's in Madras had created a stir in 1916, with Jinnah playing a leading role in the initiative. Gandhi attended and acquired with ease a major role in the Bombay Provincial Conference in Ahmedabad that October, 'discovering' few other lifelong colleagues—

Vallabhbhai Patel in October in Ahmedabad and Jawaharlal Nehru in December in Lucknow, the latter who was to be named by him, many years later, his 'heir and successor'.

Gandhi's work in South Africa had drawn him to all classes of people throughout India, including the so-called 'untouchables'. So, while matching graciousness with gratitude at receptions, he also spoke bluntly about the practice of untouchability and said Home Rule for India would not be that, if in Indian society one group dominated another.

But it was 1919 that placed Gandhi at the vanguard of India's political awakening, with Madras being the venue of his flash-decision to call a nationwide protest against the newly-promulgated Rowlatt Acts which curbed civil liberties.

Forty-year-old Tamil lawyer Rajagopalachari was his host in Madras when 'in that twilight condition between sleep and consciousness' Gandhi decided that the whole country should be roused to mass but non-violent protest. The response was electric. But it presaged a cathartic development. In early April 1919 at Amritsar in the Punjab, five or six Europeans were killed by a mob and an Englishwoman assaulted. On 13 April 1919 came General Dyer's horrific retaliation by firing at Jallianwala Bagh, Amritsar, that left an official figure of 379 dead and over 1000 injured within a space of a few minutes.

Gandhi flayed the Raj but did not spare himself saying he had launched a movement before training it in non-violence. Tagore had cautioned him about this.

Unprecedented repression was unleashed in India in the summer of 1919. If the 'Punjab wrongs' had angered the whole country, so did the betrayal by Britain of promises made to the Indian Muslims concerning the Ottoman Empire and the places held holy by the Islamic world. Gandhi's 'faith in the British Empire' was shaken. Estranged from the Government of India which he felt was hopelessly indifferent to the welfare of the people, Gandhi organized and led the great non-cooperation movement in which tens of thousands of people courted imprisonment. But, unlike in South Africa, his insistence on non-violence was not easy to comply with in India. Spontaneous protests turned violent in different parts of the country. Anguished, he called off the satyagraha, speaking of the need to start movements only after careful preparation. The period became one of intensities, both inner and outer. And also of some loneliness, with Gokhale and then Tilak having died. But the Jallianwala Bagh massacre and the Khilafat Movement cemented the constructive solidarity between Hindus and Muslims. By 1920–1, Gandhi had, in fact, become not only a bridge between India's principal communities but also India's foremost mass leader: a leader, however, whose ability to non-cooperate and organize civil disobedience was equalled only by an uncompromising adherence to non-violence, even at the risk of irritating his colleagues and leading to self-chastisement when his ideal was violated.

The 'moderate' elements in the Indian National Congress soon dissociated themselves from Gandhi's programme of non-cooperation, while the formidable unity between Hindus and Muslims forged in the wake of 'the Punjab wrong' and 'the Khilafat wrong' was weakened by events turning in a different direction in Kemal Ataturk's Turkey. Communal riots also disfigured the country in various places and Gandhi withdrew substantially, if tactically, from political work.

This Part shows how Hindu–Muslim unity over the Khilafat question, the strains in that unity, his retreat from politics to 'constructive work', especially hand-spinning, his fasts, his asceticism, made Gandhi an enigmatic as well as an iconic figure. His travels over the decade 1915 to 1925 saw all these aspects of his personality. They saw his friendship with Tagore ripen, with Motilal Nehru, [1] Lala Lajpat Rai and Deshbandhu C.R. Das[2] deepen, and with the forty-seven-years old Bengali wife of a Punjab nationalist, Saraladevi, quicken into an indefinable intensity before it ceased forever to hold any significance. But, as Gandhi wrote to his former secretary in South Africa, Sonja Schlesin, he missed his South African colleagues. 'I do not know the people here; nor they me.' But then he dismissed brooding as wrong. 'I have not the time for it.'

Arrested at Sabarmati in March 1922 on a charge of sedition, Gandhi was handed his first jail sentence—six years. He had spent two years out of the six in the Yeravda prison house at Poona when he was stricken with appendicitis necessitating emergency surgery. The Government decided to release him prematurely. While in jail, Gandhi dictated to Indulal Yajnik[3] the major part of *Satyagraha in South Africa*, his gripping account of the campaign conducted by him in that country which had culminated successfully in the Smuts–

Gandhi Agreement and the Indians Relief Act, 1914. But South Africa's Indians were not out of their travails. They would have longed to have their Gandhibhai in their midst. But he had been returned to India, where he was now 'Mahatma Gandhi'.

Gandhi observed in the conclusion to the book: 'When one considers the painful contrast between the happy ending of the satyagraha struggle and the present condition of the Indians in South Africa, one feels for a moment as if all this suffering had gone for nothing, or is inclined to question the efficacy of satyagraha as a solvent of the problems of mankind ...'

The Swaraj Party had by now become a factor as a formation that was close to and yet distinct from the Congress, with C.R. Das and Motilal Nehru becoming defining figures in Indian politics.

Gandhi introspected a great deal in this phase, sometimes on his own and sometimes when prodded by others like Maganlal. 'I have lost my former fire', Gandhi wrote to him. 'My best time is over.' Only he could have evaluated his 'best'. His most 'active' time was, of course, yet ahead of him.

To India Via England And The War

NOT MUCH time had elapsed since my fast[4] when we started on our voyage. I had not regained my normal strength. I used to stroll on the deck to get a little exercise, so as to revive my appetite and digest what I ate. But even this exercise was beyond me, causing pain in the calves, so much so that on reaching London I found that I was worse rather than better.

In Madeira we heard that the Great War might break out at any moment. As we entered the English Channel, we received the news of its actual outbreak. We were stopped for some time. It was a difficult business to tow the boat through the submarine mines which had been laid throughout the Channel, and it took about two days to reach Southampton.

War was declared on the 4th of August. We reached London on the 6th.

A, pp. 210–11; G

'Who Else Dare Be So Irreverent?

Kensington, London
5 August 1914[5]

MKG: Ah, you must be Mrs Naidu! Who else dare be so irreverent? Come in and share my meal.

Sarojini Naidu: No thanks; what an abominable mess it is.

Sengupta Padmini, Sarojini Naidu: A Biography *(London, 1966)*

At London's Reception[6] To Him

8 August 1914

To YOU, Mr Basu, and to Mrs Sarojini Naidu, I can only say that you have both overwhelmed me; I do not even know that I can struggle through what I have to say ...

I have called the Settlement[7] the Magna Charta of the British Indians of South Africa; after due deliberation I repeat my statement. It is the Magna Charta of British Indians, not only because of its substance, which is great enough, but for its spirit, which indicates a change of attitude on the part of South Africa and the South African Government. The sufferings of our countrymen sealed the settlement. The discovery was made that the ancient force could be applied in South Africa; conviction came after the sufferings of eight long-drawn-out years. They saw that Indians, when in earnest, were irresistible; that they would not take a bit less than the minimum they demanded.

Mr Cartwright is here; he has been our staunch friend throughout and I honour him for his help. But I tell him here that he almost tried to weaken us. I remember, and he will remember how he came to me in Johannesburg Gaol, and said: 'Will not this letter do?' 'No Mr Cartwright,' was my reply, 'not until this alteration is made.' 'But everything is achieved by compromise', he urged. 'There can be no compromise on principles', I answered. There never was any compromise on principles from 1906 to 1914.

... I thank again on behalf of Mrs Gandhi and myself, Mr Basu and Mrs Naidu for all their kind words. But you have only seen the bright side; you do not know our weaknesses. Indians are altogether too generous, they overlook faults and magnify virtues; this had led us to incarnating our heroes. I think of what is written in our scriptures—that it is our duty to fly away from praises, we must lay them all at the feet of the Almighty. I hope we have enough courage, and courage to lay them at His feet, in whose name and in the name of Mother India we have endeavoured to do our duty, but nothing but our duty.

Indian Opinion, 30-9-1914; CWMG Vol. 12, pp. 523–6; E

London
14 August 1914

To
The Under Secretary of State For India

(Sir,)

It was thought desirable by many of us that, during the crisis that has overtaken the Empire and whilst many Englishmen, leaving their ordinary vocation in life, are responding to the Imperial call, those Indians who are residing in the United Kingdom and who can at all do so, should place themselves unconditionally at the disposal of the Authorities.

... We would respectfully emphasize the fact that the one dominant idea guiding us is that of rendering such humble assistance as we may be considered capable of performing, as an earnest of our desire to share the responsibilities of membership of this great Empire, if we would share its privileges[8] ...

M.K. Gandhi

and others

Indian Opinion, *16 October 1914;* CWMG *Vol. 12, pp. 527–8; E*

... As soon as the news reached South Africa that I along with other Indians had offered my services in the war, I received two cables. One of these was from Mr Polak who questioned the consistency of my action with my profession of ahimsa ...

As a matter of fact the very same line of argument that persuaded me to take part in the Boer War had weighed with me on this occasion. It was quite clear to me that participation in war could never be consistent with ahimsa. But it is not always given to one to be equally clear about one's duty. A votary of truth is often obliged to grope in the dark ...

Then again, because underlying ahimsa is the unity of all life, the error of one cannot but affect all, and hence man cannot be wholly free from himsa. So long as he continues to be a social being, he cannot but participate in the himsa that the very existence of society involves.

... I know that even then I could not carry conviction with all my friends about the correctness of my position. The question is subtle.

A, pp. 212–14; G

Gokhale's Charity[9]

Dr Jivraj Mehta treated me. He pressed me hard to resume milk and cereals, but I was obdurate. The matter reached Gokhale's ears. He had not much regard for my reasoning in favour of a fruitarian diet and he wanted me to take whatever the doctor prescribed for my health.

The first question he asked me was: 'Well, have you decided to accept the doctor's advice?'

I gently but firmly replied: 'I am willing to yield on all points except one about which I beg you not to press me. I will not take milk, mik-products, or meat. If not to take these things should mean my death, I feel I had better face it.'

'Is this your final decision?' asked Gokhale.

'I am afraid I cannot decide otherwise', said I. 'I know that my decision will pain you, but I beg your forgiveness.'

With a certain amount of pain but with deep affection, Gokhale said: 'I do not approve of your decision. I do not see any religion in it. But I won't press you any more.' With these words he turned to Dr Jivraj Mehta and said: 'Please don't worry him any more. Prescribe anything you like within the limit he has set for himself.' ...

Meanwhile Gokhale left for home, as he could not stand the October fog of London.

A, pp. 215–16; G

At The London Farewell

18 December 1914

[*These are excerpts from a Reuters dispatch published in* India and Indian Opinion.]

'MR GANDHI, who was received with cheers, said that his wife and himself were returning to the motherland with their work unaccomplished and with broken health, but he wished, nevertheless, to use the language of hope ... Indians had shown themselves thereby capable of doing their duty, if they received recognition of their rights and privileges. (*Cheers*) The whole idea of the Corps arose because he felt that there should be some outlet for the anxiety of Indians to help in the crisis which had come upon the Empire. (*Hear, hear*) ... He had been practically an exile for 25 years, and his friend and master, Mr Gokhale, had warned him not to speak on Indian questions, as India was a foreign land to him. (*Laughter*)... .'

CWMG Vol. 12, pp. 564–5; E

Homeward

Dr Jivraj Mehta had bandaged my ribs with 'Mede's Plaster' and had asked me not to remove it till we reached the Red Sea. For two days I put up with the discomfort, but finally it became too much for me. It was with considerable difficulty that I managed to undo the plaster and regain the liberty of having a proper wash and bath.

My diet consisted mostly of nuts and fruits. I found that I was improving every day and felt very much better by the time we entered the Suez Canal ...

A few days more and we reached Bombay. It was such a joy to get back to the homeland after an exile of ten years.

Gokhale had inspired a reception for me in Bombay, where he had come in spite of his delicate health. I had approached India in the ardent hope of merging myself in him, and thereby feeling free. But fate had willed it otherwise.

A, pp. 219–20; G

An Invitation From Lord Willingdon[10]

Bombay
14 January 1915

The moment I reached Bombay Gokhale sent me word that the Governor was desirous of seeing me, and that it might be proper for me to respond before I left for Poona. Accordingly I called on His Excellency. After the usual inquiries, he said:

'I ask one thing of you. I would like you to come and see me whenever you propose to take any steps concerning Government.'

I replied: 'I can very easily give the promise, in as much as it is my rule, as a satyagrahi, to understand the viewpoint of the party I propose to deal with and to try to agree with him as far as may be possible. I strictly observed the rule in South Africa and I mean to do the same here.'

Lord Willingdon thanked me and said: 'You may come to me whenever you like, and you will see that my Government do not willfully do anything wrong.'

To which I replied: 'It is that faith which sustains me.'

A, Part V; G

January–February 1915

I went to Rajkot[11] and Porbandar,[12] where I had to meet my brother's widow and other relatives.

A, Part V; G

Santiniketan And Gokhale's Death

FROM RAJKOT I proceeded to Santiniketan. The teachers and students overwhelmed me with affection.

As is my wont, I quickly mixed with the teachers and students, and engaged them in a discussion on self-help. I put it to the teachers and students and teachers that, if they and the boys dispensed with the services of paid cooks and cooked their food themselves, it would enable the teachers to control the kitchen from the point of view of the boys' physical and moral health, and it would afford to the students an object-lesson in self-help ... When I invited the Poet to express his opinion, he said that he did not mind it provided the teachers were favourable. To the boys he said, 'The experiment contains the key to Swaraj.'

I had intended to stay at Santiniketan for some time, but fate willed otherwise. I had hardly been there a week when I received from Poona a telegram announcing Gokhale's death. Santiniketan was immersed in grief. All the members came over to me to express their condolences. A special meeting was called in the Ashram temple to mourn the national loss. It was a solemn function. The same day I left for Poona with my wife and Maganlal. All the rest stayed at Santiniketan.

A, Part V; G

AT BURDWAN we came face to face with the hardships that a third class passenger has to go through even in securing his ticket. 'Third class tickets are not booked so early,' we were told. I went to the Station Master, though that too was a difficult business. Someone kindly directed me to where he was, and I represented to him our difficulty. He also made the same reply. As soon as the booking window opened, I went to purchase the tickets. But it was no easy thing to get them. Might was right, and passengers, who were forward and indifferent to others, coming one after another, continued to push me out. I was therefore about the last of the first crowd to get a ticket.

The train arrived, and getting into it was another trial. There was a free exchange of abuse and pushes between passengers already in the train and those trying to get in. We ran up and down the platform, but were everywhere met with the same reply: 'No room here.' I went to the guard. He said, 'You must try to get in where you can or take the next train.'

'But I have urgent business', I respectfully replied. He had no time to listen to me. I was disconcerted. I told Maganlal to get in wherever possible, and I got into an inter-class compartment with my wife. The guard saw us getting in. At Asansol station he came to charge us excess fares. I said to him: 'It was your duty to find us room. We could not get any, and so we are sitting here. If you can accommodate us in a third class compartment, we shall be only too glad to go there.'

'You may not argue with me,' said the guard. 'I cannot accommodate you. You must pay the excess fare, or get out.'

The woes of third class passengers are undoubtedly due to the high-handedness of railway authorities. But the rudeness, dirty habits, selfishness and ignorance of the passengers themselves are no less to blame. The pity is that they often do not realize that they are behaving ill, dirtily, or selfishly. They believe that everything they do is in the natural way. All this may be traced to the indifference towards them of us 'educated' people.

We reached Kalyan dead tired. Maganlal and I got some water from the station water-pipe and had our bath. As I was proceeding to arrange for my wife's bath, Sjt. Kaul of the Servants of India Society recognizing us came up. He too was going to Poona. He offered to take my wife to the second class bathroom. I hesitated to accept the courteous offer. I knew that my wife had no right to avail herself of the second class bathroom, but I ultimately connived at the impropriety. This, I know, does not become a votary of truth. Not that my wife was eager to use the bathroom, but a husband's partiality for his wife got the better of his partiality for truth. The face of truth is hidden behind the golden veil of *maya*, says the Upanishad.

A, *Part V; G*

Kumbha

April 1915

THIS YEAR—1915, was the year of the Kumbha fair, which is held at Haridvar once every 12 years. I was by no means eager to attend the fair, but I was anxious to meet Mahatma Munshiramji[13] who was in his Gurukul.

The journey[14] from Calcutta to Haridvar was particularly trying. Sometimes the compartments had no lights. From Saharanpur we were huddled into carriages for goods or cattle. These had no roofs, and what with the blazing midday sun overhead and the scorching iron floor beneath, we were all but roasted. The pangs of thirst, caused by even such a journey as this, could not persuade orthodox Hindus to take water, if it was 'Musalmani' ...

But this was no enviable position to be in. I felt as though I was between the devil and the deep sea. Where no one recognized me, I had to put up with the hardships that fall to the lot of the millions in this land, e.g., in railway travelling. Where I was surrounded by people who had heard of me I was the victim of their craze for darshan. Which of the two conditions was more pitiable, I have often been at a loss to determine. This at least I know that the *darshanvalas'* blind love has often made me angry, and more often sore at heart. Whereas travelling, though often trying, has been uplifting and has hardly ever roused me to anger.

A, *Part V; G*

HERE I saw a cow with five feet! I was astonished, but knowing men soon disillusioned me. The poor five-footed cow was a sacrifice to the greed of the wicked. I learnt that the fifth foot was nothing else but a foot cut off from a live calf and grafted upon the shoulder of the cow! The result of this double cruelty was exploited to fleece the ignorant of their money. There was no Hindu but would be attracted by a five-footed cow, and no Hindu but would lavish his charity on such a miraculous cow.

A, *Part V; G*

'See Me ...'

8 May 1915

SEE ME please in the nakedness of my working, and in my limitations; you will then know me.

Reply at Civic Reception, Bangalore. CWMG, Vol. 13, p. 82; E

This Is My India

Ahmedabad
21 May 1915[15]

I SEE around me on the surface nothing but hypocrisy, humbug, degradation, yet underneath it, I trace a divinity I missed there as elsewhere. This is my India.

Hermann Kallenbach—Mahatma Gandhi's Friend in South Africa
by Isa Sarid and Christian Bartolf, Selbstverlag; 1997

'Losing My Temper At Ba'

8 October 1915

GOT EXCITED again and lost temper with Ba. I must find a medicine for this grave defect.

Diary entry, CWMG Vol. 13, p. 181; G

Bluntness At Benares

6 February 1916

... IF A stranger dropped from above on to this great temple[16] and he had to consider what we as Hindus were, would he not be justified in condemning us? Is not this great temple a reflection of our own character? I speak feelingly as a Hindu. Is it right that the lanes of our sacred temple should be as dirty as they are? The houses round about are built anyhow. The lanes are tortuous and narrow. If even our temples are not models of roominess and cleanliness, what can our self-government be? Shall our temples be abodes of holiness, cleanliness, and peace as soon as the English have retired from India, either of their own pleasure or by compulsion, bag and baggage?...I compare with the richly bedecked noblemen the millions of the poor. And I feel like saying to these noblemen: 'There is no salvation for India unless you strip yourselves of this jewellery and hold it in trust for your countrymen' ...

... Sir[17], whenever I hear of a great palace rising in any great city of India, be it in British India or be it in India which is ruled by our great chiefs, I become jealous at once and I say: 'Oh, it is the money that has come from the agriculturists.' ...

CWMG Vol. 13, pp. 212–14; E

... WE MAY foam, we may fret, we may resent, but let us not forget that the India of today in her impatience has produced an army of anarchists. I myself am an anarchist, but of another type. But there is a class of anarchists amongst us, and if I was able to reach this class, I would say to them that their anarchism has no room in India if India is to conquer the conqueror. It is a sign of fear. If we trust and fear God, we shall have to fear no one, not Maharajahs, not Viceroys, not the detectives, not even King George. I honour the anarchist for his love of the country. I honour him for his bravery in being willing to die for his country; but I ask him: Is killing honourable? Is the dagger of an assassin a fit precursor of an honourable death? I deny it. There is no warrant for such methods in any scriptures ... The bomb-thrower creates secret plots, is afraid to come into the open, and when caught pays the penalty of misdirected zeal. ...

CWMG Vol. 13, pp. 214–15; E

... I HAVE been told: 'Had we not done this, had some people not thrown bombs, we should never have gained what we have got with reference to the partition movement[18]'. (Mrs Besant: 'Please stop it.') This was what I said[19] in Bengal when Mr Lyons presided at the meeting. I think what I am saying is necessary. If I am told to stop, I shall obey. (Turning to the Chairman) I await your orders. If you consider that by my speaking as I am, I am not serving the country and the Empire, I shall certainly stop. (Cries of 'Go on'). (The Chairman: 'Please explain your object.') I am explaining my object. I am simply (another interruption.) My friends, please do not resent this interruption. If Mrs Besant this evening suggests that I should stop, she does so because she loves India so well, and she considers that I am erring in thinking audibly before you young men. ...

CWMG *Vol. 13, p. 215; E*

Vinoba[20]

I DO not know in what terms to praise you ... You seem almost to have met a long-felt wish of mine. In my view, a father is, in fact, a father only when he has a son who surpasses him in virtue. ...

CWMG *Vol. 14, p. 188*

Measure Of Progress

Ahmedabad
17 December 1916[21]

THE MEASURE of progress is the measure of resistance to temptations. The world may judge us by a single fall.

Hermann Kallenbach—Mahatma Gandhi's Friend in South Africa
by Isa Sarid and Christian Bartolf, Selbstverlag; 1997

Indigo

December 1916

RAJKUMAR SHUKLA caught hold of me at Lucknow, where I had gone for the Congress[22] of 1916. 'Vakil Babu will tell you everything about our distress', he said, and urged me to go to Champaran. 'Vakil Babu' was none other than Babu Brajkishore Prasad[23], who became my esteemed co-worker in Champaran.

So early in 1917[24], we left Calcutta for Champaran, looking just like fellow rustics.

A, *Part V; G*

CHAMPARAN IS a district of the Tirhut division and Motihari is its headquarters. Rajkumar Shukla's place was in the vicinity of Bettiah, and the tenants belonging to the *khotis* in its neighbourhood were the poorest in the district. Rajkumar Shukla wanted me to see them and I was equally anxious to do to. So I started with my co-workers for Motihari the same day.

A, *Part V; G*

IT SHOULD be remembered that no one knew me in Champaran. The peasants were all ignorant.

The world outside Champaran was not known to them. And yet they received me as though we had been age-long friends. It is no exaggeration, but the literal truth, to say that in this meeting with the peasants I was face to face with God, Ahimsa, and truth.

A, Part V; G

THE WORK of recording statements of the ryots' grievances was progressing apace. Thousands of such statements were taken, and they could not but have their effect. The ever growing number of ryots coming to make their statements increased the planters' wrath, and they moved heaven and earth to counteract my inquiry.

Sir Edward Gait, the Lieutenant Governor, asked me to see him expressed his willingness to appoint an inquiry and invited me to be a member of the Committee ...

The Committee found in favour of the ryots, and recommended that the planters should refund a portion of the exactions made by them which the Committee had found to be unlawful, and that the tinkathia system should be abolished by law.

The tinkathia system which had been in existence for about a century was thus abolished, and with it the planters' raj came to an end.

A, *Part V; G*

Motihari Court Room
18 April 1917
... I HAVE disregarded the order served upon me, not for want of respect for lawful authority, but in obedience of the higher law of our being— the voice of conscience.

CWMG *Vol. 13, p. 375; E*

Way Of Peace

Ahmedabad
30 April 1917[25]

MY REASON tells me that the peace which we shall have will be a mockery; it will be an armed truce, it will be the outcome not of one party admitting being in the wrong but both being fairly exhausted and desiring rest. Such a peace is bound to lead to a bloodier strife unless the intervening period brings about a change of hearts.

Hermann Kallenbach—Mahatma Gandhi's Friend in South Africa
by Isa Sarid and Christian Bartolf, Selbstverlag; 1997

Mahadev Desai

September 1917

IT TAKES me only a little while to judge people. I have found in you the person I have been looking for, the one person to whom I will one day be able to entrust my work. I need you for myself personally, not for the ashram or for any other work.

Gandhi to Mahadev Desai, RP, p. 322; G

To Kallenbach

Motihari
21 December 1917

My dear friend,

I have been irregular of late. I have been wandering so much that I never have the leisure to write love letters especially when they get lost. From you I had had only three letters during the past three months. Polak has however written to me about you and so has Miss Winterbottom[28]. How often do I not want to hug you. Daily do I have novel experiences here which I should like you to share with me. But this monstrous War never seems to be ending. All the peace talk only enhances the agony. However, like all human institutions it must have an end, and our friendship must be a poor affair if it cannot bide its time and be all the stronger and purer for the weary waiting. And what is this physical form after all? As I was whizzing through the air yesterday and looking at the trees, I saw that beneath all the change that these mighty trees daily underwent, there was a something that persisted. Every leaf has its own separate life. It drops and withers. But the tree lives on. Every tree falls in process of time or under the cruel axe, but the forest of which the tree is but a part lives and so with us leaves of the human tree. We may wither, but the eternal in us lives on, changeless and endless. I derived much comfort last evening as I was thus musing. The thoughts went on to you and I sighed, but I regained self-possession and said to myself, 'I know my friend not for his form but for that which informs him.'

With love,
Your old friend,
The Diary of Mahadev Desai *Vol. 1, p. 4*

'Wear My Mantle'

2 February 1918[27]

DEVA (A short loving form), if you equip yourself fittingly enough to wear my mantle, nobody dare come in your way. Only, I wish you became strong enough to bear the burden. But don't be under the delusion that you have no innate fitness for the aspiration. Work itself is the best teacher, and, as we take up one task after another, we grow more fit to tackle our work ever more successfully.

The Diary of Mahadev Desai *Vol. 1. p. 21*

'Talking Publicly Of My Activities'

12 February 1918[28]

My dear West,

... The Ashram[29] is beautifully situated on the banks of the Sabarmati river. We daily bathe in it. All the children can swim now. The school is under an able Principal, who was a distinguished Professor of the Gujarat College. The Ashram, of course, is under Maganlal's management. I do not know what is in store for the Ashram or the school. They are at the present moment popular institutions.

In all these activities, I often wish for the co-operation of the fellow-workers there. But I know it cannot be. But believe me, there is not a moment, when I do not think of one or the other of you.

News of your exploits serve as apt illustrations for me. I am building on the experience gained there.

Please tell Mrs West that she is not to consider, for one moment, that I have forgotten her or Granny. Nor have I forgotten the assurances given by me. New ties and new acquaintances cannot make me forget old ones.

This letter is not for publication. I do not wish to talk publicly of my activities.

With love,
Yours' ever,
M.K. Gandhi

The Diary of Mahadev Desai Vol. 1, pp. 32-3

'I Would Nestle You'

27 February 1918

Chiranjivi Ramdas,

I am worrying over you these days. I read disappointment writ large in your letters. With a painful inferiority-complex, you feel that you are uneducated and are nowhere in the world. Were you here with me, I would nestle you under my wings and give you solace and strength. I think it is due to my own defect that I cannot satisfy you. Knowing that all my faults were committed unconsciously, you will please forgive me. ...

Bapu's blessings.

The Diary of Mahadev Desai Vol. 1, pp. 50-1; G

To Ambalal Sarabhai[30]

1 March 1918

EARLY THIS morning, as I was getting up, I fell into a reverie. Whither are we going? What would be the results of my activity, if it was continued for long? And what of yours? In the former case, you would either accept the demands of the labourers or, if you are adamant, the labourers may take to some other occupation. If they give up their resolve and accept the wages you offer, it will be my defeat. But the public will not feel morally shocked at my success or defeat.

But what about your activity? If you win, the labourers will be all the more suppressed; they will sink into deeper depths in cowardice and despair, and they will be convinced that Mammon is the real Ruler, who can triumph over everything in this world. If, despite your efforts, the labourers get an increment, you and those with you will consider yourselves beaten. But is your victory really desirable? Would you wish the rich to get even more purse-proud? Would you like labourers to become utterly helpless, before the might of wealth? What would you prefer? To let the workers grovel in the dust, or to consider it as your victory, not theirs merely, if they get their due or even a little more? Don't you see that in your defeat lies your true victory, and that your seeming victory is dangerous even to yourself?...My effort, therefore is a form of Satyagraha. Please consider deeply. I appeal to you to listen to the still small voice within you and follow its dictates. Will you have the goodness to dine with us here?'

The Diary of Mahadev Desai *Vol. 1, pp. 55–6; G*

'I Feel Bored At The Blind Adoration'

3 March 1918[31]

I FEEL bored at the blind adoration of the people for me. If they know my views and even then respected me, I could utilize their regard for me for national work. I do not wish to gain any popularity at the cost of hiding my religious views. If I become an object of universal contempt for sticking to the right course, I would hail that too.

The Diary of Mahadev Desai, *Vol. 1, p. 58; G*

Ahmedabad Mill-Hands' Strike

15 March 1918[32]

THE STRUGGLE is not merely for a 35 per cent increase; it is to show that workers are prepared to suffer for their rights. We are fighting to uphold our honour. We have launched on this struggle in order to better ourselves.

Today the employers believe that the workers will not do any manual labour and so are bound to succumb soon. If the workers depend on others' money for their maintenance, the mill-owners will think that the source is bound to be exhausted sooner or later, and so will not take the workers seriously. If, they begin to do manual work (elsewhere) the employers will see that they will lose their workers unless they grant the 35 per cent increase forthwith. Thus, it is for us to shorten or lengthen the struggle. We shall be free the sooner by enduring greater suffering just now. If we flinch from suffering, the struggle is bound to be protracted. Those who have weakened will, we hope, consider all these points and become strong again.

CWMG Vol. 14, pp. 254–5; G

'Unbidden, The Words Came'

Ahmedabad
15 March 1918

ONE MORNING—it was at a mill-hands' meeting—while I was still groping and unable to see my way clearly, the light came to me. Unbidden and all by themselves the words came to my lips: 'Unless the strikers rally,' I declared to the meeting, 'and continue the strike until a settlement is reached, or until they leave the mills altogether, I will not touch any food.'

The labourers were thunderstruck. Tears began to pour down Anasuyabehn's[33] cheeks. The labourers broke out: 'Not you, but we shall fast. It would be monstrous if you were to fast. Please forgive us for our lapse, we shall now remain faithful to our pledge to the end.'

At A War Conference—On My Terms

April 1918

THE VICEROY[34] had invited various leaders to a war conference[35] in Delhi.

In response to the invitation I went to Delhi. I had, however, objections to taking part in the conference, the principal one being the exclusion from it of leaders like the Ali Brothers ...[36]

A, Part V; G

THE VICEROY was very keen on my supporting the resolution about recruiting. I asked for permission to speak in Hindi-Hindustani. The Viceroy acceded to my request, but suggested that I should speak also in English. I had no speech to make. I spoke but one sentence to this effect: 'With a full sense of my responsibility I beg to support the resolution.'

Many congratulated me on my having spoken in Hindustani. That was, they said, the first instance within living memory of anyone having spoken in Hindustani at such a meeting. The congratulations and the discovery that I was the first to speak in Hindustani at a Viceregal meeting hurt my national pride. I felt like shrinking into myself.

A, Part V; G

WE HAD meetings[37] wherever we went. People did attend, but hardly one or two would offer themselves as recruits. 'You are a votary of Ahimsa, how can you ask us to take up arms?' 'What good has Government done for India to deserve our co-operation?' These and similar questions used to be put to us.

A, Part V; G

To Devadas Gandhi

Nadiad
12 April 1918

Chiranjivi Devadas,

Your letter. You must have received mine also. You are silent as regards your health. ...

... I consider the fast[38] as my greatest achievement in life till now. I had an experience of supernal serenity while it lasted ...

... Uneasiness lurks in the mind and sometimes agitates it. I do often see that the people have grasped fully the spirit of the struggle, but what makes me worried is a passing appearance in their behaviour which suggests that they have not understood it. As for the work itself, there is no doubt it goes on in full swing, but my mind feels exhausted. The fight for Mohammad Ali's release is a crushing burden, though, I know, it has but to be borne. However, I have completely made my own the faith that God is going to give me the power to lift the load, how-so heavy, and so, deep down in me, there is peace also. Ba, besides, is with me here. ...

The Diary of Mahadev Desai, Vol. 1, pp. 91–3; G

Mahadev Or Harilal?

On the Train from Delhi to Bombay
1 May 1918

BHAI MAHADEV has redeemed what was your lapsed purpose[39]. But 'how nice it would have been if, indeed, you had filled that place' is a thought my attachment does not free me from.

Letter to Harilal, CWMG *Vol. 14, p. 385; G*

Sorabji Adajania's Death

29 July 1918

ONE OF the best Indians has just passed away in Johannesburg in the person of Sorabji Shapurji[40] of Adajan, near Surat, at the age of thirty-five. And it is my mournful duty to pay a humble tribute to a fellow-worker. Mr Sorabji, though known to a select company of friends, was unknown to the Indian public. His work lay in South Africa. He was a prince among passive resisters. ...

Bombay Chronicle, 29 July 1918; CWMG *Vol. 14, p. 507; E*

Our Duty In The War

1 August 1918

[Millie Graham Polak visited India during the war. She recalls the following conversation during the recruitment campaign: '*We talked of the War. Mr Gandhi was perplexed as to his exact position in regard to it. War and bloodshed filled him with horror ...*'.]

MKG: To refrain from action because you are afraid of the act or the results it may bring to you is not virtue.

MGP: Then what do you advise?

MKG: To take part in the work until you have learned your lesson from it. When you have really learned that, you will no longer need to take part in it; you will be above it.

MGP: That almost sounds like saying war is right ...

MKG(sadly): Yes, I know but I see that my countrymen are refraining from acts of physical violence not because of love for their fellows but from cowardice, and peace with cowardice is much worse than a battlefield with victory. I would rather they died fighting than cringe with fear.

Millie Graham Polak in Mr Gandhi: The Man

(Millie Graham Polak recounts another conversation in the course of her stay in India during the First World War: '*Once, feeling greatly depressed, I told him ...*')

MGP: I can now understand the worship of Kali in India; death seems so near and easy everywhere and life so difficult.

MKG(smiling sadly): But you would not (be able to) escape it (life). You would have to come back again. I once thought that I could finish the wheel of rebirth in this incarnation. I know now that I can't and that I shall have to return to it. We cannot escape it, but I hope it will be only once more that I come back to it.

MGP: It is not that I am tired of living. There is always something beautiful in life itself to me. The thought of birth and re-birth does not sadden me, but death stalks grey and naked here.

MKG: That is not like you. You are letting your imagination make you a coward. Where is your faith?

Millie Graham Polak in Mr Gandhi: The Man, pp. 285–6

'I Must Correct The Inaccuracies'

Nadiad

17 August 1918

Dear Mr Henderson,

... I rarely take notice of incorrections (*sic*) in my reported speeches. I have so little opportunity even of reading them, but as this one in *The Times*[41] was, I knew, calculated to do so much mischief I felt I must correct the inaccuracies. I am glad I did so, for it has silenced the evil tongue and provided [me] an opportunity of becoming acquainted with you.

Yours sincerely,

M.K. Gandhi

CWMG Vol. 15, pp. 21–2; E

To The Lokamanya[42]

25 August 1918

I HAVE your letter. I am grateful to you for your sympathy. How can you not be concerned about my health? God be thanked I am now well.

I do not propose to attend the Congress or the Moderates' Conference either. I see that my views are different from those of either. I have already told you about them.

I am strongly against any attempt to bring about a compromise between the Moderate and the Extremist parties by the method of give and take. There are two clear-cut parties in the country. No harm could be done if the parties clearly stated their individual convictions before the public and the government. That is why I do not like any patched-up agreement between the two.

I can be patient.

May God help you in your work!

Yours,
Mohandas
Letter to Lokamanya Tilak, CWMG, *Vol. 15, p. 31; H*

Unbearable Mysteries

September 1918

I VERY nearly ruined my constitution during the recruiting campaign. In those days my food principally consisted of groundnut butter and lemons. I knew that it was possible to eat too much butter and injure one's health, and yet I allowed myself to do so. This gave me a slight attack of dysentery. I did not take serious notice of this, and went that evening[43] to the Ashram, as was my wont every now and then. I scarcely took any medicine in those days. ... Within an hour the dysentery appeared in acute form.

All the friends surrounded me were deeply concerned. They were all love and attention, but they could not relieve my pain. And my obstinacy added to their helplessness. I refused all medical aid. I would take no medicine, but preferred to suffer the penalty for my folly. So they looked on in helpless dismay. I must have had thirty to forty motions in twenty-four hours. I fasted, not taking even fruit juices in the beginning. The appetite had all gone. I had thought all along that I had an iron frame, but I found that my body had now become a lump of clay. It had lost all power of resistance ...

Whilst I was thus tossing on the bed of pain in the Ashram, Sjt. Vallabhbhai[44] brought the news that Germany had been completely defeated and that the Commissioner had sent word that recruiting was no longer necessary. The news that I had no longer to worry myself about recruiting came as a very great relief.

This protracted and first long illness in my life thus afforded me a unique opportunity to examine my principles and to test them.

A, *Part V; G*

ONE NIGHT I gave myself up to despair. I felt that I was at death's door.

A, *Part V; G*

17 August 1918

[Millie Graham Polak records: *'I often tried to talk with him of what happened after death but his mind never speculated about the next condition ... he would not talk of what might happen minutes after a man is called dead ...'*]

MGP: There are three friends of mine who have had some psychic experience ...

MKG(impatiently): It is altogether a waste of time to want to know about after death conditions.

MGP: They feel more interested in trying to pierce the veil of death than they are about life.

MKG: But their duty lies in making the conditions of their fellows more happy.

MGP: And don't you think it would make them more happy if they could know more about death?

MKG: They have not to worry about that. Death does not matter.

MGP: Yet we cry about that most.

[Millie Polak says at this point Gandhi changed the subject. He would not carry it further.]

Millie Graham Polak in *Mr Gandhi: The Man*

'Harilal—Don't Run After Money'

9 September 1918

Chiranjivi Harilal,

I want you not to be too eager to get rich quickly.

Think of Sorabji's death, of Dr Jivraj's being on his death-bed, of the passing away of Sir Ratan Tata. When life is so transitory, why all this restlessness? Why this running after money? Get whatever money you can earn by ordinary but steady efforts. Resolve in mind, though, that you will not forsake the path of truth in pursuit of wealth. Make your mind as firm as you can and then go ahead making money.

The Diary of Mahadev Desai *Vol. 1, p. 249;* CWMG *Vol. 15, p. 47; G*

'Harilal—The Check Over You Has Disappeared'[45]

Ahmedabad
26 November 1918

Chiranjivi Harilal,

It will be good if you come over before I leave. Whatever you wish to say, you may pour out before me without any hesitation. If you cannot give vent to your feelings before me, before whom else can you do so? I shall be a true friend to you. What would it matter if there should be any difference of opinion between us about any scheme of yours? We shall have a quiet talk. The final decision will rest with you. I fully realize that your state at present is like that of a man dreaming. Your responsibilities have increased, your trials have increased and your temptations will increase likewise. To a man with a family, the fact of being such, that is, having a wife, is a great check. This check over you has disappeared.

CWMG *Vol. 15, p. 65; G*

Kasturba's Ingenuity

8 January 1919

... I FELT an excruciating pain at the time of evacuation, so that the very idea of eating filled me with dread ... Shankerlal Banker[46] now constituted himself the guardian of my health, and pressed me to consult Dr Dalal. Dr Dalal was called accordingly. His capacity for taking instantaneous decisions captured me.

He said: 'I cannot rebuild your body unless you take milk. If in addition you would take iron and arsenic injections, I would guarantee fully to renovate your constitution.'

'You can give me the injections,' I replied, 'but milk is a different question; I have a vow against it.'

'What exactly is the nature of your vow?' the doctor inquired.

I told him the whole history and the reasons behind my vow, how, since I had come to know that the cow and the buffalo were subjected to the process of *phooka*, I had conceived a strong disgust for milk. Moreover, I had always held that milk is not the natural diet of man. I had therefore abjured its use altogether. Kasturbai was standing near my bed listening all the time to this conversation.

'But surely you cannot have any objection to goat's milk then', she interposed. The doctor too took up the strain. 'If you will take goat's milk, it will be enough for me', he said.

I succumbed. My intense eagerness to take up the Satyagraha fight had created in me a strong desire to live, and so I contented myself with adhering to the letter of my vow only, and sacrificed its spirit. For although I had only the milk of the cow and the she-buffalo in mind when I took the vow, by natural implication it covered the milk of all animals. Nor could it be right for me to use milk at all, so long as I held that milk is not the natural diet of man. Yet knowing all this I agreed to take goat's milk. The will to live proved stronger than the devotion to truth, and for once the votary of truth compromised his sacred ideal by his eagerness to take up the Satyagraha fight.

A, *Part V; G*

Harilal's Children

Sabarmati Ashram
Ahmedabad
23 February 1919
[After the death of Harilal's wife, Gandhi and Kasturba had Harilal's four children brought over to the Sabarmati Ashram. In this letter,

remarkable for its tone of relaxed grand-parenthood, Gandhi gives Devadas a picture of his grandchildren's life in the Ashram.]

MANU[47] HAS been stealing fat from all and sundry in the Ashram, except from me, so that she looks like the largest water melon in the Ashram. When there is an occasion for installing Ganapati, an elephant's trunk should be secured and stuck on her face, and she would indeed look quite a beauty. Her radiance is ever growing brighter, with the result that she has become everyone's doll. Rasik[48] (full of zest) often demonstrates his zestfulness by employing the stick. Kanti[49] is growing calmer. Rami's[50] health continues so-so. Ba's time is taken up in ministering to them all. I notice that she even finds the thing irksome and, in consequence, her temper is often snappy, and just as the potter, when angry, twists the ears of his donkey, his wife, I infer, must be doing the same to the donkey's master.

Enough for today.

Probably this too will go all right as a saying:

'Rasiklal Harilal Mohandas Karamchand Gandhi,
Had a goat in his keeping;
The goat would not be milked
And Gandhi would not stop his weeping.'

CWMG Vol. 15, pp. 99–100; G

Rowlatt's[51] Black Bills

Sabarmati Ashram
Ahmedabad
Before 26 February 1919

THESE BILLS have come to be known as the Black Bills. A strong agitation has been going on against them all over India and the Bills have been felt to be so oppressive that Satyagraha has been started against them. Several men and women have taken the Satyagraha Pledge. A body known as the Satyagraha Sabha has been formed and the people in general have also been advised to take this Pledge.

CWMG Vol. 15, p. 110; G

'As If In A Dream'

March 1919

THE BILL had not yet been gazetted as an Act. I was in a very weak condition, but when I received an invitation from Madras I decided to take the risk of the long journey ...

Rajagopalachari[52] had then only recently left Salem to settle down for legal practice in Madras ... It was with him that we had put up in Madras.

We daily discussed together plans of the fight, but beyond the holding of public meetings I could not then think of any other programme. I felt myself at a loss to discover how to offer civil disobedience against the Rowlatt Bill if it was finally passed into law.

While these cogitations were still going on news was received that the Rowlatt Bill had been published as an Act. That night I fell asleep while thinking over the question. Towards the small hours of the morning I woke up somewhat earlier than usual. I was still in that twilight condition between sleep and consciousness when suddenly the idea broke upon me—it was as if in a dream. Early in the morning I related the whole story to Rajagopalachari:

The idea came to me last night[53] in a dream that we should call upon the country to observe a general *hartal*. Satyagraha is a process of self-purification, and ours is a sacred fight, and it seems to me to be in the fitness of things that it should be commenced with an act of self-purification. Let all the people of India, therefore, suspend their business on that day and observe the day as one of fasting and prayer.

Rajagopalachari was at once taken up with my suggestion.

The whole of India from one end to the other, towns as well as villages, observed a complete hartal on that day. It was a most wonderful spectacle.

The Diary of Mahadev Desai *Vol. 4, pp. 41–2;* A, *pp. 280–1;* G

Bombay
11 April 1919

ANASUYA BEHN, TOO, had received news of disturbances in Ahmedabad. Someone had spread a rumour that she also had been arrested. The mill-hands had gone mad over her rumoured arrest, struck work and committed acts of violence, and a sergeant had been done to death.

I proceeded to Ahmedabad. I learnt that an attempt had been made to pull up the rails near the Nadiad railway station, that a Government officer had been murdered in Viramgam, and that Ahmedabad was under martial law. The people were terror stricken. They had indulged in acts of violence and were being made to pay for them with interest.

A Part V; CWMG Vol. 39 p. 372; E

I Am Sorry ... I Embarked Upon A Mass Movement

Bombay[54]
18 April 1919

IT IS not without sorrow that I feel compelled to advise the temporary suspension of civil disobedience. I give this advice not because I have less faith now in its efficacy, but because I have, if possible, greater faith than before. It is my perception of the law of satyagraha which impels me to suggest the suspension. I am sorry, when I embarked upon a mass movement, I underrated the forces of evil and I must now pause and consider how best to meet the situation ...

My attitude towards the Rowlatt legislation remains unchanged. Indeed, I do feel that the Rowlatt legislation is one of the many causes of the present unrest. But in a surcharged atmosphere, I must refrain from examining these causes. The main and only purpose of this letter is to advise all satyagrahis to temporarily suspend civil disobedience, to give government effective co-operation in restoring order and by preaching and practice to gain adherence to the fundamental principles mentioned above.

The Hindu, 21-4-1919; CWMG Vol. 15, pp. 241–5; E

'A Himalayan Miscalculation'

Nadiad
24 April 1919

... IT WAS here that I first used the expression 'Himalayan miscalculation' which obtained such a wide currency afterwards. ...

A Part V; CWMG Vol. 39, p. 373; E

'Himalayan Blunder'

Sabarmati
April 1919

AT THE time of the Rowlatt Act satyagraha, I had to confess my Himalayan blunder, to fast myself and invite others to do so.

CWMG *Vol. 15, pp. 220–4*

'Harilal—How Can You ...'

Bombay
5 May 1919

MADHAVDAS[55] TOLD me of your financial difficulties. He has accepted my advice. It was that you should go forward without monetary help from anyone, that is what I would have you do ... How can you, in this situation, invest others' money? In a country where injustice prevails, there is no dignity except in poverty. It is impossible, in the prevailing condition, to amass wealth without being a party, directly or indirectly, to injustice.

Blessings from
Bapu
CWMG *Vol. 15, p. 278; G*

'Lonelier Here Than In South Africa'

Ahmedabad
2 June 1919

Dear Miss Schlesin,

... Satyagraha is going on merrily. Civil disobedience is expected to commence very soon. How I often wish you were here for more reasons than one! But I must plough the lonely furrow. It often makes me sad when I think of all my helpers of South Africa. I have no Doke here. I have no Kallenbach. Don't know where he is at the present moment. Polak in England. No counterpart of Kachhalia or Sorabji. Impossible to get the second edition of Rustomji. Strange as it may appear, I feel lonelier here than in South Africa. This does not mean that I am without co-workers. But between the majority of them and me, there is not that perfect correspondence which used to exist in South Africa. I do not enjoy the same sense of security which you all gave me there. I do not know the people here; nor they, me. This is all gloomy, if I were to brood over it. But I do not. I have not the time for it. ...

CWMG *Vol. 15, p. 341; E*

'You Must Learn Gujarati'

Bombay
28 June 1919

Dear Mr Jinnah[56],

I was delighted to receive your letter. I shall certainly keep you informed of the doings here. I cannot say anything about the Reforms[57] Bill. I have hardly studied it. My preoccupation is Rowlatt legislation; add to that the Punjab, Kalinath Roy[58], Transvaal and swadeshi. ...

Pray tell Mrs Jinnah that I shall expect her on her return to join the hand-spinning class that Mrs Banker Senior and Mrs Ramabai, a Punjabi lady, are conducting. And, of course, I have your promise that you would take up Gujarati and Hindi as quickly as possible. May I then suggest that like Macaulay[59] you learn at least one of these languages on your return voyage? You will not have Macaulay's time during the voyage, i.e., six months, but then you have not the same difficulty that Macaulay had. I hope you will both keep well during your stay. ...

Yours sincerely,
M.K. Gandhi
CWMG *Vol. 15, pp. 398–9; E*

Jallianwala Bagh

4 November 1919

IT IS true that a large number of our people were killed in Jallianwala Bagh. But we ought to have maintained peace even if everyone present had been killed. It is not right, in my opinion, to take blood for blood.

CWMG *Vol. 16, p. 286; H*

River Of Holy Blood

Lahore
Sunday, 21 December 1919[60]

I ACCOMPANIED the Hon'ble Pandit Madan Mohan Malaviya[61] and Mr Neville[62] to Amritsar, Jallianwala Bagh and the streets where passers-by were made to crawl on their stomachs ...

... The name Bagh is a misnomer. Jallianwala is a surname and belonged to the original owner of the Bagh. This Bagh is now the property of about 40 people. It is not a garden but a rubbish dump. It is flanked on all sides by the backs of houses and people throw refuse on to it from their rear windows. It contains three trees and one small tomb. It is an open space which can be approached by a narrow lane. It was through this that General Dyer made his entry. Hence the people who had collected there on 13 April were virtually trapped. There are 3 or 4 exits, but to use them one has to jump over a wall. It was in this way that thousands that day saved their lives.

There flowed in this Bagh a river of blood, the holy blood of innocent people. Because of this the spot has become sanctified. Efforts are being made to obtain this plot for the nation. It will, indeed, be a matter of shame for us if we do not succeed.

Navajivan, *28-12-1919*; CWMG, *Vol. 16, pp. 354–5; G*

Evidence Before Disorders Inquiry Committee

Ahmedabad
9 January 1920

[*A Disorders Inquiry Committee was appointed by His Majesty's Government to go into the sequence of events that rocked India in 1919. The Committee was presided over by Lord Hunter. The Committee consisted of Justice Rankin, W.F. Rice, Major-General Sir George Barrow, Pandit Jagat Narayan, Thomas Smith, Sir Chimanlal H. Setalvad, Sultan Ahmad Khan, and N. Willamson as Secretary. The Committee first met at Delhi on 31 October and then from 3 to 10 November 1919. Later, it collected evidence at Lahore ... Brigadier-General Dyer appeared before the Committee at Lahore. The session at Ahmedabad lasted from 5 to 10 January*

1920. Chief among non-official witnesses who testified before the Committee was Gandhi.]

CWMG Vol. 16, p. 378; E

President (Lord Hunter): Mr Gandhi, we have been informed that you are the author of the satyagraha movement?
MKG: Yes, Sir.
President: I would like you to give us an explanation of what that movement is.
MKG: It is a movement intended to replace methods of violence.

CWMG Vol. 16, p. 378; E

The Hon'ble Mr Justice Rankin: ... I think the satyagraha vow was settled somewhere about the third week in February?
MKG: I think that is very nearly right.
Rankin: I think what has been called your *hukm*[63] was dated somewhere about the 23rd of February?
MKG: Yes.

CWMG Vol. 16, p. 399; E

Sir C.H. Setalvad: With regard to your satyagraha doctrine, as far as I am able to understand it, it involves a pursuit of truth?
MKG: Yes.

CHS: Now in that doctrine, who is to determine the truth? That individual himself?
MKG: Yes, that individual himself.

CHS: You recognize, I suppose, Mr Gandhi, that in order properly to follow in the right spirit in which you conceive the doctrine of satyagraha, pursuit after truth, in the manner, you describe, the person must be equipped with high moral and intellectual equipment?
MKG: Certainly, a man who wants to pursue truth independently has to be equipped with high moral and intellectual equipment.
CHS: Now do you expect that standard of moral and intellectual equipment in the ordinary man?

MKG: It is not necessary for me to have that standard from all who accept the thing. If, for instance, A has evolved a conception of truth which B, C, and 50 others accepted (it) implicitly from him, then, I need not expect from them that high standard which I would expect from A, but the others will follow that. They will know that they are not to inflict any violence, and (then) you create a large body.

CWMG Vol. 16, pp. 408–9; E

The Khilafat[64]

... WHAT HAS hurt seven crores of Muslims ought to hurt Hindus too.

CWMG Vol. 17, p. 1; G

Saraladevi Choudhurani[65]

SARALADEVI HAS been in Ahmedabad for some time and hence it will not be out of place to give some additional information about her to readers of *Navajivan*. In a general way, all have heard of Saraladevi, but only as an erudite lady doing public service. To be more specific about her, she is a niece of Sir Rabindranath Tagore, daughter of the well-known former secretary of the Congress, Mr Ghosal, and wife of the famous Pandit Rambhuj Dutt Chowdhari of the Punjab. She completed her B.A. at the age of 19, and from then onwards has been engaged in public service in one form or another. It was she who started the Bengali monthly, named *Bharati*[66], and it is said that she showed in it the great power of her pen. Her poetic power is of a high order and her sweet song 'I bow to India', which was sung in Banaras, is known all over the country. Shrimati Saraladevi took a leading part in establishing committees in Bengal and, when the War broke out, and it came to telling the educated Bengalis that they should join the army and do their duty, few were as effective as this lady. We see her hand in the public movement in the Punjab too. Her musical talent perhaps exceeds her gift for poetry and she is, therefore, in demand at every Congress. ...

Navajivan 29-2-1920; CWMG Vol. 17, pp. 62–3; G

Joining Issues With Tilak[67]

Delhi
After 18 January 1920

Lokamanya's creed is *shatham prati shathyam (wickedness unto the wicked)* ...

... In any case I pit the experience of a third of a century against the doctrine underlying *shatham prati shathyam*. The true law is *shatham prati satyam (Truth even unto the wicked)*.

CWMG *Vol. 16, pp. 490-1; E*

Pilgrimage To Kashi

16 February 1920

IT WAS time moreover that the report[68] was finalized. The question was where the Commissioners should assemble to read it over. Kashi was likely to suit Pandit Motilal Nehru, Mr C.R. Das, and Pandit Malaviya. It was decided, therefore, that all should go to Kashi. ...

Navajivan *29-2-1920;* CWMG *Vol. 17, p. 55; E*

WE WERE staying with Panditji[69] on the banks of the Ganga. Dawn and sunrise are impressive everywhere, but from these banks the sight was simply sublime. As the clouds brightened with the light of dawn, a golden sheen would appear on the waters of the Ganga and, when the sun had come into view over the horizon, there seemed to stand in the water of the river a great pillar of gold. It was a scene on which the eyes would rest with supreme satisfaction and make the pious devotee burst forth spontaneously into the *gayatri*[70] hymn. After witnessing this magnificent sight, I felt I understood a little better the worship of the sun, the adoration of the rivers and the significance of the gayatri hymn.

... but at the same time ... I observed people defecating on the very banks of the river. We no more go out to the jungle but, instead, go to the river bank. In this holy spot, it should be possible for us to walk barefoot with our eyes closed, whereas one has to walk here with the greatest caution. One also feels disgust to sip the Ganga water at this spot. ...

CWMG *Vol. 17, p. 56; G*

To Mrs Jinnah

30 April 1920

PLEASE REMEMBER me to Mr Jinnah and do coax him to learn Hindustani or Gujarati. If I were you, I should begin to talk to him in Gujarati or Hindustani. There is not much danger of you forgetting your English or your misunderstanding each other. Is there?

Will you do it? Yes, I would ask this even for the love you bear me.

From the manuscript of Mahadev Desai's Diary,

CWMG *Vol. 17, p. 361; E*

'Maganlal, Why Are You Unhappy?'

2 May 1920

I CASUALLY asked Mahadev yesterday whether he knew why you were unhappy. He thereupon reported the conversation about the car and all that you poured out on the occasion ...

... I should certainly like to say something to calm you. I shall do so only after I hear from you.

Blessings from
Bapu
CWMG *Vol. 17, pp. 380–1; G*

'Maganlal—Let Me Explain ...'

Sinhgadh
4 May 1920[71]

... As YOU have had no time, however, to write to me, I shall say something on the basis of what I heard from Mahadev, wishing to give you as much peace as I can. (You ask or say) ...

I am no more as scrupulously firm as I used to be ...

The power which was mine, in virtue of which everyone was obliged to listen to what I said, has disappeared.

I think it is natural that these and similar doubts should arise in your mind ...

My staunchness has not disappeared. My ideas have grown stronger and more piercing. My indifference to worldy pleasures has increased. What I used to see but dimly has now become clearer to me. I have grown more tolerant, so that I am less particular about others (doing what I want them to do). ...

It is quite true that I have lost my former fire. My illness has disabled me. I have myself observed that, ever since I lost the strength to stand beside you all and work, I have lost my fire. The steel-like strength of my body having given place to softness, I put up with many things. Did anyone ever see me going for a change of air? Well, that is what I do now. When I think of the expenditure which has been incurred over me I get still more nervous. I feel ashamed when travelling second class. My soul suffers on such occasions and, to be sure, it loses its lustre. There is no way out of this. My best time is over. People may take now what they can from my ideas. I have ceased to be the 'ideal man of action' which I used to be. I am to be pitied for being in this state. ...

Blessings from
Bapu
CWMG *Vol. 17, pp. 385–8; G*

Saint Or Politician?

12 May 1920

A KIND friend has sent me the following cutting from the April number of *East and West*:

MR GANDHI has the reputation of a saint but it seems that the politician in him often dominates his decisions ...

... Now I think that the word 'saint' should be ruled out of present life. It is too sacred a word to be lightly applied to anybody, much less to one like myself who claims only to be a humble searcher after truth, knows his limitations, makes mistakes, never hesitates to admit them when he makes them, and frankly confesses that he, like a scientist, is making experiments about some of 'the eternal verities' of life, but cannot even claim to be a scientist because he can show no tangible proof of scientific accuracy in his methods or such tangible results of his experiments as modern science demands. But though by disclaiming sainthood I disappoint the critic's expectations, I would have him to give up his regrets by answering him that the politician in me has never dominated a single decision of mine, and if I seem to take part in politics, it is only because politics encircle us today like the coil of a snake from which one cannot get out, no matter how much one tries. I wish therefore to wrestle with the snake, as I have been doing, with more or less success, consciously since 1894, unconsciously, as I have now discovered, ever since reaching the years of discretion. ...

Young India; CWMG *Vol. 17, pp. 405–6*

On Weddings

May 1920

A WEDDING having taken place in the Satyagraha Ashram, I could not help making a comparison between this wedding in the Ashram and the weddings outside. I take the liberty to place before the reader some of my reflections on this.

Imam Saheb Abdul Kadir Bawazeer[72] is an earnest Muslim of a noble family. His father was the Muezzin in the Jumma Masjid in Bombay for several years ...

And now came the wedding of his eldest daughter, Fatima. We held consultations. Fatima, over twenty, is a wise girl. After having consulted her and the Imam Saheb, we decided to have a wedding which would become the Ashram and our life of poverty. We dropped the marriage procession, the band and all other pomp; we dropped even the feast ...

Next morning I went to the city. There I saw numberless marriage processions. The bandsmen, in a variety of strange costumes, deafened one's ears with their noises. Children and youngmen, loaded with ornaments and velvet clothing in this intolerable heat, were dripping with perspiration. The bridegroom was veiled in a profusion of flowers. I saw in this no religion, nor real joy nor any grandeur. If we really wish to have band music, why foolishly ape the West? If we would follow the West, we should see that we have the genuine thing. Any person even with ordinary knowledge of music will say that there is no sweetness at all nor any music in the bands which we order ...

My complaint is not against pomp and splendour. Those who have money and no high aim in life will no doubt have them. They must have occasions to use their wealth. But I wish to see in all these things some discrimination and thought, some restraint and art. ...

Navajivan, *9-5-1920*; CWMG *Vol. 17, pp. 399–400; G*

The Savarkar Brothers

26 May 1920

... THANKS TO the action of the Government of India and the Provincial Governments, many of those who were undergoing imprisonment at the time have received the benefit of the Royal clemency. But there are some notable 'political offenders' who have not yet been discharged. Among these I count the Savarkar brothers ...

Mr Ganesh Damodar Savarkar...had done no violence. He was married, had two daughters who are dead, and his wife died about eighteen months ago.

The brother[73] was born in 1884, and is better known for his career in London[74]. His sensational attempt to escape the custody of the police and his jumping through a porthole in French waters[75], are still fresh in the public mind. He was educated at the Fergusson College, finished off in London and became a barrister. He is the author of the proscribed history of the Sepoy Revolt of 1857. He was tried in 1910, and received the same sentence as his brother on 24th December 1910. He was charged also in 1911 with abetment of murder[76]. No act of violence was proved against him either. He too is married, had a son in 1909. His wife is still alive.

Both these brothers have declared their political opinions and both have stated that they do not entertain any revolutionary ideas and that if they were set free they would like to work under the Reforms Act[77], for they consider that the Reforms enable one to work thereunder so as to achieve political responsibility for India. They both state unequivocally that they do not desire independence from the British connection. On the contrary, they feel that India's destiny can be best worked out in association with the British. Nobody has questioned their honour or their honesty, and in my opinion the published expression of their views ought to be taken at its face value. What is more, I think, it may be safely stated that the cult of violence has, at the present moment, no following in India ...

... There is no question about the brothers being political offenders. And so far the public are aware there is no danger to public safety....

Young India, 26-5-1920; CWMG Vol. 17, pp. 460–2; E

The Prince Of Wales' Visit

11 July 1920

MR BAPTISTA[78] has asked in *The (Bombay) Chronicle* whether, in our present suffering, we are in a position to accord a cordial reception to the eldest son of King-Emperor George V when he visits India. He has spoken of my views and, therefore, I think it my duty to state them.

... By refusing to welcome the Prince, we express our strong displeasure at the misdeeds of the Government. We have a right to do this. If we do not do it, we shall proclaim ourselves cowards. ...

CWMG Vol. 18, pp. 30–1; E

My Inner Voice

19 July 1920

... IF YOU believe that what I am telling you is only what God tells me through my inner voice, then give me the assurance, I beg you, that you will restrain your passion and will not boil over even if they sentence me. ...

CWMG Vol. 18, p. 66; G

Non-Cooperation

28 July 1920

... MANY PEOPLE dread the advent of non-cooperation, because of the events of last year. They fear madness from the mob and consequent repetition of last year's reprisals almost unsurpassed in their ferocity in the history of modern times. Personally I do not mind governmental fury as I mind mob fury. The latter is a sign of national distemper and therefore more difficult to deal with than the former which is confined to a small corporation. It is easier to oust a government that has rendered itself unfit to govern than it is to cure unknown people in a mob of their madness. ...

Young India, *28-7-1920;* CWMG *Vol. 18, p. 92; E*

Returning The 'Kaiser-I-Hind'

1 August 1920[79]

Sir[80],

It is not without a pang that I return the Kaiser-i-Hind gold medal, granted[81] to me by your predecessor[82] for my humanitarian work in South Africa, the Zulu War medal granted in South Africa for my war services as officer in charge of the Indian Volunteers Service Corps in 1906, and the Boer War medal for my services as Assistant Superintendent of the Indian Volunteer Stretcher-Bearer Corps during the Boer War of 1899. I venture to return these medals in pursuance of the scheme of non-co-operation, inaugurated today in connection with the Khilafat movement. Valuable as these honours have been to me, I cannot wear them with an easy conscience so long as my Mussulman countrymen have to labour under a wrong done to their religious sentiments. Events, which have happened during the past month, have confirmed me in the opinion that the Imperial Government have acted in the Khilafat matter in an unscrupulous, immoral, and unjust manner and have been moving from wrong to wrong in order to defend their immorality ... No doubt the mob excesses were unpardonable. Incendiarism, the murder of the five innocent Englishmen and the cowardly assault on Miss Sherwood[83] were most deplorable and uncalled for but the punitive measure taken by General Dyer, Col. Frank Johnson, Col. O'Brien, Mr Bosworth Smith, Rai Shri Ram Sud, Mr Malik Khan, and other officers were out of all proportion to the crime of the people and amounted to a wanton cruelty and inhumanity, almost unparalleled in modern times.

I remain,
Sir,
Your faithful servant,
M.K. Gandhi

Lord Chelmsford
Viceroy of India
Delhi

CWMG *Vol. 18, pp. 104–6; E*

Lokamanya's Death

4 August 1920[84]

... A GIANT among men has fallen. The voice of the lion is hushed. ...

CWMG *Vol. 18, p. 110; E*

The Cow And The Caliphate

4 August 1920

... I AM as eager to save the cow from the Mussulman's knife as any Hindu. But on that very account I refuse to make my support of the Mussulman claim on the Khilafat conditional upon his saving the cow. The Mussulman is my neighbour. He is in distress. His grievance is legitimate and it is my bounden duty to help him to secure redress by every legitimate means in my power even to the extent of losing my life and property. ...

Young India, *4-8-1920;* CWMG *Vol. 18, p. 118; E*

After An Age, To Kallenbach

10 August 1920

My dear Lower House,

After how long a time have I the good fortune to write to you? After the greatest search, I have now got your address. Never has a day passed but I have thought of you ...

How I wish I could go over to see you and hug you. For me you have risen from the dead. I had taken it for granted that you were dead. I could not believe that you would keep me without a letter for so long ... I have come in closest touch with a lady[85] who often travels with me. Our relationship is indefinable. I call her my spiritual wife. A friend has called it an intellectual wedding. I want you to see her. It was under her roof that I passed several months at Lahore in the Punjab. Mrs Gandhi is at the Ashram. She has aged considerably but she is as brave as ever. She is the same woman you know her with her faults and virtues. Manilal and Ramdas are in Phoenix looking after *Indian Opinion.* Harilal is in Calcutta doing his business. He has lost his wife. And Mrs G is looking after his children ...

And now I shall stop. I was two years ago in death's grip. If you are free I want you to resume correspondence. My life is simpler than ever. My food is not fruit and nuts. I am living on goat's milk and bread and raisins. I am under a vow not to take more than five things. Cow's milk I would not like because of the vows I took in London. Salt I do not abjure because I find that we take inorganic salt in water and inhale it from the sea.

With love and expectation of seeing your own writing soon.

Yours ever,
Upper House

From the manuscript of Mahadev Desai's Diary;
CWMG *Vol. 18, pp. 129–31*

'There Is No Rest To Be Had'

22 September 1920

... WE WERE travelling to Madras by the night train leaving Bangalore. We had been taking meetings at Salem during the day, motoring to Bangalore, a distance of 125 miles from Salem, taking there a meeting in drenching rain and thereafter we had to entrain. We needed night's rest but there was none to be had. At almost every station of importance, large crowds had gathered to greet us. About midnight we reached Jalarpet junction. The train had to stop there nearly forty minutes or stopped that night all those terrible minutes. Maulana Shaukat Ali requested the crowd to disperse. But the more he argued, the more they shouted '*Maulana Shaukat Ali ki Jai*', evidently thinking that the Maulana could not mean what he said. They had come from twenty miles' distance, they were waiting there for hours, they must have their satisfaction. The Maulana gave up the struggle, he pretended to sleep. The adorers thereupon mounted the footboards to have a peep at the Maulana. As the light in our compartment was put out they brought in lanterns. At last I thought I would try. I rose, went to the door. It was a signal for a great shout of joy. The noise tore me to pieces. I was so tired. All my appeals proved fruitless in the end. They would stop for a while to renew the noise again. I shut the windows. But the crowd was not to be baffled. They tried to open the windows from outside. They must see us both. ...

CWMG *Vol. 18, pp. 274–5; E*

To Dr Muhammad Iqbal

Before 27 November 1920

Dear Dr Iqbal[86],

The Muslim National University[87] calls you. If you could but take charge of it, I am sure that it will prosper under your cultured leadership. Hakimji Ajmal Khan and Dr Ansari[88] and of course the Ali Brothers desire it. I wish you could see your way to respond. Your expenses on a scale suited to the new awakening can be easily guaranteed. Please reply Allahabad[89], care Pundit Nehru.

Yours sincerely,
CWMG *Vol. 19, p. 34; E*

To Saraladevi Choudhurani

On way to Bhagalpur
11 December 1920

I HAD two letters from you, one scrap, the other a longish letter which shows that you do not understand my language or my thoughts. I have certainly not betrayed any annoyance over your complex nature, but I have remarked upon it. If a person is born with a deformation [sic] one may not quarrel with nature for it, but one may pardonably take note of it and try to remove it. And that is what I have done. I refuse to call an indefinable complexity a piece of art. All art yield to patient analysis and shows a unity of design behind the diversity on the canvas. You are hugging your defects even when they are pointed out by a friend in a friendly manner. I do not feel vexed but it makes my task of helping difficult. What art can there be in moods, in fits and starts? The simplest natures are certainly complex in a sense. But they are easily analysed. But they are called simple because they are easily understandable and readily yield to treatment. But I do not want to quarrel with you. In you I have an enigma to solve. I shall not be impatient. Only bear with me whenever I try to point [out] what to me appear to be your obvious limitations. We all have them. It is the privilege of friendship to lay the gentle finger on the weak spots. Friendship becomes a divine institution only when it educates friends. Let us try to elevate each other.

From the manuscript of Mahadev Desai's Dairy, CWMG *Vol. 19, p. 93; E*

The Sin Of Untouchability

19 January 1921

IT IS worthy of note that the Subjects Committee[90] accepted without any opposition the clause regarding the sin of untouchability.

... Have we not practised Dyerism and O'Dwyerism on our own kith and kin? We have segregated the 'pariah' and we are in turn segregated in the British Colonies. We deny him the use of public wells; we throw the leavings of our plates at him. His very shadow pollutes us. Indeed there is no charge that the 'pariah' cannot fling in our faces and which we do not fling in the faces of Englishmen. ...

CWMG *Vol. 19, p. 242; E*

To Andrews

Calcutta
29 January 1921[91]

My dearest Charlie,

You have inundated me with love-letters and I have neglected you. But you have been ever in my thoughts and prayer. You had no business to get ill[92]. You had therefore be better up and 'doing'. And yet on your sick-bed you have been doing so much[93]. For I see more and more what praying is doing and that silence is the best speech and often the best argument. And that is my answer to your anxiety about the untouchables.

... I may talk glibly of the Englishman's sin in Jallianwala. But as a Hindu, I may not talk about the sin of Hinduism against the untouchables. I have to deal with the Hindu Dyers. I must act and have ever acted. You act, you do not speak, when you feel most ...

... I am attacking the sacerdotalism of Hinduism. That Hindus consider it a 'sin' to touch a portion of human beings because they are born in a particular environment! I am engaged as a Hindu in showing that it is not a sin and that it is sin to consider that touch a sin ...

... I feel as keenly about the Kalighat[94] as I do about the untouchables. Whenever I am in Calcutta the thought of the goats being sacrificed haunts me and makes me uneasy. I asked Harilal not to settle in Calcutta on that account. The pariah can voice his own grief. He can petition. He can even rise against Hindus. But the poor dumb goats? I sometimes writhe in agony when I think of it. But I do not speak or write about it. All the same I am qualifying myself for the service of these fellow creatures of mine who are slaughtered in the name of my faith. I may not finish the work in this incarnation. I shall be born again to finish that work or someone who has realized my agony will finish it. ...

Yours
Mohan
CWMG *Vol. 19, pp. 288–90; E*

A Question

30 January 1921

A FRIEND writes from Surat:

Q. Like the Lokamanya, are you not born before your time?

A. No one ever comes or goes before his time. But people feel so about every reformer in the world. When we, who are accustomed to one way, are shown another by somebody, initially we always feel shocked.

CWMG *Vol. 19, pp. 296–301; E*

Goading The Bullock

5 April 1921

IN THE course of my tours, I get experiences, both sweet and sour. I shall remember my tour through the Central Provinces for a long time ... It was decided to proceed thence in a bullock-cart. The journey commenced at 1 a.m. I was tired and felt sleepy too. Why should I bother to see what manner of bullocks they were and who the driver was? Even in my drowsiness I could judge that the bullocks were running at the speed of horses. At times, they would move slowly, but mostly they kept running. Who does not like to see bullocks running? I said to myself: 'Good. We shall reach home so much the earlier. The bullocks of this region must be good.'

Morning broke and I woke up. To my dismay, I found that the driver's goad had a sharpened nail fixed in it and he made the bullocks run by frequently piercing their backs with it. Because of this torture, the bullocks had been shedding liquid excreta all along the route.

... I put up with it for about two minutes. Then I asked for the goad from the owner of the bullocks, which he handed over to me.

... We Hindus hold cow protection to be as important as safeguarding one's life. We fight the Muslims as enemies in order to save the cow. What right have we to ask them not to kill cows, when we ourselves prod our bullocks with a goad, load them excessively, give them as little to eat as possible, and extract milk from the cow until she bleeds, resorting to blowing for the purpose? Muslims consider it no sin to kill a cow for food. Will the Hindus contend that there is no sin in piercing the bullocks with a goad?...

CWMG Vol. 19, pp. 516–18; G

Orissa, Gopabandhu Das, And Jagannath Puri

10 April 1921

AT THE time of the famine in Orissa, I realized the poverty of the province but my impression has been that nowhere else were the people likely to be so poor as in Champaran.[95] But I am afraid Orissa beats Champaran in this respect. The difference between the two is that in Champaran the ryots had been impoverished by the oppression of the indigo-planters, whereas in Orissa the suffering is due to the wrath of Nature. Either the crops do not grow through lack of rains or there are floods following excessive rains and the crops and houses are washed off; hence there is always a near-famine in this province.

In this godforsaken region, the one real leader is Gopabandhu Das ...

GOPABANDHU BABU has started a Seva Samaj[96] ...

AFTER VISITING Gopabandhu Babu's school, we went on to Jagannath Puri ... Thick darkness reigns in the recess where the images are installed. There is neither air nor light. One or two lamps burn dimly, that is all.

... As at other places, here too the priests are a terror. They fleece the devout pilgrims. How is it that Jagannath remains a silent witness to all this wickedness? ...

CWMG Vol. 19, pp. 549–51; G

Burning Foreign Cloth

1 September 1921

THE READER, I am sure, will appreciate my sharing with him the following (from a) pathetic and beautiful letter from Mr Andrews:

'I know that your burning of foreign cloth is with the idea of helping the poor, but I feel that there you have gone wrong. ...'

... If the emphasis were on all foreign things, it would be racial, parochial and wicked. The emphasis is on all foreign *cloth*. The restriction makes all the difference in the world. I do not want to shut out English lever watches or the beautiful Japanese lacquer work. ...

... Destruction is the quickest method of stimulating production. By one supreme effort and swift destruction, India has to be awakened from her torpor and enforced idleness. ...

Young India; CWMG *Vol. 21, pp. 41–4; E*

The Loin-Cloth

Madura
22 September 1921

... LET THERE be no prudery about dress. India has never insisted on full covering of the body for the males as a test of culture.

I give the advice under a full sense of my responsibility. In order therefore to set the example I propose to discard at least up to the 31st October my topi and vest and to content myself with only a loin-cloth and a *chaddar* whenever found necessary for the protection of the body. I adopt the change because I have always hesitated to advise anything I may not myself be prepared to follow, also because I am anxious by leading the way to make it easy for those who cannot afford to change on discarding their foreign garments. I consider the renunciation to be also necessary for me as a sign of mourning and a bare head and a bare body is such a sign in my part of the country. That we are in mourning is more and more being borne home to me as the end of the year is approaching and we are still without swaraj. ...

CWMG, *Vol. 21, pp. 180–1; E*

13 October 1921

To A people famishing and idle, the only acceptable form in which God can dare appear is work and promise of food as wages. ...

Young India, 13 October 1921; CWMG *Vol. 21, p. 289*

Passions

1 November 1921

... I CAN control my passions no doubt, but I have not yet become completely free from them. I can control the palate, but the tongue has not yet ceased relishing good food. ...

Letter to Mathuradas Trikumji, Bapuni Prasadi, *pp. 38–9;*
CWMG *Vol. 21, p. 376; G*

A Deep Stain

Bombay
18 November 1921

... LITTLE DID I know that at the very time that the Prince was passing through the decorated route and the pile of foreign cloth was burning, in another part of the city ... a swelling mob[97] was molesting peaceful passengers in the tram-cars and holding up the tram traffic, that it was forcibly depriving those that were wearing foreign caps of their head-dresses and pelting inoffensive Europeans. As the day went up, the fury of the mob now intoxicated with its initial success rose also. They burnt tram-cars and a motor, smashed liquor shops and burnt two.

I heard of the outbreak at about 1 o'clock. I motored with some friends to the area of disturbance and heard the most painful and the most humiliating story of molestation of Parsi sisters. Some few were assaulted, and even had theirs saris torn from them. No one from among a crowd of over fifteen hundred who had surrounded my car denied the charge as a Parsi with hot rage and quivering lips was with the greatest deliberation relating the story. An elderly Parsi gentleman said, 'Please save us from this mob rule.' This news of the rough handling of Parsi sisters pierced me like a dart. I felt that my sisters or daughters had been hurt by a violent mob! Yes, some

Parsis had joined the welcome. They had a right to hold their own view free of molestation. There can be no coercion in swaraj. The Moplah fanatic who forcibly converts a Hindu believes that he is acquiring religious merit. A non-cooperator or his associate who uses coercion has no apology whatsoever for his criminality.

As I reached the Two Tanks I found a liquor shop smashed, two policemen badly wounded and lying unconscious on cots without anybody caring for them. I alighted. Immediately the crowd surrounded me and yelled *Mahatma Gandhi ki jai*. That sound usually grates on my ears, but it has grated never so much as it did yesterday when the crowd unmindful of the two sick brethren choked me with the shout at the top of their voices. I rebuked them and they were silent. Water was brought for the two wounded men. I requested two of my companions and some from the crowd to take the dying policemen to the hospital. I proceeded then to the scene a little further up where I saw a fire rising. They were two tram-cars which were burnt by the crowd. On returning I witnessed a burning motor car. I appealed to the crowd to disperse, told them that they had damaged the cause of the Khilafat, the Punjab, and swaraj. I returned sick at heart and in a chastened mood. ...

Young India, *24-11-1921;* CWMG *Vol. 21, pp. 462–3; E*

... THE MUSSULMANS have to my knowledge played the leading part during the two days of carnage.

I must refuse to eat or drink anything but water till the Hindus and Mussulmans of Bombay have made peace with the Parsis, the Christians, and the Jews, and till the non-cooperators have made peace with the cooperators.

RP, *p. 357*

The People Of Madras

MY TOUR of Madras was something of a disappointment. ... I think there are two reasons for this. In the first place, so deep has been the influence of the English language on the region that a person in Madras who knows English cares very little for Tamil. The Bengalis too love English, but that has not made them give up Bengali ...

The other important reason for my disappointment is that, their genuine regard for dharma notwithstanding, people in Madras have allowed blind religious orthodoxy to take such complete possession of them that mere outward forms of religion remain and the inner spirit has vanished ... no other region makes such abundant use of sacred ash, sandalwood paste and vermillion powder.

CWMG *Vol. 21, pp. 232–3; G*

'Well Done, Harilal'

11 December 1921

WELL DONE[98], God bless you. Ramdas, Devadas, and others will follow you.

CWMG *Vol. 21, p. 567; E*

Chauri Chaura

19 February 1922

[The non-cooperation movement of 1921 was electrifying the country when at Chauri Chaura in the Gorakhpur district of U.P. a group of peasants attacked a police station and setting fire to it, killed 23 policemen. Gandhi called off the movement.]

I ASSURE you that if the thing had not been suspended, we would have been leading not a non-violence struggle, but essentially a violent struggle. It is undoubtedly true that non-violence is spreading like the scent of the otto of roses throughout the length and breadth of the land, but the foetid smell of violence is still powerful, and it would be unwise to ignore or underrate it. The cause will prosper by this retreat.

Letter to Jawaharlal Nehru; A Bunch of Old Letters, *Asia, 1958, p. 24; E*

A Warning

... ATONEMENT SHOULD not be advertised. But I have publicized mine, and there is a reason. My fast is atonement for me but, for the people of Chauri Chaura, it is a punishment ...

This time I have been content with a fast of five days. If, however, the people refuse to take the warning, five days may become fifteen and fifteen become fifty and I may even lose my life. ...

Navajivan *19-2-1922;* CWMG *Vol. 22, pp. 425–6; G*

Shaking The Manes[99]

How can there be any compromise whilst the British Lion continues to shake his gory claws in our faces? Lord Birkenhead[100] reminds us that Britain has lost none of her hard fibre. Mr Montagu[101] tells us in the plainest language that the British are the most determined nation in the world, who will brook no interference with their purpose. Let me quote the exact words telegraphed by Reuter:

If the existence of our Empire were challenged, the discharge of responsibilities of the British Government to India prevented and demands were made in the very mistaken belief that we contemplated retreat from India—then India would not challenge with success the most determined people in the world, who would once again answer the challenge with all the vigour and determination at its command.

... India cannot and will not answer this insolence with insolence, but if she remains true to her pledge, her prayer to God to be delivered from such a scourge will certainly not go in vain. No empire intoxicated with the red wine of power and plunder of weaker races has yet lived long in this world, and this 'British Empire', which is based upon organized exploitation of the physically weaker races of the earth and upon a continuous exhibition of brute force, cannot live if there is a just God ruling the universe.... It is high time that the British people were made to realize that the fight that was commenced in 1920 is a fight to the finish, whether it lasts one month or one year or many months or many years and whether the representatives of Britain re-enact all the indescribable orgies of the Mutiny days with redoubled force or whether they do not. ...

Young India, 23-2-1922; CWMG *Vol. 22, pp. 457–8; E*

To Devadas

Sunday, 5 March 1922

Chiranjivi Devadas,

... I AM an *anekantavadi*[102]. I can see many sides of a question. ...

Blessings from
Bapu
CWMG *Vol. 23, pp. 18–19; G*

To Manilal

Sabarmati Jail
17 March 1922

... I CANNOT imagine a thing as ugly as the intercourse of man and woman ...

Having said all this, I regard you as quite free [to act as you please]. I have written this merely as a friend. I have not given any command as a father. 'Be you good', this is my only injunction. However, do what you wish, not what I wish. If you simply cannot do without marrying, do think of marriage by all means.

Please write to me in detail what your innermost thoughts are.

Blessings from
Bapu
CWMG *Vol. 23, pp. 101–2; G*

The Great Trial

18 March 1922

[*On 11th March 1922, Gandhi and Banker, printer and publisher of* Young India *were produced before Mr Brown, Assistant Magistrate, the Court being held in the Divisional Commissioner's Office at Shahibag, Ahmedabad. The prosecution was conducted by Rao Bahadur Girdharilal, Public Prosecutor.*

The Superintendent of Police, Ahmedabad, first witness, placed before the Magistrate, the Bombay Government's authority to lodge a complaint for four articles published in Young India *dated 15 June 1921 entitled 'Disaffection a Virtue', dated 29 September, 'Tampering* with Loyalty', *dated 15 December*, 'The Puzzle and its Solution', *and dated 23 February 1922*, 'Shaking the Manes'.]

... I WISH to endorse all the blame that the learned Advocate-General[103] has thrown on my shoulders in connection with the Bombay, the Madras, and the Chauri Chaura occurrences. Thinking over these deeply and sleeping over them night after night, it is impossible to dissociate myself from the diabolical crimes of Chauri Chaura or the mad outrages in Bombay and Madras. He is quite right when he says that, as a man of responsibility, a man having received a fair share of education, having had a fair share of experience of this world, I should have known the consequences of every one of my acts. I knew that I was playing with fire ...

... I want to avoid violence. Non-violence is the first article of my faith. It is also the last article of my creed. But I had to make my choice. I had either to submit to a system which I considered had done an irreparable harm to my country, or incur the risk of the mad fury of my people bursting forth when they understood the truth from my lips. I know that my people have sometimes gone mad; I am deeply sorry for it. I am, therefore, here to submit not to a light penalty but to the highest penalty. I do not ask for mercy. I do not ask for any extenuating act of clemency. I am here to invite and cheerfully submit to the highest penalty that can be inflicted upon me for what in law is a deliberate crime and what appears to me to be the highest duty of a citizen. The only course open to you, the Judge, is as I am just going to say in my statement, either to resign your post, or inflict on me the severest penalty, if you believe that the system and the law you are assisting to administer are good for the people of this country and that my activity is therefore injurious to the public weal. I do not expect that kind of conversion, but by the time I have finished with my statement, you will perhaps have a glimpse of what is raging within my breast, to run this maddest risk that a sane man can run.

Young India, 23-3-1922; CWMG Vol. 23, p. 85 and pp. 114–15; E

Jail Diary, 1922—Excerpts

17 May, Wednesday

FINISHED READING *Tom Brown's Schooldays*. Some portions of it are beautiful.

The Holy Supper is kept indeed
In whatso we share with another's need—
Not that which we give, but what we share,
For the gift without the giver is bare;
Who bestows himself with his alms feeds three,
Himself, his hungering neighbour, and Me.

—Lowell

—from the same book as above.

20 MAY, SATURDAY

Finished reading Bacon's *The Wisdom of the Ancients*. Have given up chapatis since Wednesday. I am living, as an experiment, on four seers of milk, two ounces of raisins, four oranges, and two lemons. Haji was taken to a dark cell yesterday.

28 MAY, SUNDAY

Read the history of India up to the Moghul dynasty. Went through Morris's grammar.

17 JUNE, SATURDAY

Finished reading Kipling's *Second Jungle Book*.

21 JUNE, WEDNESDAY

Finished reading *Faust*.

7 AUGUST, MONDAY

Finished reading Gibbon, Vol. I. Started reading Vol. II.

28 AUGUST, MONDAY

Finished reading *Manusmriti*. Started reading *Ishopanishad*.

30 AUGUST, WEDNESDAY

Finished reding *Sabhaparva*. Started reading *Vanaparva*.

1 September, Friday

Finished reading Gibbon, Vol. II. Finished reading *Ishopanishad.*

2 September, Saturday

Started reading Gibbon, Vol. III

13 September, Wednesday

I have decided to observe silence from 3 p.m. today up to 3 p.m. on Tuesday, with Major Jones's[104] consent. The following exceptions will be made:
1. When others or I suffer.
2. When friends from outside come to see me.
3. If, in the meanwhile, I am removed to the ward of my Dharwar friends.
4. If an official like Mr Hayward[105] happens to visit us.
5. If Major Jones wishes to have a talk with me.

CWMG Vol. 23, pp. 146–50; G

Jail Diary, 1923—Excerpts

3 January, Wednesday

Finished reading *Steps to Christianity* yesterday. Started reading Trine's *My Philosophy and Religion.* Today the Major[106] gave me a copy of the notification that the Inner Temple had removed my name from its Roll.

4 February, Sunday

Finished reading Rajchandra's writings and *Ishopanishad* with a commentary. Reading *Kena.* Completed the second reading of Urdu Book III. Finished reading *Auto-suggestion.* Ba came and saw me on 27 January. Released Shankerlal from his vow on the 28th.

5 February, Monday

Finished reading *Helps to Bible Study*. Started reading Max Muller's translation of the Upanishads as also Wells' History.

2 March, Friday

Finished reading Wells' History, Part II, on 28 February. Started reading the Bible yesterday. Finished reading the leaflet on the worship of Vishnu. Started reading Wells's History, Part I.

11 March, Sunday

Applied, on Wednesday, caustic soda to the eye for conjunctivitis.

17 April, Tuesday

Finished reading James's *Our Hellenic Heritage*. Devadas came and saw me yesterday. Shankerlal was released today.

19 April, Thursday

Sufishah Mullah Shah, when he was advised to flee from the wrath of Shah Jehan, is reported to have said:

I am not an impostor that I should seek safety in flight. I am an utterer of truth. Death and life are to me alike. Let my blood in another life also redden the impaling stake. I am living and eternal; death recoils from me, for my knowledge has vanquished death. The sphere where all colours are effaced has become my abode.

Mansuri Hallaj said:

To cut off the hands of a fettered man is easy, but to sever the links that bind me to the Divinity would be a task indeed.

—*Claude Field in* Mystics and Saints of Islam

Received today five seers of raisins.

CWMG *Vol. 23, pp. 178–80; G*

Unnatural Crimes At Yeravda

...I WILL not shock the reader with any details. In spite of my many jail experiences, I did not think that such crimes were possible in jails. But the Yeravda experience gave me more than one painful shock. The discovery of the existence of unnatural crimes produced one of the greatest of shocks. All the officials who spoke to me about them said that, under the existing system, it was impossible to prevent them. Let the reader understand that, in a majority of cases, the consent of the victim is lacking....

Young India *1-5-1924;* CWMG *Vol. 23, pp. 508–9; E*

Adan, The Somali

ADAN WAS a young Somali soldier who was sentenced to ten years' hard labour for desertion from the British Army, which he had joined during the War. He was transferred by the Aden Jail authorities. Adan had served four years when we were admitted. He was practically illiterate. He could read the Koran with difficulty, but could not copy it correctly, if at all. He was able to speak Urdu fairly fluently and was anxious to learn Urdu. With the permission of the Superintendent, I tried to teach him, but the learning of the alphabet proved too great a strain upon him and he left it. With all that he was quick-witted and sharp as a needle. He took the greatest interest in religious matters. He was a devout Mussalman, offered his prayers regularly including the midnight one, and never missed the *Ramzan* fast. The rosary was his constant companion. When he was free, he used to recite selections from the Koran. He would often engage me in a discussion on complete fasts according to the Hindu custom as also on ahimsa. He was a brave man. He was very courteous, but never cringing. He was of an excitable nature and, therefore, often quarreled with the *bardasi* or his fellow warder. We had, therefore, sometimes to arbitrate between them. Being a soldier and amenable to reason, he would accept the award, but he would put his case boldly and cogently. Adan was the longest with us. I treasure Adan's affection. He was most attentive to me. He would see to it that I got my food at the appointed time. He was sad if I ever became ill and anticipated all my wants. He would not let me exert myself for anything. He was anxious to be discharged or at least to be transferred to Aden. I tried hard. I drew up petitions for him. The Superintendent too, tried his best. But the decision rested with the Aden authorities. Hope was held out to him that he would be discharged before the end of last year. I do hope he is already discharged. The little service I rendered gave rise to deep personal attachment. It was a sad parting when Adan was transferred to another part of the prison. I must not omit to mention that, when I was organizing spinning and carding in the jail, Adan, though one of his hands was disabled, helped most industriously at making slivers. He became very proficient in the art which he had come to like. ...

Young India 10-7-1924; CWMG *Vol. 24, pp. 366–7; E*

Interview With Sir V.S. Srinivasa Sastri

Sassoon Hospital
Poona
12 January 1924

SASTRI RECORDS: ... the Yeravda authorities had removed Mr Gandhi to the Sassoon Hospital, ... He was about to be operated for appendicitis[107].

... As the operation room was being got ready, the doctors went out and I found myself nearly alone with the Mahatma. After a remark or two of a purely personal nature, I asked him whether he had anything particular to say ...

... I then pressed him again for a message to his people, his followers or the country. He was surprisingly firm on this subject. He said he was a prisoner of Government and he must observe the prisoner's code of honour scrupulously. He was supposed to be civilly dead. He had not knowledge of outside events and he could not have anything to do with the public. He had no message.[108] ...

The Hindu 14-1-1924; CWMG *Vol. 23, pp. 189–90; E*

7 February 1924[109]

My dear friend and brother,

I send you as President of the Congress a few words which I know our countrymen expect from me on my sudden release. I am sorry that the Government have prematurely released me on account of my illness. Such a release can bring me no joy for I hold that the illness of a prisoner affords no ground for his release. ...

I am,
Your sincere friend and brother
M.K. Gandhi
The Diary of Mahadev Desai *Vol. 4, pp. 51–2*

To Jawaharlal Nehru

Delhi
15 September 1924[110]

My dear Jawaharlal,

... Shall I try to arrange for some money for you? Why may you not take up remunerative work? After all you must live by the sweat of your brow even though you may be under Father's roof. Will you be correspondent to some newspapers? Or will you take up a professorship?

Yours sincerely,
M.K. Gandhi
A Bunch of Old Letters, CWMG *Vol. 25, pp. 148–9; E*

Englishmen

I CANNOT and will not hate Englishmen; nor will I bear their yoke[111].
Nanda, Gandhi, *p. 408*

Discussions At Vykom

10 March 1925

MKG: There is nothing in the scriptures to prohibit anyone, because of his birth, from the use of public roads or public places or even of semi-public roads. A robber or dissolute character may not be prohibited.

Nambudiri: They are worse than these because of actions of their past birth.

MKG: Who is to punish them? God or Men?

Nambudiri: Their birth is the punishment of God. We are only instruments for their punishment in the hands of God.

MKG: Let us invert the process. If they say we are instrument to punish you, will you allow that?

Mahadev Desai's Diary

Capital And Labour

8 August 1925

... I HAVE had much to do with the capitalists and workmen, and I have always said that my ideal is that capital and labour should supplement and help each other. They should be a great family living in unity and harmony, capital not only looking to the material welfare of the labourers but their moral welfare also—capitalists being trustees for the welfare of the labouring classes under them.

Speech at Indian Association, Jamshedpur; Young India
20 August 1925; CWMG *Vol. 28, p. 47*

Mira

7 November 1925

YOU SHALL be my daughter[112].

Madeleine Slade's autobiography, The Spirit's Pilgrimage
(New York, 1960) p. 66

Part Eleven

1926-32

Mahatma Gandhi with C.F. Andrews and
Devadas Gandhi in London, 1931

CIVIL DISOBEDIENCE

I must admit that wherever I go I am sought out by fools,
cranks, and faddists.

The first decade spent by Gandhi in India saw him become its undisputed leader, with the Non-cooperation and Khilafat movements bringing him to the heart of India's political and social tensions. He was, as in South Africa, addressing the State as well as society—the latter, in fact, even more stridently on its 'wrongs'. In 1924, for the first and last time in his life, he served as President of the Indian National Congress.

Part Eleven of the compilation contains writings essential to Gandhi's consolidation of his political and social aims, the two sometimes criss-crossing his work and sometimes running on parallel tracks. It also includes footprints of his visit to Ceylon where his mission was self-proclaimedly non-political—it had to do with raising funds for his khadi programme in India but, unsurprisingly, went on to include some bitter prescriptions for all the communities in that island—Sinhala Buddhists, Tamil Christians, Tamil Hindus, Parsis, plantation workers, aristocratic socialites. Presciently, he reminded the Buddhists not to forget that Gautama was born into the Hindu fold and he told Hindus in Jaffna about their 'duty towards the predominant population in this island'.

In the midst of his incessant travelling and campaigns, he did not omit to check with colleagues 'back home' about their health and welfare, e.g., with Rajagopalachari about his daughter Lakshmi's health, with Jawaharlal about Kamala Nehru's recuperation, with Jayaprakash Narayan's wife Prabhavati about her attacks of depression and about JP's health, and with Padmaja Naidu about her illness.

And his inquisitive mind ticked away, as always, in myriad directions. Writing to the agricultural expert Sam Higginbottom he asked questions about 'a contrivance whereby you heated your water by the sun heat' and seemed to anticipate photo-voltaic technology by enquiring if Higginbottom 'concentrated by some mechanical contrivance the rays of the sun on to the tank'.

Gandhi was being sought by people other than politicians no less than those in the thick of politics. Sarvepalli Radhakrishnan wrote from Calcutta where he was Professor of Philosophy, asking for an article. Gandhi declined ('I am so thoroughly washed out'). Bidhan Chandra Roy wrote from Calcutta asking him to deliver the prestigious Kamala Lecture instituted by Sir Asutosh Mookerjee in memory of his daughter. Gandhi declined again ('I do not possess the literary attainment ... You are asking me to shoulder a responsibility which my shoulders cannot bear. I am biding my time and you will find me leading the country in the field of politics when the country is ready. I have no false modesty about me. I am undoubtedly a politician in my own way, and I have a scheme for the country's freedom. But my time is not yet.').

In between his national preoccupations, occurred incidents of seemingly local value but which swelled into an all-India discourse. Gandhi's decision to put an ailing heifer out of its agony at Sabarmati became an opportunity for deep cogitation within him, inside the Ashram, and beyond. It gave Gandhi cause to remind his friend Polak in South Africa about his having had a maggot-infested cat put down by drowning. Even more significantly, it elicited from him a clear statement in favour of euthanasia for humans (though he does not use the phrase).

And there were deaths—political as in the case of Swami Shraddhananda at the hands of an assassin and of Lala Lajpat Rai, from injuries received at the hands of an officer of the State, as well as within the family. Maganlal Gandhi, his nephew and invaluable colleague, died suddenly in April 1928. 'But for a living faith in God I should become a raving maniac for the loss of one who was dearer to me than my own sons ...' he wrote in *Young India*.

And then his grandson, Rasik, Harilal's promising son died of typhoid at the age of seventeen. 'I still have enough attachment to know from you,' he wrote to his son Devadas under whose care Rasik had been, 'about the last days of Rasik's life. Do not disappoint me in that.'

The 'essentiality' of Gandhi's writings emerges imperceptibly but unmistakably in all these. One generally stumbles upon that essentiality, as in a sentence from his letter to Devadas on Rasik's death: 'Dharma lies in doing one's duty, not in making no mistake at all.' And it comes in the context of both his personal and the public aspects.

The decade between 1925 and 1935 was marked by great interventions by him in politics and, equally great retreats.

Martin Green writes in *Gandhi* (1993): 'On 3 January 1926, Gandhi announced that he was retiring from public life for a year, to concentrate upon the ashram. He suffered a breakdown from strain that March, and in the second half of the year wrote: "I still have enough strength to be left alone to think and do my work, but the ability to talk to a group, to guide and to explain things to a succession of people coming to me, to humour them, to get angry and get work out of them, has all but left me".'

Lord Irwin took over as Viceroy in 1927 from Lord Reading. Gandhi had set a deadline for Swaraj—1928—but it was crossed. Rajmohan Gandhi's *Mohandas* says: 'The chance for a battle came in 1928, when land revenue in Bardoli taluka was enhanced by 22 per cent. Simultaneously, twenty-three Bardoli villages were placed in a higher tax category. The peasants wanted to defy what for many was a double blow and approached the ashramites, who in turn approached Gandhi and Patel. Gandhi gave the green light; and Patel agreed to lead the fight ... The battle was won because of Vallabhbhai's leadership, which was confident, earthy, blunt, and forceful, the solidarity of the peasants, and the work over the years of the taluka's ashrams.'

During the four summer months of 1928, the peasants showed exceptional steadfastness, refusing to pay the enhanced tax. Their properties were confiscated but the struggle held out. Finally, the increase had to be cancelled and in many cases, the seized properties were returned. The victory of the movement in Bardoli lay, of course, in the fact that they had 'won' the struggle against tax-enhancement. But, more significantly in that 'they had not hit back nor taken a single life'.

A victory for non-violent non-cooperation. Supported as it was by Abbas Tyabji, and Imam Bawazir from Sabarmati, Bardoli also consolidated Hindu–Muslim unity.

'Why not Bardolize the rest of the movement in India?' was a question on many minds, with Motilal Nehru suggesting to Gandhi that Patel be made the next Congress President, with Jawahar as the next best choice. Gandhi's response was, as usual, unpredictable. He asked Motilal to chair the session himself, as Motilal's committee had painstakingly produced the 'Nehru Report' as it came to be called, recommending Dominion Status.

When Motilal Nehru arrived in Calcutta, his chariot was pulled by horses to the venue of the Calcutta Congress. Jawaharlal was there as a future leader. But so was Subhas Bose, six years younger than Jawaharlal. Both had by then become not just popular but charismatic figures.

If Jawaharlal wore a dhoti-kurta for the Session, Bose appeared in a military officer's uniform, and was designated its 'Commander'. Motilal Nehru's Dominion Status concept was turned down by Jawaharlal and Subhas who demanded Complete Independence. Gandhi, characteristically, suggested a *via media* to give the British two years to concede Dominion Status and the rest of the Nehru Report's recommendations. If it failed to do so, Gandhi said, let the Congress recommence its struggle and ask for Complete Independence.

Bose had many supporters at the Calcutta session that year but his amendment was lost, securing 973 votes, compared with 1350 that were with Gandhi.

For Jawaharlal a two years wait was intolerable. Gandhi then said the waiting period could be reduced to one year. Jawaharlal and Bose accepted the modified compromise. Moving a resolution at the open session, Gandhi mentioned a deadline of 31 December 1929 for Dominion Status. But, contrary to the earlier agreement, Bose returned to his earlier position and moved an amendment asking for a complete break with the British. Jawaharlal backed Bose. Gandhi berated the young leaders: '*You may take the name of independence on your lips but all your muttering will be an empty formula if there is no honour behind it. If you are not prepared to stand by your words, where will independence be?*'

But, in a way that was uniquely his, he said at that meeting '... my brain is muddled.'

When in 1929 Irwin announced that a Round Table Conference would take place in London to discuss India's future, Gandhi's response was guarded.

Green writes: 'Gandhi ... (to Nehru's displeasure) ... saw Irwin on 23 December to ask for some guarantees that such a conference would accept as a starting point the idea of Dominion Status. The viceroy could give no such assurance, and so, at the Congress meeting soon after, total independence was made India's goal, and the Round Table was boycotted ... Gandhi, moreover, was charged with devising some form of civil disobedience.'

This 'form' turned out to be extraordinary—it had to with something no one had dreamed of: salt. Because of the tax imposed on it by the government, Gandhi said he would march to the seacoast, where salt would be illegally lifted. The great Salt March awoke India. Gandhi was imprisoned. In a letter to Irwin dated 2 March 1930 he asked rhetorically: 'And why do I regard the British rule as a curse? It has impoverished the dumb millions by a system of progressive exploitation and by a ruinously expensive military and civil administration which the country can never afford ...' Departing from his tenets of personal courtesy, he then made a personal statement to Irwin: 'Take your own salary. It is over Rs 21,000 per month, besides many other indirect additions. The British Prime Minister gets £5000 per year, i.e., over Rs 5400 per month at the present rate of exchange. You are getting over Rs 700 per day against India's average income of less than annas 2 per day. The Prime Minister gets Rs 180 per day against Great Britain's average income of nearly Rs 2 per day. Thus you are getting much over five thousand times India's average income. The British Prime Minister is getting only ninety times Britain's average income. On bended knees I ask you to ponder over this phenomenon.'

Gandhi described Irwin's reply as stony. 'On bended knees I asked for bread and I have received stone instead.'

The Mahatma's instructions to the organizers of the march contained an injunction to obtain village-level data *en route*.

Gandhi wrote on 9 March 1930 (*CWMG* Vol. 43, pp. 33–5):

'The march will begin at 6.30 on the 12th morning ... It is

desirable that information under the following heads should be kept ready for each village: (1) Population: Number of women, men, Hindus, Muslims, Christians, Parsis, etc., (2) Number of untouchables, (3) If there is a school in the village, the number of boys and girls attending it, (4) Number of spinning-wheels, (5) The monthly sale of khadi, (6) Number of people wearing khadi exclusively, (7) Salt consumed per head; salt used for cattle, etc., (8) Number of cows and buffaloes in the village, (9) The amount of land revenue paid; at what rate per acre, (10) The area of the common grazing-ground, if any, (11) Do the people drink? How far is the liquor shop from the village?, and (12) Educational and other special facilities, if any, for the untouchables.

It will be good if this information is written out on a sheet of paper neatly and handed to me immediately on our arrival.'

Watching him raise that fistful of salt, the world did not know that a statistical survey had preceded that climacteric and had, in fact, prepared the ground for it.

'I want world sympathy in this battle of Right against Might', he said on 5 April 1930 in Dandi. The statement is justly regarded as a great clarion call. But there again, the 'essentiality' of Gandhi lay in the small print no less than in the great epigrams. Telling his co-marchers that they must keep an account of their expenses, he said: 'I have no right to criticize the Viceregal salary if we are costing the country, say, fifty times seven pice, the average daily income of our people. I have asked the workers to furnish me with an account of the expenses. And the way things are going, I should not be surprised if each of us is costing something near fifty times seven pice. What else can be the result if they will fetch for me from whatever source possible, the choicest oranges and grapes, if they will bring 120 when I should want 12 oranges, if when I need one pound of milk, they will produce three?'

Seventy-nine satyagrahis, including one Christian and two Muslims went with sixty-one-year-old Gandhi on the salt march. Sixty thousand people followed Gandhi into jails all over India as life in several Indian cities came to a standstill.

Gandhi's second spell at Yeravda jail, Poona from 5 May 1930 to 26 January 1931, following his midnight arrest after the salt march was again used by him to read, reflect, and—to the extent the prison rules on correspondence permitted it—to write to people 'big' and 'small' on things ranging from the personal to the public. To Narandas Gandhi, he wrote on the uses and limitations of the *pranayama*, to Mira Behn to 'take care not to burn yourself with the primus', to Ghanshyamdas Birla on Jayaprakash Narayan's need for a regular income through 'absorption' in some suitable position with the rider 'but I do not wish that a post be created where none exists today.'

Are these 'essential writings' a reader may well ask? To Gandhi's way of thinking, if these were not essential, nothing else could be.

Giving Vanamala Parikh a lesson in arithmetic ('If a girl spins 252 rounds in an hour, how many would she spin in twenty minutes') was as important for the 'spinner of India's destiny' (Sarojini Naidu's phrase) as was preparing for talks with Lord Irwin and the possibility of joining the Round Table Conference's second session in London.

Within a month of his release, Gandhi's parleys with Irwin began. They were as candid as they were cordial and the prospect of Gandhi joining the London discussions was central to the talks. The Viceroy asked, tantalizingly: 'If you attend the Round Table Conference and the results are not to your satisfaction, must you resume civil disobedience?' Gandhi replied: 'I will have to unless we feel that we shall get something from the changes proposed. Otherwise I shall have no choice but to resume the movement.'

Looming over the discussion with Irwin was the issue of the impending execution of Bhagat Singh[1]. Gandhi asked the Viceroy to 'suspend' it. Irwin said the suggestion was 'worth considering'.

Gandhi was asked in March 1931 by the Press:

Q. Do you expect to hold the National Congress to the terms of the truce with Lord Irwin?

A. Yes, but if Bhagat Singh is hanged, as it now seems almost certain, it may have highly unfavourable repercussions upon the younger element in the Congress who may attempt to split the Congress.

Q. Do you entertain any hope that Bhagat Singh may be saved at the last minute?

A. Yes, but it is a very distant hope.

He made to Irwin on 23 March 1931, a 'last-ditch appeal':

Political murders have been condoned before now. It is worth while saving these lives, if thereby many other innocent lives are likely to be saved and may be even revolutionary crime almost stamped out ... Execution is an irretrievable act. If you think there is the slightest chance of error of judgment, I would urge you to suspend for further review an act that is beyond recall.

Irwin did not agree. Gandhi was criticized for not doing enough.

Gandhi's response to Bhagat Singh's ideals and practice of patriotism will never be free of controversy. That he admired the young patriot's revolutionary courage was beyond doubt. But the use of violence was totally outside Gandhi's scheme and he used the phrases 'Bhagat Singh worship' and 'Bhagat Singh cult' which no one with admiration for that martyr can quite stomach. But then Gandhi's truth, like his diet, was more often than not, alien to normal stomachs.

'There are two men,' he wrote to Rajagopalachari before leaving for the Second Round Table Conference in London, 'I would like by my side in London, you and Jawaharlal'. But he went, consistently with Congress' decision as its sole representative, aided by his two secretaries, Mahadev Desai and Pyarelal and his son Devadas as well as Mira Behn.

Gandhi's visit to London in 1931, his last one to the city he greatly admired and felt at home in, was a political failure but a personal success.

Midway during the Conference, a question put to him in Oxford elicited an 'essential' nugget from Gandhi.

Q. How far would you cut India off from the Empire?
A. From the Empire entirely: from the British nation not at all.

But the Mahatma's contribution at the RTC itself will be best remembered for his speech at the Plenary on 1 December 1931. A masterpiece of political exposition, it belongs to that order of redemptive messages only visionaries are capable of (*CWMG* Vol. 48):

I live under no illusion. I do not think that anything that I can say this evening can possibly influence the decision of the Cabinet ... All the other parties at this meeting represent sectional interests. Congress alone claims to represent the whole of India, all interests ... It may not always have lived up to the creed. I do not know a single human organization that lives up to its creed ... But the worst critic will have to recognize ... that ... its message penetrates the remotest village of India ...

Congress ... has been accused of running or desiring to run a parallel Government and in a way I have endorsed the charge ... [You should] welcome an organization which could run a parallel Government and show that it is possible for an organization, voluntarily, without any force at its command, to run the machinery of Government even under adverse circumstances. ...

I heard several speakers ... saying what a dire calamity it would be if India was fired with the spirit of lawlessness, rebellion, terrorism, and so on ... As a schoolboy I had to pass a paper in history also, and I read that the page of history is soiled red with the blood of those who have fought for freedom ...

The dagger of the assassin, the poison bowl, the bullet of the rifleman, the spear, and all these weapons and methods of destruction have been up to now used by what I consider blind lovers of liberty and freedom, and the historian has not condemned [them].

The Congress then comes upon the scene and devises a new method not known to history, namely, that of civil disobedience ...

A nation of 350 million people does not need the dagger of the assassin, it does not need the poison bowl, it does not need the sword, the spear or the bullet. It needs simply a will of its own, an ability to say 'No', and that nation is today learning to say 'No' ...

He ended by expressing thanks:

My thanks to all—from Their Majesties down to the poorest men in the East End, where I have taken up my habitation ... They have accepted me ...

Although ... the Lancashire people had perhaps some reason for becoming irritated against me, I found no irritation, no resentment even in the operatives. The operatives, men and women, hugged me ... I shall never forget that.

I am carrying with me thousands upon thousands of English friendships. I do not know them, but I read that affection in their eyes as early in the morning I walk through your streets. All this hospitality, all this kindness will never be effaced from my memory no matter what befalls my unhappy land. I thank you for your forbearance.

Sir Samuel Hoare, the Secretary of State for India was to say, 'With an eye and mind as pointed as a needle, he penetrated in a moment any sham.' It was clear that arrest awaited Gandhi's return to India.

The party stopped at Villeneuve in Switzerland to meet the savant Romain Rolland who at that point was tilting towards Marx. 'I follow the Russian experiment with a fundamental distrust', Gandhi said to Rolland (*CWMG*, Vol. 48). In Rome, acting contrary to Rolland's advice Gandhi met Mussolini whose eyes he found 'cat-like' but tarried at the Sistine Chapel, particularly beside a crucifix on the altar. He wrote in *Young India* on 31 December 1931, 'It was not without a wrench that I could tear myself away ... I saw there at once that nations like individuals could only be made through the agony of the Cross and in no other way.'

By the time the *Pilsna* brought Gandhi back to Bombay, Jawaharlal and the Khan brothers had already been arrested. Kasturba was at the pier to receive him, as were Patel and Rajagopalachari. Addressing a mammoth crowd at Azad Maidan the same evening, he said Congress condemned 'assassination' and 'methods of terrorism' but that it would also resist 'Government terrorism'. On 4 January 1932 the police came for him at Mani Bhavan, Bombay. Gandhi and Patel were taken to Yeravda jail, Kasturba and Devadas also being arrested and taken to Sabarmati and Gorakhpur jails respectively.

His life in jail followed a well-beaten path. Letters to and from Kasturba were not always delivered but a letter from Harilal, now a prisoner of alcohol and brothels, was given to Gandhi. Gandhi replied to Harilal (*CWMG* Vol. 49):

... 27 April 1932. Contrary to my usual practice, I am preserving your letter so that, when you have awakened, you may see the insolence of your letter and weep over it and laugh at your folly ... not to throw it in your face then, but only that I may laugh at it ...

To Devadas, he wrote on 23 June 1932:

Harilal's glass is always red. When he was conceived, I lived in ignorance. The years when he grew up were a time of self-indulgence. I certainly did not drink, but Harilal has made up for that. I sought my pleasure only with one woman. Harilal seeks his with many. It is only a difference of degree, not of kind.

Kasturba was very much on his mind and in a letter to Ramdas, he wrote (*CWMG*, Vol. 50):

I would not like any of you to behave towards his wife as I did towards Ba. ... She could not be angry with me, whereas I could with her. I did not give her the same freedom of action which I enjoyed. ...

A communication from Gorakhpur informed him that Devadas was down with typhoid. Memories of Rasik's death by typhoid stirred in the father who asked for Devadas to be shifted to another jail.

Gandhi practised his Urdu and through a telescope loaned by Premlila Thackersey[2] in whose Poona house, some months later, the long-postponed Devadas–Lakshmi wedding was to take place, he studied the stars.

If he made the acquaintance of stars in Yeravda he also made friends with a cat and its litter. He was also to experience a snake crawl over him. Gandhi received in jail letters from people on matters unpolitical and even other-worldly. In replying to one he gave his opinion on astrology—not dismissing its basis but questioning its impact. In reply to another, he gave an insight into God in the context of human suffering. It was simple: '... if we knew all the laws of God we should be able to account for the unaccountable.' Gandhi's friend and associate of nearly four decades, Dr Pranjivan Mehta, died in Rangoon during this period of incarceration, eliciting a pained but philosophic reflection.

Patel's presence in the prison was a source of laughter to Gandhi. If humour is one of the essences of life, Mahadev Desai's diary entry of 24 November 1932 gives us an example of it:

Today there was an open letter (to Gandhi) from a correspondent who signed himself as 'one who had the misfortune of living in your age'.
Bapu: Tell me, what sort of reply should I send him?
Patel: Tell him to poison himself. ...

Bapu: Would it not be better to say that he should poison me?

Patel: I am afraid that will not help him. If he poisons you and you die, he would be sentenced to death. Then he would take his chance of rebirth along with you. It is much better that he poison himself ...

But humour could not prevent him, in mid-September 1932, from deciding to go on an indefinite fast.

The immediate 'occasion' was the announcement on 17 April 1932 by Prime Minister Ramsay MacDonald that there would be separate electorates for the 'depressed classes' under the new Constitutional arrangements for India. This was precisely what Gandhi had resisted at the RTC in London. Gandhi wrote to Tagore on 20 September 1932, a few hours before commencing the fast asking for his blessing. Dr B.R. Ambedkar, who had championed the case for separate electorates at the RTC in London, commenced discourses with the fasting Mahatma on 22 September. The record of those discussions has an essentiality to it that places it on a special footing. 'You should not care for my life,' Gandhi said to Ambedkar, 'but do not be false to Harijans.' Tagore went to Poona to be with Gandhi on 24 September. After intensive sessions between Gandhi and Ambedkar the 'Yeravda Pact' or the 'Poona Pact' was signed on 24 September, under which the demand for separate electorates was given up and replaced by a provision for a representation of seats for the 'depressed classes' with the electorates being undivided. The pact was concluded on 26 September with Gandhi saying:

'The fast taken in the name of God was broken in His name in the presence of Gurudev ...'

The fast breaking was preceded by the Poet himself singing one of his Bengali hymns: *When the heart is hard and parched up, come upon me with a shower of mercy ...* (*Gitanjali*: 39).

Tenacious Questions From D.B. Khoja[3]

The Ashram
Sabarmati
11 July 1926

Bhaishri Dharmashi Bhanji,

It is only today[4] I am able to answer your tenacious questions. It is not right, I think, to discuss so many questions in *Navajivan*. I am quite pleased with your questions. I now answer them one by one.

One who is ready to immolate himself for the sake of truth should not bother about protecting his body, but he should do so to the extent necessary for the purpose of realizing truth ...

... What I regard as the truth is not dependent on its acceptance as such by the world. That alone I believe [as truth] which I have experienced myself. A Shastra which condones *adharma* while upholding dharma is to that extent unworthy of honour.

... That a man may indulge in sex pleasures with one woman and none other and that too for the sake of progeny and similarly a woman with one man is, I believe, the farthest limit that he or she can have.

Time goes on doing its work. Our manliness lies in foreseeing its changes and putting in the right efforts.

... I have remained absolutely free from the habit of masturbation. Even today I am not able to understand it. I shudder at the thought of it. I have no doubt whatever that a man who practises it would become weak in body and mind. I know of many such cases. The remedy for it is that those who wish to reform themselves should shun solitude and as far as possible keep both their hands as well as their body busy. They should take *sattvika* food, which is easy to digest, go for walks in the open air and repeat Ramanama.

Marriage is no remedy for bad habits ...

Vandemataram from
Mohandas Gandhi
CWMG *Vol. 31, pp. 121–4; G*

Swami Shraddhananda

23 December 1926
I CANNOT mourn over his death[5]. He and his are to be envied.

Tendulkar *Vol. II, p. 227*

DEATH[6] IS certain for every body, but rare is the man who is blessed with a death like this!? ... this glorious death will create a far deeper effect than his death from ordinary illness might have. I have not sent a single wire or letter of condolence to Sri Indra. I could not tell him anything but this: 'The death your father has met with is one of supernal bliss.'

The Diary of Mahadev Desai *Vol. 9, p. 28*

Drain Inspector's Report

15 September 1927
... SEVERAL CORRESPONDENTS have sent me cuttings containing reviews of, or protests against, Miss Mayo's[7] *Mother India* ...

The book is cleverly and powerfully written. The carefully chosen quotations give it the appearance of a truthful book. But the impression it leaves on my mind is, that it is the report of a drain inspector sent out with the one purpose of opening and examining the drains of the country to be reported upon, or to give a graphic description of the stench exuded by the opened drains. If Miss Mayo had confessed that she had gone to India merely to open out and examine the drains of India, there would perhaps be little to complain about her compilation. But she says in effect with a certain amount of triumph, 'The drains are India' ...

Young India *15-9-1927*, CWMG *Vol. 34, pp. 539–40; E*

To Nattukkottai Chettiars

Kanadukathan
22 September 1927

... WHEN I saw your houses choked with foreign furniture, your houses furnished with all kinds of foreign fineries and foreign things, your houses containing many things for which in this holy land of ours there should be no room whatsoever I told you at the outset that I had felt both glad and sad. I tell you that I have felt oppressed with this inordinate furniture. There is, in the midst of this furniture, hardly any room to sit or to breathe free. Some of your pictures are hideous and not worth looking at. I recall the many signs and the many descriptions of the simplicity of even the rich men in the time of the Mahabharata. Let us not wear our wealth so loudly as we seem to be doing here. This temperate atmosphere and climate of our country really does not admit of this lavish display of all these things. It obstructs the free flow of pure air and it harbours dust and so many million germs that float in the air. If you give me a contract for furnishing all these palaces of Chettinad I would furnish them with one-tenth of the money but give you a much better accommodation and comfort than you enjoy today and procure for myself a certificate from the artists of India that I had furnished your houses in a much more artistic fashion than you have done.

I say also that all these palaces are really built anyhow without any sense of co-operation amongst yourselves and any sense of social effect and social welfare. If you will but form a union of Chettis for the common welfare and for the welfare of the peasantry that is living in your midst you can really make Chettinad a fairyland that would attract all the people of India who would come, see and be satisfied with the ordinary life that you would be then leading. ...

CWMG, *Vol. 35, pp. 19–20; E*

The Voice Of A 'Nayadi'

Palghat
15 October 1927

... As SOON as I arrived in Palghat, I heard a shrill voice in the neighbourhood of the house where I have been accommodated. In my innocence I thought that as this was a business centre this was the sound of some labourers working in a factory in order to ease themselves of the burden of carrying heavy loads as I am used to in Ahmedabad and Bombay. Within an hour after we reached Palghat, Mr C. Rajagopalachari came to me and asked me whether I was hearing any strange sounds. I told him, yes. And he straightway asked me whether I knew what it was. He told me that that was the voice of a Nayadi and he added that that was the sign that a Nayadi at a distance was begging. I asked him how far he could be. On hearing that he was within a stone's throw I hastened out to see who this man could be who was making all that sound. Well, you all know where I could have found him. He was not walking along the road, but he was at some distance from the hedge that guarded the road. I asked him to come near and he came near but not at the roadside of the hedge and told me that he dared not come on the roadside. He added that he never walked along the roads of Palghat. The rest of the story of this miserable case I don't need to recite to you. ...

The Hindu *18-10-1927;* CWMG *Vol. 35, pp. 144–5; E*

To C. Rajagopalachari

Bombay
5 November 1927

C. Rajagopalachari
Gandhi Ashram
Tiruchengodu

Sailing tomorrow early morning. Reaching Colombo about Tenth. Wire Colombo. Bring Lakshmi[8].

Bapu
CWMG *Vol. 35, p. 215; E*

Reply To Municipal Address

Colombo
15 November 1927

Chairman and friends,

... I know that you have got a very beautiful harbour. I have passed through your cinnamon gardens, a credit to any city in the world. I have noticed some of your palatial buildings. They are very good indeed. But then do the dwellers in cinnamon gardens or those who reside in this city and do business in it require trustees to look after their welfare? I fancy not. They are trustees for those who cannot look after themselves. They are trustees, therefore, for the welfare of the labouring population.

I have not yet been able to visit your slums to be able to say at first hand what the condition of these slums is. But if you are able to tell me that your slums will be just as sweet-smelling as cinnamon gardens I will take it on trust and will advertise your city throughout my wanderings and I will say: 'Go to Colombo if you want to see an ideal municipality ...'

The Ceylon Observer 15-11-1927; CWMG Vol. 35, p. 240; E

Reply To Buddhists' Address

Colombo
15 November 1927

... I HAVE heard it contended times without number and I have read in books also, claiming to express the spirit of Buddhism, that Buddha did not believe in God. In my humble opinion such a belief contradicts the very central fact of Buddha's teaching. In my humble opinion the confusion has arisen over his rejection, and just rejection, of all the base things that passed in his generation under the name of God. ...

Young India; CWMG, Vol. 35, pp. 243, 245–6; E

At The Y.M.C.A.

Colombo
15 November 1927

... I KNOW that the world is not waiting to know my opinion on Christianity.

... I can tell you that in my humble opinion, much of what passes as Christianity is a negation of the Sermon on the Mount ... When I began as a prayerful student to study the Christian literature in South Africa in 1893, I asked myself, 'Is this Christianity?' and have always got the Vedic answer, *neti neti* (not this, not this). And the deepest in me tells me that I am right. ...

Young India 18-12-1927; CWMG Vol. 35, pp. 248–9; E

To Ceylon's Parsis

Kandy
18 November 1927

... SOME OF you good Parsis never smoke, and you make it a point, whenever you have a number of boys in your care, to train the boys not to foul their mouths by smoke.

If any of you are smoking, you will henceforth give up that bad habit. Smoking fouls one's breath. It is a disgusting habit ...

Smoking clouds one's intellect, and it is a bad habit. If you ask doctors, and they happen to be good doctors, they will tell you that smoke has been the cause of cancer in many cases, or at least that smoke is at the bottom of it ...

CWMG Vol. 35, pp. 268–9; E

A Public Meeting

Badulla
19 November 1927

... As I was passing today from Kandy to this place, I passed through some of the finest bits of scenery that I have ever witnessed in my life. Where nature has been so beneficent and where nature provides for you eternal and innocent intoxication in the grand scenery about you, surely it is criminal for men or women to seek intoxication from that sparkling but deadly liquor. ...

CWMG Vol. 35, pp. 272, 275–6; E

A Women's Meeting

Colombo
22 November 1927

... MY HUNGRY eyes rest upon the ornaments of sisters, whenever I see them heavily bedecked ...

Do you know the hideous condition of your sisters on plantations? Treat them as your sisters, go amongst them and serve them with your better knowledge of sanitation and your talents. Let your honour lie in their service ...

CWMG Vol. 35, pp. 288–9; E

At The Young Men's Buddhist Association

Colombo
25 November 1927

... WHY DO they sacrifice thousands of sheep and goats to the Goddess Kali in Calcutta—be it said to their discredit and the discredit of Hinduism—in spite of having received this message from the Hindu of Hindus—Gautama? Do they throw the carcasses away in the Hoogly? No, they eat every bit of the meat with the greatest delight, thinking that it has been sanctified because of the presentation to Kali. So the Buddha said, if you want to do any sacrifice, sacrifice yourself, your lust, all your material ambition, all worldly ambition. That will be an ennobling sacrifice. ...

Young India *8-12-1927;* CWMG *Vol. 35, pp. 310 and 313; E*

To Ceylon Hindus

Jaffna[9]
27 November 1927

FIRST OF all I want to speak to you about your duty towards the predominant population in this island. And I wish to suggest to you that they are your co-religionists. They will, if they choose to, repudiate the claim. For they will say that Buddhism is not Hinduism and they will be partly right. Many Hindus certainly repudiate the claim of Buddhism to be part and parcel of Hinduism. On the contrary, they delight in saying that they successfully drove Buddhism out of India. But I tell you that they did nothing of the kind. Buddha himself was a Hindu. He endeavoured to reform Hinduism. And he succeeded in his attempt to a very great extent and what Hinduism did at that time was to assimilate and absorb all that was good and best in the teachings of the Buddha. ...

Young India *15-12-1927;* CWMG *Vol. 35, pp. 334–5; E*

To Surendra[10]

Jaffna
28 November 1927

DEVADAS' STATE is extremely pitiable. Rajaji is not likely at all to let him marry Lakshmi, and rightly so. Lakshmi will not take one step without his consent. She is happy and cheerful, whereas Devadas has gone mad after her and is pining for her and suffering. If he had such love for God, he would have been revered as a saintly man and become a great dedicated worker.

But how can even Devadas act against his nature? He wishes to obey me, but his soul rebels against him. He seems to believe that I stand in the way of his marriage with Lakshmi and so feels angry with me. I do not know at present how he can be brought out of this condition. Try and see if you can help him recover peace of mind and explain to him his dharma. It is possible that I have not understood him and am, therefore, doing him injustice. See if you can give him peace of mind through a letter. I of course write to him frequently. ...

From the manuscript of Mahadev Desai's Dairy;
CWMG *Vol. 35, pp. 339–40; G*

To Jawaharlal Nehru[11]

The Ashram
Sabarmati
17 January 1928

My dear Jawaharlal,

... The differences between you and me appear to me to be so vast and radical that there seems to be no meeting-ground between us. I can't conceal from you my grief that I should lose a comrade so valiant, so faithful, so able, and so honest as you have always been; but in serving a cause, comradeships have got to be sacrificed. The cause must be held superior to all such considerations. But this dissolution of comradeship—if dissolution must come—in no way affects our personal intimacy. ...

With love,
Bapu
A Bunch of Old Letters; CWMG *Vol. 35, pp. 469–70; E*

Speech At Morvi[12]

24 January 1928

I SINCERELY thank the Maharaja Saheb, the people, and members of the Modh[13] community for having welcomed my companions and myself and for presenting me with an address. I should, at any rate, tell my brothers belonging to the Modh caste that I have no right whatsoever to accept an address of welcome from them ...

... I am clear in my mind that there is no room for castes in the Hindu faith; I say this to those belonging to the Modh or any other caste who happen to be present here. In the true Shastras there is no reference to castes; there is a reference only to the four *varnas*. God has washed his hands off after creating these four *varnas*. There is not even a trace of castes in the *varnadharma*. ...

Navajivan *29-1-1928;* CWMG *Vol. 35, p. 487; G*

At The Wedding Of Ramdas Gandhi[14]

Sabarmati
27 January 1928

... YOU WILL guard your wife's honour and be not her master, but her true friend. You will hold her body and her soul as sacred as I trust she will hold your body and your soul. To that end you will have to live a life of prayerful toil, and simplicity and self-restraint. Let not either of you regard another as the object of his or her lust. ...

Young India, *2-2-1928;* CWMG *Vol. 35, pp. 499–500; G*

To C. Rajagopalachari

Satyagraha Ashram, Sabarmati
28 January 1928

My dear C.R.,

I have your letter. I wish you will cease to worry about me. I can only give you my assurance that I shall do nothing wilfully to impair my health. But you know my nature. I cannot exist without dietetic experiments if I am fixed up at any place for any length of time. You know too that it has always been my intense longing to revert to fruit and nut diet or at least a milkless diet if I at all could. I find now that I can easily do so and so I have done it ...

What has given Lakshmi her fever? I hope that she is all right now. I hope to send you Rs 5000/- for untouchability work soon.

Bapu
CWMG *Vol. 35, pp. 501–2; E*

To Jawaharlal Nehru

Satyagraha Ashram, Sabarmati
26 February 1928

My dear Jawahar,

... Do come as early as possible. I hope Kamala is keeping up her strength, if not actually adding to it. I wonder if Father has told you that, before you came, when Father was with me in Bangalore, he and I had contemplated your stay in Bangalore because of its magnificent climate during summer. There are just four weeks of somewhat trying weather, but you could always go to Nandi Hill only 35 miles from Bangalore where you have delightfully cool weather. In no case should Kamala be allowed to lose what she gained in Switzerland.

Yours Sincerely,
CWMG *Vol. 36, p. 58; E*

To C. Rajagopalachari

Ashram, Sabarmati
19 March 1928

My dear C.R.,

... Many are grieved that I did not die on the 17th[15] ... Perhaps I am one among them. Perhaps I did die a kind of death. We shall see.

CWMG *Vol. 36, pp. 117–18; E*

Removal Of Exploitation

Satyagraha Ashram, Sabarmati
20 March 1928

THERE CAN be no living harmony between races and nations unless the main cause is removed, namely, exploitation of the weak by the strong. We must revise the interpretation of the so-called doctrine of 'the survival of the fittest'.

M.K. Gandhi
Message to Marcelle Capy; CWMG *Vol. 36, p. 121; E*

Letter To Sam Higginbottom[16]

The Ashram, Sabarmati
28 March 1928

Dear Friend,

When I had the pleasure of being shown over your farm on the banks of the Jumna, I remember having seen a contrivance whereby you heated your water by the sun heat. Will you please tell me whether it was merely the tank put on your building and exposed to the full sun or whether you concentrated by some mechanical contrivance the rays of the sun on to the tank?

Yours sincerely,

Sam Higginbottom, Esq.,
Agricultural Institute,
Allahabad.

CWMG *Vol. 36, p. 151; E*

Indians And South Africans[17]

5 April 1928

INDIANS HAVE too much in common with the Africans to think of isolating themselves from them. They cannot exist in South Africa for any length of time without the active sympathy and friendship of the Africans. I am not aware of the general body of the Indians having ever adopted an air of superiority towards their African brethren, and it would be a tragedy if any such movement were to gain ground among the Indian settlers of South Africa.

Gandhi writing in Young India
(courtesy: Rabindra Bhavana, Santiniketan)

To S. Radhakrishnan

The Ashram, Sabarmati
6 April 1928

Dear Friend,

I thank you for your kind letter. Nothing is yet certain about the proposed European visit. It is difficult for me to make up my mind.

As to the article you want, I would ask you to take pity on me. I am so thoroughly washed out and have to give so much time to *Young India* and *Navajivan* that I have very little left for managing any more writing.

Yours sincerely,

Prof. S. Radhakrishnan
49/I.C. Harish Mukerji Rd.,
Bhawanipur,
Calcutta.

CWMG Vol. 36, p. 198; E

My Best Comrade Gone

26 April 1928

HE WHOM I had singled out as heir to my all is no more. Maganlal K. Gandhi, a grandson of an uncle of mine had been with me in my work since 1904. Maganlal's father had given all his boys to the cause. The deceased went early this month to Bengal with Seth Jamnalalji and others, contracted a high fever whilst he was on duty in Bihar and died under the protecting care of Brijkishore Prasad in Patna after an illness of nine days and after receiving all the devoted nursing that love and skill could give.

Maganlal Gandhi went with me to South Africa in 1903 in the hope of making a bit of fortune. But hardly had he been store-keeping for one year, when he responded to my sudden call to self-imposed poverty, joined the Phoenix settlement and never once faltered or failed after so joining me. If he had not dedicated himself to the country's service, his undoubted abilities and indefatigable industry would have made him a merchant prince ...

He was my hands, my feet and my eyes. The world knows so little of how much my so-called greatness depends upon the incessant toil and drudgery of silent, devoted, able, and pure workers, men as well as women. And among them all Maganlal was to me the greatest, the best, and the purest.

As I am penning these lines, I hear the sobs of the widow bewailing the death of her dear husband. Little does she realize that

I am more widowed than she. And but for a living faith in God, I should become a raving maniac for the loss of one who was dearer to me than my own sons. ...

Young India 26-4-1928; CWMG *Vol. 36, pp. 261–3; E*

'My Time Is Not Yet'

The Ashram, Sabarmati
1 May 1928

Dear Dr Bidhan[18],

Your letter flatters me, but I must not succumb to my pride. Apart from the fact that as a non-co-operator I may have nothing to do with the University that is in any way connected with Government, I do not consider myself to be a fit and proper person to deliver Kamala lectures. I do not possess the literary attainment which Sir Asutosh[19] undoubtedly contemplated for the lecturers.

You are asking me to shoulder a responsibility which my shoulders cannot bear. I am keeping fairly fit. I am biding my time and you will find me leading the country in the field of politics when the country is ready. I have no false modesty about me. I am undoubtedly a politician in my own way, and I have a scheme for the country's freedom. But my time is not yet and may never come to me in this life. If it does not, I shall not shed a single tear. We are all in the hands of God. I therefore await His guidance.

Yours sincerely,
CWMG *Vol. 36, p. 287; E*

Monkeys

Ahmedabad
8 July 1928

... THE SLAUGHTER of animals even for the sake of saving fields involves violence. That some such forms of violence are part and parcel of human life and are unavoidable is a fact that we encounter at every step. It is difficult to say when the killing of monkeys becomes actually inescapable, but it is not difficult to find out ways to spare ourselves this slaughter. If in spite of those remedies the nuisance does not diminish, each should work out his own dharma. ...

Navajivan; CWMG *Vol. 37, pp. 32–3; G*

No Miraculous Powers

Satyagraha Ashram, Sabarmati
13 July 1928

Dear Friend,

I have your letter. I don't know how the story about miraculous powers possessed by me has got abroad. I can only tell you that I am but an ordinary mortal susceptible to the same weakness, influences and the rest as every other human being and that I possess no extraordinary powers.

Yours sincerely,

Miss Barbara Bauer
Big Spring, Texas, USA

CWMG *Vol. 37, p. 48; E*

Crown Of Thorns

Ahmedabad
26 July 1928

THE CONGRESS crown has ceased to be a crown of roses. The rose petals are year by year falling off and the thorns are becoming more and more prominent. Who should wear such a crown? The father or the son? Pandit Motilalji the weather-beaten warrior or Pandit Jawaharlal Nehru, the disciplined young soldier who by his sterling worth has captured the imagination of the youth of the country? Sjt. Vallabhbhai Patel's name is naturally on everybody's lips. Panditji[1] says in a private letter that he as the hero of the hour should be elected and the Government should be made to know that he enjoys the fullest confidence of the nation. Sjt. Vallabhbhai is however out of the question just now. His hands are too full to allow his attention being diverted from Bardoli. And before December comes upon us he may be a guest in one of His Majesty's innumerable prisons. My own feeling in the matter is that Pandit

Jawaharlal should wear the crown. The future must be for the youth of the country. ...

Young India *26-7-1928;* CWMG *Vol. 37, pp. 91–2;* E

'The Fiery Ordeal'[20]

Ahmedabad
30 September 1928

... SOME DAYS back a calf having been maimed lay in agony in the Ashram. Whatever treatment and nursing was possible was given to it. The surgeon whose advice was sought in the matter declared the case to be past help and past hope. The suffering of the animal was so great that it could not even turn its side without excruciating pain.

In these circumstances I felt that humanity[21] demanded that the agony should be ended by ending life itself. I held a preliminary discussion with the Managing Committee most of whom agreed with my view. The matter was then placed before the whole Ashram. At the discussion a worthy neighbour vehemently opposed the idea of killing even to end pain and offered to nurse the dying animal. The nursing consisted in co-operation with some of the Ashram sisters in warding the flies off the animal and trying to feed it. The ground of the friend's opposition was that one has no right to take away life which one cannot create. His argument seemed to me to be pointless here. It would have point if the taking of life was actuated by self-interest. Finally in all humility but with the clearest of convictions I got in my presence a doctor kindly to administer the calf a quietus by means of a poison injection. The whole thing was over in less than two minutes[22].

I knew that public opinion especially in Ahmedabad[23] would not approve of my action and that it would read nothing but himsa in it.

... I admit that there is always a possibility of one's mistaking right for wrong and *vice versa* but often one learns to recognize wrong only through unconscious error. On the other hand if a man fails to follow the light within for fear of public opinion or any other similar reason he would never be able to know right from wrong and in the end lose all sense of distinction between the two. That is why the poet has sung:

The pathway of love is the ordeal of fire,
The shrinkers turn away from it.

The pathway of ahimsa, that is, of love, one has often to tread all alone.

But the question may very legitimately be put to me: Would I apply to human beings the principle I have enunciated in connection with the calf? Would I like it to be applied in my own case? My reply is yes; the same law holds good in both the cases. The law of 'as with one so with all' admits of no exceptions, or the killing of the calf was wrong and violent. In practice however we do not cut short the sufferings of our ailing dear ones by death because as a rule we have always means at our disposal to help them and because they have the capacity to think and decide for themselves. But supposing that in the case of an ailing friend I am unable to render any aid whatever and recovery is out of the question and the patient is lying in an unconscious state in the throes of fearful agony, then I would not see any himsa in putting an end to his suffering by death. ...

Navajivan *30-9-1928;* CWMG *Vol. 37, pp. 310–11; G*

I Have Learnt Much From The West

I HAVE nothing to be ashamed of if my views on Ahimsa are the result of my Western education. I have never tabooed all Western ideas, nor am I prepared to anathematize everything that comes from the West as inherently evil. I have learnt much from the West and I should not be surprised to find that I had learnt something about ahimsa too from the West ...

Young India *11 October 1928*

The Assault On Lalaji[24]

4 November 1928

... I CONGRATULATE Lalaji. He has been well known for many years as the 'Lion of the Punjab'. The Government's police have themselves helped on this occasion to add to his prestige and the above assault is an addition to the many services he has rendered to the country. ...

Navajivan *4-11-1928;* CWMG *Vol. 38, pp. 16–17; G*

The Lion Of The Punjab Sleeps

Ahmedabad
18 November 1928

As THE pages of *Navajivan* were going to the printing machine on Saturday, the following telegram was received from Lala Lajpat Rai's son: 'Following a heart attack this morning, Lalaji has fallen asleep'. Lalaji's death means the dissolution of a great planet from India's solar system. ...

Navajivan *18-11-1928;* CWMG *Vol. 38, p. 70; G*

Letter To Prabhavati[25]

Silence Day
Wardha
26 November 1928

Do YOU expect a letter from me by every post? What a girl! Well, I shall try to write.

Blessings from
Bapu
CWMG *Vol. 38, p. 95; H*

Letter To J. Krishnamurti[26]

Satyagraha Ashram, Wardha
29 November 1928

Dear Friend,

I have your letter[27] for which I thank you. I hope that you are completely restored. It will certainly give me much pleasure to see you whenever you can find the time. I am in Wardha up to the 20th December at least, then I shall be in Calcutta for about a week and then I hope to find myself in Sabarmati.

Yours sincerely,

Sjt. J. Krishnamurti
C/o R.D. Morarji, Esq.
Vasant Vihar, Mount Pleasant Road, Bombay.

CWMG *Vol. 38, pp. 119–20; E*

Letter To Hanna Lazar[28]

As at the Ashram, Sabarmati
29 November 1928

Dear Friend,

... generally speaking, I would say 'no divorce'. But if your temperaments are incompatible, you should live in voluntary separation.

In any case, I hope you will have mental peace.

Yours sincerely,

Mrs Hanna Lazar
West Bank, Victoria Street, Oudtobaara, C.P.

CWMG *Vol. 38, p. 121; E*

To Jawaharlal Nehru

Wardha
3 December 1928

My dear Jawahar,

My love to you. It was all done bravely. You have braver things to do. May God spare you for many a long year to come and make you His chosen instrument for freeing India from the yoke[29].

Yours,
Bapu

CWMG *Vol. 38, p. 150; E*

Being A Good Daughter

Satyagraha Ashram, Wardha
4 December 1928

My dear Padmaja[30],

You must not mind this dictated letter. It is better that I dictate than that I delay writing to you. What on earth are you doing with your health? Is it not more your mind that is at fault? Why can't you make up your mind to be and remain healthy? This set-back in your health is bound to trouble the poor old songstress[31] in America. You must become a good daughter.

Shrimati Padmaja Naidu
Hyderabad.

CWMG Vol. 38, p. 154; E

To Polak

Wardha
7 December 1928

My dear Bhai,

The calf incident has provided me with much instruction and an equal amount of amusement ... You may not remember that when West[32] brought to me a cat whose head was full of maggots and was living in torture, I endorsed his suggestion that the poor animal's life should be ended by drowning and it was done immediately. And at the Ashram too I allowed Maganlal to destroy rabid dogs.

Yours sincerely,
CWMG Vol. 38, pp. 175–6; E

My Writings

Satyagraha Ashram, Sabarmati
7 December 1928

Dear Friend[33],

I have your letter as also copy of the Macmillan Company's. I must confess that I do not like the tone of their letter. But I suppose they cannot look at this transaction in any other light but that of a business job, whereas I think I have told you I have never entered into any business transactions about my writings. Nor did I enter into this transaction from any pecuniary motive.

Mr Andrews is in direct correspondence with you and

between you two you may do what you can with the Macmillan Company.

Yours sincerely,

Rev. John Haynes Holmes
12 Park Avenue, New York City.

CWMG *Vol. 38, p. 178;* E

Revolvers For Jawaharlal?

DESCRIBING THE incidents of Lucknow in a private letter Pandit Jawaharlal Nehru writes:

An incident which took place yesterday morning might interest you. I have not mentioned it in my statement. Soon after the mounted and foot police had driven us back near the station, a young man, whom I took to be a student, came to me and said that he could bring me two revolvers immediately if I wanted to use them. We had just experienced the baton and lathi charges and there was a great deal of anger and resentment in the crowd. I suppose he thought that it was a favourable moment to make the offer. I told him not to be foolish. Soon after I found out quite casually that this particular person was known to be in the C.I.D.

Pandit Jawaharlal was safe as he has no secrets. If he finds any use for revolvers in his scheme for the freedom of the country, he will not need the offer from the outsider to lend him one. He will carry it himself openly and use it effectively when in his opinion the occasion has arrived. So he was safe from the blandishments of the C.I.D. ...

Young India 13-12-1928; CWMG *Vol. 38, p. 209;* E

Capitalists Of India

Wardha
Before 20 December 1928

GOD FORBID that India should ever take to industrialism after the manner of the West. The economic imperialism of a single tiny island kingdom (England) is today keeping the world in chains. If an entire nation of 300 millions took to similar economic exploitation, it would strip the world bare like locusts. Unless the capitalists of India help to avert that tragedy by becoming trustees of the welfare of the masses and by devoting their talents not to amassing wealth for themselves but to the service of the masses in an altruistic spirit, they will end either by destroying the masses or being destroyed by them.

Young India *20-12-1928;* CWMG *Vol. 38, pp. 243–4; E*

Curse Of Assassination

8, Pretoria Street
Calcutta
December 1928

THE ASSASSINATION[34] of the Assistant Superintendent Mr Saunders of Lahore was a dastardly act apart from whether it had a political motive behind it or not. Violence being in the air, there will no doubt be silent and secret approbation of the act, especially if it is discovered to have had any connection with the assault on Lalaji and his utterly innocent comrades. The provocation was great and it became doubly great by the death of Lalaji which was certainly hastened by the nervous shock received by him from the disgraceful conduct of the police. Some will insist, not without considerable justification, on ascribing the death even to the physical effect of the injury received by the deceased in the region of the heart. The provocation received also additional strength from the Punjab Government's defence of the police conduct. I should not wonder if the assassination proves to be in revenge of the high-handed policy of the Punjab Government.

I wish however that it was possible to convince the hot youth of the utter futility of such revenge. Whatever the Assistant Superintendent did was done in obedience to instructions. No one person can be held wholly responsible for the assault and the aftermath. The fault is that of the system of Government. What requires mending is not men but the system. And when the youth of the country have the real determination they will find that it is in their power as it is in nobody else's to kill the system. ...

Young India *17-12-1928;* CWMG *Vol. 38, pp. 274–6; E*

On Jawaharlal Nehru[35]

Congress Session,
Calcutta
28 December 1928

... HE HAS become impatient to throw off the yoke. Every twenty-four hours of his life he simply broods upon the grievances of his countrymen. He is impatient to remove the grinding pauperism of the masses ... I do not share his belief that what we are doing at the present moment is not sufficient for the present needs of the country. But how can he help feeling dissatisfied? He would not be Jawaharlal if he did not strike out for himself an absolutely unique and original line in pursuance of his path ...

Now you understand why he is absent[36]. ...

Amrita Bazar Patrika *29-12-1929;* CWMG; *Vol. 38, pp. 283–5; E*

[Gandhi then moved the following:]

This Congress, having considered the constitution recommended by the All-Parties Committee Report (Nehru Report) welcomes it as a great contribution towards the solution of India's political and communal problems, and congratulates the Committee on the virtual unanimity of its recommendations, and, whilst adhering to the resolution relating to Complete Independence passed at the Madras Congress, approves of the constitution drawn up by the Committee as a great step in political advance, especially as it represents the largest measure of agreement attained among the important parties in the country. ...

Gandhi added:

Friends, I don't want to inflict a long speech upon you but I must confess to you that I have not been able to collect my thoughts, my brain is muddled and I have got to put my thoughts together as I proceed. ...

Amrita Bazar Patrika *29-12-1928;* Foreward *29-12-1928;*
CWMG *Vol. 38, p. 287; E*

To Manilal And Sushila Gandhi

29 January 1929

... TODAY I am writing this letter in a great hurry. Rasik[37] has caught typhoid in Delhi. Kanti has been down with fever for the past three days. Such are the ups and downs over here.

I cannot advise the closing of *Indian Opinion*. A journal that has survived till this day cannot be allowed to close down. I would not mind if both of you had to spend your whole life there[38]. That is how great tasks are accomplished. That is what single-minded devotion means ...

I was sorry to learn about Charlie[39]. That is the way the world goes.

Blessings from
Bapu
CWMG *Vol. 38, p. 411; G*

To Ashram Women

Karachi
4 February 1929

Sisters,

... Rasik's condition can be described as really very serious. I do not know whether he will be alive when this letter reaches you. But we try to learn everyday that birth and death are two facets of the same thing. He who is born dies, and he who dies is born again. Some do escape this cycle, but neither they nor the others need rejoice at birth or grieve over death. I realize this and, therefore, remain unconcerned. Rasik has recently become a votary of the *Ramayana*, and we feel, therefore, that he enjoys complete peace inwardly. ...

Blessings from
Bapu
CWMG *Vol. 39, pp. 403-4; G*

At D.J.S. College Hall, Karachi

5 February 1929

Sisters and Brothers,

... I am told that as soon as marriage is proposed to a Sindhi young man he wants to be sent to England at the expense of his prospective father-in-law and that even after marriage misses no opportunity of exacting money from the bride's father. You think yourselves very clever. You get a good lot of money and try to become barristers or I.C.S. Now what is the meaning of all this? You thereby tyrannize over your own women, over your wives. Wife in our language has been described as *ardhangini* or the better half of man. But you have reduced her to the position of mere chattel to be bought and sold ...

You read your Milton, your Browning, and your Whittier, all right. Is this what you have learnt from them to reduce your wives who should be the queens of your hearts and your homes into *londis*[40]? Shame, shame on you! ...

CWMG *Vol. 39, pp. 412, 415–16; H*

Rasik's Death

Larkana
9 February 1929

Chiranjivi Devadas[41],

I have just now got your two telegrams here at Larkana. I also got Dr Ansari's telegram. The telegram arrived while food was being brought in for me. I took my meal as usual and kept on working as I ate. Now I sit down to write this. My programme here will remain as already fixed. This is what I feel now. Rasik's death certainly pains me, but that is only because of selfishness. I loved the boy. I had placed high hopes on him. God will in some mysterious way fulfil through him the hopes we had of him. But how are we, human beings, to remain steadfast in such faith? Our pain at his departure is the result of our selfishness. As for Rasik he has been freed from the pains to which the body is subject. I have no doubt that he is in a better state in the other world, for he was a devotee of Rama.

You will feel the greatest pain of all, though you may not show it. What you did is beyond praise. You will have the reward of your services to him. Your fortitude will lead to your progress. Rasik died through no fault of yours. He went to Delhi to collect the debt owing to him, and departed when it had been paid. You did your duty well. God will certainly bless you.

Let me tell you what I feel inwardly. It is of course God's will that prevails, and human intelligence follows the law of karma. Man is however entitled to use his reason. Accordingly, it appears to me that the best remedies are the remedies I or we employ and are based on nature-cure methods. It seems to me that both Maganlal and Rasik could perhaps have been saved if simple remedies had been applied. One may put the same idea in another way. If Rasik had been destined to live, he would have been put in such circumstances that only nature-cure methods would have been used in his treatment. This thought, however, is no consolation, nor do we seek any. By saying all this, I do not express regret at having sent him to Delhi or at his being put under a doctor's treatment. You did what was proper for you to do, as Brijkishore Babu had done what was proper for him in respect of Maganlal. We should never grieve over anyone's death. Dharma lies in doing one's duty, not in making no mistake at all. But after all, mine is only a conjecture. What was best Rama alone knows.

Incidentally, I have to go to Delhi on 17 February, and that is exactly as I would have it. I shall be able to see you. Detain Ba. But let her go if she wishes to. I know you must be comforting Kanti. I shall expect a full account from you then. I still have enough attachment[42] to be eager to know from you about the last days of Rasik's life. Do not disappoint me in that.

Blessings from
Bapu
CWMG *Vol. 39, pp. 432–3; G*

Burning Cloth

Calcutta to Rangoon
5 March 1929

... SOME MAY ask: Can burning of clothes be dharma? ...

... Some say that it should be given away to the poor ... Do not the poor have self-respect? Do they not want swaraj? Why should we give to the poor a thing which we regard as infected? We do have the mean habit of offering to the poor left-overs from our plates. Shall we add to that meanness by giving them the clothes which we ourselves have discarded?

Let us consider what sort of clothes they are. The clothes I have burnt till today comprised handkerchiefs, clean or unclean black caps, neckties, collars, socks, thin long shirts, blouses, fine saris, etc. What clothes out of these could one give to the poor? And how strange would it be to create in the poor a fondness for them? If we do so, how shall we seek to boycott foreign cloth? ...

Navajivan 17-3-1929; CWMG *Vol. 40, pp. 84–5; G*

To Indians In Rangoon

10 March 1929

THERE HAS been a complaint against you to which I want to draw your attention. It is that the Indians do not share the Burmans' lot, but they cause them harm. I hope that there is exaggeration in this complaint but I am afraid that there is some grain of truth in it. For I noted such a habit in the Indians in Ceylon and also those in South Africa. Therefore I am not very much surprised to hear of it here. I must ask you to have due regard for the people of the country which enables you to earn your bread and more than that— to amass wealth. ...

From the manuscript of Mahadev Desai's diary in Gujarati,
CWMG *Vol. 40, pp. 116–17; G*

Questions[43] On Burma

Rangoon
10 March 1929

... Q. Do you think that it is in the interest of Burma that it should be part of India for ever?

A. It is a difficult question for me to answer. All I can say is that it will be worth the while of Burma to remain part of India if it means a partnership at will on a basis of equality with full freedom for either party to secede whenever it should wish. The main thing is that Burma should have an absolute right to shape her destiny as she likes.

... Q. What protection should be given to minorities in Burma?

A. The same protection should be given to Indian minorities in

Burma as it is to be given to minorities in India, nothing more. If we cannot stay here on our merits, we should retire. ...

Young India 28-3-1929; CWMG Vol. 40, pp. 122–3; E

Fads

16 June 1929

SOME LOOK upon me as a fool, a crank, or a faddist. I msut admit that wherever I go I am sought out by fools, cranks, and faddists. One can conclude from this that I must be having the characteristics of all these three types ...

... I have believed for many years that one should not eat cooked food. I had given up cooked food at the age of 20, but that state could not last beyond 15 days ...

... I have lived on raw fruit and dry fruit continuously for six years. But I have not lived for a long on uncooked cereals and pulses and I have believed that a man like me could not digest it at all ...

... None should hastily copy my experiment. He who has no experience of such experiments should never do so ...

... Now I shall describe my diet: Eight *tolas* of germinating wheat, eight tolas of almonds ground to a paste, eight tolas of green leafy vegetable crushed, eight sour lemons, five tolas of honey.

When I do not take wheat, I take an equal quantity of germinated gram. From this week I have started taking wheat and gram together. I sometimes take the grated kernel of the coconut in place of almonds, and, if there is scope, I take dried grapes or some other fruit in addition to the five constituents.

Navajivan 16-6-1929; CWMG Vol. 41, pp. 52–4; G

Accident At Almora

20 June 1929

... MY HEART is with Padam Singh—the man who was crushed under the car when he came to see me. The doctor had hoped that he would survive and I had shared this hope. But his life-thread has snapped ... I have always felt that riding in cars makes men proud. The chauffeurs who drive are vain and hot-tempered. One should beware of drivers with a hot temper. But under the illusion that I will be able to serve better I continue to use cars. I have reaped the fruit today. And yet I cannot promise to give up the use of cars, as I cannot give up the fond desire to serve the country. ...

Aaj, 4-7-1929; CWMG *Vol. 41, p. 70; H*

To Jawaharlal Nehru

Ahmedabad
7 August 1929

My dear Jawaharlal,

I do not like the title 'Dawn of History'. 'A Father's Letters to His Daughter' may be a better title than 'Letters to Indira', though I do not mind the latter.

I wish Kamala would be freed from these recurring pains. I should risk the operation, if the doctors would perform it. ...

Yours,
Bapu
Gandhi–Nehru Papers, 1929; CWMG *Vol. 41, p. 256; E*

A Ruinous Vice

While on a U.P. tour
Late September–Early October 1929

WE CAN call this (spitting in public places) a national vice. It betrays our rudeness and apathy towards our neighbours. That this vice still persists despite the awakening among us shows our indolence. It of course spreads diseases and we are rightly maligned for it in the West.

This vice is contrary to religion. When I returned to our country in the year 1915, this filthy habit had caught my attention well enough and I tried to find out what the various religions had to say about it. I do not remember where the collection of extracts is at the moment. But during this tour I came across one or two stanzas from the Hindu Shastras whose gist I give below:

No one should urinate or defecate or spit into rivers, ponds, etc.
—*Krishnayajurveda*

No one should urinate or defecate in the middle of a village or a town or in temples, cremation grounds, open spaces, watering places, or on roads.

—*Charaka*
Navajivan *13-10-1929;* CWMG *Vol. 41, pp. 557-8; G*

Khadi And Honesty

SJT. C. Rajagopalachari sends me an interesting letter, which with the omission of personal references and one or two redundant passages I publish below[44]:

... I admit that till now I have been indifferent regarding khadi. But I have now realized that khadi men are men who follow truth. The day before yesterday I went to Coimbatore khadi depot ... I had with me notes of the value of Rs 10,000 ... which I placed ... on the table. I quite forgot about the money and left the depot. After some time, your manager saw the money and in the hot sun came to Podanur ... handed over the money to me ...

This letter shows how unreasoning and illogical we are. Surely there is no necessary connection between honesty and khadi. Even rogues must cover themselves and therefore may wear khadi. I am sorry also to have to confess that not all the workers in the employ of the A.I.S.A. have always been found to be honest ...

The other reflection the foregoing letter gives rise to is somewhat humiliating. Why should anyone run into ecstasies because someone is found to possess the ordinary honesty of not stealing other people's property? Have we fallen so low that a man forgetfully leaving valuables in a shop may not feel as safe about them as if they were in his possession? At any rate this letter has a lesson for men and women in khadi service. Their honesty may bring rich votaries to the altar of *Daridranarayana*. And he needs them all.

Young India *5-12-1929;* CWMG *Vol. 42, pp. 241-2; E*

'Hajam' Or 'Valand'?

A GENTLEMAN from Palitana writes[45]:

The contemptible implication underlying the word *hajam* is actually directed towards that profession. This word isused with reference to persons whose profession is to shave or cut the hair. If this word is not approved of, I shall only use the word '*Valand*' in *Navajivan*. However, it is my confirmed opinion that this is no remedy for the basic problem. The real remedy consists in ending the prejudice against those professions which are essential but are concerned with the removal of dirt. Thereafter, we can remain indifferent to names that may be used to indicate them ...

In this age of reforms, everyone has learnt to shave himself and the sting in the barber's profession will easily disappear—it has already half disappeared. For me, words like *Valand*, Bhangi Chamar, Dhed, etc., have no repugnance. I myself do the work of all those professions and inspire others to do so and I find pleasure in it. ... We have had Chamars, weavers, cobblers, and Dheds, etc., among us who had attained the highest knowledge and had become *bhakta*s. Should it then be surprising if one of them, by virtue of the strength of his services, becomes the President of the State? Persons who follow such a profession can maintain the highest degree of integrity in their conduct and can also sharpen their intellect. The sorry part of the story is that when persons who practise such trades happen to be intelligent individuals, they are ashamed of their professions and finally give them up. The President of my imagination will be one who while earning a livelihood by practicing a barber's or a cobbler's profession, will also be guiding the ship of the State. It is possible that because of the burden of national work he will be unable to ply his trade regularly but that is a different question.

Navajivan *22-12-1929;* CWMG *Vol. 42, pp. 309–10; G*

The Cult Of The Bomb

Lahore
2 January 1930

... LET US think then for a moment what would have happened if the Viceroy[46] had been seriously injured or killed. There certainly would have been no meeting of 23rd ultimo and therefore no certainty as to the course to be adopted by the Congress. That surely would have been, to say the least, an undesirable result. Fortunately for us the Viceroy and his party escaped unhurt, and with great self-possession he went through the day's routine as if nothing had happened ...

... From violence done to the foreign ruler, violence to our own people whom we may consider to be obstructing the country's progress is an easy natural step. ...

Young India 2-1-1930; CWMG Vol. 42, pp. 361–2; E

To English Friends

Ahmedabad
23 January 1930

... 'BUT YOU are not fit for independence', say some. Surely it is for us to judge whether we are fit or not. And granting that we are not, there is nothing wrong or immoral in our aspiring after independence and in the attempt rendering ourselves fitter day by day. We shall never be fit by being taught to feel helpless and to rely upon the British bayonet to keep us from fighting among ourselves or from being devoured by our neighbours. ...

Young India 23-1-1930; CWMG Vol. 42, pp. 424–6; E

To Lord Irwin

Satyagraha Ashram
Sabarmati
2 March 1930

Dear Friend,

Before embarking on civil disobedience and taking the risk I have dreaded to take all these years, I would fain approach you and find a way out.

My personal faith is absolutely clear. I cannot intentionally hurt anything that lives, much less fellow human beings, even though they may do the greatest wrong to me and mine. Whilst, therefore, I hold the British rule to be a curse, I do not intend harm to a single Englishman or to any legitimate interest he may have in India.

I must not be misunderstood. Though I hold the British rule in India to be a curse, I do not, therefore, consider Englishmen in general to be worse than any other people on earth. I have the privilege of claiming many Englishmen as dearest friends. Indeed much that I have learnt of the evil of British rule is due to the writings of frank and courageous Englishmen who have not hesitated to tell the unpalatable truth about that rule.

And why do I regard the British rule as a curse?

It has impoverished the dumb millions by a system of progressive exploitation and by a ruinously expensive military and civil administration which the country can never afford ...

The iniquities sampled above are maintained in order to carry on a foreign administration, demonstrably the most expensive in the world. Take your own salary. It is over Rs 21,000 per month, besides many other indirect additions. The British Prime Minister gets £5000 per year, i.e., over Rs 5400 per month at the present rate of exchange. You are getting over Rs 700 per day against India's average income of less than annas 2 per day. The Prime Minister gets Rs 180 per day against Great Britain's average income of nearly Rs 2 per day. Thus you are getting much over five thousand times India's average income. The British Prime Minister is getting only ninety times Britain's average income. On bended knees I ask you to ponder over this phenomenon ...

This letter is not in any way intended as a threat but is a simple and sacred duty, peremptory on a civil resister. ...

> I remain,
> Your sincere friend,
> M.K. Gandhi

H.E. Lord Irwin,
Viceroy's House,
New Delhi 3

> Young India *12-3-1930;* CWMG *Vol. 43, pp. 3, 5, and 8; E*

The Salt March

> Ahmedabad
> 9 March 1930

... THE MARCH will begin at 6.30 on the 12th morning ...

It is assumed that the village people will provide us food.

If provisions are supplied, the party will cook its own meal. The food supplied, whether cooked or uncooked, should be the simplest possible. Nothing more that *rotli* or *rotla* or kedgeree with vegetables and milk or curds, will be required. Sweets, even if prepared, will be declined. Vegetables should be merely boiled, and no oil spices and chillies, whether green or dry, whole or crushed, should be added or used in the cooking ...

The people should incur no expense on account of betel leaves, betel-nuts, or tea for the party.

... It is desirable that information under the following heads should be kept ready for each village:

1. Population: Number of women, men, Hindus, Muslims, Christians, Parsis, etc.
2. Number of untouchables.
3. If there is a school in the village, the number of boys and girls attending it.
4. Number of spinning-wheels.
5. The monthly sale of khadi.
6. Number of people wearing khadi exclusively.
7. Salt consumed per head; salt used for cattle, etc.
8. Number of cows and buffaloes in the village.
9. The amount of land revenue paid; at what rate per acre.
10. The area of the common grazing-ground if any.
11. Do the people drink? How far is the liquor shop from the village?
12. Educational and other special facilities, if any, for the untouchables.

It will be good if this information is written out on a sheet of paper neatly and handed to me immediately on our arrival.

Navajivan *9-3-1930;* CWMG *Vol. 43, pp. 33–5; G*

11 March 1930

THIS IS a battle to the finish. The Divine Hand is guiding it. It must be prolonged till the last man offers himself for satyagraha.

The Hindu *14-3-1920;* CWMG *Vol. 43, p. 38; E*

11 March 1930[47]

... LET NOBODY assume that after I am arrested there will be no one left to guide them. It is not I but Pandit Jawaharlal who is your guide. He has the capacity to lead. Though the fact is that those who have learnt the lesson of fearlessness and self-effacement need no leader, but if we lack these virtues, not even Jawaharlal will be able to produce them in us. ...

Young India *20-3-1930;* CWMG *Vol. 43, pp. 46–7*

12 March 1930

GOD WILLING, we shall set out exactly at 6.30. Those joining the march should all be on the spot at 6.20. If our first step is pure, all our subsequent steps will be good and pure ...

We are entering upon a life-and-death struggle, a holy war; we are performing an all-embracing sacrifice in which we wish to offer ourselves as oblation. If you prove incapable, the shame will be mine, not yours. You too have in you the strength that God has given me. The Self in us all is one and the same. In me it has awakened; in others, it has awakened partially.

From the manuscript of Mahadev Desai's Diary,
CWMG *Vol. 43, pp. 59–60; G*

... THE SALT tax must be repealed now. The fact that a sea of humanity has gathered and showered blessings upon us—for a distance of seven miles from the Ashram to the Chandola lake—a sight for the gods to see—that is a good omen. And, if we climb even one step, we shall readily be able to climb the other steps leading to the palace of Independence.

Navajivan *16-3-1930;* CWMG *Vol. 43, p. 63; G*

21 March 1930

... THERE ARE three hundred districts in India and in all these districts the Collector reigns supreme. It is truly a matter of shame to them and to all of us, if we only stop to think that these three hundred men should rule over 30 crore of us.

Navajivan *30-3-1930;* CWMG *Vol. 43, p. 116; G*

27 March 1930

... NONE SHOULD arrogantly believe that because everything has gone on well so far, we have as good as arrived at Dandi. Who knows what will happen tomorrow or the very next moment? ...

From today, the first batch will form the rear and the line will begin with the batch which is at the tail end now. ...

Navajivan *13-4-1930;* CWMG *Vol. 43, p. 140; G*

... I HAVE no right to criticize the Viceregal salary if we are costing the country, say, fifty times seven pice, the average daily income of our people. I have asked the workers to furnish me with an account of the expenses. And the way things are going, I should not be surprised if each of us is costing something near fifty times seven pice. What else can be the result if they will fetch for me from whatever source possible, the choicest oranges and grapes, if they will bring 120 when I should want 12 oranges, if when I need one pound of milk, they will produce three? What else can be the result if we would take all the dainties you may place before us under the excuse that we would hurt your feeling if we did not take them? You give us guavas and grapes and we eat them because they are a free gift from a princely farmer. ...

CWMG Vol. 43, p. 147; G

... I OBSERVED that you had provided for the night journey a heavy kerosene burner mounted on a stool which a poor labourer carried on his head. This was a humiliating sight. This man was being goaded to walk fast. I could not bear the sight. I therefore put on speed and outraced the whole company. But it was no use. The man was made to run after me. The humiliation was complete. If the weight had to be carried, I should have loved to see someone among ourselves carrying it. We would then soon dispense both with the stool and the burner. No labourer would carry such a load on his head. We rightly object to *begar* (forced labour). But what was this if it was not begar? Remember that in swaraj we would expect one drawn from the so-called lower class to preside over India's destiny. If then we do not quickly mend our ways, there is no swaraj such as you and I have put before the people.

From my outpouring you may not infer that I shall weaken in my resolve to carry on the struggle. It will continue no matter how co-workers or others act. For me there is no turning back whether I am alone or joined by thousands. I would rather die a dog's death and have my bones licked by dogs than that I should return to the Ashram a broken man.

(Turning to the women in the gathering) I admit that I have not well used the money you have given out of the abundance of your love. You are entitled to regard me as one of those wretches described in the verses sung in the beginning. Shun me.

Young India 3-4-1930; CWMG Vol. 43, p. 149; G

Chhaprabhatha
1 April 1930

EVERY DAY people tell me, 'Today you will certainly be arrested'. However, the tiger does not appear! The newspapers claim that I have become impatient at the Government not arresting me. This is partially true. ...

Prajabandhu *6-4-1930;* CWMG *Vol. 43, p. 161; G*

Dandi
5 April 1930

I WANT world sympathy in this battle of Right against Might.

CWMG *Vol. 43, p. 180*

Aat
8 April 1930

... WHEN YOU have collected the salt, do not waste a single grain of it. You should be determined to eat only that salt upon which no tax has been levied ...

Do not let go of salt when the police tries to snatch it from your hands. So long as your wrists are intact, do not let your fists be loosened. Your fists will acquire the strength of iron if you have faith in satyagraha.

Prajabandhu *13-4-1930;* CWMG *Vol. 43, p. 213; G*

Arrest At Midnight

Karadi
5 May 1930

The Bombay Chronicle reported on 6-5-1930:

THE MAGISTRATE proceeded to Gandhiji's hut and woke him up[48]. 'I have a warrant for your arrest, Mr Gandhi', said the Magistrate. Gandhiji asked politely:

I am not surprised, but will you read out the warrant to me?

The Magistrate complied with this request and read the following which was signed by Sir Frederick Sykes, Governor of Bombay.

'Whereas the Government view with alarm the activities of Mr M.K. Gandhi, they direct that he should be placed under restraint under Regulation 25 of 1827 and suffer imprisonment during the pleasure of the Government and be immediately removed to the Yeravda Central Jail.'

Gandhiji was smiling when the warrant was being read. He said:

I am prepared to accompany you, but will you allow me to have a wash and clean my teeth?

'With pleasure', said the Magistrate.

In the meantime, the whole Ashram was up, and everyone was anxious to have a parting 'darshan' of Gandhiji. Having finished his wash, Gandhiji came out of the cottage to say his prayers. The whole Ashram knelt down to recite the prayers while the police officers watched. Gandhiji himself led the chorus. He then collected his papers and gave them in charge of a volunteer whom he had chosen as Captain during his incarceration.

The Bombay Chronicle 6-5-1930; CWMG *Vol. 43*, p. *399*; E

Interview To 'The Daily Telegraph'[49]

Borivli
5 May 1930

Gandhi seemed surprised when he saw my companion and myself, for both of us were known to him. He greeted us in the most friendly manner.

'Have you a farewell message you would like to give, Mr Gandhi?' I asked. He replied:

Shall I give it now or shall I wait?

'You had better give it now', I replied.

He paused, seeming to be at a loss for words and somewhat dazed by events. Then he answered:

Tell the people of America to study the issues closely and to judge them on their merits.

'Have you any bitterness or ill-will towards anyone?' I asked.

None whatsoever; I had long expected to be arrested.

Do you think your arrest will lead to great disturbances throughout India?

No, I do not; in any case I can honestly say that I have taken every possible precaution to avert disturbances. ...

The Hindu 27-5-1930; CWMG Vol. 43, p. 400; E

Letter To E.E. Doyle[50]

Yeravda
10 May 1930

Dear Major Doyle,

Having thought over our conversation, I have come to the conclusion that I must avoid, as much as possible, the special privileges offered to me by the Government.

Books and newspapers I do not want through the government. Of newspapers I would send for these if permitted:

The Bombay Chronicle,
The Times of India,
Indian Social Reformer,
Modern Review,
Young India and *Navajivan* (Hindi and Gujarati).

If these are allowed, I take it that they will not be mutilated.

... Again, I hold radical views about prison treatment.

I have never taken kindly to the classification recently made. I hold that a murderer is just as much entitled to have his needs supplied as any other prisoner. What is therefore needed is not a mechanical makeshift, but a human adjustment.

One thing I must mention. I do feel the necessity of contact with the satyagrahi prisoners who are in this jail. It is wholly unnecessary, it is cruel, to isolate me from them.

Yours truly,
M.K. Gandhi
CWMG Vol. 43, pp. 401–2; E

To Devadas Gandhi[51]

Yeravda Mandir
13 May 1930

SINCE I do not know where you are, I write to you at the Ashram address. There is God to worry for us all and we need not, therefore, worry on account of one another. You know about me, that ultimately

I never come to harm. God always clears my path. Where else in the world would you find a sweeper like Him?. ...

Blessings from
Bapu
CWMG, *Vol. 43, p. 410; G*

To Kamala Nehru

Yeravda Mandir
30 June 1930

I WAS very happy to have your letter. You must not let your body become weak. It has to render much service. How is Indu[52] keeping now? Has she grown up a little?

My *pranam* to Mother and blessings to Sarup[53] and Krishna[54].

Blessings from
Bapu
Gandhi–Nehru Papers, *1930;* CWMG *Vol. 43, p. 452; H*

To Jayaprakash Narayan

Yeravda Mandir
27 September 1930

PRABHAVATI WRITES that you are not keeping well. After acquiring so much learning, why can't you keep your body perfectly healthy? It is essential to make an effort in this direction. What are you doing now?

Blessings from
Bapu
CWMG *Vol. 44, p. 176; H*

To Mira Behn

Yeravda Mandir
13 October 1930

... I AM still at the Gandiv[55] wheel, and my rapture continues, if anything, it has increased. I am spinning scientifically now, i.e., with a yard measure underneath the track of the yarn as it is drawn. I can draw 8 threads in one minute and I pull at least two feet to each draw. This means 240 rounds or 300 yards per hour. But of course, I do nothing of the sort in an hour but that is not because of any defect in the Gandiv. The less output is due to breakages and consequent waste of time. But since adopting the method of concentration, breakages have very considerably reduced. I therefore often reach 200 yards per hour which for me is very good ...

For the past two days I have gone back to raisins and dates just to see if the cold I have had anything to do with the vegetables. Whether it is a coincidence or what, it is as good as gone today. In any event health is quite good. Weight 104.

Love.

Bapu

CWMG Vol. 44, pp. 216–17; E

To Upton Sinclair[56]

Yeravda Central Prison
30 October 1930

Dear Friend,

I read your *Mammonart*[57] with absorbing interest and *Mental Radio*[58] with curiosity. The former has given me much to think, the latter did not interest me. Nobody in India would, I think, doubt the possibility of telepathy but most would doubt the wisdom of its material use.

I will now avail myself of your kind offer and ask you to send me your other volumes or such as you think I should read.

Yours sincerely,
M.K. Gandhi

Upton Sinclair, Esq.
Station P., Pasadena,
California.

CWMG Vol. 44, p. 263; E

To G.D. Birla

Yeravda Mandir
1 November 1930

Bhai Ghanshyamdasji,

This letter concerns Bhai Jayaprakash Narayan. He belongs to a respectable family of Bihar and he is also the son-in-law of Brijkishore

Babu, the noble worker of Bihar. Till now he was with Jawaharlal in the Congress office. He has studied in America for seven years. Now, after his mother's death, he feels the necessity of earning some money. He needs Rs 300 per mensem. In my opinion, Bhai Jayaprakash is a worthy young man. If possible, absorb him somewhere and pay him his requirements. ...

Yours,
Mohandas
CWMG *Vol. 44, p. 266; H*

Yeravda Mandir
16 December 1930

Bhai Ghanshyamdasji,
  ... Jayaprakash informs me that, although you are not recruiting any new people just now, he will be absorbed somewhere because of my recommendation. I certainly hold that Jayaprakash is a worthy young man but I do not wish that a post be created where none exists today. ...

Yours Mohandas,
CWMG *Vol. 45, p. 5; H*

To Narandas Gandhi

Tuesday Morning, 16 December 1930
... ASANAS AND pranayama may be of some slight help in steadying the mind and making it single-purposed, provided that they are practised to that end. Otherwise they are no better than other methods of physical training. They are very useful indeed as physical exercise and I believe that this type of exercise is good for the soul, and may be performed from a bodily standpoint. ...
CWMG *Vol. 45, pp. 2 and 3; G*

To Vanamala Parikh[59]

Yeravda Mandir
Saturday, 17 January 1931
WHAT AN intelligent girl you are! A sum which would seem difficult to other children, you found quite easy. Here is another, a little more

difficult, sum. If a girl spins 252 rounds in an hour, how many would she spin in twenty minutes?

Blessings from
Bapu
CWMG *Vol. 45, p. 97; G*

To Narandas Gandhi

Yeravda Mandir
Afternoon, Monday, 26 January 1931

WE WERE informed this morning that Pyarelal and I are to be released. When, therefore, you get this letter, we shall have been released, but I don't know where I shall be. My present feeling is that I shall be leaving peace and quiet and going into the midst of turmoil.

Blessings from
Bapu
CWMG *Vol. 45, p. 124; G*

Interview With The Viceroy—I

New Delhi
17 February 1931

THE VICEROY[60] had impressed me very well. He had impressed me as much as Lord Reading had done, except that Lord Reading was clever and he took undue advantage of my discussions with him. Lord Irwin talked to me in a friendly way and frankly admitted that it was his mistake that we had not met so far. The second thing he admitted was that the British public had been aroused the most by my movement. This attitude of his shows that he wants to make peace. He desires peace because he has been touched by the struggle. He is wondering how long he can allow the struggle to continue and feels that now he would be obliged to rely on the gun alone. ...

From the manuscript of Mahadev Desai's Diary;
CWMG *Vol. 45, p. 188; G*

Interview With The Viceroy—II

New Delhi
18 February 1931

... Viceroy: You think any Government in the world can tolerate disobedience of its laws?

MKG: I may enunciate a counter-proposition to it: No government in the world can enforce all its laws. Take the Sarda Act and Act III of 1885 of South Africa and the Gold Law ... I know that you have issued a circular that no action should he taken under the Sarda Act.

Viceroy: That is a confidential circular.

MKG: I do not want you to issue a public circular. We shall tell our people quietly that they can make and collect salt without any fear.

Viceroy: I am seized of your position. When you have your own government, you could repeal the Salt Act.

... If you attend the Round Table Conference and the results are not to your satisfaction, must you resume civil disobedience?

MKG: I will have to unless we feel that we shall get something from the changes proposed. Otherwise I shall have no choice but to resume the movement.

Viceroy: On further thought, I find this position dangerous for the government. How can we stultify ourselves like that? In that case, would it not be better that you do not attend the Round Table Conference?

... Suppose a committee of military experts proves to your satisfaction that India cannot defend herself without British troops, even then would you wish that that safeguard should be removed?

MKG: What do you mean by 'proving to my satisfaction'? I would invite German, American, and other experts and confront your military experts with them. If, after their discussions, I feel that we must retain the British army for some time, I would definitely agree to do so.

From the manuscript of Mahadev Desai's Diary;
Adapted from CWMG Vol. 45, pp. 197–199; G

A Discussion

New Delhi
18 February 1931

G.D. Birla: Did today's discussions give any cause for disappointment?

MKG: No, he was as sweet as before. We had a few sharp exchanges, but they were of little moment. There were one or two small but rich titbits which cannot be made public, but which will give you an idea of how cordial the talks had been. Once he told me that it was his dream to take me to England and introduce me to members of all the parties there. He appealed to me to forget about civil disobedience and to have faith in their sincerity and proceed accordingly. Then as I was going to his bathroom, he accompanied me and said: 'Now tell me whether I did not do well in not arresting you in your Ashram?' I said: 'How do we know it? A crowd of thousands had assembled in the Ashram, and I heard that a special was waiting for me and that I would be arrested at 12 o'clock. So I peacefully went to sleep.' At this, the Viceroy had a hearty laugh. I continued: 'Many friends had thought that this salt movement would fizzle out, and said that Mahatma Gandhi would get tired in 20 days or so and that the Government would not take any notice of the movement. But who knew what was going to happen?' The Viceroy said: 'You planned a fine strategy round the issue of salt'. ...

CWMG *Vol. 45, pp. 199–200; G*

Interview With The Viceroy—III

19 February 1931

Viceroy: ... I shall repeat this in your presence so that you can correct me if I make a mistake anywhere: You have promised that even though the conference were to break up as a result of your being dissatisfied with the progress, you would not resume civil disobedience until after the conclusion of the conference.

MKG: Yes, I have.

Viceroy: I am very glad; now could I have a further promise from you that you would not resume civil disobedience until after the conclusion of the proceedings in the Parliament?

MKG: I am afraid I cannot promise that. ...

From the manuscript of Mahadev Desai's Diary;
CWMG *Vol. 45, p. 206; G*

Smuts And Irwin

New Delhi
February 1931

'AH, NOW Your Excellency treats[61] me like General Smuts treated me in South Africa. You do not deny that I have an equitable claim, but you advance unanswerable reasons from the point of view of the Government why you cannot meet it. I drop the demand.'

Halifax's memoirs Fulness of Days, *pp. 148–9; E*

Drafting For Irwin

New Delhi
February 1931

'I have that reputation[62]'.

Quoted in Mira Behn's The Spirit's Pilgrimage, *p. 123; E*

To The Viceroy[63]

1 Daryaganj, Delhi,
7 March 1931

Dear Friend,

Your very affectionate letter has touched me very deeply. It will always be a joy to me to renew the heart-to-heart talks, only now, let us hope, under less trying circumstances. Your kindly nature made the trial itself a pleasing work to which I had learnt to look forward. I heartily join in your prayer—may God answer it.

I am,
Your sincere friend,
M.K. Gandhi
CWMG *Vol. 45, p. 268; E*

A Discussion[64]

... I TALKED about Bhagat Singh. I told him: 'This has no connection with our discussion, and it may even be inappropriate on my part to mention it. But if you want to make the present atmosphere more favourable, you should suspend Bhagat Singh's execution.' The Viceroy liked this very much. He said: 'I am very grateful to you that you have put this thing before me in this manner. Commutation of sentence is a difficult thing, but suspension is certainly worth considering.'

I said about Bhagat Singh ... 'I am putting this matter before you as a humanitarian issue and desire suspension of sentence in order that there may not be unnecessary turmoil in the country. I myself would release him, but I cannot expect any Government to do so. I would not take it ill even if you do not give any reply on this issue' ...

CWMG *Vol. 45, p. 200; G*

Interview To The Press

Delhi
21 March 1931

... Q. Do you expect to hold the National Congress to the terms of the truce with Lord Irwin?

A. Yes, but if Bhagat Singh is hanged, as it now seems almost certain, it may have highly unfavourable repercussions upon the younger element in the Congress who may attempt to split the Congress.

Q. Do you entertain any hope that Bhagat Singh may be saved at the last minute?

A. Yes, but it is a very distant hope.

... Q. How long do you expect to live?

A. Until eternity.

Q. Do you believe in immortality?

A. Yes, reincarnation and transmigration of souls are fundamentals of the Hindu religion. ...

The Hindu *22-3-1931;* CWMG *Vol. 45, pp. 318–20; E*

To The Viceroy

1 Daryaganj, Delhi
23 March 1931

Dear Friend,

It seems cruel to inflict this letter on you, but the interest of peace demands a final appeal. Though you were frank enough to tell me that there was little hope of your commuting the sentence of death on Bhagat Singh and two others, you said you would consider my submission of Saturday ...

Political murders have been condoned before now. It is worth while saving these lives, if thereby many other innocent lives are likely to be saved and may be even revolutionary crime almost stamped out.

Since you seem to value my influence such as it is in favour of peace, do not please unnecessarily make my position, difficult as it is, almost too difficult for future work.

Execution is an irretrievable act. If you think there is the slightest chance of error of judgment, I would urge you to suspend for further review an act that is beyond recall.

If my presence is necessary, I can come. Though I may not speak[65] I may hear and write what I want to say.

'Charity never faileth'.

I am
Your sincere friend
CWMG *Vol. 45, pp. 333–4; E*

The Execution Of Bhagat Singh And Comrades

New Delhi
23 March 1931

BHAGAT SINGH and his companions have been executed and have become martyrs. Their death seems to have been a personal loss to many. I join in the tributes paid to the memory of these young men. And yet I must warn the youth of the country against following their example. We should not utilize our energy, our spirit of sacrifice, our labours and our indomitable courage in the way they have utilized theirs. This country must not be liberated through bloodshed. ...

CWMG Vol. 45, pp. 335–6; G

The Revolutionary Road

23 April 1931

THE OPEN letter written by 'One of the Many' is the late Sukhdev's letter. Sjt. Sukhdev was Sardar Bhagat Singh's comrade. The letter was delivered to me after his death. Want of time prevented me from giving the letter earlier publication ...

The writer is not 'one of the many'. Many do not seek the gallows for political freedom. However condemnable political murder may be, it is not possible to withhold recognition of the love of the country and the courage which inspire such awful deeds ...

The writer does me less than justice when he says that I have made no more than sentimental appeals to the revolutionaries to call off their movement, and I claim on the contrary that I have given them hard facts which, though they have been often repeated in these columns, will bear recapitulation:

1. The revolutionary activity has not brought us near our goal.
2. It has added to the military expenditure in the country.
3. It has given rise to reprisals on the part of the Government without doing any good.
4. Whenever revolutionary murder has taken place, it has for a time and in that place demoralized the people.
5. It has in no way contributed to mass awakening.
6. Its effect on the masses has been doubly bad in that they had to bear the burden ultimately of additional expense and the indirect effect of Government wrath.
7. Revolutionary murder cannot thrive in the Indian soil, Indian tradition, as history teaches us, being unfavourable to the growth of political violence.
8. If the revolutionaries seek to convert the masses to their

method, we would have to wait for an indefinitely long time for it to permeate the masses and then to gain freedom.

9. If the method of violence ever becomes popular, it is bound to recoil, as it has done in other countries, on our own heads.

10. The revolutionaries have an ocular demonstration of the efficacy of the opposite method, i.e., non-violence, which has gone on in spite of sporadic cases of violence on their part and in spite even of violence occasionally done by the so-called votaries of non-violence.

11. Revolutionaries should accept my testimony when I tell them that their activity has not only not done any good to the movement of non-violence, but it has on the contrary harmed the cause. In other words, if I had a completely peaceful atmosphere we would have gained our end already. ...

Young India 23-4-1931; CWMG Vol. 46, pp. 29–30; E

Interview To The Press

17 May 1931

Q. Supposing you or the Congress do not attend the Round Table Conference and the Conference produces a constitution which is approved by Parliament. What would be the attitude of the Congress?

A. I may speak on behalf of the Congress that it will examine the scheme and if good, will certainly work it.

Q. Do you believe in self-determination?

A. Yes.

Q. Would you allow any province to exercise self-determination and separate herself from India?

A. I shall fight through reason but shall not impose my will by force of arms.

... Q. So you will really go to the Round Table Conference, whether early or late, when those two problems are out of the way?

A. Yes, certainly. And I shall be very pleased to go, because I hope that when I get to England I shall find the British people not uninterested in what I have to say and open to conviction by what I tell them. Or, at the worst, I hope I shall persuade them that I am only a harmless lunatic ...

The Hindustan Times *20-5-1931 and* The Statesman *19-5-1931;*
CWMG *Vol. 46, pp. 164–6; E*

Letter To M. Rebello & Sons

31 May 1931

Gentlemen,

I have your letter of 22nd instant[66]. I have no copyright in my portraits but I am unable to give the consent you require.

Yours faithfully,
CWMG *Vol. 46, p. 262; E*

Save Me From My Admirers

Bardoli
4 June 1931

A CORRESPONDENT writes from far off Cape Comorin:

... In the car festivals here the Image is placed in the car and taken in procession. One set of people want that your photo should be placed side by side with the Image and taken in procession. Another set of riper men say that you would not like to be treated as God ...

Another from Mathura sends me a horrible portrait representing me as lying stretched on the coil of the thousand-mouthed serpent with the roll of non-co-operation in one hand and the spinning-wheel suspended on the other arm. My poor wife is massaging my legs. The other celebrities have also been pressed into service. I must not violate the reader's feelings by describing the other features. Suffice it to say that the picture is a caricature of the Vaishnavite legend representing Vishnu resting on the coil of Sheshanag ... If they have any regard for my feelings, let the organizers of the car festival who would put my portrait in the car and the publishers of the offending picture desist from their activity. There are many other healthy ways of giving expression to and promoting patriotic sentiment. ...

Young India *4-6-1931,* CWMG *Vol. 46, p. 304; E*

To Amtussalam[67]

8 June 1931

My dear Amtul,

Never mind your incorrect English. But you must soon write Hindi. If you write a clear Urdu hand I can read it. You must cultivate a brief style.

Love.
Bapu
CWMG Vol. 46, p. 352; E

A Discussion[68]

When talking about members of the Working Committee, Subhas Bose[69] was mentioned.

The Viceroy said: 'Subhas is not a member of the Working Committee.' I said, 'No, he is not. And he is my opponent and will denounce me; still, if he wants to attend, we must give him a chance to do so'.

The Viceroy said that he would think about this suggestion too.

CWMG Vol. 45, p. 200; G

A Countryman's Advice

... If I go to England I shall go as a representative and nothing more, nothing less. I must, therefore, appear not as the English would have me but as my representative character demands ... I can therefore appear neither in English costume nor in that of the polished Nehrus. In spite of the closest bond between us it would have been just as ludicrous for me to dress as Pandit Motilalji did as it would have been for him to appear in loin cloth ...

Young India 9-7-1931; CWMG Vol. 47, pp. 119–20; E

To The Press

Before 15 July 1931

Q. Will you be taking some advisers?

A. My adviser is God. I am going to take no advisers. If I had any idea to take advisers, I would have taken them as delegates. I

would take with me my son Devadas Gandhi, Mahadev Desai,
Pyarelal, Miss Slade, and none else.

The Hindu 20-7-1931; CWMG Vol. 47, pp. 133–4; E

Foul Play

THE WORST feature of the attempted assassination[70] of Sir Ernest
Hotson the Acting Governor of the Bombay Presidency was, that the
act was done by a student of the College which had invited His
Excellency when as its honoured guest he was being shown round
the College premises. It was as though a host was injuring his guest
under his own roof. The canon recognized throughout the world
is that the deadliest enemy, when he is under one's roof as guest,
is entitled to protection from all harm. The act of the student was
therefore essentially foul play without a single redeeming feature ...

The Congress is a power in the land, but I warn Congressmen that
it will soon lose all its charm if they betray their trust and encourage
the Bhagat Singh cult whether in thought, word or deed. ...

Young India 30-7-1931, CWMG Vol. 47, pp. 231–32; E

To C. Rajagopalachari

Ahmedabad
15 August 1931

YOU ARE going through a terrible trial. But I know that in the midst
of it all you can remain cheerful and unruffled. I would not think of
tearing you away from Papa[71]. So long therefore as she needs your
personal nursing, I have no doubt that your duty is to be by her.

What shall I write to you about the dramatic developments? I hope
your reasoning fully endorses the decision. I have personally not a
shadow of a doubt about it. I wish you would be able to attend the
next meeting of the Working Committee[72], if I am free till then. ...

Syt. C. Rajagopalachariar
C/o Syt. A.V. Raman
Lloyd Corner
Royapettah (Madras)

CWMG Vol. 47, pp. 296–7; E

To C. Rajagopalachari

On the Frontier Down Mail
28 August 1931

Dear C.R.,

What shall I write to you? Do you know that not a day has passed but I have thought of you and also felt the need of your presence? But I was not to have it and as ill luck will have it, I cannot have even a few words with you before sailing. There are two men whom I would like by my side in London, you and Jawaharlal. ...

How is Papa? I do hope she is better.

CWMG *Vol. 47, p. 372; E*

On Leaving For London

MKG: What's all this?[73]

Mira: Bapu, these have been put together in haste and in the last-minute confusion before our departure ...

MKG: If you want to travel with such luggage you should live with those who live like that. All these suitcases and the camp-bed should be offloaded at Aden and shipped back to Bombay.

The Spirit's Pilgrimage, *p. 123; E*

On Arriving In London[74]

September 1931

I REPRESENT, without any fear of contradiction, the dumb, semi-starved millions of my country, India.

G.D. Birla[75]: I suppose you have thought of what you want to say.

MKG: I am absolutely blank. But perhaps God will help me in collecting my thoughts at the proper time. After all, we have to talk like simple men. I have no desire to appear extra intelligent. Like a simple villager all that I have to say is: 'We want independence'.

I have an invitation to attend His Majesty's reception[76]. I am feeling so heartsick and sore about the happenings in India that I have no heart in attending such functions, and if I had come in my own right I should not have hesitated to come to a decision. But, as I am a guest, I am hesitating.

King: Why did you boycott my son?[77]

MKG: Not your son, Your Majesty, but the official representative of the British Crown.

King: I won't have you stirring up trouble in my empire. My government won't stand for it.

MKG: Your Majesty must not expect me to argue the point.

Tendulkar Vol. III, p. 126

Encouragement[78] is given not by Kings but by God.

Interview To 'The Evening Standard'

London

12 September 1931

IF INDIA gains her freedom through truth and non-violence, I feel convinced it will be the largest contribution of the age to the peace of the world.

... Why do I come here? Because I have given my word of honour to Lord Irwin. No man ever lost anything by keeping his word of honour. I have kept mine. What do I mean by peace? The dictionary will tell you it is the opposite of war. We have had enough turbulence and strife in India. Now we want peace. ...

CWMG Vol. 48, p. 1; E

Speech At Federal Structure Committee[79]

London

15 September 1931

Lord Chancellor, Your Highnesses and Friends,

... I am but a poor humble agent acting on behalf of the Indian National Congress. And it might be as well to remind ourselves of what the Congress stands for and what it is. You will then extend your sympathy to me, because I know that the burden that rests upon my shoulders is really very great ...

... I said to myself whilst I was nearing the shores of your beautiful island, perchance it might be possible for me to convince the British Ministers that India as a valuable partner, not held by force but by the silken cord of love—an India of that character—might conceivably be of real assistance to you in balancing your Budget, not for one occasion but for many years. What cannot two nations do—one a handful, but brave, with a record for bravery perhaps unequalled, a nation noted for having fought slavery, a nation that has at least claimed times without number to protect the weak—and another a very ancient nation, counted in millions, with a glorious and ancient past, representing at the present moment two great cultures, the Islamic and Hindu cultures; if you will, also containing not a small but a very large number of Christian population; and certainly absorbing the whole of the splendid Zoroastrian stock, in numbers almost beneath contempt, but in philanthropy and enterprise almost unequalled and certainly unsurpassed. ...

CWMG *Vol. 48, pp. 13, 14, and 19*

A Race Half Way

London
1931

Ben Platten, who works with Miss Lester ... came one day with a book in which he wanted Gandhiji's autograph:

MKG:　How many children have you?
Platten:　Eight, sir, four sons and four daughters.
MKG:　I have four sons so I can race with you half way.

The Nation's Voice—Part II, *by Mahadev Desai,* Navajivan, *1931*

Interview With Charlie Chaplin[80]

London
22 September 1931

... THE VERY first question Chaplin asked was why Gandhi was against machinery. The question delighted Gandhi who explained to him in detail why the six months' unemployment of the whole peasant population of

India made it important for him to restore them to their former subsidiary industry (of hand-spinning).

Charlie Chaplin: Is it then only as regards cloth?

MKG: Precisely. In cloth and food every nation should be self-contained. We were self-contained and want to be that again. England with her large-scale production has to look for a market elsewhere. We call it exploitation. And an exploiting England is a danger to the world, but if that is so, how much more so would be an exploiting India, if she took to machinery and produced cloth many times in excess of its requirements.

CC: So the question is confined only to India? But supposing you had in India the independence of Russia, and you could find other work for your unemployed and ensure equitable distribution of wealth, you would not then despise machinery? You would subscribe to shorter hours of work and more leisure for the worker?

MKG: Certainly.

CC: Naturally I am in sympathy with India's aspirations and struggle for freedom. Nonetheless, I am somewhat confused by your abhorrence of machinery.

MKG: I understand. But before India can achieve those aims, she must first rid herself of English rule. Machinery in the past has made us dependent on England, and the only way we can rid ourselves of the dependence is to boycott all goods made by machinery.

Young India *8-10-1931*; *Chaplin's* My Autobiography;

CWMG *Vol. 48, pp. 47–8; E*

To Ujjal Singh[81]

88 Knightsbridge

London, W.

1 October 1931

Dear Sardar Ujjal Singh,

I have to acknowledge with thanks your letter of the 30th ult.

... It has been a belief of a lifetime with me that he who will serve the national cause should demand no rights and make room for rights for those who demand rights, but I never meant that the blank cheque to the Mussalmans should mean a neglect, wholly or partially, of Sikhs or any other just claims.

Yours sincerely,

Sardar Ujjal Singh
St. James' Court
Buckingham Gate, S.W. 1

CWMG Vol. 48, pp. 98–9; E

Extracts From Proceedings Of Minorities Committee Meeting

London
1 October 1931

Mr Gandhi: ... I let out no secret when I inform this Committee that His Highness and the other friends with whom I was closeted last night laid upon my shoulders the burden of calling representatives of the different groups together and holding consultations with a view to arriving at some final settlement. If this proposal of mine commends itself to you, Prime Minister, and to the rest of the members of this Committee, I shall be glad ...

H.H. The Aga Khan: I have pleasure in seconding the proposal.

Sardar Ujjal Singh: I rise to give my whole-hearted support to this proposal, and I share the hope that by this means we may come to some understanding, given goodwill on both sides.

Dr Ambedkar: I do not wish to create any difficulty in our making every possible attempt to arrive at some solution of the problem with which this Committee has to deal, and if a solution can be arrived at by the means suggested by Mahatma Gandhi, I, for one, will have no objection to that proposal.

But there is just this one difficulty with which I, as representing the Depressed Classes, am faced. I do not know what sort of committee Mahatma Gandhi proposes to appoint to consider this question during the period of adjournment, but I suppose that the Depressed Classes will be represented on this Committee.

Mr Gandhi: Without doubt[82] ...

CWMG Vol. 48, pp. 102–3; E

At A Birthday Luncheon[83]

London
2 October 1931

... IT IS imagined that you have attended a lunch. My sympathies are wholly with you. I am accustomed to English lunches not through the taste but through the eyes, and when I saw this fruit-laden table, I realized what a sacrifice it was for you to take what is an apology for a luncheon. I hope that the spirit of sacrifice will forbear until tea-time comes and you provide yourselves with any little delicacies that English hotels and restaurants provide for you. But behind this apparent joke there is also seriousness. I know that you have sacrificed something. Some of you have sacrificed much for advocating the cause of India's independence—understanding the word 'independence' in its full English sense. But it may be that you will be called upon, if you continue your advocacy of India's cause, to make much larger sacrifices. ...

Young India *15-10-1931;* CWMG *Vol. 48, p. 108; E*

Interview With Maria Montessori[84]

London
October 1931

MKG (greeting her): We are members of the same family.

Madame Montessori: I bring you the greetings of children.

MKG: If you have children I have children too. Friends in India ask me to imitate you. I say to them, no. I should not imitate you but should assimilate you and the fundamental truth underlying your method. ...

Young India *22-10-1931;* CWMG *Vol. 48, p. 128; E*

Interview To Evelyn Wrench[85]

London
(On or after) 17 October 1931

... Q. I have been very much struck with your wonderful vitality. Few men of sixty-two can be so full of energy. I have read in the papers some of the things about your diet. Would you tell me just what your daily bill of fare is?

A. Certainly. I am sure that most people eat much too much. I have never felt better than I do on my present regimen and I have a horror of drugs and medicines. This is my daily bill of fare: For my breakfast at 8 o'clock I have sixteen ounces of milk and four oranges, for my luncheon at 1 o'clock I again have sixteen ounces of milk, grapes, pears, or other fruit. My evening meal is between 5 and 6 o'clock. I eat a teaspoonful of almond paste, twenty or thirty dates, several tomatoes, and a lettuce or other salad. This avoids indigestion. As you will note, I eat no starch and no cereals. ...

The Spectator *24-10-1931*; CWMG *Vol. 48, pp. 175, 180–1; E*

To Albert Einstein[86]

London
18 October 1931

Dear Friend,

I was delighted to have your beautiful letter sent through Sundaram[87]. It is a great consolation to me that the work I am doing finds favour in your sight. I do indeed wish that we could meet face to face and that too in India at my Ashram.

Yours sincerely,
M.K. Gandhi
CWMG *Vol. 48, p. 182; E*

'You Are No Better Than Doorkeepers'

1931[88]

WHO IS it that can say that you have conferred benefits on India? We or you? The toad beneath the harrow knows where the harrow pinches. A series of men, Dadabhai Naoroji, Pherozeshah Mehta, Ranade, Gokhale—who used to dote on you, who were proud of the British contact and of the benefits conferred by your civilization— do you know that they are all agreed in saying that you have on the whole done harm to India? When you go, you will have left us an impoverished and emasculated people, and the shades of all who loved you will ask, what have you done during these years of tutelage? You must realize that we cannot afford to have doorkeepers at your rate of wages, for you are no better than doorkeepers and a nation with an income of two pence a day per head cannot pay those wages.

The Nation's Voice—Part II, *by Mahadev Desai*, Navajivan, *1931*

At The Majlis[89]

Oxford
24 October 1931

... I HAVE the highest regard for Dr Ambedkar. He has every right to be bitter. That he does not break our heads is an act of self-restraint on his part. He is today so very much saturated with suspicion that he cannot see anything else. He sees in every Hindu a determined opponent of the untouchables, and it is quite natural. The same thing happened to me in my early days in South Africa where I was hounded out by the Europeans wherever I went. It is quite natural for him to vent his wrath. But the separate electorates that he seeks will not give him social reform. He may himself mount to power and position, but nothing good will accrue to the untouchables. I can say all this with authority, having lived with the untouchables and having shared their joys and sorrows all these years.

Young India *12-11-1931,* CWMG *Vol. 40, pp. 232–4; E*

Answers To Questions[90]

Eton and Oxford
On or after 24 October 1931

... Q. Do you say that you are completely fit for independence?
A. If we are not, we will try to be. ...

Young India *12-11-1931;* CWMG *Vol. 48, pp. 223–5; E*

Q. How far would you cut India off from the Empire?
A. From the Empire entirely: from the British nation not at all.
Q. How would you distinguish exploitation from trading with a nation?
A. There are two tests: (1) The other nation must want our goods which should in no case be dumped on it against her will. (2) The trade should not be backed by the navy.

CWMG *Vol. 48, p. 229; E*

Q.[91, 92] Why are you so uncharitable to those who drink?
A. Because I am charitable to those who suffer from the effects of the curse.

Q. Do you ever suffer from nerves?[93]

A. Ask Mrs Gandhi. She will tell you that I am on my best behaviour with the world but not with her.

Q. Is not the charkha a mediaeval device?

A. We were doing many things in the middle ages which were quite wise.

Q. What is the chief obstacle in the way of swaraj?

A. It is the unwillingness of the British officials to part with power.

Young India 12-11-1931; CWMG Vol. 48, p. 231; E

Q.[94] Could you please tell us how an Englishman going to India can co-operate with Indians and serve India?

A. Well, the first thing he should do is to see Charlie Andrews and ask him what he did and what he has gone through to serve India ...

The Hindu 2-11-1931; Young India 19-11-1931;
CWMG Vol. 48, p. 265; E

London
10 November 1931

A Negro student:[95] You love Englishman as much as an Indian and yet you dislike the British Government. Now British people make up the Government.

MKG: ... I have learnt from domestic law that, if I have humanity in me, I should love the Britisher whom God has made. And yet I detest his method and am doing my best to destroy his method. ...

From the manuscript of Mahadev Desai's Diary;
CWMG Vol. 48, pp. 279 and 281; E

Telegram To Lord Irwin

London
13 November 1931

CONFERENCE CRUMBLING down. Leaving London next Thursday[96].

The Hindustan Times 16-11-1931; CWMG Vol. 48, p. 291; E

Speech At Minorities Committee Meeting

London
13 November 1931

Prime Minister and Fellow Delegates,

It is not without very considerable hesitation and shame that I take part in the discussion on the minorities question. I have not been able to read with the care and attention that it deserves the memorandum[97] sent to the Delegates on behalf of certain minorities and received this morning.

... At the present moment if you were to examine the register of the Congress, if you were to examine the records of the prisons of India, you would find that the Congress represented and represents on its register a very large number of Mohammedans. Several thousand Mohammedans went to jail last year under the banner of the Congress. The Congress today has several Mohammedans on its register. The Congress has thousands of untouchables on its register. The Congress has Indian Christians also on its register. I do not know that there is a single community which is not represented on the Congress on its register. With all deference to the Nawab Sahib of Chhatari, even landlords and even mill-owners and millionaires are represented there ...

... I would not sell the vital interests of the untouchables even for the sake of winning the freedom of India. I claim myself in my own person to represent the vast mass of the untouchables. Here I speak not merely on behalf of the Congress, but I speak on my own behalf, and I claim that I would get, if there was a referendum of the untouchables, their vote, and that I would top the poll ...

... Those who speak of the political rights of untouchables do not know their India, do not know how Indian society is today constructed, and therefore I want to say with all the emphasis that I can command that, if I was the only person to resist this thing, I would resist it with my life.

CWMG *Vol. 48, pp. 293, 295–8; E*

Answers To More Questions[98]

London
22 November 1931

Q. Is the Conference certainly doomed to failure?

A. It is ungrateful to say so. But I see very little warrant for success.

Q. Don't you think the Government having allowed the discussion will now do something? Will the change in the Government make any difference?

A. I expected them to do certainly better, but I do not know that they have made up their minds to transfer power. ...

Young India 3-12-1931; CWMG Vol. 48, p. 331; E

At The Plenary Session

London
1 December 1931[99]

Prime Minister and friends,

... the National Congress of India is a daily-growing organization ... (its) message penetrates the remotest villages of India ...on given occasions the Congress has been able to demonstrate its influence over and among these masses who inhabit 700, 000 villages.

And yet here I see that the Congress is treated as one of the Parties. I do not mind it; I do not regard it as a calamity for the Congress; but I do regard it as a calamity for the purpose of doing the work for which we have gathered together here ...

... I shall hope against hope, I shall strain every nerve to achieve an honourable settlement for my country if I can do so without having to put the millions of my countrymen and countrywomen and even children through this ordeal of fire. It can be a matter of no joy and comfort to me to lead them on again to a fight of that character, but if a further ordeal of fire has to be our lot, I shall approach that with the greatest joy and with the greatest consolation that I was doing what I felt to be right, the country was doing what it felt to be right, and the country will have the additional satisfaction of knowing that it was not at least taking lives, it was giving lives; it was not making the British people directly suffer, it was suffering. ...

CWMG *Vol. 48, pp. 356–7, 360; E*

Interview To Edmond Demeter

London
Before 5 December 1931

Q. I thought you were the sworn enemy of all machines. How does it happen that you use a watch?[100]

A. I must know what time it is ... If I use a watch, that does not mean that I am its slave. But when it is a question of the organized machine, man becomes its slave and loses all of the values with which the Lord endowed him.

Q. Excuse me, if I interrupt you. You speak of God. Your God is not mine.

A. But your God is also mine for I believe in your God, in spite of the fact that you do not believe in mine.

Q. In your opinion, what world figure has exercised the greatest and best influence upon the twentieth century?

A. Tolstoy. He alone.

The Hindustan Times *17-12-1931;* CWMG *Vol. 48, pp. 386–8; E*

... Perhaps, there is no nation on earth equal to the British in the capacity for self-deception. ...

Gandhi in London, James D. Hunt, *Promilla & Co.,*
New Delhi, 1978, p. 228; CWMG *Vol. 48, p. 435; E*

Diary, 1931

On the way to Rome, 11 December Friday
SPUN 178 rounds. Talk with Rolland; Sir Cowasji met me. Left Villeneuve at 2.30. Girls from Indu's school called. Was provided a State car in Milan. Large crowds had gathered on the way.

CWMG *Vol. 48, p. 466; G*

Rome, 12 December Saturday
SPUN 204 rounds. Arrived at Rome at 8.30 in the morning. Received letter to the effect that the Pope could not receive me. Three of us

stayed with General Moris, the others in a hotel. Went to see the Vatican in the afternoon.[101] At 6 o'clock Mussolini. £20 to Maud.

CWMG *Vol. 48, p. 466; G*

13 December, Sunday
IT WAS not without a wrench that I could tear myself away from that scene[102] of living tragedy. I saw there at once that nations like individuals could only be made through the agony of the Cross and in no other way.

CWMG *Vol. 48, p. 434*

On The Way to Brindisi, 13 December, Sunday
SPUN 180 rounds. Tolstoy's daughter came in the morning. ...

CWMG *Vol. 48 p. 466; G*

Discussion With Sukhotina Tolstoy

Rome
13 December 1931[103]

Sukhotina Tolstoy[104]: I have been long looking forward to an opportunity of meeting you. If my father had been alive, he would have been delighted to hear of your non-violent battle for freedom.

MKG: I am sure. And are you the daughter who wrote that famous letter of your father to me?

(That was another daughter, a fact which led to inquiry about Tolstoy's children.)

ST: Six of us are still living. The two daughters accept my father's principles, but the four sons do not. You know my father allowed every one of us the fullest liberty of thought and action and, whilst these brothers of mine revered my father, they were not prepared to accept his principles. I was a friend of Romain Rolland.

MKG: Why 'was?' Are you not a friend now?

ST: No, I used to be a great friend of his until two years ago. He wrote to me fairly frequently and I also used to write to him.

MKG: But now?

ST: But now I find that he is in sympathy with Bolshevism and

Bolshevik methods. I do not quarrel with their goal, but their doctrine that the end justifies the means seems to me to be frightful. How can Romain Rolland, a believer in non-violence, have any sympathy with them?

MKG: Supposing what you say is true, is it not all the more necessary that you should write to him and tell him what you feel about his views?. ...

Young India 14-1-1932; CWMG Vol. 48, pp. 422–3; E

Diary, 1931

On Board Ship, 14 December, Monday
Spun 137 rounds. Reached Brindisi in the morning. Evans[105], Rogers[106] returned. S.S. *Pilsna* sailed at 12.30. The deck is no good, hence there will be some inconvenience. It is quite cold here. Vithalbhai is with me.

On Board Ship, 15 December, Tuesday
Spun 172 rounds. A little conversation with the Captain.

CWMG Vol. 48, p. 466; G

To Romain Rolland

S.S. *'Pilsna'*
20 December 1931

Dear Friend and Brother,

I beg you to write to the daughter of Tolstoy and satisfy her curiosity concerning Bolshevism ... Mussolini is a riddle to me. ...

With deep love,

Yours,
M.K. Gandhi

CWMG Vol. 48, pp. 429–30; E

Diary, 1931

On Board Ship, 21 December, Monday
Spun 170 rounds. We are nearing Aden. Was able to sleep a little less during the day today. Wrote an article for *Indian News*. Wrote letters. Completed the one to Mussolini.

On Board Ship, 22 December, Tuesday

SPUN 175 rounds. Arrived at Aden at 12.30 in the morning; went ashore; there was a meeting; visited Suraj's residence. Met the Residence Col. Riley. Returned to the ship at 4.30. Collected about Rs 4,000. Today I have pain in the left side of the chest. The steamer weighed anchor at 5 o'clock.

On Board Ship, 23 December Wednesday

SPUN 171 rounds. Did not feel all right today. Ate only figs in the afternoon, took nothing in the evening. Slept well during the day. Completed an article for *Young India*. A Bulgarian artist came to paint my portrait.

CWMG *Vol. 48, p. 467; G*

Interview To Reuters

S.S. *'Pilsna'*
27 December 1931

AS I approach the shores of India, I am weighed down with a sense of the tremendous responsibility even as I was upon approaching London. Only this time the responsibility is a thousandfold greater.

I shall therefore take no hasty step. I shall exhaust every resource at my disposal before advising India once more to go through the fire of suffering. ...

The Hindu *28-12-1931;* CWMG *Vol. 48, p. 440; E*

To Rabindranath Tagore[107]

Laburnum Road
Bombay
3 January 1932

Dear Gurudev,

I am just stretching my tired limbs on the mattress and as I try to steal a wink of sleep I think of you. I want you to give your best to the sacrificial fire that is being lighted.

With love,

M.K. Gandhi
CWMG *Vol. 48, p. 489; E*

Interview To 'The Bombay Chronicle'

Bombay
3 January 1932

WHAT I would ask the nation to do after my arrest[108], is to wake up from its sleep; ...

The Bombay Chronicle *4-1-1932;* CWMG *Vol. 48, p. 490; E*

To Mira Behn

Yeravda Prison[109]
5 January 1932

Chiranjivi Mira,

... Please send me the larger size flask. It will be useful for keeping hot water, saving the labour of warders early morning. ...

Bapu
CWMG *Vol. 49, p. 2*

A Parrot In A Cage

Yeravda
3 February 1932

Bhai Valji[110],

No one in the Ashram can keep a parrot in a cage.

If someone happens to do it, the manager will free the parrot which is bound to fly away once it gets an opportunity.

Blessings from
Bapu
CWMG *Vol. 49, p. 60; H*

To M.G. Bhandari[111]

6 March 1932

Dear Major Bhandari,

You have kindly given me a copy of the fresh instructions issued by the Government about the weekly visits.

... there should be a common definition of the adjective 'political' between the Government and me. I take 'political' to mean those who are politically minded and are actually taking part in politics as *apart from civil resistance*. For if by 'political' is meant those who have been heretofore imprisoned as civil resisters or are believers in the doctrine of civil resistance, then there is no non-political inmate in the Ashram. If, however, the meaning is (as) I have given it, there are only three political inmates. I mean Sjts. Mahadev Desai, Pyarelal, and Devadas Gandhi. But if I may not see the first two, I may not see Devadas Gandhi for they are like Devadas to me. ...

Yours sincerely,

M.K. Gandhi

CWMG *Vol. 49, p. 182; E*

To Indu N. Parekh[112]

Yeravda,

24 March 1932

Yours is an interesting question.

The Mahabharata is a poem and not history.

Blessings from

Bapu

Mahadevbhaini Diary *Vol. 1;* CWMG *Vol. 49, p. 232; G*

A Talk About Santiniketan

Yeravda

25 March 1932

MKG: As for Tagore, we can never say enough about him. There is hardly a type of literature at which he has not tried his hand, and tried it with supreme success. We have not in our midst any other man so highly gifted as he. And I doubt whether there is any such man in all the world besides.

Vallabhbhai Patel: What about his Shantiniketan? How is it going to fare, now that he is old and there is no one who can take his place?

MKG: Yes, but one never can tell. When God has had the grace to *send* such a genius to flourish in our midst, He cannot have wished that the institution he has founded should come to grief.

The Diary of Mahadev Desai *[1932], p. 27*

To Devadas Gandhi

Yeravda
26 March 1932

I RECEIVED today permission to write to fellow-prisoners, and hence this letter. I think of you every day. Mahadev has been brought here. All three of us are well. More after I hear from you in reply to this. Give me news about your health, your reading and your companions. I write to Lakshmi[113] regularly and receive her letters written in beautiful Hindi.

Blessings from
Bapu
CWMG *Vol. 49, p. 239; G*

Dagger Practice In The Ashram[114]

Yeravda
3 April 1932

... I HAVE received a beautiful question from Indu[115]: 'Can we practice sword and dagger exercises in the Ashram?' I don't know or remember when swords and daggers were introduced in the Ashram. Nor do I remember whether, if they were introduced when I was there, I had been consulted. Whether or not I was, I now think that these things have no place in the Ashram. All of you should sit together and think over this matter and, if you feel that their introduction cannot be defended in any way, get rid of them immediately. It seems to me that keeping lathis is the utmost limit to which we can go. ...

Blessings from
Bapu
CWMG *Vol. 49, pp. 259–60; G*

Harden Your Heart Towards Harilal[116]

Yeravda
4 April 1932

... NOTHING IS beyond God's power. If there is still some merit to Harilal's credit earned through good deeds in the past, it will bear fruit one day. We should not pamper him or have false pity on him, but should make our hearts purer day by day. That will have an effect on Harilal too. You have got to harden your heart and write to him and tell him plainly that, as long as he does not give up drinking, he will have to assume that you do not exist. If all of us adopt such a course, Harilal might take heed. Often a drunkard gives up his evil habit when he is greatly shocked. ...

Blessings from

Bapu

CWMG *Vol. 49, pp. 269–70; G*

Yeravda

10 April 1932

I AM happy that you[117] write to me. You should give up fear of Harilal and forget him altogether. Bali[118] is a brave woman. Her slapping (your father) was not an act of violence, but showed her deep love.

Blessings from

Bapu

CWMG *Vol. 49, pp. 292–3; G*

Watching The Stars

Yeravda[119]

24 April 1932

Chiranjivi Devadas

... I HAVE of late fallen in love with watching the stars ... During this jail term, I do not generally ask for books from the Ashram. Friends have been sending me enough for me to live on. In fact they are too many already—over two hundred, as I guess. Not that all of them are worth reading. I liked very much Upton Sinclair's latest book which he sent me. In the form of a novel, it gives a very good account of the working of the American Prohibition Law. I am sending you the book, which is named *Wet Parade*. Others of his books are there in the Ashram, but I believe that this new book has probably not arrived there. Mahadev told me a story of how you lost some books. I was not surprised to hear it, as I think I know well enough your capacity for losing things. ...

Blessings from

Bapu

CWMG *Vol. 49, pp. 359–61; G*

Your Church Is In Your Heart[120]

Yeravda
25 April 1932

I WISH you will not take to heart what the Bishop has been saying. Your church is in your heart. Your pulpit is the whole earth. The blue sky is the roof of your church. And what is this Catholicism? It is surely of the heart. The formula has its use. But it is made by man. If I have any right to interpret the message of Jesus as revealed in the Gospels, I have no manner of doubt in my mind that it is in the main denied in the churches, whether Roman or English, High or Low. Lazarus has no room in those places. ...

The Diary of Mahadev Desai, *Vol. I;* CWMG *Vol. 49, p. 367; E*

Urmila's Grief

Yeravda
26 April 1932

Bhai Maithilisharanji[121],

I have your letter. It is hardly a letter, it is sheer poetry. You have won me over. I follow your point and from that viewpoint Urmila's grief is pertinent ... I shall preserve it and read it again; which means that I must re-read *Saket* from the viewpoint expounded by you. Although your language is pretty easy, I occasionally find it difficult to understand it fully, owing to my scanty knowledge of Hindi. Yet another reason of my difficulty is my limited Hindi vocabulary. Is there any dictionary of Hindi wherein I may find the meanings of all the difficult words used in *Saket* and such other books? I know that a determined effort will by itself make many things clear. ...

Yours,
Mohandas
CWMG *Vol. 49, pp. 372–3; H*

To Harilal Gandhi[122]—A Fragment Of A Letter

Yeravda
27 April 1932

I WILL still not give up hope of your reformation, for I have not given up hope about myself. I have always believed that I was a bad man when Ba carried you in her body, but after your birth I have been doing greater and greater penance for my former life. How can I, therefore, give up all hope? I will continue to hope as long as you and I are alive. And hence, contrary to my usual practice, I am preserving your letter so that, when you have awakened, you may see the insolence of your letter and weep over it and laugh at your folly. I am not preserving this letter to throw it in your face then, but only that I may laugh at it, if God wills that I should see that day. All of us are full of short-comings. But it is our dharma to overcome them. I pray that you do so.

Mahadevbhaini Diary, *Vol. I;* CWMG *Vol. 49, pp. 374–5; G*

Jail Food

Yeravda[123]
4 May 1932

... I AM afraid I may not have been able to explain in my last letter what I wanted to say. It has always been my view that a satyagrahi should never fight about his food. He should thank God for whatever he gets and eat it.

... One may discuss the matter courteously with the official but one cannot fight about it.

People can get many things, have got many things, by creating trouble for the authorities. But we ought not to adopt such methods.

I, therefore, believe that you should not protest at all regarding the bhaji which is being served. Those who wish may eat it and others may leave it. We should thank God even if we get only rotlas and dal.

Mahadevbhaini Diary, *Vol. I;* CWMG *Vol. 49, pp. 397–8; G*

God Gives Me The Appropriate Word

Yeravda
8 May 1932

MKG: The acquisition of such power is a stage in the pilgrim's progress. But he should not be aware of it, nor should he use it.

It might however be working without any effort on his part.

Superintendent: How can a man be unaware of his power?

MKG: Well, I was thus unaware myself.

S: Do you possess any such power?

MKG: Yes. Not the power of working miracles, but of another kind.
I have no idea what I am going to say on any occasion but God
gives me the appropriate word. This is power indeed, but it should
be generated spontaneously.

The Diary of Mahadev Desai, Vol. 1 [1932], p. 103

Maintaining A Diary

Yeravda[124]
16 May 1932

IT (A diary) should be comprehensive, and place on record even the
most secret thoughts. We must not have anything to hide from
others. Therefore we need not be anxious about anyone else reading
our diary. However we must not note down the faults of others or
anything they have told us in confidence. Our diary may be inspected
by the Ashram secretary or his deputy, but nothing in it is to be
kept back from anybody else.

... To[125] work and produce goods in jail means adding to the wealth
of the nation. The fact that the Government is manned by foreigners
does not affect my argument ...

The Diary of Mahadev Desai, Vol. 1 [1932], pp. 113–14

Roughness Of Life

Yeravda[126]
17 May 1932

LIFE WITHOUT a ruffle would be a very dull business. It is not to be
expected. Therefore it is wisdom to put up with all the roughnesses
of life, and that is one of the rich lessons we learn from the Ramayan.

The Diary of Mahadev Desai Vol. 1 [1932], pp. 114–15

The Cat—A Teacher[127]

Yeravda
22 May 1932

OBSERVING HER and her kittens' ways, I feel that she is an ideal teacher.
Whatever they have to be taught, she teaches quietly and without
any fuss. The method is quite easy. She demonstrates to them by

her own example what she wishes to teach, and the kittens learn the thing very quickly. In this manner they learnt to run, climb trees and come down again carefully to eat, to kill a prey and to lick their bodies and clean them. In a very short time they have learnt to do all that their mother can do.

The cat does not leave the kittens alone for long. Her love for them is just like that of a woman's for her children. She sleeps with the kittens clinging to her. When they indicate a desire to suck, she lies down and lets them do it. If she has killed a prey, she brings it to them. Vallabhbhai gives them some milk every day. All three of them lick it from a saucer. Sometimes the mother only looks on without sharing the milk. She plays with them as if she were their own age, and even engages in a sort of wrestling with them.

I have drawn a lesson from all this, namely, that if we wish to educate children properly we should ourselves do what we want to teach them to do. Children have a great capacity for imitating others. They do not easily understand what is explained to them orally. If we wish to teach them truthfulness, we ourselves should be scrupulously truthful. ...

CWMG Vol. 49, p. 466; G

Marriage

Yeravda[128]
24 May 1932

CHILDREN SHOULD be married only when they have grown up. The parties to a marriage should arrange it themselves and obtain their parents' consent. Thus there is no artificial restriction. But I look upon marriage between two persons who follow different faiths as a risky experiment. For if they believe in and practise their faiths, difficulties are likely to crop up. Thus I think that that Bhatia girl has incurred great risk, but her marriage is not irreligious in my opinion. She and her Muslim husband may have pure love for each other, and each may be able to follow his or her own faith. Again I would not oppose such a marriage if the parties to it have the same ideas about food. But I would not approve of it as I approve of inter-caste marriage. Nor would I agitate against it. It is something that everyone should think out for oneself. The same law cannot be laid down for all.

The Diary of Mahadev Desai, Vol. 1 [1932], p. 125

Collyrium[129]

Yeravda
3 June 1932

COLLYRIUM SHOULD not be applied to the eyes for beautifying them. It can, however, be used as medicine for some eye-complaints.

Bapu
CWMG Vol. 50, p. 12; G

My Fingers Have Gone Weak

Yeravda[130]
3 June 1932

Chiranjivi Bhau,

... Both my hands are disabled for plying the *takli*. The fingers have grown so weak that for the present I am unable to use them for manipulating the takli. The future rests with God. ...

Bapu
CWMG Vol. 50, p. 12; H

The Right To Suicide[131]

Yeravda
3 June 1932

IT GRATIFIES me greatly that you are bearing with the disease so cheerfully. This is what I expected of you all.

... Have you quoted that saying in reference to suicide from some book? My opinion in this matter is as follows: A person suffering from an incurable disease has the right to commit suicide if he cannot perform any service whatsoever and lives only as a result of the ministrations of others. Fasting unto death is infinitely superior to drowning oneself. A person's strength of character is tested in fasting, moreover it leaves scope for changing one's mind, which is both proper and necessary. But as long as he can perform the least bit of service, he is not justified in putting an end to his life. Although physical activity is an important and necessary feature of yajna, a physically disabled person can certainly perform mental *yajna* which is not totally unfruitful. A man by his pure thoughts alone can render service. He can also be engaged in giving useful advice and such like. The thoughts of a man possessing a pure heart are an activity by themselves and can produce far-reaching results.

Mahadevbhaini Diary Vol. I, CWMG, Vol. 50, p. 13; H

Mechanized Farming

Yeravda[132]
4 June 1932

IF MR Cooper's plough is what he claims it to be, I should have no objection to its use merely because it is a steel plough and therefore the village carpenter will be deprived of a portion of his work. I do not mind the partial deprivation of the carpenter if the plough increases the earning capacity of the farmer. But I have very grave doubts about the claims made by Mr Cooper for the invention. At Sabarmati we have tried almost all improved ploughs manufactured in India and I think even others, but the claims made for each variety have not proved true in the long run. An experienced man has said that the indigenous plough is specially designed for the Indian soil. It conserves the soil, because it ploughs deep enough for the farmer's crops but never so deep as to do damage. Of course I do not claim to understand agriculture. I am simply giving you the testimony of those who have had considerable experience in these matters. What we have to remember is that all improved implements have to meet the peculiar conditions of India. ...

I do not believe in the doctrine of the greatest good of the greatest number. It means in its nakedness that in order to achieve the supposed good of 51 per cent the interest of 49 per cent may be, or rather, should be sacrificed. It is a heartless doctrine and has done harm to humanity. The only real, dignified, human doctrine is the greatest good of all, and this can only be achieved by uttermost self-sacrifice.

The Diary of Mahadev Desai, Vol. 1, 1932, pp. 148–9;
CWMG Vol. 50, p. 14

Some Day ...

Yeravda[133]
11 June 1932

MKG: Some day or other one must mount the shoulders of the bearers.

Sardar Patel: No, no. Don't leave us in the lurch. Bring the ship to shore, and then go where you like. And I will go with you.

The Diary of Mahadev Desai Vol. 1, 1932, p. 159

Devadas Ill

Yeravda[134]
16 June 1932

... I SUPPOSE you know that Devadas is down with fever. The telegram received says there is nothing serious. I have wired for more particulars. ...

Bapu
CWMG Vol. 50, pp. 46–7; E

Yeravda
16 June 1932

Chiranjivi Devadas,

I did fear some such thing. I had a feeling the day before yesterday that there would be bad news from somewhere. And then I got your wire yesterday. I immediately asked Vallabhbhai what the wire contained, and on opening it he read the news about your illness. It was not likely that you would escape fever in Gorakhpur. But I assume that it will have left you before you get this letter. I think that, according to your nature, you would like to be surrounded by friends and relations at such a time. You would deserve such care because you have looked after many people in their illness. But I myself am a hard-hearted man. I, therefore, would not like to ask anybody from the western part to run up to Gorakhpur. ...

After saying this, I suggest that, if you want anybody from the Ashram to be near you, send a wire there. But my hope is that by the time you get this letter your illness will have been a thing of the past. You always have the blessings of us all.

CWMG Vol. 50, p. 50; G

Snake

Yeravda[135]
16 June 1932

THE STORY about the snake is correct only to a certain extent. The snake was passing over my body. At such a moment what could I or anyone else do except to remain still? I don't see that this deserves any such praise as the writer has given me. And how do we know if the snake was poisonous or not?. ...

Mahadevbhaini Diary; CWMG Vol. 50, p. 51; H

Yeravda[136]
17 June 1932

... THERE IS need for reform in the administration of prisons. A prison should be a house of correction and not punishment. If that is so, why should a forger have fetters on his legs in prison? The fetters will not improve his character. To my mind it is intolerable that anyone should be fettered if there is no likelihood of his trying to escape or becoming unmanageable or wishing to make a nuisance of himself. But if a political prisoner is an athlete like you, always thinking about means of escape and unable to control his tongue and hands, it will be the duty of the authorities to put him in fetters....

Mahadevbhaini Diary Vol. 1; CWMG Vol. 50, p. 56; G

Telegram To Sir Malcom Hailey[137]

His Excellency Governor
United Provinces

Yeravda
18 June 1932

OVER THREE months ago my son Devadas was tried Delhi and Meerut as Civil Resister and sometime after conviction transferred Gorakhpur Jail. Gorakhpur climate notoriously Malarial. Cause for removal companionless to such out of the way jail unknown. He is suffering from sixth instant from suspected mild enteric though he seems to be recovering. Request his removal to healthier and more accessible place preferably to Dehradun to join Pandit Jawaharlal with whom he is close friends or to Yeravda to join me if removal here at all possible.

M.K. Gandhi
Prisoner, Yeravda Central Prison
Bombay Secret Abstracts, Home department Special Branch,
File No.800(40) (3), Pt. I, p. 283,
Mahadevbhaini Diary Vol. I; CWMG Vol. 50, p. 57; E

To Devadas About Harilal

Yeravda
23 June 1932

HARILAL'S GLASS is always red. He goes about drunk and begs from people. He holds out threats to Bali and Manu. Even in this, his motive is to force Bali to give him money. To me also he has written letters holding out very insolent threats. He has threatened that he will file a suit against Bali for control of Manu. I don't feel hurt by all this. I only feel pity for him, and smile too. There are many other people like him. What about them? Shouldn't I feel for them as much as I do for Harilal? They all obey their nature. What else can they do? If we behave in the right manner towards Harilal, he will come round in the end. I think I am not a little responsible for what he is. When he was conceived, I lived in ignorance. The years when he grew up were a time of self-indulgence. I certainly did not drink but Harilal has made up for that. I sought my pleasure only with one woman. Harilal seeks his with many. It is only a difference of degree, not of kind. I should, therefore, atone for my sinful life, and that means self-purification. It is an extremely slow process ...

Mahadevbhaini Diary *Vol. 1;* CWMG *Vol. 50, p. 92; G*

A Prison Death

Yeravda
24 June 1932

Mahadev Desai: I was very angry to find how indifferent the Superintendent was as regards the boy's death in jail.

MKG: Men tend to become callous in service.

MD: In the other jail he was a bad fellow, but took care of sick prisoners, felt for them, and talked about them everyday.

MKG: That was because the officer was addicted to drink. Drink addicts have tender feelings.

MD: I wonder how.

MKG: In Tolstoy's story the man drinks but still has not the courage to murder his victim; he has some vestige of feeling left. He then smokes a cigar, which blunts his sensibilities. A man is capable of anything when once his intellect is clouded.

Mahadev Desai's Diary, p. 191; G

Hardy, Zola, And Sinclair

Yeravda
29 June 1932

... RAJAJI SEEMS to be rather prejudiced against American writers[138]. I have read nothing of Hardy or Zola. And I have always felt the loss of not reading the latter. But Upton Sinclair is not a writer to be despised. A propagandist novel cannot be dismissed from an idea that propaganda as such is a fault in it. A propagandist devotes all his powers to the production of his work. He makes no secret of his purpose, and still does not let the interest flag in his story. *Uncle Tom's Cabin* is propaganda pure and simple, but its art is inimitable. ...

Mahadevbhaini Diary Vol. I, pp. 258–60; CWMG Vol. 50, p. 110; G

Astrology

Yeravda[139]
30 June 1932

... PUT NO trust in the predictions of astrologers. Do not take any interest in the matter at all. Even if such predictions come true, there is no benefit in knowing them. The harm is plain. ...

Bapu
CWMG Vol. 50, p. 118; G

Death Of Rajaji's Son-in-Law

Yeravda
5 July 1932

Papa[140]
Gandhi Ashram, Tiruchengodu

Devadas wires news your husband's[141] death. We are all deeply stirred but you will not grieve over death which is common lot of humanity. Remember you are daughter of brave father. May God give you peace. Love from us all.

Bapu
CWMG *Vol. 50, p. 151; E*

To Saraladevi Choudhurani

Yeravda
5 July 1932

Dear Sister[142],

I was grieved to note from the papers that your mother was no more. My sympathies go out to you and Dipak[143] in your sorrow. Sardar and Mahadev join me in sending you condolences.

Yours sincerely,
M.K. Gandhi
CWMG *Vol. 50, p. 153; E*

To Prema Behn Kantak

Yeravda
17 July 1932

... WE NEVER know how a person feels in his heart. It is the heart which matters; all else is false. ...

Bapu
CWMG *Vol. 50, p. 248; G*

'Of Death We Simply Do Not Know'[144]

Yeravda
26 July 1932

My dear Sister,

I received your disconsolate letter only today. It had to pass through so many hands before coming to me. My whole heart goes out to you and your aged mother. God suffers us to blame Him, to swear at Him and deny Him. We do it all in our ignorance ...

... The fact is if we knew all the laws of God we should be able to account for the unaccountable. Why should we think that the withdrawal of your brother from our midst is an affliction? We simply do not know. But we do, or ought to know that God is wholly good and wholly just. Even our illnesses such as your other brother's may be no misfortune. Life is a state of discipline. We are required to go through the fire of suffering. I do so wish that you and your mother could really rejoice in your suffering. May you have peace. ...

Mahadevbhaini Diary; CWMG Vol. 50, pp. 294–295

To Kamala Nehru

Yeravda
1 August 1932

Kamala Nehru
Anand Bhawan,
Allahabad

Alarming account press about health. Wire exact condition.

Bapu
CWMG Vol. 50, p. 323; E

Death Of Dr Pranjivan Mehta

Yeravda
4 August 1932

Chhaganlal Mehta[145]
8 Pagoda Road
Rangoon

God's will be done[146] consolation to you and mother. Hope you will fully carry on all noblest traditions left by father for commercial integrity lavish hospitality and great generosity. Sardar and Mahadev join me in condolences. For me I feel forlorn without lifelong faithful friend. Continue keep me informed of everything. May God bless you all.

Gandhi.
Mahadevbhaini Diary Vol. I, p. 342; Bombay Secret Abstracts,
Home Department, Special Branch, File No.800(40)(3), pt. II,
p. 441; CWMG Vol. 50, p. 327; E

To Sarojini Naidu

Yeravda
8 August 1932

Dear Bulbul,

... It is naughty of Padmaja[147] to neglect me for so long. I hope she is better. Do you hear from your bearded[148] son? If you write to him, please give him my love.

Have the ladies there[149] told you that Sardar is seriously studying Sanskrit? He has made much progress during the four weeks he has been at it. His application would shame a youthful student.

Love from us all.

Yours,
Little Man[150]
CWMG *Vol. 50, p. 348; E*

'My Strictness Has Gone'[151]

Yeravda
11 August 1932

... I DO not regret the strictness which I imposed on the occasions which you mention. It was justified at that time. Now I feel the slightest degree of strictness to be as heavy as the weight of the Himalayas. Formerly, I had to fast in order to make people do what I can now persuade them to do with a mere rebuke; and other people, too, had to act more or less similarly. If I continue to act as I used to do, I would be a cruel man ...

... I would not like any of you to behave towards his wife as I did towards Ba ... she could not be angry with me, whereas I could with her. I did not give her the same freedom of action which I enjoyed ...

My behaviour towards Ba at Sabarmati progressively became in line with this attitude, and the result was that she changed. Her old fear of me has disappeared mostly, if not completely. Even if I feel angry with her, I turn the anger on myself. The cause of anger is my attachment to her. ...

CWMG *Vol. 50, pp. 353–5; G*

To Kasturba

Yeravda
20 August 1932

YOU WILL soon be released now. But you will feel unhappy that you cannot see me. I also feel unhappy. ...

Mahadevbhaini Diary Vol. 1; CWMG, Vol. 50, p. 391; G

Action—Thoughtful And Thoughtless[152]

Yeravda
28 August 1932

... WE CLEAN lavatories. If we don't think about it, we would feel the work to be low and degrading and eagerly wish that we could be saved from it. If, however, we think about it, we would realize that it was our moral duty to do it. To clean it means to make the place perfectly clean, to bury the contents of the bucket carefully, to keep in a clean condition the things with which we do the work, and to examine the contents. If there is any blood or the stink is very offensive or if there are worms, we may conclude that somebody is ill. We should then find out who that person is. We would of course know who uses a lavatory. ...

CWMG Vol. 50, pp. 436-7; G

Sardar Patel

Yeravda[153]
28 August 1932

VALLABHBHAI IS running with the speed of an Arab horse. He is never found without a book about Sanskrit in his hands. I had not hoped for this. Nobody can equal him in the art of making envelopes. He makes them without using measurements and is guided only by his eyes in cutting the paper, and still he does not seem to take much time. His orderliness is simply wonderful. If there is anything which he has to do, he does not leave it to his memory. He does it immediately. From the time that he started spinning, he always spins at the fixed time, and so the quantity of yarn spun and the speed of spinning are increasing daily. He rarely forgets anything which he takes up. With such orderliness, there can be no confusion any time.

Mahadevbhaini Diary Vol. 1; CWMG Vol. 50, p. 440; G

To Narandas Gandhi

Yeravda
7/11 September 1932

IT IS the morning of Wednesday, and the goats are being milked, singing to us the while ...

You will find my Will lying in some place there. Send me a copy of it. If it is sealed in a cover, break open the seal. If you wish to make any suggestion about it, send it to me. I suppose it will be necessary now to revise the names of the trustees. Imam Saheb is no more. ...

CWMG Vol. 51, pp. 45 and 47; G

To Devadas Gandhi

Yeravda
13 September 1932

THE COUNTRY now knows about my intention to go on an indefinite fast. I assume that the news has not upset you in the slightest degree. One does not get such a unique opportunity by seeking it. It comes rarely, and only to a fortunate man. I believe that such an opportunity has come to me, and anybody who believes that he has got a unique opportunity would welcome it heartily. Hence you need not feel agitated. ...

Mahadevbhaini Diary Vol. II, p. 22; CWMG, Vol. 51, p. 51; G

To Kasturba

Yeravda
13 September 1932

I HAVE your letter. You have probably heard about my fast. Do not get frightened in the slightest degree by the news and also do not let the other women get frightened. Indeed, you should rejoice that God has granted me an opportunity to go through such an ordeal for the sake of dharma. I also hope that you have understood the meaning of this fast. I shall not have to start the fast if my demands regarding the *Antyajas* are accepted, and even if I have started it I can end it. If, however, I have to carry it on till the end, you should indeed thank God. Only one in millions meets the death for which he has prayed. What a good fortune it would be if I meet such a death! And if I do not die, it is clear as daylight that it would then be my moral duty to purify myself still further and to devote myself more to service. I think that after having lived with me for fifty years you will be able clearly to understand this simple thing and willingly follow me.

Mahadevbhaini Diary Vol. II, pp. 22–3; CWMG Vol. 51, p. 52; G

The Epic Fast

MY FAST[154] I want to throw in the scale of justice. This may look childish to the onlookers, but not so to me. If I had anything more to give, I would throw in that also to remove this curse, but I have nothing more than my life.

Pyarelal: The Epic Fast, p. 32

WHAT I want[155], what I am living for, and what I should delight in dying for, is the eradication of untouchability root and branch. (If untouchability is really rooted out) it will not only purge Hinduism of a terrible blot but its repercussion will be world-wide.

Pyarelal: The Epic Fast, p. 120

To Rabindranath Tagore

20 September 1932

Dear Gurudev,

This is early morning 3 o'clock of Tuesday. I enter the fiery gate at noon. If you can bless the effort, I want it. You have been to me a true friend because you have been a candid friend often speaking your thoughts aloud. I had looked forward to a firm opinion from you one way or the other. But you have refused to criticize. Though it can now only be during my fast I will yet prize your criticism, if your heart condemns my action. I am not too proud to make a confession of my blunder, whatever the cost of the confession, if I find myself in error. If your heart approves of the action I want your blessing. It will sustain me. I hope I have made myself clear.

My love,

M.K. Gandhi

CWMG *Vol. 51, p. 101;* E

Discussion With Dr B.R. Ambedkar

22 September 1932

Ambedkar: We must accept that in the country there are two groups belonging to two different ideologies and act accordingly, and I should get my compensation. I also want that a clear understanding should be arrived at which would recompense me in other respects also. The decision of the Government gives me seventy-one seats and I feel that is a just, reasonable, and definite allocation.

MKG: According to you.

A: Over and above that I get the right to vote and contest elections in the general constituencies. I also have a franchise in the labourers' constituencies. We do realize that you are of immense help to us.

G: Not to you personally.

A: But I have only one quarrel with you, that is, you work for the so-called national welfare and not for our interests alone. If you devoted yourself entirely to the welfare of the Depressed Classes, you would then become our hero.

G: Very sweet of you to say so.

A: I want political power for my community. That is indispensable for our survival. The basis of the agreement therefore should be: I should get what is due to me. I wish to tell the Hindus that I should be assured of my compensation.

G: ... I want to serve the untouchables. That is why I am not at all angry with you. When you use derogatory and angry words for me, I tell myself that I deserved that. I will not get angry even if you spit on my face. I say this with God as witness. I know that you have drunk deep of the poisoned cup. However, I make a claim which will seem astounding to you. You are born an untouchable but I am an untouchable by adoption ... I learnt the lesson of democracy at the tender age of 12. I quarrelled with my mother for treating the domestic sweeper as an untouchable. That day

I saw God in the form of a Bhangi. You spoke the truth when you said that the welfare of untouchables is dearer to you than my own life. Now be honest and stick to it. You should not care for my life. But do not be false to Harijans. My work will not die with me ... A person who is regarded as 'unseeable' today should also have the opportunity to become the Viceroy of India. I had said, in the first political speech I made on coming to India that I would like to make a Bhangi the President of the Congress.

So I appeal to you not to haggle. Do not bring to me something which is so bad that I would not even like the look of it. Bring to me some nice present which would inspire life into a person who is willingly courting death. However you will do that only if you are convinced that my co-operation has some value.

Mahadevbhaini Diary *Vol. 1;* CWMG *Vol. 51, pp. 458–60; G*

To Jawaharlal

24 September 1932

Pandit Jawaharlal Nehru
Jail Dehradun

During all these days of agony you have been before minds' eye. I am most anxious to know your opinion[156]. You know how I value your opinion. Saw Indu [157], Sarup's[158] children[159]. Indu looked happy and in possession of more flesh. Doing very well. Wire reply.

Love.

Bapu
CWMG *Vol. 51, p. 134; E*

To The Press

25 September 1932

IF THE Premier accepts the settlement *in toto* I would be bound to break the fast. ...

The tremendous awakening that has taken place in the country during the five days fills me with hope that orthodoxy will surpass itself and rid Hinduism of the canker of untouchability which is eating into its vitals.

I suppose the future plan is in the hands of Government.

The Epic Fast; CWMG *Vol. 51, p. 141; E*

To Great Britain[160]

25 September 1932

... The Cabinet decision was to me a timely warning from God that I was asleep when He was knocking at the door and waking me up. The settlement[161] arrived at is to me but the beginning of the work of purification. The agony of the soul is not going to end until every trace of untouchability is gone. I do not want the British Cabinet to come to any hasty decision. I do not want them for saving my life or for appearing to be right with the world to accept it in a niggardly spirit. If they have not realized the true inwardness of the Agreement, they must summarily reject it, but if they have, they will not alter one word or comma of it, but they will implement every condition that is implied in the great settlement which the so-called untouchables and the so-called touchables have arrived at with all their heart and with God as their witness. ...

CWMG *Vol. 51, p. 140*

Telegram To Mira Behn

26 September 1932

Mira Behn
Arthur Road Jail
    No letter sent today. Thank God fast broken 5.15 presence gurudev other loving friends. Love.

Bapu
CWMG *Vol. 51, p. 143*

To The Press

26 September 1932

... The settlement is but the beginning of the end. The political part of it, very important though it no doubt is, occupies but a small space in the vast field of reform that has to be tackled by caste Hindus during the coming days, namely, the complete removal of social and religious disabilities under which a large part of the Hindu population has been groaning. ...

The Hindu *27-9-1932;* CWMG *Vol. 51, pp. 143–4; E*

A Soul-Destroying Sin

10 October 1932[162]

My dear Suresh,

Why have you kept me in suspense about your health? I know your views of old on caste and untouchability. I quite agree with you that caste has got to go. But whether it would do so in my generation I do not know. Only let us not mix up the two and spoil both causes. Untouchability is a soul-destroying sin. Caste is a social evil. Anyway you get thoroughly well and work away against caste with your usual vigour. You will find in me a good supporter.

With love and all good wishes,

Bapu

Advance 15-10-1932; Mahadevbhaini Diary *Vol. II;* CWMG *Vol. 51, p. 219; E*

Discussion With B.R. Ambedkar

17 October 1932

Ambedkar: I have not come to discuss untouchability but political matters.

Gandhi: That is true. I cannot talk about it with you; even if you do I shall not be able to express an opinion—my mind does not work in that direction.

A: I have come here for this. I want to request you to give up civil disobedience and to join the Round Table Conference. The point is that if you do not come, we shall get nothing in England and everything will be upset. People like Iqbal who are enemies of the country will come to the forefront. We have to work any sort of constitution. Hence though I am a small man, I request you to come.

G: If you elaborate your argument, I shall think over it. I suggest you go and write about it at length in the newspapers. I shall think over it.

A: It is not a thing that can be put down in writing. In it I shall have to say a lot that will hurt the Muslims and I cannot say that publicly. But I shall write anonymously or have someone write in a different way. Please have a look at it and, taking it to be mine, think over it.

G: It will be good if you write under your own name. But of course you may do as you wish.

A: I must honestly say that I have no interest in the temples being thrown open, common dinners and the like, because we suffer thereby. My people have to put up with beatings and bitterness increases. After the common dinner at Vile Parle, the Maratha workers went on strike. If the caste Hindus had the strength they would have engaged untouchables as servants. But that has not been so. Hence I do not feel interested in the thing. I only want that social and economic hardships should end.

G: Give examples.

A: The untouchables do not get houses to live in; they continue to suffer injustice and oppression. In one case, an untouchable was accused of having murdered a Maratha. I could have taken the case to Sessions and got him acquitted, but the magistrate changed the charge of murder to one of grievous injury. Now he will receive some punishment. You may not know what even I have to face. I do not get any other place to live in Bombay except the Port Trust chawl. In my village, I have to stay in the midst of the Mahars. In Poona, all others stay with their friends. I have to stay at the National Hotel and have to spend Rs 7 and transport fare.

G: Servants of India?

A: Yes, I can perhaps stay there. But only perhaps. You will know if you ask Vaze. Once Vaze's servant insulted me in his presence. I want to do away with all these hardships.

G: I am at one with you ...

Mahadevbhaini Diary *Vol. II;* CWMG *Vol. 51, p. 462; G*

Part Twelve

1933–6

Receiving gifts for the Harijan movement in Calcutta
in July 1934

The Personal and the Public

*Mary Chesley: How do you understand what is God's guidance for
you when it is a question of choosing between two good things?*
*MKG: I use my intellect on the subject and if I don't get any strong
feeling as to which of the two I should choose, I just leave the
matter, and before long I wake up one morning with the perfect
assurance that it should be A rather than B.*

On 8 May 1933—one year and four months after he had been taken
in—Gandhi was released, weakened by his fasting but strengthened
by his reflections. A touch of familial joy was to give him and
Kasturba pleasure: Devadas and Lakshmi were married in Premlila
Thackersey's Poona home. Addressing his daughter-in-law whom
he had known since the time she was a seven year old, Gandhi said,
'I believe Devadas will prove himself a worthy husband to you ... Let
your marriage strengthen, if possible, the bond of affection that
has ever been growing between Rajagopalachari and me.'

The Harijan issue dominated Gandhi's essential thinking,
speaking, and writing in 1934, rather more than the issue of
independence. He undertook an all-India 'Harijan tour' from
November 1933 to February 1934 raising funds in support of his
Harijan work.

This Part includes a talk with Mary Chesley (who had devoted
the later part of her life to the service of 'untouchables' in India)
which reveals something of his inner life. It also includes incisive
letters to Prema Kantak. And Harilal's waywardness keeps featuring
in his thoughts, sometimes with hope, sometimes with despair but
always with the 'scorching love' that was unique to him. Did Harilal
feel scorched or loved? We cannot know.

Gandhi's own searchlight remained, as always, turned 'inward'. His introspective article in *Harijan* on his practice of walking with his hands on the shoulders of boys and girls belongs to the 'essential' genre.

If 1933 began politically with the activating of the 'Poona Pact', it was also to become 'constructive'. Gandhi founded the Harijan Sevak Sangh and the weekly journal in English *Harijan*, initially edited by Ramchandra Shastri. From this point onwards that journal became the vehicle for his 'essential' thoughts and writings. One of the first major revelations of his thinking—autobiographical as well as conceptual—was to appear in the shape of a patient reply that Gandhi sent to Ranchhoddas Patwari, a former Diwan of the state of Morvi who had put his questions that bordered on the insolent.

In an important letter dated 5 February 1933, to Bill Lash, an American missionary, Gandhi reverted to the Saraladevi Choudhurani episode saying that his 'flesh was pulling hard' and had been saved from 'perdition' and 'hell-fire'.

To the same *genre* belongs his January 1936 letters to Prema Kantak in which he describes the arising in him of sexual desire.

The personal and the public alternate classically in this phase of Gandhi's life. The death of his valued associate, Dr M.A. Ansari, his asking Zakir Saheb to 'be to me what the doctor was on the Hindu Muslim question', his letter to Jawaharlal on the young leader's insistence on Complete Independence, and his letter to Ghanshyamdas Birla who had written a critical article on Jawaharlal Nehru disagreeing with the young leader, belong to the highest order of public correspondence.

This Part also has a conversation with Sir C.V. and Lady Raman in which Sir C.V. concedes he 'cannot speak Hindi' and ascribes it to 'conceit', adding 'I am full of [it] as much as you'. Gandhi takes humorous irreverence well.

The irreverence from Harilal also exhibited in this phase belongs, however, to another *genre* of independence. Harilal converted formally on 19 May 1936, to Islam at one of Bombay's prominent mosques. Gandhi wrote philosophically to Ramdas: 'We should indeed feel satisfied if he truly practices in his life what is best in Islam.' He issued a public statement on 2 June 1938: 'I do not mind whether he is known as Abdulla or Harilal if by adopting one name for the other he becomes a true devotee of God, which both the names mean.' But Gandhi did not hide his misgivings. In the same statement he told his 'numerous Muslim friends' that they should 'examine Harilal in the light of his immediate past and, if they find that his conversion is a soulless matter, to tell him so plainly ...' No one was surprised when, before a year was out, Harilal returned to the Hindu fold via the Arya Samaj altering the spelling of his name to 'Hiralal'. The inner agonies of those criss-crossings of identity, name, and belonging were best known to Harilal. But the 'essential' mother in Kasturba understood them too, in her own way, retaining her son's love.

Gandhi remained the sail-mast on the family's little vessel, taking the blast unmoved while the others held on to the deck-railings of family-bonding for support.

Gandhi was on a nationwide tour to raise money for his Harijan Fund when, on 15 January 1934, an earthquake of great intensity shook Bihar and neighbouring regions. His mind preoccupied with the Harijan question, Gandhi said: 'You may call me superstitious if you like; but a man like me cannot but believe that this earthquake is a divine chastisement sent by God for our sins. Even to avowed scoffers it must be clear that nothing but Divine Will can explain such a calamity. It is my unmistakable belief that not a blade of grass moves but by the Divine Will.' This elicited from Tagore a swift riposte. The essentiality of Gandhi emerges in that dialogue between the two.

To Ranchhoddas Patwari

Yeravda
11 January 1933

Respected Ranchhodbhai[1],

I was pained to read your letter. Is it not strange that you should write to me in English? Or that you should frame questions as if you wanted to catch in your trap a witness who was trying to escape it? ...

I will now reply to your questions[2].

... During your stay in England you took meals in hotels or in the house of Englishmen?

At both places.

... Are you of the opinion that a Hindu does not cease to be a sanatanist Hindu by this?

That is my considered view.

Even now you have no objection to take the food prepared in European hotels or by a Christian or a Mohammedan?

I would have no objection if I otherwise regarded the article as acceptable food.

... Are you in favour of intermarriages between the Brahmins, Kshatriyas, and Vaishyas on the one hand and the untouchables on the other?

If the bride and bridegroom are a suitable pair, if their lives are pure, and they believe in the ideal of self-control in married life, I would certainly approve of such unions. But I do not regard interdining and intermarrying between Harijans and other Hindus as a necessary part of the movement for the eradication of untouchability.

Do you keep any idol or any picture of Shri Rama or Shri Krishna when you offer prayers in the morning and at night?

No.

Do you believe that it is necessary to go to a temple for darshan of the image for attaining emancipation and for acquiring supreme love for God?

No.

How often have you visited the Hindu temples for the darshan of the idols during the last sixteen years?

I have visited them so often in the course of my tours that I cannot count the number of times.

What amount have you sent as bhet or samagri to temples from the funds collected by you?

I had no right to spend anything on temples from the money I had collected.

Do you believe that a Dhed, Bhangi, or Chamar cannot attain emancipation or acquire supreme love for God unless he gets an opportunity to go into the Hindu temple for darshan?

I don't believe so at all. ...

CWMG Vol. 53, pp. 13 and 16–19; G

'I Had All But Fallen'

Yeravda
5 February 1933

Dear Father Lash[3],

... Some have God to rely upon; others, poor mortals, have their parents; and yet others, like me, have their wives, sons, and friends to lean on. I had, not very many years ago, all but fallen, but the thought of Devadas, who was then living with me, of Mahadev, Mathuradas, and others[4] who were at that time surrounding me and whom I believed to be themselves leaning on me, and the thought of my wife, kept me from going to perdition. It was their love which chained me so tightly and strongly that I could not burst through the bond although the flesh was pulling hard enough to tear the chains to bits and rush into hell-fire. ...

Yours sincerely,
Bapu
CWMG Vol. 53, pp. 228–9; E

Why 'Harijan'

Yeravda

MANY PEOPLE have asked me why I have used the name 'Harijans' for people whom we commit the sin of regarding as untouchables. Years ago a Kathiawari *Antyaja* had written to me that names like *antyaja, achhut, asprishya* hurt his community. I could appreciate their feelings. For me they were neither antyajas nor untouchables. It was this correspondent who had pointed out to me that the poet-devotee Narasinh Mehta in one of his *bhajan*s had referred to the antyajas as 'Harijans'. In my view the bhajan he had sent to me to support his contention did not yield the meaning which he thought it did. All the same I liked the name 'Harijan' immensely. 'Harijan' means a devotee of God, beloved of God. It is God's promise that He is the Protector of the oppressed, an ocean of compassion, the strength of the weak, the Refuge of the helpless, the Support of the lame, and the Eye of the blind. One may therefore expect Him to bestow especial grace on the oppressed. Looked at from this point of view, I am sure the name, 'Harijan' is appropriate in every way for the antyaja brethren. ...

Harijan Sevak *23-2-1933;* CWMG *Vol. 53, pp. 374–5; H*

On B.R. Ambedkar

Yeravda

7 February 1933

DR AMBEDKAR is bitter. He has every reason to feel so. He has received a liberal education. He has more than the talents of the average educated Indian. Outside India he is received with honour and affection, but, in India, among Hindus, at every step he is reminded that he is one of the outcastes of Hindu society. It is nothing to his shame, for, he has done no wrong to Hindu society. His exterior is as clean as that of the cleanest and the proudest Brahmin. Of his interior, the world knows as little as of that of any of us. In spite of all this, he believes that 'it will be a most unwarranted presumption on his part to suppose that he has sufficient worth in the eyes of the Hindus which would make them treat any message from him with respect'. This is the caste Hindus' shame, not his ... The attack on untouchability is thus an attack upon this 'high-and-low'ness. The moment untouchability goes, the caste system itself will be purified, that is to say, according to my dream, it will resolve itself into the true varnadharma, the four divisions of society, each complementary of the other and none inferior or superior to any other, each as necessary for the whole body of Hinduism as any other. How it can be and what that varnashrama is, it is not necessary to examine here. But, such being my faith, I have always respectfully differed from those distinguished countrymen, Dr Ambedkar among them, who have held that untouchability will not go without the destruction of varnashramadharma. ...

Harijan 11-2-1933; CWMG Vol. 53, pp. 260-1

To Verrier Elwin

Yeravda
23 February 1933

My dearest Son[5],

Son you have become of your own choice. I have accepted the responsible position. And son you shall remain to the end of time. The tie between you and me is much thicker and tougher than of blood. It is the burning love of Truth at any cost. Therefore whatever you may do will not disappoint me. But I was sad.

I am not thinking of the superiority of celibacy over marriage. I am thinking of what you had intended, almost pledged yourself to be. But I know that you had to be true to yourself and appear as you were.

I showed your letter to Jamnalalji and he too felt the same as I did.

But whilst I was trying to make time to write to you, in came Ala[6], tears dropping from her eyes. She put into my hands your letter and said, 'How can I bear this? It was agreed between us that we were both to remain single, or if we could not, we were to marry each other.' I consoled her and advised her to send you her blessings. I do not know what she has done or written. You will tell me what understanding there was between you and her.

But taking it for granted that your word was never given to Ala as she imagines it was, you and Mary[7] have my blessings. I have met her. I have a vivid recollection that the innocence of her face stamped itself upon my mind. I know that your joint life will be one of complete dedication to service. But if there is the slightest possibility of a breach (moral) of word given to Ala, you must both—you and Mary—be prepared to bear what will be the heaviest cross and sacrifice your cherished hope on the altar of Truth which is God ...

May God guide you and Mary.

With my deep love to you and Mary,

Yours,
Bapu
CWMG Vol. 53, pp. 376–7; E

'Ba—Why Do You Worry About Harilal?'

Yeravda[8]
11 March 1933

WHY DO you worry about Harilal? He will not write. If God suffers his drunkenness, what can we do? God will reform him when He wills.

Mahadevbhaini Diary Vol. III; CWMG Vol. 54, p. 61; G

'Manilal—Do Not Leave Phoenix'

Yeravda
15 April 1933

... YOU SEEM even to have forgotten how quickly and with what difficulties I turned my back on city life and established Phoenix. You grew up in Phoenix. It was there you atoned for your errors, lived an independent life. Sita was born there too. That you should forget all this in a moment and think of leaving Phoenix for ever—imagine the weakness and the pitiable condition of mind it reveals ...

There is Miss Schlesin entertaining beautiful dreams about you, and you are thinking of filthy Durban. You must have sufficient pride in you to be determined that, if you cannot bring glory to your father's legacy, you will at any rate not disgrace it. Do you know the objects of Phoenix, or have you forgotten them as well? Read them again ...

Please don't take this letter as a rebuke to you. I have written to wake up both of you. Indecision is a very bad thing....

Blessings from
Bapu
CWMG *Vol. 54, pp. 419–21; G*

Homoeopathy[9]

Yeravda
28 April 1933

My dear Titus,

... You have missed my point about 'Allopathic' and 'Homoeopathic'. Personally I would prefer Homoeopathy any day to Allopathy. Only I have no personal experience of its efficacy and I have told you so. ...

Yours sincerely,
CWMG *Vol. 55, p. 56; E*

Devadas–Lakshmi Wedding[10]

Poona
16 June 1933

... DEVADAS, YOU know my expectations about you. May you fulfil them, and I assure you that if you do so all the objections raised again the match will melt away. Since I reached the age of discretion, I have tried to understand the meaning of dharma and live up to it as best as I could. I do not think that in celebrating this marriage anything has been done against the dictates of dharma. ...

What a piece of good fortune for you that you should have so many friends and elders to bless you on the occasion! May you prove worthy of all these blessings! You have today robbed Rajagopalachari of a cherished gem. May you be worthy of it! May you treasure it! She is a real Lakshmi. Guard her, protect her as you would Lakshmi, the goddess of the good and beautiful. ...

Devadas, you have always looked upon Rajagopalachari as a respected elder. From today, he is as good as your father. Tender to him the same loyalty and obedient devotion that you have been tendering to me.

To you, Lakshmi, I need not say much. I believe that Devadas will prove himself a worthy husband to you. Ever since I have seen and known you, I have felt that you have justified your name. Let your marriage strengthen, if possible, the bond of affection that has ever been growing between Rajagopalachari and me. ...

The Hindu 17-6-1933; also The Hindustan Times 17-6-1933,
CWMG Vol. 55, pp. 200–1; G and H

'Ramdas Is A *Bhakta*'

3 July 1933

... RAMDAS IS unfortunate[11]. He cannot be either happy or at peace, and his health is deteriorating ... Ramdas is a bhakta and of a trustful nature. He is always anxious to know what his duty is and tries his best to do it. I believe, therefore, that ultimately he will be happy. ...

Blessings from
Bapu
CWMG Vol. 55, pp. 240–1; G

Before The District Magistrate[12], Ahmedabad

1 August 1933

THERE HAS never been the slightest desire on my part to disturb the public peace, as I think[13]. In my opinion, I have never done a single thing consciously to disturb the public peace. On the contrary, I make bold to say that I have made the best endeavour possible to promote public peace and I can show several instances in which I have attained very considerable success in preserving and promoting public peace. Being a lover of peace all my life, nothing can be remoter from my thought than to disturb public peace.

CWMG Vol. 55, p. 336; E

Trial At Poona[14]

4 August 1933

(*To a question put by the Court, Gandhi stated that his age was 64, and that he was a Hindu by caste. ...*)

Magistrate: What is your occupation?

MKG: (*Hesitatingly*) I am by occupation a spinner, a weaver, and a farmer.

M: Your residence?

MKG: Yeravda Jail now. (*Laughter*)

M: Now, of course, but otherwise?

MKG: Otherwise, Sabarmati in Ahmedabad district.

The Bombay Chronicle 5-8-1933; CWMG *Vol. 55, pp. 341–2; E*

The Breath Of My Life

Parnakuti, Poona
23 August 1933

... How I shall use this life out of prison, I do not know[15]. But I must say this that whether in prison or outside prison, Harijan service will be always after my heart and will be the breath of life for me, more precious than the daily bread. I can live for some days at least without the daily bread, but I cannot live without Harijan service for one single minute. ...

Harijan 26-8-1933; CWMG *Vol. 55, p. 366*

'I Have To Die A Heroic Death'

MKG: Anand, [16] what do you think I should do in my present predicament? This time I did not expect to be released. I thought I would be allowed to die. In fact, I had fully prepared myself for such an eventuality, so much so that I had even given away my little personal things to the nurses and the other attendants in the hospital only a day previous to my release. I do not know how my death by fasting would have been regarded by people.

Anand Hingorani: Why, it would have been a most glorious death, Bapu.

MKG: Nonsense. You consider that a glorious death—dying by fasting? I don't. Where is the glory in it? But do you know it is written in my horoscope that I have to die a heroic death?

AH: But, Bapu, even this death by fasting is a heroic one. To allow oneself deliberately to die by inches is not an easy thing. It means courage of the highest order.

MKG: No, I do not think so. My death is to come about either on the gallows or by shooting. And that indeed would be a truly heroic death, not the one by fasting in bed.

Harijan 15-2-1948

To Jawaharlal Nehru

'Parnakuti', Poona,
14 September 1933

My dear Jawaharlal,

I am glad you have written so fully and frankly.

... With much of what you have said in your letter I am in complete agreement. The experience gained after the Karachi Congress has, if possible, strengthened my faith in the main resolution and the economic programme referred to by you. I have no doubt in my mind that our goal can be no less than 'Complete Independence' ... Nor have I the slightest difficulty in agreeing with you that in these days of rapid intercommunication and a growing consciousness of the oneness of all mankind, we must recognize that our nationalism must not be inconsistent with progressive internationalism. India cannot stand in isolation and unaffected by what is going on in other parts of the world. I can, therefore, go the whole length with you and say that 'we should range ourselves with the progressive forces of the world'. But I know that though there is such an agreement between you and me in the enunciation of ideals, there are temperamental differences between us...I feel too that our progress towards the goal will be in exact proportion to the purity of our means. If we can give an ocular demonstration of our uttermost truthfulness and non-violence, I am convinced that our statement of the national goal cannot long offend the interests which your letter would appear to attack ...

Now about the secret methods. I am as firm as ever that they must be tabooed. I am myself unable to make any exceptions. Secrecy has caused much mischief and if it is not put down with a firm hand, it may ruin the movement ...

Finally, if I can say so without incurring the risk of your accusing me of egotism, that I have no sense of defeat in me and the hope in

me that this country of ours is fast marching towards its goal is
burning as bright as it did in 1920. ...

Yours,
Bapu
Jawaharlal Nehru
Poona

CWMG *Vol. 55, pp. 426–30; E*

Brandy

Wardha[17]
11 October 1933

... You CANNOT be blamed for the doctor having given you an injection
of brandy. You did not drink the thing for pleasure. Moreover, an
injection of brandy is not as objectionable as a vaccine. ...

Blessings from Bapu
CWMG *Vol. 56, pp. 82–3; G*

To Mathuradas Trikumji

Wardha
11 October 1933

You SEEM to have forgotten one rule, namely, that one should never
read what has been scored out by the writer of a letter. If one reads
it by chance, one should not pay any attention to it. A person must
be permitted to revise his ideas. It is lack of understanding to think
ill of a person for even the most wicked thought, after he has
corrected himself. If all of us revealed all our thoughts to one
another, people wouldn't be happy even for a minute. ...

CWMG *Vol. 56, p. 84; G*

'Charlie—Tell Me About Red Indians'

Wardha
17 October 1933

My dear Charlie,
    I think you told me that you visited the Booker Washington
Institution at Tuskegee. For the sake of Harijans I have been reading

literature about that wonderful institute. Does your personal inspection confirm what appears in the books about it? Will you write a brief account under the title 'What I saw in Tuskegee'? Did you meet any of the Red Indians? Can you give me your impression of them? The United States Government seem to be spending large sums on their education and general improvement.

Love.

Mohan

Rev. C.F. Andrews
Anand Bhawan
Allahabad

CWMG Vol. 56, p. 103; E

Hindu Sabha

Wardha
1 November 1933

My dear Jawaharlal,

... I do not follow the Hindu Sabha activities. They are vicious. It is most unscrupulous if they are making use of my name in connection with *shuddhi*[18] ...

Love.

Bapu

Gandhi–Nehru Papers, 1933; CWMG Vol. 56, pp. 167–8; E

Speech To Harijans

Nalwadi
Before 7 November 1933

... DR AMBEDKAR is pained and enraged by the oppression of Harijans by caste Hindus. Why should he not feel angry at the oppression which caste Hindus have perpetrated on Harijans? Why, then, do you make such distinctions of high and low among you? If the position that only the Bhangis may remove night-soil and dead animals is accepted, the work being done among Harijans will stop Brahmana, Kshatriya, Vaishya, and Shudra were the four varnas and some others were regarded as belonging to the fifth varna, or as falling outside the varna system. These varnas have not retained their original character. What survives is the distinction of high and low. God has not made anybody high or low. If, living here, we serve you as your Bhangis, you should not be angry. How can we serve Harijans? Should we serve the Mahars but not the Bhangis? Should we make distinctions among Harijans? Hinduism will perish unless these distinctions are wiped out. ...

Harijanbandhu 12-11-1933; CWMG Vol. 56, pp. 189-90; G

Harijan Tour

Amaravati
16 November 1933

(*Gandhi undertook a nationwide tour for raising funds in support of his Harijan work from November 1933 to February 1934. Addressing public meetings, he appealed for cash and jewellery gifts and also auctioned gifts for him brought to those meetings.*)

MKG: This is a small silver-box, very useful. The price is Rs 5.

A European: Thirty rupees!

MKG: Go ahead (*chaliye*).

The European: Forty.

MKG: Not only men, but women can also bid.

The European: Forty-five.

MKG: Sold!

(*The European wants an autograph*)

MKG: Where's the paper?

(*A page from a notebook is torn and given*)

MKG writes:

'With kind regards
        M.K. Gandhi'
        16.11.1933

Akola, 18 November 1933

MKG: Come on with your questions.

Kandare: I have many questions to put, but don't be sorry for my questions, or get angry with me.

MKG: Please do put me your questions. I shall not be sorry or angry.

Kandare: (*Taking his question paper from his pocket*): You posed at the Round Table Congress as a Harijan leader and denied the leadership of Dr Ambedkar.

MKG: No, I said there that I was the representative of millions of people of India. I said there I shared along with Dr Ambedkar the responsibility of looking after the Harijans' interest.

Kandare: Dr Ambedkar opposed you at the Round Table Conference. By doing so did he do justice or injustice to the country?

MKG: He thought he did justice, but I was of opinion that he did injustice.

Laungi (Central Province), 28 November 1933
(*A welcome address and a silver umbrella are presented.*)

MKG: I am going immediately.

(*The hosts are perplexed. MKG points to the welcome address which says* 'Shubhgaman'[19], *instead of* 'Shubhagaman'!)

Saugor, 2 December 1933
(*A child presents him with a purse and a flower. Gandhi thanks her for the presents and strokes her hair, which is dishevelled and has not a trace of oil.*)

MKG: Why don't you comb your hair?

(*The child looks down*)

MKG: (*To the father of the child*) Why don't you give her a bath? Look what a lot of dirt is in her eyes! Why do you not give her a bath daily?

Father: Yes, I give her baths.

MKG: (*Holding her tiny fingers in his hand*) What a lot of dirt there is in her finger nails!

(*The father blinks. Then turning to the others ...*)

MKG: Have you all given up drink?

Men: Yes, given it up.

MKG: Don't eat beef.

Men: We have left that habit long ago.

MKG: Don't drink. Don't eat beef or carrion. Be clean. Do you understand?

(*Picking on a man*)

Tell the women what I said just now.

(*The man stands up, puts his hands to the turban to adjust it, and beginning with 'Mahatmaji says ...', he fumbles ...*)
    (*Picking another*) You tell them.

Man: Mahatmaji advises us not to drink.

(*'Beef' say the people in the gathering*)

Man: Mahatmaji says this also. We must not eat beef.

(*'Carrion', suggests another*)

Man: Yes, we must not eat carrion also.

MKG: (*Turning to the women*) Do you understand?

Women: Yes, sir.

Excerpted from *Flashes in Harijan Tour* by S. Mahadevan, 1936

At Jain Mandir, Madras[20]
22 December 1933

Now I proceed to business. You people go to far-off lands exploiting people and amassing wealth. I am now going to exploit you.

The audience greeted this statement with laughter and cheers. Putting up for auction an ivory casket, Gandhi said:

What will you give for this?

The first bid for the casket which would be worth roughly Rs 15, was Rs 101 by Mr Ramnath Goenka.

Get along, Rs 101 is nothing for you, Gujaratis assembled here. *Rs 201 was the next bid.*

Shall I let it go ... once ... twice, ... I will not yet say 'thrice' ... There is yet time ... A few hundred is nothing to you ...

The Hindu *22–12–1933,* CWMG *Vol. 56, p. 371; E*

Somanahalli, 6 January 1934

(*The auction sale over, Gandhi is about to leave the platform, when a boy rushes to him.*)

Boy: I want your autograph, please.
MKG: What will you give? I want rupees.
Boy: One rupee.
MKG: (*Seeing and touching his earrings*) What are these?
Boy: You can take them.
MKG: Have you your father's permission?
Boy: Yes. He will not object to my giving them to you.
MKG: You have so much independence!

(*And then taking the earrings*) You don't want them. Do not put on earrings hereafter. Do not ask your parents for new ones.
    (*Giving him the autograph*)
    What is your name?

Boy: B.V. Thammappa.
MKG: How old are you?
Boy: Thirteen.
MKG: So you have independence at thirteen. I had not.

Bangalore, 4 January 1934

At a public meeting a girl, 18 years old, comes to him with a request for his autograph. As he takes the pen to write, she makes another request: 'Please give me a motto also.'
    (*Laughing*) 'Truth at any cost'.
    (*She is very pleased and touches his feet with her head.*)

Badagara, Malabar, 13 January 1934

... I CANNOT recall a scene more touching than that of the Harijan cause. I had just finished my speech at Badagara. In it I had made a reasoned appeal to the women present for jewellery. I had finished speaking and was selling the presents received when gently walked up to the platform Kaumudi, a girl 16 years old. She took out one bangle and asked me if I would give my autograph. I was preparing to give it, when off came the other bangle. She had only one on each hand. I said, 'You need not give me both, I shall give you the autograph for one bangle only.' She replied by taking off her golden necklace. This was no easy performance. It had to be disengaged from her long plait of hair ... 'But have you the permission of your parents?' I asked. There was no answer. She had not yet completed her renunciation. Her hands automatically went to her ears and out came her jewelled ear-rings amid the ringing cheers of the public, whose expression of joy was no longer to be suppressed. I asked her again whether she had her parents' consent to the sacrifice. Before I could extract any answer from the shy girl, someone told me that her father was present at the meeting, that he was himself helping me by bidding for the addresses I was auctioning and that he was as generous as his daughter in giving to worthy causes. I reminded Kaumudi that she was not to have the ornaments replaced. She resolutely assented to the condition. As I handed her the autograph, I could not help prefacing it with the remark, 'Your renunciation is a truer ornament than the jewellery you have discarded.' May her renunciation prove to have been an earnest of her being a true Harijan *sevika*.

Harijan *19-1-1934;* CWMG *Vol. 57, pp. 18–19*

At Public Meeting, Calicut[21]
14 January 1934

Friends,

... I have said from many a platform after entering Malabar, if there was a map of untouchability made for the whole of India, Malabar would be marked as the blackest spot in all the land; and as matters stand today, I suppose you will admit that you will have to plead guilty to the charge. ...

Harijan *2-2-1934;* CWMG *Vol. 56, p. 489*

Alwaye, 17 January 1934
Speech at Union Christian College, Alwaye

... My message is simply this that *savarna* Hindus, who have been considering themselves superior to those whom they have called untouchables, unapproachables, invisibles or *avarna* Hindus, should realize that this arrogation of superiority has no sanction whatsoever in the Shastras. If I discovered that those scriptures, which are known as Vedas, Upanishads, Bhagavad Gita, *Smritis*, etc., clearly showed that they claimed divine authority for untouchability as I have described it to you, then nothing on this earth would hold me to Hinduism. I should throw it overboard as I should throw overboard a rotten apple.

Harijan *26-1-1934*

Trivandrum, 20 January 1934

Gandhi visits the Harijan Hostel in Trivandrum and enquires of the gentleman-in-charge details as to how it is run. He is told the meals cost Rs 9.

MKG: It can't cost Rs 9.

(*After looking into the accounts for a few minutes*)

   Whose writing is this?
Ans.: It is the clerk's.
MKG: How much does he get?
Ans.: The clerk is a part time worker.
MKG: Are vouchers kept here?
Ans.: There are no vouchers.
MKG: This is extraordinary. The cost of food does not come to Rs 4. There are other expenses also. Does Rs 9 include all expenses such as rent?
Ans.: Yes, all expenses, but not rent.
MKG: Then Rs 9 is too much.
MKG: Do you have curd?
Ans.: Only buttermilk.
MKG: It does not cost much.

Tirunelveli [22], 24 January 1934

... YOU MAY call me superstitious if you like; but a man like me cannot but believe that this earthquake[23] is a divine chastisement sent by

God for our sins. Even to avowed scoffers it must be clear that nothing but divine will can explain such a calamity. It is my unmistakable belief that not a blade of grass moves but by the Divine Will. ...

Harijan 2-2-1934; CWMG *Vol. 57, p. 44*

... YOU MUST show to your brethren and sisters of Bihar, by your sharing your food and clothing with them, that the same blood courses in your veins as in the veins of the Biharis. You can send your contributions to Babu Rajendra Prasad, or you can send them to me and I shall see to it that every pie you give reaches the proper quarters.

Harijan 2-2-1934; CWMG *Vol. 57, p. 45*

FOR ME there is a vital connection between the Bihar calamity and the untouchability campaign. The Bihar calamity is a sudden and accidental reminder of what we are and what God is; but untouchability is a calamity handed down to us from century to century. It is a curse brought upon ourselves by our own neglect of a portion of Hindu humanity. Whilst this calamity in Bihar damages the body, the calamity brought about by untouchability corrodes the very soul.

Harijan 2-2-1934; CWMG *Vol. 57, pp. 45–6*

Tuticorin[24], 24 January 1934

... I WANT you to be 'superstitious' enough with me to believe that the earthquake is a divine chastisement for the great sin we have committed and are still committing against those whom we describe as untouchables, *Panchamas*, and whom I describe as Harijans. ...

CWMG *Vol. 57, p. 46*

Madurai, 25 January 1934

Chiranjivi Prabhavati,

I have not heard from you recently. I feel worried because of the terrible earthquake. Where is Jayaprakash[25]? How are you both? Following the earthquake I had expected a detailed letter from you. ...

Blessings from

Bapu

CWMG *Vol. 57, p. 48; G*

Bihar And Untouchability

... I AM not affected by posers such as 'why punishment for an age-old sin', or 'why punishment to Bihar and not to the South', or 'why an earthquake and not some other form of punishment'. My answer is: I am not God. ...

Harijan 2-2-1934; CWMG *Vol. 57, p. 87*

'Gurudev—I Cannot Help Myself'

2 February 1934

Dear Gurudev,

I received your letter only just now. There is a campaign of vilification of me going on. My remarks on the Bihar calamity were a good handle to beat me with. I have spoken about it at many meetings. Enclosed is my considered opinion. I see from your statement that we have come upon perhaps a fundamental difference. But I cannot help myself. I do believe that super-physical consequences flow from physical events. How they do so, I do not know.

If after reading my article, you still see the necessity of publishing your statement, it can be at once published either here or there just as you desire. I hope you are keeping well.

Yours sincerely,

M.K. Gandhi

(P.S.) The last lines are disgracefully written but I was tired out and half asleep. Please forgive. If I am to catch the post today, I may not wait to make a fair copy.

CWMG *Vol. 57, p. 95; E*

In Bihar

Motihari, 15 March 1934

THIS IS no time for talking. I have come to see and help you, and not to talk. But there are just two things I want to say to you. The first is this. The relief committees have the money, and either beggars or workers will take it. And I want no beggars. It would be deplorable if this earthquake turned us into mendicants. Only those without eyes, or hands, or feet, or otherwise unfit for work, may ask for alms. For the able-bodied to beg is, in the language of the Gita, to become thieves.

The second thing is this, that God had Himself sent us this gift. We must accept it as a gift from Him, and then we shall understand its meaning. What is the meaning? It is this, that untouchability must go, that is to say, nobody must consider himself higher than another.

The Searchlight 18-3-1934; CWMG Vol. 57, p. 283; H

To Kasturba

Patna
20/21 March 1934

Ba,

... I visited Motihari and other places. Even big mansions have been reduced to heaps of brick and mortar. Everywhere in the streets we saw heaps of bricks and ruins of buildings. The fields are covered with sand ejected with water from the bowels of the earth. Till this sand is removed, no crops can grow, and removing it is no easy work. For it is not only one or two *bighas* that are so covered. Thousands of bighas have been covered and in some places the layers are six inches thick or even thicker. The people's misery, therefore, is beyond measure. ...

Blessings to you all from
Bapu
CWMG Vol. 57, p. 293; G

At Sonepur[26]

28 March 1934

... YESTERDAY, AS the motor was passing along the Gandak embankment, I received a note from the Doms[27] of a village close by, telling me that they were suffering terribly from want of water, as the villagers would not allow them to take water from the common well. I drew the attention of the Headman to the note and he promised to put the thing right, if it was found that the Doms' complaint was justified. God's wrath was felt equally by the rich and the poor, the Hindu and the Mussalman, the caste man and the outcaste. Shall we not learn God's terrible impartiality that it is criminal to consider any human being untouchable or lower than ourselves? If a single Dom or any other human being is denied the use of village wells, surely, the lesson of the fifteenth of January will have been lost upon us. ...

Harijan 6-4-1934; CWMG Vol. 57, pp. 320–1

The Shame Of It[28]

Karachi
10 July 1934

... DR AMBEDKAR is such an intelligent and clever lawyer that he puts to shame many others. He is able to touch the hearts of many people by his sharp intelligence. The magnitude of his sacrifice is great. He is absorbed in his own work. He leads a simple life. He is capable of earning one to two thousand rupees every month. He is also in a position to settle down in Europe if he so desires. But he doesn't want to stay there. He is only concerned about the welfare of the Harijans. But what is the condition of even a man like him in our society today? He says: 'If I go to Poona to attend the Assembly session, I have to stay in a hotel and spend the entire amount of the daily allowance of Rs 10, whereas the others can stay with their friends and save that money. There is no Hindu family in Poona which would accept me as a colleague or a friend.' Whose shame is this?. ...

Harijanbandhu 22-7-1934; CWMG Vol. 58, p. 166; G

'I Have Not Abandoned Harilal'

Kanpur
23 July 1934[29]

... I HAVE not abandoned Harilal, nor given up hope about him. I am serving him by not yielding to him ... I am extremely doubtful about the rightness of the course which has now been adopted. He has always lived thus up to now. He used to be brave, but friends have deprived him of his capacity for self-reliance. And now he has thought of (business in) patent medicines. But as all of you have approved of this solution, I need not criticize it. What seems right to one, that is one's dharma. Keep writing to me.

Blessing from
Bapu
CWMG Vol. 58, p. 233; G

'A Dog Can Drink From A Reservoir But ...'

Benares[30]
31 July 1934

... A DOG can drink from a reservoir, but a thirsty Harijan boy may not. If he goes, he cannot escape being beaten. Untouchability as practiced today considers man worse than a dog.

A Harijan was down with pneumonia. A sanatanist doctor was called on payment. He accepted the fees but how could he touch the patient? He sent for a Muslim, gave him a watch and told him: 'Please tell me how many times his pulse beats in a minute.' The doctor was given the pulse-count, he wrote the prescription and left. A second doctor was then called. He examined the patient's lungs and heart carefully and then prescribed medicine; the sick man then recovered. ...

Harijan Sevak *10-8-1934;* CWMG *Vol. 58, pp. 266–7; H*

To Jawaharlal

Wardha
14 August 1934

My dear Jawaharlal,

Though you are now under distressing circumstances, your release[31] takes a great load off my mind, as it is three-fourths medicine for Kamala ...

This is however to suggest to you that you should not make any public political pronouncement. I have felt that in cases of domestic illness or sorrow the Government has acted in a becoming manner. I do feel therefore that we ought to recognize this fact by not using the liberty thus obtained for any other purpose not inconsistent with that of the Government. ...

Bapu
CWMG *Vol. 58, p. 303; E*

Socialism

17 August 1934

My dear Jawaharlal,

... I have looked up the dictionary meaning of socialism. It takes me no further than where I was before I read the definition.

What will you have me read to know its full content? I have read one of the books Masani[32] gave me and now I am devoting all my spare time to reading the book recommended by Narendra Deva. ...

Bapu
CWMG Vol. 58, pp. 317–18; E

Fasting

Wardha
28 August 1934

... DURING ALL the four fasts undertaken for the Harijan cause, I have noticed a particular dislike for water, whether with or without soda or salt, and whether hot or cold. I have been able to bear, but only just bear, aerated water. This inability to drink water has been the greatest drawback in my fasts. I must mention that, being largely a fruitarian and having abstained from condiments of every description, except salt, practically for the past forty years, I rarely drink water even in the ordinary course. All the liquid I need comes from the fresh juicy fruit and the non-starch vegetables and honey and hot-water drinks. ...

Harijan 24-8-1934; CWMG Vol. 58, pp. 355–6

'We Have Turned The Congress Into A *Tamasha*'

Wardha[33]
4 September 1934

... WHAT IS this about music and cinema? Do they wish to turn the Congress session into a Felix Circus or Barnum show? But, then, what can I say in this matter? I do love music, but everything is good in its place. If the three or four days of the Congress session are crowded with such activities, the atmosphere of seriousness will disappear. Even if they wish to arrange such programmes, somebody may be given a contract for them. I am of the view, however, that no such programmes can be arranged at the place where the [nation's] parliament meets. But we have turned the Congress into a tamasha. Inclusion of genuine Indian music in a cent per cent swadeshi exhibition is legitimate. But only traditional instruments should be used in such a programme. I can see no room at all for a band. You may show this to Sardar[34]. ...

Bapuni Prasadi, p. 252; CWMG Vol. 58, pp. 398–9; G

'Ramdas[35]—God Will Restore You'

Wardha

12 September 1934

... GOD WILL restore you. Keep repeating the name of Him whose <i>das</i> you are considered to be, that is, to whom your name signifies that you have been dedicated. Know that Ramanama is the only remedy that never fails. There is no remedy like peace of mind. Who has ever escaped birth, death, old age, and disease? They are inseparable from the body. If, however, we preserve equality of mind towards them, they will seem the same though in fact different. ...

CWMG Vol. 58, p. 441; G

To Harilal

Wardha

3 October 1934

... I WOKE up at 2.30 and started thinking about my dharma towards you. I couldn't go to sleep again and left the bed at 2.45. After cleaning my teeth and drinking warm water with honey, I have set down to write this.

... I do not yet believe in your regeneration. I must have independent proof of that. I, therefore, do not wish to ask you for an assurance to that effect. However, I wish to assure myself through your conduct ...

1. Have you touched liquor any time after you wrote our first letter to me from there?
2. Have you indulged in sexual pleasure through mind, speech, or body?
3. Do you smoke?
4. Have you any other addiction?

Let there be this understanding between you and me. If at any time you break your word to me or if it is proved that you have deceived me, I should fast for at least seven days. I may fast even longer, if I wish and have the strength to do so, in case your breach of promise or misdeed pains me very much.

... Whatever you do, do after full deliberation. Do not do any thing that is beyond your strength, nor anything that does not appeal to your heart or reason ...

May you attain the highest good. May God dwell in you. He alone is your true Guru. 'Friends of the body but care for their own interests; they will keep away at the end.' You should, therefore, do as the self within bids you, with God as witness. It will not hurt me in the least if you do not accept my advice. But it will hurt me very much indeed if you deceive me. I am an old man now, and you are not a child.

Blessings from
Bapu
From the manuscript of Mahadev Desai's Diary;
CWMG *Vol. 59, pp. 110–12; G*

Wardha
11 October 1934

I LIKED your letter very much. I hope the changes in you will endure. You should have patience. Since you have come to trust me, there will be no difficulty. ...

Blessings from
Bapu
From the manuscript of Mahadev Desai's Diary;
CWMG *Vol. 59, p. 162; G*

Wardha
17 October 1934

YOU ARE constantly in my thoughts. If I had time, I would go on inflicting long letters on you. If the change that you have described endures, a painful episode in my life would end and I would be extremely happy in this the last stage of my life.

I do not wish that you should do anything beyond your strength. Only as much as your reason and heart accept will endure and seem natural. I am sure that if you followed rules of diet, etc., you would be completely all right. Do not regard yourself as an old man.

... I see that you have not been able to give up smoking. So long as you find it absolutely necessary to smoke, you may do so as if you were taking medicine. Perhaps you do not know that it is not in the least difficult to give up smoking. It can be done by adopting a simple diet. What do you eat? Are you ready to make changes in your diet?. ...

From the manuscript of Mahadev Desai's Diary;
CWMG *Vol. 59, pp. 187–8; G*

My Supposed Inconsistency

Wardha
9 November 1934

THE EDITOR (of *Harijan*) has sent the following received by him for answer:

In the *Harijan* of the 9th March Gandhiji is reported to have said that 'there was no warrant in the Shastras for untouchability' ... [This] does not seem to accord with his previous statement, which was that there is such sanction but he did not accept the authority of such passages because they were immoral.

Will you kindly explain the apparent inconsistency, through the columns of the *Harijan*?

I make no hobgoblin of consistency. If I am true to myself from moment to moment, I do not mind all the inconsistencies that may be flung in my face. But in the letter quoted, there is no inconsistency. ...

Harijan 9-11-1934; CWMG *Vol. 59, p. 308; E*

To M. Visvesvaraya

Wardha
10 December 1934

Dear Friend,
... I have no difficulty whatsoever in endorsing your remarks about heavy industries. I know that the heavy industries cannot be

organized without power driven machinery. I can have no quarrel with such use of machinery. My objection comes in when such machinery displaces human labour without providing displaced hands with a substitute at least as good as displaced labour.

Yours sincerely,
M.K. Gandhi
CWMG *Vol. 59, p. 435*

Talk With Mary Chesley

Wardha
On or before 15 December 1934[36]

Mary Chesley: Do you believe your guidance comes from subconscious reasoning or from God?

MKG: From God—but subconscious reasoning may be the voice of God ...

MC: Then does following conscience lead to mystical experiences?

MKG: It may or it may not. But one thing is sure that the humility which feels itself nothing before God is necessary for mystical experiences, such as those of Saint Francis and Saint Augustine ...

MC: How do you understand what is God's guidance for you when it is a question of choosing between two *good* things?

MKG: I use my intellect on the subject and if I don't get any strong feeling as to which of the two I should choose, I just leave the matter, and before long I wake up one morning with the perfect assurance that it should be A rather than B ...

MC: From what sources do you get your conception of God?

MKG: From my childhood, remembering my mother's constant visits to the temple. Sometimes these were as many as four or five a day, and never less than two. Also my nurse used to tell me I must repeat the name of God if I felt afraid.

MC: Have you had any mystical experiences?

MKG: If, by mystical experiences, you mean visions, no. I should be a fraud if I claimed to have had such. But I am very sure of the voice which guides me ...

MC: You have said sometimes that consciousness of sin brings a feeling of separation from God. Did you feel any such separation before your fast?

MKG: No. I felt only great uneasiness and restlessness. I could not joke even in my usual way.

CWMG *Vol. 59, pp. 459-62; E*

Revising Drafts

Wardha
16 December 1934

Chiranjivi Prema,

... By writing 'not revised'[37] I ensure—and do—justice to myself and to the person to whom the letter is addressed. If by chance I have written '*aaj mar gaya*' instead of 'Ajmer gaya', the other party may correct the mistake or, in case of doubt, ask me. A letter which has not been revised should always be regarded as incomplete. But I would prefer, and so would you, that I write an incomplete letter to you rather than not write any. ...

Blessings from
Bapu
CWMG *Vol. 60, pp. 1-2; G*

'I Am No Judge Of Prose'

Wardha
24 December 1934

Dear Friend[38],

Surely the friends have perpetrated a joke. I am no representative of the domain of literature. I have no University qualifications. I cannot write after my name even a 'failed B.A.', having never gone beyond the London Matriculation. Nor can I call myself a literary man by training. I am no judge of prose, much less of poetry. Some of the latter I cannot understand. My ignorance is really appalling in the domain of literature. I had therefore to send you a negative telegram which I hope you received in time. Though therefore I cannot propose your name, I can at least hope that you will win the prize.

With greetings of the season and regards to you and Mrs Cousins.

Yours sincerely,

M.K.G.

From the manuscript of Mahadev Desai's Diary*; CWMG Vol. 60, p. 27; E*

Discussion At A Harijan Home

Kingsway Camp, Delhi

29 December 1934

MKG: Is this the hut that I was told was being hurriedly erected for me? Why this height of 16 feet, and these heavy pillars and this high plinth? A simple cutcha hut with grass-thatched roof was the one I had in mind and had expected to find here. It should not have cost more than Rs 500, whereas this has cost Rs 2500.

Malkani: The thing had to be hurriedly arranged ... We went in for iron beams and rafters, as wooden ones would have taken much time.

MKG: No excuse at all. If you knew that this thing was going to cost so much, why did you not give up the idea altogether? I should have been perfectly comfortable in a tent. The pity is that you forgot that you were the representative of Harijans and villagers. You acted as Sjt. Ghanshyamdas's representative ... And why this spiral staircase? You might easily have procured a wooden staircase!

Malkani: No Bapu, it has been borrowed and will be returned as soon as we do not need it.

... It was bed-time. Beds were being brought.

MKG: No bed-stead necessary. The cotton mattress over the mat is quite enough. Not that I should not use it if health made it imperative, but I should do without it as long as I could.

Brijkrishna: But, Bapu, even the poorest villagers have got their *charpais*.

MKG: I know, I know. Does that mean that we should imitate them in that convenient matter, when we cannot possibly imitate them in other things? ...

Harijan 11-1-1935; CWMG Vol. 60, pp. 35–6

Contraception

Delhi
8 January 1935

Mrs C. Kuttan Nair[39]: ... Will not the teaching of sex hygiene in schools in the most scientific and informal manner be really beneficial to our boys and girls?

MKG: Yes. And there should be no reason why one should not be able to talk freely on this matter.

Mrs Nair: ... For the sake of the mother, whose health is drained away by the bringing forth of too many children, and for the sake of children themselves, who should be a joy to us but who now come forth unwanted in such large numbers, may not birth control through contraceptives be resorted to, as the next best thing to self-control, which is too high an ideal for the ordinary man or woman?

MKG: Do you think that the freedom of the body is obtained by resorting to contraceptives? Women should learn to resist their husbands ...

Mrs Nair: Are you, under these conditions, in favour of sterilization as is being done in Germany under Hitler?

MKG: Sterilization is a sort of contraceptive and though I am against the use of contraceptives in the case of women, I do not mind voluntary sterilization in the case of man, since he is the aggressor. ...

The Hindustan Times *11-11-1935;* CWMG *Vol. 60, pp. 66–9; E*

To Khurshed Captain[40]

Wardha
7 February 1935

... I WISH you to overcome your objection to eggs. I think I told you that it was possible now to have sterile eggs. ... These eggs are obtained without the hens having to be mated. As an article of daily food, from the spiritual standpoint, that would be perhaps objectionable. But as a medical agent, sterile eggs might not be objected to.

Perhaps you know that Kamala[41] had a set-back and lost 2 lb. last week.

CWMG *Vol. 60, p. 185; E*

To Feroze Gandhi[42]

Wardha
7 February 1935

My dear Feroze,

Your postcard of the 2nd instant is somewhat disturbing. Kamala has no weight to lose. Yet I suppose there will be these ups and downs whilst she is still convalescing.

Are you getting the fruit and vegetables in the manner wanted?

CWMG *Vol. 60, p. 187*

The Jamia Has A Great Future

Wardha
20 February 1935

Dear Zakir[43],

It is a great idea to have the foundation of the Jamia[44] laid by its youngest child. My congratulations on the originality of the conception. I know that the Jamia has a great future. Through it I expect the seed of Hindu-Muslim union to grow into a majestic tree. ...

Yours,
Bapu
CWMG *Vol. 60, p. 244*

'Anger Is A Madness'

Wardha
11 March 1935

PRABHAVATI SHOWED me your[45] letter to her. It grieved me. I knew you had a temper but I had never imagined that you could get so angry without there being any occasion for it. I am the cause of your anger, am I not? After all Prabhavati only conveyed to you what instructions I had given her. You ought to understand that a vow if taken must be observed too. And why such contempt for the Ashram? Can anyone contemptuous of the Ashram have any respect for me? If there is no love for the Ashram, how can there be any love for me? But can one argue against anger?

Anger is a kind of madness and when it subsides you will laugh at yourself. ...

Blessings from
Bapu
From the manuscript of Mahadev Desai's Diary;
CWMG *Vol. 60, pp. 296–7; H*

Polished And Unpolished Rice[46]

Wardha
On or before 18 March 1935

Member: Unpolished rice does not cook easily, and when cooked, it all becomes a lump and scares people away.

MKG: That it takes more time to cook is true, that it is delicious, and more delicious than polished rice, has been proved beyond doubt; and after all, what is handsome to the eye may not be handsome after all. Handsome is that handsome tastes.

Goshi Behn[47]: Don't you murder good age-old proverbs, Bapu, in the heat of your argument.

MKG: Well, what else can I do, when I am out to murder age-old prejudices and superstitions?

adapted from Harijan *22-3-1935;* CWMG *Vol. 60, pp. 311–12; E*

'A Fellow Crank'

Wardha,
29 March 1935

Dear Agatha[48],

... I remember Josiah Oldfield[49] well. He was of the greatest help to me when I went to London as a lad. He is a fellow crank. ...

Bapu
CWMG *Vol. 60, p. 357; E*

'Harilal—You Crave For Sex'

Ramanawami, Wardha
12 April 1935

... I UNDERSTAND your problem. You don't wish to deceive yourself or me. You still crave for sex pleasure. If so, you must satisfy your craving. You can suppress it only when you feel a strong aversion to worldly pleasures. ...

Blessings from
Bapu
CWMG *Vol. 60, p. 410; G*

Harijans And The Killings Of Pigs

Wardha
13 April 1935

SETH ACHALSINGH of Agra wrote to me two months ago a letter describing a scene he had witnessed for the first time in his life. He had seen pigs, with their mouths gagged, being roasted alive by Harijans. I was horrified by the description. But I know that pigs are used as food by Sikhs, and also by thousands of Hindus in Andhra Desha. It is possible that pig-flesh is eaten in the other parts of India by non-Harijans. The only thing that can be said with certainty is that, apart from vegetarians, Mussalmans alone never eat pig's flesh.

... If one is to consider the degrees of cruelty, the pig seems to require the most cruelty before it can be killed. My purpose in writing this is to show that Harijans are the least offenders in this matter, not, I admit, from choice but from sheer necessity. The question raised by Seth Achalsingh therefore resolves itself into one not of Harijan reform but of broad humanitarian reform. We must not take up any stick that comes our way to beat the poor Harijan with. ...

Harijan 13-4-1935; CWMG *Vol. 60, pp. 416–17*

To Harilal

Indore
22 April 1935

THERE IS no need at all to be in a hurry to come to a decision about Amala's[50] letter. I think you will have to drop the idea. You should write and tell her plainly that any children that may be born will have to be brought up in a simple manner. And whatever means of livelihood the Lord provides will probably be in Wardha. If you start going to women or drinking, she should be free to leave you immediately. And even this you may write only if you are sure that you wish to marry her. Amala's letter seems a good one to me, but I didn't know her as she reveals herself in it. I am, therefore, of the view that you will not be happy unless she comes to feel strongly that she cannot live without you.

It is certainly a good thing that you have not become impatient. Have patience and do only what is proper.

Blessings from
Bapu
CWMG *Vol. 60, pp. 456–7; G*

To S. Satyamurti[51]

Wardha
16 May 1935

YOU ARE a tempter. I must not succumb. You will be all right without my blessings. As you have well said, you will succeed if you deserve success.

The Hindu *20-5-1935*; CWMG *Vol. 61, p. 66*

The King And The Viceroy

Wardha
24 May 1935

My dear Agatha[52],

... The King there is, or may be, above party strife. The King-Emperor is here identified with the Services. He is the ruler through his Viceroy. ...

Love.

Bapu
CWMG *Vol. 61, p. 96*

To The Press

Borsad
31 May 1935

(Asked as to why he selected Wardha as his headquarters)

BECAUSE WARDHA is in the centre of India, and it was in Wardha that I was able to get a rich piece of land with buildings and plenty of water, land worth over two lakhs. There are nearly 700 fruit trees on the land. I selected Wardha also because Sheth Jamnalal Bajaj was most anxious that the land which he had contemplated as donation for the Maganlal Gandhi Memorial should be taken up by the All-India Village Industries Association. ...

The Bombay Chronicle 1-6-1935; CWMG Vol. 61, p. 122; E

Which Jesus?

Poona
19 June 1935

Dear Sister[53],

... Which Jesus am I to believe? Him of your conception or mine? You will say, 'Jesus of the Bible'. Then the question is: 'According to whose interpretation?' I solve the difficulty by going the way God takes me.

From the manuscript for Mahadev Desai's Diary; *CWMG Vol. 61, p. 180*

Vaids

Poona
21 June 1935

Bhai Vallabhbhai,

... I can't put my faith in *vaids*. Their remedies are like black magic. They are just a shot in the dark. Are they worth trying even if they help? ... They do have some effective drugs, but when their power is exhausted you are where you were. I would quake with fear to put you in their hands. I see that even Malaviyaji and Motilalji went ultimately to doctors. ...

Blessings from
Bapu
CWMG Vol. 61, pp. 184–5; G

A Discussion[54]

Before 22 June 1935

MKG: Is not this spinning wheel a machine?[55]

Socialist: I do not mean this machine, but I mean bigger machinery. ... You would have nothing to do with electricity?

MKG: Who said so? If we could have electricity in every village home, I should not mind villagers plying their implements and tools with the help of electricity. ...

Harijan *22-6-1935;* CWMG *Vol. 61, p. 187*

To Narandas Gandhi

Wardha
25 June 1935

IT SEEMS that Harilal is off the rails again. ...

CWMG *Vol. 61, p. 199; G*

Wardha
27 June 1935

THE BOND of blood-relationship also has its limits. It shouldn't make us violate moral principles. Harilal cannot have greater claims on you than a stranger placed in similar circumstances. We should rather be more generous towards a stranger and more miserly towards Harilal. That is, the more intimate the blood-relationship, the stricter should our attitude be. Only thus can we do pure justice.

CWMG *Vol. 61, pp. 206–7; G*

Wardha
1 July 1935

... IF HARILAL does not confess his faults, then, you cannot keep him at all. In no circumstances can anything be given to him in the shape of help from public funds. ...

Blessings from
Bapu
CWMG *Vol. 61, p. 219; G*

To Prabhavati

Wardha
5 July 1935

... HOW LONG would it have taken to drop me a postcard with two lines? ...

CWMG *Vol. 61, p. 229; G*

A Lesson In English Grammar

Wardha
5 July 1935

IF YOU[56] do not follow the corrections and the notes, do ask me. Please improve your handwriting. Make the letters large and keep your words separate.

I do not have any trouble (in correcting your lessons). But I will appoint another teacher. Meanwhile keep on sending (your lessons) to me.

1. Normally we can say that 's' is used for living things and 'of' for non-living things; e.g., 'a man's leg' but 'a leg of a table'.

2. 'Had' is used for an action which is already over before another; e.g., 'He had eaten when I went to him'; but 'He ate at 10 o'clock'. 'Had eaten' is past perfect tense; 'ate' is simple past tense.

3 'Have' is used as an auxiliary verb as well as the main verb. As the main verb it denotes possession or relationship, e.g., 'He has a box'—possession; 'He has a son'—relationship.

When an action is complete, forms of 'have' are used but when it is intended merely to suggest the past tense, forms of 'be' are used. ...

Blessings from
Bapu
CWMG *Vol. 61, pp. 229–30; G and E*

On Press Reports

Wardha
Monday, 8 July 1935

... NEVER BELIEVE what the papers say of me unless you[57] have confirmation from here. I did howl from pain for 45 minutes. When it was over, there was no weakness felt, no weight lost. It was an overdose of *neem* leaf. I was trying its maximum capacity. Such experiments must be tried on self. My experiments have never done permanent harm ...

Believe me, I am quite fit. ...

Bapu
CWMG *Vol. 61, pp. 240–1; E*

Advice To Keisho[58]

Wardha
Before 13 July 1935

... 'IN ROME do as the Romans do' is not a meaningless saying. We must try to observe the manners and customs of the country whose salt we eat. When I was in Africa, I tried to use as many things as I could, made by African hands. So unless you have any special objection, I would ask you to use khadi. Khadi is no doubt dearer, but then you may try to do with less cloth than you need.

Harijan 13-7-1935; CWMG *Vol. 61, p. 247*

Harilal Has Crossed All Limits

Wardha[59]
22 July 1935

... HARILAL HAS gone to the last extreme. For the whole day he is found in a drunken state. This time he has crossed all limits. ...

Blessings from
Bapu
CWMG *Vol. 61, p. 276; G*

Snake Poisoning

Wardha
17 August 1935

DR SOKHEY, Director of Haffkine Institute, has kindly supplied me with a note on Indian snakes ...

Since nine-tenths of snakes are non-poisonous and are valuable protectors of fields against rats, etc., it would be a good thing if a simple key for distinguishing poisonous from non-poisonous snakes can be had ...

Though Col. Sokhey has warned me that there is no sure remedy against bites of poisonous snakes except injections of anti-venom serum, I cannot resist giving the remedy claimed to have been successfully tried by Just, the author of *Return to Nature.* I have tried it successfully in two or three cases of snake-bites and numerous cases of scorpion stings. It consists in applying an ample earth bandage to the affected part. Take as much clean earth as possible, add cold water to it, and make a cold poultice of it. Spread the composition an inch as a pack on a wet linen piece, fold, apply, and bandage. If it is a toe that is bitten, the leg should have the poultice up to the knee, if a finger, the whole arm should be bandaged, the more the better. All the other treatment as described in the foregoing note should undoubtedly be taken. And if the serum injection is taken, the earth treatment may be quite superfluous. I was assured that if the injection was given in time, it was a sure antidote. Nor can I vouch for the absolute efficacy of the earth treatment. For I have no knowledge that the bites treated by me were highly poisonous. I suggest the earth treatment as being harmless and most easily available in villages and as being highly acclaimed by its author.

Harijan *17-8-1935;* CWMG *Vol. 61, pp. 338–9*

To Kasturba

Wardha
24 August 1935

Ba,

Don't you feel that you were prompted by God to go there[60]? Moreover Manu also is with you. And so I am not worrying at all. You are a lioness and illness has no terrors for you. Face the situation courageously, therefore. Put your trust in Rama. Ask Manu[61] to write to me everyday. ...

CWMG *Vol. 61, p. 361; G*

To Manu Harilal Gandhi

Wardha
24 August 1935

KEEP ME informed daily about Devadas' condition. ...

Blessings from
Bapu
CWMG *Vol. 61, p. 362; G*

To Devadas

Wardha
26 August 1935

... IT IS good that I have a detailed letter from Ba. She writes and says that you have become panicky. But why should you be alarmed because of the illness? When we know the ultimate result and are prepared for it, why should you feel frightened? But there is still plenty of time before you take leave. You have to render a lot of service through your body. So resolve and get well. I can only advise you as regards diet and so on. May God protect you.

Blessings from
Bapu
CWMG *Vol. 61, pp. 369–70; G*

Telegram To Viceroy

Wardha
30 August 1935

REGARDING KAMALA Nehru's health have just received express cable Germany. 'Condition serious owing to persistent nausea and vomiting.' In view of this serious news may I appeal for Pandit Jawaharlal Nehru's unconditional discharge enabling him if at all possible to catch Dutch Air Mail flying next Tuesday?[62, 63]

The Leader *5-9-1935;* CWMG *Vol. 61, p. 375; E*

To Jawaharlal

Wardha
12 September 1935

My dear Jawaharlal,

How well you have joined Kamala! It is the best tonic for her ...

Rajagopalachari has just dropped in with Lakshmi and her baby boy[64]. Devadas was badly ill. Ansari has packed him off to Simla. I have Mira on my hands prostrate with bad fever.

I would like you to allow yourself to be elected President for the next year. Your acceptance will solve many difficulties. If you think fit, send me a wire.

Has Indu been fixed up? ...

Love from us all.

Bapu

CWMG Vol. 61, p. 406; E

A Practice Of Mine—And Its Risk

Wardha

21 September 1935

In 1891 after my return from England, I virtually took charge of the children of the family and introduced the habit of walking with them—boys and girls—putting my hands on their shoulders. These were my brothers' children. The practice continued even after they grew old. With the extension of the family, it gradually grew to proportions sufficient to attract attention ...

Recently two co-workers who came to Wardha suggested that the practice was likely to set a bad example to others and that I should discontinue it on that account. Their argument did not appeal to me. Nevertheless I did not want to ignore the friends' warning. I, therefore, referred it for examination and advice to five inmates of the Ashram. Whilst it was taking shape a decisive event took place. It was brought to my notice that a bright university student was taking all sorts of liberties in private with a girl who was under his influence, on the plea that he loved her like his own sister and could not restrain himself from some physical demonstration of it. He resented the slightest suggestion of impurity. Could I mention what the youth had been doing, the reader would unhesitatingly pronounce the liberties taken by him as impure. When I read the correspondence, I and those who saw it came to the conclusion that either the young man was a consummate hypocrite or was self-deluded.

Anyway the discovery set me a-thinking. I recalled the warning of the two co-workers and asked myself how I would feel if I found that the young man was using my practice in its defence ... Whilst I do not believe in a brahmacharya which ever requires a wall of protection against the touch of the opposite sex and will fail if exposed to the least temptation, I am not unaware of the dangers attendant upon the freedom I have taken. ...

Harijan *21-9-1935;* CWMG *Vol. 61, pp. 436–7*

Soya Beans

Wardha
19 October 1935

IT HAS been found that soya beans can be cooked whole and eaten like any other beans. Shri Narhar Bhave of Baroda, who has given his three gifted and gentle sons, Vinoba, Balkrishna and Shivaji, to national service, is himself a careful observer, 61 years old. He is living almost wholly on milk and six ounces of soya beans and is keeping perfect health and strength ...

Let those who are interested in food-reform from the poor man's point of view try the experiment. It should be remembered that soya beans are a most nutritious diet. ...

Harijan *19-10-1935;* CWMG *Vol. 62, p. 42*

About Snake-Bites

Wardha
20 October 1935

Question: Is there any risk involved in making vertical and horizontal cuts over a snake-bite?

MKG: There is no risk at all in making a cut over the bite. It would have been easier to follow if the translator had used the word 'incision' instead of 'cut'. The only purpose of making an incision is to drain some blood out ...

Question: What is meant by 'using the blade of the safety razor after passing it over a flame'?

MKG: The blade should be passed back and forth over a lighted match until the latter burns out. This would take only a few seconds.

Question: Is there no danger of death to the person who sucks [the poison]?

MKG: If he has no ulcers in his mouth, there is no danger of death or of any other harm.

Harijanbandhu *20-10-1935;* CWMG *Vol. 62, pp. 50–1*

The Buddha[65]

Before 2 November 1935

... Visitor: You would judge the Buddha?

MKG: I never said so. I simply said, if I had the good fortune to be face to face with one like him, I should not hesitate to ask him why he did not teach the gospel of work, in preference to one of contemplation. ...

Harijan 2-11-1935; CWMG Vol. 62, p. 85

Caste Has To Go[66]

Wardha
16 November 1935

... THE SOONER public opinion abolishes it, the better. ...

Harijan 16-11-1935; CWMG Vol. 62, pp. 121–2

If Only Women Will Learn To Say 'No'

Segaon, Wardha[67]
3 December 1935

... MY WIFE I made the orbit of all women. In her I studied all women. I came in contact with many European women in South Africa, and I knew practically every Indian women there I worked with them. I tried to show them they were not slaves either of their husbands or parents, not only in the political field but in the domestic as well. But the trouble was that some could not resist their husbands. The remedy is in the hands of women themselves. The struggle is difficult for them and I do not blame them. I blame the men. Men have legislated against them. Man has regarded woman as his tool ... I have felt that during the years still left to me if I can drive home to women's minds the truth that they are free, we will have no birth control problems in India. If they will only learn to say 'no' to their husbands when they approach them carnally! I do not suppose all husbands are brutes and if women only know how to resist them all will be well. I have been able to teach women who have come in contact with me how to resist their husbands. The real problem is that many do not want to resist them. ...

CWMG Vol. 62, p. 157; Tendulkar Vol. 4, p. 45

Jawaharlal's Autobiography

Wardha
19 December 1935

IT IS needless to say that it[68] is a brilliantly written book, and a great literary production. There are parts where I have my fundamental differences with you and which I would like to criticize, but I will not do so as it is scarcely necessary or useful ...

There is just one thing where perhaps I might make a helpful suggestion. The attack on the Liberals seems to have been overdone. It seems to obtrude on the reader's attention over and over again and sometimes mars the grace and beauty of the narrative. ...

CWMG Vol. 62, pp. 171–2; E

Temptation

Bombay
January 1936

... I HAVE been trying to follow brahmacharya consciously and deliberately since 1899. My definition of it is purity not merely of body but of both speech and thought also. With the exception of what must be regarded as one lapse, I can recall no instance, during more than thirty-six years' constant and conscious effort, of mental disturbance such as I experienced during this illness. I was disgusted with myself. The moment the feeling came I acquainted my attendants and the medical friends with my condition. They could give me no help. I expected none. I broke loose after the experience from the rigid rest that was imposed upon me. The confession of the wretched experience brought much relief to me. I felt as if a great load had been raised from over me. It enabled me to pull myself together before any harm could be done[69]. ...

Harijan 29-2-1936; CWMG *Vol. 62, pp. 210–12*

Bombay
January 1936

MY DARKEST hour was when I was in Bombay[70] ... It was the hour of my temptation. Whilst I was asleep I suddenly felt as though I

wanted to see a woman. Well, a man who had tried to rise superior
to the instinct for nearly forty years was bound to be intensely pained
when he had this frightful experience. I ultimately conquered
the feeling, but I was face to face with the blackest moment of
my life and if I had succumbed to it, it would have meant my
absolute undoing.

Louis Fischer, The Life of Mahatma Gandhi, *p. 337;*
Tendulkar Vol. 4, p. 52

A Conversation With African Americans[71]

Bardoli
21 February 1936[72]

MKG: Is the prejudice against colour growing or dying out?

Dr Thurman[73]: ... Among many of the Southern white students
there is a disposition to improve upon the attitude of their
forbears ...

MKG: Is union between Negroes and the whites recognized by law?

Carrol[74]: Twenty-five States have laws definitely against these
unions. ...

Dr Thurman: But there has been a lot of intermixture of races as
for 300 years or more the Negro woman had no control over
her body. ... Did the South African Negro take any part in your
movement?

MKG: No, I purposely did not invite them. It would have endangered
their cause. They would not have understood the technique of
our struggle nor could they have seen the purpose or utility of
non-violence. ...

Harijan 14-3-1926; CWMG *Vol. 62, p. 198, 199; E*

Kamala Nehru's Death

Wardha
28 February 1936

Kamala's death is a great national loss. I had the privilege of knowing
her intimately for years. I have not known a truer, braver, and more
God fearing woman. May her life be a pattern for us all to follow.

The Bombay Chronicle 29-2-1936; CWMG *Vol. 62, p. 209; E*

To Prabhavati

Delhi
8 March 1936

... IT WILL be the greatest service you render to Jayaprakash if you lay before him your correct position with the utmost firmness and calm of mind. I am afraid you have not fully stated your case to Jayaprakash and if you have, it did not make any impression on him, that is, he does not take the statement to be correct. He will calm down without doubt, if he is convinced that you have in you no such thing as sexual desire. Your freedom from desire should put out the fire of his, just as water puts out any fire. ...

From the manuscript of Mahadev Desai's Diary;
CWMG *Vol. 62, p. 250; G*

To Jawaharlal

Delhi[75]
9 March 1936

So YOU return leaving Kamala for ever in Europe. And yet her spirit was never out of India and will always be your precious treasure as it will be of many of us. I shall never forget the final talk that wetted our four eyes.

Heavy responsibility awaits you here. ...

Bapu
CWMG *Vol. 62, p. 251; E*

To Jayaprakash

12 March 1936

I READ your book carefully and liked it although the attack on me which it carries betrays considerable ignorance regarding me. That can be removed but I am enchanted with your study. After these preliminaries I may say that I find in it no remedy for our problem. Your solution does not suit the conditions in this country at least for the present. The goal you aim at is almost the same as that desired by me and many Congressmen. But our method of attaining it differs from yours. Your method in my opinion is not practicable in this country. I am not so attached to my own method that I cannot see the merits of anyone else's. But I am unable to appreciate your solution in spite of all sincere effort. ...

Blessings from
Bapu
From the Manuscript of Mahadev Desai's Diary;
CWMG *Vol. 62, pp. 258–9; H*

Sexual Union

A CORRESPONDENT writes:

... the scriptures (Prashnopanishad) have said, there is brahmacharya where sexual union occurs only at night (i.e., as opposed to abnormal cohabitation during the day time). Here normal sex-life itself is spoken of as brahmacharya. ...

I gladly publish this letter as I should any such letter that is not full of declamation, abuse, or insinuations. The reader should have both the sides of the question to enable him to come to a decision. ... I can bear ample testimony from my own experience and that of many friends. I am not aware of any of us having derived any benefit, mental, spiritual, or physical (from sexual union). Momentary excitement and satisfaction there certainly was. But it was invariably followed by exhaustion. And the desire for union returned immediately the effect of exhaustion had worn out ... I have no manner of doubt that the self-restraint is responsible for the comparative freedom from illness that I have enjoyed for long periods and for my output of energy and work both physical and mental which eye-witnesses have described as phenomenal. ...

CWMG *Vol. 62, pp. 309–10; E*

Savli
28 March 1936

THE OPINIONS I have formed, and the conclusions I have arrived at, are not by any means final; I may change them tomorrow if I find better ones.

Quoted by Madeleine Slade in The Spirit's Pilgrimage
[New York, 1960], p. 200

To Prabhavati

Wardha
30 April 1936

... How DOES it matter what the world says? You alone have to settle your account with Jayaprakash. His is a different case[76]. Hence it will not do if you fall ill under the stress of worry. The true follower of the Gita is one who can remain calm and composed in any situation whatever, and you have to become such a one. For the present, write to me regularly. ...

Bapu
CWMG *Vol. 62, pp. 355-6; G*

To Prema Kantak

Segaon
6 May 1936

... I HAD a discharge, but I was awake and the mind was under control. I understood the cause and from that time stopped taking rest as prescribed by the doctors. And my state now is better than it was, if such a state could be imagined. If you wish to ask me more questions about this you may, for I have cherished high hopes of you. You may, therefore, know from me anything concerning myself that you wish to. ...

CWMG *Vol. 62, p. 372; G*

Indian Culture

Nagpur
9 May 1936

... THE INDIAN culture of our times is in the making. Many of us are striving to produce a blend of all the cultures which seem today to be in clash with one another. No culture can live if it attempts to be exclusive. There is no such thing as pure Aryan culture in existence today in India. Whether the Aryans were indigenous to India or were unwelcome intruders, does not interest me much. What does interest me is the fact that my remote ancestors blended with one another with the utmost freedom and we of the present generation are a result of that blend. Whether we are doing any good to the country of our birth and the tiny globe which sustains us or whether we are a burden, the future alone will show. ...

Harijan *9-5-1936;* CWMG *Vol. 62, pp. 383 and 385*

Discussion With C.V. Raman And Dr Rahm[77]

On or after 10 May 1936[78]

'He has discovered,' said Sir Chandrashekhara, introducing Dr Rahm, 'an insect that can live without food and water for 12 years, and has come to India for further researches in biology.'

MKG: When you discover the secret at the back of it, please pass it on to me.

Sir C.V. Raman: ... The growing discoveries in the science of astronomy and physics seem to me to be further and further revelations of God. (But) Mahatmaji, religions cannot unite. Science offers the best opportunity for a complete fellowship. All men of science are brothers.

MKG: What about the converse? All who are not men of science are not brothers?

CVR: But all can become men of science.

MKG: You will have to present a *kalma*[79] of science as Islam presents one.

CWMG *Vol. 62, pp. 387–9; E*

Telegram To Associated Press[80]

Nandi Hill
11 May 1936

Dr Ansari's death is a stunning blow. He was one of the best among Mussalmans as also Hindus. For me his death is a personal loss. He was my infallible guide on Hindu-Muslim questions. He and I were just planning an attack on the growing social evils. He was the poor man's Physician if he was also that of the Princes'. His death will be mourned by thousands for whom he was their sole consolation and guide.

The Hindu *12-5-1936;* CWMG *Vol. 62, pp. 389–90*

Nandi Hills

Nandi Hill[81]
11 May 1936

... I WALKED up the hill from the base. It took me $2^1/_2$ hours, the distance covered was over 5 miles. I walked very slow. Hence there was no fatigue. It was Dr Ansari who wanted the Sardar to pass the summer on a hill. And he himself is no more. Evidently his death was quite sudden. For me it is a very personal loss. I relied upon his advice in so many matters.

... Well, Nandi Hill is really a model of sanitation, of course enforced from above. The air is beautiful. The calmness is divine. No cars or carts or even rickshaws. Only 30 families can live here comfortably. More are not allowed. I do not know a more secluded, cleaner, quieter hill. Sardar is in raptures over the stillness. I know you will love it, if you were here. ...

CWMG Vol. 62, pp. 391–2; E

To Prema Kantak

Nandi Hill
21 May 1936

... You HAVE put the question very well. You could have put it still more plainly. I have always had involuntary discharges. In South Africa they occurred at intervals of several years. I do not remember exactly. Here in India they have been of months. I have mentioned the fact of my getting discharges in a few articles of mine. If my brahmacharya had been completely free from discharges, I would have been able to place before the world very much more than I have succeeded in doing. But it seems practically impossible that a person who has indulged in sex gratification from the age of 15 to 30, may be with his own wife only, can, on taking a vow of brahmacharya, control the discharge of his vital fluid completely. One whose capacity for retention has progressively weakened from day to day for fifteen years cannot recover it fully all at once. Both his body and mind will have become too weak for that. I, therefore, consider myself a very imperfect *brahmachari*. But my position is like that of the castor oil plant which looks big on a heath where there are no trees. People know this shortcoming of mine.

The experience which tormented me in Bombay was a strange and painful one. All my discharges so far had occurred in dreams and they never troubled me. I could forget them. But the experience in Bombay occurred while I was fully awake and had a sudden desire for intercourse. I felt of course no urge to gratify the craving, there was no self-forgetfulness whatever. I was completely master of my body. But despite my best efforts the organ remained aroused. This was an altogether strange and shameful experience. I have already explained the cause. As soon as that cause was removed the state of remaining aroused came to a stop, that is, during the waking state.

Despite my imperfection, one thing has always come easily to me, viz., that thousands of women have remained safe in my company. There have been occasions in my life when certain women, though aroused, were saved by God, or say, I was saved. I am a hundred per cent certain that it was God who saved us and, therefore, take no pride in the fact. It is my unceasing prayer to God that I might remain in the same condition till the very end of my life. ...

CWMG Vol. 62, pp. 428-9; G

Bribery

Harijan, 23 May 1936

BRIBERY IN the name of *mamul*[82] and the like to railway officials and the others is not as unusual occurrence in Indian life. Any official with whom the public has anything to do is generally said to be open to receive bribes even for the performance of his duty, not to speak of committing breach thereof. I have had to suffer in my time for refusing to pay a paltry anna at the third-class ticket windows for getting my ticket in my turn which would never come because favourites had to be served first. I have had to wait for hours sometimes before I could get a chance of buying my ticket. The customs and the railways are the two departments with which the general public have to come in frequent touch. And it is there that the public suffer most ... It is difficult to advise in this matter. Obviously no bribe[83] may possibly be given. Equally obviously public work must not be allowed to suffer. There is no quick remedy against a petty official who misuses his brief authority ...

If they are ill paid, let them demand a higher pay, but they may

not take bribes from the public whom they are paid to serve. I hope
the higher authorities will see these lines and deal effectively with
the evil which they know does flourish widely.

Harijan 23-5-1936; CWMG *Vol. 62, pp. 434–5*

To Zakir Husain

25 May 1936

... I ASK, will you take Dr Ansari's place? In answer, do not think of
your status in society. If you have self-confidence, you must say
'Yes'. If you have not, you must say 'No'. I shall not misunderstand
you. I know and love you too well to misunderstand you. ...

Bapu

From the manuscript of Mahadev Desai's Diary;
CWMG *Vol. 62, pp. 441–2*

To Jawaharlal

Nandi Hills
29 May 1936

... YOUR EXPLANATION about the omission of a woman on the Working
Committee does not give me satisfaction. If you had shown the slightest
desire to have a woman on the Committee, there would have been no
difficulty whatsoever about any of the older ones standing out. ...

Bapu

CWMG *Vol. 62, p. 454; E*

To Ramdas

Saturday, 30 May 1936

... JUST READ in the paper about Harilal's exploit[84]. There could be no
harm in his being converted to Islam with understanding and selfless
motives. But he suffers from greed for wealth and sensual pleasures ...
He had ceased to belong to any faith and now he has taken on the
label of Islam. That does not make him a follower of the faith, though
we should indeed feel satisfied if he truly practices in his life what
is best in Islam. And if this is a mere show, it does not deserve to
be lamented.

This instance should make us all alert and we should [try to] understand whatever religion we follow and bring credit to it ...

From the manuscript of Mahadev Desai's Diary;
CWMG *Vol. 62, pp. 461–2; G*

Harilal To 'Abdulla'

Bangalore, 2 June 1936
... I DO not mind whether he is known as Abdulla or Harilal, if by adopting one name for the other he becomes a true devotee of God, which both the names mean.

Published in Harijan *6-6-1936*

To Devadas

3 October 1936
... As THE banyan so its fruit, as the father so the son. When such thoughts occur, I don't feel like finding fault with Harilal. What is the use of being angry with myself? I know how useful I was then. I do not know anything else. But who can understand the inscrutable ways of God? We can only deduce principles from well-known illustrations.

Let me know if you have received any comments on Ba's letter[85] whether through public or private correspondence.

Blessings from
Bapu
CWMG *Vol. 63, pp. 344–5; G*

Segaon, Wardha
10 October 1936
I AM glad to learn that the whole line of thought has been Ba's own. She certainly has that power, and the letter is indeed a good one. ...

Blessings from
Bapu
CWMG *Vol. 63, p. 364; G*

Segaon, Wardha
12 November 1936
THE ACCOMPANYING letter will tell you[86] if you do not already know of Harilal's latest exploit[87]. I do not attach any value to his letter. It seems

he is not getting any money from there either. May be, too, he is tired of the whole thing. After I had torn up the letter it occurred to me that probably you had not come across it, so I decided to send you the pieces.

Write to me about your health and Lakshmi's. Hope the children are well. Nimu has been quite ill at Bombay.

Do you go for walks? Do you take your meals regularly? These two things you must not fail to do.

Blessings from
Bapu
CWMG *Vol. 64, pp. 23–4; G*

Discussion With John R. Mott[88]

Segaon, Wardha
13/14 November 1936

JRM: What is the cause of your greatest concern, your heaviest burden?

MKG: My greatest worry is the ignorance and poverty of the masses of India, and the way in which they have been neglected by the classes, especially the neglect of the Harijans by the Hindus ...

JRM: What affords you the greatest hope and satisfaction?

MKG: Faith in myself born of faith in God.

JRM: The greatest thing you have ever done is the observance of your Monday silence. You illustrate thereby the storing up and releasing of power when needed. What place has it continued to have in the preparation of your spiritual tasks?

MKG: It is not the greatest thing I have done, but it certainly means a great thing to me. ...

Harijan *19-12-1936, 26-12-1936;* CWMG *Vol. 64, pp. 33 and 38–40*

Piercing The Nose And The Ears

Segaon
6-12-1936

... IN BOTH my ears, taken together, there were six holes. These are still there and I do not like them. But how am I to close these up? My wife's nose and ears were pierced. She must have resented taking off her ornaments. Neither of us feels that either one of us looks less comely for having taken them off ...

Women, as it is, are slaves. In the act of piercing their noses and ears, I have never seen anything but a symbol of their slavery. By tying a string to her ear-rings, a woman can be pulled like a bullock. Instances exist of cruel husbands having cut off both the ears and the noses of their wives along with the ornaments in them.

I invite those who advocate the piercing of the nose and the ears to look at the frightful ornaments on the noses and ears of Indian women and the dirt in them and then advise me as to what I should do. ...

Harijanbandhu *6-12-1936;* CWMG *Vol. 64, pp. 108 and 109–10; G*

Part Thirteen

1937-42

Gandhi and Kasturba with Tagore at Amra Kunja
in Santiniketan, 1940

War Within and Without

Acharya Kripalani is quite correct in saying that there is no such thing as 'Gandhism'.

Illness never spared Gandhi, nor anxiety about the state of the Congress, of the struggle, and of the nation's future.

The countrywide elections held in 1937 gave Congress the mandate to form ministries on its own in eight provinces—UP, Madras, Bihar, the Central Provinces, and Orissa. With alliances, it could also do so in Bombay, Assam, and the North West Frontier Province (NWFP). The 'untouchables' voted for the Congress overwhelmingly except for Bombay's Maharashtra part where Ambedkar's party won several seats. The Muslim League under Jinnah won most of the Muslim votes (except in the NWFP). Jinnah sent word to Gandhi suggesting a Congress–League coalition in Bombay, but, Rajmohan Gandhi writes in *Mohandas*:

Gandhi was reluctant. May be he was put off by Jinnah's retort to Nehru. May be he felt he could not discuss office-sharing with Jinnah before the Congress had decided on accepting office. In any case he sent Jinnah a written answer in general but discouraging terms:

'Mr Kher has given me your message. I wish I could do something, but I am utterly helpless. My faith in unity is as bright as ever; only I see no daylight ...' (22 May 1937; *CWMG* Vol. 65).

Nehru who was the Congress president, was against taking office. While keeping options open, the Congress had in fact resolved to 'wreck' the 1935 Act under which provincial ministries would be formed, for that Act also provided for a federal assembly where unelected princes (or their nominees) could vote. At Nehru's initiative, the UP Congress Committee passed a resolution opposing office-acceptance.

None in the Congress liked the federal part of the 1935 Act, but Patel was for acceptance of provincial office, as was Rajagopalachari, now the leader of the Congress party in the Madras legislature, to which he had been elected from a university seat. The question went to the 'retired' Gandhi, who said he would counsel acceptance of office provided the Viceroy, Lord Linlithgow, gave an assurance that governors would not overrule elected ministers.

Congress ministries came to be installed and Gandhi described the step as 'an unwritten compact between the British Government and the Congress ... a gentleman's agreement, in which both sides are expected to play the game'.

But as Congress moved towards office, Jinnah asked for the inclusion of two League legislators in the Bombay ministry.

In the UP, Khalilquzzaman and Nawab Ismail Khan commenced talks with the Congress represented by Nehru, Azad, Pant (leader of the Congress legislature party in the UP), Kripalani, and Acharya Narendra Deva. In both Bombay and the UP, Congress said League members could join provided they merged with the Congress.

On 21 July Nehru wrote to Prasad: 'We came to the conclusion that we should offer stringent conditions to the UP Muslim League group and if they accepted them in toto then we would agree to two ministers from their group.' One condition, said Nehru, was 'the winding up of the Muslim League group in the UP and its absorption in the Congress'. Jinnah was not going to let the Muslim League accept such a self-effacement.

While the Congress took office in most of the Provinces of India, it did not in Bengal where its leadership was in the hands of Netaji Subhas Chandra Bose, for the first three years of the period covered in this part of the compilation. (The Muslim League took office in Bengal.)

Bose's ascent to the Presidentship of the Congress in 1938–9 and his subsequent resignation are major enactments in this phase of Gandhi's life and his 'essentiality', as a person and as the de facto leader of the Congress emerges strongly in his writings and statements of the period. From the telescope to the microscope, was an easy movement for Gandhi's mental eye.

We have him write letters scolding Amtussalaam, upbraiding Mira Behn, writing with anguish at the loss of Jamnalal Bajaj, telling Patel on 23 February 1942 about Mahadev Desai's illness in a manner that anticipated Desai's death—some six months later. And in the midst of these events of subcontinental scale, the 'seconds' hand' of Gandhi's pocket-watch ticked away on home ground. If the outbreak of World War II brought from Gandhi important statements on the impact of world powers' fighting with each other and on subject people, on India's role in the proceedings, on violent and non-violent resistance to aggression, it did not come in the way of his corresponding with strangers and his grandchildren. Manilal's twelve-year-old daughter Sita had her English spelling corrected, a Chinese visitor had communism discussed with him, a correspondent complimented on serving a blind dog, H.G. Wells engaged on the 'Rights of Man', the subject of beef, test-tube babies, widows' taboos discussed, and a simple opinion—relevant for all time—expressed on capital punishment.

This phase saw Manilal Gandhi, then editing *Indian Opinion* in Durban being told his attack on 'Jinnah Sahib in *Indian Opinion*' was 'not proper', while Sevagram workers were treated to a protracted discussion—including the possibility of his going on a fast—over the theft of a letter and a pen from inside the ashram precincts. Letters were written and Rajkumari Amrit Kaur on the desirability of their meeting Ramana Maharshi, to Prabhavati about Jayaprakash in which Gandhi describes JP as 'a fakir ... and lost in his own dream', to Devadas to not neglect writing to Kasturba.

Meanwhile, the clouds of World War II hovered over the world menacingly, as nationalist opinion in India reached fever pitch. The Muslim League's demand for the partition of India on religious lines acquired irresistible proportion. Congress ministries were in office in some provinces in India, strengthening Indian self-governance. But the Congress and Muslim League drifted irreconcilably apart. The League alleged injustices on Muslims in Congress-governed provinces, while parties representing extreme Hindu opinion criticized Gandhi and the Congress bitterly for 'pandering to Muslim intransigence' and 'betraying Hindu interests'.

The relationship between the Viceroy and his Executive Council on the one hand soured, as the Congress and Muslim League drifted further apart.

The 'strait' between him and 'his own' political associates in the Working Committee grew steadily into a 'gulf'. 'I now represent a totally different mentality from that of the Working Committee', said Gandhi to Rajagopalachari in July 1940 during a meeting of the Committee.

When Britain declared war on Germany, India had not been consulted. The Congress ministries resigned in protest in 1939. Jinnah and the Muslim League promptly celebrated the day as a 'Day of Deliverance'. The two-nation theory was now, officially, part of political discourse.

This part contains excerpts from Gandhi's discussions with his colleagues on the War, with the British authorities in India, and his controversial letter to Adolf Hitler dated 24 December 1940. Gandhi makes in it a misjudgment astonishing in one of his perspicacity. 'We have no doubt about your bravery or devotion to your fatherland,' he wrote to Hitler, 'nor do we believe you are the monster described by your opponents.' This piece of appreciation is only partially mitigated by the sentiment that follows: 'But your own writings and pronouncements ... leave no room for doubt that many of your acts are monstrous and unbecoming of human dignity ...'

Between March and August 1942, the Congress High Commission saw Rajagopalachari leading the dissent against Gandhi's approach to Britain at war. By then, Norway, Denmark, Holland, Belgium, and France had fallen, Churchill had replaced Chamberlain as Prime Minister. With the world caught in a clash of arms, and though still unknown to anyone heading for an atomic denouement, Gandhi's belief that India should defend liberty 'with the force of non-violence' was cutting no ice with the Congress Working Committee.

With a majority in the Working Committee, including Congress President Azad and Patel, disagreeing with him, Gandhi sought to be excused. He was not implored to stay. Four days' deliberations ensued, concluding in a statement that 'they are unable to go the full length' with Gandhi. They recognized that he 'should be free to pursue his great ideal in his own way' but they absolved him from responsibility for the programmes the Congress had to pursue ... 'in regard to external aggression and internal disorder'. The seventy-three year old Gandhi was now distanced from the working of Patel, now sixty-five, Rajagopalachari sixty-two, Prasad fifty-six, Azad fifty-two, and Nehru fifty-one.

Responding to a Viceregal invitation, Gandhi went to Simla at the end of June 1942 but he told the Viceroy that 'this was [his] last interview' and that the Viceroy 'should send for the president of the Congress if he must have an offer on behalf of the Congress', in the future.

But outside of the Working Committee, Gandhi maintained his loyalty to the party. Addressing the All India Congress Committee in its open session, Gandhi asked AICC's endorsement of the Working Committee's offer to Britain. C.R., he said, had shown 'persistency, courage, and skill' (*The Hindu*, 9 July 1940), and Vallabhbhai had held 'fast to his convictions'. Gandhi did not agree with his team but was not going to let it down or see Congress breaking up.

By this time, Subhas Bose and Jayaprakash, strongly opposed to any overtures to the British, were in jail. Prior to his arrest Bose asked for mass defiance and for the formation of a 'provisional national government'. Rammanohar Lohia was jailed in August. Gandhi spoke against the arrests of these two young socialists in the Congress.

Gandhi crafted, with Nehru's help, a two-sentence statement:

It is wrong to help the British war effort with men or money. The only worthy effort is to resist all war with non-violent resistance.

This was enough for the stage to be set for the campaign of individual civil disobedience (ICD). ICD lashed, between October 1940 and before the summer of 1941. More than 15,000 Indians were in prison. The ICD candidates were chosen or approved by Gandhi personally, on the basis of their commitment to non-violence, spinning, caste equality, and Hindu–Muslim friendship.

Each resister was to recite the slogan as he or she walked until arrested by a police officer, who was often intimated in advance. No violence occurred, and on Christmas satyagraha was started. This was one of the most disciplined of the many all-India campaigns Gandhi had initiated.

For the first ICD volunteer Gandhi selected Vinoba Bhave, thereby bringing to national and global attention his most prominent 'non-political' associate.

Jawaharlal was chosen to follow Vinoba. But before he could even utter the two sentences, he was arrested and on 31 October, charged with sedition for earlier speeches, and sentenced for four years. By the year-end, Rajaji, Patel, Prasad, Azad, and many other nationally known Congress leaders among hundreds of unknown 'foot soldiers' were in jail. ...

During all this Gandhi remained, in his words, 'buried in Sevagram'.

It was during this 'burial' that occurred one of the most important and best-known conversations of Gandhi with a writer from overseas, Louis Fischer[1]. For sheer clarity of thought and expression, few interviews can match those. While the war and India's role in it was the 'urgent' element in that set of 'essential' interviews, other matters of non-urgent importance figured in them.

In between his vigorous opposition to India's joining the war effort without a corresponding gesture from the British, Gandhi showed what being Gandhi meant. He took to task 'nationalists' in Bombay who had heckled Rajagopalachari for his views on the War, flinging tar on the dissenting statesman. 'Those who tarred him and created a disturbance have disgraced themselves', he said.

Gandhi's ability to surprise people by a new interpretation of his beliefs or by a constructive caveat to his ideas never ceased. In a letter to President Roosevelt, Gandhi made a startling offer: '... if the Allies think it necessary, they may keep their troops at their own expense in India, not for keeping internal order but for preventing Japanese aggression and defending China.' But certain sub-themes never lagged behind the mega ones. In a letter to Viceroy Lord Linlithgow Gandhi said, 'the military must not slaughter milch cows and plough cattle for beef'; Linlithgow concurred.

Meanwhile, the war lurched eastwards.

A 'twist' of bitter truths into the beverage of his public statements was essential. In a letter 'To Every Japanese', on 18 July 1942, Gandhi said, 'make no mistake about the fact that you will be sadly disillusioned if you believed that you will receive a willing welcome from India'.

'Quit India' was taking shape slowly but unmistakably. Rajmohan Gandhi tells us in *Mohandas*:

Quit India. The two-word phrase was not his own and first used by him only on 3 August, in a letter to American friends. But the idea behind it came to him in the middle of April (1942) ...

From the 4th to the 8th the Working Committee met daily, and there were numerous smaller meetings. On 6 August Gandhi said in a public statement: 'I have definitely contemplated an interval between the passing of the Congress resolution and the starting of the struggle ... (A) letter will certainly go to the Viceroy, not as an ultimatum but as an earnest pleading for avoidance of a conflict. If there is a favourable response, then my letter can be the basis for negotiation.' The Gowalia Tank grounds in central Bombay bore an electric atmosphere and an immense throng when, on 7 August, the AICC began its two-day session there ...

In his speech at the mammoth meeting on 7 August, Gandhi started with non-violence:

'I must tell you that there is no change in me. I stick to the principle of non-violence as I did before. If you are tired of it then you need not come with me.'

He added:

'Time was when every Mussalman claimed the whole of India as his motherland. During the years that the Ali Brothers were with me, the assumption underlying all their talks and discussions was that India belonged as much to the Mussalmans as to the Hindus.'

Turning to Hindu extremists, he said:

'Those Hindus who, like Dr Moonje and Shri Savarkar, believe in the doctrine of the sword may seek to keep the Mussalmans under Hindu domination. I do not represent that section. I represent the Congress. You want to kill the Congress which is the goose that lays golden eggs. If you distrust the Congress, you may rest assured that there is to be a perpetual war between the Hindus and the Mussalmans, and the country will be doomed to continue warfare and bloodshed. If such warfare is to be our lot, I shall not live to witness it ... 'I ... want freedom immediately, this very night, before dawn, if it can be had. Freedom cannot now wait for the realization of communal unity ...'

And on 8 August he said the lines that belong to history:

'Here is a mantra, a short one, that I give you. You may imprint it on your hearts and let every breath of yours give expression to it. The mantra is: "Do or Die". We shall either free India or die in the attempt ...'

The Quit India Movement of 1942 saw Gandhi, his wife Kasturba, and some of his associates behind prison bars, in the Aga Khan Palace, Poona.

Before sunrise on 9 August, Gandhi, Mahadev Desai, and Mira Behn were removed from Birla House. Working Committee members and many local Congressmen, likewise, were shifted from their lodgings in Bombay. Kasturba and Pyarelal were told that they could, if they choose, join Gandhi in jail.

Kasturba opted to join her husband. Mahadev Desai, who had been told by his son Narayan when about to get inside the police car, 'We will meet again in free India', died on 15 August 1942.

Ayyankali

Venganoor
14 January 1937[2]

... IN AYYANKALI[3], whom you half in jest and half in endearment call
the *Pulaya Rajah*, you have an indefatigable worker. I understand
that under his leadership you have been making steady progress and
I have no doubt that this gracious Proclamation will quicken the
progress you are making. ...

CWMG *Vol. 64, p. 240*

Not My Intention To Judge Mahomed and Jesus

Segaon, Wardha[4]
25 February 1937

Dr Crane[5]: Does not Mahomed prescribe the use of the sword in
   certain circumstances?

MKG: ... if I came to the conclusion that the Koran teaches violence,
   I would still reject violence, but I would not therefore say that
   the Bible is superior to the Koran or that Mahomed is inferior
   to Jesus. It is not my function to judge Mahomed and Jesus. It
   is enough that my non-violence is independent of the sanction
   of scriptures. ...

Harijan *6-3-1937;* CWMG, *Vol. 64, pp. 397 and 399; E*

To Sampurnanand[6]

Segaon, Wardha
February 1937

HOW IS it that the majority of you Socialists keep such bad health?
Narendra Dev[7] is a chronic sufferer from asthma, Meherally[8] is

down with heart trouble, Jayaprakash is ill and now you, who seemed to be the healthiest of the lot, are also confined to bed. Evidently none of you can look after himself. Come to Wardha for some time and stay with me. I promise to send you back fully cured.

CWMG Vol. 64, p. 409; H

A National Language For India

Madras
26 March 1937[9]

... A STRONG and virile national language requires healthy development of the provincial languages. If the latter be weak and anaemic, how can the former at all grow?

Gujarati, I said to myself, cannot be the language. Not more than a thirtieth part of the people of the country speaks it. How am I to find Tulsi Ramayana therein? What about Marathi, then, I wondered. I love Marathi. I claim among the Marathi-speaking people some staunch co-workers. I know the Maharashtrians' efficiency, capacity for self-sacrifice, and their learning. And yet I did not think Marathi— the language that Lokamanya Tilak wielded so wonderfully well— could be our *rashtrabhasha*. When I was thus reasoning this out, let me tell you that I did not know the actual number of people speaking Hindi, and yet I instinctively felt that only Hindi could take that place, and no other ...

I certainly congratulate you on what you have achieved. ...

The Hindu 27-3-1937; Harijan 3-4-1937; CWMG Vol. 65, pp. 19–21; F

To C. Rajagopalachari

Tithal[10], Bulsar
Gujarat
17 May 1937

My dear C.R.,

... If what I am doing does not carry conviction to you, you should strive with me and resist me. For it is you who have to bear the brunt, not I. And if you act merely as an advocate no matter how brilliant—

but without conviction, the battle will be lost. I write not a line without deep conviction. ...

Bapu

CWMG *Vol. 65, p. 215; E*

To M.A. Jinnah

Tithal

22 May 1937

Dear Shri Jinnah,

... I wish I could do something, but I am utterly helpless. My faith in unity is as bright as ever; only I see no daylight out of the impenetrable darkness and, in such distress, I cry out to God for light.

Yours sincerely,

M.K. Gandhi

CWMG *Vol. 65, p. 231; E*

To Amrit Kaur

Tithal

24 May 1937

... POOR TOFA[11]! In spite of your references to him in every letter, I have not even thought of him. My apologies to you and him. In spite of my regarding dogs and human beings as equal, I cannot feel the same in respect of illness of dogs as of men. But I hope for your sake that he is fully restored. The moral from this domestic illness may be that you cannot serve man and dogs at the same time and therefore dogs should not be kept as pets ...

Love.

CWMG *Vol. 65, p. 239; E*

Jawaharlal

Segaon, Wardha[12]

10 July 1937

... JAWAHARLAL WAS more than good throughout[13]. His innate nobility asserted itself every time a difficulty cropped up. He is truly a warrior, *sans peur et sans reproche.* The more I see him, the more I love him. I had long chats with him and the Maulana. It will be most difficult to replace him next year. ...

To C. Rajagopalachari

Before 15 July 1937[14]

Shri Rajagopalachari
Senate House
Madras

Private. Deepest prayer has been the Spring on which I have drawn for guiding committee[15]. You know how my hope is centred on you. May God bless your effort. Don't publish this. Have no right to send message members. You must ask Jawaharlal. Love.

Bapu
CWMG *Vol. 65, p. 394; E*

Congress Ministries

Segaon
17 July 1937

... How will Congress Ministers discharge themselves? Their Chief, the President of the Congress, travels third class. Will they travel first? The President is satisfied with a coarse khadi dhoti, kurta, and waistcoat. Will the Ministers require the Western style and expenditure on Western scale? ... If the Ministers will simply refrain from copying the Governors and the secured Civil Service, they will have shown the marked contrast that exists between the Congress mentality and theirs.

... There is a beauty and an art in simplicity which he who runs may see. It does not require money to be neat, clean and dignified. Pomp and pageantry are often synonymous with vulgarity. ...

Harijan; CWMG *Vol. 65, pp. 406–8; E*

To Vallabhbhai Patel

Segaon,
19 July 1937

Bhai Vallabhbhai,

The suggestion to fix the salary[16] at Rs 500 is worth thinking over seriously. I can't understand house-rent allowance in addition to Rs 500 and the distinction between Personal Assistant and Secretary. But if you hold different views, please let me know. ...

Blessings from
Bapu
CWMG Vol. 65, p. 419; G

To Jawaharlal

Segaon, Wardha
30 July 1937

My dear Jawaharlal,

... Your calling khadi the 'livery of freedom'[17] will live as long as we speak the English language in India. It needs a first-class poet to translate into Hindi the whole of the thought behind that enchanting phrase. For me it is not merely poetry but it enunciates a great truth whose full significance we have yet to grasp.

Love.

Bapu
CWMG Vol. 65, pp. 445–6; E

To C. Rajagopalachari

Segaon, Wardha
2 August 1937

My dear C.R.[18],

... I do hope you won't pay the Members for twelve months. I should regard (as enough) Rs 2 per day *whilst* the Assembly is sitting plus 3rd class travelling and actual out-of-pocket for coolies and tonga not exceeding Rs 2. But you know best ...

> Blessings from
> Bapu
> CWMG *Vol. 66, p. 4; E*

To C. Rajagopalachari

> Segaon, Wardha
> 6 August 1937

My dear C.R.,

What nonsense! Why should you feel sorry or disappointed because I hold certain views about salaries? I do not at all resent your not enforcing them. I have said, my views need not be accepted if found unworkable. We all marvel at the way you are managing things there. You have approached your task with faith and religious zeal. You must not feel the slightest disappointment. You know my deepest feeling. Then why should you worry? I hope you will be able to spare yourself for 17th[19]. My prayers and best wishes are with you always. ...

> Bapu
> CWMG *Vol. 66, p. 13–14*

Interview To William B. Benton[20]

> Segaon, Wardha
> Before 13 September 1937

... *Have you ever seen an American movie or heard American jazz? These are our two most famous exports.*

No, no, I haven't.

There's a good story for you. Do what you can with it. I've never been to a moving picture.

Hasn't one ever been brought to you, I query.

No, I have never seen one. ...

> The Hindustan Times *13-9-1937;* CWMG *Vol. 66, pp. 127–9; E*

Export Of Monkeys

Segaon, Wardha
18 September 1937

I HAVE before me nearly fifty letters from America asking me to do what I can to prevent the export of Macacus Rhesus monkeys from India to America for purposes of vivisection ...

My sympathies are wholly with my correspondents. If I had the power I would not send a single monkey abroad for vivisection or slaughter. ...

Harijan 18-9-1937; CWMG *Vol. 66, p. 139; E*

To E.M.S. Namboodiripad[21]

Segaon, Wardha
21 September 1937

My dear Namboodiripad,

I have your letter. It is right that you have written to the Premier, but before doing so you should have written to the police authorities and gone step by step. Don't expect that from top to bottom the Permanent Service has become angelic. And why do you say you cannot condemn even bad actions of Congress Ministries? I think it is not only a right, but a duty for any Congressman to openly criticize acts of Congress officials, no matter however highly placed they may be. The criticism has got to be courteous and well-informed.

Yours sincerely,
M.K. Gandhi

Sjt. E.M.S. Namboodiripad
Post Cherukara, via Shoranur
S. Malabar.

CWMG *Vol. 66, p. 155; E*

Notes

Segaon, Wardha,
September 1937

LEGALIZED PROSTITUTION

DR MUTHULAKSHMI Reddi[22] furnishes one more proof of the very high expectations formed of Congress Ministries. People have a right to form such expectations ... Dr Muthulakshmi has issued a public appeal to the Madras Ministry to pass her bill which puts a stop to the immoral custom of dedicating *devadasis*[23] to a life of shame. I have not examined the bill. But the idea behind is so sound that it is a wonder that it has not yet found a place in the statute-book of the Southern Presidency. I wholly agree with Dr Muthulakshmi that the reform is as urgent as prohibition ... And I hope with her that before many months have passed the devadasi system will cease to have legal sanction. ...

Harijan *25-9-1937;* CWMG *Vol. 66, pp. 164–5; E*

Maulana Azad

Before 30 September 1937[24]
... ON QUESTIONS relating to Mussalmans, the Congress is solely guided by Maulana Abul Kalam Azad. ...

The Hindu *2-10-1937;* CWMG *Vol. 66, pp. 181–2; E*

To M.A. Jinnah

Segaon, Wardha
19 October 1937

Dear Friend,

I carefully went through your speech at Lucknow[25], and I felt deeply hurt over your misunderstanding of my attitude ...

Of course, as I read it, the whole of your speech is a declaration of war. Only I had hoped you would reserve poor me as a bridge between the two. I see that you want no bridge. I am sorry. Only it takes two to make a quarrel. You won't find me one, even if I cannot become a peace-maker.

This is not for publication, unless you desire it. It is written in all good faith and out of an anguished heart.

Yours sincerely,
M.K. Gandhi
CWMG *Vol. 66, p. 257; E*

A Foreword[26]

Segaon, Wardha
27 November 1937

ONE CAN at once perceive in Acharya Kripalani's way of thinking and writing a quality of uniqueness. Anyone who has known him will recognize at once any piece of writing as his and his alone. This is the impression I had while reading this collection.

... Acharya Kripalani is quite correct in saying that there is no such thing as Gandhism. ...

M.K. Gandhi
CWMG *Vol. 66, p. 308; G*

To Ramdas

Segaon, Wardha
10 January 1938[27]

... How CAN one eat one's fill without a sense of guilt in this poverty-stricken country?. ...

From the manuscript of Mahadev Desai's Diary;
CWMG *Vol. 66, pp. 334–5; G*

To Subhas Chandra Bose

Segaon
23 January 1938

WELCOME HOME[28]. God give you strength to bear the weight of Jawaharlal's mantle. Love.[29]

The Bombay Chronicle *26-1-1938;* CWMG *Vol. 66, p. 346*

Letter To M.A. Jinnah

Segaon, Wardha
3 February 1938[30]

Dear Mr Jinnah,
... You seem to deny that your speech was a declaration of war, but your later pronouncements too confirm the first impression. How can I prove what is a matter of feeling? In your speeches I miss

the old nationalist. When in 1915 I returned from the self-imposed exile in South Africa, everybody spoke of you as one of the staunchest of nationalists and the hope of both Hindus and Mussalmans. Are you still the same Mr Jinnah? If you say you are, in spite of your speeches I shall accept your word.

Lastly, you want me to come forward with some proposal. What proposal can I make except to ask you on bended knees to be what I had thought you were. But the proposal to form a basis of unity between the two communities has surely got to come from you.

This is again not for publication but for your eyes. It is the cry of a friend, not of an opponent.

Yours sincerely,
M.K. Gandhi

The Bombay Chronicle 16-6-1938; CWMG Vol. 66, pp. 349–50; E

Gandhi Seva Sangh

Delang
District Puri, Orissa
26 March 1938

MKG: ... I know there are quite a few Muslims who regard the Hindus as infidels and do not wish to associate with them. But all Muslims do not harbour such hatred in their hearts. There are enough Muslims who consider the Hindus as their compatriots and believe that it is only by living in amity that both these communities can look after their interests and make progress. But we should not be frightened even by those Muslims whose hands hold knives and whose hearts are filled with hatred ...

Kripalani: You say you should go and allow yourself to be killed. But you must remember that if the Muslims completely lose their heads that they kill you, the Hindus will not forget this thing for the next two thousand years ...

MKG: This consideration is irrelevant. ...

CWMG Vol. 66, pp. 430–2; H

Kasturba At The Puri Temple

Calcutta[31]
2 April 1938

... BA FOOLISHLY entered the Puri[32] temple and it upset me terribly. I must not give you the whole history. I have not yet got over the shock. The (blood) pressure therefore has now steadied round 175–80 ...

CWMG *Vol. 67, pp. 2–3*

To Jawaharlal Nehru

On the train to Peshawar[33]
30 April 1938

My dear Jawaharlal,
... My handicap today is that I do not move about the country, as you do, and a still more serious handicap is the inner despondency that has overtaken me. I am carrying on, but it is galling to me to think that I have lost the self-confidence that I possessed only a month ago. I hope that this is but a temporary phase in my life. ...

Bapu
CWMG *Vol. 67, p. 56; E*

Violence And The CPI

Segaon(Wardha)
21 May 1938

My dear C.R.[34],
I had two hours and a half with friend Jinnah yesterday[35]. The talk was cordial but not hopeful, yet not without hope. I must not enter into the details of the conversation, but he complained bitterly of Hindi having been imposed in particular areas of Madras in primary schools. What is exactly the position? Are Mussalman boys affected? Please send me as early a reply as possible and one that I could publicly use.

I had a long chat with Jawaharlal about the Communist Party. I think we understand each other better than before on this particular question. He says (in) the Communist Party's programme, there is no violence, there is no secrecy. Why should it (be) banned therefore as such? If any communist or party resorts to violence openly or secretly or incites to violence they must be dealt with not because of allegiance to a particular party, but because of violence. Thus the author of the writing that you showed me can clearly be dealt with under law, not because there is a ban on the Communist (Party) but because the writing itself has a criminal taint. Have you anything against this argument? ...

Love.

Bapu
CWMG Vol. 67, pp. 90–1; E

Jinnah—A Tough Customer

Segaon[36]
22 May 1938

I MUST send you a copy of what happened between Jinnah and me. He is a very tough customer. If the other members of the League are of the same type a settlement is an impossibility. ...

CWMG Vol. 67, p. 92; E

Ramana Maharshi

Segaon, Wardha
30 July 1938

... I WISH you to visit Ramana Maharshi as early as possible[37].

Blessings from
Bapu
CWMG Vol. 67, p. 214; G

20 August 1938[38]

... I HOPE you will keep well and drive to the Cape[39] if you have time. Would like you to drop in at Tiruvannamalai for a day to see the Maharshi[40] on your return. ...

CWMG Vol. 67, p. 269

If I Were A Czech[41]

Peshawar
6 October 1938

... I WANT to speak to the Czechs because their plight moved me to the point of physical and mental distress and I felt that it would be cowardice on my part not to share with them the thoughts that were welling up within me ... If I were a Czech, therefore, I would free these two nations (England and France) from the obligation to defend my country. And yet I must live. I would not be a vassal to any nation or body. I must have absolute independence or perish. To seek to win in a clash of arms would be pure bravado. Not so, if in defying the might of one who would deprive me of my independence I refuse to obey his will and perish unarmed in the attempt. In so doing, though I lose the body, I save my soul, i.e., my honour ...

But, says a comforter, 'Hitler knows no pity. Your spiritual effort will avail nothing before him.'

My answer is, 'You may be right. History has no record of a nation having adopted non-violent resistance ... But as a believer in non-violence, I may not limit its possibilities. Hitherto he and his likes have built upon their invariable experience that men yield to force. Unarmed men, women and children offering non-violent resistance without any bitterness in them will be a novel experience for them. Who can dare say that it is not in their nature to respond to the higher and finer forces? They have the same soul that I have.' ...

Harijan 15-10-1938; CWMG Vol. 67, pp. 404–6

Talk With Abdul Ghaffar Khan

Utmanzai
On or before 15 October 1938[42]

Abdul Ghaffar Khan: There are some Pathans in the villages here who persecute Khudai Khidmatgars beyond endurance. They beat them, seize their lands, and so on. What are we to do against them?

MKG: We have to meet their high-handedness with patience and forbearance. We have to meet their atrocities in the same way as we used to meet the Britishers', not answer violence by violence, nor abuse by abuse, nor harbour anger in our hearts. If we do that it is sure to melt their hearts ...

AGK: Would it be permissible for us to lodge a complaint against them before the police and get them punished?

MKG: A true Khudai Khidmatgar won't go to a law-court. Fighting in a law-court is just like physical fighting. ...

CWMG Vol. 68, pp. 4–5; H

To Kasturba

Peshawar
15 October 1938

Ba,

You are causing me a good deal of worry this time. I keep swinging between my concern for you and my sense of dharma. The mind prompts me to run down to you. Dharma tells me to remain where I am and finish the work here. If you get well soon now, my worry may end.

Blessings from
Bapu
CWMG Vol. 68, p. 8; G

Speech At Hoti Mardan[43]

16 October 1938

I KNOW it is difficult; it is no joke for a Pathan to take an affront lying down. ...

CWMG Vol. 68, p. 13; E

To Kasturba

Peshawar
2 November 1938

Ba,

Only nine days remain now, and God willing, we shall meet. We shall leave for Segaon the same day. I forgot to reply to one remark in your letter. You said that while leaving I did not even put my hand on your head. As the motor started I also felt that, but you were away from me. Do you require outward signs? Why do you believe that because I do not show my love by outward signs, it has dried up? I assure you that my love has increased and goes on increasing. Not that it was less before, but what was there is becoming purer day by day. I do not look upon you merely as a clay doll. What more need I say? ...

CWMG Vol. 68, p. 85; G

The Jews

Segaon, Wardha,
20 November 1938

SEVERAL LETTERS have been received by me asking me to declare my views about the Arab-Jew question in Palestine and the persecution of the Jews in Germany ...

My sympathies are all with the Jews. I have known them intimately in South Africa. Some of them became life-long companions. Through these friends I came to learn much of their age-long persecution. They have been the untouchables of Christianity. The parallel between their treatment by Christians and the treatment of untouchables by Hindus is very close ...

But my sympathy does not blind me to the requirements of justice. The cry for the national home for the Jews does not make much appeal to me. The sanction for it is sought in the Bible and the tenacity with which the Jews have hankered after return to Palestine. Why should they not, like other peoples of the earth, make that country their home where they are born and where they earn their livelihood?

... I have no doubt that they are going about it the wrong way. The Palestine of the Biblical conception is not a geographical tract. It is in their hearts. But if they must look to the Palestine of geography as their national home, it is wrong to enter it under the shadow of the British gun. A religious act cannot be performed with the aid of the bayonet or the bomb. They can settle in Palestine only by the goodwill of the Arabs. They should seek to convert the Arab heart. The same God rules the Arab heart who rules the Jewish heart. ...

Harijan 26-11-1938; CWMG Vol. 68, pp. 137–40; E

JP

Segaon, Wardha[44]
29 November 1938

JAYAPRAKASH ... IS a fakir, absorbed in himself and lost in his own dreams. How can I expect him to pass some time with me? He will not be able to get anything from me and he may not even like some aspects of my life. What is the remedy? I am glad that you remain busy in his service. My health is fine.

Blessings from
Bapu
CWMG *Vol. 68, pp. 156–7; G*

My Reading

Segaon, Wardha[45]
5 December 1938

My dear Malkani,
    I rarely read anything outside my beat. ...

Bapu
CWMG *Vol. 68, p. 178*

To Devadas Gandhi

Segaon, Wardha
5 December 1938

YOU OR Lakshmi should drop a few lines to Ba from time to time. She yearns, and naturally, for the love of you all. ...

CWMG *Vol. 68, p. 180; G*

Interview To Timothy Tingfang Lew[46]

Segaon, Wardha
31 December 1938

(*Rev. Lew, in conveying thanks for the Indian Medical Mission*[47] *to help the Chinese, remarked*):

L: We appreciate it as an expression of India's sympathy and goodwill towards China. China's struggle is not merely for China but for the whole of Asia ... We want your message ... We look to you for spiritual guidance.

MKG: ... I should love to be able say to the Chinese definitely that their salvation lay only through the non-violent technique. But then it is not for a person like me, who is outside the fight, to say to a people who are engaged in a life-and-death struggle, 'Not this way, but that' ...

L: I am of opinion that only the economic collapse of Japan could save China. How are the prospects of a boycott of Japanese goods by India?

MKG: ... Our sympathies are with you but they have not stirred us to our very depths, or else we should have boycotted all Japanese goods, especially Japan's cloth. Japan is not only conquering you but it is trying to conquer us too by its cheap, flimsy machine-made goods. The sending of the Medical Mission was good as a gesture of friendship and goodwill which there are in abundance. But that does not give me much satisfaction when I know we could do much more. We too are a big nation like you. If we told the Japanese: 'We are not going to import a single yard of your calico nor export any of our cotton to you', Japan would think twice before proceeding with its aggression.

Adapted from Harijan *28-1-1939;* CWMG *Vol. 68, pp. 262–4; E*

Islamic Culture

Bardoli
23 January 1939

Q. Let me be plain. I do not believe in Akbar's dream. He aimed at fusing all religions into one and producing a new faith. Do you have some such aim?

A. I do not know what Akbar dreamt. I do not aim at any fusion. Each religion has its own contribution to make to human evolution. ...

Harijan *28-1-1939;* CWMG *Vol. 68, p. 323; E*

Bose's Victory

Bardoli[48]
31 January 1939

SHRI SUBHAS Bose has achieved a decisive victory over his opponent, Dr Pattabhi Sitaramayya. I must confess that from the very beginning I was decidedly against his re-election for reasons into which I need not go. I do not subscribe to his facts or the arguments in his manifestos. I think that his references to his colleagues were unjustified and unworthy. Nevertheless, I am glad of his victory. And since I was instrumental in inducing Dr Pattabhi not to withdraw his name as a candidate when Maulana Saheb withdrew, the defeat is more mine than his. I am nothing if I do not represent definite principles and policy. Therefore, it is plain to me that the delegates do not approve of the principles and policy for which I stand.

I rejoice in this defeat. ...

Harijan 4-2-1939; CWMG Vol. 68, p. 359; E

To Jawaharlal Nehru

Segaon, Wardha
3 February 1939

My dear Jawaharlal,

After the election and the manner in which it was fought, I feel that I shall serve the country by absenting myself from the Congress at the forthcoming session[49]. Moreover, my health is none too good. I would like you to help me. Please do not press me to attend. ...

Bapu
CWMG Vol. 68, p. 368; E

To Subhas Bose

Segaon
5 February 1939

My dear Subhas,

... So far as I can judge the old colleagues whom you consider as rightists will not serve on your cabinet. You can have their resignations now, if that would be more convenient for you. Their presence would be unfair to you and to them. You should be left free to frame your own programme and expect the rightists (I wish you would choose better and indigenous terms to designate the parties of your imagination) to support where they can and abstain without obstructing where they cannot see eye to eye with you ...

Love.

Bapu

CWMG Vol. 68, pp. 382–3; E

A Statue For The Mahatma

Segaon, Wardha
6 February 1939

... IT WILL be waste of good money to spend Rs 25,000 on erecting a clay or metallic statue of the figure of a man who is himself made of clay. ...

Harijan 11-2-1939; CWMG Vol. 68, p. 386; E

To Subhas Bose

On the Train
Address as at Birla House, New Delhi
24 March 1939

My dear Subhas,

I do hope this will find you steadily progressing towards complete recovery.

... Anyway, the anarchy at the Centre should end. In accordance with your request, I am keeping absolutely silent, though pressure is being put upon me to give my opinion on the crisis.

I saw the resolution[50] for the first time in Allahabad. It seems to me to be quite clear. The initiative lies with you. I do not know how far you are fit to attend to national work. If you are not, I think you should adopt the only constitutional course open to you.

I shall have to be in Delhi still for a few days.

Love.

Bapu

The Hindustan Times 14-5-1939; CWMG Vol. 69, p. 80; E

New Delhi
30 March 1939

My dear Subhas,

... Yes, I adhere to the view expressed by me at Segaon at our February meeting that I would not be guilty of being party to any self-suppression by you, as distinguished from voluntary self-effacement. ...

So far as the Gandhi-ites (to use that wrong expression) are concerned, they will not obstruct you. They will help you where they can, they will abstain where they cannot. There should be no difficulty whatsoever, if they are in a minority. They may not suppress themselves if they are clearly in a majority.

What worries me, however, is the fact that the Congress electorate is bogus and that, therefore, majority and minority lose their full meaning. Nevertheless, till the Congress stable is cleansed, we have to manage with the instrument we have for the time being. The other thing worrying me is the terrible distrust among ourselves. Joint work is an impossibility where the workers distrust one another.

I think there is no other point in your letter that needs answering.

In all you do, may you be guided by God. Do be well quickly by obeying the doctors.

Love.

Bapu

The Hindustan Times *14-5-1939;* CWMG *Vol. 69, pp. 90–1; E*

Rajkot
10 April 1939

My dear Subhas,

... I cannot, will not, impose a Cabinet on you. You must not have one imposed on you, nor can I guarantee approval by A.I.C.C. of your Cabinet and policy. It would amount to suppression. Let the members exercise their own judgment. If you do not get the vote, lead the opposition till you have converted the majority. ...

The Hindustan Times *14-5-1939;* CWMG *Vol. 69, pp. 125–6; E*

Questions At Gandhi Seva Sangh

Brindaban
5 May 1939

Question: What was the difficulty in giving the names when Subhas Babu himself had agreed to accept any names you suggested?

MKG: ... When there was such a gulf between me and Subhas Babu, would it have been civilized behaviour to inflict some names on him merely by virtue of that right? Having a right surely does not mean that I should exercise that right in utter disregard of my sense of proportion ...

Question: You have mentioned in one of the letters to Subhas Babu that there are fundamental differences between you and him. What are those differences?

MKG: ... He holds that we possess enough resources for a fight. I am totally opposed to his views. Today we possess no resources for a fight ... If today I am asked to start the 'Dandi March', I have not the courage to do so. How can we do anything without the workers and peasants? The country belongs only to them ...

The same is true of the corruption in the Congress. There the difference between me and him is one of degree. He also agrees that there is corruption. But he feels that it is not of such proportion as to cause worry. But in my view, we shall not be able to do anything so long as this corruption persists ... Thus my point of view and assessment of the situation are altogether different from his. He does not mean the same thing by satyagraha as I do. Hence, sometimes even the difference of degree becomes a fundamental difference.

Question: Are not your differences with the socialists and Jawaharlalji also fundamental? Would you take up a similar attitude with regard to them?

MKG: No. My differences with the socialists are of a different kind. Do not confuse the two ... Moreover, we cannot put the socialists and Jawaharlal in the same category. Jawaharlal does not lend his name to any socialist group. He believes in socialism. He mixes with the socialists and consults them. But there is considerable difference between their methods of work ... There are certainly differences between Jawaharlal and me. But they are not significant. Without him I feel myself a cripple. He also feels more or less the same way. Our hearts are one. This intimate relationship between us has not started with politics. It is very much older and deeper. We shall leave it at that. ...

CWMG *Vol. 69, pp. 206–11; H*

Jawaharlal And I

Bombay[51]
23 June 1939

JAWAHARLAL ... THINKS I am impossible for an organization. He is right there. But I am helpless. Of course there is this thing possible. I can voluntarily retire from all activity. It may come but only by a call from God. I am praying.

... Love.

CWMG *Vol. 69, p. 369; E*

Vandemataram[52]

Bombay
27 June 1939

... NO MATTER what its source was and how and when it was composed, it had become a most powerful battle-cry among Hindus and Mussalmans of Bengal during the partition days. It was an anti-imperialist cry. As a lad, when I knew nothing of *Anandmath* or even Bankim, its immortal author, *Vandemataram* had gripped me, and when I first heard it sung, it had enthralled me. I associated the purest national spirit with it. It never occurred to me that it was a Hindu song or meant only for Hindus. Unfortunately now we have fallen on evil days. All that was pure gold before has become base metal today. In such times it is wisdom not to market pure gold and let it be sold as base metal. I would not risk a single quarrel over singing *Vandemataram* at a mixed gathering. It will never suffer from disuse. It is enthroned in the hearts of millions. It stirs to its depth the patriotism of millions in and outside Bengal. Its chosen stanzas are Bengal's gift among many others to the whole nation. The flag and the song will live as long as the nation lives.

Harijan *1-7-1939,* CWMG *Vol. 69, pp. 379–81; E*

On Jawaharlal

Vishram Vatika, Juhu[53]
P.O. Santa Cruz, Bombay
29 June 1939

... I HAVE advised you about Jawaharlal Nehru's invitation. In my opinion the whole of his planning[54] is a waste of effort. But he can't be satisfied with anything that is not big. ...

CWMG *Vol. 69, pp. 383–4*

Cable To General J.C. Smuts[55]

Abbottabad
On of after 7 July 1939[56]

WHY IS the Agreement of 1914 being violated with you as witness? Is there no help for Indians except to pass through fire?

CWMG *Vol. 69, p. 399; E*

To Hitler

Abbottabad
23 July 1939

FRIENDS HAVE been urging me to write to you for the sake of humanity. But I have resisted their request because of the feeling that any letter from me would be impertinence. Something tells me that I must not calculate and that I must make my appeal for whatever it is worth.

It is quite clear that you are today the one person in the world who can prevent a war which may reduce humanity to the savage state. Must you pay that price for an object however worthy it may appear to you to be? Will you listen to the appeal of one who has deliberately shunned the method of war not without considerable success?

Anyway, I anticipate your forgiveness, if I have erred in writing to you.

Tendulkar Vol. V, *p. 160*

Discussion With Charles Fabri[57]

Abbottabad,
On or before 26 July 1939[58]

... Fabri: What would you say to the right of man to dispose of his life? Life as life I hold of very little importance.

MKG: I think that man has a perfect right to dispose of his life under certain circumstances ...

... supposing I have a cancer, and it is only a question of time for me to pass away, I would even ask my doctor to give me a sleeping draught and thereby have the sleep that knows no waking[59] ....

Harijan *19-8-1939*; CWMG *Vol. 70, pp. 26–30; E*

To Amtussalaam

Segaon
29 July 1939[60]

You hurt me and I hurt you. This is a good bargain, isn't it? ...

Yes, it will indeed be good if you visit Ramana Maharshi. ...

Blessings from
Bapu
CWMG *Vol. 70, p. 43; H*

Threat Of Famine[61]

Segaon
2 August 1939

THERE HAVE been no rains yet at many places in Kathiawar.

This news is alarming. We do hope that Kathiawar will escape this calamity; but if it does not, my second hope is that those who have foodgrains and fodder, or can manage them, will not take advantage of the situation and make profits, and will sell them at cost price. My third hope is that the Rulers will fulfil their duty by rendering the people as much help as possible, and the fourth hope is that the volunteers will rush out to offer help at various places ...

CWMG Vol. 70, p. 54

To Lord Linlithgow

Segaon
29 August 1939

Dear Lord Linlithgow,

I thank you for your letter[62] of 26th instant. I reciprocate your wish that the world will be spared the calamity of war. But if it comes and you think my presence necessary in Simla, of course I shall come.

I am,
Yours sincerely,
M.K. Gandhi
CWMG Vol. 70, p. 137

To V.A. Sundaram

Wardha
31 August 1939

My dear Sundaram,

It is great thing that Sir Radhakrishnan has become Vice Chancellor[63]. ...

Bapu
CWMG Vol. 70, p. 147; E

To Lord Linlithgow

Wardhaganj
2 September 1939

SORRY TERRIBLE news.[64] Taking earliest train. Arriving Simla fourth morning.

CWMG Vol. 70, p. 152; E

Statement To The Press[65]

Simla
5 September 1939

... I TOLD His Excellency that my own sympathies were with England and France from the purely humanitarian standpoint. I told him that I could not contemplate without being stirred to the very depth the destruction of London which had hitherto been regarded as impregnable. And as I was picturing before him the Houses of Parliament and the Westminister Abbey and their possible destruction, I broke down. I have become disconsolate. In the secret of my heart I am in perpetual quarrel with God that He should allow such things to go on. My non-violence seems almost impotent. ...

CWMG Vol. 70, pp. 161–2; E

Oxford Group[66]

Segaon, Wardha
23/24 September 1939

... WHEN WE say we are listening to God and getting answers, though we say it truthfully, there is every possibility there of self-deception ...

I say this in order to warn you how unwise it may be to believe that you are always listening to God. ...

Harijan 7-10-1939; CWMG Vol. 70, pp. 195–6; E

Thanks

On The Train To Delhi[67]
1 October 1939

SIR SARVEPALLI Radhakrishnan has made much of my seventy-first birthday. He has sent me his book[68] of praises from friends, known and unknown to me. ... To Sir Sarvepalli and all those who have sent me their blessings and greetings, I return my thanks hereby. It is impossible for me to send personal acknowledgements.

One warning I should like to issue to my admirers. Some would like to erect my statues in public places, some others would have portraits, yet others would proclaim my birthday as a public holiday. C. Rajagopalachari knows me well and so he has wisely vetoed the proposal to declare my birthday a public holiday. ...

Harijan 7-10-1939; CWMG Vol. 70, p. 221; E

India And The War

Segaon, Wardha
9 October 1939

THE WORLD is looking for something new and unique from India. The Congress will be lost in the crowd if it wears the same old outworn armour that the world is wearing today. The Congress has a name because it represents non-violence as a political weapon *par excellence*. If the Congess helps the Allies as a representative of non-violence, it will give to the Allied cause a prestige and a power which will be invaluable in deciding the ultimate fate of the war. But the members of the Working Committee have honestly and bravely not made the profession of such non-violence.

My position is, therefore, confined to myself alone. I have to find out whether I have any fellow-traveller along the lonely path. ...

Harijan *14-10-1939;* CWMG, *Vol. 70, p. 245; E*

Savarkar

Segaon[69]
12 October 1939

My dear Haribhau,

... I have walked to Savarkar's[70] house. I have gone out of my way to win him over. But I have failed. ...

Yours,
Bapu
CWMG *Vol. 70, p. 248; E*

To Subhas Bose

Anand Bhavan, Allahabad
23 November 1939

My dear Subhas,

... Your way is not mine. For the time being you are my lost sheep. Some day I shall find you returning, to the fold, if I am right and my love is pure.

Ever yours,
Bapu
From the manuscript of Mahadev Desai's Diary;
CWMG *Vol. 70, pp. 373–4; E*

To Devadas

Segaon, Wardha
8 December 1939[71]

WHERE IS the need to guide you? You are not likely to neglect anything in Ba's service. Who can charge you with neglect if anything happens to Ba? She will pass away wherever she is destined to. No one protects another. God alone protects all. Ba will give you the details about the death of Ashalata's child. She was present there at the time. Gopalrao's[72] son died in a matter of a few minutes. He was stung by a black scorpion. He screamed and fell down dead. All of us live in the jaws of death. As long as it does not swallow us we may go about dancing.

J. has written to Jinnah. Now one may say this too is over.

Blessings from
Bapu
CWMG *Vol. 71, pp. 15–16; G*

Tossing A Coin

Segaon, Wardha
15 December 1939

... I CLING to an old superstition, if it may be so called. When in doubt on a matter involving no immorality either way, I toss and actually read in it divine guidance. I have no other scientific basis. To attribute residuary powers to God is a scientific mode in my opinion ...

Harijan *23-12-1939;* CWMG *Vol. 71, p. 38; E*

Dissent

Segaon
16 January 1940

... I AM not spoiling for a fight. I am trying to avoid it. Whatever may be true of the members of the Working Committee, I wholly endorse Subhas Babu's charge that I am eager to have a compromise with

Britain if it can be had with honour. Indeed satyagraha demands it. Therefore I am in no hurry. ...

Harijan *20-1-1940;* CWMG *Vol. 71, p. 114; E*

Dear Quaid-e-Azam[73]

16 January 1940

I HATE to write 'Mr' before any Indian name. It is so unnatural. Hence I have been writing of you as 'Janab Jinnah Sahib', according to the usage taught to me by the later Hakim Sahib. But Abul Kalam tells me that in the League circles you are always called 'Quaid-e-Azam' ...

The purpose of writing this letter is to send you the enclosed advance copy of the article I have sent to the *Harijan*. I have written it to further the end I have read in your recent messages and actions. I know you are quite capable of rising to the height required for the noble motive attributed to you. I do not mind your opposition to the Congress. But your plan to amalgamate all the parties opposed to the Congress at once gives your movement a national character ...

Yours sincerely,
M.K. Gandhi
CWMG *Vol. 71, pp. 117–18; E*

Speech At Santiniketan[74]

17 February 1940[75]

MY UPPERMOST feelings on arriving here are about Deenabandhu[76]. Perhaps you do not know that the first thing I did yesterday morning on alighting from the train at Calcutta was to pay him a visit in the hospital. Gurudev is a world poet, but Deenanbadhu too has the spirit and temperament of a poet in him. ...

... I have often claimed myself to be an accomplished beggar. But a more precious gift has never dropped into my beggar's bowl than Gurudev's blessings today. I know his blessings are with me always. But it has been my privilege today to receive the same from him in

person, and that fills me with joy. Words are useless when the
relation is one of love[77].

Harijan *9-3-1940;* Amrita Bazar Patrika *18-2-1940;*
CWMG *Vol. 71, pp. 220–1; E*

JP's Arrest[78]

Sevagram
12 March 1940

THE ARREST of Shri Jayaprakash Narayan is unfortunate. He is no
ordinary worker. He is an authority on socialism. It may be said
that what he does not know of Western socialism nobody else in
India does. He is a fine fighter. He has forsaken all for the sake of
the deliverance of his country. His industry is tireless. His capacity
for suffering is not to be excelled. I do not know what speech has
brought him within the law. But if 124A or the highly artificial
Sections of the Defence of India Act are to be inspanned for catching
inconvenient persons, then any person whom the authorities want
can be easily brought within the law. ...

Harijan *16-3-1940;* CWMG *Vol. 71, p. 322; E*

The London Assassination

Ramgarh[79]
17 March 1940

FURTHER DETAILS that have come through the Press of the assassination
of Sir Michael O'Dwyer and the attempted assassination of Lord
Zetland, Lord Lamington, and Sir Louis Dane confirm my opinion
that it was a work of insanity. It is none the less reprehensible on
that account. We had our differences with Sir Michael O'Dwyer, but
that should not prevent us from being grieved over his assassination
or condoling with Lady O'Dwyer and her family. I would like every
Indian patriot to share with me the shame of the act and the joy
that the lives of the three distinguished Englishmen were saved.
We have our grievance against Lord Zetland. We must fight his
reactionary policy. But there should be no malice or vindictiveness
in our resistance. ...

Harijan *23-3-1940;* CWMG *Vol. 71, p. 346; E*

At Congress Subjects Committee

Ramgarh
18 March 1940

OURS HAS been both a democratic organization and a fighting one, ever since we reorganized it in 1920. We have used even military language, though in a non-violent sense. Well, then, I want to repeat what I have said times without number that, if you will be soldiers in my army, understand that there is no room for democracy in that organization. The army may be a part of a democratic organization, but there can be no democracy in it, as there can be none in its ranks, as there is none in our various organizations, A.I.S.A, A.I.V.I.A., and so on. In an army the General's word is law, and his conditions cannot be relaxed.

I am supposed to be your General, but I do not know a more feeble General in history. I have no sanctions. My only sanction is the love and affection in which you hold me. But it has its weakness as it has its strength. I know that you love me. Does your love translate itself in action? If it does not, if it does not mean ever-incresing discipline and ever-increasing response to what I say, let me declare to you that I cannot launch civil disobedience, and you must select another General. ...

Harijan 30-3-1940; Congress Bulletin *12-4-1940;*
CWMG *Vol. 71, pp. 350–1; H*

My Answer To Quaid-e-Azam

Sevagram
26 March 1940

Quaid-e-Azam Jinnah is reported to have said:[80]

... Why should Mr Gandhi not be proud to say: 'I am a Hindu and the Congress is a Hindu body'? I am not ashamed of saying that I am a Muslim and that the Muslim League is the representative of Muslims. Why all this camouflage, why this threat of civil disobedience, and why this fight for a Constituent Assembly?

Why should not Mr Gandhi come as a Hindu leader and let me meet him proudly representing the Mussalmans?

My position is and has been clear. I am proud of being a Hindu, but I have never gone to anybody as a Hindu to secure Hindu-Muslim unity. My Hinduism demands no pacts. My support of the Khilafat was unconditional. I am no politician in the accepted sense. But whatever talks I had with Quaid-e-Azam or any other have been on behalf of the Congress which is not a Hindu organization. Can a Hindu organization have a Muslim divine as President, and can its Working Committee have four Muslim members out of 15? ... If the vast majority of Indian Muslims feels that they are not one nation with their Hindu and other brethren, who will be able to resist them? But surely it is permissible to dispute the authority of the 50,000 Muslims who listened to Quaid-e-Azam to represent the feelings of eight crores of Indian Muslims.

Harijan *30-3-1940;* CWMG *Vol. 71, pp. 371–2; E*

A Brave Statement

Sevagram
30 March 1940

SHRI JAYAPRAKASH Narayan sent me a copy of his statement before the court which is printed below. It is worthy of him, brave, brief, and to the point ...

... He has no malice in him. He wants to end Imperialism and Nazism. He has no quarrel with Englishmen or Germans and says truly that, if England were to shed imperialism, not only India but the freedom-loving people of the whole world would exert themselves to see the defeat of Nazism and the viceroy of freedom and democracy.

Harijan *30-3-1940;* CWMG *Vol. 71, p. 372; E*

On Andrews' Death[81]

Sevagram
5 April 1940

IN THE death of C.F. Andrews not only England, not only India, but humanity has lost a true son and servant ... He will live through those thousands who have enriched themselves by personal contact or contact with his writings. In my opinion Charlie Andrews was one of the greatest and best of Englishmen. And because he was a good son of England he became also a son of India. And he did it all for the sake of humanity and for his Lord and Master, Jesus Christ. I have not known a better man or a better Christian than C.F. Andrews. India bestowed on him the title of Deenabandhu. He deserved it because he was a true friend of the poor and downtrodden in all climes.

Harijan *13-4-1940;* The Hindu *5-4-1940;* CWMG *Vol. 71, p. 394; E*

Discussion With A Chinese Visitor

Sevagram

Before 7 April 1940[82]

... Q. In China we used to think that communism would never take any root, but it has now got a definite hold. Can the same be said of India?

MKG: I may say that communists have not made much headway yet in India, and I somehow feel that the character of our people will not easily lend itself to communist methods.

Q. Is it true that an Indian is a Hindu or a Muslim first and an Indian afterwards?

MKG: It is not true, generally speaking, though neither will sell his religion for his country.

... Q. India is a nation of so many races. Do you think that should prove to be an obstacle to unity?

MKG: None whatever ...

Harijan *13-4-1940;* CWMG *Vol. 71, pp. 397 and 399; E*

Jayaprakash's Picture

Sevagram[83]

14 April 1940

... SHRI JAYAPRAKASH's propositions about land may appear frightful. In reality they are not. No man should have more land than he needs for dignified sustenance. Who can dispute the fact that the grinding poverty of the masses is due to their having no land that they can call their own? ...

Harijan *20-4-1940;* CWMG *Vol. 71, pp. 422 and 424–5; E*

Cable To H.G. Wells[84]

Sevagram
Before 16 April 1940

RECEIVED YOUR cable[85]. Have carefully read your five articles[86]. You will permit me to say you are on the wrong track. I feel sure that I can draw up a better charter of rights than you have drawn up. But of what good will it be? Who will become its guardian? If you mean propaganda or popular education you have begun at the wrong end. I suggest the right way. Begin with a charter of Duties of Man (both D and M capitals) and I promise the rights will follow as spring follows winter. ...

The Hindustan Times *16-4-1940;* CWMG *Vol. 71, p. 430; E*

Interview To *The New York Times*

Sevagram
Before 22 April 1940

... Q. Supposing India does become free in your lifetime, what will you devote the rest of your years to?

MKG: If India becomes free in my lifetime and I have still energy left in me, of course I would take my due share, though outside the official world, in building up the nation on a strictly non-violent basis.

Harijan *27-4-1940;* CWMG *Vol. 72, pp. 10–12; E*

Death Sentence

Sevagram
22 April 1940

Q. Do you consider death sentence to be against your principle of ahimsa? If so, what form of punishment would you advocate as a substitute in a free India?

MKG: I do regard death sentence as contrary to ahimsa. Only He takes life who gives it. All punishment is repugnant to ahimsa. Under a State governed according to the principles of ahimsa, therefore, a murderer would be sent to a penitentiary and there given every chance of reforming himself. All crime is a kind of disease and should be treated as such.

Harijan *27-4-1940;* CWMG *Vol. 72, pp. 13–14; E*

An English Suggestion

Sevagram
29 April 1940

An English Friend writes thus:

... *The crux of the matter is who is to control power at the Centre— Hindus or Muslims? Over this the Congress must be prepared to make great concessions* ...

... My life is made up of compromises, but they have been compromises that have brought me nearer the goal. Pakistan cannot be worse than foreign domination. ...

Harijan 4-5-1940; CWMG *Vol. 72, pp. 26–7*

A Briton's Question

Sevagram
30 April 1940

Q. Would you prefer Muslim rule to British rule?

MKG: The question is badly put. You, being British, cannot get out of the habit of thinking that India is fit only to be ruled by someone. Muslim rule is equivalent to Indian rule. ... It makes no difference to me that some Muslims regard themselves as a separate nation. It is enough for me that I do not consider them as such. They are sons of the soil. ...

Harijan 4-5-1940; CWMG *Vol. 72, pp. 32–3*

To Margarete Spiegel

Sevagram, Wardha
11 May 1940

I HAVE your letter. I was very happy. It is good you are serving the blind dog. ...

Blessings from
Bapu

Dr Margarete Spiegel
Ivanhoe, Opp. Backbay Baths
Fort, Bombay

CWMG *Vol. 72, p. 59; G*

To Manilal

Sevagram, Wardha
14 May 1940

YOUR ATTACK on Jinnah Saheb in *I(ndian) O(pinion)* was not proper.
You should never discuss our quarrels here. This is only the impression
I have formed from this end. I do not know whether you have any
special reason for such severe criticism. ...

Blessings from
Bapu
CWMG Vol. 72, pp. 67–8; G

To Master Tara Singh[87]

Before 21 May 1940[88]

THE CONGRESS will stick to its resolution passed at the Lahore session
of the Congress regarding communal rights of the Sikhs, meaning
thereby that no communal solution will be accepted by the Congress
which will not be acceptable to the Sikhs.

The Hindustan Times 23-5-1940; CWMG Vol. 72, p. 84

Question Box

Sevagram
17 June 1940

TEST-TUBE BABIES

Q. You say that motherhood is sublime but sex is bad. From the
spiritual and eugenic point of view don't you agree that the test-
tube technique of begetting babies is ideal since it altogether
eliminates lust and carnality from procreation?

MKG: So long as I hold to the view that carnality prevents man
or woman from rising to the fullest height possible, so long must
I rebel against these artificial methods of procreation. Your
method, as far as I can see, can only result in multiplying idiots or
monsters, not human beings, thrown into the sea of passions ...
But I own I belong to an age that is perhaps dying.

CWMG Vol. 72, p. 185

At Congress Working Committee Meeting

New Delhi
3/7 July 1940[89]

MKG: I have been oppressed all the time by the fact that I now represent a totally different mentality from that of the Working Committee. When I asked for absolution it was not a formal thing ...

C. Rajagopalachari: I cannot go with Gandhiji in his conception of the State. Ours is a political organization not working for non-violence but for the political ideal. We are working in competition with other political parties.

Jawaharlal Nehru: I agree with Rajaji in his understanding of violence and non-violence; else we cannot function on the political plane.

CWMG *Vol. 72, pp. 235 and 237*

Draft Resolution For The Working Committee

New Delhi
4/6 July 1940

MKG: ... Rajaji is right that if I believe that the Congress is with me I am living in a fool's paradise. ...

... I don't want to be instrumental in militarizing the masses. ...

Wardha Office, *Satyagraha File* 1940-1; CWMG *Vol. 72, pp. 244-5; E*

To Manilal And Sushila Gandhi

Sevagram
19 July[90] 1940

I GOT your letter. Nanabhai had telegraphed to me at Delhi the news of Sushila's delivery. It is good that everything was over without much suffering. You have found a nice name. Did you find a good astrologer or did you consult an almanac for the sign of the Zodiac? Whisper my blessings in Ila's[91] ear and say: 'Be a credit to the family'. ...

Blessings from
Bapu
CWMG *Vol. 72, pp. 293-4; G*

Question Box[92]

Sevagram
30 July 1940

PAKISTAN AND AHIMSA

A GUJARATI Mussalman correspondent writes:

Q. I am a believer in ahimsa as well as Pakistan. How can I use the ahimsa principle for the realization of my ideal?

MKG: It is not possible to attain an iniquitous end by non-violent means. For instance, you cannot commit theft non-violently. ...

Harijan 4-8-1940; CWMG Vol. 72, pp. 333–4; E

The Case Of My First Son[93]

Sevagram
5 August 1940

Q. You have failed to take even your own son with you, and he has gone astray. May it not, therefore, be well for you to rest content with putting your own house in order?

MKG: This may be taken to be a taunt, but I do not take it so. For the question had occurred to me before it did to anyone else. I am a believer in previous births and rebirths. All our relationships are the results of the *samskaras* we carry from our previous births. God's laws are inscrutable and are the subject of endless search. No one will fathom them.

　　This is how I regard the case of my son. I regard the birth of a bad son to me as the result of my evil past whether of this life or previous. My first son was born when I was in a state of infatuation. Besides, he grew up whilst I was myself growing and whilst I knew myself very little. I do not claim to know myself fully even today, but I certainly know myself better than I did then. For years he remained away from me, and his upbringing was not entirely in my hands. That is why he has always been at a loose end. His grievance against me has always been that I sacrificed him and his brothers at the altar of what I wrongly believed to be public good. My other sons have laid more or less the same blame at my door, but with a good deal of hesitation, and they have generously forgiven me. My eldest son was the direct victim of my experiments—radical changes in my life—and so he cannot forget what he regards as my blunders. Under the circumstances I believe I am myself the cause of the loss of my son, and have therefore learnt patiently to bear it. And yet it is not quite correct to say that I have lost him. For it is my constant prayer that God may make him see the error of his ways and forgive me my short-comings, if any, in serving him. It is my firm faith that man is by nature going higher, and so I have not at all lost hope that some day he will wake up from his slumber of ignorance. Thus he is part of my field of experiments in ahimsa. When or whether I shall succeed I have never bothered to know. It is enough for my own satisfaction that I do not slacken my efforts in doing, what I know to be my duty. 'To work thou hast the right, never to the fruit thereof' is one of the golden precepts of the *Gita*.

Harijan 18-8-1940; CWMG Vol. 72, pp. 354–5; E

Creation

Sevagram
6 August 1940

Q. You say that God has a hand in the creation of the world. Why is then there this frightful war? Why aren't they inspired by God? Millions of men, women, and children are being killed. It seems that God loves it. What are the things inspired by God? Can't He prevent bad deeds?

MKG: If we knew this should we not become God? ...

CWMG Vol. 72, p. 362; H

To Rabindranath Tagore[94]

Delhi
1 October 1940

Dear Gurudev,

You must stay yet awhile. Humanity needs you. I was pleased beyond measure to find that you were better.

With love.

Yours,
M.K. Gandhi
CWMG Vol. 73, p. 73; E

Speech At Wardha[95]

2 October 1940

IN THIS *Kali Yuga*, you get more fruit for less work. ...

The Bombay Chronicle *3-10-1940*; CWMG *Vol. 73, p. 74*

Lord Linlithgow

Sevagram

5 October 1940

... I THINK it is necessary for my purpose to say a few words regarding Lord Linlithgow. He is straight in his talk, always deliberate, and economical in his language ...

I went to Simla in the capacity of a representative and as a friend. As a friend I presented him with my doubts as to certain acts of the British Government ...

I failed to get any satisfaction on the points raised. The Viceroy would not be drawn into a discussion. ... There is a certain cold reserve about the British official world which gives them their strength and isolation from surroundings and facts. They do not want to be too frank. They politely refuse to enter into embarrassing argument. They leave you to draw what inferences you like while they continue to maintain their inflexible attitude. I suppose that is what is meant by the steel frame ...

Nevertheless, I will not accept defeat. ...

Harijan *13-10-1940;* CWMG *Vol. 73, pp. 77–80; E*

Civil Disobedience[96]

Sevagram

15 October 1940

... DIRECT ACTION will be commenced by Shri Vinoba Bhave and for the time being confined to him only. ...

Who is Vinoba Bhave and why has he been selected? He is an undergraduate having left college after my return to India in 1915[97]. He is a Sanskrit scholar. He joined the Ashram[98] almost at its inception. He was among the first members. In order to better qualify himself he took one year's leave to prosecute further studies in

Sanskrit. And, practically at the same hour at which he had left the Ashram a year before, he walked into it without notice. I had forgotten that he was due to arrive that day. He has taken part in every menial activity of the Ashram from scavenging to cooking. Though he has a marvellous memory and is a student by nature, he has devoted the largest part of his time to spinning in which he has specialized as very few have ...

He believes in the necessity of the political independence of India. He is an accurate student of history ...

It was necessary to introduce Vinoba at length to the public in order to justify my choice. ...

Harijan 20-10-1940; CWMG Vol. 73, pp. 102–5

To Jawaharlal

Wardha
24 October 1940[99]

... IF YOU are ready, you may now ceremonially declare your civil disobedience. I would suggest your choosing a village for your audience. I do not suppose they will allow you to repeat your speech. They were not ready with their plans so far as Vinoba was concerned. But should they let you free I suggest your following the plan laid down for Vinoba. But if you feel otherwise, you will follow your own course. Only I would like you to give me your programme ... I know what strain you are bearing in giving me your loyalty. I prize it beyond measure. I hope it will be found to have been well-placed, for it is 'do or die'. There is no turning back. ...

Love.

Bapu
CWMG Vol. 73, pp. 126–7; E

To Adolf Hitler

Wardha
24 December 1940

Dear Friend,

That I address you as a friend is no formality. I own no foes. My business in life has been for the past 33 years to enlist the friendship of the whole of humanity by befriending mankind, irrespective of race, colour, or creed.

I hope you will have the time and desire to know how a good portion of humanity who have been living under the influence of that doctrine of universal friendship view your action. We have no doubt about your bravery or devotion to your fatherland, nor do we believe that you are the monster described by your opponents. But your own writings and pronouncements and those of your friends and admirers leave no room for doubt that many of your acts are monstrous and unbecoming of human dignity, especially in the estimation of men like me who believe in universal friendliness. Such are your humiliation of Czechoslovakia, the rape of Poland, and the swallowing of Denmark ...

Is it too much to ask you to make an effort for peace during a time which may mean nothing to you personally but which must mean much to the millions of Europeans whose dumb cry for peace I hear, for my ears are attuned to hearing the dumb millions? I had intended to address a joint appeal to you and Signor Mussolini, whom I had the privilege of meeting when I was in Rome during my visit to England as a delegate to the Round Table Conference. I hope that he will take this as addressed to him also with the necessary changes.

I am,
Yours sincere friend,
M.K. Gandhi
CWMG *Vol. 73, pp. 253–5; E*

To Tej Bahadur Sapru

Sevagram, Wardha
16 February 1941[100]

Dear Sir Tej Bahadur
... Quaid-e-Azam Jinnah's letter confirms my fear. He would see me if I go 'on behalf of the Hindu community'. This I cannot do. I do not represent the Hindu community. ...

Yours sincerely,
M.K. Gandhi
CWMG *Vol. 73, p. 337*

To Rabindranath Tagore[101]

Wardha
12 April 1941

Gurudev
Santiniketan
Four score not enough. May you finish five. Love.[102]

Gandhi
CWMG Vol. 73, p. 438; E

Communal Riots

Sevagram
4 May 1941

HINDU–MUSLIM riots that have broken out in many important places in the country must have saddened all sane people. My grief however is special. The Congress influence seems to have been practically unfelt during the dark days.

We have proved ourselves barbarians and cowards in these places. Arson, loot, and killing of innocent people including children, have been common in almost all the places. Thousands have run away from their homes for fear of their lives. ...

A.I.C.C. File 1941, CWMG *Vol. 74, p. 26; E*

Tribute To Rabindranath Tagore

Sevagram
7 August 1941[103]

IN THE death of Rabindranath Tagore, we have not only lost the greatest poet of the age, but an ardent nationalist who was also a humanitarian. There was hardly any public activity on which he has not left the impress of his powerful personality. In Santiniketan and Sriniketan, he has left a legacy to the whole nation, indeed, to the world. May the noble soul rest in peace and may those in charge at Santiniketan prove worthy of the responsibility resting on their shoulders.

The Bombay Chronicle *8-8-1941;* CWMG *Vol. 74, p. 218; E*

Letter To S. Radhakrishnan

Sevagram
12 October 1941

... HAVING YIELDED to you I cannot interfere with your announcement[104]. Please do what you think best. Do however spare me the degree. These honours must be reserved for those who really deserve them. How can a law-breaker be a doctor of laws? ...

Yours sincerely,
M.K. Gandhi

Sir S. Radhakrishnan
30 Edward Elliot's Road,
Mylapore, Madras.

CWMG *Vol. 75, p.* 3

At A.I.C.C. Meeting

Wardha
15 January 1942

... PLEASE DO not think that I am speaking to you from a high pedestal. The simple question is why are we prepared today to discard a thing which we have cherished for so many years. No doubt, you have not discarded it yet, but you will if your terms are accepted. This much I am able to see. I do not raise the question of what we shall do after swaraj. I am myself not aware what I will do after swaraj. But today you are eager to barter away ahimsa for swaraj. You had taken a pledge that you would win swaraj only through ahimsa, and through no other means. Today you are ready to depart from it. I want to tell you that this bargain will not bring you complete independence ...

... Somebody suggested that Pandit Jawaharlal and I were estranged. This is baseless. Jawaharlal has been resisting me ever since he fell into my net. You cannot divide water by repeatedly striking it with a stick. It is just as difficult to divide us. I have always said that not Rajaji, nor Sardar Vallabhbhai,[105] but Jawaharlal will be my successor. He says whatever is uppermost in his mind, but he always does what I want. When I am gone he will do what I am doing now. Then he will speak my language too. After all he was born in this land. Every day he learns some new thing. He fights with me because I am there. Whom will he fight when I am gone? And who will suffer his fighting? Ultimately, he will have to speak my language. Even if this does not happen, I would at least die with this faith.

... This is not the resolution as drafted by Jawaharlal. His draft has been materially amended. Rajaji also had a hand in revising it. People have an erroneous impression about Jawaharlal that he never budges from his views. Today at least he cannot get that certificate. He argues vehemently, but when the time for action arrives, he can make considerable compromises. ...

Harijan Sevak *25-1-1942;* Harijan *25-1-1942;*
CWMG *Vol. 75, pp. 22–5; H*

At Benares Hindu University

21 January 1942

... I AM afraid our universities are the blotting-sheets of the West. We have borrowed the superficial features of the Western universities, and flattered ourselves that we have founded living universities here. Do they reflect or respond to the needs of the masses? Now I am told that a special feature of your University is that engineering and technology are taught here as nowhere else. I should not consider this a distinguishing feature. Let me make a suggestion to you. Have you been able to attract to your University youths from Aligarh? Have you been able to identify yourselves with them? That, I think, should be your special work, the special contribution of your University. ...

CWMG *Vol. 75, pp. 244–5; H*

To Prema Kantak

Sevagram
30 January 1942

... YOU DID well to draw my attention to my habit of talking too much. I will continue to call you silly, but I will bear in mind your criticism ...

I plead completely guilty to your second charge. I am in no position now to write long and interesting letters. I can do that only if I went to jail. Nor can I talk interestingly. The pressure on my time has become much too heavy for that.

Blessings from
Bapu
CWMG *Vol. 75, p. 271; G*

Seth Jamnalal Bajaj

Sevagram
11 February 1942[106]

IN SETH Jamnalal Bajaj, death has taken a mighty man. Whenever I wrote of wealthy men becoming trustees of their wealth for the common good I always had this merchant prince principally in mind. If his trusteeship did not reach the ideal, the fault was not his. I deliberately restrained him. I did not want him in his enthusiasm to take a single step which in his cool moments he might regret. His simplicity was all his own. Every house he built for himself became a dharmashala ... Janakidevi, the widow, has decided to take up the work to which he had dedicated himself. She has divested herself of all her personal property valued at about two and a half lacs. May God enable her to fulfil the trust she has undertaken.

Harijan *15-2-1942;* CWMG *Vol. 75, p. 306; E*

Fiery Ordeal

Sevagram
16 February 1942

TWENTY-TWO years ago a young man of thirty came to me and said, 'I want to ask something of you'.

'Ask, and it shall be given, if it is at all within my power to give', I replied with some surprise.

'Regard me as your son Devadas', the young man said.

'Agreed', I replied. 'But what have you asked of me? You are the giver, I am the gainer.'

The young man was no other than Jamnalal Bajaj. People know something of what this sacrament meant. But few know the extent of the part played by the self-adopted son. Never before, I can say, was a mortal blessed with a 'son' like him. ...

Harijan Sevak 22-2-1942; CWMG *Vol. 75, p. 323; H*

To Jayaprakash

Sevagram

17 February 1942

... THERE IS no danger in practicing pranayama[107] Western style. Breathe slowly through the nose in and out sitting erect or standing in the open air. Doing it on an empty stomach daily morning and evening will make you feel better. ...

Blessings from

Bapu

From the manuscript of Mahadev Desai's Diary; CWMG *Vol. 75, p. 331; H*

To Vallabhbhai

Sevagram

23 February 1942

MAHADEV HAS had a serious attack. Yesterday he left with Ghanshyamdas for a seven-day visit to Nasik, but felt giddy on the way to the station. He, therefore, wisely decided not to proceed further and went to the Civil Surgeon instead. After getting himself treated there for a while, he returned home. He is better now. The blood-pressure has come down to normal. But he had a narrow escape. This is an indication that he needs a long rest. Do not worry. ...

Blessings from

Bapu

CWMG *Vol. 75, p. 354; G*

'Blessings In Every Way'[108]

Sevagram

27 February 1942

WHAT THE papers announced you have confirmed. May your union prove a blessing in every way.

Yours,

M.K. Gandhi

સેવાગ્રામ   SEVAGRAM,   سیواگرام
વર્ધા સી.પી.   WARDHA, C.P.   وردا۔سی۔پی

27 2 42

Dear Uday Shankar,
        what the papers
announced you
have confirmed.
may your union
prove a 'blessing
in every' way.
                yours,
                M K Gandhi

From a copy of the letter given to the editor by Smt Amala Shankar

Indira Nehru's Engagement

Sevagram
2 March 1942

I HAVE received several angry and abusive letters and some professing to reason about Indira's engagement with Feroze Gandhi. Not a single correspondent has anything against Feroze Gandhi as a man. His only crime in their estimation is that he happens to be a Parsi. I have been, and I am still, as strong an opponent of either party changing religion for the sake of marriage. Religion is not a garment to be cast off at will. In the present case there is no question of change of religion. Feroze Gandhi has been for years an inmate of the Nehru family. He nursed Kamala Nehru in her sickness. He was like a son to her. During Indira's illness in Europe he was of great help to her. A natural intimacy grew up between them. The friendship has been perfectly honourable. It has ripened into mutual attraction. But neither party would think of marrying without the consent and blessing of Jawaharlal Nehru ... I had also talks with both the parties. ...

Harijan 8-3-1942; CWMG Vol. 75, p. 375; E

Interview To Bertram Stevens[109]

Delhi
On of before 4 April 1942[110]

MKG: ... You have vast living spaces, you can absorb millions and millions of human beings. But I know what you are doing. I have followed the history of your country for over 35 years. White Australia is your policy, and as a result you are without the wonderful accession of strength that would have been yours if you had followed a policy of brothering all.

B.S.: I agree. But our country is only 150 years old. Prejudices die hard, but they are dying.

MKG: You might very well have absorbed our people. Wherever they have gone they have been able to show that they are businesslike, able, and quite competent to take care of themselves. Your country with its infinite resources would have been a different country with these Indian settlers.

B.S.: Yes, Australia is half as big again as India. But it is not quite so fertile as India. But I agree with what you say. ...

Harijan 3-5-1942; CWMG Vol. 76, p. 4; E

To Kantilal Harilal Gandhi

6 April 1942

... I saw Harilal[111]. He had a fracture in the hand. I sent him to a hospital and got the fracture set. He started talking about coming back to

me, but that was only a ruse for getting money out of me. He has no
sense of truth and falsehood. He is always drunk. You need not worry.

Blessings from
Bapu
CWMG *Vol. 76, p. 10; G*

11 April 1942
ABOUT HARILAL I have talked to Devadas and asked him to tell Harilal
that if he is ready I will get him admitted to some jail or asylum for
some time. But he is not likely to accept any reasonable suggestion ...
He is devoid of human feelings.

Blessings from
Bapu
CWMG *Vol. 76, p. 19; G*

Linguistic Basis

Sevagram
12 April 1942
... I BELIEVE that the linguistic basis is the correct basis for demarcating
provinces. I should not mind two provinces speaking the same
language, if they are not contiguous ... If Kerala and Kashmir were
speaking the same language, I would treat them as two distinct
provinces.

Harijan *19-4-1942;* CWMG *Vol. 76, pp. 20–1*

That Ill-Fated Proposal[112]

Sevagram
13 April 1942
IT IS a thousand pities that the British Government should have sent
a proposal for dissolving the political deadlock, which, on the face of
it, was too ridiculous to find acceptance anywhere. And it was a
misfortune that the bearer should have been Sir Stafford Cripps,
acclaimed as a radical among radicals and a friend of India. I have no
doubt about his goodwill. He believed that no one could have brought
anything better for India. But he should have known that at least the

Congress would not look at Dominion Status even though it carried the right of secession the very moment it was taken. He knew too that the proposal contemplated the splitting up of India into three parts each having different ideas of governance. It contemplated Pakistan, and yet not the Pakistan of the Muslim League's conception. And last of all it gave no real control over defence to responsible ministers.

The fact is that Sir Stafford Cripps[113], having become part of the Imperial machinery, unconsciously partook of its quality. ...

Harijan 19-4-1942, CWMG Vol. 76, p. 28; E

To Vallabhbhai Patel

Sevagram
13 April 1942

... Jawaharlal now seems to have completely abandoned ahimsa. You should go on doing what you can. Restrain the people if you can.

His speech[114] reported today seems terrible. I intend to write to him ...

Blessings from
Bapu
CWMG Vol. 76, p. 31; G

To Jawaharlal

Sevagram, Wardha
15 April 1942

The Professor[115] is here. He has told me everything. I also heard about your Press interview. Whereas we have always had differences of opinion it appears to me that now we also differ in practice ...

The more I think of it the more I feel that you are making a mistake. I see no good in American troops entering India and in our resorting to guerrilla warfare.

It is my duty to caution you.

I hope Indu and Feroze are well.

Blessings from
Bapu
CWMG Vol. 76, p. 40; E

To Kantilal Harilal Gandhi

Sevagram
21 April 1942

... IF HARILAL could be legally put in jail, I would have got it done long ago. But there is no such law and he also knows it. That can be done only if one day he himself yields. I do cherish the hope that he will. But the stratagem that he attempted this time has weakened my hope. Devadas continues to do his best.

Blessings from
Bapu
CWMG *Vol. 76, p. 58; G*

To Every Briton

Bombay[116]
11 May 1942

BRITISH STATESMEN talk glibly of India's participation in the war. Now India was never even formally consulted on the declaration of war. Why should it be? India does not belong to Indians. It belongs to the British. It has been even called a British possession. The British practically do with it as they like. They make me—an all-war resister—pay a war tax in a variety of ways. Thus I pay two pice as war tax on every letter I post, one pice on every postcard, and two annas on every wire I send. This is the lightest side of the dismal picture. But it shows British ingenuity. If I was a student of economics, I could produce startling figures as to what India has been made to pay towards the war apart from what are miscalled voluntary contributions. ...

Harijan *17-5-1942;* CWMG *Vol. 76, p. 98–9; E*

Interview To Bombay Suburban And Gujarat Congressmen[117]

Bombay
15 May 1942

... I DISAGREE with Rajaji. Rajaji is an old colleague of mine, and my love for him remains as strong as ever. But I do not feel like Rajaji that of the two Britain is better and can be dealt with later—now, Japan. For me an exploiter of other nations is an exploiter, whether he be imperialist or a totalitarian. Names do not matter. Besides, who says the British are better? I do not want to say for a moment that Rajaji will accept National Government outside the Congress, i.e., without its sanction. But have the British offered it? Rajaji is prepared to help them in every way against the Japanese. Then why the hitch? Simply because they do not want us to get the power.

They will not give it. They are what they are and nothing will change them. Yes, Cripps has gone back. But why do not they negotiate again? Through Sapru or Jayakar or even Rajaji? Because, as I said, they do not want to. Their time to go has come. Rajaji concedes Pakistan. But has Jinnah even moved an inch to discuss matters with him? No. For Jinnah's game is to bring Government pressure on the Congress, and Congress pressure on the Government, or both. Rajaji says, let India be split up. But I cannot agree. I cannot swallow the splitting of India. I alone know what pain the thought has caused me. Rajaji is an old friend and an astute politician. And only I know what I suffered to let him go. But he is strong-willed ... Rajaji still hopes to achieve that which the British have determined will not be achieved: Hindu-Muslim unity. What really is Pakistan? Jinnah has never really explained. Can you tell me? Yes, yes, who denies that?[118] But what is the demand? The masses are duped. Good Mussalmans have failed to explain it to me. Indeed, when I am asked to solve the deadlock, I admit I can't do anything about it. The British make us fight although I don't hide for a moment that we too want to fight ... I therefore ask the British to give us the gift of anarchy. If the British withdraw it will be given automatically. If not, then we will create anarchy, by launching satyagraha. I know the general confusion. You find Maulana says one thing, Jawahar another, Rajaji a third, and now I a fourth thing. What are we to do? My advice to you is to weigh all the four and decide which to accept for yourself. I have not yet met Jawahar nor Maulana. But as you know well, although Jawahar and myself have differed quite often, he has always been with me as far as action goes. And I hope to win him to me. As for Maulana, we have always stood together since years. So I hope to reduce the four different notes to two. Then there will be only my voice and the voice of Rajaji and you can decide which of the two to follow.

B.G. Kher: But will such a mass civil disobedience not mean direct help to the Japanese?

MKG: Oh, no! We are driving the British. We do not invite the Japanese. No, I disagree with those who think them liberators. Chinese history points that out. In fact I advised Chiang Kaishek when he came here to fight the Japs my way. In fact I believe that Subhas Bose will have to be resisted by us ...

Q. I want to ask just this: A man is strangling me. Meanwhile another man comes to strangle him. Should I not help the other fellow to strangle my strangler?

MKG: I am a non-violent person, and I say by all means struggle for your freedom but then stop. My self-esteem will not allow me to help in strangling my strangler. No, I cannot help the Japanese ...

G.P. Hutheesing: But Bapu ...

MKG: Sorry, I didn't know you were here (*loud laughter*).

G.P.H.: But Bapu, some people say that one's outlook should be wider. That India should not think of her own freedom, but should stand by the international forces of freedom ...

MKG: None could be greater fools (*loud laughter*). But where is India? India as India does not exist. It is in Britain's pocket. How can such India help? And why? The British give us nothing while they demand everything. ... Can we depend upon Britain and America, both whose hands are stained with blood? India's name can be found nowhere in the Atlantic Charter. Even before the Communists ever said it, I have been thinking of a new mode of life. But it is impossible unless Britain withdraws to let the Indian and the Negroes[119] be free. Then talk to me of a new mode of life. ...

The Transfer of Power 1942–7, *Vol. II;* CWMG *Vol. 76, pp. 107–11; E*

Question Box

Sevagram
23 May 1942

OUT OF TOUCH

Q. Do you know, being confined in Sevagram, how much you are out of touch with the public? ...

MKG: I cannot endorse your proposition that I am out of touch with the public. Though I am confined in Sevagram I see all sorts of people and receive correspondence from every nook and corner of India. Probably, therefore, I am more in touch with the people than you can be though living in a big town. ...

Harijan *31-5-1942;* CWMG *Vol. 76, p. 139; E*

Interview With Louis Fischer[120]

LF: Can not the Indians immediately organize a government?

MKG: Yes, there are three elements in the political situation here: the Princes, the Muslims, and Congress. They could all form a provisional government.

LF: In what proportion would power and the posts be divided?

MKG: I do not know. Congress being the most powerful unit might claim the largest share. But that could be determined amicably.

LF: If you demand that the British pack up and go bag and baggage, you are simply asking the impossible; you are barking up a tree. You do not mean, do you, that they must also withdraw their armies?

MKG: No, Britain and America, and other countries too, can keep their armies here and use Indian territory as a base for military operations. I do not wish Japan to win the war. I do not want the Axis to win. But I am sure that Britain cannot win unless the Indian people became free. Britain is weaker and Britain is morally indefensible while she rules India. I do not wish to humiliate England.

LF: Could the terms of this collaboration be set forth in a treaty of alliance?

MKG: Yes, we could have a written agreement with England.

LF: Or with Britain, America and the others? Why have you never said this? ... I see complete darkness for the world if the Axis win. I think we have a chance for a better world if we win.

MKG: There I cannot quite agree. Britain often cloaks herself in a cloth of hypocrisy, promising what she later doesn't deliver. But I accept the proposition that there is a better chance if the democracies win.

LF: Why have you not communicated your plan to the Viceroy? He should be told that you have no objection now to the use of India as a base for Allied military operations.

MKG: No one has asked me ... Jawaharlal told me about you before you came. He said you were honest and had no axe to grind. You don't have several irons in the fire. He said you were a solid man. I can see that by looking at you.

LF: Yes, solid, at least physically.

6 JUNE 1942

I asked him what was the theory behind his weekly day of silence.

MKG: What do you mean by theory?

LF: I mean the principle, the motivation.

MKG: It happened when I was being torn to pieces. I was working very hard, travelling in hot trains incessantly, speaking at many meetings, and being approached in trains and elsewhere by thousands of people who asked questions, made pleas, and wished to pray with me. I wanted to rest for one day a week. So I instituted the day of silence. Later of course I clothed it with all kinds of virtues and gave it a spiritual cloak. But the motivation was really nothing more than that I wanted to have a day off.

Silence is very relaxing. It is not relaxing in itself. But when you can talk and don't, it gives you great relief—and there is time for thought.

LF: It was sad that Congress leaders and Muslim Leaguers came to New Delhi to talk to Cripps, and talked to Cripps but did not talk to one another.

MKG: It was not only sad, it was disgraceful. But it was the fault of the Muslim League. Shortly after this war broke out, we were summoned to meet the Viceroy at New Delhi. Rajendra Prasad and I went to speak for Congress, and Mr Jinnah for the Muslim League. I asked Jinnah to confer with us in advance and face the British Government unitedly. We agreed to meet in New Delhi, but when I suggested that we both demand independence for India he said, 'I do not want independence.' We could not agree. I urged that we at least make the appearance of unity by going to the Viceroy together; I said he could go in my car or I would go in his. He consented to have me go in his car. But we spoke to the Viceroy in different tones and expressed different views.

In actual life, it is impossible to separate us into two nations. We are not two nations. Every Muslim will have a Hindu name if he goes back far enough in his family history. ...

LF: The Muslim bartender in my hotel in New Delhi said to me—although he is a member of the Muslim League and an advocate of Pakistan—that communal troubles always started where Muslims were a minority and never where the Hindus were a minority.

MKG: Fischer, you have been here only for a short time. You cannot study everything. But if you make any investigations and find that we are wrong or guilty, please say so in a loud voice ...

LF: Doesn't the fact that Congress gets its money from the moneyed interests affect Congress politics? Doesn't it create a kind of moral obligation?

MKG: It creates a silent debt ...

LF: I have been told, and I read in the Simon report that one of the great curses of India is the village money-lender to whom the peasant is often in debt from birth to death ... Why could not some of your rich friends start a land bank on a purely business basis except that, instead of getting 40–70 per cent interest per year, they would get 2 or 3 per cent? Their money would be secure, they would earn a small profit, and they would be helping their country.

MKG: Money-lending is an ancient institution and it is deeply rooted in the village. What you advocate cannot be done before we are free.

LF: What would happen in a free India? What is your programme for the improvement of the lot of the peasantry?

MKG: The peasants would take the land. We would not have to tell them to take it. They would take it.

LF: Would the landlords be compensated?

MKG: No. That would be fiscally impossible. You see, our gratitude to our millionaire friends does not prevent us from saying such things. The village would become a self-governing unit living its own life.

LF: ... I would like to talk to you for a few moments about Subhas Chandra Bose, who has escaped to Axis territory. I was rather shocked when I heard that you had sent a telegram of condolence to Bose's mother on the receipt of the report[121], since proved false, that Bose had died in an airplane accident.

MKG: Do you mean because I had responded to news that proved to be false?

LF: No, but that you regretted the passing of a man who went to Fascist Germany and identified himself with it.

MKG: I did it because I regard Bose as a patriot of patriots. He maybe misguided. I think he is misguided. I have often opposed Bose. Twice I kept him from becoming president of Congress. Finally he did become president, although my views often differed from his. But suppose he had gone to Russia or to America to ask aid for India. Would that have made it better?

LF: Yes, of course. It does make a difference to whom you go.

MKG: I do not want help from anybody to make India free. I want India to save herself. ...

Adapted

7 JUNE 1942

LF: ... Do you believe in the transmigration of the soul?

MKG: Of course. I cannot admit that the soul dies with the body. When a man's house is blown away, he builds himself another. When his body is taken away, his soul finds another. Nor do I accept the view that when the body is laid in the ground the soul remains suspended somewhere waiting for judgment day when it will be brought to the bar and confronted with its crimes. No, it immediately finds itself a new home.

LF: This is obviously another form of man's eternal striving for immortality. Does it not all arise from the weak mortal's fear of death? Tolstoy was irreligious until his old age, when he started dreading the end.

MKG: I have no fear of death. I would regard it with relief and satisfaction. But it is impossible for me think that that is the end. I have no proof. People have tried to demonstrate that the soul of a dead man finds a new home. I do not think this is capable of proof. But I believe it.

LF: I believe that faith in one's immortality, if it is distinct from one's acts, is really fear of death and an attempt to find comfort in an illusion. ...

8 JUNE 1942

LF: India's population is increasing by five million each year. ... How are you going to deal with that?

MKG: One of the answers might be birth control. But I am opposed to birth control

LF: I am not, but in a backward country like India birth control could not be very effective anyway.

MKG: Then perhaps we need some good epidemics.

LF: Or a good civil war ...

MKG: You want to force me into an admission that we would need rapid industrialization. I will not be forced into such an admission. Our first problem is to get rid of British rule. Then we will be free, without restraints from the outside, to do what India requires ...

LF: Well, how do you actually see your impending civil disobedience movement? What shape will it take?

MKG: In the villages, the peasants will stop paying taxes. They will make salt despite official prohibition. This seems a small matter; the salt tax yields only a paltry sum to the British Government. But refusal to pay it will give the peasants the courage to think that they are capable of independent action. Their next step will be to seize the land.

LF: With violence?

MKG: There maybe fifteen days of chaos, but I think we could soon bring that under control.

LF: You feel then that it must be confiscation without compensation?

MKG: Of course. It would be financially impossible for anybody to compensate the landlords.

LF: That accounts for the villages. But that is not all of India.

MKG: No. Working men in the cities would leave their factories. The railroads would stop running.

LF: General strike. I know that you have in the past had a large following among the peasants, but your city working-class support is not so big.

MKG: No, not so big. But this time the workingmen will act too, because, as I sense the mood of the country, everybody wants freedom. ...

LF: What about the time factor? When you launch your civil disobedience movement, and if the British yield, will it be a matter of the immediate transfer of political power?

MKG: The British would not have to do that in two days or in two weeks. But it must be irrevocable and complete political withdrawal.

LF: Suppose the British say they will withdraw completely after the war?

MKG: No. In that case my proposal loses much of its value....

LF: Have you any organization with which to carry on this struggle?

MKG: The organization is the Congress Party. But if it fails me, I have my own organization, myself. I am a man possessed by an idea. If such a man cannot get an organization, he becomes an organization ...

LF: So you intend to tell the British in advance when you will launch your movement?

MKG: Yes.

LF: You had better not tell them too far in advance.

MKG: Is that a tip from you?

LF: No.

MKG: They will know in good time.

LF: If you look at this in its historic perspective, you are doing a novel and remarkable thing—you are ordaining the end of an empire.

MKG: Even a child can do that. I will appeal to the people's instincts. I may arouse them. ...

LF: Have I your authority to say this to the Viceroy?

MKG: Yes, you have my permission ...

LF: Do you expect drastic action when you launch the movement?

MKG: Yes. I expect it any day. I am ready. I know I may be arrested. I am ready.

A Week With Gandhi *by Louis Fischer, George Allen & Unwin, 1942,*
CWMG Vol. 76, pp. 427–51; E

Interview To Preston Grover[122]

Wardha
10 June 1942

MKG: ... *You* have yet to abolish slavery!

Q.: In United States, you mean?

MKG: Yes, your racial discrimination, your lynch law and so on. But you don't want me to remind you of these things.

Harijan 21-6-1942; CWMG *Vol. 76, p. 212; E*

Question Box

Sevagram
12 June 1942

WHAT ABOUT RADIO MESSAGES?

Q. You do not hear the radio messages. I do most assiduously. They interpret your writings as if your leanings were in favour of the axis powers and you had now veered round to Subhas Babu's views ...

MKG: ... Better the enemy I know than the one I do not. I have never attached the slightest importance or weight to the friendly professions of the Axis powers. If they come to India they will come not as deliverers but as sharers in the spoil. There can therefore be no question of my approval of Subhas Babu's policy. ...

Harijan 21-6-1042; CWMG *Vol. 76, p. 216; E*

India And China

Sevagram
14 June 1942

Dear Generalissimo[123],

I can never forget the five hours' close contact I had with you and your noble wife in Calcutta. I had always felt drawn towards you in your fight for freedom, and that contact and our conversation brought China and her problems still nearer to me. Long ago, between 1905 and 1913, when I was in South Africa, I was in constant touch with the small Chinese colony in Johannesburg. I knew them first as clients and then as comrades in the Indian passive resistance struggle in South Africa. I came in touch with them in Mauritius also. I learnt then to admire their thrift, industry, resourcefulness, and internal unity. Later in India I had a very fine Chinese friend living with me for a few years and we all learnt to like him.

I have thus felt greatly attracted towards your great country and, in common with my countrymen, our sympathy has gone out to you in your terrible struggle. Our mutual friend, Jawaharlal Nehru, whose love of China is only excelled, if at all, by his love of his own country, has kept us in intimate touch with the developments of the Chinese struggle.

... Very soon you will have completed five years of war against Japanese aggression and invasion and all the sorrow and misery that these have brought to China. My heart goes out to the people of China in deep sympathy and in admiration for their heroic struggle and endless sacrifices in the cause of their country's freedom and integrity against tremendous odds. I am convinced that this heroism and sacrifice cannot be in vain; they must bear fruit. To you, to Madame Chiang and to the great people of China, I send my earnest and sincere wishes for your success. I look forward to the day when a free India and a free China will co-operate together in friendship and brotherhood for their own good and for the good of Asia and the world. ...

CWMG Vol. 76, pp. 223 and 225; E

Hooliganism

Sevagram
28 June 1942

THE REPORT of hooliganism[124] at Rajaji's meeting in Matunga makes painful reading. Has Rajaji lost every title to respect because he has taken what seems to be an unpopular view? He went to Matunga on invitation. He was entitled to a patient hearing. Those who did not share his views might have abstained from attending the meeting, but having gone there they should have given him a hearing. They might have cross-questioned him. Those who tarred him and created a disturbance have disgraced themselves and have harmed their cause. Their way is neither the way to swaraj nor 'Akhand Hindustan'. It is to be hoped that the hooliganism at Matunga will be the last exhibition of barbarism. The calmness, good humour, presence of mind and determination that Rajaji showed at that trying time were worthy of him. These must bring him many admirers, if not even followers. For people generally do not weigh the pros and cons of a problem. They follow their heroes. And Rajaji has never lacked the qualities that go to make a hero.

Harijan 5-7-1942; CWMG *Vol. 76, p. 255; E*

Letter To Franklin D. Roosevelt

Sevagram, via Wardha (India)
1 July 1942

Dear Friend,

I twice missed coming to your great country. I have the privilege (of) having numerous friends there both known and unknown to me. Many of my countrymen have received and are still receiving higher education in America. I know too that several have taken shelter there. I have profited greatly by the writings of Thoreau and Emerson. I say this to tell you how much I am connected with your country ... You will therefore accept my word that my present proposal, that the British should unreservedly and without reference to the wishes of the people of India immediately withdraw their rule, is prompted by the friendliest intention. I would like to turn into goodwill the ill will which, whatever may be said to the contrary, exists in India towards Great Britain and thus enable the millions of India to play their part in the present war. ...

I remain,
Yours sincerely,
M.K. Gandhi
CWMG *Vol. 76, p. 264; E*

Guru Gobind Singh

Sevagram
4 July 1942

AT LAST after diligent search Mahadev Desai and others have traced the writing in which I have referred to Guru Gobind Singh[125].

It appears in *Young India* of 9th April 1925. It is headed 'My Friend the Revolutionary'. I would commend it to my Sikh friends and, for that matter, others the whole of the article ... Here I must content myself with only relevant extracts from that article. Here they are:

I shall ask you to answer these questions: Was Guru Gobind Singh a misguided patriot because he believed in warfare for a noble cause? What will you like to say about Washington, Garibaldi, and Lenin? What do you think of Kamal Pasha and De Valera? Would you like to call Shivaji and Pratap well-meaning and sacrificing physicians who prescribed arsenic when they should have given fresh grape-juice? Will you like to call Krishna Europeanized because he believed also in the *vinasha* of *dushkritas*?

This is a hard or rather awkward question. But I dare not shirk it. In the first instance Guru Gobind Singh and the others whose names are mentioned did not believe in secret murder. In the second, these patriots knew their work and their men, whereas the modern Indian revolutionary does not know his work. He has not the men, he has not the atmosphere, that the patriots mentioned had. Though my views are derived from my theory of life I have not put them before the nation on that ground. I have based my opposition to the revolutionaries on the sole ground of expedience. Therefore, to compare their activities with those of Guru Gobind Singh or Washington, or Garibaldi or Lenin would be most misleading and dangerous. But by test of the theory of non-violence I do not hesitate to say that it is highly likely that, had I lived as their contemporary and in the respective countries, I would have called every one of them a misguided patriot, even though a successful and brave warrior. As it is, I must not judge them. I disbelieve history so far as details of acts of heroes are concerned. I accept broad facts of history and draw my own lessons for my conduct.

I reverted to the same subject in another article written a short time after, from which I need take only the following lines:

My belief about the Sikh Gurus is that they were all deeply religious teachers and reformers, that they were all Hindus, and that Guru Gobind Singh was one of the greatest defenders of Hinduism. I believe too that he drew the sword in its defence. But I cannot judge his actions nor can I use him as my model so far as his resort to the sword is concerned.

It must be clear even to him who runs that I never applied the word 'misguided patriot', to the Great Guru and that I have not written a word in disrespect or of which I have any reason to be ashamed or to repent. I abide by every word I have said in that article. I hope that now that the source of the mischief has been traced it will abate entirely and the Sikhs will count me, though a humble Hindu, as a fellow devotee of the Panth.

Harijan 12-7-1942; CWMG *Vol. 76, pp. 268–71*

To Jawaharlal

Sevagram, Wardha
13 July 1942

... BUT I do desire that, as far as possible, all of us should interpret the appeal in the same way. It will not be good if we speak in different voices.

... This is my plea about Maulana Saheb. I find that the two of us have drifted apart. I do not understand him nor does he understand me. We are drifting apart on the Hindu–Muslim question as well as on other questions. I have also a suspicion that Maulana Saheb does not entirely approve of the proposed action. No one is at fault. We have to face the facts. Therefore I suggest that the Maulana should relinquish Presidentship but remain in the Committee, the Committee should elect an interim President and all should proceed unitedly. This great struggle cannot be conducted properly without unity and without a President who comes forth with a hundred per cent cooperation.

Please show this letter to Maulana Saheb. At the moment it is intended for you two only. If you do not like either or both of my suggestions, you may reject them. ...

Blessings from
Bapu
CWMG *Vol. 76, pp. 293–4; E*

To Every Japanese[126]

Sevagram
18 July 1942

... I GRIEVE deeply as I contemplate what appears to me to be your unprovoked attack against China and, if reports are to be believed, your merciless devastation of that great and ancient land.

... I would ask you to make no mistake about the fact that you will be sadly disillusioned if you believe that you will receive a willing welcome from India. ...

I am,
Your friend and well-wisher,
M.K. Gandhi
Harijan *26-7-1942;* CWMG *Vol. 76, pp. 309–11*

For Muslim Friends

Sevagram
20 July 1942

... IF THE Quaid-e-Azam really wants a settlement, I am more than willing and so is the Congress. He will forgive me for suggesting that ... he does not want a settlement. If he wants one, why not accept the Congress President's offer that Congress and League representatives should put their heads together and never part until they have reached a settlement. Is there any flaw or want of sincerity in this offer?

Harijan *26-7-1942;* CWMG *Vol. 76, p. 316; E*

Question Box

Sevagram
On or before 2 August 1942[127]
WHAT ABOUT NEPAL?

Q. When India is free will she treat Nepal as an independent country that she is now or will she be annexed to free India?

MKG: If I know India's mind at all, having tasted the bitter fruit of dependence, she will not want to annex or steal any country. She can have no imperial ambition. Nepal therefore will be an honoured and independent neighbour. ...

Harijan 9-8-1942; CWMG *Vol. 76, p 351; E*

Speech At A.I.C.C. Meeting[128]

Bombay

8 August 1942

... QUAID-e-Azam Jinnah himself was at one time a Congressman. If today the Congress has incurred his wrath, it is because the canker of suspicion has entered his heart. May God bless him with long life, but when I am gone, he will realize and admit that I had no designs on Mussalmans and that I had never betrayed their interests ...

... To demand the vivisection of a living organism is to ask for its very life. It is a call to war. The Congress cannot be party to such a fratricidal war. Those Hindus who, like Dr Moonje and Shri Savarkar, believe in the doctrine of the sword may seek to keep the Mussalmans under Hindu domination. I do not represent that section. I represent the Congress. You want to kill the Congress which is the goose that lays golden eggs. If you distrust the Congress, you may rest assured that there is to be a perpetual war between the Hindus and the Mussalmans, and the country will be doomed to continue warfare and bloodshed. If such warfare is to be our lot, I shall not live to witness it.

... I, therefore, want freedom immediately, this very night, before dawn, if it can be had. Freedom cannot now wait for the realization of communal unity. If that unity is not achieved, sacrifices necessary for it will have to be much greater than would have otherwise sufficed. But the Congress must win freedom or be wiped out in the effort. And forget not that the freedom which the Congress is struggling to achieve will not be for the Congressmen alone but for all the forty crores of the Indian people. Congressmen must forever remain humble servants of the people.

... You may take it from me that I am not going to strike a bargain with the Viceroy for ministries and the like. I am not going to be satisfied with anything short of complete freedom. May be, he will propose the abolition of salt tax, the drink evil, etc. But I will say: 'Nothing less than freedom.'

Here is a *mantra*, a short one, that I give you. You may imprint it on your hearts and let every breath of yours give expression to it. The mantra is: 'Do or Die.' We shall either free India or die in the attempt; we shall not live to see the perpetuation of our slavery. Every true Congressman or (Congress) woman will join the struggle with an inflexible determination not to remain alive to see the country in bondage and slavery. Let that be your pledge ... Take a pledge with God and your own conscience as witness, that you will no longer rest till freedom is achieved and will be prepared to lay down your lives in the attempt to achieve it. He who loses his life will gain it; he who will seek to save it shall lose it. Freedom is not for the coward or the faint-hearted.

... I will now write to the Viceroy. You will be able to read the correspondence not just now but when I publish it with the Viceroy's consent. But you are free to aver that you support the demand to be put forth in my letter. ...

There is much I should yet like to say. But my heart is heavy. I have already taken up much of your time. I have yet to say a few words in English also. I thank you for the patience and attention with which you have listened to me even at this late hour. ...

CWMG *Vol. 76, pp. 384–5; H*

Part Fourteen

1942-8

Gandhi in Bihar, 1947

The Ending of an Epoch

I fancy I know the art of living and dying non-violently.
But I have yet to demonstrate it by one perfect act.

The first communication of the 'essential' nature to emanate from Gandhi's incarceration was to Governor Lumley, dated 10 August 1942, and spoke of his determination to 'no longer accept special privileges' which hitherto he had accepted 'though reluctantly'.

When Kasturba was brought to the place of detention, it was a relief of sorts to both. But on 15 August, a shock of monumental proportions was dealt to Gandhi. Mahadev Desai, of whose health Gandhi had been worrying for long, collapsed and died within minutes. And, not long thereafter, Kasturba's health began to wane. By December 1943, Gandhi was in no doubt that she was 'a dying woman'.

Kasturba fell grievously ill in February 1944 and on 22 February 1944, passed away, a prisoner of the British Raj. But a prisoner who had shaken the prison house to its foundations.

Subhas Chandra Bose issued on 22 February 1944 a statement on Kasturba's death (*Chalo Delhi—Writings and Speeches of Subhas Chandra Bose—1943-5*):

'Shrimati Kasturba Gandhi is dead. She has died in British custody in Poona at the age of 74. With 388,000,000 of my countrymen at home and with my compatriots abroad, I share the deepest bereavement over the death of Kasturba. She died under tragic circumstances, but for a member of an enslaved nation no death could have been more honourable or more glorious. India has suffered a personal loss ...

I pay my humble tribute to the memory of that great lady who was a mother to the Indian people, and I wish to express my deepest sympathy for Gandhiji in his bereavement. I had the privilege of coming into frequent personal contact with Shrimati Kasturba, and I would sum up my tribute to her in a few words. She was the ideal of Indian womanhood, strong, patient, silent, and self-sufficient. Kasturba was a source of inspiration to the millions of India's daughters among whom she moved and whom she met in the struggle for the freedom of her motherland ...'

Gandhi was released on 6 May 1944, after twenty-one months in prison.

Wavell became Viceroy of India in 1945, as the war was nearing its close. Gandhi did not hesitate to communicate with communists who had stayed away from the Quit India movement as it was seen by them as assisting the Axis cause. He wrote to Mohan Kumaramangalam and saying he knew Rajani Palme Dutt 'both by name and fame' wished 'RPD' success in the latter's parliamentary campaign against America in Britain.

Robert Payne writes in *The Life and Death of Mahatma Gandhi* (1969):

Gandhi rebelled against the thought of partition; it was 'an untruth', a denial of God, a vivisection on the living flesh of India, and therefore a sin. India divided against itself would be a denial of his whole lifework, and his task therefore was to wean Jinnah from his dream of Pakistan. Jinnah fell ill, and the meeting was delayed until September 9. It took place in Jinnah's palatial residence on Malabar Hill in Bombay, and from the beginning it was stormy. They spoke politely with one another, pretending that they were discussing realities. They spoke in English, the only language they had in common; the house was guarded by Indian bayonets; the servants tiptoed in and placed a glass of orange juice on the table. They pretended to be talking about formulas, constitutions, methods of forming a government, but in fact they were deliberating about the destruction of an empire, the birth of new empires, new nations. Asked after the first meeting whether he had brought anything from Jinnah, Gandhi answered bitterly: 'Only flowers.'

What was terrible was that these two men, both educated in London, possessed no common language of ideas. They could not communicate, perhaps because Jinnah had no desire to communicate ...

The Jinnah–Gandhi conversation failed. The failure was to lead to the partitioning of India. Though Gandhi thought of another fast, he did not undertake it just then. He moved ill and worn, to his ashram, observing his weekly silence, spinning daily, and meeting visitors both political and non-political. Some even speculated that his political life had come to an end.

The War was, of course, reaching its predestined end, with its complications for India. Indian troops were spread across the theatres of combat in Malaya, Burma, North Africa, and Italy. Subhas Chandra Bose also had stunned India by his dramatic exiting from India and commandeered the Indian National Army which became a force—but on the doomed side.

In a message broadcast on 6 July 1944 Bose addressed the man whose path he had crossed so famously, as 'Father of our Nation':

Mahatmaji,
... I would like to inform you of the feelings of deep anxiety which Indians throughout the world had for several days after your sudden release from custody on grounds of ill-health. After the sad demise of Shrimati Kasturbaji in British custody, it was but natural for your countrymen to be alarmed over the state of your health. It has, however, pleased providence to restore you to comparative health, so that 388 millions of your countrymen may still have the benefit of your guidance and advice. I should next like to say something about the attitude of your countrymen outside India towards yourself ... Ever since you sponsored the Independence Resolution at the Lahore Congress in December 1929, all members of the Indian National Congress have had one common goal before them. For Indians outside India, you are the creator of the present awakening in our country ... For the world-public, we Indian nationalists are all one—having but one goal, one desire, and one endeavour in life. In all the countries free from British influence that I have visited since I left India in 1941, you are held in the highest esteem, as no other Indian political leader has been, during the last century. Each nation has its own internal politics and its own attitude towards political problems. But that cannot affect a nation's appreciation of a man who served his people so well and has bravely fought a first-class modern power all his life. In fact, your worth and your achievements are appreciated a thousand times more in those countries that are opposed to the British Empire than in those countries that pretend to be the friends of freedom and democracy. The high esteem in which you are held by patriotic Indians outside India

and by foreign friends of India's Freedom, was increased a hundred-fold when you bravely sponsored the 'Quit India' Resolution in August 1942 ...

Father of our nation: In this holy war for India's liberation, we ask for your blessings and good wishes.

Jai Hind.

In regular correspondence with Wavell on Congress's power-sharing with the Muslim League, Gandhi began touring India intensively.

Arriving in Calcutta on 1 December 1945 from Sevagram by Bombay Mail and detraining at Maurigram level crossing, Howrah, he motored immediately to Sodepur Khadi Pratisthan by car. Bengal Nagpur Railway had made special arrangements to stop the Bombay Mail at Maurigram for Gandhi since Bombay Mail was not scheduled to stop there. He was warmly greeted by large crowds throughout the journey. At Raipur, a lady came to Gandhi's compartment and presented him her gold bangles for the Kasturba Memorial Fund. She said these bangles were presented to her by her father-in-law at the time of her marriage and that she wore them for the last twenty-five years ...

Explaining the object of his visit to Bengal and Assam while addressing the congregation after prayer at Sodepur Ashram in the evening, Gandhi said that it was to offer consolation to the victims of the famine and to do whatever he could to relieve their distress.

He engaged Governor Richard G. Casey[1] in discussions at Calcutta's Government House. *The Statesman* in an editorial on the visit and meeting said:

With Mr Gandhi's arrival in Bengal, the stage begins to be set for momentous events. The Congress Parliamentary Board and Working Committee will meet this week in Calcutta. Within a few days, H.E. the Viceroy is expected to arrive. Opportunity is provided by these overlapping visits and we trust it will be taken. Recent events in Calcutta cannot properly be regarded in isolation. There are wider aspects which are unlikely to be comprehended even by a public inquiry, but raise issues of importance to all India ...

The discussions with Governor Casey continued on 2 December, the meeting lasting ninety minutes.

Discussions with Governor Casey resumed on 4 December, the meeting lasting seventy-five minutes. This was Gandhi's day of silence and it was not broken at the meeting. *The Statesman* reported:

Vital Bengal issues discussed. Mr Gandhi had a third meeting with H.E. Mr R.G. Casey, Governor of Bengal at Government House ... Now that the Gandhi–Casey conversations have continued for three days, there is no doubt that the talks deal with very vital issues for Bengal and India ...

R.G. Casey was to record in his book *Personal Experience: 1939–46* (published by Constable & Company Ltd in 1962):

'On April 9th 1945, I had a message from Mahatma Gandhi that he would like to visit Bengal later in the year, if it would be agreeable to me. In the months that followed, I exchanged a number of letters with him, in the course of which he said that he wanted to come 'to help and not to hinder'. In due course I said we would be glad to see him in Bengal and would be glad to offer him transport by road, river, and train.

He arrived in Bengal on December 1st and I had my first discussion for $2^{1}/_{2}$ hours with him that day.

In December and January, I was to see him many times. We had thirteen hours' discussion in the course of the seven times he came to see me—as well as a voluminous correspondence in between meetings. We discussed many matters of consequence—political prisoners in Bengal, the differences between Congress and the Muslim League, civil disturbances in Calcutta, the possibility of widespread violence, the food situation in Bengal, terrorist activities in Bengal carried out 'in the name of the Congress', the release of the terrorists, home spinning and weaving, sales tax on salt and home-woven cloth, the 'iniquities' of the I.C.S., and much else.

Gandhi was the most interesting individual I met in India. Although he was then about seventy-six years old, he showed no outward signs of age. His personality was lively and he had great charm. He was innately courteous, tactful, and a good listener. He had a good sense of fun, and I think probably also a good sense of humour. His physical gestures were simple and dramatic. A discussion with him was enlivened by a good deal of relevant and entertaining reminiscence. I believe he had the useful attribute of political sense in high degree. He knew when to use his undoubted influence with the people, and when not to. He had a keen appreciation of the use of words. He could be clear-cut and specific in public statements when he wanted to, or he could command expressions that meant something different to each group within his following. He could make his point publicly with an opponent, yet leave him without any feeling of bitterness, when he liked. He knew the things that would advance his cause and those that would not. He seldom, if ever, spoke ill of any man. I discussed several men with him who had used him harshly, but he managed to find some good to say of them and no ill.

In my many talks and correspondence with Gandhi, there was one subject which clearly dominated his mind—the encouragement of cottage industries to absorb the great deal of idle time of the tens of millions of the Indian peasantry. He was impatient of any proposals for irrigation schemes to enable them to grow more crops, or of industrialization to absorb redundant labour. Home cotton-growing, home spinning and weaving, and the like (encourage the cultivator to grow his own clothes) filled his mind and he talked and wrote to me at great length about it. He said it was no use my talking 'economics' to him. On most other subjects he was susceptible to what I believed were logical arguments, but not on this.

Another subject on which he was not open to argument was the very small excise duty that we imposed on salt, on which he said there should be no tax at all. He was deaf to the argument about the need for public revenues and that the burden of the salt tax was so small on each individual as to be negligible. He just kept on saying that the whole thing was wrong and should be abolished and that's all there was to it.

When Gandhi came to see me on December 3rd it was one of his self-imposed days of silence. I talked and he wrote what he wanted to say on a pad of paper. It slowed up but did not inhibit discussion ...

One incident emphasized Gandhi's standing with his fellow-countrymen. We had had a great deal of trouble a little time before with some bad men in one of the districts of Bengal (Midnapore) who were terrorizing other Indians of consequence in the district and were extorting money from them 'in the name of the Congress', failing which they were assaulted and victimized and sometimes killed. The police in Bengal were unable to discover the malefactors and the terror went on. We had caused the story to be canalized to Gandhi and asked him, when he had convinced himself through his own channels of the facts, if he would exert his influence in an effort to have it stopped, which he said he would do. Within a short time, he had sent messages through his own channels into the district concerned that those concerned were to give themselves up 'even if it meant hanging'. This happened. The terror ceased and a number of the malefactors gave themselves up to the police.

When I thanked Gandhi in sincere terms for what he had done, he said that it was not necessary to do so, as he would have been grievously wrong not to have done what he did in the circumstances. He said that a man was not only responsible for what he did, but for what he did *not* do, and if he had not exerted his influence in the matter, he would personally have been doing a great wrong himself.

There was another example of the affection and respect in which Gandhi was held by the ordinary people of India. When we had finished our first long talk together in my office, I escorted him to his car. We walked together through the long corridors of Government House, which were lined on each side by a hundred or more of Government House servants, Hindus, Muslims, and others—each of whom made his customary salute. The gathering was informal and unorganized, but was to me very impressive.

While the release of political prisoners was at the heart of the Gandhi-Casey talks, so were—potatoes!

Gandhi wrote to Governor Casey (*CWMG*, Vol. 82, p. 181):

Khadi Pratisthan
Sodepur

Immediate

8 December 1945

Dear Friend,

I write this with the greatest hesitation. The more I see and hear, the greater is the grief over the happenings in Bengal. Here is a sample demanding immediate attention.

Satish Babu brings me the story that potato-growers cannot get seed potatoes and the planting season will be over in a week's time. Seed potatoes are there in the market under Government control. But the grower cannot get them.

There is evidently something radically wrong if the news brought by Satish Babu is true. I wonder if you can do anything. You were telling me about the clever Mr Dey whose services you have enlisted for such matters. Can you make him over to me or some other officer who can attend to this immediate affair?

I am having this letter delivered at once. The question is small enough on the large Bengal canvas but is all in all to the poor growers whose livelihood is at stake.

Yours sincerely,
M.K. Gandhi
Gandhiji's Correspondence with the Government, 1944–7

On 18 December Gandhi left for Santiniketan where he was received by the Poet's son, Rathindranath Tagore. Speaking at a prayer meeting there, he said:

Gurudev (Rabindranath Tagore) was like a great bird, wide and swift of wings, under which he gave protection to many.

During the last few years, India has passed through a great ordeal and none has suffered so greatly as this province of Bengal. The news of Bengal's agonies[2] reached me when I was in jail—powerless to do anything. I all along prayed to God to send me to serve Bengal and to help the distressed people. My visit this time, therefore, was undertaken with a view to serve and to work for Bengal. That is why I am very sorry that I shall not be able to prolong my stay. I shall take my sustenance of peace and inspiration from this place and then go away. I hope you will understand and forgive me.

Visva-Bharati was going through something like an identity crisis. Gandhi said at a discussion with Heads of Department, Santiniketan:[3]

Regard me as a blank slate. So far I have had only hearsay and hearsay has very little place in my life. Solid facts are what I want. Without a full knowledge of facts I shall be able to do little to help you.

It is not that you have nothing to say. That would mean that the institution is perfect. But nothing in this world is perfect. Speak to me freely about the shortcomings. Good things speak for themselves, not the bad things, at any rate, not to me. I have followed every word of what you have said with the keenest interest and I have learned a lot from it. I do not propose to make detailed observations on what has been said or to give expression to all that is welling up in me just now but shall confine myself to one or two remarks of a general character. As I listened while Nanda Babu and Kshitmohan Babu were speaking, I said to myself: 'Here is a real difficulty; but it is a difficulty of our own making.' If a person conducts a big department he is expected to transmit what he stands for to someone who can be termed as his successor. Yet it is the dominant cry of the two stalwarts that they are unable to find a suitable successor for their respective departments. True, these are departments of a special character. I know these departments and I know too Gurudev's views about them.

It is my conviction, which I arrived at after a long and laborious struggle, that Gurudev as a person was much superior to his works or even this institution where he soared and sang. He poured his whole soul into it and nurtured it with his life's blood and yet I dare say that his greatness was not fully expressed by it or through it. That is perhaps true of all great and good men—they are better and greater than their works. If, then, you are to represent that goodness or greatness for which Gurudev stands but which he could not express fully even through this institution, you can do it only through *tapascharya*.

Yours[4] is a common difficulty. You cannot ride two horses at the same time. If you mix day-scholars with full-time students, the former will overshadow and spoil the training of the latter. Your institution was not designed for the mixture.

Gandhi visited Alipore Presidency Jail on 15 January 1946 and met, among others, two women prisoners Lila Roy[5] and Ujjwala Mazumdar.[6]

On 18 January he met Governor Casey for the final time at a meeting that lasted 135 minutes. Lady Maie Casey in her memoirs *Tides & Eddies*, published in London by Michael Joseph in 1966, records:

Out of Dick's office, which he described as being about the size of a tennis-court, a concealed spiral staircase of iron lace led upstairs to my sitting-room. I came down it to meet Mr Gandhi after his first visit, when his business with Dick was over.

It was winter then so he was wrapped up in a fine white Kashmir shawl. His lean golden-brown legs showed beneath it and on his feet he wore a pair of sandals of unusual pattern. He afterwards had a similar pair made for me; they were of cowhide, but from a cow that had died a natural death, for cows are semi-sacred in India and are protected.

I could not keep away once I had met Gandhi and hurried down the little staircase to greet him before he left, on every occasion except on his day of silence when any exchange of thought was conducted by him on slips of paper.

I found his strong gentle personality irresistible. His gestures and speech were clear and dramatic though he was able if he wished to wrap himself in a cocoon of words impossible to penetrate. He spoke of interesting matters and asked interesting questions. He had no particular sympathy with the scientific age, still less with the industrial age. Life was better and happier, he believed, if it was simple; he could not see why the western pattern of living should be imposed upon the east. I was reminded that, of the nearly three thousand million human beings in the world, not more than a third of them were aware of the industrial age and of western civilization. This age and civilization touched only a crust of persons and gave them toys rather than happiness.

I was not the Governor. I was only his wife, therefore my conversations with Gandhi flowed in unrestricted freedom. His eyes behind thick lenses were shrewd and kind and comforting. I had the feeling that if I were in trouble I would like to go to him for advice, which though it might not be for me entirely functional would be wise and human.

Mahatma Gandhi had an extraordinary power over Indian people. Persons of his own Hindu religion revered and obeyed him even if it meant exposing themselves to death, but respect for him was universal. When he came and went through the portals of Government House all our staff, clerks, domestics, gardeners, of whatever religion or caste—all living creatures—crowded the entrance hall on his arrival and departure, greeting him reverently after their own fashion. This happened to no one else who visited us. I went with Dick to see him out on his last visit and noticed that even the independent Misr[7], who differentiated between persons, had appeared from somewhere to watch him go.

A great man came and went and the aura of peace and patience that surrounded him remained with us for a while after he had gone.

To quote Payne again:

'On August 15 (1946) an English journalist who met Jinnah in Bombay found him seething with rage. In an immaculate white suit, his eyeglass swinging on a black ribbon, he attacked the Hindus for all the crimes they had committed and would continue to commit. He found no extenuating circumstance anywhere. They were treacherous, weak-willed, dirty, slovenly, incapable of governing themselves and still less of governing others. The bewildered journalist asked why he was so vehemently opposed to the Hindus. Surely there were some good ones among them? 'There are none!' Jinnah replied. When he was asked whether there was any message he cared to give to the West, he answered: 'There is only one message to give to the West—that is, that they pay the least possible attention to Indian affairs, and let us settle the issues ourselves. He had spoken menacingly of "Direct Action" for many weeks. On the following day "Direct Action" began in Calcutta. On that day, and for three more days, the streets of Calcutta ran with blood.'

The Muslim League's declaration of 16 August 1946 as 'Direct Action Day' elicited from Gandhi the simple statement 'We are not in the midst of Civil War. But we are nearing it.' And he asked for Wavell to be replaced.

With the change of Government in London, events moved quickly in India and an interim government was formed in Delhi. But Gandhi was drawn irresistibly towards Noakhali in Bengal where riots of a ferocious magnitude had broken out, Hindus being butchered on a mass scale. Bihar responded in kind, with Muslims being killed with a barbarism that surpassed Noakhali.

This Part goes on to describe the Noakhali tour in Gandhi's words as taken down mainly by his devoted secretary Pyarelal and by the anthropologist Nirmal Kumar Bose, who acted as Gandhi's interpreter in Noakhali. This was a period of introspection, of inner turmoil. There were bouts of illness, anger, remorse. But then there was also humour, resignation. He was regularly contacted by the Congress leadership and local leaders like Premier Suhrawardy and Fazlul Huq, not always in pleasant tones.

On the third anniversary of the death of Kasturba, Gandhi was in Birampur. He observed the day by fasting. At 7.35 p.m. the party assembled for a recitation of the Gita. In front of the prayer spot was placed a portrait of Kasturba, decorated with flowers and garlands. Gandhi sat through the reading of the first six chapters, in deep meditation. He then lay down to rest. The rigorous penance he had been putting himself through seemed to have heightened psychic sensitivity and he had the experience of a mystic reunion with Kasturba for the first time. Describing it in one of his letters, he wrote: 'During the Gita recitation, the whole scene of Ba's last moments three years ago came back and stood before my mind's eyes in all its vividness. I felt as if her head was actually resting on my lap.' [Quoted by Pyarelal in *Mahatma Gandhi, The Last Phase* Vol. I] Birampur was a fishermen's village. The river Meghna, which at one time used to skirt it had since shifted its course to a place six miles away. But the fishermen families had remained.

On 20 February at Birampur—Bishkatholi, the Muslim opposition had reached its culmination—a small village with a Hindu population of 306 souls in the midst of a Muslim population of 4,694. The greater part of those who had left during the disturbances have still not returned to their homes. The owner of the house, where Gandhi stayed, had temporarily returned because of the visit. The house had a fine library containing a number of handwritten books on religion—a symbol of the old cultural tradition of the district. During the disturbances the library had been burnt. Along the route a number of handwritten posters were found stuck on the trees. Some of them read:

Remember Bihar
And leave Tipperah immediately.
We have warned you many times
Still you are here.
Go back; otherwise it would be the worse for you.

* * *

Go where you are wanted.
Give up your hypocrisy and
Accept Pakistan.

* * *

Muslim League Zindabad.
Quaid-i-Azam Zindabad
Let there be Pakistan
Down with the Congress.

On 21 February at Bishkatholi—Kamalapur—news comes of fresh violence in Bihar.

It was while Gandhi was in Noakhali that Prime Minister Attlee's announcement came of 'HMG's definite intention to ... effect the transfer of power to responsible hands by a date not later than June 1948.'

And it was again while in Noakhali that something other than political freedom seemed suddenly to obsess Gandhi: his brahmacharya. A well-publicized 'experiment' in his self-control became the subject of much 'essential' thinking and writing in Noakhali.

Soon after Gandhi's arrival at Haimchar, on the 25 February 1947, Thakkar Bapa asked:

'Why this experiment here?'

Gandhi: 'You are mistaken, Bapa; it is not an experiment but an integral part of my *yajna*. One may forgo an experiment, one cannot forgo one's duty. Now if I regard a thing as a part of my yajna—a sacred duty—I may not give it up even if public opinion is wholly against me. I am engaged in achieving self-purification.'

Rajmohan Gandhi writes in *Mohandas*:

Observing him from close quarters, (Nirmal Kumar) Bose concluded that it was Gandhi's 'questioning attitude towards his own perfection' that brought him close to ordinary men and women. It was a factor, Bose thought, in Gandhi's 'tenderness' which 'soothed' men and women and 'lifted them above their sorrows'.

As the visit to Noakhali seemed to douse communal flames in that part of the country, Gandhi's presence in Bihar was urgently entreated. So to Bihar he went to becalm where he could not heal. And thence, for a brief spell, to Delhi where the Attlee announcement was being fast-tracked by the new Viceroy Lord Louis Mountbatten and where Jawaharlal Nehru had organized an Inter-Asian Relations Conference. He was soon, back in Bihar.

The Gandhi–Mountbatten parleys led to the Viceroy's taking a measure of the Mahatma's moral stature which he found to be higher than he expected. But it also enabled him to see that the Mahatma's political influence was now weak. Partition was now not just a prospect but a plan with the Congress which was getting into it.

Gandhi left for Bihar, this time for a brief visit, as Nehru wanted him back in Delhi. He met Jinnah in Delhi on 6 May 1947, despite contrary advice from Patel and others, saying he would go to Jinnah 'seventy times seven' if necessary. The details of that meeting are not recorded. Both leaders agreed that 'what we talk should remain between us'.

On 12 April, just before he left for Bihar, Gandhi signed with Jinnah not the 'solution' he had envisaged but a joint appeal for peace proposed by Mountbattan:

We deeply deplore the recent acts of lawlessness and violence that have brought the utmost disgrace on the fair name of India ... We denounce for all time the use of force to achieve political ends, and we call upon all the communities of India, to whatever persuasion they may belong, not only to refrain from all acts of violence and disorder, but also to avoid both in speech and writing any words which might be construed as an incitement to such act.

In a statement issued by Jinnah with Gandhi's concurrence, the League leader said their discussions had covered

... the question of division of India into Pakistan and Hindustan and Mr Gandhi does not accept the principle of division. He thinks division is not inevitable, whereas, in my opinion, not only is Pakistan inevitable but this is the only practical solution of India's political problem.

In his prayer-meeting talk the next day, Gandhi said:

I claim to have (Jinnah's) friendship. After all he also belongs to India. Whatever happens, I have to spend my life with him.

On 20 April Jawaharlal publicly conceded Pakistan: 'The Muslim League can have Pakistan, if they wish to have it, but on the condition that they do not take away other parts of India that do not wish to join Pakistan.' Nine days later, Prasad, who chaired the Constituent

Assembly, spoke to it of the likelihood of 'not only a division of India but a division of some provinces'.

Unwilling as yet to declare it in public, Patel conveyed his acceptance of Pakistan to Mountbatten. 'I for one cannot agree to Pakistan on any account', said Gandhi on 7 May, but it was also clear that his dissent would take the form of dissociation, not defiance. 'When I say that I cannot bear it,' explained Gandhi, 'I mean that I do not wish to be a party to it.'

Invited to sessions of the Working Committee held on 31 May and 1 and 2 June to consider the plan (its elements were known to the Congress negotiators), Gandhi told the Committee that he 'disagreed' with it 'but would not stand in the way'.

This Part also deals with Gandhi's little-studied visit to Kashmir and then his journey to Calcutta where he was on 15 August 1947, the day India became free. He was also there when riots broke out in the city obliging him to commence a fast which was to be termed the 'Miracle of Calcutta', for it led to the riot's abatement.

Gandhi arrived in Calcutta on 9 August from Patna accompanied by Horace Alexander[8], Manu Gandhi, and Abha Gandhi[9], was met by Dr Prafulla Chandra Ghosh[10], the first Chief Minister designate of West Bengal, and Professor Nirmal Kumar Bose. Initially he stayed at Satis Chandra Das Gupta's Khadi Pratisthan, Sodepur. His intention was to go to Noakhali to resume work for Hindu–Muslim amity there but events in Calcutta were worrisome. Dr P.C. Ghosh had an exclusive interview for an hour.

At 3.30 p.m. Gandhi met Governor Frederick Burrows, who requested him to stay over in Calcutta and help quell its riot-like situation. Dr Prafulla Chandra Ghosh accompanied Gandhi to Government House and was present at the meeting with the Governor.

On his return from Government House, Gandhi had an interview with Syed Mohammed Usman[11], former Mayor of Calcutta, who also requested Gandhi to postpone his departure for Noakhali and 'save Calcutta'.

At his prayer meeting that evening Gandhi said, 'This is the time of our real test. We must show our strength to the whole world. If India is to be enslaved again, I do not wish to live to see it, as my soul will weep at the sight. But I pray to God that such a time does not come.' An officer of the Information Department met him and asked for a message to the nation for 15 August; Gandhi declined to give one. He was importuned, it will be bad (*kharab*) if he does not give any message. *Hai nahin koi message; hone do kharab,* ('There is no message; if that is bad, let it be bad') was his terse reply. BBC sought a message for 15 August again, in vain.

On 10 August Gandhi was up for prayers at 3.30 a.m. and wrote for *Harijan.* M. Baron, Governor of French Territories in India visited Gandhi that day. Soon, reports came of riots in the city, initiated this time by Hindus. Again Usman Saheb urged him to postpone going to Noakhali and save Calcutta instead. A large Muslim deputation accompanied him. They entreated Gandhiji to stay on in Calcutta even if it were only for two more days: 'We Muslims have as much claim upon you as the Hindus. For you yourself have said you are as much of Muslims as of Hindus.'

Gandhi replied: 'I am willing, but then you have to guarantee the peace of Noakhali. If I do not go to Noakhali before the 15th on the strength of your guarantee and things go wrong there, my life will become forfeit; you will have to face a fast unto death on my part[12]'.

Gandhi toured the riot-affected areas from 2.30 p.m. to 5.15 p.m. with Chief Minister-designate Prafulla Chandra Ghosh and Usman Saheb. Suhrawardy, outgoing Premier came at 9 p.m. and stayed till 11 p.m. urging Gandhi to remain in Calcutta indefinitely. Gandhi said he will do so if Suhrawardy also agreed to live and work with him for the same cause.

On 12 August Suhrawardy sent a message agreeing to Gandhi's precondition. Manu Gandhi has recorded in *The Miracle of Calcutta* (Navajivan Publishing House):

In the afternoon, Usman, the ex-Mayor of Calcutta, brought Suhrawardy's message which was that he and Bapuji should stay together in the same bungalow in the area where Muslims dared not enter. Both should go there with open minds. Neither should have secret interviews. Both should issue joint statements. Both should stay and eat together. Suhrawardy took upon himself to take care of Noakhali. Bapu launched on a frightening venture, for the locality in which he was asked to stay was thought to be very dangerous. Not a single Muslim had been spared there. One has to rely on God for the future.

Gandhi attended a prayer meeting in Sodepur. *Harijan* reported on 24 August 1947:

Gandhiji said that the 15th instant was to be a landmark in India's history. It was a day when India would be declared free of the foreign yoke. It was to be an independent nation. He had explained how the day was to be observed, but he was probably alone in the view. Already there was an announcement that the Muslims of Calcutta were to observe it as a day of mourning. He hoped that it was not true. No man could be compelled to observe the day in a particular manner. It was to be a perfectly voluntary act. He would ask his Muslim countrymen not to mourn over the freedom. The present distemper was to go. What were the Hindus in Pakistan to do? They should salute the Pakistan Flag if it meant the freedom and equality of all in every respect, irrespective of caste, colour, or creed.

Gandhi left Sodepur on 13 August at 2.30 p.m. by car and reached Hydari Manzil[13], selected for his stay in Beliaghata, a predominantly Muslim area. Manu Gandhi records:

It was a very shabby house without any sort of facility. It was open on all sides, thus being easy of access to outsiders. The doors and windows were broken. There was only one latrine which was used by hundreds of people, including a number of volunteers, policemen, and visitors. Every inch of the place was covered with dust. In addition, rain had made the passages muddy. Bleaching powder having been profusely sprinkled, the acrid smell caused great discomfort. There was only one usable room where everybody and everything had to be accommodated, including Bapu himself, his luggage, and guests.

Hindu demonstrators raised black flags and asked him why he is not going to Hindu quarters to save them. Many demonstrators heckled him and Suhrawardy to their faces. Gandhi told Nirmal Kumar Bose such boldness was to be admired.

Manu has written:

The youths were excited. They said to Bapu, 'Why have you come here? The slight suffering on the part of the Muslims has caused you to hasten to their succour. Where were you when we suffered?' But they did not prevent Bapu from entering the house. Shaheed Saheb, who came later on, was stopped at the door. It was feared that he might be killed. Bapu sent Nirmalbabu and others to bring a few representatives of the rioting mobs to meet him. When they came inside, the rest of the mob remained calm. Suhrawardy was then allowed to enter the house.

On 14 August N. C. Chatterjee of the Hindu Mahasabha, Acharya Kripalani, Renuka Ray, Surendra Mohan Ghose[14], Tushar Kanti Ghosh[15], called; Acharya Kripalani, Aruna Asaf Ali[16], Dr Suresh Chandra Banerjee, and Hemchandra Naskar[17] then called on Gandhi separately. Scenes of camaraderie were witnessed in parts of Calcutta, with Hindus and Muslims embracing each other. Gandhi was driven by Suhrawardy in a closed car, sitting between two or three passengers for privacy to observe the emotional scenes.

He visited the Marwari Club[18] and said to them: 'Tomorrow we will be free from bondage to the British, but from midnight tonight Hindustan will be broken into two pieces. So tomorrow will be both a day of happiness and of sorrow.'

Manu Gandhi has recorded:

On the return journey Bapu was perturbed. He protested, 'I spend only half an hour walking, and I have wasted an hour in a car to reach the place and return. How can I afford to waste time like this? It is bad business. It is past ten now. When will the girls eat?' Suhrawardy replied, 'It is not very late; it is just ten o'clock.' Bapu: 'It may be early for you, but for me it is like midnight.'

We returned home at 10.45 p.m. and Bapu retired at 11. He was worried because we remained hungry till so late. People disturbed us throughout the night. They kept coming in great numbers as the following day was the 15th of August. The whole city was being decorated with flags and the noise of the bustle reached our ears from all sides.

Gandhi announced at the prayer meting that he would undertake a twenty-four-hour fast holding prayer and spinning on 15 August.

A delegation of large number of ladies from Chittagong met Gandhi in the evening. The group included the revolutionary Bina Das, Kamala Dasgupta[19], and Ashoka Gupta.

On 15 August itself Gandhi observed Mahadev Desai Day. He then held talks with Communist Party leaders Bhupesh Gupta and Jyoti Basu. In a reminiscence in early 2007 Jyoti Basu has written: 'It was in Beliaghata that Comrade Bhupesh Gupta, our Party leader (later MP) and myself went to meet Gandhiji. He was sitting on the floor with a few people. We introduced ourselves. We said we were Communists and we have come to take your advice. What do we do in these circumstances when everything had gone out of hand. He said very calmly, "In my experience, in such a situation it is not possible to have a mass meeting but if you could bring out a small procession with people of all religions—Hindus, Muslims, Sikhs, and so on, that may be the beginning of the peace process." We thanked him and then we came back and the next day we organized the meeting near Park Circus. I think there were about fifty to sixty people, both Hindus and Muslims but it was dispersed within ten minutes. At one stage we took out a march, it was attacked and dispersed. So nothing actually happened by these activities then. Many people went to see him in Beliaghata.'

Nirmal Kumar Bose records:

At 2, there was an interview with some members of the Communist Party of India to whom Gandhiji said that political workers, whether Communist or Socialist, must forget today all differences and help to consolidate the freedom which had been attained. Should we allow it to break into pieces? The tragedy was that the strength with which the country had fought against the British was failing them when it came to the establishment of Hindu–Muslim unity. With regard to the celebrations, Gandhiji said:

I can't afford to take part in this rejoicing, which is a sorry affair. [*My Days with Gandhi* by N.K. Bose]

On 16 August the new Governor, C. Rajagopalachari paid a visit and congratulated him on the miracle he had wrought.

Rev. John Kellas[20] of the Scottish Church College came to meet him and asked, 'What is the relation between a nation and religion?' Gandhi replied, 'A nation does not belong to any particular religion or sect. It should be absolutely independent of either religion or sect. Every person should be free to follow the religion of his choice.'

Bapu went to bed at 10.30 p.m.

On 17 August, Manu tells us:

The morning programme was gone through as usual, after which Bapu spent his time in meeting workers, advising people, and writing articles for *Harijan*, this being the last day for dispatching the material.

Shaheed Suhrawardy was the first to speak at the prayer meeting[21] which was held today at Narkeldanga. It was a vast assemblage of people. Shaheed Saheb said: 'During the riots Hindus and Musulmans could not pass through each other's localities even in motor vehicles. But, today, even a small child can walk without fear wherever it likes. Remember that we owe all this to Gandhi.'

Referring to his place of residence Bapuji said,

'People now seem to think that they are not bound to obey any one's orders. People who visit my place of residence indulge in shouting and abusing the police. The latter fold their hands in return. The police are no doubt our servants, but they receive orders only from the Government, not from private individuals. If each one of us start to order the police they will be crushed. If we continue to behave in this unruly manner, we shall surely lose our freedom. You are free to complain if the police try to rule instead of serving. But it is their duty to arrest all those who commit crimes. I have, therefore, requested the Government to withdraw the police force. It is really painful that they should have to listen to your abuse for our sake. Now it is in your hands to kill us or save us. I do not deny your love for me. But I am afraid it may prove to be merely an effervescence similar to that of a soda water bottle. All things are good within their proper limits.'

The prayer grounds were covered with mud. Shaheed Suhrawardy was carried to the car, but Bapu walked. His legs were covered with the mud by the time he reached the car. We got back from the prayer meeting at 9 p.m. Bapu went to bed at 10 p.m. after an hour's discussion with Shaheed Suhrawardy.

On 18 August occurred the festival of Eid. Congress workers from Khulna, now in East Pakistan, called on Gandhi. They had hoisted the tricolour on 15 August thinking Khulna will go to India but the Boundary Commission awarded it to East Pakistan. What is to be done to the hoisted tricolour, they asked. It was Gandhi's day of silence and so he wrote: 'There can be no two opinions, the Union Flag must go, Pakistan's must be hoisted without demur and with joy if possible. Award is award, good or bad.'

On 31 August, Manu records:

Prayer and other routine matters were observed from 3.30 a.m. onwards. Bapu carried on his daily work in spite of his cold. He has decided to go to Noakhali. He discussed the matter with Shri Charubabu Choudhari and Pyarelalji who had come to meet him.

There were visitors continuously from 10 a.m. to 3 p.m. He went to the Grand Hotel at 3.30 p.m.

Muslims present a felicitatory message. But then things suddenly took a turn for the worse. Manu records:

A wounded man came here tonight. He had fallen down from a tram and had been injured. But people beat him and forced him to state that he had been assaulted by Musulmans. Some boys brought him here in procession at 10 p.m. Bapuji was sleeping. I woke up due to the noise and went outside. Abhaben was already there at the door trying to pacify the crowd. I joined her in pacifying them and said, 'Your noisy demonstration is painful both to the wounded man and Bapuji. Besides, we cannot hear what you have to say. You may, therefore, select two representatives from amongst you to explain matters to Abhaben, who being a Bengali will understand you fully. And then we shall communicate your message to Gandhi.' But it was impossible to check the boys.

It was 10 o'clock at night. There were only three of us in the whole building—Bapuji, Abhaben, and myself. Shaheed Suhrawardy had gone out. Pyarelalji, Nirmalbabu, and Charubabu—who had come to request Bapu to go to Noakhali—had also gone out. We were busy preparing for our trip to Noakhali, the following morning. But what was proposed by man was to be disposed by God.

The boys soon increased in numbers. They started breaking things. Stones were hurled at lamps and window panes, shattering them to pieces, there were two Musulmans in the house who were our hosts. The boys wanted to catch and kill them. They were running helter-skelter.

Bapuji had a very bad cold, and he was also observing silence. He got up and came out. Abhaben and I were surrounded by the crowd. But a few among them, kindly disposed, suggested that we go inside the house. They were trying to save us from the anger of the crowd. Bapuji in the meantime arrived at the door and we immediately went to him. Bisenbhai[22] was with us. The crowd mistook him for a Musulman and tried to assault him. The boys in the meantime saw Bapuji; this added to their excitement. They began to shout even more loudly than before. Bapuji broke his silence and shouted thrice: 'What is all this? Kill me, kill me I say; why don't you kill me?' With these words he tried to rush amidst the crowd. We stood in his way to stop him going. In the meantime one of the Musulmans staying in the house ran and stood behind Bapu. Seeing him one or two boys threw brick-bats at him. Fortunately, they did not hit anyone; otherwise the hands of Hindu boys might have shed Bapu's blood. When I consider how Bapu ultimately met his death at the hands of a Hindu, I feel that this incident was an indication.

Bapu said with a voice full of extreme grief, 'My God is asking me "where are you?" I am extremely grieved. Is this the peace you have preserved from the 15th of August?'

A fast followed, restoring peace.

Gandhi left Calcutta on 7 September 1947. The 146 days that were left to Gandhi on this earth were spent in Delhi. This Part contains his 'essential' words of that period which, too, saw him undertake another miraculously healing fast—his last—in Delhi.

Pyarelal wrote a letter to Rajagopalachari on 29 January. It said 'Bapu is OK in every respect.'

The next day was to be different. It was to be Gandhi's last.

To Sir Roger Lumley, Governor Of Bombay

The Aga Khan's Palace, Poona
10 August 1942

AFTER THE train that carried me and other fellow prisoners reached Chinchwad on Sunday, some of us were ordered to alight. Shrimati Sarojini Devi, Shrimati Mirabai, Shri Mahadev Desai, and I were directed to get into a car. There were two lorries lined up alongside the car. I have no doubt that the reservation of the car for us was done out of delicate considerations. I must own too that the officers incharge performed their task with tact and courtesy.

Nevertheless I felt deeply humiliated when the other fellow-prisoners were ordered to occupy the two lorries. I realize that all could not be carried in motor-cars. I have been before now carried in prison vans. And this time too we should have been carried in prison vans. And this time too we should have been carried with our comrades. In relating this incident my object is to inform the Government that in the altered conditions and the altered state of my mind, I can no longer accept special privileges which hitherto I have accepted though reluctantly. ...

I am,
Yours sincerely,
M.K. Gandhi
CWMG *Vol. 76, p. 404; E*

To Lord Linlithgow

The Aga Khan's Palace, Poona
14 August 1942

... THE GOVERNMENT of India should have waited at least till the time I inaugurated mass action. I had publicly stated that I fully contemplated sending you a letter before taking concrete action. It was to be an appeal to you for an impartial examination of the Congress case. ... They should surely have waited for an authentic report of my speeches on Friday and on Saturday night after the passing of the resolution by the All-India Congress Committee. You would have found in them that I would not hastily begin action ...

Anyway the summary rejection of the demand has plunged the nation and the Government into confusion. The Congress was making every effort to identify India with the Allied cause.

The Government resolution says:

The Governor-General-in-Council has been aware too for some days past of dangerous preparations by the Congress Party for unlawful and in some cases violent activities, directed among other things to interruption of communications and public utility services, the organization of strikes, tampering with the loyalty of Government servants, and interference with defence measures including recruitment.

This is a gross distortion of the reality. Violence was never contemplated at any stage. ...

I am,
Yours sincerely,
M.K. Gandhi
CWMG Vol. 76, pp. 406 and 407

To Chimanlal N. Shah[23]

15 August 1942

Chimanlal, Ashram
Sevagram
Wardha

Mahadev died suddenly gave no indication. Slept well last night had breakfast walked with me Sushila. Jail doctors did all they could but God had willed otherwise. Sushila and I bathed body. Body lying peacefully covered with flowers, incense burning. Sushila and I reciting Gita. Mahadev has died Yogi's and Patriot's death. Tell Durga, Babla[24], and Sushila no sorrow allowed. Only joy over such noble death. Cremation taking place front of me. Shall keep ashes[25].

Advise Durga remain ashram but she may go to her people if she must. Hope Babla will be brave and prepare himself fill Mahadev's place worthily. Love.

Bapu

CWMG Vol. 76, pp. 410–11; E

To Secretary, Home Department, Government Of Bombay

Detention Camp
27 August 1942

Dear Sir,

With reference to the Government orders about the writing of letters by the security prisoners, it seems that the Government do not know that for over thirty-five years, I have ceased to live a family life and have been living what has been called Ashram life in association with persons who have more or less shared my views. Of these Mahadev Desai, whom I have just lost, was an associate beyond compare. His wife and only son have lived with me for years sharing the Ashram life. If I cannot write to the widow and her son or the other members of the deceased's family living in the Ashram, I can have no interest in writing to anyone else ...

I hope that even if the Government cannot extend the facilities for correspondence in terms of this letter, they will appreciate my difficulty.

I am,
Yours sincerely,
M.K. Gandhi

CWMG Vol. 76, pp. 412–13; E

To Lord Linlithgow

Detention Camp[26]
New Year's Eve, 1942

Personal

YOU HAVE placed me in a palace where every reasonable creature comfort is ensured. I have freely partaken of the latter purely as a matter of duty, never as a pleasure, in the hope that some day those that have the power will realize that they have wronged innocent men. I had given myself six months. The period is drawing to a close, so is my patience. The law of satyagraha, as I know it, prescribes a remedy in such moments of trial. In a sentence it is: 'Crucify the flesh by fasting.' That same law forbids its use except as a last resort. I do not want to use it if I can avoid it. This is the way to avoid it: convince me of my error or errors, and I shall make ample amends. You can send for me or send someone who knows your mind and can carry conviction. There are many other ways, if you have the will. May I expect an early reply? May the New Year bring peace to us all.[27]

I am,
Your sincere friend,
M.K. Gandhi
CWMG *Vol. 77, pp. 49–51; E*

To Sir Richard Tottenham[28]

Detention Camp, Poona
8 February 1943

... IF THE temporary release is offered for my convenience, I do not need it. I shall be quite content to take my fast as a detenu or prisoner ...

... In order to give the Government enough time, I shall suspend the fast, if necessary, to Wednesday next, 10th instant.[29]

Yours sincerely,
M.K. Gandhi
CWMG *Vol. 77, pp. 61–2*

An Explanation[30]

Detention Camp
26 February 1943

I HAD to choose between death on the one hand and sweet lime-juice on the other. I had promised to live; I must try to live and hence mixed sweet lime-juice with water on Sunday[31] to enable me to drink water and get over nausea.

The Hindu, *27-2-1943*; CWMG *Vol. 77, pp. 68–9; E*

Talk With Mira Behn[32]

Detention Camp
27 February 1943

... No FAST of mine has ever had such a wonderful ending as this one is having. I do not mean what is going on in the outside world, but what is going on inside me. There is a heavenly peace.[33]

('Correct', 7 March 1943.[34])
CWMG *Vol. 77, p. 69; E*

To M.G. Bhandari[35]

Detention Camp
2 March 1943

YOU WERE good enough yesterday, my day of silence, to tell me that the Government had restricted to my two sons the admission of outsiders at the breaking of the fast tomorrow. Whilst I am thankful for the concession, I am unable to avail myself of it. For, as the Government know, I make no distinction between sons born to me and numerous others who are as dear to me even as they are.

Your sincerely,
M.K. Gandhi
CWMG *Vol. 77, p. 70; E*

Talk Before Breaking The 21-Day Fast[36]

Detention Camp
3 March 1943

I DO not know why Providence has saved me on this occasion. Possibly, it is because He has some more mission[37] for me to fulfil.

CWMG *Vol. 77, p. 70; E*

Answers To Questions[38]

After 3 March 1943[39]

Q: How do you then reconcile your faith in non-violence with the allegations made against you and the Congress that all these acts of sabotage and violence that took place after the 8th of August so happened because of some secret instructions issued by you or by the Congress?

MKG: There is absolutely no truth in it. I never issued any secret or overt instructions in favour of sabotage or any other kind of violence. Had Congress issued instructions, I would have known it ...

Q: Do you then disapprove of these acts of sabotage and violence?

MKG: I definitely disapprove of them. I have made it clear to all those friends who have met me during the period of my fast ...

Q: It has been suggested that you started this movement under the notion that the Allies were going to be defeated ... You are not only not pro-German or pro-Japan, but you are anti-Nazi and anti-Fascist. Am I right?

MKG: ... I have called the Nazis and Fascists the scum of the earth. I wrote a letter some time in May 1942 to Mira Behn while she was in Orissa. I cannot give you a copy of that letter since I am in jail. I understand Mira Behn has sent a copy of that letter to the Government. You can ask the Government to supply you with a copy of it and satisfy yourself. I have given in that letter complete instructions as to how to resist the Japanese, if they at all invade India. No one after reading that letter could charge me with any sympathy with Nazism and Fascism or with Japan.

CWMG *Vol. 77, pp. 71–2; E*

To M.A. Jinnah

Detention Camp
4 May 1943

Dear Quaid-e-Azam,

When some time after my incarceration the Government asked me for a list of newspapers I would like to have, I included the *Dawn* in my list. I have been receiving it with more or less regularity. Whenever it comes to me, I read it carefully. I have followed the proceedings of the League as reported in the *Dawn* columns. I noted your invitation[40] to me to write to you. Hence this letter.

I welcome your invitation. I suggest our meeting face to face rather than talking through correspondence. But I am in your hands.

I hope that this letter will be sent to you and, if you agree to my proposal, that the Government will let you visit me.

One thing I had better mention. There seems to be an 'if' about your invitation. Do you say I should write only if I have changed my heart? God alone knows men's hearts. I would like you to take me as I am.

Why should not both you and I approach the great question of communal unity as men determined on finding a common solution, and work together to make our solution acceptable to all who are concerned with it or are interested in it?[41]

Yours sincerely,
M.K. Gandhi

Quaid-e-Azam M.A. Jinnah
Mount Pleasant Road
Bombay

CWMG *Vol. 77, pp. 75–6; E*

To Lord Linlithgow

Personal   Detention Camp
                                    27 September 1943[42]

Dear Lord Linlithgow,

On the eve of your departure from India, I would like to send you a word.

Of all the high functionaries I have had the honour of knowing, none has been the cause of such deep sorrow to me as you have been. It has cut me to the quick to have to think of you as having countenanced untruth, and that regarding one whom, at one time, you considered as your friend. I hope and pray that God will some day put it into your heart to realize that you, a representative of a great nation, had been led into a grievous error.

With good wishes,[43]

I still remain,
Your friend,
M.K. Gandhi
CWMG *Vol. 77, p. 201; E*

Unbecoming

December 1943

IT IS unbecoming of the Government to impose such conditions[44] on a dying woman. Supposing she wants the bed-pan when Dr Dinshaw Mehta is there, who is to give it to her if the nurses are not to be near her? Supposing I want to ask the nature cure doctor how my wife is progressing, am I to do so through someone else? This is a curious situation. I would far rather the Government sent me away to another prison, instead of worrying me with pinpricks at every step. If I am away, my wife would not expect any help from me and I will be spared the agony of being a helpless witness to her suffering.

Sushila Nayar, Kasturba: A Personal Reminiscence, *p. 81*

To Ardeshir E. Kateli

Detention Camp
6 January 1944[45]

Bhai Khan Bahadur,

After the talk I had with my son Devadas today, I have ascertained Kasturba's wishes which are as follows:

... In case Kanu Gandhi[46] cannot stay here during patient's illness, he should be allowd to visit her for about an hour daily so that he can sing her some *bhajan*s and also do some little nursing. As you are aware, the patient is insistent upon having Kanu as a whole-time nurse ...

... Shrimati Prabhavati Jayaprakash Narayan has done a lot of nursing for the patient before. She is like a daughter to us. Her father himself sent her to stay in the Ashram when she was quite young. If she is sent here, she will be of great help.

I am,
Yours,
M.K. Gandhi
CWMG *Vol. 77, pp. 215–16; G*

Letter To Secretary, Home Department, Government Of Bombay

Detention Camp
31 January 1944

Sir,

... The patient is no better. The attendants are about to break down. Four only can work—two at a time on alternate nights. All the four have to work during the day. The patient herself is getting restive, and inquires: 'When will Dr Dinshaw come?' ...

I hope it may not have to be said that the relief came too late.[47]

I am etc.,
M.K. Gandhi
CWMG *Vol. 77, p. 222; E*

To Lord Wavell

17 February 1944[48]

Dear Friend,

Although I have not had the pleasure of meeting you, I address you on purpose as 'dear friend'. I am looked upon by the representatives of the British Government as a great, if not the greatest, enemy of the British. Since I regard myself as a friend and servant of humanity including the British, in token of my goodwill I call you, the foremost representative of the British in India, my 'friend'.

... The speeches recently made on behalf of the Government in the Assembly on the release motion[49], and on the gagging order[50] on Sarojini Devi, I consider to be playing with fire. I distinguish between defeat of Japanese arms and Allied victory. The latter must carry with it the deliverance of India from the foreign yoke. The spirit of India demands complete freedom from all foreign dominance and would, therefore, resist Japanese yoke equally with British or any other ...

... It is no pleasure for me to be in this camp, where all my creature comforts are supplied without any effort on my part, when I know that millions outside are starving for want of food. But I should feel utterly helpless, if I went out and missed the food by which alone living becomes worth while.

I am,
Yours sincerely,
M.K. Gandhi
CWMG *Vol. 77, pp. 232–3; E*

Kasturba's Death

21 February 1944

Why don't you trust God? Why do you wish to drug your mother even on her death bed?

(To Devadas Gandhi who wanted a chance to be given to penicillin)
Sushila Nayar, Kasturba: A Personal Reminiscence, *p. 96*

Request To Government On Kasturba's Funeral[51]

22 February 1944[52]

1. Body should be handed over to my sons and relatives which would mean a public funeral without interference from Government.
2. If that is not possible, funeral should take place as in the case of Mahadev Desai[53]; and if the Government will allow relatives only to be present at the funeral, I shall not be able to accept the privilege unless all friends who are as good as relatives to me are also allowed to be present.
3. If this also is not acceptable to the Government, then those who have been allowed to visit her will be sent away by me and only those who are in the camp (detenus) will attend the funeral.

It has been, as you will be able to bear witness, my great anxiety not to make any political capital out of this most trying illness of my life companion. But I have always wanted whatever the Government did, to be done with good grace which, I am afraid, has been hitherto lacking. It is not too much to expect that now that the patient is no more, whatever the Government decide about the funeral will be done with good grace[54].

CWMG *Vol. 77, p. 236; E*

To Additional Secretary, Home Department Government of India

Detention Camp
4 March 1944

Sir,

It is not without regret and hesitation that I write about my dead wife. But truth demands this letter.

According to the newspapers, Mr Butler[55,56] is reported to have said in the House of Commons on 2nd March 1944:

'... She was receiving all possible medical care and attention, not only from her regular attendants but from those desired by her family ...'

The deceased herself had repeatedly asked the Inspector-General of Prisons for Dr Dinshaw Mehta's help during practically a month previous to that. He was allowed to come only from 5 February 1944. Again, the regular physicians Drs. Nayar and Gilder made a written application for consultation with Dr B.C. Roy of Calcutta on 31st January 1944. The Government simply ignored their written request and subsequent oral reminders.

Mr Butler is further reported to have said:

No request for her release was received and the Government of India believe it would be no act of kindness to her or her family to remove her from the Aga Khan's Palace.

Whilst it is true that no request was made by her or by me (as satyagrahi prisoners it would have been unbecoming), would it not have been in the fitness of things, if the Government had at least offered to her, me, and her sons to release her? The mere offer of release would have produced a favourable psychological effect on her mind. But unfortunately no such offer was ever made.

As to the funeral rites, Mr Butler is reported to have said:

'I have information that the funeral rites took place at the request of Mr Gandhi in the grounds of the Aga Khan's Palace at Poona, and friends and relatives were present'.

The following, however, was my actual request which the Inspector-General of Prisons took down in writing from dictation at 8.07 p.m. on 22 February 1944. ...[57]

Government will perhaps admit that I have scrupulously avoided making any political capital out of my wife's protracted illness and the difficulties I experienced from the Government. Nor do I want to make any now. But in justice to her memory, to me, and for the sake of truth, I ask the Government to make such amends as they can. If the newspaper report is inaccurate in essential particulars or the Government have a different interpretation of the whole episode, I should be supplied with the correct version and the Government interpretation of the whole episode. If my complaint is held to be just, I trust that the amazing statement said to have been made in America by the Agent of the Government of India in U.S.A. will be duly corrected.

I am, etc.,
M.K. Gandhi.
CWMG *Vol. 77, pp. 242–3; E*

'We Were A Couple Outside The Ordinary'

Detention Camp
9 March 1944

Dear Friend[58],

I must thank you for your prompt reply to my letter of 17th February. At the outset, I send you and Lady Wavell my thanks for your kind condolences on the death of my wife. Though for her sake I have welcomed her death as bringing freedom from living agony, I feel the loss more than I had thought I should. We were a couple outside the ordinary. ...

I am,
Yours sincerely,
M.K. Gandhi
CWMG *Vol. 77, p. 244; E*

To Ardeshir E. Kateli

Detention Camp
16 March 1944

You have given me the following memorandum:

Mr Gandhi may reply to messages from his relatives, and Government will, if he so wishes, inform other correspondents that their messages have been delivered to him.

In reply, I beg to say that unless I can write to senders of condolences irrespective of relatives, I would not care to exercise the facility Government have been pleased to give me. ...

Yours etc.,
M.K. Gandhi

Khan Bahadur Kateli
Superintendent, Detention Camp

CWMG Vol. 77, pp. 250–1; E

Release

Poona
5 May 1944

ACCORDING TO *The Transfer of Power*, Vol. IV, in a cable dated 4 May 1944, to the Secretary of State for India, the Viceroy reported: 'Latest reports show progressive deterioration in Gandhi's anaemia, blood-pressure and kidney functions, all of which in opinion of Dr B.C. Roy shared by Surgeon-General Candy, have tendency to produce coronary or cerebral thrombosis. ... This is a case in which I consider we must be guided by medical opinion. Deterioration in Gandhi's health appears such that his further participation in active politics is improbable and I have no doubt that death in custody would intensify feeling against Government. ... I am accordingly instructing Bombay Government to release Gandhi unconditionally at 8 a.m. on Saturday, 6 May, with announcement that release is entirely on medical grounds and am informing all Governors accordingly.

Pyarelal Writes:

Col. Bhandari, the Inspector General of Prisons, Bombay, had turned up suddenly in the evening—a rather unusual time for such a visit—at the

Aga Khan Palace Detention Camp at Poona, where Gandhiji was being kept incommunicado, and told him that he and his party were to be unconditionally released at 8 o'clock the next morning.

MKG: Are you joking?

Bhandari: No. I am serious. I received the order just today. You can continue to stay here for some time for convalescence, if you like. But the guards will be removed at 8 tomorrow morning.

MKG: What happens to my railway fare?

B: You will have it whenever you leave Poona.

MKG: All right. Then I will stay in Poona for two or three days.

B: Now, please, do not come back again. See, my hair has turned grey with worry.

Pyarelal concludes:

Thus ended the spell of twenty-one months of prison life—Gandhiji's last—for giving the British Government the ultimatum on the night of 8 August 1942, to declare India independent and quit, so that India could defend herself against the Japanese invasion and effectively play her part in the defence of democracy.

P, MG: LP *Vol. I, B1, p.* 3

Telegram To Inayatullah Khan Mashriqui[59]

Juhu

On or before 15 May 1944[60]

MY LAST year's request to Quaid-e-Azam Jinnah still stands and I will be ready to discuss the question of Hindu-Muslim understanding as soon as I get better[61].

The Hindu *17-5-1944;* CWMG *Vol. 77, p. 272; E*

To Narandas Gandhi

Juhu

20 May 1944

... THIS TIME, while in jail, I read about Marx and whatever literature I could get about the great experiment in Russia. ...

CWMG *Vol. 77, p. 277; G*

To Aruna Asaf Ali

9 June 1944

I HAVE been filled with admiration for your courage and heroism. I have sent you messages that you must not die underground.[62] You are reduced to a skeleton. Do come out and surrender yourself and win the prize offered for your arrest. Reserve the prize money for the Harijan cause.

CWMG *Vol. 77, p. 306; E*

To P.C. Joshi[63]

Juhu
11 June 1944[64]

I HAD expected a prompt reply to the questions I had raised at our meeting. Meanwhile some additional questions have arisen which please, answer when you answer my first questions.

1. What is the meaning of 'people' in 'people's war'? Does it mean war on behalf of India's millions, or the Negroes in East, South or West Africa, or the Negroes of America, or all of them? Are the Allies engaged in such a war?
2. Are the finances of the Communist Party, represented by you, subject to public audit? If they are, may I see them?
3. It is stated that the Communist Party has actively helped the authorities to arrest leaders and organizers of labour strikes during the last two years.
4. The Communist Party is said to have adopted the policy of infiltrating the Congress organization with a hostile intent.
5. Is not the policy of the Communist Party dictated from outside?

Yours sincerely,
M.K. Gandhi
CWMG *Vol. 77, p. 310*

To Acharya P.C. Ray

On or before 12 June 1944[65]

HOPE YOU will insist on finishing at least a century[66].

The Hindu *14-6-1944;* CWMG *Vol. 77, p. 311; E*

To Kanu Ramdas Gandhi

Juhu
14 June 1944

...WE WILL certainly play odds-and-evens when we meet. But shouldn't you play games involving vigorous physical exercise? Your English handwriting also needs improvement. How can one believe in both violence and non-violence? Can one ride two horses simultaneously?

Blessings from
Bapu
CWMG Vol. 77, p. 315; G

To Ziauddin Chaudhari

Panchgani
On or after 10 July 1944[67]

Ziauddin Chaudhari[68]
Care Emdessons
Karachi

Rajaji's offer supersedes previous writing if contrary.

CWMG Vol. 77, p. 365

To S. Zaheerul Mujahid

Panchgani
11 July 1944

Dear Friend,

I feel wholly unable to undertake the task[69] you have entrusted me with.

Yours sincerely,
M.K. Gandhi
CWMG Vol. 77, p. 366; E

Interview To The Press

Panchgani
13 July 1944

... I MYSELF feel firmly that Mr Jinnah does not block the way, but the British Government do not want a just settlement of the Indian claim for independence which is overdue, and they are using Mr Jinnah as a cloak for denying freedom to India. ...

CWMG *Vol. 77, pp. 376–7; E*

To Winston Churchill

'Dilkhusha', Panchgani
17 July 1944

Dear Prime Minister,

You are reported to have a desire to crush the simple 'naked fakir' as you are said to have described me. I have been long trying to be a fakir and that naked—a more difficult task. I, therefore, regard the expression as a compliment though unintended. I approach you then as such and ask you to trust and use me for the sake of your people and mine and through them those of the world.

Yours sincere friend,
M.K. Gandhi
CWMG *Vol. 77, pp. 391–2; E*

Talk With C. Rajagopalachari

Panchgani

CR: I am afraid, your letter[70] will be misunderstood; it is a naughty letter.

MKG: I don't think so. I meant it seriously.

CR: You have touched him on the raw by rubbing in a past utterance of his, of which he is probably not very proud.

MKG: I have taken out the sting by appropriating his remark as an unintended compliment.

CR: I hope you are right.

MKG: I am sorry, but I think you are wrong!

CWMG *Vol. 77, p. 478; E*

To M.A. Jinnah

'Dilkhusha', Panchgani
17 July 1944

THERE WAS a time when I was able to persuade you to speak in our mother tongue. Today I venture to write in the same. I had already invited you while I was in jail. After my release I have not written to you so far. But today I am prompted to do so. Let us meet when you wish to. Please do not regard me as an enemy of Islam and the Muslims here. I have always been a friend and servant of yours and of the whole world. Do not dismiss me. I am enclosing a translation of this letter in Urdu.

Your brother,
Gandhi

(P.S.) Please write in Urdu ...[71]

CWMG *Vol. 77, pp. 393–4; G*

Answers To Questions[72]

Panchgani
20 July 1944

Q. Do you agree with inferences being drawn in London following the publication of your interview that you favour full entry of free Indian government into war against Japan?

MKG: Yes.

Q. Regarding Pakistan there is a tendency here to interpret your last contact with Mr Jinnah as indicating your acceptance of Pakistan. Is this so?

MKG: Mr Rajagopalachari's Formula indicates my way of meeting the communal difficulty. I am indifferent whether it is called Pakistan or not.

The Bombay Chronicle *22-7-1944;* CWMG *Vol. 77, pp. 410–11; E*

Interview To The Press

Panchgani
30 July 1944

... THE RAJAJI Formula is intended as a help to all lovers of the country. It is the best we could conceive, but it is open to amendment, as it is open to rejection or acceptance. ...

The Hindu *1-8-1944;* CWMG *Vol. 77, pp. 438–9; E*

To B.R. Ambedkar

Sevagram
6 August 1944

... I WOULD love to find a meeting ground between us on both the questions. I know your great ability and I would love to own you as a colleague and co-worker. But I must admit my failure to come nearer to you. If you can show me a way to a common meeting ground between us I would like to see it. Meanwhile, I must reconcile myself to the present unfortunate difference.

The Bombay Chronicle *3-1-1945;* CWMG *Vol. 78, p. 13; E*

To K.M. Munshi

Sevagram
12 August 1944

... IT DOES not matter if others do not understand me. You are among those who do know me. I am sure you know that, in spite of my accepting *Akhand*[73] Hindustan on principle, I am the originator of the Congress principle of self-determination. A believer in non-violence, I can maintain the unity of India only if I accept the freedom of every part. ...

Blessings from
Bapu
CWMG *Vol. 78, p. 25; G*

To A Deputation Of The Duty Society[74]

Sevagram
15 August 1944

I WANT that myself and the Quaid-e-Azam should be locked up and should not be allowed to come out till we come to some decision to remove this deadlock ...

I wish to see a free India in my lifetime, for God knows what will happen when I am no more.

The Bombay Chronicle *20-8-1944;* CWMG *Vol. 78, p. 32; E*

To M.A. Jinnah

18 August 1944

HOW WAS it you fell ill all of a sudden? The whole world was looking forward to our meeting. I had entertained high hopes, although, I must admit, I had my own apprehensions. Hence when Fatimabehn[75] conveyed to me the news of your illness, I was shaken. I hope God will soon restore you to health, hasten the meeting to which the whole world is looking forward and that the meeting will lead to the welfare of India.

I hope Fatimabehn or someone else will keep me informed about your health.

Your brother,
M.K. Gandhi
CWMG *Vol. 78, p. 39; G*

On The First Day's Talk With Jinnah

Bombay
7 September 1944

(Asked after the first meeting whether he had brought anything from the Quaid-e-Azam)

Only flowers.

Robert Payne 'The Life And Death of Mahatma Gandhi', *p. 511*

Description Of Talk With Jinnah[76]

Bombay
9 September 1944[77]

IT WAS a test of my patience ... I am amazed at my own patience. However, it was a friendly talk.

His (Jinnah's) contempt for your Formula (Rajaji Formula) and his contempt for you is staggering. You rose in my estimation that you could have talked to him for all those hours and that you should have taken the trouble to draw up that formula.

He says you have accepted his demand and so should I. I said, 'I endorse Rajaji's Formula and you can call it Pakistan if you like. ...'

He said I should concede Pakistan and he would go the whole length with me. He would go to jail, he would even face bullets. I said, 'I will stand by your side to face them.' 'You may not', he said. 'Try me', I replied.

We came back to the Formula. He wants Pakistan now, not after independence. 'We will have independence for Pakistan and Hindustan', he said. 'We should come to an agreement and then go to the Government and ask them to accept it, force them to accept our solution:' I said I could never be a party to that. I could never ask the Britishers to impose partition on India. 'If you all want to separate, I can't stop you. I have not got the power to compel you and I would not use it if I had.' He said, 'The Muslims want Pakistan. The League represents the Muslims.' I said, 'I agree the League is the most powerful Muslim organization. I might even concede that you as its President represent the Muslims of India, but that does not mean that all Muslims want Pakistan. Put it to the vote of all the inhabitants of the area and see.' He said, 'Why should you ask non-Muslims?' I said, 'You cannot possibly deprive a section of the population of its vote. You must carry them with you, and if you are in the majority why should you be afraid?' I told him of what Kiron Shankar Roy had said to me: 'If the worst comes to the worst, we in Bengal will all go in Pakistan, but for goodness sake do not partition Bengal. Do not vivisect it.'

... In the end he said, 'I would like to come to an agreement with you.' I answered, 'You remember that I have said that we should meet not to separate till we had come to an agreement'. He said, yes, he agreed. I suggested, 'Should we put that also in our statement?' He said, 'No, better not. Nevertheless that will be the understanding between us and the cordiality and friendliness of our talk will be reflected in our public utterances, too.'[78]

CWMG Vol. 78, pp. 87–90; E

Talk With M.A. Jinnah[79]—II

12 September 1944

HE DREW a very alluring picture of the government of Pakistan. It would be a perfect democracy. ...

CWMG Vol. 78, p. 96; E

Discussion With C. Rajagopalachari

Bombay
12 September 1944

CR: Find out what he[80] wants.

MKG: Yes, that is what I am doing. I am to prove from his own mouth that the whole of the Pakistan proposition is absurd. I think he does not want to break. On my part I am not going to be in a hurry. But he can't expect me to endorse an undefined Pakistan.

CR: Do you think he will give up the claim?

MKG: He has to, if there is to be a settlement. He wants a settlement, but what he wants he does not know. I want to show him that your Formula is the only thing that he can reasonably ask for.

Reconstructed from CWMG *Vol. 78, p. 97*

13 September 1944

(*To the Press*) ... Yesterday you read something in our faces. Here are we both. I would like you not to read anything in our faces except hope and nothing but hope.

At this stage Gandhi turned to Jinnah and asked:

MKG: Am I right? Have you seen the papers this morning?

M.A.J.: Why bother. They have written so much that is terrible.

MKG: (*Turning round to the Pressmen again*): You do not know what people who are bent on mischief will do. ...

Reconstructed from The Bombay Chronicle *14-9-1944;*
CWMG *Vol. 78, p. 98; E*

Bombay
14 September 1944[81]

... WE SHOULD take nothing for granted. I should clarify your difficulties in understanding the Rajaji Formula and you should do likewise regarding yours, i.e., the Muslim League Lahore Resolution of 1940.

... Perhaps at the end of our discussion, we shall discover that Rajaji not only has not put the Lahore Resolution out of shape and mutilated it but has given it substance and form.

Indeed, in view of your dislike of the Rajaji Formula, I have, at any rate for the moment, put it out of my mind and I am concentrating on the Lahore Resolution in the hope of finding a ground for mutual agreement.

... You ask for my conception of the basis for a provisional interim government. I would have told you if I had any scheme in mind ...

Rajaji tells me that 'absolute majority' is used in his Formula in the same sense as it is used in ordinary legal parlance wherever more than two groups are dealt with. I cling to my own answer. But you will perhaps suggest a third meaning and persuade me to accept it.

The form of the plebiscite and franchise must be left to be decided by the provisional interim government unless we decide it now. I should say it should be by adult suffrage ...

... supposing that the result of the plebiscite is in favour of partition, the provisional government will draft the treaty and agreements as regards the administration of matters of common interest, but the same has to be confirmed and ratified by the governments of the two States. The machinery required for the settlement and administration of matters of common interest will, in the first instance, be planned by the interim government, but subsequently will be the matter for settlement between the two governments acting through the agencies appointed by each for that purpose. ...

Yours sincerely,

M.K. Gandhi

The Hindu *29-9-1944;* CWMG *Vol. 78, pp. 99–100*

Bombay

15 September 1944

... FOR THE moment I have shunted the Rajaji Formula and with your assistance am applying my mind very seriously to the famous Lahore Resolution of the Muslim League.

... Pakistan is not in the Resolution. Does it bear the original meaning Punjab, Afghanistan, Kashmir, Sind, and Baluchistan, out of which the name was mnemonically formed? If not what is it?

Is the goal of Pakistan pan-Islam?

I know that you have acquired a unique hold on the Muslim masses. I want you to use your influence for their total welfare, which must include the rest.

In this hastily written letter, I have only given an inkling of my difficulty.

Yours sincerely,
M.K. Gandhi
The Hindu *29-9-1944;* CWMG *Vol. 78, pp. 101–3; E*

15 September 1944

... THE FORMULA was framed by Rajaji in good faith. I accepted it in equal good faith. The hope was that you would look at it with favour. We still think it to be the best in the circumstances. You and I have to put flesh on it, if we can. I have explained the process we have to go through. You have no objection to it. Perhaps, you want to know how I would form the provisional government if I was invited thereto. If I was in that unenviable position, I would see all the claimants and endeavour to satisfy them. My co-operation will be available in that task. ...

Yours sincerely,
M.K. Gandhi
The Hindu *29-9-1944;* CWMG *Vol. 78, pp. 103–4; E*

Bombay
19 September 1944

... WHY CAN you not accept my statement that I aspire to represent all the sections that compose the people of India? Do you not aspire? Should not every Indian? That the aspiration may never be realized is beside the point. ...

Yours sincerely,
M.K. Gandhi
The Hindu *29-9-1944;* CWMG *Vol. 78, pp. 116–17; E*

Bombay
22 September 1944

THE MORE I think about the two-nation theory the more alarming it appears to be ... I am unable to accept the proposition that the Muslims of India are a nation, distinct from the rest of the inhabitants of India. ... Once the principle is admitted there would be no limit to claims for cutting up India into numerous divisions, which would spell India's ruin. I have, therefore, suggested a way out. Let it be a partition as between two brothers, if a division there must be. ...

Yours sincerely,
M.K. Gandhi
The Hindu *29-9-1944;* CWMG *Vol. 78, pp. 122–3; E*

Bombay
23 September 1944

LAST EVENING's talk has left a bad taste in the mouth. Our talks and our correspondence seem to run in parallel lines and never touch one another. We reached the breaking point last evening but, thank God, we were unwilling to part. We resumed discussion and suspended it in order to allow me to keep my time for the evening public prayer.

In order that all possibility of making any mistake in a matter of this great importance may be removed I would like you to give me in writing what precisely on your part you would want me to put my signature to[82].

I adhere to my suggestion that we may call in some outside assistance to help us at this stage.

Yours sincerely,
M.K. Gandhi
The Hindu *29-9-1944;* CWMG *Vol. 78, p. 124; E*

Bombay
Id (23 September 1944)[83]

I WAS wondering what I shall send you today. It should be fair on my part to let you and your sister[84] share equally the crisp chapatis they make for me. Here is your share. Please regard it as a token of my love and do please help yourself to it.

Id greetings from
M.K. Gandhi
CWMG *Vol. 78, p. 125; E*

Bombay
24 September 1944

... DIFFERING FROM you on the general basis, I can yet recommend to the Congress and the country the acceptance of the claim for separation contained in the Muslim League Resolution of Lahore, 1940, on my basis and on the following terms:

The areas should be demarcated by a commission, approved by the Congress and the League. The wishes of the inhabitants of the area demarcated should be ascertained through the votes of the adult population of the areas or through some equivalent method.

If the vote is in favour of separation, it shall be agreed that these areas shall form a separate State as soon as possible after India is free from foreign domination and can, therefore, be constituted into two sovereign independent States.

There shall be a treaty of separation, which should also provide for the efficient and satisfactory administration of Foreign Affairs, Defence, Internal Communications, Customs, Commerce and the like, which must necessarily continue to be matters of common interest between the contracting parties.

The treaty shall also contain terms for safeguarding the rights of minorities in the two States. ...

Yours sincerely,
M.K. Gandhi

The Hindu *29-9-1944;* CWMG *Vol. 78, pp. 126–7; E*

Bombay[85]
24 September 1944

Jinnah: If you want defence and so many things in common, that means that you visualize a centre?

Gandhi: No, but I must say, in practice, there will have to be a body selected by both parties to regulate these things.

... You can refer the matter to a lawyer of eminence impersonally and take his opinion whether there is anything in it which could be considered inimical to the Muslim League or the Muslims.

Jinnah: Why should I want another's opinion when I know it for myself? ...

CWMG *Vol. 78, p. 128; E*

Bombay
25 September 1944

... YOU ARE too technical when you dismiss my proposal for arbitration or outside guidance over points of difference. If I have approached you as an individual, and not in any representative capacity, it is because we believe that if I reach an agreement with you, it will be of material use in the process of securing a Congress-League settlement and acceptance of it by the country. Is it irrelevant or inadmissible to supplement our efforts to convince each other without help, guidance, advice, or even arbitration?

Yours sincerely,
M.K. Gandhi
The Hindu *29-9-1944;* CWMG *Vol. 78, pp. 130–1; E*

Bombay
26 September 1944

... I CONFESS I am unable to understand your persistent refusal to appreciate the fact that the Formula presented to you by me in my letter of the 24th as well as the Formula presented to you by Rajaji give you virtually what is embodied in the Lahore Resolution, providing at the same time what is absolutely necessary to make the arrangement acceptable to the country ...

Your constant references to my not being clothed with representative authority are really irrelevant. I have approached you so that, if you and I can agree upon a common course of action, I may use what influence I possess for its acceptance by the Congress and the country. If you break, it cannot be because I have no representative capacity, or because I have been unwilling to give you satisfaction in regard to the claim embodied in the Lahore Resolution.

Yours sincerely,
M.K. Gandhi.
The Hindu *29-9-1944;* CWMG *Vol. 78, pp. 131–2; E*

To M.S. Subbulakshmi[86]

Bombay
28 September 1944

RAJAJI HAS told me everything about your good work in connection with Kasturba Memorial Fund by using your musical gifts. May God bless you.

Yours,
M.K. Gandhi[87]
CWMG *Vol. 78, p. 136; E*

Interview To The Press[88]

28 September 1944

IT IS a matter of deep regret that we two could not reach an agreement. But there is no cause for disappointment. The breakdown is only so-called. It is an adjournment *sine die*. ...

CWMG *Vol. 78, pp. 136–7; E*

Interview To 'News Chronicle'[89]

Bombay
29 September 1944[90]

I COULD not accept the two nations basis. This was Mr Jinnah's demand. He wants immediate recognition of the North-West Frontier Province, Sind, the whole of the Punjab, Bengal, and Assam as a sovereign and completely independent Pakistan.

... I want to make it clear that I believe Mr Jinnah is sincere, but I think he is suffering from hallucination when he imagines that an unnatural division of India could bring either happiness or prosperity to the people concerned. ...

CWMG *Vol. 78, pp. 142–3; E*

Interview To *The Hindu*

2 October 1944

... I WANT life for 125 years. But Malaviyaji cut it down by 25 years when he wired to me in Poona at Parnakuti that I must live for a hundred years.

The Hindu *4-10-1944;* CWMG *Vol. 78, p. 149; E*

Interview To N.G. Ranga[91]

Sevagram
29 October 1944

NGR: You say that the earth rightly belongs or should belong to the peasant. By this do you mean only that the peasant ought to gain control over the land ...?

MKG: I do not know what has happened in Soviet Russia. But I have no doubt that if we have democratic swaraj, as it must be if freedom is won through non-violence, the *kisan* must hold power in all its phases including political power.

NGR: Am I right in interpreting your statement that land should not belong 'to the absentee landlord or zamindar' and that ultimately the zamindari system has to be abolished, of course through non-violent means?

MKG: Yes. But you should remember that I visualize a system of trusteeship regulated by the State. In other words I do not want to antagonize the zamindars (and for that matter any class) without cause.

NGR: Are we right in thinking that you stand for the abolition of this process of exploitation of the producers of primary commodities and the agricultural masses of the world?

MKG: Root and branch.

> The Hindu *23-1-1945;* CWMG *Vol. 78, pp. 246 and 251; E*

Cable To V.K. Krishna Menon[92]

> Sevagram
> 12 November 1944

JAWAHARLAL IS a jewel among men. Happy is the land that owns him. Something is radically wrong with the system that has no better use of persons like him than as prisoners.

> The Hindu *14-11-1944;* CWMG *Vol. 78, p. 289; E*

A Thought For The Day[93]

> 1 December 1944

... THE TREE bears the heat of the sun, yet provides cool shade to us. What do we do?

> CWMG *Vol. 78, p. 392; H*

> 13 December 1944

A SISTER said: 'I used to pray, but have now given it up.' I asked: 'Why?' She replied: 'Because I used to deceive myself.' The reply is of course correct. But let her give up deceiving. Why give up praying?

CWMG *Vol. 78, p. 393; H*

21 December 1944

THE POET-saint Narsinh[94] says: 'A man of God seeks not deliverance from birth and death; he asks to be born again and again.' Viewed from this angle, *mukti* takes on a somewhat different form.

CWMG *Vol. 78, p. 394; H*

Letter To Sumitra Gandhi

Sevagram
4 January 1945

THOUGH THERE is no letter from you Ramdas wrote to me about you.

First, about your eyes. You should not be in a hurry to pass the examination. You may do as much work as you can, while taking care of your health and your eyes. It should be enough for you that you are not idling away.

Then, about gold bangles. What will you do with them? There can be bangles made of yarn, sea shells, glass, copper, silver, gold, pearls, diamonds, and so on. But what use are they to you? Your bangles should be in your heart. That alone is the real lasting adornment. All else is false. If nevertheless you cannot do without them you may put on any kind of bangles that you want and your parents can get for you. Consider how it will affect the poor. Do what your heart prompts you to do. Only hear what I say. Write to me.

Blessings from
Bapu

Sumitra Ramdas Gandhi
Pilani

CWMG *Vol. 79, p. 7; G*

To Kanu Ramdas Gandhi[95]

Sevagram
16 January 1945

... I DON'T believe in ghosts. I have had no such experience. It is all right if Bhansalibhai believes in them. That does not detract from his saintliness. But there is no reason to believe that everything a saint says must be true. No one is omniscient. The planchette business is pure fraud. Do not get involved in it.

Blessings from
Bapu
CWMG *Vol. 79, p. 35; G*

Note To Sub-Inspector Of Police, Wardha[96]

Sevagram
4 February 1945

HE (THE wanted person) came and said he believed in me and my teachings and had decided to surrender himself. Hence the note he wrote. I must add that even if he had admitted his guilt to me I would be bound not to disclose it to the police. I could not be reformer and informer at the same time.

CWMG *Vol. 79, p. 93*

Speech At Prayer Meeting

Sevagram
22 February 1945

THIS DAY marks the end of a solar year since Ba's departure from the earth. According to the lunar calendar, the anniversary fell on Mahashivarati Day. This is no occasion for mourning. On the contrary, it should be celebrated with the same joy as a day of birth. I do not make much distinction between birth and death. The atman has neither birth nor death. We loved Ba's atman which is immortal.

There was a marriage celebration yesterday. Five minutes before (the function) I went to inspect the latrine. It smelled. I found excreta uncovered. Is this not a sign of our outer sin? We are guilty of a great error in keeping the latrine thus. We might have committed other sins as well. ...

CWMG *Vol. 79, pp. 153–4; H*

Speech At All-India Hindustani Prachar Sabha Conference—III

Wardha
27 February 1945

... I DON'T want Hindi to die nor Urdu to be banished. What I wish is that both should become useful to us ...

I live for Hindu-Muslim unity. I know the propagation of Hindustani will bring about this unity ...

I say, let Hindi and Urdu both prosper. I have to take work from both. Even today, Hindustani exists but we do not utilize it. This is the age of Hindi and Urdu. These are two streams from which the third will flow. Hence it will not do if the first two dry up.

The villagers will follow my language. They will not be able to follow a language which is full of Sanskrit and Arabic-Persian words. If those in the Hindi Sahitya Sammelan should say that they are going to sponsor a Sanskritized language, then, as far as I am concerned, the Sammelan does not exist. The language of the villages is only one. They cannot have two languages. The champions of Hindi want me to blow the trumpet for Hindi only and to forget Urdu. But I am a satyagrahi believing in ahimsa. How can I do this? ...

The Hitavada *1-3-1945;* CWMG *Vol. 79, p. 179; H*

All Is Dust

Sevagram[97]
15 March 1945

... LIFE IS only a short spell of moonlight. In the end all is dust.

Blessings from
Bapu
CWMG *Vol. 79, p. 250; G*

Sleep

Sevagram[98]
21 March 1945

WHY SHOULD you have even a piece of wood under the head? Sleep in *shavasana*,[99] as I do. If you must have something, have a stone or a brick. ...

Blessings from
Bapu
CWMG *Vol. 79, p. 283; H*

To Vinayak D. Savarkar

Sevagram
22 March 1945

I WRITE this after reading the news of the death of your brother. I had done a little bit for his release and ever since I had been taking an interest in him. Where is the need to condole with you? We are ourselves in the jaws of death. I hope his family are all right.

Yours,
M.K. Gandhi

Vir Savarkar
Ratnagiri

CWMG *Vol. 79, p. 287; H*

On The Death Of Hermann Kallenbach[100]

Sevagram
25 March 1945

SOUTH AFRICA has lost a most generous-minded citizen and the Indians of that subcontinent a very warm friend.

In Hermann Kallenbach's death I have lost a very dear and near friend. He used to say to me often that when I was deserted by the whole world, I would find him to be a true friend going with me, if need be, to the ends of the earth in search of Truth. He used to spend at one time £75 per month on his person alone. But he so revolutionized his life that his monthly personal expenses amounted to under £8. This lasted while we lived together in a cottage seven miles from Johannesburg. When I left South Africa, he reverted in large part to his original life though mostly eschewing the things of life he had deliberately left. ...

The Hindu *27-3-1945;* CWMG *Vol. 79, p. 301; E*

'True' History

27 March 1945

HE CAN serve by writing a true and original history of the people. If there is progress he will describe the progress; if he finds there is decline he will record that decline[101].

Blessings from
Bapu
CWMG *Vol. 79, p. 318; H*

Brahmacharya

Bombay[102]
9 April 1945

... MY WORK has increased. My endeavour now is to see that no one expects any money from me and the institutions I have created become self-supporting. This will, of course, take some time and meanwhile I shall have to find money for them. The institutions are All-India Spinners' Association, Village Industries Association, Nayee Talim, Hindustani Prachar, and the Ashram. The second, third, fourth, and fifth need the money now. So far as the fifth, the Ashram, is concerned it will never be self-supporting ...

Now for my relationship with women and my experiment. I have suspended the experiment for the sake of co-workers. I did not see anything improper in it. I am the same who took a vow of brahmacharya in 1906 and have been observing brahmacharya since 1901. Today I am a better brahmachari than I was in 1901. What my experiment has done is to make me more firm in my brahmacharya. The experiment was designed to make of myself a perfect brahmachari and if God so wills it will led to perfection. You wanted to talk to me and question me on the subject. You may do both.

Please do not hesitate. It will be unbearable if there is any hesitation in one with whom I have such intimate relations and whose money I have been so freely spending. ...

Blessings from
Bapu

(P.S.)

I had thought of writing a short letter, but it has become somewhat lengthy: After all it covers three points. ...

Bapu
CWMG *Vol. 79, pp. 359–60; H*

Questions From K.R. Narayanan[103]

Bombay
10 April 1945

KRN: All great men have a passion for simplification. You have simplified the nature of human conflict as between violence and non-violence, truth and untruth, right and wrong. But in life, is not the conflict between one right and another right or between one truth and another truth? How can non-violence deal with such a situation?

MKG: That is a matter of application.

KRN: In the Hindu–Muslim question where the conflict is between the rights of the Hindus and the rights of the Muslims, what technique of non-violence can be employed to solve the problem, especially when these rights seem to be irreconcilable?

MKG: That awful situation can only be dealt with properly through satyagraha.

Your questions show that you have not studied it. If I am right, Pyarelal will give you a list of the books. My advice to you is that you should seriously study the literature on the subject.

KRN: How can a Harijan who goes abroad[104] best serve his country and community from abroad?

MKG: He cannot serve the one without the other. Abroad you will say it is a domestic question which you are determined to solve for yourselves.

CWMG *Vol. 79, pp. 363–4; E*

To Eleanor Roosevelt

Bombay
6 p.m., 16 April 1945

Mrs Roosevelt
Hyde Park
New York (U.S.A.)

My humble condolence and congratulations[105]. Latter because your illustrious husband died in harness and after war had reached a point where allied victory had become certain[106]. He was spared humiliating spectacle of being party to peace which threatens to be prelude to war bloodier still if possible.

Gandhi

The Hindu 10-5-1945; CWMG Vol. 79, p. 384; E

Hindi + Urdu = National Language

Bombay[107]
19 April 1945

... IT BECOMES your duty and mine—and of other patriots also—to know both the scripts and their styles. We include Urdu-knowing people in taking account of the supporters of the national language. Therefore the national language is = Hindi + Urdu. Hindi will be an incomplete national language if we take it in its narrow sense ...

The poison cannot spread if supporters of Hindi put up with and take kindly to the popularization of Hindustani.

Yours,
M.K. Gandhi

CWMG Vol. 79, pp. 397–8; H

On Harilal

Bombay[108]
19 April 1945

I WAS very happy to receive your letter. God will grant you success. The victory over Harilal, which was denied me, has come to you two. You are correct in saying that if he can get rid of the two vices he can be the best of all brothers. Let us see what you people can do. Kanti is very confident. Faith is a great thing. ...

Blessings from
Bapu
CWMG *Vol. 79, p. 399; H*

The Big Powers And Peace

Mahabaleswar[109]
Before 25 April 1945[110]

Ralph Coniston: Why do you feel so sceptical about the possibility of a lasting peace emerging from the defeat of the Axis Powers?

MKG: The reason is patent. Violence is bound sooner or later to exhaust itself but peace cannot issue out of such exhaustion ...

RC: While the representatives of the big powers who would be meeting at San Francisco were what they were, the people at large, after the experience of the horrors of war, would force the hands of their respective Governments.

MKG: I know the European mind well enough to know that when it has to choose between abstract justice and self-interest, it will plump for the latter ...

RC: So, you don't think that the average man in Europe or America cares much for the high ideals for which the war is professed to be fought?

MKG: I am afraid, I do not ...

RC: Then, you don't think the Big Five or the Big Three can guarantee peace?

MKG: I am positive. If they are so arrogant as to think that they can have lasting peace while the exploitation of the coloured and the so-called backward races goes on, they are living in a fool's paradise.

RC: You think they will fall out among themselves before long?

MKG: There you are stealing my language. The quarrel with Russia has already started ...

RC: What about the war criminals?

MKG: What is a war criminal? ... Hitler was 'Great Britain's sin'. Hitler is only an answer to British imperialism, and this I say in spite of the fact that I hate Hitlerism and its anti-Semitism.

England, America, and Russia have all of them got their hands dyed more or less red—not merely Germany and Japan. The Japanese have only proved themselves to be apt pupils of the West. They have learnt at the feet of the West and beaten it at its own game.

RC: What would you see accomplished at San Francisco?

MKG: Parity among all nations—the strongest and the weakest— the strong should be the servants of the weakest not their masters or exploiters.

RC: Is not this too idealistic?

MKG: May be. But you asked me what I would *like* to see accomplished ...

RC: Would you not go to the West to teach them the art of peace?

MKG: ... If I go there I shall be like a stranger. Probably I shall be lionized but that is all. I shall not be able to present to them the science of peace in language they can understand. But they will understand if I can make good my non-violence in India.

RC: If you were at San Francisco, what would you be advocating there?

MKG: ... I react to a situation intuitively. Logic comes afterwards, it does not precede the event. The moment I am at the Peace Conference, I know the right word will come. But not beforehand. This much, however, I can say that whatever I say there will be in terms of peace, not war.

RC: What kind of world organization would promote an enduring peace or preserve it?

MKG: Only an organization based predominantly on truth and non-violence.

CWMG Vol. 79, p. 421; E

125 Years

Mahabaleshwar
25 April 1945[111]

... I HOPE to live for 125 years but there are many obstacles in the way. Even supposing I survived, it seems to me I shall only be an adviser. It is true that if the Congress comes into power, I will suggest changes in the field of education. ...

CWMG Vol. 80, p. 4; G

To Sarojini Naidu

Mahabaleshwar
30 April 1945

Sarojini Devi Naidu
Hyderabad Deccan

Telegram worthy of you. Death[112] is deliverance. Love.

Spinner[113]
CWMG Vol. 80, p. 40; E

On Nehru

Mahabaleshwar[114]
4 May 1945

THESE ARE the remarks attributed to Sir Firoz Khan Noon[115] as having been made by him at San Francisco.

Gandhi is in the hands of the reactionary and orthodox Hindus. He would be doing a great service to the country if, at this moment, he were to retire in favour of a younger man. I feel Nehru would be an excellent successor to Gandhi. He has quite a large support among the Muslims and is not so bigoted as Gandhi, who is at a dead-end. The only solution is for Nehru to come to the forefront. But Nehru respects Gandhi so much that he would not come forward.

He should know that I have called the Pandit my successor. He does not need to come to the front. He is in the front ...

Let him make no capital out of my supposed bigotry or orthodoxy. He may not know that I have never been a bigot or known as such since my youth. And orthodoxy would not have me for my uncompromising and radical attitude on untouchability and general social reform. Sir Firoz is on safer ground when he accuses me of being out of date. For no one knows what or who is out of date. ...

The Hindu 6-5-1945; CWMG Vol. 80, pp. 64–5; E

'A Thought For The Day'

Mahabaleswar
5 May 1945

JUST AS only others can see a man's back while he himself cannot, we too cannot see our own errors.

Mahabaleswar
27 May 1945

I TOOK off my spectacles to wash my face. I had intended to pick them up later, but forgot to do so. Why? Because something else engrossed my attention and so I became negligent. This is called disorganization which is a dangerous thing.

Mahabaleswar
21 June 1945

IF WE stopped talking about useless things and talked of things that matter in as few words as possible, much of our time as well as that of others could be saved.

CWMG Vol. 80, pp. 431, 433 and 436; H

We Are Not God

14 May 1945[116]

... WHY SHOULD we observe anybody's face? We may even make a mistake in judging a person from his face. We are not God. We might even do him injustice. And moreover, when one has made up one's mind not to fear anybody, why need one know the other person's mind?

CWMG Vol. 80, pp. 134–5; G

Draft Amendment To Rule 72
Of Kasturba Gandhi National Memorial Trust

Mahabaleshwar
19 May 1945

THE TRAVELLING expenses shall be third-class fare provided that it will be open to the local chairman to sanction second-class fare owing to sickness or other valid reason which he shall record in the minute-book.

This is my suggestion.

CWMG Vol. 80, p. 149

Mohan Kumaramangalam's Release

Mahabaleshwar
21 May 1945

My dear Subbaroyan,[117]

I was glad to have your letter. Regard me as a partner in your joint joy on the restoration of your son to liberty. May he soon join you! Mohan ought to see me this week. I like him ...

Love.

Bapu
CWMG Vol. 80, p. 154; E

To Sumati S. Morarjee[118]

Mahabaleswar
22 May 1945[119]

Chiranjivi Jamna *alias* Sumati,

Why should a woman be given a different name when she goes to live with her husband and why not a man? This custom irks me very much. I think I came to know only here that your real name is Jamna. ...

Blessings from
Bapu
CWMG Vol. 80, p. 163; G

A Name For A New Grandson

Mahabaleswar,
22/23 May 1945

Chiranjivi Lakshmi,

I have your letter. I was very glad. Let the new grandson[120] be named Govind and also Madhav. If you want to keep only one name, let it be the one suggested by Anna[121]. Ba has gone, her love remains. The body has got to perish, but even if it does so the love of Him who dwells in the body cannot die.

... What will happen to your studies now? Let one of the boys at least occasionally write to me.

Blessings from
Bapu
CWMG *Vol. 80, p. 166; H*

To Mohan Kumaramangalam[122]

Mahabaleshwar
24 May 1945

... MANY HONEST Congressmen come to me or write to me from the various provinces that communists have no principles save of keeping their party alive and beating their opponents with any stick that came to their hands. I am not going to base my opinion on this evidence either ... I do not want to pass judgment against a political party. I tell friends to be guided by their own knowledge and not by my judgment which may be erring for want of complete evidence.

CWMG *Vol. 80, p. 175; E*

My English

Mahabaleshwar
28 May 1945

My dear Bharatan[123],

... My English is not perfect. It may be relatively better than Hindustani. I must try to make it equal to my English, if it is not. I reach the masses only through Hindustani, however imperfect it may be, never through English, however perfect it may be ...

Love.

Bapu

CWMG Vol. 80, p. 192; E

Marriage

Mahabaleshwar
29 May 1945

YOU MUST firmly refuse to marry the person whom your parents want you to marry.

Marry the man with whom you are so much in love after informing your parents. Do not seek my blessings. ...

Blessings from
M.K. Gandhi

Sushila
(C/o) Shri Guruprasad Srivastava
R.M.S. Office
Charbagh Junction
Lucknow

CWMG Vol. 80, p. 207; H

Working With Communists

Panchgani[124]
2 June 1945

... I HAVE no difficulty in working side by side with communists. One must depend upon one's own experiences.

CWMG Vol. 80, p. 238

What Are You?

Panchgani
9 June 1945

My dear Singer,

... Your letter brings out a mother's affection at its best. I do not know whether to love you best as a poetess, philosopher, or mother? Tell me.

Love

Spinner

Shrimati Sarojini Naidu
Hyderabad, Deccan

CWMG *Vol. 80, p. 282; E*

On Rajani Palme-Dutt

Panchgani
9 June 1945

My dear Mohan,

Of course I know Palme-Dutt[125] both by name and fame. I do wish him success in his campaign.

Love.

Bapu

Shri Mohan Kumaramangalam
Raj Bhavan
Sandhurst Road, Bombay—4

CWMG *Vol. 80, p. 283; E*

Panchgani
9 June 1945

... PALME-DUTT is a well-known figure. He will be able to give a fight to Amery. Patel[126], I do not know. Nor do I wish that too many Indians should stand for election. ...

CWMG *Vol. 80, p. 283; G*

To The Last Anna

Panchgani[127]
9 June 1945

YOUR LETTER is good. It is bad to use the expression 'two or four'. The shifting of the latrine will cost either Rs 2 or Rs 4. Truly speaking, we should calculate to the last anna. ...

Blessings from
Bapu

CWMG *Vol. 80, p. 286; H*

To Hamid Khan

Panchgani
10 June 1945

... I KNEW Ganesh Shankar Vidyarthi[128] well. I had great regard for him. I have already given my view on the question of a memorial. You must know it. Go through it if you have not already done so. You can't raise a memorial by constructing a building or spending money. A man thinks that having given the money he has done his duty. Therefore, in my opinion, it will be a true memorial to Ganesh Shankar Vidyarthi if, at least in Kanpur, and as far as possible throughout India, Hindus and Muslims should unite and instead of cutting each other's throats be prepared to lay down their lives for each other. ...

CWMG *Vol. 80, p. 292; H*

Two Posers

Panchgani
On or before 12 June 1945[129]

SHRI SAILENDRA Nath Chattopadhyaya of the United Press puts the following posers before me: 'Why do you wish to live for 125 years, and what is Ram Rajya?'

... I know that, medically speaking, the chances are against me for I have not always followed nature's way. I began to adopt it fairly strictly in South Africa in 1903 or thereabout. Want of brahmacharya in early married life must also weigh against the full span.

... Thus, though I wish and even hope to live up to 125 years, what does it matter, if I die tomorrow? There is no sense of regret or frustration in me. And there will be no anguish in me over an early death.

... Now for Ram Rajya. It can be religiously translated as Kingdom of God on Earth; politically translated, it is perfect democracy in which inequalities based on possession and non-possession, colour, race or creed, or sex vanish; in it, land and State belong to the people, justice is prompt, perfect and cheap and, therefore, there is freedom of worship, speech, and the Press—all this because of the reign of the self-imposed law of moral restraint.

... It is a dream that may never be realized. I find happiness in living in that dreamland. ...

The Hindu 12-6-1945; CWMG Vol. 80, pp. 299–300; E

To Harilal Gandhi

Panchgani
14 June 1945

I GOT your letter. I do get news of you from time to time. I would not at all like your going away from there. Kanti and Saraswati serve you so well, keep you with them so lovingly. It is, therefore, your duty to stay with them. How can you be a burden on them? Moreover, you are able to keep yourself in control there. You should not, therefore, think just now of going away anywhere else. ...

Blessings from
Bapu
CWMG Vol. 80, p. 321; G

Express   Panchgani
17 June 1945

H.E. Viceroy
New Delhi

... I suggest immediate invitation to Congress president attend conference or depute Congress nominee. If fixity of parity between caste Hindus and Muslims unchangeable religious division will become officially stereotyped on eve of independence. Personally I can never subscribe to it nor congress if I know its mind. In spite of having overwhelmingly Hindu membership Congress has striven to be purely political. I am quite capable advising Congress to nominate all non-Hindus and most decidedly non-caste hindus. You will quite unconsciously but equally surely defeat purpose of conference if parity between caste Hindus and Muslims is unalterable. Parity between Congress and League understandable. I am eager to help you and British people but not at sacrifice of fundamental and universal principles. For it will be no help. ...

Gandhi
Telegram; CWMG Vol. 80, p. 341

Letter To Usha Ramdas Gandhi

Panchgani
18 June 1945

Chiranjivi Usha,

I have your postcard. Your demand is crazy. My going to Simla is uncertain and even if I go it will only be for work. It is therefore not proper to take children along. It is a different thing if there is some occasion. One can say that you have considerably improved your handwriting. My handwriting will improve on its own if all the children write a pearl-like hand. You should therefore stand first in that.

Blessing from
Bapu
CWMG *Vol. 80, p. 347; G*

Express

Panchgani
18 June 1945[130]

H.E. Viceroy
New Delhi

Grateful for your prompt frank and full reply also for directly inviting Maulana Saheb ... Congress has never identified itself with caste or non-caste Hindus and never can, even to gain independence which will be one-sided untrue and suicidal. Congress to justify its existence for winning independence of India must remain for ever free to choose best men and women from all classes and I hope always will. That it has for sake of conciliating minorities chosen men to represent them though they have been less than best redounds to its credit but that can never be pleaded to justify or perpetuate distinction based on caste or creed.

Telegram; CWMG *Vol. 80, p. 345; E*

Letter To Lord Wavell

'Manor Ville', Simla West
28 June 1945

Dear Friend,

Some hangings—an aftermath of the disturbances of 1942—are impending. I have some cases given to me by Dr Rajendra Prasad of the Working Committee. The Chimur cases you perhaps know. I do not quite know how the last stages of the conference are shaping. Be that as it may, I suggest that all such hangings be commuted to life sentences without further public appeal or agitation and whether judicial proceedings are going on or not. If you think that this is beyond you, may I suggest that these be postponed so as to be dealt with by the national government that is coming into being?[131]

Yours sincerely,
M.K. Gandhi
CWMG *Vol. 80, p. 379*

Interview To Associated Press of India

Simla
30 June 1945

Correspondent: What will be the composition of the interim government if you have your way?

MKG: (*laughing*) The interim government will consist of top men, irrespective of caste, creed, or colour. If I became the Viceroy of India, I would startle the world with my list and yet make it acceptable.

Of course, nobody will take the trouble of appointing me the Viceroy of India. ...

CWMG *Vol. 80, p. 389; E*

To Kishorelal G. Mashruwala

'Manor Ville', Simla West
2 July 1945

...THOUGH I am engaged here in an important work, all the same the mind is filled with supreme peace. My window opens on the Himalaya. As soon as it was known that I would have to stay here for fifteen days, the mind turned to this spectacle. Since the house was built for men accustomed to sitting in chairs, one can see nothing if one squats on the floor. I, therefore, became shameless and seated myself on a bench. Now the eyes are stuck on the scene, so is the mind. Even while lying on the bench I can see something of the spectacle. On a clear day, the hills are covered with snow. ...

Blessings from
Bapu
CWMG *Vol. 80, p. 397; G*

To Amrit Kaur

Sevagram
19 July 1945

WE REACHED yesterday 2.30 Wardha and 4 p.m. Sevagram. We walked most of the way. This I am writing before the morning prayer.

You—all—surrounded us with lavish affection. May God bless you for it. I hope there is no more grief over Tofa's[132] departure from you. There should be none. ...

Bapu
CWMG *Vol. 81, p. 5*

23 July 1945[133]

... I HOPE you no longer grieve over Tofa's death. Don't have another pet animal if you can restrain yourself.

... Well, I hear today from the Viceroy that the Bihar young man[134] is to hang. It is a bad augury. I had forebodings as you know but had hoped otherwise. Let us see.

My love to you all.

Blessings from
Bapu
CWMG *Vol. 81, pp. 19–20; E*

Letter To Sucheta Kripalani[135]

Sevagram
27 July 1945

I HAVE gone through your Urdu letter. I like it; you should not understand it to mean that you are to give up writing in Hindi. You should write in both according to the occasion. Why did you fall ill?

It will be good if you go to Gulmarg first and get well. ... I do not write to the Professor[136]. This for him: He should write to me in Hindi or Urdu or Sindhi. Why does he write in English? Is it because he is a 'professor'?

Blessings from
Bapu

Swaraj Bhavan
Allahabad

CWMG *Vol. 81, p. 40; H*

To Abul Kalam Azad

Sevagram,
2 August 1945[137]

I AM not aware of any public service rendered by Begum Azad. If what I believe is true, there should not be any public memorial in her name. Some persons came to me. I told them to do whatever they wanted. I did not have the courage to say anything more to them. But I can speak to you. I would advise you to issue a nice Press statement saying that since Begum Azad had not rendered any public service you would not like any public memorial in her name. If my advice does not appeal to you, you will please reject it. The love we hold for each other demands no less.

CWMG *Vol. 81, p. 63; H*

To Kantilal Gandhi

Sevagram
5 August 1945

... YOU TWO have spared no effort in the service of Harilal. I had felt all along that Harilal would ultimately act as he had always done ... If you do not show the slightest softness to Harilal, he will leave Mysore. Try to find out, if you can, how he managed to obtain Rs 200 from the Maharaja of Mysore. ...

CWMG *Vol. 81, pp. 76-7; G*

Advice To Engineers[138]

Sevagram
On or before 16 August 1945

HOW USEFUL it would be if the engineers in India were to apply their ability to the perfecting of village tools and machines. This must not be beneath their dignity.

The Hindu *25-8-1945;* CWMG *Vol. 81, p. 130; E*

Telegram To Dipak Datta Choudhuri

Bombay
20 August 1945

GLAD MOTHER[139] passed away from pain to peace leaving you free to shoulder responsibility to country. Wrote you yesterday. Love.

Bapu
CWMG *Vol. 81, p. 145; E*

Telegram To Amiyanath Bose[140]

Poona
27 August 1945

I HAVE approached report[141] with suspicion. If you share suspicion announce and avoid ceremony.

Gandhi
CWMG *Vol. 81, p. 170; E*

To Dr Jivraj Mehta

Poona
3 September 1945

NOWADAYS THE villages around Sevagram are in the grip of cholera ...

What funeral rites can be performed for thousands of villagers? How to find wood for burning so many? Who can burn a hundred or two hundred daily and how much time will it take? If they

are buried, how much space will be required? How to cope with
the situation? ...

Blessings from
Bapu
CWMG *Vol. 81, p. 222; G*

To Manahar Diwan

Poona
7 September 1945

Bhai Manahar,

I have your telegram regarding Shastriji's[142] (death). I am very
happy that he has been released. My faith grown stronger that
it cannot be dharma to live or to keep someone alive somehow
or other.

Blessings from

Bapu
CWMG *Vol. 81, p. 235; H*

To Jawaharlal Nehru

Poona
5 October 1945

... I WANT that we two should understand each other fully. And this
for two reasons. Our bond is not merely political. It is much deeper.
I have no measure to fathom that depth. This bond can never be
broken. I therefore want that we should understand each other
thoroughly in politics as well. The second reason is that neither of
us considers himself as worthless. We both live only for India's
freedom, and will be happy to die too for that freedom. We do not
care for praise from any quarter. Praise or abuse are the same to us.
They have no place in the mission of service. Though I aspire to
live up to 125 years rendering service, I am nevertheless an old
man, while you are comparatively young. That is why I have said
that you are my heir. It is only proper that I should at least

understand my heir and my heir in turn should understand me. I shall then be at peace. ...

Blessings from
Bapu
CWMG Vol. 81, pp. 319–21; H

To Shamaldas Gandhi[143]

Poona
After 1 November 1945[144]

... YOU DID know about his (Sardar Patel) birthday[145]. If you did not, it is a grave offence.

I had thought you were a skilled journalist but you don't seem to be one. In a well-organized office, blocks of photographs are always kept ready. And so also most of the write-ups. Have a look at the special issue of *Janmabhoomi*. It is a very good.

'Vandemataram' Karyalaya
Bombay

CWMG Vol. 82, pp. 5–6; G

To K.M. Munshi

Poona
2 November 1945

Bhai Munshi,

On your recommendation I read *Prithvivallabh*[146]. According to me it owes its popularity not to the interest it sustains but to the meaning it contains. Besides, you have beautifully blended the beautiful languages descended from Sanskrit. But, as you have not been able to forget that history[147], can you, as a historian, forget the whole of Muslim history? Even if you can do so, can you make the whole of India forget it? Can you reverse the flow of water and make it go upward? After the British have left, will it be possible to wipe all the consequences of the British connection off history?

I have placed these two ideas before you with some hesitation, for I do not regard myself either as an expert on art or as a student of history. I, however, felt it was my duty to place before you the experience I have gained as, with my eyes open, I have wandered around the world. ...

CWMG *Vol. 82, pp. 9–10; G*

The Ganapati Festival

Poona[148]
2 November 1945

THE GANAPATI festival, and such others, are entirely of a political character and have nothing to do with religion. We cannot, therefore, celebrate them. But celebrations which are part of religious practice must be observed. For instance, in the Ashram Imam Saheb used to give, at my instance and request, the call to the faithful and we used to pray. The call is an essential practice in Islam. ...

... I do not approve of any leader's photograph being worshipped or of *arati* being performed in front of it, but I have not always opposed these things publicly though I did oppose them in my mind. Since such worship of human beings runs in the blood of Hindus, I have remained indifferent to them. In this matter I am the greatest culprit, as it is the worship of my image that has become most widespread. Since it cannot be prevented, do what I will, I derived a kind of false consolation when the worship of other leaders also started. This, of course, does not mitigate my guilt. It is very difficult to say where this thing will take us. There is some basis of truth in this practice, namely, that man himself being, in a sense, an image, he will always remain an image-worshipper. ...

Blessings from
Bapu
CWMG *Vol. 82, pp. 10–12; G*

Arun And Ila

Poona
8 November 1945

I GOT your letter and postcard. Arun[149] has taken away your letter and has not returned it. He is always in high spirits these days. He soon makes friends with everybody who comes here. So I do not now worry about him. Though he makes not effort, he does learn a little. There is, therefore, no need for any of you to worry about him just now.

... Tell Ila[150] I have no reason to remember her. She does not keep a single promise. She had said she would not leave me, but she went away. And she does not make haste to learn to write so that she can at least write to me. I hope she will now lose no time to learn to write letters to me in a beautiful hand. ...

Blessings from
Bapu
CWMG *Vol. 82, p. 44; G*

To Jawaharlal Nehru

Poona
13 November 1945

I was very happy with our talks yesterday. We could not have discussed more yesterday and it is my view that we shall not be able to finish our work at a single sitting. We must meet from time to time. I am so made that if I had the strength to travel about, I would seek you out, stay with you for a day or two, have some talk and then leave. Though I am not in a position to do that now, you may know I have done such things before. I want that people should know us as we know each other. If in the end we find that our paths are different, then so be it. ...

CWMG *Vol. 82, p. 71; H*

Asanas

Poona[151]
16 November 1945

... You can go up to 108 *namaskars*. Many asanas can be performed while doing *suryanamaskar*. It is largely for you to see which ones will suit you best. Consider also whether you should go up to 108 namaskars. There is no point in losing weight by starving. One has to reduce weight if one has put on any because of some disease, but that too not by starving oneself. If even with regular exercise and balanced diet you put on weight, let it be so. You need not worry about it in the least. ...

Blessings from
Bapu
CWMG *Vol. 82, pp. 83–4; G*

A 'Message'

Poona
19 November 1945

Bhai Khandubhai,

What message can a labourer give to a labour union? I have not heard of anyone sending a message to himself.

Blessings from
Bapu

Shri Khandubhai Desai
Majoor Mahajan Sangh
Lal Darwaja
Ahmedabad

CWMG *Vol. 82, p. 97; G*

To The Aga Khan

Khadi Pratishthan
Sodepur (Nr. Calcutta)
6 December 1945[152]

Dear Friend,

I write this about the little crematorium on your ground. You know perhaps that when I was a prisoner in the Aga Khan Palace in Yeravda the ashes of Mahadev Desai first and then of my wife were buried in your compound. The remains were cremated there at the Government's instance. They would not let me cremate them outside at the usual crematorium. Through Government's good grace and your people's forbearance, friends have been able to have access to the above crematorium. I have been pleading with the Government that they acquire the little plot and some right of way for devotees.

Now that you are in India, may I look to you to facilitate my request in the manner you think proper?

I hope you are keeping well and that we shall meet before you leave India again.

Yours sincerely,
M.K. Gandhi

H.H. The Aga Khan

CWMG Vol. 82, p. 169; E

Santiniketan And Politics

Santiniketan
20 December 1945

Q. Should Santiniketan allow itself to be drawn into political work?

A. I have no difficulty in saying that Santiniketan and Visva-Bharati ought not to be mixed up with politics. Every institution has its limitations. This institution should set limitations upon itself unless it is to be cheap. When I say that Santiniketan should not get mixed up with politics, I do not mean that it should have no political ideal. Complete independence must be its ideal, as it is that of the country. But that very ideal would require it to keep out of the present-day political turmoil ...

Q. In order to make Visva-Bharati really an international University, should we not try to increase the material resources of the university ...?

A. By material resources I suppose you mean finance. Let me then say that your question is addressed to a person who does not swear by material resources. 'Material resources' is after all a comparative term. For instance, I do not go without food and clothing. In my own way I have tried—more than perhaps any other man—to increase the level of material resources of the average man in India. But it is my firm conviction that Visva-Bharati will fail to attract the right type of talent and scholarship if it relies on the strength of the material resources or material attractions that it can offer. Its attraction must be moral or ethical, or else it will become just one out of the many educational institutions in India.

CWMG *Vol. 82, pp. 242–3; E*

To Rathindranath Tagore[153]

Khadi Pratishthan, Sodepur
22 December 1945

Chiranjivi Rathi,

Music in Santiniketan is charming, but has the professor there come to the conclusion that Bengali music is the last word in that direction? Has Hindustani music, i.e., music before and after Muslim period, anything to give to the world of music? If it has, it should have its due place at Santiniketan. Indeed, I would go so far as to say that Western music which has made immense strides should also blend with the Indian. Visva-Bharati is conceived as a world university. This is merely a passing thought of a layman to be transmitted to the music master there.

One question about music. I have a suspicion that perhaps there is more of music than warranted by life, or I will put the thought in another way. The music of life is in danger of being lost in the music of the voice. Why not the music of the walk, of the march, of every movement of ours, and of every activity? It was not an idle remark which I made at the Mandir service about the way in which boys and girls should know how to walk, how to march, how to sit, how to eat, in short how to perform every function of life. That is my idea of music. So far as I know, Gurudev stood for all this in his own person. ...

CWMG *Vol. 82, pp. 250–1; E*

A Thought For The Day

In Train on Way to Madras
20 January 1946

WITHOUT THE maximum possible non-attachment, it is inconceivable for anyone to live up to the age of 125 years.

On Nearing Madras
21 January 1946

IF THERE is any hope for a man, whose mind remains impure in spite of himself, it is Ramanama.

Madras
22 January 1946

ONLY THAT work which is done after anger has subsided can bear fruit.

Madras
23 January 1946

A FOREIGNER deserves to be welcomed only when he mixes with the indigenous people as sugar does with milk.

CWMG *Vol. 83, p. 407*

Silence

28 January 1946

... THE JOY one derives from silence is unique. How good it will be, if everyone observed silence for some time every day! Silence is not for some great men; I know that whatever one person is able to do can be done by everyone, given the effort. ...

Speech Read out at Prayer Meeting, Madras;
The Hindu *30 January 1946;* CWMG *Vol. 83, p. 44*

Canalizing Hatred

Sevagram
15 February 1946

HATRED IS in the air, and impatient lovers of the country will gladly take advantage of it, if they can, through violence, to further the cause of independence. I suggest that it is wrong at any time and everywhere ... The hypnotism of the Indian National Army has cast its spell upon us. Netaji's name is one to conjure with. His patriotism is second to none. (I use the present tense intentionally.) His bravery shines through all his actions. He aimed high but failed. Who has not failed? Ours is to aim high and to aim well. It is not given to everyone to command success. My praise and admiration can go no further. For I knew that his action was doomed to failure, and that I would have said so even if he had brought his I.N.A. victorious to India, because the masses would not have come into their own in this manner. The lesson that Netaji and his army brings to us is one of self-sacrifice, unity irrespective of class and community, and discipline. If our adoration will be wise and discriminating, we will rigidly copy this trinity of virtues, but we will as rigidly abjure violence. I would not have the I.N.A. man think, or say, that he and his can ever deliver the masses of India from bondage by force of arms. But, if he is true to Netaji and still more so to the country, he will spend himself in teaching the masses, men, women, and children to be brave, self-sacrificing, and united. Then we will be able to stand erect before the world. But, if he will merely act the armed soldier, he will only lord it over the masses and the fact that he will be a volunteer will not count for much. I, therefore, welcome the declaration made by Capt. Shah Nawaz that, to be worthy of Netaji, on having come to Indian soil, he will act as a humble soldier of non-violence in Congress ranks.

Harijan *24-2-1946;* CWMG *Vol. 83, pp. 133 and 135; E*

At Prayer Meeting

Bombay
18 February 1946

THERE IS a time for laughing and shouting and a time for observing silence and being serious. I have often said that a people who want to be free should learn to mount to the gallows with a smile upon the face. But laughter becomes an offence against decorum, if it is out of season. Similarly shouting out of season is an exhibition of bad manners. It becomes a man to remember his Maker all the twenty-four hours ...

... In this land of ours, fabulously rich in natural resources, there is the lofty Himalayas with its everlasting snows where, they say, dwells the Lord of the Universe. It has mighty rivers like the Ganges. but owing to our neglect and folly, the year's rains are allowed to run down into the Bay of Bengal and the Arabian Sea. If all this water was trapped and harnessed to irrigational purposes by the construction of dams[154] and tanks, there should be no famine or food shortage in India Similarly cloth shortage can immediately be remedied by planting a miniature mill in every home in the form of a spinning-wheel or a takli. That would give us all the cloth that we need almost for nothing. I have cried myself hoarse in pressing this solution on the Government ...

... There is an inexhaustible reservoir of water in the bowels of the earth. It should be tapped, even though we may have to dig two thousand feet deep for it, and used for growing food. We may not blame fate before we have exhausted all available means for combating a threatening calamity. ...

Harijan *3-3-1946;* CWMG *Vol. 83, pp. 151–3*

Fisheries

Nature Cure Clinic
6 Todiwala Road, Poona
21 February 1946

Dear Mr Abell[155],

Here are a few more suggestions to meet the food situation. ...

... Fish abounds in the seas around the coasts of India. The war is over; there are innumerable small and medium-sized vessels which were used for doing patrol and guard duties along our shores for the last five years. The Royal Indian Navy could arrange about staffing these with the Department of Fisheries giving all assistance. If everything and anything can be done during a war, why not a peace-time war effort? Dry fish does even now form part of the normal diet of a great number of people who are very poor that is when it is available and they can afford to buy it.

All public gardens should immediately by law made to start growing vegetables. Squads of army personnel should be put to work here too ...

The distribution of food should be through co-operative societies or similar organizations.

All food parcels to friends or relatives in Britain or elsewhere abroad should be stopped as also the export of groundnuts, oils, oil-cakes, etc.

All stocks of foodstuffs in the hands of the military should be released forthwith and no distinction should be made between military and civil ranks. ...

Yours sincerely,
M.K. Gandhi
CWMG *Vol. 83, pp. 161–2; E*

Two Requests[156]

Poona
25 February 1946

A FRIEND suggests that I should resume writing my autobiography from the point where I left off and, further, that I should write a treatise on the science of ahimsa.

I never really wrote an autobiography. What I did write was a series of articles narrating my experiments with truth which were later published in book form. More than twenty[157] years have elapsed since then. What I have done or pondered during this interval has not been recorded in chronological order. I would love to do so but have I the leisure? I have resumed the publication of *Harijan* in the present trying times as a matter of duty. It is with difficulty that I can cope with this work. How can I find time to bring the remainder of my experiments with truth up to date? But if it is God's will that I should write them, he will surely make my way clear.

To write a treatise on the science of ahimsa is beyond my powers. I am not built for academic writings. ...

Harijan 3-3-1946; CWMG *Vol. 83, pp. 179–80; G*

Statement To The Press

Poona
26 February 1946

I CONGRATULATE Shrimati Aruna Asaf Ali on her courageous refutation[158] of my statement on the happenings in Bombay[159]. Except for the fact that she represents not only herself but also a fairly large body of underground workers, I would not have noticed her refutation, if only because she is a daughter of mine not less so because not born to me or because she is a rebel. I had the pleasure of meeting her on several occasions while she was underground. I admired her bravery, resourcefulness, and burning love of the country. But my admiration stopped there. I did not like her being underground. I do not appreciate any underground activity. I know that millions cannot go underground. Millions need not. A select few may fancy that they will bring swaraj to the millions by secretly directing their activity. ...

Harijan 3-3-1946; CWMG Vol. 83, p. 182; E

To C. Rajagopalachari

Poona
11 March 1946

IT IS just 6.15 a.m. I am to be off to Bombay by 7.30 a.m.

If we discover a mistake, must we continue it?[160] We began making love in English—a mistake. Must it express itself only by repeating the initial mistake? You have the cake and eat it also.

Love is love under a variety of garbs—even when the lovers are dumb. Probably it is fullest when it is speechless. I had thought, under its gentle unfelt compulsion, you will easily glide into Hindustani and thus put the necessary finishing touch to your service of Hindustani. But let it be as you will, not I.[161]

I do not like your despondence. You have to be thoroughly well. Why not come to me? I hope to return in five or six days.

This *tamasha* will vanish leaving the water of life cleaner for the agitation. If it does not, what then?

Ambudan.[162]

Bapu[163]
CWMG Vol. 83, pp. 238–9

Talk With Agatha Harrison

Bombay
On or before 16 March 1946

Agatha Harrison: Won't you ask people to grow flowers on a small piece of land? Colour and beauty are necessary to the soul as food is to the body[164].

MKG: No, I won't. Why can't you see the beauty of colour in vegetables? And then there is beauty in the speckless sky. But no, you want the colours of the rainbow which is a mere optical illusion. ...

Harijan 7-4-1946; CWMG Vol. 83, p. 265; E

The British Cabinet Mission

Birla House[165]
Bombay
11, 15, and 16 March 1946

MKG (at prayer meeting): The British Cabinet Delegation will soon be in our midst. To suspect their *bona fides* in advance would be a variety of weakness. As a brave people, it is our duty to take at its face value the declaration of the British Ministers, that they are coming to restore to India what is her due. If a debtor came to your house in contrition to repay his debt, would it not be your duty to welcome him? Would it not be unmanly to treat him with insult and humiliation in remembrance of an injustice?

P. MG: LP *Vol. I, B1, pp. 163–4*

To C. Rajagopalachari

Poona
17 March 1946

YOUR DEAR letter. The Tamil lesson is good. I hope I shall not forget *anbu* and *ambu*.[166] Does not the latter also mean lotus? What is the meaning of *anbudan*? Or is the final letter 'm'? ...

When are you coming to Poona?

Romba anbudan[167]

Bapu

(P.S.) Can you use romba as I have?

CWMG *Vol. 83, pp. 275–6; E*

Cable To J.C. Smuts

Poona
18 March 1946

Field Marshal Smuts
Union of South Africa, Cape Town

Your Asiatic policy requires overhauling. It ill becomes you. ...

Your and South Africa's sincere friend,
Gandhi
CWMG *Vol. 83, p. 280; E*

Telegram To Lord Wavell

Express   Poona
                                                    18 March 1946

H.E. Viceroy

Viceroy's Camp

Please accept my sympathy in your loss[168] which may God enable you and Lady Wavell and your daughter bear with fortitude.

Gandhi

CWMG *Vol. 83, p. 280; E*

Cable To J.C. Smuts

Poona

22 March 1946

Field Marshal Smuts

Cape Town

Union of South Africa

Thanks for wire. India is expected to get independence this year. If you believe it wait till then. Cloistered civilisation like cloistered virtue. Your good intention undoubted. Premise appears faulty. India's protest against inferior status. Proposed franchise doubtful privilege. Land tenure is segregation. Shall respect your wish avoid publicity. ...

Gandhi

CWMG *Vol. 83, p. 298*

Talk With Army Men

Uruli-Kanchan[169]

After 22 March 1946[170]

Army Men: We are soldiers, but we are soldiers of Indian freedom.

MKG: I am glad to hear that. For, so far you have mostly been instrumental in the suppression of Indian freedom. Have you heard of Jallianwala Bagh?

Q.: Oh yes. But those days are past. ... What would be our position when India is Independent?

MKG: Why, you will fully share that Independence and breathe the air of freedom with your countrymen. Independent India will have need of you. You have had military training. You will give India the benefit of that training. You have learnt the lesson of *camaraderie* under common danger. It would be a bad day, if the moment that peril is lifted, the lesson is lost. But in free India you won't be pampered as you are today. You won't have these lavish privileges with which a foreign Government bribes you at the expense of India's poor. India is destitute. You cannot serve her unless you are prepared to share her destitution. ... Unless you are prepared to forgo your privileges, you will feel sorry when Independence comes, and sigh for the return of old times and old masters.

Q.: There was a time when we were not allowed to read any civil newspaper. And now we go and tell our officers that we are going to see our greatest leader, and no one dares to stop us.

MKG: I know, there is a new ferment and a new awakening among all the army ranks today. Not a little of the credit for this happy change belongs to Netaji Bose. I disapprove of his method, but he had rendered a signal service to India by giving the Indian soldier a new vision and a new ideal.

Q.: How anybody can think of dividing India into two, three, or more parts, we army men are at a loss to understand. We know only one India for which we have fought and shed our blood.

MKG: Well, it requires all sorts to make the world.

Q.: May we shout slogans?

MKG: Well, you may.[171]

Harijan 7-4-1946; CWMG Vol. 83, pp. 303–4; E

Why One More Burden?[172]

Uruli-Kanchan
25 March 1946

WHY HAVE I got involved in nature cure in the evening of my life? This question is being asked of me by several people. Had I not enough work on my hands already? Could anyone expect me to add to my existing burdens? All these are pertinent questions demanding any careful consideration. But they do not evoke any echo within me. The still small voice within me whispers: 'Why bother about what others say? ...

Harijan 31-3-1946; CWMG Vol. 83, p. 318

Vithabai

I would advise this, she should take sun-bath in the nude, followed by a hip-bath and a friction-bath in cold water ... Complete cure is rather difficult.

Hira

She should chew fruit and throw away the residue; take milk or butter-milk; also hip-bath and friction-bath; mud-poultice on the abdomen ...

Arjun

Urine will pass regularly, if he is seated in hot and cold water by turns.

Salu

Had she come yesterday? She should be given sun-bath even in this heat so that she perspires and the boils dry up. I feel that she might derive some benefit, if she lies down naked with a wet towel on her head. While doing so—lying down—she should constantly utter Ramanama. ...

Vithu

... His asthma can be brought under control, if he does regular pranayama[173].

Hirunana

Fruit-juices for two days; then fruit-juice mixed with milk. Sun-bath, hip-bath, and friction-bath. If the motion is not clear, he should try the syringe after two days. Mud-poultices. Tomato juice, if tomatoes are available. ...

CWMG Vol. 83, pp. 320–1; G

Netaji[174]

Uruli-Kanchan
30 March 1946

SOME YEARS ago it was announced[175] in the newspapers that Subhas Chandra Bose had died. I believed the report. Later the news was proved to have been incorrect. Since then I have had a feeling that Netaji could not leave us until his dream of swaraj had been fulfilled.

... On the other hand, there is strong evidence[176] to counteract the feeling. The British Government is party to that evidence. Capt. Habibur Rahman has said, he was present at the time of Netaji's death and has brought back his charred wrist watch. Another of his companions, Shri Iyer, met and told me that my instinct was wrong and I should abandon the feeling that Subhas Chandra was alive. In the face of these proofs I appeal to everyone to forget what I have said and, believing in the evidence before them, reconcile themselves to the fact that Netaji has left us. All man's ingenuity is as nothing before the might of the One God. He alone is Truth and nothing else stands.

Harijan 7-4-1946; CWMG Vol. 83, p. 339

At Prayer Meeting

New Delhi[177]
5 April 1946

... NETAJI WAS like a son to me. I came to know him as a lieutenant full of promise under the late Deshabandhu Das. His last message to the I.N.A. was that whilst on foreign soil they had fought with arms; on their return to India, they would have to serve the country as soldiers of non-violence under the guidance and leadership of the Congress. The message which the I.N.A. has for India is not adoption of the method of appeal to arms for settling disputes (it has been tried and found wanting), but of cultivating non-violence, unity, cohesion, and organization.

Though the I.N.A. failed in their immediate objective, they have a lot to their credit of which they might well be proud. Greatest among these was to gather under one banner men from all religions and races of India and to infuse into them the spirit of solidarity and oneness to the utter exclusion of all communal or parochial sentiment. It is an example which we should all emulate. ...

Far more potent than the strength of the sword is the strength of satyagraha. I said so to the I.N.A. men and they were happy to tell me, as I was to hear, that they had realized this and would hereafter strive to serve India as true soldiers of non-violence under the Congress flag.

New Delhi, 8 April 1946; CWMG Vol. 83, pp. 370–1; E

Discussion With Woodrow Wyatt[178]

New Delhi
13 April 1946

Woodrow Wyatt: Do you think we are getting off your backs at last?

MKG: I have no doubt as to the sincerity of your intention. The question is whether you will have the strength and courage needed for it.

WW: We must not precipitate a solution. We must let India decide for herself. At the same time, one does not want to leave the country to chaos when an unprecedented famine threatens it.

MKG: Your difficulty will remain so long as you retain the belief that your rule has benefited India. None of us believes it.

WW: One or two have testified to the contrary.

MKG: That is neither here nor there. I too believed it once. Such benefit as has really accrued to India is not part of foreign rule but is the result of contact with a robust people. The good is incidental, the evil of foreign rule is inherent and far outweighs the good. Communal divisions in India can be demonstrably proved to be a British creation. Even famine as we know it today is your creation[179].

... Famines in India today are not due to rain or lack of it merely, but due to the fact that India is ill-equipped to tide over the dry periods. Nothings has been done to safeguard her population against the threat of recurring famines.

WW: Would India have been better equipped, if Britain had not been here?

MKG: Yes, there would have been no railways[180]. If there were no railways, etc., we would be living in a natural state as they used to in England and Europe in the Middle Ages when every feudal baron had his castle with its stocks of grain and water. Before the advent of railways in India, every village had its granary. In that sense we were better equipped. Moreover we had our system of domestic crafts to fall back upon, if crops failed. Now railways have depleted the country side of its stocks and killed the handicrafts. Whatever cash the cultivator gets in return for his produce runs through his fingers like water, thanks to the invasion of his economy by the revenue collector and the imported foreign goods without which he thinks he can no longer do. The British have told him: 'Do not stock grain, do not hoard silver.' There is no provision made for a deficit period. Railways have become a snare, cheap transport, a trap.

    ... A few lakhs might be killed in internecine warfare but, real peace will come at last.

WW: But it is a big responsibility to leave India faced with anarchy.

MKG: Not a bigger responsibility than you were prepared to face during the war out of strategic considerations.

WW: Supposing we imposed what we considered to be a just solution and went?

MKG: All would be upset.

WW: So it must be left to India's decision?

MKG: Yes, leave it to the Congress and the League.

WW: And what happens after the British leave?

MKG: Probably there will be arbitration ... But thee might be a blood-bath. It will be settled in two days by non-violence, if I can persuade India to go my way, or the ordeal may last longer. Even so it would not be worse than what it is under the British rule ...

WW: Suppose we set up an Interim Government and went? ... If the Congress concedes Pakistan, it will then be their job.

MKG: That will be a good beginning. Even if the whole of India goes under the League in this way, it won't matter. It won't be the Pakistan of Jinnah's conception. India would then have something to live for and die for.

WW: Whom shall we put in the place of the present Government?

MKG: You can ask the elected legislators of nominate their representatives. ... Or, as I have already said, you let Jinnah nominate out of the present legislators.

WW: Supposing the Muslim League starts destruction, will you jail them?

MKG: I won't. But, may be, the Congress will decide to fight. It will then be a clean fight, not the cowardly hit-and-run that you see today or the taking of a hundred lives for one *a la* the British[181].

Harijan *19-5-1946;* CWMG *Vol. 83, pp. 404–6*

Question Box

New Delhi
14 April 1946

Q. On what principle is the question of the salaries of ministers in Congress majority provinces going to be settled this time? Does the Karachi resolution in this regard still hold? If the question is to be settled on the basis of the present high prices, is it possible, within the limits of their revenues, for the provincial budgets to increase the pays of all their servants threefold? If not, will it be proper for the ministers to be paid Rs 1,500 while a *chaprasi* or a teacher is told to make the two ends meet on Rs 15 and 12 p.m. and not make a fuss about it because Congress has to run the administration?

A. The question is apt. Why should a minister draw Rs 1500 and a chaprasi or a teacher Rs 15 p.m.? But the question cannot be solved by the mere raising of it. Such differences have existed for ages. Why should an elephant require an enormous quantity of food and a mere grain suffice for the ant? The question carries its own answer. God gives to each one according to his need. If we could as definitely know the variations in the needs of men as those of the elephant and the ant, no doubts would arise. Experience tells us that differences in requirements do exist in society. But we do not know the law governing them. All therefore that is possible today is to try to reduce the differences as far as possible. ...

Harijan *21-4-1946;* CWMG *Vol. 84, pp. 5–6*

Talk With A Zamindar

Before 23 April 1946

Zamindar: Where shall we stand when India is independent?
MKG: You will be as free as any scavenger ...

Z: Many ancient *zamindaris*[182] existed long before the advent of the British ...

MKG: Anything that is ancient and consistent with moral values has a title to be retained. *Per contra* anything that does not conform to moral values has to go. Wrong has no prescriptive right to exist merely because it is of long standing.

Z: We have no objection to an independent Indian Government abolishing all manner of vested interests. But let there be no discrimination against the zamindars especially.

MKG: A just man need have no fear of any kind from an independent India. India may, however, fall into unjust hands. Every Congressman is not an angel, nor is everyone who is not a Congressman a devil. Let us hope that, if Congress comes into power, it will try to be more than just.

Z: We only wish that nothing should be done without consulting us.

MKG: That goes without saying[183].

CWMG Vol. 84, pp. 50–1

On Independence

New Delhi
29 April 1946

... INDIA WILL have to decide whether attempting to become a military power she would be content to become, at least for some years, a fifth-rate power in the world without a message ... or whether she will by further refining and continuing her non-violent policy prove herself worthy of being the first nation in the world using her hard-won freedom for delivery of the earth from the burden[184] which is crushing it in spite of the so-called victory[185].

Harijan 5-5-1946; CWMG Vol. 84, pp. 80–1; E

Letter To Manilal Gandhi

Simla
9 May 1946

... PARTING IS such a sweet sorrow. I felt moved to tears when bidding good-bye to you all, but soon calmed myself. My step, however, was perfectly right. I am experiencing its sweet fruits. I have no time to write at length about it.

... Your dharma is to return to South Africa ...

Blessings from
Bapu
CWMG *Vol. 84, p. 130; G*

Valmikis Of Simla

Simla
13 May 1946

READERS MUST know that Valmiki is another word for Bhangi. Their living quarters in Simla are deplorable. No one bothers about them. ...

Harijan *19-5-1946;* CWMG *Vol. 84, p. 148; H*

Breakdown At Simla

New Delhi
16 May 1946

(THE CABINET Mission held many rounds of discussions with Indian leaders across the political divide. Though it could not obtain a consensus, it announced an award for the long term. Rejecting Pakistan as also Jinnah's demand for Hindu-Muslim parity in the proposed Central Assembly, it envisaged a Union dealing with Foreign Affairs, Defence, and Communications. Other subjects and powers were to vest with the provinces. Existing provincial legislators and rulers of princely states were to send representatives to a Constituent Assembly, the former reflecting Hindu-Muslim ratios. But most significantly, the award envisaged a grouping together of Muslim majority States, with the right to, as the League interpreted it, to secede from the Union. The award was, therefore, not without dangers and ambiguities.)

After four days of searching examination of the State Paper issued by the Cabinet Mission and the Viceroy on behalf of the British Government, my conviction abides that it is the best document the British Government could have produced in the circumstances.

My compliment, however, does not mean that what is best from the British standpoint is also best or even good from the Indian. Their best may possibly be harmful. ...

P. MG: LP *Vol. I, B1, pp. 204–5*

Talk With A Friend

Mussoorie
After 28 May 1946

An English friend: If all nations were armed with the atom bomb would not they refrain from using it as it would mean absolute destruction for all concerned.

MKG: They would not. The violent man's eyes would light up with the prospect of the much greater amount of destruction and death which he could now wreak.

Harijan *23-6-194;* CWMG *Vol. 84, p. 225; E*

Talk With Foreign Press Correspondents[186]

Mussoorie
After 28 May 1946

Q: What about the big cities like Bombay and Calcutta?

MKG: ... The blood of the villages is the cement with which the edifice of the cities is built. ...

Q: What would you do if you were made a dictator of India for one day?

MKG: I would not accept it in the first place, but if I did become a dictator for one day I would spend it in cleaning the hovels of the Harijans in Delhi. It is disgraceful that under the very nose of the Viceroy such poverty and squalor should exist as there is in the Harijan quarters, which are, virtually, the stables of the Viceroy's House. And why does the Viceroy need such a big house? If I had my way I would turn it into a hospital.

(He then gave the instance of South African President Kruger whose residence in Pretoria was not even as good as Birlaji's 'Hermitage' in which he was staying in Mussoorie).

Q: Well, sir, suppose they continue your dictatorship for the second day?

MKG: The second day would be a prolongation of the first ...

Adapted from CWMG Vol. 84, pp. 226–7; E

Snakes And Scorpions

Mussoorie
29 May 1946

... A correspondent asks:

Q: You had put 27 questions to Shri Raichandbhai from Durban. One of these questions was: 'What should a seeker do when a snake attacks him?' His answer was: 'He should not kill the snake and, if it bites, he should let it do so.' How is it that you speak differently now?

MKG: ... My non-violence is not merely kindness to all living creatures. The emphasis laid on the sacredness of subhuman life in Jainism is understandable. But that can never mean that one is to be kind to this (subhuman) life in preference to human life ...

Raichandbhai's advice to me was that if I had courage, if I wanted to see God face to face, I should let myself be bitten by a snake instead of killing it. I have never killed a snake before or after receiving that letter. That is no matter of credit for me. My ideal is to be able to play with snakes and scorpions fearlessly. But it is merely a wish so far. Whether and when it will be realized I do not know. Everywhere I have let my people kill both. I could have prevented them if I had wished. But how could I? I did not have the courage to take them up with my own hands and teach my companions a lesson in fearlessness. I am ashamed that I could not do so. But my shame could not benefit them or me. ...

Harijan 9-6-1946; CWMG Vol. 84, pp. 230–2

Question Box—Is Lying Ever Justifiable?

Mussoorie
31 May 1946

Q. What do you say to the following from Bertrand Russell? 'I once in the course of a country walk saw a tired fox at the last stages of exhaustion still forcing himself to run. A few minutes afterwards I saw the hunt. They asked me if I had seen the fox, and I said I had. They asked me which way he had gone, and I lied to them. I do not think I should have been a better man if I had told the truth.'

A. Bertrand Russell is a great writer and philosopher. With all respect to him I must dissent from the view attributed to him. He made the initial mistake of admitting that he had seen the fox. He was not bound to answer the first question. He could even refused to answer the second question unless he deliberately wanted to put the hunt off the track. I have always maintained that nobody is bound always to answer quetions that may be put to him. Truth-telling admits of no exceptions.

CWMG Vol. 84, p. 243

Take Care Of Pennies

Mussoorie
8 June 1946

I HAVE discovered honourable members of Assemblies using most expensive embossed notepaper even for private use. So far as I know, office stationery cannot be used for private purposes such as writing to friends or relatives or for letters from members of Assemblies to constituents outside matters of public business. So far as I know, this is a universal objection in every part of the world.

But for this poor country my objection goes deeper. The stationery I refer to is too expensive for us. Englishmen belonging to the most expensive country in the world and who had to flourish on the awe they could inspire in us introduced expensive and massive buildings for offices and bungalows requiring for their upkeep an army of servants and hangers-on. If we copy their style and habits we will be ruined ourselves and carry the country in this ruin. And what was tolerated in the case of the conquerors will not be tolerated in ours. There is, too, paper shortage. ...

Harijan 16-6-1946; CWMG Vol. 84, p. 308

A Nameless Fear[187]

New Delhi
Before 12 June 1946[188]

A NAMELESS fear has seized me that all is not well. As a result, I feel paralysed. But I will not corrupt your mind by communicating my unsupported suspicions to you.

Harijan 23-6-1946; CWMG Vol. 84, p. 319

'Soldier—Dare To Do The Right'

Bhangi Colony, Reading Road,
New Delhi
13 June 1946[189]

Dear Friend[190],

... You are a great soldier—a daring soldier. Dare to do the right. You must make your choice of one horse or the other. So far as I can see you will never succeed in riding two at the same time. Choose the names submitted either by the Congress or the League. For God's sake do not make an incompatible mixture and in trying to do so produce a fearful explosion: Anyway, fix your time limit and tell us all to leave when that limit is over.

I hope I have made my meaning clear.

Yours sincerely,
M.K. Gandhi
CWMG Vol. 84, pp. 328–9; E

To Sir Stafford Cripps

New Delhi
13 June 1946

Dear Sir Stafford,

... You are handling the most difficult task of your life. As I see it the Mission is playing with fire. If you have courage you will do what I suggested from the very beginning ... Everyday you pass here coquetting now with the Congress, now with the League and again with the Congress, wearing yourself away. This will not do. Either you swear by what is right or by what the exigencies of British policy may dictate. In either case bravery is required. ...

Your sincerely,
M.K. Gandhi
CWMG Vol. 84, pp. 330–1; E

At Prayer Meeting

New Delhi
16 June 1946

WHAT IS surprising is that instead of following the democratic procedure of inviting the one or the other party to form a national government, the Viceroy and the Cabinet Mission have decided to impose a government of their choice on the country. The result may well be an incompatible and explosive mixture. There are, however, two ways of looking at a picture. You can look upon it from the bright side or you can look upon it from the dark.

The Bombay Chronicle *17-6-1946;* Harijan, *23-6-1946;*
CWMG Vol. 84 p. 340; H

New Delhi
16/17 June 1946

PERSONALLY, I believe in looking at the bright side. Thus regarded, what appear to be blemishes in the Viceregal announcement would be seen to be really its beauty. You should bear with the Mission, too. They have inherited the tradition of imperialism which they cannot outgrow all at once ... We must not blame them for not throwing it overboard overnight. Let us trust their *bona fides*. Let us not act upon mere suspicion.

(At night he woke up at half past one and dictated for the Working Committee the draft of a letter to the Viceroy. He particularly emphasized in it four points[191].)

(1) The League being avowedly a Muslim organization could not include any non-Muslim representative in its list; (2) the Congress would include a Congress Muslim in its list; (3) the

League could not have any say in the selection of any names outside those belonging to its quota of five Muslims. This would mean that, in the event of a vacancy occurring among the seats allotted by the Congress to the minorities, the Congress alone would have the right to select names to fill up those vacancies as it claimed to represent all sections; and (4) the Interim Government should be regarded as being responsible to the elected representatives in the Assembly.

(The Working Committee, in its afternoon session on the 17th, was un-enamoured by the Viceroy's proposal but did not quite say 'No' to it.)

P, MG: LP *Vol. I, B1, p. 219*

At Congress Working Committee Meeting

New Delhi
18 June 1946

CONGRESS IS a national organization and it should not give up its national character. In view of that character it must have a right to put forward its claim to suggest names of six Congressmen in the list of fourteen. Amongst the Congressmen there must be one nationalist Muslim and one woman. ...[192]

CWMG *Vol. 84, p. 345; H*

At Prayer Meeting

New Delhi
19 June 1946

IF I were appointed dictator for a day in the place of the Viceroy, I would stop all newspapers.

He added with a smile and a wink:

With the exception of *Harijan* of course.

Incidentally, if I were to rename my weekly I would call it not *Harijan* but 'Bhangi' i.e., sweeper, that being more in tune with my present temper and the need of the hour as I understood it. ...

CWMG *Vol. 84, p. 347; H*

Draft Letter To Lord Wavell[193]

New Delhi
24 June 1946

I HAVE just received the telephone message sent on your behalf asking me to communicate immediately the decision of the Congress Working Committee in regard to the proposals for the Provisional Government[194]. The decision was in fact taken yesterday but we felt that it would be better if we wrote to you fully on all aspects of the proposals made by you and the Cabinet Delegation The Working Committee have been sitting almost continuously and will be meeting at 2 p.m. again today. After full consideration and deliberation they have been reluctantly obliged to decide against the acceptance of the Interim Government proposals as framed by you. ...

CWMG *Vol. 84, p. 364; E*

At Congress Working Committee Meeting—II[195]

24 June 1946

My mind is in a fog. ...

CWMG *Vol. 84, pp. 364–5; H*

At Prayer Meeting[196]

New Delhi
24 June 1946

NEWS HAS been received from South Africa that hooligans have attacked the satyagrahis again. A reverend English clergyman tried to dissuade them but without success. No satyagrahi was seriously hurt. The police, according to Reuter, have not arrested any of the hooligans. Let us put up with these things patiently. It is also reported that the satyagrahis have not retaliated. This is pure satyagraha. If the satyagrahis remain firm till the end they are sure to come out victorious.

Hindustan *25-6-1946;* CWMG *Vol. 84, p. 366; H*

Jayaprakash Narayan[197]

New Delhi
Before 25 June 1946

JAYAPRAKASH IS an outstanding general in India's fight for freedom. Any country will be proud of such jewels among men. Like Jawahar and Subhas, he too is impatient to a degree, but this is a virtue considering the prevailing circumstances. I adore Jayaprakash.

CWMG *Vol. 84, p. 368; H*

Dr Lohia In Goa

New Delhi
26 June 1946

IT WOULD appear from newspaper reports that Dr Lohia[198] went to Goa at the invitation of Goans and was served with an order to refrain from making speeches. According to Dr Lohia's statement, for 188 years now, the people of Goa have been robbed of the right to hold meetings and form organizations. Naturally he defied the order. He has thereby rendered a service to the cause of civil liberty and especially to the Goans. The little Portuguese settlement which merely exists on the sufferance of the British Government can ill afford to ape its bad manners. In free India Goa cannot be allowed to exist as a separate entity in opposition to the laws of the free State. Without a shot being fired, the people of Goa will be able to claim and receive the rights of citizenship of the free State. ...

Harijan *30-6-1946;* CWMG *Vol. 84, p. 373; E*

With Louis Fischer Again

New Delhi
26 June 1946

LF: You should turn your attention to the West.
MKG: I? I have not convinced (even) India. There is violence all around us. I am a spent bullet.

LF: Since the end of the Second World War, many Europeans and Americans were conscious of a spiritual emptiness. You might fill a corner of it.

MKG: But I am an Asiatic. A mere Asiatic.

(*He laughed, then after a pause*)

Jesus was an Asiatic.

Reconstructed from Fischer's The Life of Mahatma Gandhi, *p. 454, CWMG Vol. 84, p. 377; E*

At The Working Committee

New Delhi

25 June 1946

GANDHI ATTENDED the Working Committee meeting. He asked Pyarelal to read out the note which he had written to Cripps last night and then addressed the Members as follows:

I admit defeat. You are not bound to act upon my unsupported suspicion. You should follow my intuition only if it appeals to your reason. Otherwise you should take an independent course. I shall now leave with your permission. You should follow the dictates of your reason.

Pyarelal writes in *Mahatma Gandhi: Last Phase*, Vol. I, pp. 227–8: A hush fell over the gathering. Nobody spoke for some time. The Maulana Saheb with his unfailing alertness at once took in the situation. 'Is there any need to detain Bapu any further?' he asked. Everybody was silent. Everybody understood. In that hour of decision they had no use for Bapu. They decided to drop the pilot. Bapu returned to his residence ... The final phase of negotiations with the Cabinet Mission marked the beginning of that cleavage between Gandhiji and some of his closest colleagues which in the final phase of the transfer of power left them facing different ways ...

On Jinnah

New Delhi

25 June 1946

THE QUAID-E-AZAM was not invited to form the Interim Government without the Congress, something he had expected the Cabinet Mission and the Viceroy to do. He was informed that para 8 of the statement would take effect. (This para had said that if either of the two major parties was unwilling to join in the setting up of a Coalition Government, the Viceroy would form an Interim Government.)

MKG: They (the Cabinet Mission) should not have dealt with him (Jinnah) in that legalistic manner. ... He is a great Indian and the recognized leader of a great organization.

P. MG: LP Vol. I, B1, pp. 239–40

At Prayer Meeting[199]

Poona
30 June 1946

AN ACCIDENT had taken place in the middle of the night, while I was fast asleep. Some persons had placed boulders on the rails between Karjat and Neral and but for the presence of mind of the engine driver, the train would have been derailed and no one could say who would have survived to tell the tale[200]. But no one can kill you unless God wills it.

This is perhaps the seventh occasion when a merciful Providence has rescued me from the very jaws of death. I have injured no man, nor have I borne enmity to any. Why should anyone have wished to take my life is more than I can understand. But there it was.

CWMG Vol. 84, p. 392; H

A Remark[201]

Poona
On or after 30 June 1946[202]

I SEE now how splendid I shall look when I am dead. I have already known how I shall look before my death. Such is this lucky age!

CWMG Vol. 84, p. 393; G

Atom Bomb And Ahimsa

Poona
1 July 1946

... SO FAR as I can see, the atomic bomb has deadened the finest feeling that has sustained mankind for ages. There used to be the so called laws of war which made it tolerable. Now we know the naked truth. War knows no law except that of might. ...

Harijan *7-7-1946;* CWMG *Vol. 84, pp. 393–4*

To Morarji Desai[203]

Poona
1 July 1946

I WAS somewhat alarmed on hearing about (the incidents at) Ahmedabad[204]. I was aware of the *Rath-yatra*[205] day. They must have anticipated a skirmish. Why did the police not take precautionary measures? Does not the police now belong to the people? Why did they not seek the people's co-operation before hand? Our real defence force ought to be the people. Why call the military for such tasks? The people ought to have been forewarned that they would not get the help of the military. The State too may not rule with the help of the military. This could not be. Now realize your mistake and start afresh. Withdraw the military if you can. If you find it risky to withdraw the military immediately let them do policing. They may not carry rifles, and if they carry bayonets these should be used sparingly. Don't mind if a few[206] have to die. They have been trained to act like monkeys. Under your administration they should cease to be monkeys and become human beings. Think about all this. Don't do anything only because I am saying it. Do what you are convinced about. ...

Blessings from
Bapu

Sjt. Morarji Desai
Poona

CWMG *Vol. 84, p. 396; G*

At A.I.C.C.

Bombay
7 July 1946

... A POLISH lady[207] has sent me a note just today saying that all Europeans had received secret instructions to leave India as the

British army would no longer be able to give them adequate protection. If it is so, it is a sad reflection on us. We should be unworthy of the name of satyagrahi if even an English child did not feel secure in our midst. ...

The Hindu *8-7-1946;* Harijan *14 & 21-7-1945;* CWMG *Vol. 84, p. 422; E*

Jews And Palestine

Panchgani
14 July 1946

... I DO believe that the Jews have been cruelly wronged by the world. 'Ghetto' is, so far as I am aware, the name given to Jewish locations in many parts of Europe. But for their heartless persecution, probably no question of a return to Palestine would ever have arisen. The world should have been their home, if only for the sake of their distinguished contribution to it.

But, in my opinion, they have erred grievously in seeking to impose themselves on Palestine with the aid of America and Britain and now with the aid of naked terrorism. Their citizenship of the world should have and would have made them honoured guests of any country. Their thrift, their varied talent, their great industry should have made them welcome anywhere. It is a blot on the Christian world that they have been singled out, owing to a wrong reading of the New Testament, for prejudice against them. 'If an individual Jew does a wrong, the whole Jewish world is to blame for it.' If an individual Jew like Einstein makes a great discovery or another composes unsurpassable music, the merit goes to the authors and not to the community to which they belong.

No wonder that my sympathy goes out to the Jews in their unenviably sad plight. But one would have thought adversity would teach them lessons of peace. Why should they depend upon American money or British arms for forcing themselves on an unwelcome land? Why should they resort to terrorism to make good their forcible landing in Palestine?. ...

Harijan *21-7-1946;* CWMG *Vol. 84, pp. 440-1*

Interview To Louis Fischer[208]

Panchgani
17 July 1946[209]

LF: I would go into the Constituent Assembly and use it for a different purpose—as a battle-field—and declare it to be a sovereign body. What do you say to this?

MKG: It is no use declaring somebody else's creation a sovereign body. After all, it is a British creation. A body does not become a sovereign body by merely asserting it.

LF: What do you mean by your socialism.

MKG: My socialism means 'even unto this last'. I do not want to rise on the ashes of the blind, the deaf, and the dumb. In their socialism, probably these have no place. Their one aim is material progress. For instance, America aims at having a car for every citizen. I do not. I want freedom for full expression of my personality. I must be free to build a staircase to Sirius if I want to. That does not mean that I want to do any such thing. Under the other socialism, there is no individual freedom. You own nothing, not even your body.

LF: Does not, under your socialism, the State own your children and educate them in any way it likes?

MKG: All States do that. America does it.

LF: Then America is not very different from Russia.

MKG: But socialism is dictatorship or else arm-chair philosophy. I call myself a communist also.

LF: O, don't. It is terrible for you to call yourself a communist. I want what you want, what Jayaprakash and the socialists want: a free world. But the communists don't. They want a system which enslaves the body and the mind.

MKG: Would you say that of Marx?

LF: The communists have corrupted the Marxist teaching to suit their purpose.

MKG: What about Lenin?

LF: Lenin started it. Stalin has since completed it. ...

MKG: You mean to say, you do not want communism of Stalin's type.

LF: But the Indian communists want communism of the Stalin type in India and want to use your name for that purpose.

MKG: They won't succeed.

LF: Your young men are too Indo-centric.

MKG: That is only partly true. I won't say we have become international, but we have taken up forlorn causes, e.g., the cause of the exploited nations, because we are ourselves the chief exploited nation.

LF: The growing anti-white feeling here is bad. In the Taj Mahal Hotel (Bombay) they have put up a notice 'South Africans not admitted'. I do not like it. Your non-violence should make you more generous.

MKG: That won't be non-violence. Today the white man rules in India. So, if the Taj Mahal Hotel has the gumption to put up that notice, it is a feather in its cap.

LF: That is what any nationalist will say. You must say something better.

MKG: Then I will be a nationalist for once. They have no right to be here if they do not deal with Indians on terms of equality.

LF: No right—yes. But you must give them more than their right. You must invite them.

MKG: Yes, when I am the Viceroy.

LF: You mean the President of the Indian Republic.

MKG: No. I will be quite content to be the Viceroy, a constitutional Viceroy, for the time being. The first thing I will do will be to vacate the Viceregal Lodge and give it to the Harijans. I will then invite the South African white visitors to my hut and say to them: 'You have ground my people to powder. But we won't copy you. We will give you more than you deserve. We won't lynch you as you do in South Africa', and thus shame them into doing the right. ...

Harijan 4-8-1946; CWMG Vol. 85, pp. 7–11; E

Bloodshed In Ahmedabad

Panchgani
22 July 1946

BLOODSHED HAS been going on in Ahmedabad for several days now. It is difficult to say who is at fault ... in Ahmedabad everyone must know who is the aggressor or who is more to blame. ...

... Is it not enough that three young men[210] have died in the attempt to stop the holocaust? ... Several friends have written to me about the martyrdom. If we had sense that sacrifice would have quenched the fire. That has not happened. However, that does not mean that the sacrifice was in vain. It only means that many more such sacrifices must be offered before the fire can be quelled. Or both sides must tire themselves out. Some must face police bullets, some go to jail and some hang before the flames are extinguished. This is the wrong way, because the fire thus put out has every possibility of erupting again. It will not reduce the poison, only suppress it, which will then spread in the body politic and cause immense mischief.

... Poet Iqbal has said: 'Religion does not teach us to bear enmity towards each other' ...

... I am told that nearly all the stabbings have been in the back, none or very few in the chest or the face. Why should one be frightened of such people? One should either die at their hands in the hope that they will in the end give up their madness and *goondaism,* or if one does not have that much courage one should fight to defend oneself. The question may rightly be asked how can one fight against a person who strikes from behind. It may not be possible to prevent such a person from stabbing people in the back but if the onlookers are not in collusion with him and are brave enough, they can catch hold of the culprit and hand him over to the police or to the community to which he belongs, or bring him before the *panch.* Only, they may not become judges.

Harijanbandhu 28-7-1946; CWMG Vol. 85, pp. 40–1; G

Heal Thyself

Panchgani
25 July 1946

A CORRESPONDENT has written to me about the butchery that is going on in Ahmedabad. I give below the relevant portions from his letter.

... Supposing you were in Ahmedabad today and went out to quell the riots, any number of volunteers will join you. Two of our Congress workers, Shri Vasantrao and Shri Rajabali, went out in such a quest and fell a prey to the *goonda*'s knife. They laid down their lives in the pursuit of an ideal and they deserve all praise. But no one else had the courage to follow in their footsteps ...

... I feel that unless you set an example in action, your writings and utterances will not be of any use to the ordinary people, and even Congressmen, in organizing non-violent protection of society.

I like the suggestion mentioned above. People followed my advice and took to non-violent resistance against the British Government because they wanted to offer some sort of resistance. But their non-violence, I must confess, was born of their helplessness. Therefore, it was the weapon of the weak. ...

Harijan 4-8-1946; CWMG Vol. 85, pp. 54–5; H

Being Sovereign

Panchgani
July 1946

Some Congressmen: The best use that the Congress could make of the Constituent Assembly' is to capture it, declare it to be a sovereign body and turn it to revolutionary account.

MKG: Not while I am alive ... To become sovereign you have to behave in a sovereign way ... (He then recounted the episode of three tailors on Tooley Street in Johannesburg who declared themselves as a sovereign body). It ended in nothing. It was just a farce.

P. MG: LP Vol. I, B1, p. 237

To Vallabhbhai Patel

Poona
1 August 1946

... Mine may be a voice in the wilderness. Even so I prefer it that way. Therefore, if we negotiate with Ambedkar out of fear of the League we are likely to lose on both the fronts.

Blessings from
Bapu
CWMG Vol. 85, p. 102; G

Is God A Person Or A Principle?[211]

Sevagram
8 August 1946

... Nobody knows ... and nobody is likely ever to know. ...

Harijanbandhu 18-8-1946; CWMG Vol. 85, pp. 136–7; G

Compensation For Murder

Sevagram
9 August 1946

I HAVE been asked whether the brother or other relatives of the late Rajabali should demand compensation from the Government for his murder. The deceased himself would not have considered such a death a loss. He would have held that such a murder, if allowed to go unavenged, would ultimately put an end to further murders and was therefore beneficial. To demand even the smallest compensation for the death of such a man is bound to wash away to some extent the good that it might do. ...

Harijanbandhu 18-8-1946; CWMG *Vol. 85, p. 140; G*

Bodily Labour And The Mind

Sevagram
23 August 1946

... No ONE in Government schools or colleges bothers to teach the students how to clean the roads or latrines. Here cleanliness and sanitation form the very Alpha and Omega of your training. Scavenging is a fine art you should take pains to learn. Persistent questioning and healthy inquisitiveness are the first requisite for acquiring learning of any kind. Inquisitiveness should be tempered by humility and respectful regard for the teacher. It must not degenerate into impudence. The latter is the enemy of receptivity of mind. There can be no knowledge without humility and the will to learn. ...

Address to Trainees of Basic Teachers' Camp; Harijan
8 September 1946; CWMG *Vol. No. 85, pp. 199–200*

'Direct Action'

Sevagram
24 August 1946

LET US be humble and confess that we have not got the strength today to meet all the expectations that the people entertain of us ... We are not in the midst of civil war. But we are nearing it.

P. MG: LP *Vol. I, B1, pp. 240–5*

To Lord Wavell

Valmiki Mandir
Reading Road, New Delhi
28 August 1946

Dear Friend,

I write this as a friend and after deep thought.

Several times last evening you repeated that you were a 'plain man and a soldier' and that you did not know the law. We are all plain men though we may not all be soldiers and even though some of us may know the law. It is our purpose, I take it, to devise methods to prevent a repetition of the recent terrible happenings in Calcutta.[212] The question before us is how best to do it.

Your language last evening was minatory. As representative of the King you cannot afford to be a military man only, nor to ignore the law, much less the law of your own making. You should be assisted, if necessary, by a legal mind enjoying your full confidence. You threatened not to convene the Constituent Assembly if the formula you placed before Pandit Nehru and me was not acted upon by the Congress[213]. If such be really the case then you should not have made the announcement[214] you did on 12th August. But having made it you should recall the action and form another ministry enjoying your full confidence. ...

I am,
Yours sincerely,
M.K. Gandhi

H.E. The Viceroy
The Viceroy's House
New Delhi

CWMG Vol. 85, pp. 215-16; E

At Prayer Meeting

New Delhi
2 September 1946[215]

... WE SHALL have full freedom only when our uncrowned king Pandit Jawaharlal Nehru and his colleagues in the Interim Government devote themselves to the service of the poor as people expect them to do.

This is a memorable day in the history of India. There is no occasion, however, for illuminations and jubilation. We must remember that today our ministers are putting on the crown of thorns.

The Muslim League, which is the second most important organization after the Congress and represents the Muslims of India, has not joined the Interim Government. Muslims are related to us by blood, for they are the children of the same land. They are angry with the Hindus. The Muslim League contends that the Hindus have betrayed them. The followers of the League are observing this day as a day of mourning. But the Hindus should not answer anger with anger and blow with blow. Time was when the Ali Brothers were with the Hindus. So, even though the Hindus cannot join the Muslim Leaguers in observing the day as a day of mourning, they should avoid illuminations, feasting, and other forms of rejoicing. They should be patient. They should ask themselves for what failing of theirs the Muslims have come to regard them as enemies. ...

The Hindustan 3-9-1946; CWMG *Vol. 85, pp. 243–4;H*

Interim Government

New Delhi
2 September 1946

(PYARELAL—ON the 2nd September, the Congress Ministers took office after receiving Gandhij's blessing at an impressive little ceremony at his residence in Bhangi Colony. For Gandhiji it was a day of deep heart-searching. In the early hours of the morning, whilst most slept, he scribbled a short message for the members of the new Government ...)

You have been in my thoughts since the prayer. Abolish the Salt Tax. Remember the Dandi March. Unite Hindus and Muslims. Remove untouchability. Take to Khadi.

P. MG: LP, *Vol. I, B1, pp. 5–6*

At Prayer Meeting

New Delhi
7 September 1946

THE SPEECHES being made by the Quaid-e-Azam and his followers cause me much pain. They say that they will take what they want by force ...

When the Quaid-e-Azam and his followers describe Hindus

as their enemies I am surprised and pained. I am not a Muslim but I venture to say that Islam does not preach enmity towards anyone. ...

Hindustan 8-9-1946; CWMG Vol. 85, p. 276; H

Talk With An English Journalist

New Delhi
Before 24 September 1946

... Q. What do you think of Russia?

MKG: Russia is an enigma to me ...

Q. And the atom bomb?

MKG: Oh, on that point you can proclaim to the whole world without hesitation that I am beyond repair. I regard the employment of the atom bomb for the wholesale destruction of men, women, and children as the most diabolical use of science.

Q. What is the antidote? Has it antiquated non-violence?

MKG: No. It is the only thing the atom bomb cannot destroy. I did not move a muscle when I first heard that the atom bomb had wiped out Hiroshima. On the contrary, I said to myself, 'Unless now the world adopts non-violence, it will spell certain suicide for mankind. ...'

Harijan 29-9-1946; CWMG Vol. 85, pp. 370–1; E

Discussions With Wavell

New Delhi
26 September 1946

Pyarelal—Lord Wavell left the Interim Government not a moment's respite. On the 26th September, he invited Gandhiji to meet him. In the course of their meeting he again returned to his pet theme.

Viceroy: The League must be brought in somehow.

MKG: The Congress is ready provided the League is willing to come in a straight way. Let Jinnah seek an interview with Pandit Nehru and come to an honourable understanding. It will be a great day if and when the Congress and the League come together in the Interim Government after a mutual understanding, without any mental reservations, and not to non-cooperate and fight.

Viceroy: The only stumbling block is the inclusion of a nationalist

Muslim in the Interim Government. The Congress has the undoubted right to nominate a nationalist Muslim. But in view of the fact that Jinnah is obstinate on that point, where is the harm in waiving it?

MKG: One may waive a right, one cannot waive a duty.

Viceroy: But if the League refuses to come in, what happens to the Constituent Assembly?

MKG: I admit that in that event the Constituent Assembly cannot properly meet. I must, however, make it clear that in this I represent nobody but myself.

Viceroy: Let us pursue this line of thinking a little further. If the Constituent Assembly is not called, what happens next?

MKG: The National Interim Government will carry on administration as it is doing at present. If you do not allow it to continue, you will expose your *bona fides* to suspicion.

Viceroy: How can we do that?

MKG: Then, do you want to retain power for yourself under this excuse? If you do that the whole world will condemn you. All you may insist on is that the Interim Government should include the Muslim League representatives. The Congress is prepared to do that.

Viceroy: For that I shall need a mandate from the British Cabinet. I can only act according to my instructions. I admit that my sympathies are with the League. My endeavour to bring in the League will continue.

(The Viceroy denied that he had ever said that his leanings were towards the League. In some other respects, too, his recollection differed from Gandhiji's. But he declined to give his own version even when pressed: 'I think it is unwise during negotiations like those now in progress to attempt to secure agreed minutes of conversations. It was decided not to do so during the Cabinet Mission's negotiations ...')

28th September 1946

MKG to Lord Wavell: ... I understood you to say that although in some of his presentations he was unreasonable, your leanings were towards the Muslim League. But after your correction my impression loses all its value.

I would like to have your other corrections also if you have the time.

P. MG: LP *Vol. I*, B1, *pp. 261–3*

Telegram To Y.M. Dadoo

New Delhi
10 October 1946

Doctor Dadoo[216]
Durban

Glad passive resisters adhere non-violence. Hope no weakening or division among our people.

Gandhi
CWMG *Vol. 85, p. 442; E*

Dying Embrace

New Delhi
15 October 1946

IN BOMBAY a Hindu gave shelter to a Muslim friend the other day. This infuriated a Hindu mob who demanded the head of the Muslim friend. The Hindu would not surrender his friend. So both went down literally in deadly embrace. This was how it was described to me authentically. Nor is this the first instance of chivalry in the midst of frenzy. During the recent bloodbath in Calcutta, stories of Muslims having, at the peril of their lives, sheltered their Hindu friends and *vice versa* were recorded. Mankind would die if there were no exhibition any time and anywhere of the divine in man. ...

Harijan *20-10-1946;* CWMG *Vol. 85, p. 459; E*

Towards Bengal

New Delhi
27 October 1946

(GANDHI, HOUSED in Delhi's Bhangi Colony, discussed his future programme with Pandit Nehru in the light of the Great Calcutta Killings. A return to Sevagram Ashram was in his thoughts.)

If I leave Delhi, it will not be in order to return to Sevagram but only to go to Bengal. Else, I would stay here and stew in my justice.

The same evening two close friends from Bengal—Satis Chandra Das Gupta, the distinguished pupil of the great chemist Sir P.C. Ray, his devoted wife

Hemprabha Devi, came with Satin Sen, a veteran Bengal leader. 'Allow us to go to Noakhali', they urged. 'Give us a chance to do our bit and then, if necessary, you can go there.'

Sarat Chandra Bose, one of the members of the Interim Government, joined the group.

MKG: Go forth, therefore; you have my blessings. And I tell you, there will be no tears but only joy if tomorrow I get the news that all the three of you are killed.

Group: It will be pure joy to be so killed.

MKG: But mark my words. There should be no foolhardiness about it. You should go because you feel you must and not because I ask you to.

Group: That goes without saying.

P. MG: LP Vol. I, B1, pp. 302–3

Towards Noakhali

On or before 28 October 1946

When Gandhi left Delhi for Noakhali, Calcutta was ablaze. The fires had not really been doused since August 1946. Gandhi was cautioned to be prepared for acid-bulbs hurled when he detrained at Calcutta. Was it safe for him to expose himself to such risk?

I do not know what I shall be able to do there (Noakhali). All I know is that I won't be at peace with myself unless I go there.

P, MG: LP Vol. I, B2, p. 3

With The Governor Of Bengal

Calcutta
30 October 1946

The last Governor of Bengal, Fredrick Burrows, asked Gandhi what, during the interim period after the British declaration to quit, the Governor's role was. Gandhi was clear.

Governor of Bengal, Frederick Burrows: What would you like me to do?

MKG: Nothing, Your Excellency.

Chief Minister Suhrawardy suggested to Gandhi that he should extend his stay in Calcutta to help consolidate peace in the city, at least till Baqr-Id. He could proceed to Noakhali later. Not everyone trusted the Chief Minister. Moreover, many held him responsible in large measure, for the Great Calcutta Killings.

Gandhi reasoned that if he extended his stay in Calcutta the responsibility of maintaining peace in Noakhali during the interval would rest upon Chief Minister Suhrawardy. The Chief Minister gave Gandhi his solemn assurance on this score.

Gandhi had known Suhrawardy from Khilafat Days. Suhrawardy used to take pride in calling himself Gandhi's 'son'.

MKG: How is it Shaheed Saheb, everybody calls you the chief of the Goondas? Nobody seems to have a good word to say about you!

S: Mahatmaji, don't people say things about you, too, behind your back?

MKG: That may be. Still there are at least some who call me Mahatma. But I have not heard a single person calling you, Shaheed Suhrawardy, a Mahatma!

S: Mahatmaji, don't believe what people say about you in your presence!

P, MG: LP Vol. I, B2, pp. 7–8; E

In Calcutta

Calcutta
3 November 1946

Pyarelal: On the 3rd November, the *Morning News,* a Muslim League paper of Calcutta, came out with news about extensive rioting in Bihar. Immediately Gandhiji wired to Pandit Nehru, who with three of his colleagues in the Interim Government, Sardar Patel, Liaquat Ali Khan and Sardar Abdur Rab Nishtar, had proceeded to Patna, asking for details. The latter wired back that the situation was tense in many parts, but the government were doing their utmost to bring it under control.

MKG: If someone abducts my daughter, am I to abduct his or his friend's daughter? That would be infamous. I am pained beyond measure. The cry of blood for blood is barbarous. You cannot take revenge in Bihar for the happenings in Noakhali.

Prayer Meeting, Calcutta, P, MG:LP *Vol. I, B2, pp. 9–10*

Calcutta

4 November 1946

... WE ALWAYS put the blame on the goondas. But it is we who make the goondas and give them encouragement. It is not correct to say that all the wrong that has been done is the work of the goondas.

Prayer meeting, Calcutta, P, MG: LP *Vol. I, B2, p. 10*

Calcutta

4 November 1946

PRINCIPALLY FOR reasons of health, soon after coming to Calcutta, I had gone on a spare, milkless diet. Subsequent happenings in the country induced me to prolong it. Now Bihar will send me to a complete fast if things do not radically mend. There will be no time limit. Do not agitate yourself but be really glad that I feel I have the strength to go through the ordeal and live up to my creed.

Letter To Rajkumari Amrit Kaur quoted by P, in MG: LP

Vol. I, B2, pp. 10–11

Calcutta

5 November 1946

THE NEWS from Bihar has shaken me. My own duty seems to me clear ... Although I have striven hard to avert a fast, I can do so no longer ... My inner voice tells me, 'You may not live to be a witness to this senseless slaughter. If people refuse to see what is clear as daylight and pay no heed to what you say, does it not mean that your day is over?' The logic of the argument is driving me irresistibly towards a fast. I, therefore, propose to issue a statement that unless this orgy of madness ceases, I must go on a fast unto death ... You can strive with me, if you think differently. Whatever you say will carry weight with me. But knowing as you do my temperament, I am sure you will approve of my proposed step. In any event, you will go on with your work without a moment's thought about my possible death and leave me in God's good care. No worry allowed.

Letter to Jawaharlal Nehru quoted by P, in MG: LP *Vol. I, B2, p. 11*

Noakhali

Calcutta
6 November 1946

Pyarelal: Before leaving for Noakhali, on the 6th November, Gandhiji issued a statement and an appeal entitled *To Bihar*.

It is easy enough to retort that things under the Muslim League Government in Bengal were no better, if not worse, and that Bihar is merely a result of the latter. A bad act of one party is no justification for a similar act by the opposing party ... Is counter-communalism any answer to the communalism of which Congressmen have accused the Muslim League? Is it nationalism to seek barbarously to crush the fourteen per cent of the Muslims in Bihar?

I do not need to be told that I must not condemn the whole of Bihar for the sake of the sins of a few thousand Biharis. ... I am afraid, if the misconduct in Bihar continues, all the Hindus of India will be condemned by the world. That is its way, and it is not a bad way either. ...

P, MG: LP Vol. I, B2, pp. 11–12

IT IS far better to magnify your mistake and proclaim it to the whole world than leave it to the world to point the accusing finger at you. God never spares the evildoer ...

Why should people flee from their homes? Everybody knows that an unoccupied and unprotected house is bound to be looted by someone or the other. Would anyone risk the loss of all he owns just to discredit the League?

P, MG: LP Vol. I, B2, p. 14

WHAT A shame for Hindus, what a disgrace for Islam! No, I am not going to leave you in peace. Presently you will ask yourselves: 'When will this old man leave us and go?' But this old man will not go. He did not come on your invitation and he will go only on his own, but with your blessings, when his mission in East Bengal is fulfilled.

THESE DISTURBANCES are a part of the Muslim League's plan for Pakistan.

IT IS midsummer madness and they have realized it. They will soon sicken of it. They have already begun to.

EVEN IF there were only one Hindu in East Bengal, I would want him to have the courage to go and live in the midst of the Muslims and die, if he must, like a hero. He would then command the admiration even of the Muslims. There is not a man, however cruel and hard-hearted, but would give his admiration to a brave man. A goonda is not the vile man he is imagined to be. He is not without his redeeming features.

P, MG: LP Vol. I, B2, p. 16

Commentator: A goonda does not understand reason.

MKG: But he understands bravery. If he finds that you are braver than he, he will respect you. You will note that for the purpose of our present discussion I have not asked you to discard the use of arms. I cannot provide you arms. It is not for me to provide arms to the Chittagong armoury raid men. The most tragic thing about the armoury raid people is that their bravery was lop-sided. It did not infect others.

Commentator: I am an armoury raid man myself.

MKG: You are no armoury raid man or you would not have lived to tell me these things. That so many of you should have remained living witnesses to the things that have happened here is in my eyes a tragedy of the first magnitude. If you had shown the same fearlessness and courage to face death in the present crisis as at the time of that raid, you would have gone down in history as heroes. As it is, you have only inscribed a small footnote in the page of history. You will see I am not asking you just now to follow my type of heroism. I have not made it good hundred per cent even in my own case. I have come here to test it out in East Bengal. I want you to take to conventional type of heroism. You should be able to infect others, both men and women, with the courage and fearlessness that are needed to face death when the alternative is dishonour and humiliation. Thus only can the Hindus stay in East Bengal, not otherwise. After all, the Muslims are blood of our blood and bone of our bone.

Commentator: The proportion of Muslims and Hindus here is 6 to 1. How can you expect us to face such heavy odds?

MKG: When India was brought under British subjection, there were only 70,000 European soldiers against 33 crore of Indians.

Commentator: We have no arms. The hooligans have the backing of Government bayonets.

MKG: The Europeans had arms. We had none. So we forged the weapon of satyagraha. Today the Indian is respected by the white man in South Africa, not so the Zulu with all his fine physique.

Commentator: So, are we to fight those with arms anyhow?

MKG: Not anyhow. Even violence has its code of ethics. For instance, to butcher helpless old men, women, and children is not bravery but rank cowardice. Chivalry requires that they should be protected even at the cost of one's life. The history of early Islam is replete with such instances of chivalry and Islam is all the stronger for it.

Commentator: Would you permit the Hindus to take the offensive?

MKG: The people of Bihar did that and brought disgrace upon themselves and India. I have heard it said that the retaliation in Bihar has 'cooled' the Muslims down. They mean it has cowed them down for the time being. They do not know, Bihar has set the clock of Indian independence backward. The independence of India is today at stake in Bengal and Bihar.

Use your arms well, if you must. Do not ill use them. Bihar has not used its arms well ... It is the privilege of arms to protect the weak and the helpless. The best succour that Bihar could have given to the Hindus of East Bengal would have been to guarantee with their own lives the absolute safety of the Muslim population living in their midst. Their example would then have told. And I have faith that they will still do so with due repentance when the present madness has passed away. At any rate, that is the price I have put upon my life, if they want me to live.

P, MG: LP *Vol. I, B2, pp. 17–18*

Pyarelal: The next day, the 10th November, Gandhiji shifted his camp from Chaumuhani to Dattapara, in order to be able to visit more affected villages in the interior. At the evening prayer gathering at which nearly eight per cent were Muslims, he asked the Muslims to search their hearts and tell him whether they really wanted the Hindus to come back and live in their midst as friends and neighbours.

WHETHER YOU believe me or not, I want to assure you that I am a servant of both the Hindus and the Muslims. I have not come here to fight Pakistan. If India is destined to be partitioned, I cannot prevent it. But I wish to tell you that Pakistan cannot be established by force ... I ask my Muslim brethren to search their hearts and if they do not wish to live as friends with the Hindus, say so openly. The Hindus must in that case leave East Bengal and go somewhere else. The refugees cannot stay on as refugees for ever. The Government cannot go on feeding them for an indefinite period. Nor can they subsist for long, as they are subsisting at present, on less than half the daily ration of cereals to keep an able-bodied man alive; no fish, no vegetables, nor anything else to supplement it with. But even if every Hindu of East Bengal goes away, I shall still continue to live amidst the Muslims of East Bengal. I will not import any food from outside but subsist on what they give me and what I consider lawful for me to partake. If, on the other hand, you want the Hindus to stay in your midst, you should tell them that they need not look to the military for protection but to their Muslim brethren instead. Their daughters and sisters and mothers are your daughters, sisters, and mothers, and you should protect them with your lives. You should ponder what I have said and let me know what you really wish. I shall advise the Hindus accordingly.

Pyarelal: He was physically exhausted as a result of more than a week's semi-fast—the daily nourishment being less than 600 calories. To conserve strength, he had to consent to being carried to the prayer ground in an improvised chair slung over a pole and borne on the shoulders of some members of his party. The voice was feeble and the face bore marks of deep anguish. But there was not a trace of anger or impatience in the speech.

P, MG: LP *Vol. I, B2, pp. 27–8*

Pyarelal: As Gandhiji emerged from the ruined building after his grim tour of inspection, a Tibetan spaniel that was always seen roaming about the place in mournful silence came along and with a soft whimper tried to attract his attention. It would run a few steps, turn back and again beckon, if it was not followed. Gandhiji's companions were mystified by the strange behaviour of the animal and wanted to drive it away.

GANDHIJI STOPPED them, and said: 'Don't you see the animal wants to say something to us?'

He then let the dog lead him. It brought him to three human skeletons one after another and several skulls and bones that lay scattered all over the ground! It had seen its master and seven other members of the family being done to death during the riots.

P, MG: LP *Vol. I, B2, pp. 28–9*

On 20th November Gandhi decided to dismantle his camp, taking only Professor Nirmal Kumar Bose, his Bengali interpreter, with him set out to the interior. A short prayer was held before the departure, with *Vaishnavajana* being sung. A little craft bearing him passed quietly towards Srirampur. In a statement he said:

I find myself in the midst of exaggeration and falsity. I am unable to discover the truth. There is a terrible mutual distrust. Oldest friendships have snapped. Truth and ahimsa by which I swear, and which have to my knowledge sustained me for sixty years, seem to fail to show the attributes I have ascribed to them. To test them, or better to test myself, I am going to a village called Srirampur, cutting myself away from those who have been with me all these years, and who have made life easy for me. ... The other workers, whom I have brought with me, will each distribute themselves in other villages of Noakhali to do the work of peace, if it is at all possible, between the two communities ...

My ideal is to live in a local Muslim League family, but ... I must meanwhile establish such contacts with the Muslims as I can in their own villages. My suggestion to the League Ministers is that they should give me one honest and brave Muslim to accompany one equally honest and brave Hindu for each affected village ... Without some such thing it seems to me difficult to induce ... (the

Hindu refugees) to return to their villages. From all accounts ... life therefore, prefer to live as exiles from their own homes, crops, plantations, and surroundings, and live on inadequate and ill-balanced doles.

Many friends from outside Bengal have written to me to allow them to come for peace work but I have strongly dissuaded them from coming. I would love to let them come if and when I see light through this impenetrable darkness. In the meantime ... I have decided to suspend all other activities in the shape of correspondence, including the heavy work of Harijan and the allied weeklies ...

How long this suspense will last is more than I can say. This much, however, I can. I do not propose to leave East Bengal till I am satisfied that mutual trust has been established between the two communities and the two have resumed the even tenor of their lives in their villages. Without this there is neither Pakistan nor Hindustan; only slavery awaits India, torn asunder by mutual strife and engrossed in barbarity.

P, MG: LP Vol. I, B2, pp. 36–7

A wire came from Dr Rajendra Prasad appealing him to give up his semi-fast in view of the improvement in Bihar. So Gandhi announced he would revert to normal diet as soon as his system might permit.

I HAVE just been rescued from the very jaws of death.

P, MG: LP Vol. I, B2, pp. 36–7

MY PRESENT mission is the most complicated and difficult one of my life. I can sing (with Cardinal Newman) with cent per cent truth: 'The night is dark and I am far from home, Lead Thou me on.' I never experienced such darkness in my life before. The night seems long. The only consolation is that I feel neither baffled nor disappointed. I am prepared for any eventuality. 'Do or Die' has to be put to test here. 'Do' here means that Hindus and Muslims should learn to live together in peace and amity. Otherwise, I should die in the attempt. It is really a difficult task. God's will be done.

P, MG: LP, Vol. I, B2, p. 37

Srirampur, Noakhali
Between 21 November and 3 December 1946[217]

NIRMAL KUMAR Bose, outstanding anthropologist, and constant companion of Gandhi in Noakhali and Calcutta during this period, records that in the village Srirampur one day he heard Gandhi muttering to himself.

What shall I do? What shall I do?

Nirmal K. Bose's My Days with Gandhi, *pp. 99–100*

Srirampur, Noakhali
December 1946

(Gandhi to Nirmal Bose)

I DON'T want to die a failure. But I may be a failure.

Nirmal K. Bose's My Days with Gandhi, *p. 97*

On one occasion, he visited a Muslim home. The inmates spoke of their poverty. 'Why should there be poverty in Bengal?' he wondered. He recalled how he had told Governor Casey that to call Bengal a deficit Province was to own a bankruptcy of resourcefulness...He continued to practice Bengali writing, drawing squares on his exercise book like a lower form schoolboy.

THAT IS how my teacher used to teach us to draw characters of the alphabet. It is an excellent method. People think that one ceases to be a student when his schooldays are over. With me it is the other way about. I hold that so long as I live, I must have a student's inquiring mind and thirst for learning.

P, MG: LP *Vol. I, B2, pp. 43–4*

BENGAL IS in the forefront today because Bengal is Bengal. It is her proud privilege. It is Bengal that has produced Bankim Chandra and Tagore as well as the Chittagong armoury raid heroes, however misguided the latter's action. Bengal has now to show a higher type of courage. If Bengal in this juncture plays the game, it will save India. That is why leaving all my old loves, I have today become a Bengali. I have seen enough of ravages in Noakhali to make me weep my eyes out but I am not going to shed a tear for what has happened. We have a long way yet to go.

P, MG: LP *Vol. I, B2, p. 50*

MKG: Whether they are many or few, the Hindus of East Bengal have to learn the art of being brave. They should be able to live even in a minority of one, otherwise there is no hope for them in East Bengal. They must never feel ... helpless ... Courage does not depend upon numbers.

A Commentator: What if the Muslims do not play the game?

MKG: The Hindus must then be prepared to die but not turn cowards. This is the only solution that is feasible.

P, MG: LP *Vol. I, B2, p. 50*

SUPPOSE, THE Muslims of Bihar wanted to create a Muslim colony in Bihar; it would be looked upon by the Hindu population of Bihar as a potential menace. No matter what the Hindus might say, I know the authorities would not be able to guarantee the safety of the Muslim minority. But the same token, the creation of pockets can bode no good to the Hindus of East Bengal. The Bengal government would oppose it because it would amount to an admission that the minority community could not be protected unless it lived on its own strength, on fighting terms with the rest. A Government that made such an admission would stand self-condemned.

P, MG: LP *Vol. I, B2, p. 51*

IT WON'T do to live in the villages like a jinn. We must learn to live and move with the proverbial cautiousness and wisdom of a she-elephant. Then alone shall we have the fitness to live there. To live in the villages of Bengal calls for a special knack. We have all to cultivate it. You and I have to pass that test.

P, MG: LP *Vol. I, B2, pp. 73–4*

I SHALL ... (feel) confident ... (only) when I shall attain perfection so that I can cross ... (even longer) bridges of this type.

P, MG: LP *Vol. I, B2, p. 74*

I AM groping for light. I am surrounded by darkness but I must act or refrain as guided by truth. I find that I have not the patience and the technique needed in these tragic circumstances. Suffering and evil often overwhelm me and I stew in my own juice.

P, MG: LP *Vol. I, B2, pp. 75-6*

NOAKHALI HAS become a laboratory, where a crucial test is being made; the remedy will apply to situations all the world over where disputes arise between communities and nationalities and a new technique is needed for peaceful adjustment.

P, MG: LP *Vol. I, B2, p. 76*

I SEE I have not the knack. I have not yet found the key to Ahimsa. Here I am out to perform a stupendous *yajna*, but my unfitness for the task is showing at every step. There can, however, be no running away. And where can I run to? Success or or failure is not in our hands. It is enough if we do our part well. I am leaving no stone unturned. Ours is but to strive. In the end it will be as He wishes.

P, MG: LP *Vol. I, B2, p. 77*

I DON'T want to return from Bengal defeated. I would rather die, if need be, at the hands of an assassin. But I do not want to court it, much less do I wish it.

P, MG: LP *Vol. I, B2, p. 77*

5 December 1946

I NOTE that you have ... repeated the advice you have given me often enough that my place is in Bihar rather than in Noakhali ... If I could feel that my presence was at all necessary in Bihar, I assure you that I would not need any encouragement from you to go there ... You will pardon me ... for not taking your statements for gospel truth. For one thing, you have no first-hand knowledge of events. I suggest that there should be an impartial commission, appointed with the consent of the two Governments, to go into the disturbances both in Noakhali and Bihar.

P, MG: LP *Vol. I, B2, p. 103*

A letter which he wrote to Sardar Patel at this time mirrors his inner travail vividly.

I AM being tested through and through. My truth and ahimsa are being weighed in a balance more delicate than any a pearl merchant ever used ... a balance so delicate as to show the difference of even a hundredth part of a hair.

The situation here is most baffling. It is so hard to get at the truth. Himsa masquerades as Ahimsa, irreligion as religion. But is it not just under such circumstances that truth and ahimsa are truly tested? I know it, I fully realize it; that is why I am here. Do not call me away from here. If I myself run away from here like a coward defeated, it must be my fate, not India's fault. But I have no such fear. I am out to do or die. ...

P, MG: LP Vol. I, B2, p. 111

In Noakhali Gandhi became both exact and exacting. Pyarelal says, 'He converted himself and his little family of co-workers into tools of research in his spiritual laboratory and developed an extraordinary psychic sensitivity to the slightest variation in the moral atmosphere around him. Even a suggestion of hidden untruth or impurity seared him like red-hot-iron.'

HOW SHALL I cope with the multitude of problems that beset me? All around me is raging fire ... Thank god, it is my day of silence.

P, MG: LP Vol. I, B2, p. 113–14

26 December 1946

EVERYTHING SEEMS to be going awry. There is falsehood all around.

1 January 1947
P, MG: LP Vol. I, B2, p. 115

(Reports of discord with the Congress Working Committee reached Gandhi, particularly the difference in temperament between Patel and Nehru. In a letter to the Sardar, Gandhi wrote on 30 December 1996:)

I HAVE heard many complaints against you ... Your speeches are inflammatory and made to please the crowd; you have left behind all distinction between violence and non-violence; you are teaching the people to meet sword by the sword; you miss no opportunity to insult the League in season and out of season. All this is very harmful if true. They say, you talk about sticking to office. That again is very jarring, if it is true. Whatever I have heard I have passed on to you for your consideration. This is a very delicate time. If we deviate from the straight path by ever so little, we are done for. There is not that unison in the Working Committee that there should be. Root out corruption—you know how to do it. Send some trustworthy and intelligent person, if you think fit, to explain things to me and understand my mind. There is no need whatever for you to come yourself. You are no longer physically fit to run about. You seem to take no care of your health; this is bad.

P, MG: LP *Vol. I, B2, p. 132*

THE WAY to Jagatpur had been swept clean by workers assisted by some local people But some Muslims had fouled it overnight by scattering cow-dung and excreta over it. When Gandhiji's attention was drawn to it he remarked:

I like it. It does me no harm and it helps them let off pent up steam!

There was a women's meeting in the afternoon at Jagatpur. One of the women came with the half-charred thigh-bone of her murdered husband, which she carried with her as a sacred relic. Gandhiji told her that he did not like identification of the departed with their perishable remains and persuaded her to throw it away....

It astonishes me bow God is sustaining me through all this. Just think of it, I go to bed at 10 or 11 at night, get up at 2 a.m., go through the day's march at my age without fatigue and work round-the-clock without a breakdown.

P, MG: LP *Vol. I, B2, pp. 142–3*

MKG: When you think of establishing Pakistan first you think in terms of achieving it with the aid of a third power. When I think of the freedom of India, I think in terms of getting it without any foreign aid, on the basis of our own inner strength. Once freedom is secured for the country as a whole we can decide about Pakistan or Akhand Hindustan.

Q.: After the recent disturbances there is neither Pakistan nor peace. What is the solution?

MKG: That is exactly what I am in search of. As soon as it is discovered the world shall know.

P, MG: LP, Vol. I, B2, pp. 146–7

If you want to know how heartless I can be, make your body tough as steel. Have you ever seen a blacksmith at work? He takes a crude piece of iron, beats it on the anvil with vigorous hammer blows and turns it into a beautiful article of use. I can be as heartless as that blacksmith.

A couple of days later he decided, according to his practice, to put a young Muslim co-worker, who had joined him in his venture, through his initiation by asking him to take up kitchen work and latrine cleaning, beginning with the latter. The young man having never done scavenging before wrestled heroically but in vain with the rising revulsion against his new avocation. Manu was moved to compassion but wisely refrained from offering relief. When she narrated the incident to Gandhiji, he told her that she had done well in refraining or he would have taken her to task for it.

Such pity is no kindness at all but cruelty. To weaken this man's resolve by showing false pity when he was struggling to overcome his weakness would have been a distinct disservice to him. A surgeon who fights shy of performing an appendectomy, when a patient comes to him with a suppurating appendix, sends his patient to certain death. He has to be prompt and ruthless if he is to save the patient's life. I am a surgeon of that type.

P, MG: LP Vol. I, B2, pp. 147–8

On the 22nd January the party reached Kethuri. Gandhi was fatigued. While going through some papers after the morning prayer, he dozed off, papers in hand. It was time to resume the journey and people were waiting outside. But Manu did not want to remove the papers from his hands lest he be disturbed. So the start was delayed by a few minutes.

When people have been told we are to start at seven, it must be at the stroke of seven. Unpunctuality is sin.

During the march to Paniala—next halt—Manu sang a new *Ramadhun*. The second verse of the modified version ran (in translation):

Ishwar and Allah are thy names,

Do thou, O Lord, grant right understanding to all men.

Manu sang this version at the evening prayer as well; the entire audience joining. She had heard that version as a little girl, in a Vaishnava temple in Porbandar. It had remained in her sub-conscious memory but had come back to her spontaneously that morning. It stirred up early childhood memories in his mind.

That is how it used to be in olden days. The name of Allah came naturally to the lips even of orthodox Brahman priests. The present poisoned relationship between Hindus and Muslims is a recent excrescence. The more I see of the stiffening opposition around me, the firmer grows my faith in the Unseen Power. The spontaneous inspiration you had today to sing this Ramadhun is to me a sign of it.

After the prayer address at Paniala, questions were put by Muslims League hecklers.

Hecklers: You have said that the Muslim majority Provinces, if they choose, can realize Pakistan today. What do you mean by it?

MKG: Jinnah had declared that in Pakistan the minorities would, if possible, have better treatment even than the Muslims, there would be no under-dog nor upper-dog; if the Muslim majority Provinces, where it was as good as Pakistan, became wholly independent of the British Power and realized that ideal set forth by Jinnah in practice, the whole of India would welcome such an order, no matter by what name it was called, and the whole of India would be Pakistan.

H: How did your Ahimsa work in Bihar?

MKG: It did not work at all, it failed miserably. But if the reports received from responsible quarters are to be relied upon, the general population in Bihar has realized the seriousness of the crimes committed by large masses of Biharis in certain parts of the Province.

H: Who saved Hindus and Hindu property in Noakhali if not the Muslims?

MKG: The question betrays subtle conceit. Repentance ought to be humble. If the mischief in Noakhali has not been worse than it actually was, it is not man but God who is to be thanked for it. At the same time, I am free and happy to admit that there were Muslims in Noakhali who gave protection to the Hindus.

P, MG: LP Vol. I, B2, pp. 158–9

When Gandhi reached Palla next day, it was so cold that his feet nearly froze. But he contemplated the peace of the nature around him, as also what he had been witnessing day after day.

I AM in love with the huts of Bengal. They are so airy and light. Why cannot, in the midst of nature's plenty which is here scattered all around, Hindus and Muslims live together as brothers? Look at the stupidity of it. On one side there is the threat of famine and starvation; on the other they are retarding cultivation by the boycott of Hindu cultivators and thereby, in their ignorance, applying the axe to their own feet. ... That is why I daily pray, 'May God grant right understanding to all men.

P, MG: LP Vol. I, B2, pp. 161–2

27 January 1947

IF THERE are women who when assailed by miscreants cannot resist themselves without arms, they do not need to be *advised* to carry arms. They will do so. There is something wrong in this constant inquiry as to whether to bear arms or not. People have to learn to be naturally independent. If they will remember the central teaching, namely, that the real, effective resistance lies in non-violence, they will mould their conduct accordingly.

P, MG: LP Vol. I, B1, pp. 310–11

At Amki (30 January) goat's milk was not to be found. Gandhi said coconut milk was as good as goat's milk for him and coconut oil could easily take the place of goat's butter in his menu. so, instead of goat's milk he had 8 oz. of coconut milk. But this brought on a violent attack of diarrhoea and by evening he was utterly exhausted and by the time he managed to reach his room, he was collapsing. Manu gently propped up his head and called Nirmal Bose to help her. Together, they lifted him and laid him down in his bed. The thought then occurred to her that everybody would have thought her a fool if anything serious had happened as a result of her not sending for a doctor. She then wrote a note asking Dr Sushila Nayar to come and was about to hand it to the Professor when Gandhi opened his eyes.

I HAD really expected of you was that on an occasion like this, you would do nothing but take Ramanama with all your heart. I was, of course, doing it all the while ... Now, don't inform anybody about it, not even Sushila. Rama alone is my true doctor. He will keep me alive so long as He wants to take work from me, otherwise He will take me away.

P, MG: LP Vol. I, B2, pp. 167–8

Mahashivaratri fell on the 19 February when Gandhi was at Birampur. It was the third anniversary of the death of Kasturba. Gandhi observed the day fasting.

    But to all outward appearances it was just any other day. Gandhi's routine began as always at 4 a.m. and continued without pause for the rest of the day. The only allusion to the to the anniversary came in one entry in his diary:

ON THIS day, and exactly at this time (7.35 p.m.) Ba quitted her mortal frame three years ago.

At 7.35 p.m. the party assembled for a recitation of the Gita. A portrait of Kasturba, decorated with flowers was placed in front of the gathering. Gandhi sat through the reading in deep meditation.

    Describing the experience in one of his letters, he wrote:

During the Gita recitation, the whole scene of Ba's last moments three years ago came back and stood before my mind's eyes in all its vividness. I felt as if her head was actually resting on my lap. This was particularly so after the sixth chapter, when I laid myself down to rest and for a moment fell into a gentle sleep.

P, MG: LP Vol. I, B2, pp. 194–5

ON THE 20 February 1947, Prime Minister Attlee made a statement in the Parliament that it was H.M.G.'s definite intention to take necessary steps to effect the transfer of power to responsible Indian hands by a date not later than June 1948. Simultaneously with this, came the announcement of the termination of Lord Wavell's appointment as the 'war-time' Viceroy and the appointment of Lord Mountbatten as his successor. Gandhi wrote to Pandit Nehru on the 24 February:

I HAD anticipated practically the whole of it ... My interpretation of the speech (Attlee's) is this: If the British Government are (and are able to remain) sincere the declaration is good. Otherwise it is dangerous.

P, MG: LP Vol. I, B2, pp. 205–6

On the same day on that Gandhi wrote to Nehru, Nehru was writing to Gandhi from New Delhi:

MR ATTLEE's statement contains much that is indefinite and likely to give trouble. But I am convinced that it is in the final analysis a brave and definite statement ... Your advice at this critical moment would help us greatly. But you are too far away for consultation and you refuse to move out of East Bengal: Still if you could convey to us your ideas on the subject, we would be very grateful.

On 28 February Pandit Nehru again wrote:

The Working Committee is meeting here soon and all of us were anxious to have you here on the occasion. At present it is exceedingly difficult for any of us to leave Delhi even for two or three days. For several to go together would upset work completely. There is the budget in the Assembly, the Committees of the Constituent Assembly, the negotiations with the Princes, the change in Viceroys and so many other things that demand constant attention. So we cannot go away and if you will not come how are we to meet?

But Gandhi thought his allotted task was where it was. In a letter to Sardar Patel he said:

All of you veterans are there putting your shoulder to the wheel ... I am the only figure among ciphers here. Allow me, therefore, to continue here. If I can achieve something worthwhile, the whole country will be benefited; if I fail none will be any the worse for it.

To Maulana Azad, who had suggested to him to make Calcutta his headquarters if he could not come and stay at Delhi, he replied:

Your affection prompts you to say that if only I were near you, all would be well. The truth however, that so long as I cannot make good here, I can be of no use anywhere.

But Bihar called him not soon thereafter.

P, MG: LP *Vol. I, B2, pp. 206–8*

Meanwhile, an altogether new development—not from the outside but from within him—was to give a drastically unpredictable aspect to his life. Rajmohan Gandhi writes in *Mohandas* (pp. 572–3):

Gandhi resolved on a brahmacharya test in Noakhali, with Manu as his partner. He had discussed the idea with some (Pyarelal, Nirmal Kumar Bose, Devadas, C.R. and possibly others) and would later discuss it with several more, but more to inform thatn to consult. Most thought the plan dangerous or crazy; all felt he was giving himself an avoidable burden; and many believed that valuable reputations were at risk: his own and his associates', and the reputations of their common undertakings.

Gandhi himself had no doubts. To address the violence around him he had to summon his chastity. This time it would be not an experiment but a 'yagna', a sacrificial offering of his sexuality to God. He would feel equal to the Noakhali challenge, which was the challenge of violence in independence-eve India, if neither he nor Manu felt the sexual urge despite sharing the same bed. Rather than prove a distraction—a waste of time, thought and energy—the 'yagna', he claimed, would purify him, oblige him to pray more ardently, help him focus with all his being on the Noakhali task.

Pyarelal would later write extensively about Gandhi's brahmacharya in his biography, and Bose wrote frankly and critically of it in My Days with Gandhi. *Although Bose remained uneasy about the impact of Gandhi's experiments on the women who participated*

*in it, he accepted Gandhi's linkage of brahmacharya with his battle
for peace.*

*And while not convinced of the soundness of Gandhi's step, Bose
seemed satisfied as to its integrity. If it was a mask for lust, Nirmal
Bose would have been the first to know and the first to unmask
Gandhi. Fortunately for Gandhi, it was the critical forty-six-year-
old professor often disagreeing with him who recorded and analyzed
the old man's unusual doings in Noakhali.*

*Though based now in different villages, Gandhi's 'party' knew
of what was happening. The thin 'door' to his cottage-room was
always open.*

I CANNOT say I have attained the full brahmacharya of my definition
but, in my opinion, I have made substantial progress towards it. If
God wills it, I might attain even perfection in this life ... I do not
consider thirty-six years too long a period for the effort. The richer
the prize, the greater must the effort be. Meanwhile my ideas regarding
the necessity for brahmacharya have become stronger. Some of my
experiments have not reached a stage when they might be placed
before the public with advantage. I hope to do so some day if they
succeed to my satisfaction. Success might make the attainment of
brahmacharya (by others) comparatively easier.

P, MG: LP Vol. I, B2, pp. 213–14

Rajmohan Gandhi continues (*Mohandas* pp. 573–4):

*His close friends across the country also knew of his 'yagna';
Gandhi spoke of it to several of his callers and wrote about it in
many of his letters. The journalists covering him in Noakhali came
to know, and we must assume that Suhrawardy and his police, as
well as the British, now in the Empire's endgame, also knew.*

*There was an early casualty. Parasuram, whose efficient, silent
service as a stenographer Gandhi had repeatedly praised, felt he could
not continue his work unless Gandhi ceased the practice. We do not
have the text of Parasuram's evidently long letter of protest, but after
reading it between 3 and 4 a.m. on 2 January, Gandhi wrote to him:*

I HAVE read your letter ... It contains half-truths which are dangerous. ...
I cannot concede your demands. The other points you make do not

make much appeal to me ... Since such is my opinion and there is a conflict of ideals, and you yourself wish to be relieved, you are at liberty to leave me today. That will be honourable and truthful: I like your frankness and boldness. ...

P, MG: LP Vol. I, B2, pp. 216–17

RAJMOHAN GANDHI in *Mohandas* (pp. 575–6):

In her diary Manu entered Gandhi's remarks in Noakhali about chastity. He told her that the life of one who kept his body as 'a holy temple for God' would speak as 'a poem of exquisite spiritual beauty', and 'a full-blown flower of perfection' would banish communal hate. Interestingly enough, the ascetic employs metaphors of poem, flower, and beauty.

Here we must mark a resemblance between Gandhi's Noakhali trek and his march forty years earlier in the Zulu country. Both occurred amidst memorable scenes, with Noakhali's web of rivers matching Zululand's hills and glens. Both brought Gandhi face to face with wounded humanity. As in the Zulu country, people in Noakhali turned to him with appealing eyes. He saw himself as a soldier in both terrains; and both exercises involved brahmacharya, embraced in Zululand and now daringly tested in East Bengal.

In February 1947 he said to Manu: Here I want to be tested to the fullest extent possible. If I fail the examination it will be under God. I want no testimony apart from God's. If there is any deceit, even if hidden from us, the world will come to know of it.

The phrase 'fullest extent possible' hints at the drastic nature of the Noakhali 'yagna' where the two participants were at times naked together.

Rajmohan Gandhi in *Mohandas* (pp. 574–5):

For all his keenness to 'understand' the 'yagna' Nirmal Bose found himself unwilling to translate Gandhi's words into Bengali when, for the first time, he spoke publicly of it. This was at a prayer-meeting on 1 February 1947 in the village of Amishapara. Referring to 'small-talks, whispers and innuendos' going round, Gandhi said that he did not want his 'most innocent acts to be misunderstood and misrepresented'. Added Gandhi:

I have my granddaughter with me. She shares the same bed with me. The Prophet had discounted eunuchs who became such by an operation. But he welcomed eunuchs made such through prayer by God. This is my aspiration ...

I know that my action has excited criticism even among friends. But a duty cannot be shirked even for the sake of the most intimate friends.

Bose did not translate these sentences. Far away in Ahmedabad, Mashruwala and Narhari Parikh removed them from Harijan's *report of the speech. They were among the 'intimate friends' who hoped to persuade Gandhi to abandon the 'test'. Meanwhile they would put a lid on it.*

This is a very personal letter[218] but not private.

Manu Gandhi my grand-daughter, as we consider blood-relations, shares the bed with me, strictly as my very blood ... as part of what might be my last yajna. This has cost me dearest associates ... You as one of dearest and earliest comrades ... should reconsider your position in the light of what they have to say ... I have given the deepest thought to the matter. The whole world may forsake me but I dare not leave what I hold is the truth for me. It may be a delusion and a snare. If so, I must realise it myself. I have risked perdition before now. Let this be the reality if it has be.

I need not argue the point. I have simply conveyed the intensity of my thoughts.

Do not consider my feeling in the matter. I have none. All I want is to *do* the truth at all cost, as I see it.

P, MG: LP Vol. I, B2, pp. 220–1

A.V. Thakkar: Why this experiment here?

MKG: You are mistaken, Bapa; *it is not an experiment* but an integral part of my yajna. One may forgo an experiment; one cannot forgo one's duty. Now if I regard a thing as a part of my yajna—a sacred duty—I may not give it up even if public opinion is wholly against me. I am engaged in achieving self-purification. The five cardinal observances are the five props of my spiritual striving. brahmacharya is one of them. But all the five constitute an indivisible whole. They are inter-related and inter-dependent. If one of them is broken, all are broken. That being so, if in practice I resile in regard to brahmacharya to please Mrs Grundy, I jettison not only brahmacharya but Truth, Ahimsa, and all the rest. I do not allow myself any divergence between theory and practice in respect of the rest. If then I temporize in the matter of brahmacharya, would it not blunt the edge of my brahmacharya and vitiate my practice of truth? Ever since my coming to Noakhali, I have been asking myself the question, 'What is it that is choking the action of my Ahimsa? Why does not the spell work? May it not be because I have temporized in the matter of brahmacharya?

AVT: Your Ahimsa has not failed. Do not miss the wood for the trees ... Just think what would have been the fate of Noakhali if you had not come. The world does not think of brahmacharya as you do.

MKG: If I accept your contention then it would amount to this that I should give up what I hold to be right for me, for fear of displeasing the world. I shudder to think where I should have been if I had proceeded like that in my life. I should have found myself at the bottom of the pit. You can have no idea, Bapa, but I can well picture it to myself. I have called my present venture a Yajna—a sacrifice, a penance. It means utmost self-purification. How can there be that self-purification when in my mind I entertain a thing which I dare not put openly into practice?

AVT: What if your example is copied?

MKG: If there is blind imitation or unscrupulous exploitation of my example, society will not and should not tolerate it. But if there is sincere, *bona fide,* honest endeavour, society should welcome it and it will be the better for it. As soon as my research is complete, I shall myself proclaim the result to the whole world.

AVT: I for one cannot imagine anything base in you: After all, Manu is in place of a grand-daughter to you—flesh of your flesh and bone of your bone. I confess, I had my mental reservations in the beginning. I had come in all humility to press upon you my doubts. I did not understand. Only after our talk today have I been able to have a deeper understanding of the meaning of what you are trying to do.

MKG: Does that make any real difference? It does not and it should not. You seem to make a distinction between Manu and others like her. My mind makes no such distinction. To me they are all alike—daughters.

P, MG: LP *Vol. I, B2, pp. 224–6*

VERY[219] GREAT pressure is being put upon me to go to Bihar because they all say that things are not properly represented to me on behalf of the Bihar government. I am watching.

YOUR[220] LETTER ... is ... hysterical...I would like you to tell me how I can serve the Muslims better by going to Bihar. Whilst I do not endorse your remark that the atrocities committed by the Hindus in Bihar have no parallel in history, I am free to admit that they were in magnitude much greater than in Noakhali ... I would urge you, as President of the Monghyr District Muslim League, to confine yourself to proved facts which, I am sorry to say, you have not done.

YOU[221] BELONG to a great university and hold the degree of M.A. But I am sorry to have to tell you that your letter is wholly unbalanced. You will let me serve Hindus, Muslims, and others in the best manner I know. If I fail, I shall feel sorry. But I cannot change my programme according to an opinion which does not appeal to my reason ... I refuse to draw the distinction between aggressive and non-aggressive communities ... Religion is my personal concern. It ought not to interfere with my duty as a citizen of India.

P, MG: LP *Vol. I, B2, p. 247*

ARE YOU[222] not my old tireless correspondent to whom I could carry no conviction? You have started with an emphatic statement of opinion without caring to inquire how I am passing my time and telling me on what grounds you have come to a conclusion: You have condemned me guilty without even hearing me, the accused. You have also laid down the law that Bihar needs my presence more urgently than Noakhali. Since I am in a position to know more fully than any other person whether I am wasting my time in Noakhali or not, it is fair for me to assume that your conclusion about Bihar is as erroneous as about Noakhali.

P, MG: LP *Vol. I, B2, p. 248*

I HAVE seen in the newspapers a statement attributed to you[223] which reads like a jibe at me. I would not expect that from you. Therefore I give you the credit of believing that I have the inner voice to which I listen. My belief is that all mankind has it. But the outside din and noise have practically deadened it for the vast majority of people When my voice speaks I shall find myself in Bihar without any further prompting.

P, MG: LP *Vol. I, B2, p. 249*

MKG: So, if I come to Barisal, there is only the *khal*[224] for me, is it not?
Maulvi Fazlul Huq: No, no, Mahatmaji, you are always welcome. That was only a joke. I never can let go a joke—even at the expense of my father. That is my nature!
MKG: Regarding Bihar I may shortly go there. But it will not be to oblige you.

P, MG: LP *Vol. I, B2, pp. 249–51*

From what I have been hearing, it seems to me that the Bihar massacre was like the Jallianwala Bagh massacre. Dr Mahmud's wife today brought some Muslim women to me. I had no reply to their tears.

P, MG: LP *Vol. I, B2, p. 259*

Bihar

I WOULD not be hurt by the truth but I would prefer not to live and see the failure of the method of non-violence. It does not matter to me where I lay down my life in the pursuit of my cherished dream. Anywhere in India is the same to me. In the example which Bihar might set lies the future of our unhappy land.[225]

Q.[226]: In the present unsettled conditions would you advise the Muslims to go back and settle in their villages?
MKG: If you have courage and the requisite faith in God, I would ask you to go back. I confess, if similar things had happened to me, perhaps I would not have been able to go back myself. The thought of the dead would have haunted me. My ambition, however, is to be able with confidence in God, to remain even in the midst of those who may have become my deadly enemies.

P, MG: LP *Vol. I, B2, pp. 289–90*

INDIA TODAY seems an inferno of madness[227] and my heart weeps to see our homes set on fire by ourselves.

I find today darkness reigning over India and my eyes vainly turn from one direction to another to see light.

P, MG: LP *Vol. I, B2, pp. 293–4*

19 March 1947[228]

Is IT or isn't it a fact that quite a large number of Congressmen took part in the disturbances? ... How many of the 132 members of your Committee were involved? ... I have also worked in the Congress. Today I am not even a four-anna member. But there was a time when I was ... all in all. Hence I know the Congress inside out ...

I wish to ask you, how could you live to see an old woman of 110 years being butchered before your eyes? ... I will not rest nor let others rest. I will wander all over on foot and ask the skeletons what happened. There is such a fire raging in me that I will know no peace till I have found a solution for all this ...

If I find that my comrades are deceiving me, I will be furious and I shall walk barefoot on and on through hail or storm. I would throw away the soft seat and other amenities which you have offered me.

Rajmohan Gandhi, Mohandas, *p. 601*

With Lord Mountbatten

MKG[229] to Mountbatten: You have rightly gauged my difficulty about moving out of Bihar at the present moment. But I dare not resist your kind call. I am just now leaving for one of the disturbed areas of Bihar. Will you, therefore, forgive me if I do not send you the exact date of my departure for Delhi?

P, MG: LP *Vol. II, p. 76*

GANDHI PUT the following outline before the Viceroy:[230]
1. Mr Jinnah to be given the option of forming a Cabinet.
2. The selection of the Cabinet be left entirely to Mr Jinnah. The members may be all Muslims, or all non-Muslims, or they may be representatives of all classes and creeds of the Indian people.
3. If Mr Jinnah accepted this offer, the Congress would guarantee to cooperate freely and sincerely, so long as all measures that

Mr Jinnah's Cabinet bring forward are in the interests of the Indian people as a whole.

4. The sole referee of what is or is not in the interests of India as a whole will be Lord Mountbatten, in his personal capacity.

5. Mr Jinnah must stipulate, on behalf of the League or of any other parties represented in the Cabinet formed by him that, so far as he or they are concerned, they will do their utmost to preserve peace throughout India.

6. There shall be no National Guards or any other form of private army.

7. Within the frame-work hereof Mr Jinnah will be perfectly free to present for acceptance a scheme of Pakistan even before the transfer of power, provided however that he is successful in his appeal to reason and not to the force of arms, which he abjures for all time for this purpose. Thus, there will be no compulsion in this matter over a Province or a part thereof.

8. In the Assembly the Congress has a decisive majority. But the Congress shall never use that majority against the League but will give its hearty support to every measure brought forward by the League Government, provided that it is in the interest of the whole of India. Whether it is in such interest or not shall be decided by Lord Mountbatten as a man and not in his representative capacity.

9. If Mr Jinnah rejects this offer, the same offer to be made *mutatis mutandis* to Congress.

P, MG: LP *Vol. II, p. 79–80*

In Delhi

Nehru had convened an Inter-Asian Relations Conference. It was held at the Purana Qila, Delhi in the last week of March 1947. Bringing nearly 250 delegates from 22 countries, representing more than half the population of the world, the Conference has a symbol of a definite 'Asia sentiment'. Pandit Nehru was most anxious that Gandhi should attend it. 'We are having a very distinguished and representative gathering ... from all the countries of Asia', he wrote to Gandhi in the last week of February. 'If you do not come ... your absence will be keenly felt by all.' Gandhi agreed.

You, FRIENDS, have not seen real India, and you are not meeting in Conference in the midst of real India. The big cities are not the real India. The carnage which you see going on in various parts of India is certainly a shameful thing. But you are greatly mistaken and you will only mislead others if you go away with the impression that you have seen the real India when you have visited a few big cities of India. If you really want to see India, it is to be found not in her dozen or so big cities but in the seven hundred thousand villages where dwell thirty-eight crores of India's population—miserable specimens of humanity with lustreless eyes.'

P, MG: LP *Vol. II, pp. 89–1*

DID YOU[231] notice that while the delegates from other countries were befittingly dressed in simple style, reflecting the respective cultures of their countries, our own visitors and the lady volunteers on duty, attired in silk and wearing lip-stick and rouge in the western style, presented a very incongruous picture? I feel humiliated. How my heart would have danced with joy if they were seen there in the Congress women volunteers' simple Khadi uniform.

P, MG: LP *Vol. II, p. 93*

When Gandhi returned to the Bhangi Colony where he was staying from the Asian Conference for the evening prayer meeting, a Hindu Mahasabha youth stood up and shouted: 'This is a Hindu temple. We won't let you recite any Muslim prayer here.' Some tried to eject the youth from the meeting but Gandhi intervened.

I SHALL not proceed with the prayer so long as there is a single person objecting. I want to insure the fullest freedom to the dissenting minority.

The young man then tried to work his way up to the rostrum. Others prevented him. Gandhi moved halfway down to meet him saying,

Let no-one come between me and this young man.

But the crowd hustled him out of the meeting. In deep sorrow Gandhi said to the gathering:

This young man was in anger. Anger is a sort of madness. But it should be up to you and me to meet madness not with madness but with sanity. I am coming from Bihar. I have seen with my own eyes what people can do when they are seized by madness. It has bent my head with shame.

P, MG: LP *Vol. II, p. 93*

The next day, before the prayer commenced, Gandhi asked if there was any objector. Again, up sprang a young man and repeated the previous day's objection: 'It is a Hindu temple. ...'

MKG: The temple belongs to Bhangis. Only the trustees of the temple have a right to object. But they have not objected.

The young man: It is a public place of worship. You must go elsewhere if you want to read from the Koran.

The gathering: 'We want the prayer to continue. What right has one individual to hold it up against the wishes of all the rest? Proceed, please.'

MKG to the young man: Thousands want the prayer to be held. If you persist, they will be sorely disappointed. Does it behove you?

The young man sat down. But another rose: 'Why don't you go and recite the Gita verses in a mosque?'

MKG: You need not become excited. You are doing no good to Hinduism by your unreasoning fanaticism, but only encompassing its ruin. Hinduism is the acme of toleration and broadmindedness. Here is Badshah Khan, a man of God every inch of him if you want to see one in the flesh. Have you no respect even for him? But, as I have already said, even if a child objects, I shall not proceed with the prayer.

The young man: You cannot have a Muslim prayer here.

MKG: All right ... Let everyone keep calm and quiet. Tomorrow I shall again put this question and it will be open even to a little child by simply saying 'no' to prevent me from holding the prayer.

With that he left the prayer ground and prayed inside his room, with only members of his party present. Pandit Nehru entered the room while the prayer was in progress. He took his place quietly among the congregation unnoticed.

On the third day, Gandhi again asked if there were any objectors in the gathering. In reply three persons stood up.

MKG: I bow to the opposition. There will be no prayer.

He rose to go. There was again a clamour from the gathering asking him not to suspend the prayer.

MKG: Not today. The number of objectors has increased. That is good. But I cannot afford the luxury of martyrdom today. I have other important business to attend to. In Noakhali, they never prevented me from chanting *Ramadhun*. Those who had objection left the meeting ... Now let not the police harass the objectors.

A leader of Rashtriya Swayamsevak Sangh came to him that evening and assured him that there would be no more interruption at his prayer meetings. But when he again asked at the prayer meeting if there were any objectors, a youngster raised his hand.

MKG: All right. I own defeat. But it is no defeat of the gathering. Their defeat will be only when they indulge in anger, abuse, or violence against you.

The Objector: I withdraw my opposition, you can proceed with the prayer. The prayer thus did take place on the fourth day.

Let no-one imagine that we have had no prayer for the last three days. We did not pray with the lips but we prayed with our hearts, which is by far the more effective part of prayer. In this those who have opposed, have also helped, though unconsciously. Their opposition has helped me to turn the searchlight inward as never before. You might be tempted to ask what I mean by giving so much of my time and energy to such trifles, when negotiations are in progress with Lord Mountbatten on which hangs the fate of the nation. Let me tell you, for me there is no big, no small: They are all of equal importance. In Noakhali, in Bihar, in Pubjab, in Delhi, even in this prayer ground the battle of undivided India is being lost and won daily. The experience here today has provided me with the key to success elsewhere.

[Thereafter, the prayer meetings were held without any disturbance. The congregation on the 4 and 5 April was estimated to have exceeded one hundred thousand.]

P, MG: LP *Vol. II, pp. 94–6*

IF A fanatic should kill you[232], I shall dance with joy! My misfortune is that I have not many like you who would die bravely and without anger. If I had even half-a-dozen like you, the flames that threaten to devour us would be put out and peace would reign in India in no time.

P, MG: LP *Vol. II, p. 100*

1 May 1947

MAY I ask the Viceroy why he is a silent witness of all this[233]? Why does he not hold me or Jinnah Saheb, whoever is remiss in the implementation of the joint appeal, to account? And if the British cannot make the Hindus and Muslims to live at peace with one another, why do they not retire leaving them to square it out among themselves?

P, MG: LP *Vol. II, pp. 156–7*

IT WOULD be a good thing if the British were to go today[234]—thirteen months means mischief to India. I do not question the nobility of the British declaration, I do not question the sincerity of the Viceroy, but facts are facts. Neither the British Cabinet nor the Viceroy, however outstanding he may be, can alter facts. And the facts are that India has been trained to look to the British power for everything. Now it is not possible for India to take her mind off that state all of a sudden.

P, MG: LP *Vol. II, pp. 160–1*

With complete honesty behind[235] it—no mental reservations of any kind whatsoever.

P, MG: LP *Vol. II, p. 161*

On the following day the socialist leaders, Aruna Asaf Ali, Achyut Patwardhan, and Asoka Mehta, called on Gandhiji.

Socialists: Is there any alternative to Pakistan?

MKG: The only alternative to Pakistan is undivided India. There is no *via media*. Once you accept the principle of partition in respect of any Province, you get into a sea of difficulties. By holding fast to the ideal of undivided India, you steer clear of all difficulties.

Socialists: Then why does not Congress give a clear lead?

MKG: Because it feels helpless. It is not in favour of division: But it says, and with perfect logic, that if Pakistan is to be conceded, justice should be done to non-Muslim majority areas of Bengal and the Punjab, and to the Sikhs, and these Provinces should be partitioned on the same principle on which the Muslim League demands the partition of India. I do not agree with that view. In my opinion, the Congress should in no circumstance be party to partition. We should tell the British to quit unconditionally. If they do not listen and partition the country in spite of us, we shall know what to do. Why should we make ourselves accessory to what we hold to be evil?

Socialists: In other words, you think that the British power need not stay on in India for another thirteen months?

MKG: Quite so.

Socialists: What is our duty?

MKG: If you agree with my analysis, you and those over whom you have influence should join me in preparing the atmosphere for non-violence in the country. I would love to have you with me in that.

Socialists: That is our duty?

MKG: In a sense, yes. But ... tell me how many of your are with me? Is Aruna with me? Are Asoka and Achyut with me? No, you are not. The Congress is not. So I am left to plough my lonely furrow and I am content so to do. If you decide to launch forth with me, I shall take it to mean that you have pledged yourselves to die without killing, abjured the doctrine that the end justifies the means. I have admiration for what Jayaprakash, Aruna, Achyut, and others did in 1942. They thought nothing of playing with their lives. I have paid tribute to their fearlessness and courage. But you will now have to cultivate the higher courage which dying without killing calls for. In that campaign sabotage can have no place. You may not agree but it is my conviction that if the Bihar masses had not had the lesson which they had at your hands in 1942, the excesses which Bihar witnessed last year would never have occurred.

P, MG: LP *Vol. II, pp. 161–3*

ON BENDED knees I ask[236] those who want Pakistan to convince me that Pakistan is for the good of India. Let them put their case before the people and explain to them how it will benefit them. If they succeed in appealing to their reason, well and good. But let them understand that not an inch will be yielded to force.

Verily Badshah Khan is a *fakir*[237]. Independence will come but the brave Pathan will lose his. They are faced with a grim prospect. But Badshah is a man of God.

P, MG: LP *Vol. II, p. 170*

To Lord Mountbatten

8 May 1947[238]

IT STRIKES me that I should summarize what I said and wanted to say and left unfinished for want of time at our last Sunday's meeting.

1. Whatever may be said to the contrary, it would be a blunder of the first magnitude for the British to be party in any way whatsoever to the division of India. If it has to come, let it come after the British withdrawal.
2. Meanwhile the Interim Government should be composed either of Congressmen or those whose names the Congress chooses or of Muslim League men or those whom the League chooses. The dual control of today, lacking team work and team spirit, is harmful for the country.
3. Referendum at this stage in the Frontier (or any Province for that matter) is a dangerous thing in itself.
4. I feel sure that partition of the Punjab and Bengal is wrong in every case and a needless irritant for the League. This as well as all innovations can come after the British withdrawal, not before, except for mutual agreement. Whilst the British power is functioning in India, it must be held principally responsible for the preservation of peace in the country.

5. Your task as undisputed master of naval warfare, great as it was, was nothing compared to what you are called to do now. The single-mindedness and clarity that gave you success are much more required in this work.

6. If you are not to leave a legacy of chaos behind, you have to make your choice and leave the government of the whole of India including the States to one party. The Constituent Assembly has to provide for the governance even of that part of India which is not represented by the Muslim League or some States.

7. Non-partition of the Punjab and Bengal does not mean that the minorities in these Provinces are to be neglected. In both the provinces they are large and powerful enough to arrest and demand attention. If the popular Governments cannot placate them, the Governors should during the interregnum actively interfere.

8. The intransmissibility of Paramountcy is a vicious doctrine, if it means that they can become sovereign and a menace for independent India. All the power wherever exercised by the British in India must automatically descend to its successor. Thus the people of the States become as much part of Independent India as the people of British India. The present Princes are puppets created or tolerated for the upkeep and prestige of the British power.

9. Similarly, difficult but not so baffling is the question of the Civil Service. Its members should be taught from now to accommodate themselves to the new regime. They may not be partisans taking sides. The slightest trace of communalism among them should be severely dealt with. The English element in it should know that they owe loyalty to the new regime than to the old and therefore to Great Britain. The habit of regarding themselves as rulers and therefore superiors must give place to the spirit of true service of the people.

P, MG: LP Vol. II, pp. 171–2

YOU SHOULD do your duty and not be afraid of Ministers[239]. It would do you and them good. They must not ride rough-shod over rules or else democracy will go to pieces.

P, MG: LP Vol. II, p. 176

My Death

Calcutta
14 May 1947

MKG: When there is a raging fire all round, I have no desire to prolong my life by taking rest[240].

Dr Roy: Not for yourself, Bapu. People need your services more than ever.

MKG: What's the good ... Neither the people nor those in power have any use of me. 'Do or Die' becomes me more in the circumstances. I wish to die in harness, taking the name of God with my last breath. I have a feeling He will grant me that wish.

P, MG: LP Vol. II, p. 191

25 May 1947

... I would die smiling with the name of Rama on my lips. ...

CWMG Vol. 88, p. 6; H

Britain's Departure

It is not for them to give us liberty but only to get off our backs[241]. This they are under promise to do. But for retaining our freedom and giving it shape, we have to look to ourselves ... We are unable to think coherently, while the British power is still there in India. Its function is not to change the map of India. All it has to do is to withdraw and leave India in an orderly manner, if possible. But withdraw in any case on or before the promised date it must even if it means chaos.

P, MG: LP Vol. II, pp. 205–6

Let him (Jinnah) not appeal to the British power or its representative Viscount Mountbatten. The latter's function is only to quit by the end of June next year—peace or no peace. Imposed peace would be the peace of the grave of which all India and the British should be ashamed. Let it not be said that Gandhi was too late on the scene. He was not. It is never too late to mend, never too late to replace the force of the sword with that of reason. Dare the British impose Pakistan on an India temporarily gone mad?

P, MG: LP Vol. II, pp. 207–8

MKG: Who listens to me today?[242]

Co-worker: ... The people are behind you.

MKG: Even they are not. I am being told to retire to the Himalayas. Everybody is eager to garland my photos and statues. Nobody really wants to follow my advice.

Co-worker: They may not today, but they will have to before long.

MKG: What is the good? Who knows, whether I shall then be alive? The question is: What can we do today? On the eve of independence we are as divided as we were united when we were engaged in freedom's battle. The prospect of power has demoralized us.

P, MG: LP *Vol. II, p. 209*

MKG: Non-violence knows no despair. It is the hour of test for you and the Khudai Khidmatgars. You can declare that Pakistan is unacceptable to you and brave the worst. What fear can there be for those who are pledged to 'do or die'? It is my intention to go to the Frontier as soon as circumstances permit. I shall not take out a passport because I do not believe in division. And if as a result somebody kills me I shall be glad to be so killed. If Pakistan comes into being, my place will be in Pakistan.

Badshah Khan: I understand. I won't take any more of your time.

P, MG: LP *Vol. II, p. 210*

Chakrayya

New Delhi
31 May 1947[243]

... I FEEL like crying over his[244] death, but I cannot cry. For whom should I cry and for whom should I refrain from crying? ...

Prarthana Pravachan-I; CWMG *Vol. 88, p. 47; H*

... THE TIME[245] is fast approaching when India will have to elect the first President of the Republic. I would have proposed the name of Chakrayya, had he been alive. ...

Prarthana Pravachan-I; CWMG *Vol. 88, pp. 62–3; H*

Partition

Delhi
31 May 1947

... ANY PRINCE, just because he is a Muslim, would not be entitled to say that he would join Pakistan. Nor can a Hindu ruler, because he is a Hindu, say that he would be with the Congress. Either would have to follow the wishes of the people. ...

Prarthana Pravachan-I, pp. 106–11; CWMG Vol. 88, p. 47; H

Pyarelal records that on the morning of the 1 June, Gandhi woke up earlier than usual. Half an hour remained before prayer time. So he remained lying in bed and began to muse in a low voice, as Pyarelal took down the words:

THE PURITY of my striving will be put to the test only now. Today I find myself all alone. Even the Sardar and Jawaharlal think that my reading of the situation is wrong and peace is sure to return if partition is agreed upon. ...They did not like my telling the Viceroy that even if there was to be partition, it should not be through British intervention or under the British rule ... They wonder if I have not deteriorated with age ...

But in spite of my being all alone in my thoughts, I am experiencing an ineffable inner joy and freshness of mind. I feel as if God Himself is lighting my path before me. And that is perhaps the reason why I am able to fight on single-handed. People ask me to retire to Kashi or to the Himalayas. I laugh and tell them that the Himalayas of my penance are where there is misery to be alleviated, oppression to be relieved. There can be no rest for me so long as there is a single person in India lacking the necessaries of life ... I cannot bear to see Badshah Khan's grief ... His inner agony wrings my heart. But, if I gave way to tears, it would be cowardly and, the stalwart Pathan as he is, he would break down. So I go about my business unmoved. That is no small thing.

But may be all of them are right and I alone am floundering in darkness.

I shall perhaps not be alive to witness it, but should the evil I apprehend overtake India and her independence be imperilled, let it not be said that Gandhi was party to India's vivisection. But everybody is today impatient for independence. Therefore there is no other help.

P, MG: LP Vol. II, pp. 210–11

Delhi
3 June 1947

OF LATE[246] I have noticed that I very easily get irritated. That means I cannot now live for long. But my faith in God is daily becoming deeper and deeper. He alone is my true friend and companion. He never deserts even the least of His creatures.

In all probability, the final seal will be set on the partition plan during the day.

But though I may be alone in holding this view, I repeat that the division of India can only do harm to the country's future. The slavery of 150 years is going to end, but from the look of things it does not seem as if the independence will last as long. It hurts me to think that I can see nothing but evil in the partition plan.

P, MG: LP *Vol. II, p. 215*

MAY GOD protect them, and grant them all wisdom[247].

P, MG: LP *Vol. II, p. 216*

THE PARTITION has come in spite of me.[248] It has hurt me. But it is the way in which the partition has come that has hurt me more.

Delhi
10 June 1947

YOU[249] DO not know I repudiated the title of Mahatma long before you questioned it. But may be out of your concern for me, you feel it necessary to put me on my guard lest I should fall into the dotage of old age.

I say the same thing to Pakistan, too. In England they managed to survive when odds seemed all against any chance of survival. The secret of it was their wonderful unity, national discipline and organization. For betrayal of the country, father did not hesitate to send his son to the gallows. But in India, even after partition, Hindus and Sikhs are quarreling among themselves. Each wants to go his way. Nobody listens. Where shall it all end? We, old leaders, are like autumn leaves. Tomorrow you shall have to shoulder the whole burden.

P, MG: LP *Vol. II, pp. 246–7*

My Assassin

16 June 1947

... I SHALL consider myself brave if I am killed and if I still pray to God for my assassin. ...

Prarthana Pravachan-I, *pp. 166–70;* The Hindu *17-6-1947;* CWMG *Vol. 88, p. 164*

To Lord Mountbatten

Delhi
27/28 June 1947

YOU THREW out a hint that Quaid-e-Azam might not be able even to let you quit even by 15 August especially if the Congress members did not adopt a helpful attitude. This was for me a startling statement. I pointed the initial mistake of the British being party to splitting India into two. It is not possible to undo the mistake. But I hold that it is quite possible and necessary not to put a premium upon the mistake. This does not in any way impinge upon the very admirable doctrine of fair-play. Fair-play demands that I do not help the mistaken party to fancy that the mistake was no mistake but a belated and only partial discharge of an obligation.

You startled me again by telling me that, if the partition had not been made during British occupation, the Hindus being the major party would have never allowed partition and held the Muslims by force under subjection. I told you that this was a grave mistake. The question of numbers was wholly untenable in this connection. I cited the classic example of less than once hundred thousand British soldiers holding India under utter subjection. You saw no analogy between the two instances. I suggested the difference was only one of degree. ...

P, MG: LP Vol. II, pp. 289–90

As 15 August Approaches

YOU[250] ARE enunciating the doctrine of an eye for an eye and a tooth for a tooth. Only you will wait till the 15 August. Both these statements ill comform with the Congress policy. Has the Congress policy changed? Congressmen have changed, I know, but I am not aware of any change in the Congress constitution.

So far as I can see, I am a back number.[251] I have come to the conclusion that our way was non-violent only superficially, our hearts were violent. It was enough to displace the foreign power. But the violence nursed within has broken out in a way least expected. Heaven knows where it will lead us.

P, MG: LP Vol. II, p. 322

In my opinion,[252] nothing would have been lost if our councillors had never thought of interfering with the design of the original flag. ... In the defence of the improvement some say that the spinning-wheel was an old woman's solace and Gandhi's toy; but Swaraj does not belong to old women. It belongs to the warriors, and, therefore, we want Asoka's disc mounted with lions ...

Pandit Nehru, however, explained in the Constituent assembly, that, in implication, the new flag was the same as the existing tricolour. It also was to be of khadi like the old. Commenting upon it, Gandhiji wrote:

The wheel on the improved pattern bereft of the spindle and the *mal* need not be counted as a defect if it was purely due to the exigencies of art. After all every picture has to leave something for the imagination ... Some will recall though through the wheel the name of that Prince of Peace, Asoka, the founder of an empire, who ultimately gave up the pomp and circumstance of power to become the undisputed Emperor of the hearts of men and became the representative of all the known faiths. We would call it a legitimate interpretation of the wheel to seek in it the Wheel of Law ascribed to that living store of mercy and love. The spinning-wheel thus interpreted adds to its importance in the life of billions of mankind. To liken it to and to derive it from the Asoka disc is to recognize in the insignificant-looking Charkha the necessity of obeying the ever-moving Wheel of the Divine Law of Love.

P, MG: LP Vol. II, pp. 334–5

Kashmir

India will be free on the 15 of August, 'what of Kashmir?' a deputation of workers asked him at Jammu.

THAT WILL depend on the people of Kashmir.

They all wanted to know whether Kashmir would join the Union or Pakistan.

That again should be decided by the will of the Kashmiris.

P, MG: LP, Vol. II, p. 355

The more I think over it, the more I feel that as soon as the matter of Kashmir is settled, I should leave Delhi.[253]

P, MG: LP Vol. II, pp. 344–5

DURING[254] THE two interviews with the Prime Minister (of Kashmir) I told him about his unpopularity among the people ... He wrote to the Maharaja ... that on a sign from him he would gladly resign.

... The Maharaja had sent me a message ... that the Maharaja and the Maharani were anxious to see me. I met them ... The heir-apparent with his leg in plaster was also present ... Both admitted that with the lapse of British Paramountcy the true Paramountcy of the people of Kashmir would commence. However much they might wish to join the Union, they would have to make the choice in accordance with the wishes of the people. How that could be determined was not discussed at that interview ...

Bakshi (Ghulam Mohammad) was most sanguine that the result of the free vote of the people, whether on the adult franchise or on the existing register, would be in favour of Kashmir joining the Union provided of course that Sheikh Abdullah and his co-prisoners were released, all bans were removed, and the present Prime Minister was not in power. Probably he echoed the general sentiment. I studied the Amritsar treaty properly called 'sale deed'. I presume it lapses on the 15 instant. To whom does the State revert? Does it not go to the people?

HE (THE Maharaja) wishes to remove Kak. ...[255] The only question (before him) is how ... In my opinion the Kashmir problem can be solved.

P, MG: LP *Vol. II, pp. 357–8*

To A Railway Guard

MKG: What will happen to this one?[256]
Railway Guard: The passengers from the other compartment will occupy it.
MKG: If it is good enough for them, it should be good enough for me, too. How can I think of making myself comfortable at others' expense!
RG: Is there any service I can render?
MKG: Do not harass poor passengers and do not take bribes. That will be the greatest service you can render to me.

P, MG: LP *Vol. II, pp. 360–1*

Non-Violence Of The Brave

New Delhi
4 July 1947

... THE VIOLENCE we see today is the violence of cowards. There is also such a thing as the violence of the brave. If four or five men enter into a fight and die by the sword, there is violence in it but it is the violence of the brave. But when ten thousand armed men attack a village of unarmed people and slaughter them along with their wives and children it is the violence of cowards. America unleashed its atom bomb over Japan. That was the violence of the cowards. The non-violence of the brave is a thing worth seeing. I want to see that non-violence before I die. ...

Speech at Prayer Meeting; Prarthana Pravachan *Vol. 1, pp. 217–20;*
CWMG *Vol. No. 88, p. 274; H*

Leaders And Laws

6 July 1947

WE SHALL never be able to raise the standard of public life through laws. We are not made that way. Only if the lives of the leaders, both private and public, are perfect will they be able to produce any effect on the people. Mere preaching will have no effect.

A Letter; Bihar Pachhi Dilhi, *p. 285;* CWMG *Vol. No. 88, p. 285; G*

12 July 1947

... Who[257] will be responsible for the incalculable harm that will have overtaken the people of India as well as Pakistan in the meantime? Who can control the people if they go mad and launch on a course of retaliation?

CWMG *Vol. 88, p. 319*

Women Of The World Must Unite

New Delhi
18 July 1947

... IF AN ancestral treasure lying buried in a corner of the house unknown to the members of the family were suddenly discovered, what a celebration it would occasion. Similarly, women's marvellous power is lying dormant. If the women of Asia wake up, they will dazzle the world. ...

Message to Chinese Women; Bihar Pachhi Dilhi, *p. 354;*
CWMG *Vol. 88, p. 366; G*

7 August 1947

... I SHALL be alive in the grave and, what is more, speaking from it. ...
Harijan, *17-8-1947;* CWMG *Vol. 89, p. 16*

In Calcutta

Hydari Mansion[258]
Beliaghata
Calcutta
13 August 1947

To Sardar Patel

I have got stuck here and am now going to undertake a grave risk. Suhrawardy and I are going from today to stay together in a Muslim quarter. The future will reveal itself. Keep close watch. I shall continue to write.

P, MG: LP *Vol. II, p. 364*

After Gandhi moved to the house in the city's Muslim locality, demonstrators converged there. They were agitating when Horace Alexander, who had been invited by Gandhi to come and stay with him at Beliaghata, arrived. The demonstrators tried to stop him.

Some of the young agitators tried to climb onto the windowsill of the room inside which Gandhi was seated. Horace began to shut the windows. This (as he himself afterwards owned) was a 'most misguided action': Stones began being thrown through the glasspane of the window.

Gandhi asked for representatives of the demonstrators be let in. One of them began:

Demonstrator: Last year when Direct Action was launched on the Hindus on the 16 August, you did not come to our rescue. Now that there has been just a little trouble in the Muslim quarters, you have come running to their succour. We don't want you here.

MKG: Much water has flown under the bridge since August 1946. What the Muslims did then was utterly wrong. But what is the use of avenging the year 1946 on 1947? I was on my way to Noakhali where your own kith and kin desired my presence. But I now see that I shall have to serve Noakhali only from here. You must understand that I have come here to serve not only Muslims but Hindus, Muslims, and all alike. Those who are indulging in brutalities are bringing disgrace upon themselves and the religion they represent. I am going to put myself under your protection. You are welcome to turn against me and play the opposite role if you so choose. I have nearly reached the end of my life's journey. I have not much farther to go. But let me tell you that if you again go mad, I will not be a living witness to it. I have given the same ultimatum to the Muslims of Noakhali also; I have earned the right. Before there is another outbreak of Muslim madness in Noakhali, they will find me dead. Why cannot you see that by taking this step I have put the burden of the peace of Noakhali on the shoulders of Shaheed Suhrawardy and his friends— including men like Mian Ghulam Sarwar and the rest? This is no small gain.

Demonstrator: We do not want your sermons on Ahimsa. You go away from here. We won't allow the Muslims to live here.

MKG: This means that you do not want my services. If you will cooperate with me and allow me to carry on my work, it will enable the Hindus to return and to live in all the places from where they have been driven out. On the other hand, it will profit you nothing to remember old wrongs and nurse old enmities.

An eighteen years old: History shows that Hindus and Muslims can never be friends. Anyway, ever since I was born I have seen them only fighting each other.

MKG: Well, I have seen more of history than anyone of you, and I tell you that I have known Hindu boys who called Muslims 'uncle'. Hindus and Muslims used to participate in each others' festivals and other auspicious occasions. You want to force me to leave this place but you should know that I have never submitted to force. It is contrary to my nature. You can obstruct my work, even kill me I won't invoke the help of the police. You can prevent me from leaving this house, but what is the use of your dubbing me an enemy of the Hindus? I will not accept the label. To make me quit, you have to convince me that I have made a mistake in coming here. I put it to you, young men, how can I, who am a Hindu by birth, a Hindu by creed, and a Hindu of Hindus in my way of living, be an 'enemy' of Hindus? Does this not show narrow intolerance on your part?

P, MG: LP Vol. II, pp. 366–7

From tomorrow[259] (15 August) we shall be delivered from the bondage of the British rule. But from midnight today, India will be partitioned too. While, therefore, tomorrow will be a day of rejoicing, it will be a day of sorrow as well. It will throw a heavy burden of responsibility upon us. Let us pray to God that He may give us strength to bear it worthily. Let all those Muslims who were forced to flee return to their homes. If two millions of Hindus and Muslims are at daggers drawn with one another in Calcutta, with what face can I go to Noakhali and plead the cause of the Hindus with the Muslims there? And if the flames of communal strife envelop the whole country, how can our new-born freedom survive?

A shout: Where is Suhrawardy?

MKG: He is inside the house. He has with my consent kept himself away from the meeting as he wanted to avoid giving the slightest cause for irritation. But in view of the becoming tolerance which you have shown today, I shall be encouraged to bring him to the meeting from tomorrow onwards.

Another shout: Where is Suhrawardy?

Gandhi said he was inside engaged in ending the Ramzan fast and would appear before them presently. After a time, Suhrawardy, came to his side and stood in full view of the crowd. Gandhi placed his hand on Suhrawardy's shoulder.

Suhrawardy said: 'It is Bengal's great good luck that Mahatmaji is in our midst at this hour. Will Bengal realize its high privilege and stop the fratricide?'

One of the crowd (to Suhrawardy): Are you not responsible for the Great Calcutta Killing?
Suhrawardy: Yes, we all are.
Questioner: Will you answer my question, please?
Suhrawardy: Yes, it was my responsibility.

This owning of his responsibility had an effect on the crowd. 'It was the turning point', Gandhi later remarked. 'It had a cleansing effect. I could sense it.'

P, MG: LP Vol. II, pp. 368–9

FROM TODAY you[260] have to wear the crown of thorns. Strive ceaselessly to cultivate truth and non-violence. Be humble. Be forbearing. The British rule no doubt put you on your mettle. But now you will be tested through and through. Beware of power; power corrupts. Do not let yourselves be entrapped by its pomp and pageantry. Remember, you are in office to serve the poor in India's villages. May God help you.

P, MG: LP Vol. II, p. 370

RAJAJI, NOW Governor of West Bengal, came to see Gandhiji in the course of the day on 16 August. As a mark of respect he left his sandals at the entrance, and walked the whole length of the hall barefoot though other visitors had come up to Gandhi's room with their shoes on. C.R. congratulated him on the miracle he has wrought. Gandhi said he is not yet satisfied that the so-called miracle is an abiding one.

EVERYBODY IS showering congratulations on me for the miracle that Calcutta is witnessing.[261] Let us all thank God for His abundant mercy. But let us not, in this pardonable exuberance, forget that there are isolated spots in Calcutta, where all is not well. I have heard that in one place the Hindus are not prepared to welcome back the Muslim residents who were obliged to leave their homes.

P, MG: LP *Vol. II, p. 373*

I HOPE the decision not to have music in the vicinity of mosques[262] at the *namaz* time is acceptable to all and will be regarded as binding by *all* Hindus, not only those who are present on the spot. The League and the Congress have agreed to solve all differences by peaceful methods and without resort to force.

P, MG: LP *Vol. II, pp. 374–5*

SUHRAWARDY[263] AND I are living together in Beliaghata where Muslims have been reported to be sufferers ... We are living in a Muslim house and Muslim volunteers are attending to our comforts with the greatest attention ... Here in the compound numberless Hindus and Muslims continue to stream in shouting the favourite slogans. One might almost say that the joy of fraternization is leaping up from hour to hour.

Is this to be called a miracle or an accident? By whatever name it may be described, it is quite clear that the credit that is being given to me from all sides is quite undeserved; nor can it be said to be deserved by Shaheed ... This sudden upheaval is not the work of one or two men. We are toys in the hands of God. He makes us dance to His tune. The utmost, therefore, that man can do is to refrain from interfering with the dance and that he should tender full obedience to his Maker's will: Thus considered, it can be said that in this miracle He has used us two as His instruments and as for myself I only ask whether the dream of my youth is to be realized in the evening of my life.

For those who have full faith in God, this is neither a miracle nor an accident. A chain of events can be clearly seen to show that the two were being prepared, unconsciously to themselves, for fraternization. In this process our advent on the scene enabled the onlooker to give us credit for the consummation of the happy event.

Be that as it may, the delirious happenings remind me of the early days of the Khilafat movement. The fraternization then burst on the public as a new experience. Moreover, we had then the Khilafat and Swaraj as our twin goals. Today we have nothing of the kind. We have drunk the poison of mutual hatred and so this nectar of fraternization tastes all the sweeter and the sweetness should never wear out.

P, MG: LP *Vol. II, pp. 381–2*

August 1947

I WILL give you a talisman. Whenever you are in doubt, or when the self becomes too much with you, apply the following test. Recall the face of the poorest and the weakest man whom you may have seen, and ask yourself if the step you contemplate is going to be of any use to him. Will he gain anything by it? Will it restore him to a control over his own life and destiny? In other words, will it lead to swaraj for the hungry and spiritually starving millions?

Then you will find your doubts and yourself melting away.

M.K. Gandhi[264]
'A Note'; From a facsimile: Mahatma, *Vol. VIII, p. 89;*
CWMG *Vol. No. 89, p. 125*

He wrote to Jawaharlal

24 August 1947

PUNJABIS IN Calcutta have been pressing me to go to the Punjab at once. They tell me a terrible story. Thousands have been killed! A few thousand girls have been kidnapped! Hindus cannot live in the Pakistan area, nor Muslims in the other portion. Add to this the information that the two wings of the army took sides and worked havoc! Can any of this be true!

When do you think I should go to the Punjab if at all? I have still work in Calcutta, then in Noakhali and Bihar. But everything can be laid aside to go to the Punjab if it is proved to be necessary.

P, MG: LP *Vol. II, p. 385*

THIS WAS about 10 p.m.[265] They began to shout at the top of their voices. My sleep was disturbed but I tried to lie quiet, not knowing what was happening. I heard the window panes being smashed. I had ... on either side of me two very brave girls (Abha and Manu). They would not (wake me up from my) sleep, but without my knowledge—for my eyes were closed—they went among the crowd and tried to pacify them. Thank God, the crowd did not do any harm to them.

The old Muslim lady in the house endearingly called Bi Amma and a young Muslim stood near my matting, I suppose, to protect me from harm. The noise continued to swell. Some had entered the central hall, and begun to knock open the many doors. I felt that I must get up and face the angry crowd. I stood at the threshold of one of the doors. Friendly faces surrounded me and would not let me move forward.

Gandhi asked them:

What madness is this? Why do not you attack me? I offer myself for attack.

He repeated it thrice and asked his Bengali grand-niece-in-law to translate his words into Bengali.

All to no purpose. Their ears were closed against reason. I clasped my hands in the Hindu fashion. Nothing doing. More window panes began to crack.

At that point two Muslim members of the family with whom Gandhi was staying came rushing in pursued by the crowd. One of them was bleeding profusely. He took shelter behind Gandhi. A massive brickbat was aimed at him. It struck another Muslim standing by. A heavy stick narrowly missed Gandhi's head, crashing against the opposite wall without hurting anybody.
Gandhi then said:

My God asks me, 'Where do you stand?' I am deeply pained. 'Is this the reality of the peace that was established on the 15 August?'

Dr Prafulla Ghosh, the Chief Minister arrived at that point. He asked Gandhi: 'Shall we arrest Hindu Mahasabha leaders?'

MKG: No. Instead, you should put upon them the burden and responsibility of maintaining the peace. Ask them whether they want peace or fighting. Tell them you want their cooperation and wait for their reply.

P, MG: LP Vol. II, pp. 403–4

You are right. I am praying for light. May be, by nightfall I shall get a clear indication.[266]

P, MG: LP Vol. II, pp. 405–6

1 September 1947

Preparations for a fight are today in evidence everywhere.[267] I have just returned after seeing the corpses of two Muslims who have died of wounds. I hear that conflagration has burst out at many places. What was regarded as the 'Calcutta miracle' has proved to be a nine days' wonder. I am pondering what my duty is in the circumstances. I am writing this almost at 6 p.m. This letter will leave with tomorrow's post. I shall, therefore, be able to add a postscript to it. There is a wire from Jawahar that I should proceed to the Punjab. How can I go now? I am searching deep within myself. In that silence helps.

A Marwari: How can we help?

MKG: You should go in the midst of the flames and prevent them from spreading or get killed in the attempt. A number of you are businessmen of long standing in the city. At least in the localities where you carry on your business your presence should tell. But in any case do not return alive to report failure.

The Marwari: All this is the work of the Sikhs. They want to take revenge here for what is happening in the West Punjab.

MKG: Whoever is responsible for it will regret it. They do not know what it will cost them. Well, it will be as God wills.

P, MG: LP Vol. II, pp. 406–7

Governor Rajagopalachari came in at 10 p.m., Gandhi showed him a draft announcing his fast. Rajaji responded:

CR: You don't expect me to approve of your proposed step. Can one fast against the goondas?

MKG: I want to touch the hearts of those who are behind the goondas. The hearts of the goondas may or may not be touched. It would be enough for my purpose if they realize that society at large has no sympathy with their aims or methods and that the peace-loving element is determined to assert itself or perish in the attempt.

CR: Why not wait and watch a little?

MKG: The fast has to be now or never. It will be too late afterwards. The minority community cannot be left in a parlous condition. My fast has to be preventive if it is to be of any good. I know I shall be able to tackle the Punjab too if I can control Calcutta. But if I falter now, the conflagration may spread, and soon I can see clearly, two or three Powers will be upon us and thus will end our short-lived dream of independence.

CR: But supposing you die, the conflagration would be worse.

MKG: At least I won't be a living witness of it. I shall have done my duty. More is not given to a man to do.

CR: Why add sour lime juice to water if you are to put yourself entirely in God's hands?

MKG: You are right. I allowed it out of weakness. It jarred on me even as I wrote it. A satyagrahi must hope to survive his conditional fast only by the timely fulfilment of the terms of his fast.

And so the portion referring to the sour lime juice was scored out and the unadulterated venture of faith commenced.

P, MG: LP Vol. II, pp. 407–8

After referring to the disturbances at Hydari Manzil on the night of 31 August, the statement went on:

WHAT IS the lesson of the incident? It is clear to me that if India is to retain her dearly-won independence, all men and women must completely forget lynch law. What was attempted was an indifferent imitation of it ... There is no way of keeping the peace in Calcutta or elsewhere if the elementary rule of civilized society is not observed. ... The recognition of the golden rule of never taking the law into one's own hands has no exceptions ...

From the very first day of peace, that is August 14th last, I have been saying that the peace might only be a temporary lull: there was no miracle. Will the foreboding prove true and will Calcutta again lapse into the law of the jungle? Let us hope not, let us pray to the Almighty that He will touch our hearts and ward off the recurrence of insanity.

Since the foregoing was written ... some of the places which were safe till yesterday (31 August) have suddenly become unsafe. Several deaths have taken place. I saw two bodies of very poor Muslims. I saw also some wretched-looking Muslims being carted away to a place of safety. I quite see the last night's incidents, so fully described above, pale into insignificance before this flare up. Nothing that I may do in the way of going about in the open conflagration could possibly arrest it.

I have told the friends who saw me ... what their duty is. What part am I to play in order to stop it? The Sikhs and the Hindus must not forget what the East Punjab has done during these few days. Now the Muslims in the west Punjab have begun the mad career. It is said that the Sikhs and the Hindus (of Calcutta) are enraged over the Punjab happenings.

Now that the Calcutta bubble seems to have burst, with what face can I go to the Punjab? The weapon which has hitherto proved infallible for me is fasting. To put an appearance before a yelling crowd does not always work. It certainly did not last night. What my word in person cannot do, my fast may. It may touch the hearts of all the warring elements in the Punjab if it does in Calcutta. I, therefore, begin fasting from 8.15 tonight to end only if and when sanity returns to Calcutta. I shall, as usual, permit myself to add salt and soda bicarb to the water I may wish to drink during the fast.

If the people of Calcutta wish me to proceed to the Punjab and help the people there, they have to enable me to break the fast as early as may be.

In a supplementary statement to the Press, the Governor said that if trouble had not broken out in Calcutta, Gandhi would have gone to the Punjab. It was in their hands to send him to the Punjab. 'The women and children of the Punjab are eagerly looking forward to his presence in their midst and to the healing influence of his word and spirit. Let us send him with the laurels of victory round his aged brow to that afflicted Province.'

P, MG: LP *Vol. II, pp. 408–9*

2 September 1947

SINCE WRITING[268] ... yesterday, a lot more news has come. A number of people also have come and seen me. I was already pondering within me as to what my duty was. The news that I received clinched the issue for me. I decided to undertake a fast. It commenced at 8.15 last evening. Rajaji came last night. I patiently listened to all that he had to say. He exhausted all the resources of his logic ... But none of his arguments went down with me. ... Let no-one be perturbed. Perturbation won't help. If the leaders are sincere, the killing will stop and the fast end, and if the killing continues what use is my life? If I cannot prevent people from running amock, what else is left for me to do? If God wants to take work from this body He will enter into the people's hearts, bring them round to sanity and sustain my body. In His name alone was my fast undertaken. May God sustain and protect you all. In this conflagration others will not be able to help much.

P, MG: LP *Vol. II, pp. 409–10*

2 September 1947[269]

I WOULD have started for Lahore today but for the flare up in Calcutta. If the fury did not abate, my going to the Punjab would be of no avail. I would have no self-confidence If the Calcutta friendship was wrong, how could I hope to affect the situation in the Punjab? Therefore my departure from Calcutta depends solely upon the result of the Calcutta fast. Don't be distressed or angry over the fast.

P, MG: LP *Vol. II, p. 410*

Chief Minister Dr P.C. Ghosh: You have been very unfair to the Ministry in undertaking the fast without taking them into your confidence.

MKG: Perhaps you are right. But the conflagration was spreading so fast that every moment counted. Any avoidable delay would have meant further loss of innocent lives.

Dr Ghosh: One thing, however, strikes me. You have launched your fast at a time when a section of the Hindus have begun to look upon you as their enemy. They foolishly feel that by asking them to practice non-violence, when the other side has shed all scruples, you are being very unfair to them. I would have had nothing to say if you had declared a fast for anything wrong that the Ministry did.

MKG: All this is wide of the mark. Don't you see, this now gives me the right to fast against the Muslims, too. My fast is intended to serve both the communities. The moment the Hindus realize that they cannot keep me alive on any other terms, peace will return to Calcutta.

Dr Ghosh: Your fast weighs down on us more than anything else. How can we effectively set to work under the heavy weight of your fast?

MKG: It is a wrong way of looking at the thing. My fast is intended to strengthen your hands and to spur everybody to greater activity. You will be done for if you regard it as an oppression:

P, MG: LP Vol. II, pp. 413–14

Dr Shyama Prasad Mookerjee was the next to come (on 2 September 1947). He was accompanied by some other Hindu Mahasabha leaders. Before he could say anything, Gandhiji made solicitous inquiries about his health. This concern for him, by one who was himself fasting, touched Dr Mookerjee deeply.

Dr Mookerjee: The general feeling here now is in favour of peace. But there is danger of a delayed repercussion in East Bengal. The news from Dacca is disturbing. There may be a flare up there any moment.

MKG: It is inevitable if the situation here does not improve immediately.

Dr Mookerjee: From tomorrow[270] Hindusthan National Guards (of Hindu Mahasabha) will be patrolling the streets along with the Muslim National Guards.

P, MG: LP Vol. II, p. 415

The Governor sent a note at half past five. Tension had ceased in the city, he said. All was now quiet and he would come to see Gandhi at night. By 6 p.m. a deputation of the citizens of Calcutta representing all communities came.

In it were Suhrawardy himself, N.C. Chatterjee, and Sardar Niranjan Singh Talib. They told him that they had been to the affected parts of the city and found quiet everywhere. They said they would hold themselves responsible for maintaining peace thereafter and requested him to terminate his fast. Gandhiji spoke after some reflection. He deprecated the suggestion that the outbreak of violence was not communal in character but really the work of the goondas.

IT IS we who make the goondas and we alone can unmake them. Goondas never act on their own. By themselves they cannot function.

P, MG: LP *Vol. II, pp. 419 and 421*

I AM breaking this fast[271] so that I might be able to do something for the Punjab. I have accepted your assurance at its face value. I hope and pray I shall never have to regret it. I would certainly like to live to serve India and humanity, but I do not wish to be duped into prolonging my life. I hope I will not have again to fast for the peace of Calcutta. Let me therefore warn you that you dare not relax your vigilance. Calcutta today holds the key to the peace of the whole of India. If something happens here, its repercussion is bound to be felt elsewhere. You should, therefore, solemnly resolve that even if the whole world went up in a blaze, Calcutta would remain untouched by the flames. You have just heard the song 'Ishwar and Allah are thy names.' May He be witness between you and me.

PUT OUT the lights, drain every drop of *ghee* into a vessel and distribute it to the poor[272].

P, MG: LP *Vol. II, pp. 423–4*

In Death

New Delhi

9 September 1947

Pandit Nehru:　The wretches have created chaos in the whole city.[273] What can we say to Pakistan now?

MKG :　What is the use of being angry?

Pandit Nehru:　I am angry with myself. We go about with armed guards under elaborate security measures. It is a disgrace. Ration shops have been looted. Fruit, vegetables, and provisions are difficult to obtain. What must be the plight of the ordinary citizen? Dr Joshi, the famous surgeon who knew no distinction between Hindu and Muslim but served both alike, was fired upon from a Muslim house while he was proceeding to visit a patient and was killed.

P, MG: LP *Vol. II, p. 431*

'MAN PROPOSES God disposes' has come true often enough in my life, as it probably has in the case of many others.[274] When I left Calcutta on Sunday last, I knew nothing about the sad state of things in Delhi. But since my arrival in the capital city, I have been listening the whole day long to the tale of woe that is Delhi today. I have seen several Muslim friends who have recited to me their pathetic story. I have heard enough to warn me that I must not leave Delhi for the Punjab until it has once again become its former peaceful self.

I must do my little bit to calm the heated atmosphere. I must apply the old formula, 'do or die' to the capital of India. I am glad to be able to say that the residents of Delhi do not want the senseless destruction that is going on. I am prepared to understand the anger of the refugees, whom fate has driven from West Punjab. Retaliation is no remedy. It makes the original disease...worse. I, therefore, ask all those who are engaged in committing senseless murders, arson and loot, to stay their hands.

P, MG: LP *Vol. II, pp. 433–4*

MKG to the refugees:[275] Die with God's name on your lips if necessary but do not lose heart.

P, MG: LP *Vol. II, pp. 435–6*

THE WAVELL Canteen transit camp near the railway station was filled with Muslim refugees waiting to be evacuated to Pakistan. A wounded Pathan was brought into the camp while Gandhiji was there. It was a pathetic sight.

While arrangements were being made for the removal of the Pathan to the hospital Gandhiji remarked:

INDIA HAS to expiate for the massacre of the innocents.

P, MG: LP *Vol. II, p. 436*

The Sikhs were sore over the Government's decision to prohibit, on security grounds, the carrying of *kirpans* more than nine inches long. Their representatives met Gandhiji in a deputation and complained that any such restriction was an interference with their religion.

BUT I do not see religion anywhere in evidence today. And if it is a religious *symbol*, the restriction as regards its size should not matter.

P, MG: LP, Vol. II, p. 438

The head of the Rashtriya Swayamsevak Sangh also called on Gandhiji. It was common knowledge that the R.S.S., as it was called for short, had been behind the bulk of the killings in the city as also in various other parts of India. This these friends denied. Their organization was for protecting Hinduism—not for killing Muslims. It was not hostile to anyone. It stood for peace.

Gandhiji, with his boundless faith in human nature and in the redemptive power of truth, felt he must give everybody a chance to make good his *bona fide*. They should issue a public statement, he told them, repudiating the allegations against them and openly condemn the killing and harassment of the Muslims that had taken place and that still was going on in the city. They said Gandhiji could do that himself on their behalf on the strength of what they had told him. Gandhiji answered that he would certainly do that but if what they were saying was sincerely meant, it was better that the public should have it from their own lips.

A member of Gandhiji's party later interjected that the R.S.S. people had done a fine job of work at Wah refugee camp. They had shown discipline, courage, and capacity for hard work.

BOTH THE Sardar and Pandit Nehru will be rendered powerless if you become judge and executioner in one. They are tried servants of the nation. Give them a chance to serve you. Do not sabotage their efforts by taking the law into your own hands.[276]

P, MG: LP Vol. II, pp. 439–41

MKG:[277] I feel like a general without an army. To whom am I to give the marching orders?

Joshi: The general has no confidence in himself. He is not calling the army. Calcutta was a hundred times worse. In Calcutta you had *shanti sena* (peace brigades); here we shall provide Home Guards. You have made the nation, you must take it on. Give us the call.

MKG: I made it and I unmade it. You are all young men. I have not your self-assurance—and I am not sorry for that. I shall try to profit by your advice.

Reconstructed from P, MG: LP Vol. II, p. 442

IT GRIEVES[278] and hurts me that this historic city, where Indraprastha once stood, which has witnessed the rise and fall of so many dynasties and civilizations, where ruled the Kauravas and the Pandavas and the Moghuls, where the Muslims honoured Swami Shraddhanand by asking him to address them from the Juma mosque and which the Swamiji sanctified by his martyrdom, should have disgraced itself as it has today.

P, MG: LP Vol. II, pp. 444-5

These thoughts[279] have haunted me throughout these last twenty hours. My silence has been a blessing. It has made me inquire within. Have the citizens of Delhi gone mad? Have they no humanity left in them? Have love of the country and its freedom no appeal for them? I must be pardoned for putting the first blame on the Hindus and Sikhs. Could they not be men enough to stem the tide of hatred? I would urge the Muslims of Delhi to shed all fear, trust God, and discover all the arms in their possession which the Hindus and Sikhs fear they have. Either the minority rely upon God and His creature man to do the right thing or rely upon their firearms to defend themselves against those whom, they feel, they must not trust.

P, MG: LP Vol. II, pp. 445-6

MY ADVICE[280] is precise and firm. Its soundness is manifest. Trust your Government to defend every citizen against wrong-doers. ... Further, trust it to demand and get damages for every member of the minority wrongfully dispossessed. All that neither Government can do is to resurrect the dead. The people of Delhi will make it difficult to demand justice from the Pakistan Government if they take the law into their own hands. Those who seek justice must do justice, must have clean hands.

P, MG: LP Vol. II, p. 446

18 September 1947

... WHEN I go to Pakistan I will not spare them. I shall die for the Hindus and the Sikhs there. I shall be really glad to die there. I shall be glad to die here too. ...

CWMG *Vol. 89, p. 201; H*

MKG: You saw it happen with your own eyes?[281]
The Refugee: Yes, I saw it happen with my own eyes.
MKG: And you have lived to report this?

P, MG: LP *Vol. II, p. 451*

I BEGAN repeating Ramanama to myself and to expostulate with him[282] to calm him.

SLEEPING OR walking I can think of nothing else.[283]

P, MG: LP *Vol. II, pp. 453–4*

23 September 1947

I WANT to go to Lahore. I want to go to Rawalpindi. ... If you avoid fighting in Delhi I will take it that God has granted my prayer. Then with the grace of God, I will go to the Punjab. Let me tell you that once peace descends on Delhi, I shall not stay here even a day longer.

Prarthana Pravachan-I, *pp. 337–40;* CWMG *Vol. 89, pp. 223–6*

MKG: I had a dream.[284] I saw her (Kasturba) standing there (pointing her finger at vacant space). Of course I must try to sleep.

P, MG: LP *Vol. II, p. 454*

The Last Birthday

EITHER THE present conflagration should end or He should take me away.[285] I do not wish another birthday to overtake me in an India still in flames.

WHERE DO congratulations[286] come in? It will be more appropriate to say good wishes. There is nothing but anguish in my heart.

S. Radhakrishnan, Mahatma Gandhi, A Hundred Years,
New Delhi, 1968, p. 10

WHAT SIN must I have committed that He should have kept me alive to witness all these horrors?[287]

P, MG: LP *Vol. II, p. 457*

After the visitors had left, he had another spasm of coughing.

I WOULD prefer to quit this frame unless the all-healing efficacy of His name fills me. The desire to live for 125 years has completely vanished as a result of this continued fratricide. I do not want to be a helpless witness of it.

P, MG: LP *Vol. II, p. 457*

Humans And Snakes

New Delhi
3 October 1947

... TO LIKEN[288] a human being, however degraded he may be, to a snake to justify inhuman treatment is surely a degrading performance ... I have known rabidly fanatical Muslims to use the very analogy in respect of Hindus. ...

Lastly, let me, for the sake of snake-kind, correct a common error (I am say) that eighty snakes out of every hundred are perfectly harmless and they render useful service in nature.

Harijan, *12-10-1947;* CWMG, *Vol. 89, p. 276*

New Delhi
27 October 1947

My dear Shaheed,

I address you frankly. I would like you, if you can, to remove your angularity. If you think you have none, I withdraw my remarks.

Hindus and Muslims are not two nations. Muslims never shall be slaves of Hindus nor Hindus of Muslims. Hence you and I have to die in the attempt to make them live together as friends and brothers, which they are. Whatever others my say, you and I have to regard Sikhs and others as part of India. If anyone of them declines, it is their concern.

I cannot escape the conclusion that the mischief commenced with Quaid-e-Azam and still continues. This I say more to make myself clear to you than to correct you. I have only one course—to do or die in the attempt to make the two one.

Yours,
Bapu
P, MG: LP *Vol. II, pp. 483–4*

29 November 1947
BUT WHEN someone commits a crime anywhere I feel I am the culprit. You too should feel the same.

CWMG, *Vol. 90, p. 133; H*

I FANCY I know the art of living and dying non-violently. But I have yet to demonstrate it by one perfect act.[289]

P, MG: LP*, Vol. II, pp. 475–6*

On Junagadh

On the 17 August, two days after the transfer of power, it was learnt that the Nawab of Junagadh, a State of 3,300 square miles and a population of 700,000 of which 82 per cent were Hindus, had acceded to Pakistan.

Gandhi set forth his own attitude on the Junagadh issue in his prayer address on the 11 November. In free India, he said, the whole country belonged to the people, none of it belonged to Princes as individuals. Accession to Pakistan by the Junagadh Nawab against the wishes of his people was, he said, ab initio void.

A plebiscite was held in Junagadh State in February 1948. The count showed that out of the total votes polled 190,779 were in favour of accession to India; only 91 for Pakistan. The result of course was foregone.

Unfortunately, communalist groups which by and large were behind the killings in Delhi and elsewhere, had also obtained a foothold in Kathiawar and there was some killing, arson, and loot in Junagadh also, before it was brought under control.

Gandhi lost no time in condemning in the plainest language possible the alleged communal excesses in Kathiawar.

WE SHOULD never make the mistake of thinking that we never make any mistakes. The bitterest critic is bitter because he has some grudge, fancied or real, against us. We shall set him right if we are patient with him and, whenever the occasion arises, show him his error or correct our own when we are found to be in error...In the present disturbed atmosphere, when charges are hurled against one another, it would be folly to live in a fool's paradise and feel that we can do no wrong. That blissful state it is no longer possible for us to claim. It will be creditable if by strenuous effort we succeed in isolating the mischief and then eradicating it ... Nature has so made us that we do not see our backs; it is reserved for others to see them. Hence it is wise to profit by what they see.

In *Harijan* he wrote:

When it is relevant, truth has to be uttered, however unpleasant it may be ... Misdeeds of the Hindus in the Union have to be proclaimed by Hindus from the housetop, if those of the Muslims in Pakistan are to be arrested or stopped.

P, MG: LP *Vol. II, pp. 488–90*

On Kashmir Again

On the 23 October large armed bands of tribesmen from the Frontier Province came into Muzaffarabad from Abbottabad-Mansera with soldiers of the Pakistan army, said to be 'on leave'. They were fully armed with modern weapons, including Bren guns, machine guns, mortars, and flame throwers. Coming in about 100 trucks, driven by petrol issued from the Frontier Province and West Punjab rationed quota, they moved rapidly towards Srinagar, resorting to arson, murder, loot, rape and the abduction of women all along the way.

The State forces were in a panic and altogether inadequate to cope with the emergency and a most critical situation developed.

The Maharaja of Kashmir approached the Union Government with the request to send arms and troops immediately to save the situation. But under Lord Mountbatten's advice decided that the Union Government could not send their troops into Kashmir unless it became an inescapable obligation by Kashmir's accession to India. V.P. Menon, the Secretary to the Ministry of States, flew on the 25 October to convey to the Maharaja this decision of the Union Government. He returned on the 26 October with a duly signed letter from the Maharaja declaring Kashmir's accession to India.

The letter of accession read: 'With the conditions obtaining at present in my State and the great emergency of the situation as it exists, I have no option but to ask for help from the Indian dominion. Naturally they cannot send the help asked for by me without my State acceding to the Dominion of India. I have accordingly decided to do so and I attach the Instrument of Accession for acceptance by your Government.'

The raiders had spared no one. They had sacked St Joseph's Convent at Baramula, smashed hospital equipment, wounded the Mother Superior of the Order of St Francis, violated a number of nuns and shot some. The reign of terror continued for nine days at Baramula. Loot and women were the chief prizes sought by the raiders. But for their preoccupation with these, they might have overrun the whole of Kashmir before the Indian troops arrived.

Gandhi had been following the developments in Kashmir closely. He re-affirmed in one of his prayer addresses, that the real rulers of all the States were their people. The people of Kashmir, without any coercion or show of force from within or without, he said, must by themselves decide the issue.

Brigadier Usman, a Muslim officer of the Indian army, fell fighting valiantly while commanding his troops. Mir Maqbool Sherwani, a young Muslim leader of the National Conference in Baramula was captured by the invaders when they took Baramula. He was asked to repudiate the Kashmir National Conference and swear allegiance to the so-called Azad Kashmir Government. He told his captors to their face that their triumph would be short-lived as the Indian troops would be soon back in Baramula. Nails were driven through the palms of his hands and his body was riddled with fourteen bullets followed by defacement and mutilation. His dying prophecy was to be fulfilled 48 hours later, with the raiders being driven out of Baramula by Indian troops. Paying a tribute to his steadfastness and undaunted courage in one of his prayer addresses Gandhi remarked:

THIS WAS a martyrdom of which anyone—Hindu, Sikh, Muslim, or any other—would be proud.

P, MG: LP, *Vol. II*

Gandhi un-enamoured of taking any Indo-Pakistan dispute to an outside organization. It would only get them 'monkey justice', he warned. Were the Union and Pakistan always to depend on a third party to settle their disputes? He asked in the course of his post-prayer address on the 25 December.

WILL NOT the Pakistan Government and the Union Government close the ranks and come to an amicable settlement with the assistance of impartial Indians? Or, has impartiality fled from India? I am sure it has not.

P, MG: LP, Vol. II, p. 498

Following upon the Punjab upheavals, in October 1947, Muslim evacuee convoys going out of Jammu were attacked and massacred by non-Muslims. The State army played a very discreditable part in these massacres. When Gandhi came to know of this he said that the Maharaja, as the absolute ruler, could not be absolved from responsibility for such happenings; he was unfit to continue to hold power. He should, therefore, either abdicate or remain only as the titular head 'even as the British King is'; full power *de jure* and *de facto* being transferred to the true representatives of the people.

The instrument of accession stands as it is. It confers on or reserves certain rights for the ruler. I, as a private individual, have ventured to advise that he (the Maharaja) should waive or diminish the rights and perform the duty pertaining to the office of a Hindu prince. If I am wrong as to my facts, I should be corrected. If I err in my conception of Hinduism and of the duty of the Hindu prince, I am out of court.

P, MG: LP Vol. II, p. 499

IF SHEIKH Abdullah is erring in the discharge of his duty as the chief of the Cabinet or as a devout Muslim, he should certainly step aside and give place to a better man. It is on the Kashmir soil that Islam and Hinduism are being weighed. If both pull their weight correctly and in the same direction, the chief actors will cover themselves with glory and nothing can move them from their joint credit. My sole hope and prayer is that Kashmir should become a beacon light to this benighted sub-continent.

P, MG: LP Vol. II, pp. 499–500

Would the Muslims continue to look upon the Hindus and Sikhs as their 'enemies' and vice versa till the Kashmir issue was settled? He asked on the evening of 20 January 1948. The army of the Indian Union had not entered

Kashmir on their own; they had gone there at the call of the ruler of the State and the leaders of the Kashmir Muslims.

IF THE invaders, tribesmen and others, would withdraw and leave the issue to the rebels in Poonch and the rest of Kashmir without any aid from outside, it would be time to ask the Indian troops to withdraw.[290]

P, MG: LP Vol. II, pp. 500-1

Princess Elizabeth Weds

9 November 1947

Lord Mountbatten was going home on short leave to attend the wedding of Princess (now Queen) Elizabeth with his nephew, who had been brought up in the Mountbatten home. Gandhi had spoken in one of his meetings with Lord Mountbatten of sending a wedding present. Mountbatten was delighted. 'But what can I send?' Gandhi had enquired: 'You know I have no worldly possessions.' After some discussion, it was decided that he should send something made by himself. On returning to his residence he sent for some yarn of his own spinning and had it made into a tea-cloth.

THIS LITTLE thing is made out of doubled yarn of my own spinning. The knitting was done by a Punjabi girl ... Please give the bride and the bridegroom this with my blessings, with the wish that they would have a long and happy life of service of men.

P, MG: LP Vol. II, p. 514

To The Congress

WHEN WE were fighting for our freedom, we bore a heavy responsibility[291]. But today, when we have achieved freedom, our responsibility has grown a hundred-fold ... There are many places where a Muslim cannot live in security ... I would not be satisfied if you said that it could not be helped or that you had no part in it... We have to fight against this insanity and find a cure for it ... I confess that I have not yet found it. ...

As things are, we cannot hold our heads high in the world today and we have to confess that we have been obliged to copy Pakistan in its misdeeds and have thereby justified its ways ...

I repeat that it is your prime duty to treat Muslims as your brothers, no matter what happens in Pakistan ... Restraint will add to your strength ... If, on the other hand, you approve of what has happened, you must change the very creed and character of the All-India Congress Committee. This is the root issue before you. Let all Muslims who have left their homes and fled to Pakistan come back here ... Whatever Pakistan may do now, sooner or later it will be obliged by the pressure of world opinion to conform. Then war will not be necessary and you will not have to empty your exchequer ...

A hundred and fifty thousand Muslims near Gurgaon are about to be sent to Pakistan. It is said they are not better than criminal tribes and had better be sent to Pakistan. I cannot understand the logic of this argument. There were criminal tribes in India during the British regime. Was there any talk of deporting them then? It is wrong of us to send them away because they are 'criminal'. Our duty should be to reform them. How shameful it is for us that we should force them to trudge three hundred miles! I am against all such forced exodus ...

I know some people are saying, the Congress has surrendered its soul to the Muslims. Gandhi! Let him rave as he will. He is a washout. Jawaharlal is no better. As regards Sardar Patel, there is something in him. A portion of him is sound Hindu, but he, too, is after all a Congressman! Such talk will not help us ... Violent rowdyism will not save either Hinduism or Sikhism. Such is not the teaching of Guru Granth Sahib. Christianity does not teach these ways. Nor has Islam been saved by the sword. I hear many things about the R.S.S. I have heard it said that the R.S.S. is at the root of all this mischief ... Hinduism cannot be saved by orgies of murder. You are now a free people. You have to preserve your freedom. You can do so if you are humane and brave and ever vigilant, or else a day will come when you will rue the folly which made this lovely prize slip from your hands. I hope such a day will never come.

P, MG: LP Vol. II, pp. 516–18

A few days later some Hindu and Sikh refugees went out to an empty Muslim house and tried forcibly to occupy it. A scuffle ensued and a rumour was spread that four Sikhs had been killed. Retribution followed. Curfew had to be re-imposed in several parts of the city. Gandhiji sadly remarked to Rajaji that he would rather that his eyes were closed in death than that he should be a living witness to what was going on around him.

WHAT IS the use of my getting the Congress or the A.I.C.C. to pass certain resolutions if they are to be rendered nugatory in action?

P, MG: LP Vol. II, p. 521

To General Cariappa

General K.M. Cariappa of the Indian Army a statement made in England had said that non-violence was of no use in India; only a strong army could make India one of the greatest nations in the world. Gandhi joined issue with him in *Harijan*:

GENERALS GREATER than General Cariappa have been wise and humble enough frankly to make the admission that they can have no right to speak of the possibilities of the great force of Ahimsa. I make bold to say that in this age of the atom bomb, unadulterated non-violence is the only force that can confound all the tricks put together of violence. We are witnessing the tragic insolvency of military science and practice in its own home. Should a bankrupt, who has been (ruined) by the gamble in the share-market, sing the praise of that particular form of gambling?

P, MG: LP Vol. II, pp. 522-3

MKG: You know something of my having written in my paper about your statement on non-violence in London last month?[291]

General Cariappa: We soldiers are a very much maligned community. ... Even you think that we are a very violent tribe. But we are not ... Of all the peoples in this world, the one community which dislikes wars is the soldier community. It is not because of dangers and horrors in the battlefield but because of the knowledge we have of the utter futility of wars to settle international disputes. We feel one war merely leads to another. History has taught us this. In a democratic country soldiers do not initiate wars ... Governments, when they have failed to get a satisfactory solution to international problems, declare wars. ... So you see we are the innocent party ... Why blame us?

MKG: When we meet again ... I would like further to discuss this subject with you.

P, MG: LP, Vol. II, p. 523

Two days later they met again. 'He was looking very cheerful', the General recalls. 'I was in uniform on this occasion. I stood in front of him and saluted him.'

MKG: I see you have again removed your shoes outside. You had done it when you came two days ago also.

General Cariappa: It is but proper that I should do so when coming to see a godly man like you. If we have to have an army at all ... it must be a good one ... I would ... like to remind them in my own way of the need for and the value of non-violence. I cannot possibly do my duty well by the country if I concentrate only on telling the troops of non-violence all the time, subordinating their main task of preparing themselves efficiently to be good soldiers. So I ask you, please, to give me the 'Child's Guide to Knowledge' ... Tell me, please, how I can put this over, i.e., the spirit of non-violence to the troops ... without endangering their sense of duty to train themselves well professionally as soldiers. I am a child in this matter. I want your guidance.

MKG: Yes ... you are all children; I am a child too, but I happen to be a bigger child than you because I have given more thought to his question than you all have. You have asked me to tell you in a tangible and concrete form how you can put over to the troops you command the need for non-violence.

Half closing his eyes, he stretched his right arm out to emphasise his words and added:

I am still groping in the dark for the answer. I will find it and I will give it to you some day.

MKG: I will think about this seriously in the next few days and will let you know about it soon. However, I would like to see you more often so that we may further discuss this important subject more ... I have always had the greatest admiration for the discipline in the army and also for the importance you army people pay to sanitation and hygiene. I tell my people in my talks to them to copy the army in these respects.

General Cariappa: I am going to Kashmir in a few days' time.

MKG: I hope you will succeed in solving the Kashmir problem non-violently. Come and see me after your return from Kashmir.[292]

P, MG: LP *Vol. II, pp. 524–5*

The Last Fast

To the tension between India and Pakistan was now added the issue of Pakistan's share of the cash balances of undivided India amounting to Rupees 55 crore. On the ground that this money would provide Pakistan the sinews of war to be used against the Indian Union on the Kashmir soil, the Government of India deferred the payment of the amount.

Gandhi discussed the question with Lord Mountbatten on the 6 January 1948, and asked for his frank and candid opinion on the Government of India's decision. Mountbatten said, it would be the 'first dishonourable act' by the Indian Union government if the payment of the cash balance claimed by Pakistan was withheld. This set Gandhi thinking. He would have to, he felt, have to create a new moral climate.

Gandhiji had decided to launch on a fast unto death. ...

... A PURE fast, like duty, is its own reward. I do not embark upon it for the sake of the result it may bring. I do so because I must. Hence I urge everybody dispassionately to examine the purpose and let me die, if I must in peace which I hope is ensured. Death for me would be a glorious deliverance rather than that I should be a helpless witness of the destruction of India, Hinduism, Sikhism, and Islam. That destruction is certain if Pakistan ensures no equality of status and security of life and property for all professing the various faiths of the world and if India copies her. Only then Islam dies in the two Indias, not in the world. But Hinduism and Sikhism have no world outside India.

P, MG: LP *Vol. II, pp. 702–3*

Devadas ... made an impassioned attempt to dissuade him from the grave decision through a note which he drafted. The note ran: 'My chief concern and my argument against your fast is that you have surrendered to impatience, whereas your mission by its very nature calls for infinite patience. You do not seem to have realized what a tremendous success your patient labour has achieved. It has saved ... thousands of lives and may still save many more. ... By your death you will not be able to accomplish what you can by living. I would, therefore, beseech you to pay heed to my entreaty and give up your decision to fast.'

Gandhiji replied to Devadas:

... You ARE of course a friend and a friend of a very high order at that. But you cannot get over the son in you. Your concern is natural and I respect it. But your argument betrays impatience and superficial thinking ... I regard this step of mine as the acme of patience. Is patience which kills its very object patience or fully? I cannot accept the credit for what has been achieved since my arrival in Delhi. It would be sheer conceit on my part to do so. How can any mortal say with assurance that so many lives were saved as a result of his or anyone's labours? God alone could do that ...

... Your last sentence is a charming token of your affection. But your affection is rooted in attachment or delusion. Attachment does not become enlightenment because it relates to a public cause. So long as one has not shed all attachment and learnt to regard both life and death as same, it would be idle to pretend that he wants to live only because his life is indispensable for a certain cause. 'Strive while you live' is a beautiful saying, but there is a hiatus in it. Striving has to be in the spirit of detachment. Now perhaps you will understand why I cannot comply with your request. God sent this fast. He alone will end it, if and when He wills. In the meantime it behoves you, me, and everybody to have faith that it is equally well whether He preserves my life or ends it, and to act accordingly. I can therefore, only pray that He may lend strength to my spirit lest the desire to live may tempt me to a premature termination of my fast.

P, MG: LP *Vol. II, pp. 703–5*

Inside his room as Gandhi lay in his bed he heard some noise outside and asked.

MKG: What are they shouting?
Associate: They are shouting, 'Let Gandhi die'.
MKG: How many are they?
Associate: Not many.

With a sigh he began taking Ramanama.

The Cabinet of the Indian Union met on the lawn of Birla House round Gandhiji's fasting bed to consider afresh the issue of Pakistan's share of the cash balances.

At night some Sikhs from the West Punjab held a demonstration in front of Birla House, shouting, 'Blood for Blood', 'We want revenge', 'Let Gandhi die'. Pandit Nehru had just boarded his car to leave Birla House after meeting Gandhi. On hearing the shouts he got down from his car and rushed out. 'Who dares to shout "Let Gandhi die"?' he roared. 'Let him who dares repeat those words in my presence. He will have to kill me first.' The demonstrators scurried away.

P, MG: LP *Vol. II, p. 711*

On the third day of his fast (15 January) Gandhi was weak and had to be taken to his bathroom in a chair. One alarming symptom was that water was not being eliminated, the output being 28 ounces only against an input of 68 ounces. In other words, the kidneys were failing.

I AM taking my meal such as a fasting man with prescribed food can take. Don't be shocked. The food consists of 8 ounces of hot water sipped with difficulty. You sip it as poison, well knowing that in result it is nectar. It revives me whenever I take it. Strange to say, this time I am able to take about 8 meals of this poison-tasting but nectar-like meal. Yet I claim to be fasting and credulous people accept it! What a strange world! ...

Don't rush here because I am fasting. The Yajna, as I have called it, demands that everyone, wherever he or she is, should perform his or her duty. If an appreciable number do this, I must survive the ordeal. Trust God and be where you are.

P, MG: LP *Vol. II, pp. 714–15*

On the third day of Gandhiji's fast, the Government of India in a communiqué announced that it had decided to pay Pakistan immediately the sum of rupees 55 crore.

THE GOVERNMENT of India's decision has put the Pakistan Government on its honour. It ought to led to an honourable settlement not only of the Kashmir question, but of all the differences between the two Dominions. Friendship should replace the present enmity. It is never a light matter for any responsible Cabinet to alter a deliberate, settled policy. Yet our Cabinet, responsible in every sense of the term, has with equal deliberation yet promptness unsettled their settled fact ... I know that all the nations of the earth will proclaim this gesture as one which only a large-hearted Cabinet like ours could rise to. ... No Cabinet worthy of being representative of a large mass of mankind can afford to take any step merely because it is likely to win the hasty applause of an unthinking public. In the midst of insanity, should not our best representatives retain sanity and bravely prevent a wreck of the ship of State under their care?

P, MG: LP *Vol. II, p. 718*

What then was the motive behind the Union Government's decision? He asked rhetorically giving the following reply.

IT WAS my fast. It changed the whole outlook. Without the fast, they could not go beyond what the law permitted and required them to do ... There is a homely maxim of law which has been in practice for centuries in England that when common law seems to fail, equity comes to the rescue. Not long ago there were even separate courts for the administration of law and equity. Considered in this setting, there is no room for questioning the utter justice of this act of the Union Government.

P, MG: LP *Vol. II, p. 719*

I EMBARKED on the fast in the name of Truth whose familiar name is God. Without living Truth, God is nowhere. In the name of God we have indulged in lies, massacred people, without caring whether they were innocent or guilty, men or women, children or infants ... (But) I am not aware if anybody has done these things in the name of Truth. With the same name on my lips I have broken the fast. ...

Telegrams after telegrams have come from Pakistan and the Indian Union urging me to break my fast. I could not resist the counsel of all these friends. I could not disbelieve their pledge that come what may, there would be complete friendship between the Hindus, Muslims, Sikhs, Christians, Parsis, and Jews, a friendship not to be broken. ...

P, MG: LP *Vol. II, p. 733*

Towards The End

Two days after the breaking of the fast, on the 20 January 1948, while Gandhi was delivering his post-prayer address, there was a loud explosion. In an impassioned voice that can still be heard with the thud of the explosion on the sound track of All-India Radio, Gandhi upbraided the congregation for panicking.

After a little while order was restored and it was then found that a bomb had been detonated about 75 feet away from where Gandhi was seated. Madanlal Pahwa, a youth of about 25 years, who was a refugee from West Punjab, was arrested. On being searched, a hand-grenade was found on his person, he was unrepentant.

IF WE get panicked like this over nothing, what shall be our plight if something really happens? ... Listen! Listen! Listen everybody ... nothing has happened ... (a short, pained laugh and silence).

P, MG: LP *Vol. II, pp. 748–9*

A co-worker asked Gandhi whether he had not, by referring to the bomb explosion as an attempt on his life while the matter was sub judice, prejudged the issue and prejudiced the trial. For anything they knew, the whole matter might turn out to be a harmless prank of an irresponsible youth. Gandhi laughed and exclaimed.

THE FOOL! Don't you see, there is a terrible and widespread conspiracy behind it?

P, MG: LP *Vol. II, p. 750*

On the 27 of January, Gandhi attended the annual Urs at Mehrauli. Seven miles to the south of Delhi is the seat of the Dargah Sharif of Khwaja Syed Qutubuddin Bakhtiar—a shrine ranking second only to the world famous dargah of Khwaja Mohayuddin Chishti at Ajmer. It had been through some ghastly experiences.

Accompanying Gandhi were three women members of his party. As a rule, women were not allowed into the shrine beyond a certain point. Gandhi told the custodians of the dargah that the women members of his party would stop wherever the Islamic practice required. The Muslim friends who had taken him there, however, said that there was no need to leave them behind. They looked upon them 'not as women but as Mahatmaji's daughters'. The whole party was accordingly taken inside the shrine. Benedictory sweets were presented to Gandhi. These he distributed to the crowd around him. One of the Muslims requested that the women members of Gandhiji's party should sing the verses from the Muslim prayer, Fateha, just as they did daily at his evening prayer meeting. This they did with pleasure. He had heard that 130 innocent Hindus and Sikhs had been killed in Parachinar refugee camp at Peshawar by raiders from across the tribal territory. The actual casualties, it was feared, were many more. Referring to the Parachinar incident in the course of his address at the shrine Gandhi said the following:

I WANT you to take a vow that you will never again listen to the voice of Satan and abandon the way of brotherliness and peace.

P, MG: LP Vol. II, pp. 761–2

SEE WHAT India is doing.[293] See what is happening in Kashmir. I cannot deny that it is with my tacit consent. They would not lend ear to my counsel. Yet, if they were sick of it, I could today point them a way. Again, see the exhibition that the United Nations Organisation is making. Yet I have faith: If I live long enough ... they will see the futility of it all and come round to my way.

P, MG: LP Vol. II, p. 764

MKG: I cannot retire at anybody's bidding.[294] I have put myself under
    God's sole command.
Refugee: It is God who is speaking to you through us. We are beside
    ourselves with grief.
MKG: My grief is not less than yours.

P, MG: LP Vol. II, p. 765

WHERE WILL this[295] take us? How long will this last? Shall we be able at this rate to maintain our prestige in the world? Where do I stand?

What must I do to realize unruffled calm and serenity in the midst of this disquiet?

He then had a severe fit of coughing. Asked to suck penicillin lozenges to allay it, he reiterated for the last time his resolve to be cured by the power of Ramanama alone. To one of his attendants who was massaging his head, he said the following:

IF I die of a lingering illness ... it will be your duty to proclaim to the world, even at the risk of making people angry with you, that I was not the man of God that I claimed to be. If you do that it will give my spirit peace. Note down this also that if someone were to end my life by putting a bullet through me—as someone tried to do with a bomb the other day and I met his bullet without a groan, and breathed my last taking God's name, then alone would I have made good my claim.

P, MG: LP *Vol. II, pp. 765–6*

30 January 1948

On the fateful Friday, the 30 January 1948, Gandhiji woke up as usual at 3.30 a.m. One of his party had not got up for prayer.

He did not feel well enough to go out for his morning walk. So he paced up and down for a while inside his room. He used to take palm-jaggery lozenges with powdered cloves to allay his cough. The clove powder had run out. Manu, therefore, instead of joining him in his constitutional sat down to prepare some. 'I shall join you presently,' she said to him, 'otherwise there will be nothing at hand at night when it is needed.' Gandhiji did not like anyone missing his duty in the immediate present to anticipate and provide for the uncertain future.

WHO KNOWS, what is going to happen before nightfall or even whether I shall be alive? If at night I am still alive you can easily prepare some them.

P, MG: LP *Vol. II, pp. 766–7*

At 1.30 in the afternoon he had his abdominal mud pack. The sun was warm. So he slipped on his Noakhali peasant's bamboo hat to shade his face. A journalist asked him if it was true that he would be leaving for Sevagram on the 1 February.

MKG: Who says so?
Journalist: The papers have it.
MKG: Yes, the papers have announced that Gandhiji would be going on the 1st. But who that Gandhi is, I do not know.

P, MG: LP *Vol. II, p. 770*

Among those who came to see him were Dr De Silva from Ceylon and his daughter. The latter got him to give her an autograph—perhaps the last autograph given by him in his life. A French photographer came next and presented to him an album of photographs. Other interviews followed. Margaret Bourke-White of *Life* magazine was having her interview with him when I left for the city.

At 4 p.m. the interviews came to an end. He then repaired with Sardar Patel, who had come with his daughter, to his room and had a talk with him for over one hour, while spinning. Although he had previously expressed his view, he told the Sardar, that one of the two—either the Sardar or Pandit Nehru—should withdraw from the Cabinet, he had since come to the firm conclusion that the presence there of both of them was indispensable. Any breach in their ranks at that stage would be disastrous. He further said, he would make that the topic of his post-prayer speech in the evening. Pandit Nehru would be seeing him after the prayer; he would discuss the question with him, too. If necessary, he would postpone his going to Sevagram and not leave Delhi till he had finally laid the spectre of disunity between the two.

P, MG: LP *Vol. II, pp. 770–1*

I Hate Being Late

And so the talk with the Sardar continued. At 4.20 p.m. Abha brought Gandhiji his evening meal. It was practically the same as that served in the morning.

It was getting near prayer time. But the Sardar had still not finished. Poor Abha felt fidgety, knowing the great importance that Gandhiji attached to punctuality, particularly in regard to prayer time. But she dared not interrupt. At last becoming desperate, she picked up his watch and held it before him to draw attention. But it was no good. Noting her predicament, the Sardar's daughter tactfully intervened. 'I must now tear myself away', Gandhiji said to the Sardar as he rose to get ready to go to the prayer-ground. On the way, one of the attendants told him that two workers from Kathiawar had asked for an appointment. 'Tell them to come after prayer', Gandhiji replied. 'I shall then see them—if I am alive.'

He then walked to the prayer ground, his hands resting on the shoulders of Abha and Manu as he laughed and exchanged jokes with them. Referring to the raw carrot menu which Abha had served him in the afternoon, he twitted her:

MKG: So you are serving me cattle fare!

Abha: Ba used to call it horse fare!

MKG: Is it not grand of me to relish what no-one else would care for?

Abha: Bapu, your watch must have felt neglected. You would not look at it.

MKG: Why should I since you are my time-keepers?

Abha: But you would not look at the time-keepers either!

MKG: I am late by ten minutes. I hate being late. I like to be at the prayer punctually at the stroke of five.

P, MG: LP *Vol. II, p. 772*

RAJMOHAN GANDHI concludes in *The Good Boatman* redemptively thus (pp. 436–8):

With this the three and those walking behind them fell into a complete silence, for they had reached the five curved steps that gently led up to the open prayer ground. It was Gandhi's stipulation that small talk and laughter had to cease, and all thoughts turn to their sacred purpose, before they put their feet on the prayer site.

Behind their backs the winter sun was setting. A 32-yard path lay between the steps and the platform where Gandhi used to sit for the prayers. The women and men who had come for the prayers lined the path on both sides. Removing his hands from the shoulders of the girls, Gandhi brought them together to acknowledge the greetings of the congregation.

From the side to the left of Gandhi, Nathuram Godse of Pune roughly elbowed his way towards him. Godse had been on the scene ten days earlier for the abortive attempt to kill Gandhi, had slipped away, travelled to Bombay, and returned with a fresh plan of assassination. Thinking that Godse intended to touch Gandhi's feet, Manu asked Godse not to interrupt Gandhi, added that they were late already, and tried to thrust back Godse's hand.

Godse violently pushed Manu aside, causing the Book of Ashram Prayer Songs and Gandhi's rosary that she was carrying to fall to the ground. As she bent down to pick the things up, Godse planted himself in front of Gandhi, pulled out a pistol and fired three shots in rapid succession, one into Gandhi's stomach and two into his chest.

The sound 'Rama' escaped twice from Gandhi's throat, crimson spread across his white clothes, the hands raised in the gesture of greeting which was also the gesture of prayer and of goodwill dropped down, and the limp body sank softly to the ground. As he fell, Abha caught Gandhi's head in her hands and sat down with it.

Always a sharp observer and well aware, as we have seen, of a conspiracy aimed at his life, Gandhi may have perceived Godse's intention before seeing the pistol in his hand. We will never know for certain whether he forgave Godse before life left him, but his mind was on prayer when he was shot and he had prayed earlier to be able to forgive his assassin.

A haste to pray. A hush on entering holy ground. A sense of the Eternal. Lines of fellow-worshippers. A gesture of goodwill. Rude elbows. A smell of attack. The ring of three bullets. 'God! God!' Possibly a silent, 'God! Forgive them.' Loving hands underneath. Earth, moisture, grass. The open sky. Rays from the dipping sun. A perfect death.

NOTES

Part One: 1869–85

1. Published in *Partisan Review*, January 1949.
2. Going beyond the original in Gujarati, the English version of the Autobiography specifies that the Gandhis 'belong to the Bania caste'.
3. The 'Gandhi line' has been traced back by Prabhudas Chhaganlal Gandhi in *Otabapa no Vadlo* (*Uttamchand Gandhi's Family Tree*) (*Navajivan*, 1972) to Lalji Gandhi (1665–1725), an employee of the Junagarh State in Kutiyana, whose son Ramji Gandhi (1698–1753) became a Daftari (Home Minister) under the Porbandar Rana, to be succeeded by his son Rahidas (1722–74) in the same position. Rahidas had two sons Harjivan (1748–1805) and Daman (1750–1810). Both held the same office of Daftari in Porbandar. Harjivan's son Uttamchand (1786–1852) rose to be Diwan (Prime Minister) of Porbandar, being succeeded by his son Karamchand (1822–85) in the same office. Karamchand's place was taken by his younger brother Tulsidas (1824–90).
4. Karamchand alias Kaba Gandhi (1822–85), Diwan of Porbandar (1847–74), Diwan of Rajkot (1874–8 and 1879–83), Diwan of Vankaner (1878–9).
5. Kaba Gandhi's third wife was still alive, an invalid, when he married Putlibai. (P, *MG: EP*, p. 185).
6. Muli Behn (1842–1913) and Pankunvarben (1845–70).
7. Putlibai (1843–91) of village Datrana, Junagadh State.
8. Gandhi had a distaste for constricting footwear, as we will see in later accounts pertaining to South Africa and of a visit to Calcutta in 1901.
9. At being shown a pair of 3000-year old heavy silver anklets by the curator of the archaeological museum at Taxila during a visit (July 1939) to that ancient site (now in Pakistan).
10. Illness was a regular feature, as was early mortality, among females in the Kathiawar of Gandhi's childhood. While the first three of Karamchand

Gandhi's wives died at ages 20, 18, and 26 respectively, Putlibai died at a relatively later age, 47.

11. A fast in which the daily quantity of food is increased or diminished accordingly as the moon waxes or wanes.

12. The title of the ruler of Rajkot.

13. Uka, an 'untouchable' scavenger, used to clean the Gandhi home. If perchance Mohan brushed against Uka, he would have to bathe in order to cleanse himself of the 'unholy' touch.

14. A Canadian Quaker. She had come to India to visit friends with the idea of doing village work.

15. Rambha had been specially inducted to look after Mohandas after an episode. Pyarelal writes (*MG: EP I*, p. 194): On festivals, when there were crowds about, it was a job to keep Moniya from straying. Once his sister (Raliyat) took him out with her during the *Molakat* festival. This is a festival that comes in the month of *Ashadha* (July–August). For four days preceding the full moon, young girls observe a vow of taking plain food without any salt. On the last day there is a carnival of feasting, dancing, and singing, which continues far into the night. In celebration for the festival bevies of girls were going about gaily, with flowers in their hair, all over the town. Little Moniya eluded his sister's vigilance, followed one of the groups and was lost in the crowd. At dusk one of the girls brought him home. He could not eat and complained of a burning in the throat. Asked the reason, he said he had eaten some flowers which he had picked up from under a tree.

'What flowers?' the frightened mother asked.

'I do not know', Moniya answered.

A *vaidya* was immediately sent for. He administered an antidote and also applied a throat paint. His father thereafter gave strict instructions that Moniya was not to be left unaccompanied at any time, and engaged a maid-servant especially to look after him. This was Rambha, whom the Mahatma has immortalised in his autobiography. She remained with the Gandhi family till her death which occurred, according to a legend, as a result of asphyxiation, while preparing *dhupel*, a scented hair-oil, over a low fire.

16. Pyarelal says (in *MG: EP I*, p. 194): One of the members of the family who used to be in charge of him was his sister Raliyat or Gokibehn—more familiarly known as Phai Ba, i.e., auntie. She had often dandled Moniya. She vividly remembered his early childhood days. 'I used to carry him in my arms when I went out for a walk or for recreation. Mother used to be worried lest I should drop him or lose sight of him. Moniya was restless as mercury, could not sit still even for a little while. He must be either playing or roaming about. I used to take him out

with me to show him the familiar sights in the street—cows, buffaloes, horses, cats, and dogs. He was full of curiosity. At the first opportunity, he would go up to the animals and try to make friends with them. One of his favourite pastimes was twisting dog's ears.'

17. The Gujarati original has a part-line here, omitted in the English translation: 'I was fond of playing musical instruments'.

18. Rambha's contribution of a fear-subjugating arrow to Gandhi's quiver has not gained sufficient recognition, except for a dance-drama written and directed by Ramchandra Gandhi (1937–2007), with the Kathak exponent Shovana Narain in the lead role. 'Rama' was, of course, the last word to leave Gandhi's lips.

19. Karsandas Karamchand Gandhi (1867–1913).

20. Nandkunvar (1861–1925), wife of Lakshmidas Karamchand Gandhi (1860–1914).

21. Kasturbai Gandhi nee Kapadia (1869–1944) was born in Porbandar. The last letter 'i' in her name fell into disuse later. Her home was not far from that of the Gandhis' and could be seen from the terrace.

22. Sheikh Mehtab (see note 15 in the Introduction).

23. Karsandas Karamchand Gandhi.

24. Baseless suspicion against Kasturbai.

25. 'So, father, your son is now, in your eyes, no better than a common thief' (quoted in Pyarelal's *MG: EP*, p. 212, as one of the sentences of the confession written to his father after self-mortification at removing a bit of gold from an amulet belonging to his brother Karsandas to clear a debt of that brother's).

26. In Rajkot, having retired two years earlier as Diwan of Rajkot.

27. Tulsidas Gandhi (1824–90) younger brother of Karamchand Gandhi, succeeding him as Diwan of Porbandar.

28. Kasturba gave birth on 20 November 1885. See note 14 in the Introduction.

29. The Reverend Joseph J. Doke (1861–1913) Minister at the Central Baptist Church, Johannesburg author of the first biography of Gandhi (*An Indian Patriot in South Africa*—1909) observes: 'When Mr Gandhi speaks of his parents, those who listen realize that they are on holy ground.'

Part Two: 1887–91

1. The *Autobiography*.

2. Examination conducted in Ahmedabad 21 to 25 November 1887. Gandhi, then aged 18, was examined in Languages (English and Gujarati), Mathematics, and General Knowledge, securing 89/200 in English,

$45^{1}/_{2}/100$ in Gujarati, 59/175 in Mathematics, and 54/150, in General Knowledge.

3. See *Mahatma Gandhi As A Student* by J.M. Upadhyaya, Publications Division, Government of India, 1965.

4. Wine, woman, and meat. Putlibai's permission came after Mohandas was administered an oath to abjure these three, by Becharji Swami, a Jaina monk she knew and trusted.

5. The *London Diary*, of which Pyarelal says (*MG: EP*, p: 226) 'Shortly after reaching England he started keeping a journal in which he systematically wrote the full story of his going to England ... Part of it has survived.' The diarist's English is that of a 19-year old Kathiawari who, until this point, had attempted no writing in that language.

6. The S.S. *Clyde* left Bombay on 4 September and arrived in London on 29 September. Her ports of call were Aden (10 September), Suez (14th), Port Said (15th), Brindisi (18th–19th), Malta (20th), Gibraltar (23rd–24th), Plymouth (28th), Gravesend (29th), and Albert Dock, London (29th). These details have been obtained through the courtesy of Sakari Nuottimaki, a Bangalore-based novelist and theatre worker, with roots in Finland and Sweden, who is working on a biography of Mahatma Gandhi, to be published in Sweden, end-2007 and who has had the old logs of *P&O* Company checked for the dates.

7. Interestingly, the canal was inaugurated in the same year as Gandhi's birth, 1869.

8. River near Rajkot.

9. Tryambakrai Trikamrai Mazmudar, a vakil from Junagadh, who happened to sail on the same ship as Gandhi to study for the Bar in London and stayed in touch throughout their stay in England. Rajmohan Gandhi (*The Good Boatman*, Viking, 1995) quotes Mazmudar saying to Narahari Parikh in 1919 after a meeting with Gandhi 'We went to England together ... He went on rising and I just sat, doing nothing but eat ... He is a real Mahatma.' Mazmudar adds: 'Oh, I forgot one thing. He said (at the 1919 meeting) he was going to die of a blow by an Indian.'

10. Khwaja Abdul Majid Saheb was one of the earliest to join the nationalist movement and take to khadi and stuck to it; an old and dear friend of Gandhi. During the days of Khilafat once Gandhi stayed at his house. He taught Urdu to Mahadev Desai in the Naini Jail. Vice-Chancellor of the National Muslim University of Aligarh which later became Jamia Millia Islamia of Delhi. President of All-India Nationalist Muslim Majlis.

11. Dr Pranjivan Mehta (1858–1932), medical doctor and lawyer, one of Gandhi's earliest friends and benefactors.

12. Dadabhai Naoroji (1825–1917) came from Bombay to London in 1855 as a partner in the first Indian firm to be established in that city, rose by his calibre and distinction to be the first Indian—or 'man of colour'—to be elected to the House of Commons. Later, President of the Indian National Congress and venerated both in India and Britain as a sage among statesmen and the 'Grand Old Man of India'.

13. *Poverty and Un-British Rule in India* (1901).

14. The italicized portions are handwritten. It is noteworthy that Gandhi spells his first name here with a double 'ss', perhaps consistently with the way clerkdom in India (mis)spelt it on his passport. The blanks on the form have remained unfilled. The facsimile of the signature used is reproduced from the original.

15. A tonifying preparation of roots and herbs.

16. Gandhi's first London home was at 20, Baron's Court Road, West Kensington. An Anglo-Indian widow was his landlady during the winter of 1888–9 (*Gandhi in London* by James D. Hunt; Promilla & Co., Publishers, New Delhi: 1978).

17. Joseph Parker (1830–1902), Congregationalist and pastor in the City Temple, London, who 'converted to Christ' while walking from Church one summer evening. His Thursday noon service was celebrated.

18. Dr Josiah Oldfield (1863–1953), editor of *The Vegetarian*, a journal of the London Vegetarian Society, who remained a steadfast friend throughout Gandhi's life.

19. Charles Bradlaugh (1833–91), English freethinker and neo-Malthusian politician who was elected MP in 1880 but owing to his refusal to take the oath was not allowed to take his seat till 1886. Friend of Dr Annie Besant, supporter of Indian aspirations, espouser of birth control and editor of *National Reformer*. Dr Annie Besant (1847–1933) was married at 19 to Frank Besant, a clergyman from whom she separated and, rejecting Christianity, joined the Secular Society. She came to India in 1893 to serve The Theosophical Society of which she later became President; initiated the Home Rule League during World War I and was interned in Ootacamund; President of the Indian National Congress, 1917.

20. Tryambakrai Mazmudar (see note 9).

21. The Bar Finals, taken after keeping nine terms, were sat for between 15 and 20 December 1890.

22. On the S.S. *Oceana*.

23. From *Guide to London*, written for would-be barristers in 1893 'as a postscript to his own struggle for a career in law' (P, *MG: EP*, p. 285).
24. Rev. Joseph J. Doke (1861–1913).

Part Three: 1891–3

1. Rajachandra (1861–1901) on Raychandbhai, Bombay-based son-in-law of Dr Pravjivan Mehta's brother was born to a Jaina mother and a Hindu father, and chose to be a Jaina. Possessed of a formidable intellect, learning, and spiritual intelligence, apart from his skills in jewellery-retail, Raychandbhai exercised a defining influence on Gandhi. Their first meeting in Bombay should have been in July 1891.
2. Doer.
3. Non-doer.
4. He had asked Gandhi about the dictates of the 'inner voice'.
5. Sir Charles Ollivant (E.C.K Ollivant) was a senior member of the Indian Civil Service. Ollivant had arrived in India in 1881. By 1892, he was Political Agent in Rajkot. By 1899, Ollivant had become a KCIE. In 1901, he was a judicial member of the Bombay provincial government. Ollivant also became a director of the Bombay, Baroda, and Central India Railway.
6. Muhammad Ali Jinnah (1876–1948); Kathiawar barrister, initially a proponent of Hindu-Muslim unity, leading Congressman for several years, joined Muslim League in 1913, veered steadily to the concept of Two Nations and Partition; founder and first Governor-General of Pakistan. Ollivant, then Judicial Member, observing Jinnah's calibre offered to hire him at Rs 1500 per month. Jinnah declined, preferring to continue rising in the Law. Muhammad Ali Jinnah's reputation as a lawyer in Bombay became formidable at this time. After being interrupted during a hearing thrice by the Judge who said 'rubbish' on each occasion, Jinnah said, 'Nothing but rubbish has passed from Your Lordship's mouth throughout the day.'
7. Lakshmidas Gandhi.
8. Gandhi's thoughts about re-uniting with Kasturba and Harilal (1888–1948) are not recorded by him.
9. Dr Pranjivan Mehta (see note 11 of Part Two).
10. Gandhi asked Raychandbhai, who was opposed to the use of leather, to take a look at the inner lining of the cap he was wearing. It had a strip of leather common in such caps. Gandhi writes that Raychandbhai tore off the strip 'without either discussion or protest'.
11. Lakshmidas Karamchand Gandhi (1860–1914).
12. Sir Charles Ollivant.
13. This should be between 10 July 1891 and 20 April 1892.

14. A dispatch rider who could be on horseback.
15. Sir Pherozeshah Mehta (1845–1915), leading lawyer of his time, thrice Chairman of the Bombay Municipal Corporation, Member of the Bombay Legislative Council, Viceroy's Legislative Council and President of the Indian National Congress at its Calcutta session, 1890.
16. On 24 April 1893, aboard the *Safari*.
17. Manilal Gandhi (1892–1956), Gandhi's second son born on 28 May 1892.

Part Four: 1893–7

1. Many years later Gandhi wrote in *Harijan* (on 1 September 1940): God has always come to my rescue ... My courage was put to the severest test on 13th January 1897 when ... I went ashore and faced the howling crowd determined on lynching me. I was surrounded by thousands of them ... but my courage did not fail me. I really cannot say how the courage came to me. But it did. God is great.
2. Abdoola Hajee Adam Jhaveri, (Dada Abdulla) (1854–1912), proprietor of Dada Abdulla & Co., Durban, leading Indian firm, in connection with whose lawsuit Gandhi went to South Africa. Abdulla and his brother controlled the Durban Indian Committee, which protested against discrimination against Indians by submitting petitions to the government and lobbying prominent British and Indian politicians.
3. The nativity of the 'Bengal pugree', as Gandhi describes it, could have occurred him only because pugrees were famously worn by two Bengalis known outside Bengal at the time: Raja Rammohun Roy (1772–1833) and Bankim Chandra Chatterjee (1838–94).
4. Sir Harry Escombe (1838–99), leading advocate of the Supreme Court of Natal. He later successfully pleaded for Gandhi's admission to the Bar of the Natal Supreme Court. Premier of Natal in 1897.
5. Letter to Ramdas Gandhi, dated 1 June 1919.
6. The journey from Durban to Pretoria was undertaken in connection with the lawsuit. Gandhi purchased a first-class ticket for the part of the journey that had to be done by train, with the confidence of a barrister, despite contrary advice given by Abdulla Sheth.
7. 'Sami' or 'Sammy' was a term employed by the white population of South Africa, just as 'coolie' was, for Indians. Its derivation is from the common Tamil name-ending for men, 'swami', spelt in South Africa at the time as 'sammy'.
8. Michael Coates, an English-born Quaker in Pretoria, about seven years older than Gandhi.
9. Of the order of Hindus who worship Vishnu, the Protector among the

Trinity of which Brahma is regarded as the Creator and Siva as the Destroyer.

10. The sacred basil (*Ocimum sanctum*) from the stem of which beads are fashioned to be strung into a rosary or 'necklace'.

11. Traditional religious practices.

12. In Pretoria, sometime in early 1894.

13. President Stephannes Johannes Paul Kruger (1825–1904).

14. 'I had already forgiven him', Gandhi says in A, p. 114.

15. An 'Open Letter' addressed to The Hon'ble Members of The Hon'ble The Legislative Council and The Hon'ble The Legislative Assembly.

16. Report of the Natal Indian Congress.

17. On Beach Grove, Durban. 'An unpretentious semi-detached, double-storeyed building with an iron front gate, a side-entrance with a passage and a verandah under the balcony in which Gandhi lived from 1894 to 1901', Pyarelal records (*MG: EP*, p. 493). Kasturba was in India at this time.

18. Gandhi worked from 326–8 Smith Street, Durban, in 1894–5 and then shifted to 374 West Street, Durban. (*Gandhi Sites in Durban*, Paul Tichman, The Local History Museum, Durban, 1998).

19. Vincent Lawrence, Gandhi's Roman Catholic confidential clerk from South India who also lived in the house.

20. Mehtab then attached himself to a prominent Indian merchant (M.C. Camroodin) in Durban. He never again crossed Gandhi's threshold, although he remained publicly loyal to him. Later, Mehtab married and his wife joined the South African satyagraha struggle. Mehtab's two known passions in South Africa were delivering lectures and composing poems in Urdu. One of his poems, which he had entered in a prize competition for the 'best patriotic poem in an Indian language' during the satyagraha struggle, was published by Gandhi in *Indian Opinion*. He is known to have spoken in praise of Gandhi at public events.

21. The stupendous task of ameliorating the condition of Indian South Africans stretched to three years. Gandhi combined that work with his legal practice. In June 1896 he took time off to visit India and bring his family over to South Africa. He landed in Calcutta on 4 July 1896. While in India, he strove to explain to the Indian leadership and public the plight of their compatriots in South Africa. Travelling widely over six months he visited Calcutta, Allahabad (where he gave an interview to the Editor of *The Pioneer*), Rajkot (for three weeks during which, apart from reuniting with his family, he wrote the celebrated Green Pamphlet on the Indian Problem in South Africa), Bombay (where he met prominent lawyers and politicians), Madras and Poona (where he

met for the first time, Gopal Krishna Gokhale, Lokamanya Tilak and R.G. Bhandarkar.)

22. Mahadev Govind Ranade (1842–1902). Judge, author, and reformer. Founded the Prarthana Samaj, a Hindu movement inspired by the Brahmo Samaj. Founded the Poona Sarvajanik Sabha and later was one of the originators of the Indian National Congress. Mentor of Gopal Krishna Gokhale.

23. Badruddin Tyabji (1844–1906). First Indian to be called to the English Bar (1867) and then the first Indian barrister in Bombay; in public life, formed the 'triumvirate' along with Kashinath Telang and Pherozeshah Mehta, that presided over Bombay's public life. One of the founders of Anjuman-I-Islam. Justice of the Bombay High Court from 1895, acting as Chief Justice in 1902 (the first Indian to hold this post in Bombay).

24. The Natal Indian Congress had helped Gandhi with his expenses in India by advancing him £ 75.

25. This is an excerpt from a day by day statement of accounts in rupees, annas and pice, tendered by him to the Natal Indian Congress for his miscellaneous requirements during the six months' stay. He spent an additional £40 of his own.

26. On 6 May 1896, Gandhi left Calcutta for Bombay, via Allahabad. The train stopped at Allahabad for 45 minutes. Restless as ever, Gandhi decided to utilize the interval for a drive through the town. He also had to purchase some medicine at a chemist's. The chemist, half asleep, took an unconscionable time in dispensing the medicine, with the result that when Gandhi reached the station, the train had already started. The Station Master had been kind enough to detain the train for one minute for Gandhi's sake, but not seeing him coming, had his luggage taken out of the train. Gandhi took a room at Kellner's, and decided to use his enforced stay gainfully. He had heard about *The Pioneer* published from Allahabad, and had understood it to be an opponent of Indian aspirations.

27. Mr Chesney Jr.

28. The first was *An Appeal to Every Briton in South Africa*. It contained a statement, supported by evidence, of the general condition of Natal Indians. The other was entitled *The Indian Franchise An Appeal*. It contained a brief history of the Indian franchise in Natal with facts and figures.

29. Present-day readers of this passage will be relieved by the clarification that Gandhi used 'child labour' only 'when they had no school'.

30. Addressing a public meeting at Pachaiyappa Hall in Madras, 26 October 1896, presided over by the Chittoor (Andhra) born P. Ananda Charlu

(1843–1908), who was to become Congress President in 1891 at Nagpur. Gandhi was in Madras from 14 October to 27/28 October, staying at the Buckingham Hotel.

31. In Durban on the S.S. *Courland*, on 13 January 1897, with Kasturba, sons Harilal (9), Manilal (5), and nephew Gokuldas (10), son of Gandhi's sister Raliyat (1863–1960). Although the S.S. *Courland*, in which Gandhi travelled, had reached the Durban harbour on 18 December 1896, the ship was placed under an extended quarantine, along with another passenger ship the *Naderi*, ostensibly on the ground that their port of origin, Bombay, was then infested with plague. The interview took place, Gandhi says 'on the day of the landing, as soon as the yellow flag was lowered' (vide *An Autobiography*—Part III, Chapter III.) But according to *The Natal Advertiser*, 14-1-1897, it took place 'yesterday morning', viz., on 13-1-1897.

32. The assault took place in West Street, Durban near where Tudor Hotel stands at present (*Gandhi Sites in Durban*, 1998, edited by Paul Tichman). Gandhi had landed at 5 p.m. and was set upon by a section of the Durban mob. He escaped serious harm through the intervention of Mrs Alexander, the Police Superintendent's wife. Besieged later in Parsi Rustomji's house, he was rescued by Police Superintendent Alexander who suggested the device of disguising himself as an Indian constable. On 14 January, the Natal Government reported the incident to the Secretary of State for the Colonies and blamed Gandhi for having landed at an inopportune time under bad advice. Interviewed by the Attorney-General, Gandhi declined to have his assailants prosecuted and gave a written expression to his wish that the matter be overlooked. On 22 January Gandhi wrote personal letters of thanks and sent gifts to Mr and Mrs Alexander for their help during the attack.

33. The railings of the house.

Part Five: 1898–1901

1. At Beach Grove, Durban. Paul Tichman tells us in *Gandhi Sites in Durban* (1998) that Gandhi moved into this house on 7 August 1894 and Borough Records confirm his occupancy until 1902.

2. Vincent Lawrence.

3. A 'fifth', coming after the four traditional categories of Hindu society, and then regarded as an 'untouchable' caste.

4. Mr B. N. Bhajekar was a High Court pleader in Bombay. The letter is from *Swami Vivekananda in the West—New Discoveries—The World Teacher* (Advaita Ashrama, Mayavati, India: 1985) Vol. 4, pp. 507–9. The book says: ... More information came from a young Indian barrister

who was then living in Durban, Natal, and championing the rights of his people. His letter ... was forwarded to Swami Vivekananda, then in Kashmir. It found its way into the papers of Mrs Bull and thence, through the kindness of her granddaughter, Sylvea Bull Curtix, into the pages of this book. The writer's name was Mohandas K. Gandhi ... Swamiji (Swami Vivekananda) could not send Swami Shivananda to Africa and, for a variety of reasons, could not go himself—even as he could not go to China, Japan, or Russia—to spread his Master's message.

5. Swami Shivananda was Tarak Nath Ghoshal before meeting Sri Ramakrishna in the 1850s. He became after Ramakrishna's death, a wandering monk and in 1902 opened a monastery of the Ramakrishna Order in Benares.

6. Swami Vivekananda.

7. Devadas (1900–57) was born on 22 May 1900 in Durban. CWMG spells his name 'Devdas' after contemporary usage. But the owner of the name spelt it with an 'a'—Devadas.

8. The Boer War (1899–1902) by the Transvaal and Orange Free State against Britain had, at its root, British eyeing of the gold under the Transvaal soil. President Kruger and the Boer Government refused to countenance. British demands and war resulted. Indians were divided on the issue, heing ill-treated by both Boer and Briton. Gandhi reflected the dilemma, siding with the British through his ambulance corps as a sign of loyalty while his 'personal sympathies were all with the Boers'. The war ended with the annexation of the two Republics by Britain. Kruger died in Pretoria on 20 July 1901, a defeated but proud Boer.

9. Addressed to the readers of *India*, Bombay.

10. Gold chain, 'sovereign' purse, and seven gold coins presented by Mr Parsee Rustomjee.

Gold watch presented by Mr Joosub of Messrs Dada Abdoola & Co.

Diamond ring presented by the Indian community.

Gold necklace presented by the Gujarati Hindus.

Diamond pin presented by Mr Abdul Cadir and a silver cup and plate presented by the Kathiawar Hindus, Stanger.

In addition to these, Gandhi had received the following on earlier occasions:

Gold medal presented in 1896.

Gold coin presented in 1896 by the Tamil Indians.

Gold chain presented by the Johannesburg Committee in 1899.

All of these, without exception, were handed over to the Indian community. Gandhi does not say if Kasturba reminded him during this conversation that the sale of her jewellery had played a part in Gandhi's 1888 journey to London to become a barrister.

Part Six: 1901–2

1. Gandhi, accompanied by Kasturba—bereft of all jewellery—and their sons reached Bombay on 28 November 1901 and went on to Rajkot. Gandhi came to Calcutta on 23 December. The annual session of the Indian National Congress was held in that city, with Sir Dinshaw Edulji Wacha (1844–1936) presiding, on 27–8 December 1901.

2. Bhupendranath Basu (1869–1924), lawyer, who had captained the Volunteer Corps at the Calcutta Congress Session, 1886 and was to take leading part in the anti-partition of Bengal Movement 1905–11, become President of the Indian National Congress, Madras, 1914, and Vice-chancellor of Calcutta University.

3. Janakinath Ghosal (1840–1913), husband of Tagore's sister Swarnakumari Devi (1855–1932) and father of Saraladevi Choudhurani (1872–1945), nationalist and poet, figuring later in Gandhi's life. ('Sjt.' signifies 'Srijukta' an archaic honorific meaning, literally, 'Sri-added' and denoting an additionality to the respect offered.)

4. Gopal Krishna Gokhale (1866–1915) towering 'Moderate' in the Congress, President of the Congress 1905; founder of the Servants of India Society (1905); teacher in Poona, and acknowledged as an outstanding speaker in the Bombay and Central Assemblies.

5. This reference is to a Calcutta-based darbar, not to be conflated with the Delhi Durbar of 1903 at which King Edward VII was proclaimed Emperor of India.

6. A Club in Calcutta established in 1882. The credit for starting a Club, that could be a meeting ground for Europeans and natives, goes to the Maharaja of Cooch Behar. Gandhi stayed there for some days during this visit. It was located at 6 Bankshall Street (E.E. McCluskie's Directory published in 1901 by Bengal Printing Book Company, 55, Bentinck Street, Calcutta, mentions the location as 10, Strand Road). It had several commodious rooms and a fine large terrace. (This club is not the same as the Calcutta Club, founded in 1907.)
(Note Credit: *Calcutta A Hundred Years Ago* by Ranabir Ray Choudhury, published by *The Statesman* in 1988.)

7. Waiters.

8. Babu Kalicharan Banerji (1847–1907) a prominent Christian personality of Calcutta, active in the Congress.

9. Between 1 January and 28 January 1902.

10. Margaret Noble (1867–1905), charismatic Irishwoman who met Swami Vivekananda in London in 1895 and took the name of Nivedita on becoming his disciple.

11. A Parsi contemporary of Gandhi in London, noted for his erudition and more for his vegetarianism. Later, he served as Prothonotary, High Court, Bombay. He was opposed to Gandhi's working in South Africa when there was 'so much work to be done in India'.

12. Mahadev Desai records in his *Diary* on 1 June 1932, in Yeravda Prison: As we were talking about Sister Nivedita, Bapu said: 'I can never forget that when I first met her, she gave expression to a deep hatred and contempt for English people. I had felt that she was living in a grand style, but many others have testified that she lived in the most squalid of scavengers' quarters and I accept their testimony. We met once again at Padshah's house. His mother made a remark which I still remember. She said, "Tell her that having abandoned her own faith she is not in a position to expound my faith to me."'

Volume 34 of *CWMG* has the following item under 'Notes':

In Justice To Her Memory

The Modern Review (of July 1927) has a paragraph on what occurs in *The Story of My Experiments with Truth*, Chapter 19, Part III (published in *Young India*, 14 April 1927), on Sister Nivedita. After quoting my remarks, *The Modern Review* has:

The mention of 'the splendour that surrounded her' without any other details conveys a wrong idea of Sister Nivedita's mode of living. The fact is, at the time when Mr Gandhi saw her, she was the guest of Mrs Ole Bull and Miss Josephine MacLeod at the American Consulate, and, as such, was not responsible for the 'splendour'. Her ascetic and very simple style of living in a tumbledown house in Bossepara Lane, Baghbazar, is well known to all her friends and acquaintances. We do not know whether Mr Gokhale spoke to Mr Gandhi in English and actually used the word 'volatile' to describe her; for what has appeared in *Young India* is translated from the Gujarati *Navajivan*. But whoever may be responsible for the use of the word 'volatile' has wronged her memory. Sister Nivedita had her defects, as in fact even the greatest of mankind had and have, but volatile she was not in any sense of that word. As English is not our vernacular, we have consulted two dictionaries on our table to find out its exact meaning as applied to human beings. The Pocket Oxford Dictionary defined it to mean 'of gay temperament, mercurial'. In Webster's New International Dictionary the explanation given is, 'light-hearted; airy; lively; hence, changeable; fickle'. Sister Nivedita was a very serious-minded person, noted for her constancy and steadfast devotion to the cause of

Hinduism and India. The reference to 'her overflowing love for Hinduism' is quite just and accurate.

I gladly reproduce this correction. For I never knew the fact, till I saw the note in *The Modern Review* that I had met the deceased not at her own place but at a guest's. The reader has to recognize my painful limitations. My reading is so poor that I have not read, much though I should like to have, the lives even of those who have contributed to the making of modern India. My only consolation is that the poverty of my reading is not due to any laziness on my part, but a life of ceaseless action and full of tempest from early youth left not time for much reading. Whether on the whole I have lost or gained thereby is to me a debatable question. But if it is a gain, it has been achieved in spite of myself. I can therefore claim no credit for it. And if in the story that I am writing from week to week (the reference is to Gandhi's *Autobiography*, chapters of which were being published in *Navajivan* from 29 November 1925 and in *Young India* from 3 December 1925). I deal with men and women, I do so only in so far as such reference is necessary for showing the working of my mind, so far as I can, in my search for Truth. I am therefore leaving out innumerable instances in life, which would be certainly otherwise interesting, as also references to several men and women. And it will be unjust to those whom I am obliged to refer in the story and to me, if the reader concludes that the estimate that I may give about persons is my final statement or true in fact. Such references should be regarded merely as the impression left upon my mind at the time to which they may relate. I introduced Sister Nivedita, Swami Vivekananda, Maharshi Devendranath, and others in the story simply to illustrate my desperate search, and to illustrate the point, that even then my political work in South Africa was an integral part of that search, which was never once subordinated to the political work. It has therefore given me pleasure to reproduce the paragraph in *The Modern Review* at the very first opportunity after reading it.

As to the use of the word 'volatile', though the translation is not mine, I cannot dissociate myself from its use, because as a rule I revise these translations, and I remember having discussed the adjective with Mahadev Desai. We both had doubts about the use of the adjective being correct. The choice lay between volatile, violent, and fanatical. The last two were considered to be too strong. Mahadev had chosen volatile and I passed it. But neither he nor I had the dictionary meaning in view. What word Gokhale used I cannot recall. The word used in the original writing is *tej*. I have a full recollection of the conversation between Sister Nivedita and myself. But I do not propose to describe it. No fault in the translation of the original can possibly damage the memory of one who loved Hinduism and India so well. It will ever be cherished with gratefulness.

Young India 30-6-1927

13. Traditionally, a gift to the officiating priest at the completion of a rite; remuneration in general.
14. A hereditary functionary at a place of pilgrimage, ghat, or temple. Also, often, a registrar of pilgrims' genealogies.
15. Portion of Keshavji Tulsidas' house on Girgaum (Back Road), Bombay. Gandhi practiced as a lawyer in Bombay from July to November 1902, taking chambers in Frazer, Gilbert, and Sayani's offices.
16. Most likely, this was Dr Dadibarjor, the Bombay-based Parsi doctor, retained by Abdullah Sheth for his company, who had treated Gandhi in Durban on 13 January 1897 after the assault by white youths.

Part Seven: 1902–5

1. Joseph Chamberlain (1836–1914) Secretary of State for the Colonies from 1895–1903.
2. While Kasturba and the sons were left in the Santa Cruz house, Gandhi took with him to South Africa his cousin Khushalchand Gandhi's son Maganlal Gandhi (1883–1928) and his cousin Amritlal Gandhi's son Anandlal (1878–1943) in order to set them up in business there.
3. 25 December 1902.
4. Victor Alexander Bruce, 9th Earl of Elgin (Lord Elgin II) Governor General and Viceroy of India, 1894–99.
5. Kallenbach was challenged to a duel by a Volksrust European for his Indian sympathies, declined saying that he had 'accepted the religion of peace'; himself a satyagrahi, he gave, in 1910, his 1100–acre property, later named by Gandhi 'Tolstoy Farm' near Johannesburg for the maintenance of satyagrahis' families. Kallenbach became Gandhi's close friend and associate, teaching on this farm carpentry, gardening, and sandal-making, the last of which he had learnt at a Trappist monastery.
6. Gandhi settled and set up practice in Johannesburg in February 1903.
7. Sonja Schlesin (1887–1956) of Russian-Jewish descent, joined Gandhi's office in Johannesburg as a stenotypist. She made herself very useful to *Indian Opinion* and devoted herself to the Indian cause in South Africa with a rare zeal.
8. Madanjit Vyavaharik was a school teacher from Bombay who emigrated to South Africa, set up the International Printing Press in Durban in 1898 at Gandhi's suggestion. He died in 1932.
9. The first issue of *Indian Opinion* appeared from Durban on 4 June

1903. It quoted Ralph Waldo Emerson from his essay on *Self-Reliance* (1841): 'A foolish consistency is the hobgoblin of little minds, adored by little statesmen and philosophers and divines. With constancy a great soul has simply nothing to do ... Speak what you think today in words as hard as cannon-balls, and tomorrow what tomorrow thinks. ...'

10. Mansukhlal Hiralal Naazar (1862–1906). Emigrated to England and established business in London. Was also an occasional journalist. Arrived in Durban in December 1896 and became a close friend of Gandhi. After Gandhi resigned as secretary of NIC to go to India in October 1901, Naazar was appointed one of two joint secretaries (with R.K. Khan); he held this position until 1904. Served in the Indian Ambulance Corps in Anglo-Boer War. Was the first editor of *Indian Opinion*, 1903–6.

11. A gold mine near Johannesburg.

12. Dr William Godfrey, the Tamil resident of Johannesburg who associated with Gandhi in nursing plague patients in Johannesburg in 1904 was later disappointed at his non-inclusion in the deputation to London in 1906 and, therefore, counter-petitioned Secretary of State Elgin against Gandhi.

13. Henry Solomon Leon Polak (1882–1959) was born in Dover, England and came to South Africa in 1903 for a health cure. He joined *The Transvaal Critique* as Assistant Editor, met Gandhi in a vegetarian restaurant in Johannesburg and became an ardent supporter, editing *Indian Opinion*, among other forms of colleagueship. On becoming a lawyer, he served his articles with Gandhi before opening his own legal offices in Johannesburg. He survived Gandhi by eleven years, dying in London on 2 February 1959.

14. Gandhi commuted frequently between Johannesburg and Durban during this phase.

15. Albert West was a Theosophist and printer by trade, who became a settler at the Phoenix settlement and played an active role in the 1913 satyagraha. Gandhi first met him at Isaac's vegetarian restaurant. West offered to help with the plague epidemic in Johannesburg in 1904. Gandhi asked him to help him with the press and paper in Durban. When Gandhi mooted the idea of moving the press to Phoenix, in pursuit of his newly developing philosophy of Sarvodaya, or the ideal society, West supported that and became one of the foundation settlers. His wife, mother-in-law, and sister, also became Phoneix settlers.

16. The Phoenix Settlement or 'ashram' is reckoned to have been founded on 26 June 1904. Located $2^1/_2$ miles from the Phoenix railway station, the price paid for its 100 acres extent was £1000. Following his wife's death in India in July 1904 Madanjit Vyavaharik left South Africa in

October 1904. Gandhi thereupon said the responsibility for *Indian Opinion* would now be solely his own. The first issue of *Indian Opinion* appeared out of Phoenix on 24 December 1904.

17. In preparation for the family's return to South Africa, Gandhi wrote to his Johannesburg landlord to effect repairs in the house and, in view of the fall in the rents in the city, to reduce the rent as well.

18. Ramdas Gandhi (1897–1969), Gandhi's third son. Kasturba, accompanied by her sons Manilal, Ramdas, and Devadas returned to South Africa in 1904 leaving Harilal, now sixteen, to school in Bombay under the remote-controlled care of Gandhi's elder brother Lakshmidas Gandhi. Gandhi's nephew Chhaganlal Khushalchand Gandhi (1881–1970) elder brother of Maganlal Gandhi had arrived earlier on 8 April 1904. Rajmohan Gandhi writes in *Mohandas* (pp. 112–13) of Ramdas' injury:

'Daily, "Doctor" Gandhi dressed the injury in this manner; in a month the arm was healed. For his family Gandhi rented a two-storey house with a garden in Johannesburg's upscale Troyeville area. Though this home where Kastur, Manilal, Ramdas, Devadas, and Gandhi moved, and lived for about two years (1904–6) was fair-sized, modern and in an enviable location, life inside it was being drastically simplified 'in the light of Ruskin's teaching'. There was a servant in the house, living 'as a member of the family', and 'the children used to help him in his work'. A municipal sweeper removed the night-soil from the house but Gandhi and his family, rather than the servant, cleaned the toilet. Bread was not bought at a baker's. Unleavened wholemeal bread was baked at home according to Kuhne's recipe, made from flour ground at home by two males working a hand-mill that Gandhi had purchased for seven pounds. At about this time, influenced by the notion of *aparigraha*, Gandhi decided to cancel his insurance policy. He was there himself, Gandhi reasoned, to support his family. If he were to die God would look after them, or they themselves would; he should not rob them of their self-reliance. "What happened to the families of the numberless poor in the world? Why should I not count myself as one of them?" (*A*, p. 231).

More difficult was a letter he wrote in May 1905 to Laxmidas, the head of the Gandhi family and the recipient thus far of a good chunk of Gandhi's savings. By 1902, Gandhi had sent him 60,000 rupees (some of the amount settling debts incurred by brother Karsandas), apart from repaying the 13,000 rupees spent on Gandhi's studies in England.

Henceforth, Gandhi wrote, Laxmidas should not expect any money from him. Any savings now and in the future would go to *Indian Opinion* and to the Indian community in South Africa (*A*, pp. 233–4).'

Part Eight: 1906–9

1. This was a disastrous fire in the underground Electric Railway in Paris on 10 August 1903, in which 84 persons were killed and many injured.
2. The nineteenth and early twentieth century term used to denote 'native' Africans, is now universally regarded as derogatory and offensive, in the same category if not worse than 'Sammy'. Gandhi's use of it, though understandable and explicable in terms of early twentieth century usage, cannot but strike modern readers as jarring. Nelson Mandela is worth quoting here: 'All in all, Gandhi must be judged in the context of the time and the circumstances'. (*Mahatma Gandhi 125 Years*, ICCR, New Delhi, 1995). Mandela however substitutes 'Kaffir' by 'native Africans' in the quotes from Gandhi in his article. This compilation cannot exercise such an editorial privilege.
3. Chief Bambata, the Zulu chief who had advised non-payment of a new tax arbitrarily imposed on his people and had assagaied a sergeant who had gone to collect it.
4. 'Sergeant Major M.K. Gandhi' led the Corps from 15 June 1906 to 19 July 1906. As the 'rebellion' was being crushed with brutality, the Empire was officially celebrating the birth anniversary of Queen Victoria.
5. Extracted from Pyarelal's *A World in Agony*, which contains a record of Gandhi's talk with Rev. S.S. Tema, a Minister of African origin in the Dutch Reformed Mission, Johannesburg and a member of the African National Congress, who was one of the delegates to a Conference at Tambaram, Madras. The delegates came to see Gandhi after the Conference was over. They were in Segaon on 31 December and 1 January 1939. An excerpt from Pyarelal's record of the interview:

1 January 1939

Tema: How can my people make their Congress as successful as the Indian National Congress?

MKG: ... You have adopted European dress and manners, and have as a result become strangers in the midst of your own people. Politically, that is a disadvantage. It makes it difficult for you to reach the heart of the masses. You must not be afraid of being 'Bantuized' or feel ashamed of carrying an assagai or of going about with only a tiny cloth round your loins. A Zulu or a Bantu is a well-built man and need not be ashamed of showing his body. He need not dress like you. You must become Africans once more.

Tema: Of late there has been some talk of forming an Indo-African United non-white Front in South Africa. What do you think about it?

MKG: ... Yours is a far bigger issue. It ought not to be mixed up with that of the Indian. This does not preclude the establishment of the friendliest relations between the two races. ...

Tema: What sort of relations would you favour between these two races?

MKG: The closest possible. But while I have abolished all distinction between African and Indian, that does not mean that I do not recognize the difference between them. ...

CWMG *Vol. 68, pp. 272–3; E*

6. Gandhi's strong spiritual inclinations at this time found expression in a set of four lectures that he delivered at The Theosophical Society in Johannesburg on 4, 11, 18, and 25 March 1906. The venue was the Masonic Lodge, Johannesburg. Other pictures on Gandhi's office wall included those of Annie Besant, Sir William Hunter, Justice Ranade, and of the Indian contingent in the Boer War.

7. Lakshmidas Karamchand Gandhi had written a sharp letter to his younger brother to which this is the reply.

8. Harilal, who had been left behind in India, when Gandhi sent for Kasturba and the other three sons, tried to pursue studies in Rajkot but also found himself in love with Gulab alias Chanchal Vora, daughter of Haridas Vaqatchand Vora, educationist and reformer friend of Gandhi's in Rajkot. Gandhi, who knew and was fond of his friend's daughter was, nonetheless, opposed to Harilal marrying at so young an age (he was 18 and Gulab was 17). Lakshmidas, as the elder uncle and *pater familias* went ahead with arrangements for it and the wedding took place on 2 May 1906.

9. Kalyandas, was the son of Jagmohandas Kapol of Bombay, who had been introduced to Gandhi by Haridas Vora. Kalyandas' name was among those described as 'heroes of the plague' in April 1904. Kalyandas returned to India in 1910.

10. Literally, 'walking with the Creator', the term denotes abstinence from sexual activity at the minimum and all-persuasive 'chastity' and 'purity' at the maximum. Gandhi returned from the field to Phoenix on 20 July 1906 and took the brahmacharya vow the same day.

11. 'Soul Force, pure and simple'.

12. Maganlal Gandhi (1883–1928) second son of Gandhi's cousin Khushalchand Gandhi came to South Africa at Gandhi's bidding in 1902 after his matriculation. Gandhi set him up in a shop in a remote interior of Stanger, Natal. Maganlal shifted to Phoenix in 1904 and from that point became Gandhi's right hand in the ashrams set up by him in South Africa and in India. Maganlal died suddenly in 1928 in Patna at the age of 45, leaving Gandhi bereft.

13. 31 July 1907 at the Mosque, Pretoria.

14. 'Sheth' Ahmed Mahomed Kachhalia (Cachhalia) (1877–1918). President of the British Indian Association of Transvaal.

15. Gandhi and H.O. Ally went on a deputation on behalf of the Indians in South Africa to London to ask for a withholding of London's approval of the Ordinance. He stayed initially in the 'India House' hostel for Indian students founded by the extremist Shyamji Krishnavarma (1857–1930) and then in Hotel Cecil.

16. Louis W. Ritch, an articled clerk with Gandhi. Theosophist and manager of a Johannesburg firm in 1902 when Gandhi first met him.

17. This first imprisonment of Gandhi's took place on 11 January 1908 at Fort Prison, Johannesburg. The experience of being stripped, described above, was also that of Nelson Mandela whose first jail term was coincidentally, in the same prison in December 1956. Mandela writes in *Long Walk To Freedom* (1944): 'We were soon moved to the Johannesburg Prison, popularly known as the Fort, a bleak castle-like structure located on a hill in the heart of the city. Upon admission, we were taken to an outdoor quadrangle and ordered to strip completely and line up against the wall.'

18. Essentially, the settlement provided for voluntary registration as a substitute for compulsory registration under the Act.

19. Jan Christian Smuts (1870–1950), Barrister, General, statesman, and philosopher. A 'guerilla leader of exceptional talent' in the Boer War (1899–1902) he played a leading role in the Vereeneging Peace Treaty by which Great Britain annexed Transvaal and Orange Free State. Smuts believed that South Africa's future required cooperation with Britain. Defence Minister with responsibility for the Interior under President Botha, he was invited in 1917 by British Prime Minister Lloyd George to join the Imperial War Cabinet. Smuts participated in the Paris Peace Conference and signed The Treaty of Versailles (1919). Prime Minister of South Africa 1919–24; Deputy Prime Minister 1933–39, Prime Minister 1939–48 he was the only statesman to sign Peace Treaties after both World Wars. Sharing an almost identical lifespan as Gandhi, he also shared Gandhi's admiration for soldierly discipline and courage, retaining a deep spiritual bent. But Smuts and Gandhi had a definingly different sense of their discussions and 'compromises'.

20. Around midnight of 30–31 January 1908, Gandhi addressed about 1000 Indians on the grounds of a mosque in Johannesburg. He asked the Indians to register voluntarily, because the opposition was to compulsion not registration. As Gandhi finished, Mir Alam, 'fully six feet in height and of a large and powerful build', stood up. Alam, one of the Transvaal's fifty or so Pathans, asked Gandhi if they had to give

ten fingerprints. Those with difficulties of conscience do not need to, replied Gandhi.

21. This was published in *Indian Opinion* under the title: 'Why he sent his son to gaol: Mr Gandhi's Explanation'. Harilal spent a total of 398 days in jail in South Africa for his political activities: 27 July to 3 August 1908 in Johannesburg, 18 August to 17 September 1908 in Johannesburg again, 10 February to 9 August 1909 in Volksrust and Pretoria, June 23 to September 22, 1909 in Johannesburg and, finally, 10 October 1910 to 9 January 1911 in Johannesburg. Harilal thereby bettered his father's South Africa jail record (188 days).

22. On 25 October 1908.

23. King Edward's Hotel is a humorous reference to a prison. It possibly refers to the prison at Volksrust.

24. Parsi Rustomji underwent prison terms in 1908 and 1909, spending a total of 18 months there during the Passive Resistance Campaigns. Rustomji was made a trustee of the Phoenix Settlement Trust in 1912.

25. 'Dawad' is to Haji Hoosen Dawad Mohomed. Born in 1891 in Durban, he joined the Phoenix Settlement and was a passive resister, going to prison. He died in 1930.

26. Chanchal or Gulab Harilal Gandhi (1889–1918) wife of Gandhi's eldest son, Harilal Gandhi (1888–1948).

27. Gandhi was detained on this day at Volksrust on his way to Johannesburg after seeing Kasturba Gandhi, who was seriously ill, at Phoenix. Harilal was also in jail at the time.

28. Kasturba Gandhi.

29. Consequent on Harilal's incarceration and in case he was to opt for more gaol-going under satyagraha. Harilal did so opt, being jailed on five occasions of which the longest term of 180 days began less than a fortnight after this letter was written.

30. Dr R.M. Nanji was a medical practitioner who often treated sick Phoenix settlers.

31. A humorous reference by Gandhi to prison.

32. Father and son were together in Volksrust Prison from 25 February 1909 to 2 March 1909, being transferred to Pretoria Prison on 3 March 1909. Gandhi was released on 24 May 1909 after an imprisonment of 57 days, his longest prison term in South Africa. Harilal remained imprisoned there until 9 August 1909.

33. Rami Harilal Gandhi (1908–55), eldest daughter of Harilal and Chanchal Gandhi.

34. Gandhi was placed in solitary confinement during this imprisonment in Pretoria.

35. This letter to Manilal Gandhi, who was in Phoenix at the time, was

written untypically in English to accord with jail regulations facilitating surveillance. Harilal was in the same prison as Gandhi.

36. Chanchal Harilal Gandhi.

37. Pandit Nathuram Sharma of Saurashtra, translator of the Upanishads into Gujarati.

Part Nine: 1909–14

1. The reference is to the period when Gandhi was a law student in London during 1888–91. He had again visited London in 1906.

2. A reference to Mrs Alexander who rescued Gandhiji on 13 January 1897 from mob violence in Durban. One does not know what the 'promise' was.

3. To Kallenbach. Gandhi went to London on a second deputation on behalf of the Indian passive resistance in South Africa, accompanied this time by another Gujarati-speaking Muslim, Haji Habib. Gandhi was in London from 10 July 1909 to 13 November 1909.

4. Written from London to Harilal (who was in Johannesburg Prison).

5. To Kallenbach.

6. Gandhi spoke on the 'Ethics of Passive Resistance' to the Emerson Club, London on 8 October 1909.

7. In a letter to Polak about Harilal then in political incarceration.

8. From Hind Swaraj written originally in Gujarati on the ship's notepaper in nine days (the first twelve chapters on 11.12.1909 and the rest on 18.12.1909) on board *The Kildonan Castle* while returning from London to South Africa in 1909. Gandhi translated it into English himself for Kallenbach. 'Editor' speaks for Gandhi.

9. Madan Lal Dhingra (1887–1909) a disciple of Vinayak Damodar Savarkar, shot dead Sir Curzon Wyllie, political aide to the Secretary of State for India, in London on 10 July 1909. A Parsi doctor, Cowasji Lalkaka who tried to help Wyllie, was also fatally wounded. Dhingra was hanged at Brixton prison on 17 August 1909. On 13 November 1909, the day Gandhi left London, a bomb was hurled by extremists in Ahmedabad in the wake of Lord Minto, Viceroy of India, and Lady Minto.

10. Prabhudas Gandhi records that when the steamer bringing H.S.L. Polak back to Durban from his visit to India reached Durban Port, Gandhi, accompanied by Parsi Rustomji and others, including Chhaganlal Gandhi, were present to welcome Polak back. An English youth, an employee of the Port, told Chhaganlal Gandhi to move back. Chhaganlal held his ground, upon which the Port Officer lost his temper and said, 'Hey you! I am asking you to move and you are not?' Saying that he moved threateningly towards Chhaganlal Gandhi. Gandhi spoke those

five freezing words in English at that moment. Prabhudas records that the man was stunned and, advised by others, moved away.

11. Recorded by Mahadev Desai on 20 April 1932.

12. Talking to some students of the Sunav National School on 16 January 1925.

13. In a letter to Lord Wavell from a Detention Camp, dated 9 March 1944.

14. Harilal Gandhi's release referred to in the first paragraph of this letter took place on 9 January 1911. Chanchal was in Phoenix at the time.

15. Maganlal was in Phoenix.

16. There were a number of passive resisters by the name of Naidoo—Gopal Naidoo, P.K. Naidoo, and C.K. Thambi Naidoo.

17. Harilal was in Phoenix on 9 May 1911. He left home without informing any one. He travelled under a false name but was recognized at Delagoa Bay. On 15 May he returned and met his father and spoke about his future inconclusively. On 17 May he left South Africa for good. Gandhi went to the railway station to see him off and records show the father was visibly moved to see the son go. (Harilal's wife Chanchal had left South Africa in August 1910.)

18. Harilal.

19. Dr Pranjivan Mehta, Gandhi's doctor cum lawyer friend and benefactor. Sorabji Shapurji Adajania was sent to Gandhi to London to study for the Bar, in preference to Harilal or Manilal, on a stipend offered by Dr Mehta, after Chhaganlal Gandhi discontinued his studies on health grounds. Harilal protested against Adajania being sent.

20. The sand spit along which Durban Harbour was built.

21. Natal Indians boycotted the celebrations of King George V's coronation.

22. Abbreviation of *Indian Opinion*.

23. The leading article on the front page of the *Indian Opinion* of 24 June 1911. The article was entitled 'Coronation Day in Durban: Indians Boycott Official Celebrations'.

24. Andaman Islands were a British penal settlement.

25. To Kallenbach.

26. Probably Pragji Desai.

27. Umgeni Railway Station.

28. The reference is to the arrival of Harilal's and Chanchal's third child, Rasiklal Harilal Gandhi (1912–29) in India.

29. Gopal Krishna Gokhale, whom Gandhi had long wanted to welcome in South Africa, visited it from 22 October 1912 to 24 November 1912. A friend of Lord Hardinge, the Viceroy, a Member of the Viceroy's Council, President of the Servants of India Society, Gokhale was given the status of a Minister. Gandhi received him in Cape Town and saw him off at Zanzibar on 27 November 1912.

30. To Kallenbach.
31. The Cape Supreme Court Judgement invalidated all non-Christian Indian marriages unless they were registered. Some passive resisters indicated that they would resort to passive resistance against the decision.
32. Probably Inanda waterfall.
33. This is a literal rendering of the Gujarati 'baheno' which really means 'ladies' or 'women', rather than female siblings.
34. In a letter to Kallenbach.
35. 12 July 1913.
36. Jaykunvar, daughter of Dr Pranjivan Mehta and Manilal Gandhi. For details see Uma Dhupelia-Mesthrie's Gandhi's Prisoner? *The Life of Gandhi's Son Manilal* (Permanent Black, 2004).
37. From 14 July 1913.
38. To Kallenbach.
39. Kasturba and 15 others including Valliamma were detained at Volksrust on 16 August 1913, arrested on 22 August 1913, and sentenced on 23 August 1913, to three months rigorous imprisonment. Valliamma succumbed, on 22 February 1914, to the illness that bore her down in Maritzburg jail. Born in Johannesburg in 1898 she had joined the satyagraha on 29 October 1913 and crossed over to the Natal and re-crossed into the Transvaal defying the law with the party of women satyagrahis.
40. This is a cable to Gokhale
41. Charles Freer Andrews (1871–1940) came to India in 1904 as a member of the Cambridge Brotherhood, left the Order in 1913, became a lifelong friend of Gandhi and Tagore. His affinity with the Indian nationalist cause made him suspect in the eyes of the Raj which, nonetheless, did not prevent 'CFA' from acting as a bridge between the two. Andrews and Pearson were sent by Gokhale to study the S.A. Indian question.
42. William Winstanley Pearson (1881–1923); worked in Bengal as a missionary and collaborated with Andrews in Y.M.C.A. work; taught for some time at Santiniketan. While in South Africa, he studied the conditions of Indian labour on Natal sugar estates.
43. At the Durban wharf Gandhi, with several Indian associates, H.S.L. Polak, A.H. West, and a number of European clergymen met Andrews and Pearson. On landing, Andrews greeted Polak and asked: 'Where is Mr Gandhi?'. Polak turned to a figure, dressed in a dhoti and kurta of coarse material. Andrews bent swiftly down and touched Gandhi's feet.
44. Cable to Gokhale.
45. Letter to Manilal Gandhi who was serving a three months' sentence for participating in the passive resistance movement. This letter was written in English to conform to prison regulations.

46. Hurbat Singh at age 75 died on 5 January in Durban jail.
47. The funeral procession on 8 January included Europeans and Indians of different faiths.
48. Spicy, salted food; liable to stimulate the qualities of tamas or darkness, animality.
49. Manilal was asked by Gandhi to be a 'personal attendant' to Andrews who though young at 43, was recovering from malaria.
50. The reference to 'purity' can be linked to the 'comfortable "atmosphere" of the Gool home in Cape Town'.
51. Kasturba had fallen critically ill.
52. To Kallenbach.
53. Letter to Hermann Kallenbach.
54. In the event Kallenbach predeceased Gandhi, dying on 25 March 1945. He visited Gandhi in India twice, in 1937 and 1939.
55. Yusuf and Wahieda Gool. He was an Indian merchant originally from Surat, Gujarat. The Gools were Gandhi's hosts in Cape Town.
56. To Kallenbach.
57. Lakshmidas Gandhi passd away on 9 March 1914.
58. On Gandhi's release from his last jailing in South Africa (Bloemfontein, 17 December 1913) he took to wearing the dress—shirt and lungi—associated with indentured labourers (*girmitias* from '*agreement*'). He even dispensed with footwear for a while.

Part Ten: 1914–25

1. Pandit Motilal Nehru (1861–1931), lawyer in Allahabad and President of the Congress in 1919 and 1928. Founded, with C.R. Das, the Swaraj Party within the Congress and led that party in the Central Assembly 1924–6.
2. Deshbandhu Chittaranjan Das (1870–1925), outstanding barrister, joined the Congress in 1906, becoming Bengal's pre-eminent political figure, formed with Motilal Nehru the Swaraj Party in 1922, Congress President in 1922, host to Gandhi in Calcutta and Darjeeling.
3. Indulal Yajnik (1892–1972) sociologist, biographer, dramatist, novelist. Led the 'Mahagujarat' agitation after Independence and was a member of the Lok Sabha. He was a fellow prisoner with Gandhi at Yeravda and records in *Gandhi As I Knew Him*: 'One evening our Negro warder from Somaliland was bitten by a scorpion on his hand. He gave a shout. Mr Gandhi was quickly on the spot. ... He first asked for a knife to cut the wound and to let out the poison. But he found the knife dirty. So missing no moment he quickly washed the area round the wound and applying his lips to the wound began to suck out the

poison. He went on spitting after sucking and eventually stopped when Adan felt relief.'

4. A fourteen-day fast from 2 May 1914 occasioned by the episode concerning his son Manilal about which Uma Dhupelia-Mesthrie has written in detail in *Gandhi's Prisoner?* (Permanent Black, 2005).

5. Sarojini Naidu records: I had not been able to meet his ship on his arrival, but the next afternoon I went wandering around in search of the lodgings in an obscure part of Kensington and climbed the steep stairs of an old, unfashionable house, to find an open door framing a living picture of a little man with a shaven head, seated on the floor on a black prison blanket, and eating a messy meal of squashed tomatoes and olive oil out of a wooden prison bowl. Around him were ranged some battered tins of parched ground nuts and tasteless biscuits of dried plantain flour. I burst instinctively into happy laughter at this amusing and unexpected vision of a famous leader, whose name had already become a household word in our country. He lifted his eyes and laughed back.

6. After his arrival in England on 4 August, Gandhi, Kasturba, and Kallenbach were given a reception at Hotel Cecil by British and Indian friends. Among those present were Sarojini Naidu, Satchidanand Sinha, Lala Lajpat Rai, his South African acquaintance Albert Cartwright and, most significantly, Mohammed Ali Jinnah. Bhupendranath Basu President of the Indian National Congress that year, took the Chair. Sarojini Naidu paid a tribute to Gandhi and garlanded the chief guests.

7. The Gandhi-Smuts Settlement of January 1914.

8. The Under Secretary of State for India, Charles Roberts, replied to this communication, indicating government's qualified acceptance of the offer.

9. Gandhi had gone down with a severe attack of pleurisy.

10. The First Marquis of Willingdon (1866-1941), Governor of Bombay (1913-19); Governor of Madras (1919-24); Governor General of Canada (1926-31); Viceroy of India (1931-6).

11. 17 to 21 January 1915 and 27 to 31 January 1915.

12. 23 to 26 January 1915.

13. Known, after 22 January 1917 as Swami Shraddhananda.

14. 3 to 5 April 1915.

15. To Kallenbach.

16. The Kashi Vishwanath temple, Benares.

17. Addressing Sir Rameshwar Singh, Maharaja of Darbhanga in the chair. (Speech at the founding of the new University at Benares, 6 February 1916, which brought the proceedings to an end in an uproar. CWMG *Vol. 13, pp. 212-15; E.*

Resolution' in the last issue, you have represented me as holding that I considered 'everything fair in politics'. I write this to you to say that my view is not correctly represented therein. Politics is a game of worldly people and not of sadhus, and instead of the maxim 'Akkodhena jite kodham' as preached by Buddha, I prefer to rely on the maxim of Shri Krishna 'Ye yatha mam prapadyante tanstathaiva bhajamyaham'. That explains the whole difference and also the meaning of my phrase 'responsive cooperation'. Both methods are equally honest and righteous but the one is more suited to this world than the other. Any further explanation about the difference will be found in my 'Gita Rahasya'.

68. Report of the Commission appointed by the Congress to go into the Jallianwala Bagh massacre.

69. Pandit Madan Mohan Malaviya.

70. Vedic prayer to the Sun for illumination.

71. The letter also appears in *Mahadevbhaini Diary*, Vol. V, under 3 May. 4 May is the more likely date since Gandhi left Sinhgadh on that day.

72. Imam Abdul Kader Salim Bawazeer, Assistant Priest, Hamidia Mosque, Johannesburg; outstanding passive resister, first sentenced on 2 July 1908 for hawking without licence; Chairman of Hamidia Islamic Society (1910); participated in 1913 Satyagraha, settled in Phoenix, and joined Gandhi at Sabarmati ashram, India. Participated memorably in the salt satyagraha (1930) at Dharasana.

73. Vinayak Damodar Savarkar (1884–1966), a leading revolutionary who served 16 years in the Penal Settlement in the Andamans for his nationalist actions. Later became the chief leader of All-India Hindu Mahasabha and one of the accused (to be acquitted) in the Mahatma Gandhi assassination case (1948).

74. He carried on an agitation for the freedom of India from Europe, which at one time reached the stage of his sending fire-arms to India from Paris.

75. Off Marseilles, in July 1910, when he was being brought to India from England where he had been arrested under the Fugitive Offenders Act of 1881.

76. Of A.M.T. Jackson, the Collector of Nasik in December 1909. It was alleged that the pistol with which Jackson was murdered was one of the many sent by Savarkar from Europe.

77. Government of India Act, 1919.

78. Joseph 'Kaka' Baptista was a prominent personality (1864–1930) in Bombay in the early 20th century. He was active on the moderate side of the Indian freedom movement. Along with Bal Gangadhar Tilak and Annie Besant, he was a co-founder of the Indian Home Rule League and the President of its first conference at Nasik, held on 17 May 1917.

He was also a co-founder, along with Lala Lajpat Rai, of the Indian Trade Union Congress, a still functioning labour movement aligned with the Congress Party.

79. From the reference to the inauguration of non-cooperation in connection with the Khilafat movement on this date.

80. Lord Chelmsford. The text of this letter appeared in *Young India*, 4-8-1920, under the caption 'Renunciation of Medals'.

81. In 1915.

82. Lord Hardinge (1858–1944) Viceroy and Governor General of India, 1911–16.

83. An Englishwoman who served in the Mission School, Amritsar. She was brutally attacked on 10 April 1919, while cycling and was rescued by an Indian.

84. This obituary appeared on the first page of *Young India*, on 4-8-1920.

85. Saraladevi Choudhurani.

86. Sir Dr Muhammad Iqbal (1873–1938); renowned poet; took his Ph.D from Cambridge and Munich; nationalist leader during the 1920s; one of the representatives at the Second and Third Round Table Conferences, 1931–2; inspirer of Hindu–Muslim unity ideals and, ironically, later, of the Pakistan movement.

87. At Aligarh.

88. Dr Mukhtar Ahmed Ansari (1880–1936); a nationalist Muslim leader; president, Indian Muslim League, 1920; president, Indian National Congress, 1927.

89. Gandhi reached Allahabad on 28 November 1920, and stayed there for four days.

90. At the 35th session of the Congress held at Nagpur.

91. The contents suggest that the letter was written in 1921 and in that year Gandhi was in Calcutta on January 29.

92. In January 1921 Andrews had a severe attack of influenza.

93. After visiting the emigrants who had returned from Fiji and were stranded near the Calcutta docks, Andrews was confined to his bed but dictated 35 letters, telegrams, and articles in one day.

94. The famous site in Calcutta, near the temple to Kali.

95. The district in Bihar where Gandhi conducted his indigo enquiry.

96. A voluntary body for social service.

97. Violence broke out on 17 November 1921 in Bombay during the boycott of the visit of the Prince of Wales. Gandhi issued this statement as a leaflet, vide *Navajivan*, 24-11-1921.

98. A telegram sent to Harilal on his arrest joining the nationwide non-cooperation movement.

99. This is one of the articles for which Gandhi was tried and sentenced in March 1922.

100. Lord Birkenhead (1872–1930); British lawyer, politician, and scholar; Lord Chancellor and later, Secretary of State for India.
101. Edwin Samuel Montagu (1879–1924) was a liberal MP, first elected to the House of Commons in 1906, becoming Secretary of State for India from 1917 to 1922. He held that office during the Jallianwala Bagh massacre (14 April 1919) and labelled it as 'frightful'. His incumbency coincided with the zenith of Gandhi's first non-cooperation movement against the Rowlatt Acts curbing civil liberties and the Khilafat question.
102. One who believes in looking at things from more than one point of view.
103. Sir J.T. Strangman, the Advocate General of Bombay Presidency, in the Court of Justice Robert Broomfield at Ahmedabad. The following is from the text of the judgment:

'Mr Gandhi, you have made my task easy in one way by pleading guilty to the charge ... Even those who differ from you in politics look upon you as a man of high ideals and of noble and of even saintly life. I have to deal with you in one character only. It is not my duty and I do not presume to judge or criticize you in any other character. It is my duty to judge you as a man subject to the law, who has by his own admission broken the law and committed what to an ordinary man must appear to be grave offences against the State ...

... You will not consider it unreasonable, I think, that you should be classed with Mr Tilak, and that is the sentence, two years' simple imprisonment on each count of the charge, i.e., six years in all, which I feel it my duty to pass upon you and I should like to say in doing so that, if the course of events in India should make it possible for the Government to reduce the period and release you, no one will be better pleased than I.'

Gandhi, responding, said:

'I would say one word. Since you have done me the honour of recalling the trial of the late Lokamanya Bal Gangadhar Tilak, I just want to say that I consider it to be the proudest privilege and honour to be associated with his name. So far as the sentence itself is concerned, I certainly consider that it is as light as any judge would inflict on me, and so far as the whole proceedings are concerned, I must say that I could not have expected greater courtesy.'

       Young India 23-3-1922; CWMG *Vol. 23*, pp. 119–20; E
104. Superintendent of Yeravda Central Jail in the place of Col. Dalziel during the period the latter acted as Inspector-General of Prisons.
105. Sir Maurice Hayward, the then Home Member of the Government of Bombay.
106. Major Whitworth Jones. Sixty-six years later on 6 November 1988, the hundredth anniversary of his removal, Gandhi was posthumously

readmitted to the Bar of England and Wales. *The Times* (London) reported on 7 November 1988: In an unprecedented move the governing body of the Inner Temple, the Masters of the Bench, unanimously voted at a meeting last week attended by nearly 40 benchers that Gandhi should be readmitted as a gesture to mark the Nehru centenary celebrations. Captain Patrick Sheehan, sub-treasurer of the Inner Temple, said it was the first time to his knowledge that any barrister had been readmitted after his death.

107. Writing for *Young India* on 29 January 1924, Mahadev Desai describes the condition of Gandhi during his ailment as follows:

'If anyone had asked me to write anything about Bapu that day I would not have had the heart to do it. He was so emaciated, so shriveled up, that you could not bring yourself to be composed enough to say or to write anything about his condition. But, thank God, he began picking up unexpectedly fast, and I am happy to say that I feel now able to say something about what is happening in this, the greatest of our places of pilgrimage today. ...'

108. Gandhi was released 'prematurely' at 8 a.m. on 5 February 1924. Writing for *Navajivan* on 10 February 1924, Mahadev Desai says:

It was 7.30 in the morning. Andrews, who did not care to wait for his tea was already by Bapu's side ... When conversation was going on in this free and gay manner, a most unexpected thing happened. Col. Maddock approaching Bapu so early as at 7.30! His time to come for dressing the wound was 9!

How was it that he was coming up at this early hour? But he did. There was an envelope in his hand a large red-sealed one-and it seemed he was highly excited. 'Let me introduce two good-Englishmen to each other', thought Bapu. So he said 'Col. Maddock! This is my dear friend, Mr Charlie Andrews!' But almost before Bapu could finish, the surgeon broke out impatiently, 'Yes, yes, but I have not come here so early, as your doctor. I am the bearer of good news. Government has released you unconditionally.' He laid special emphasis on 'unconditionally'. 'Now you are free to go wherever you like.' Bapu was silent for a moment, and then with just a smile he said, 'I thank you. But I do hope I can continue to stay here as your patient and guest for a few days more.' The surgeon laughed in return and said, 'Most certainly. With great pleasure. But on one condition. You will continue to obey my orders as your doctor, exactly as you have been doing till now. You are no longer a prisoner, but you haven't ceased to be my patient!' Bapu also burst into a broad laugh. (After the surgeon's departure, Andrews said to Bapu, 'The surgeon was more than a match for you in his volley of answers.') After some more chat, the surgeon observed as he was leaving, 'I had the luck to be the first to give you this message, and I hope I shall be equally lucky in having to send you away from the hospital safe and sound.'

Who can describe the sense of relief that spread after this news? Andrews told me: 'Immediately they heard the news, they all flocked into the room. And there was revelry all around. Everybody was mad with joy and I the maddest. But Bapu sat still, the same unruffled figure of quiet repose and charm. As I saw him in that mood I thought he must be thinking with an indulgent smile, "These butterflies! How they flutter! And for what?"'

The Diary of Mahadev Desai Vol. 4, pp. 42–4

109. It was from the hospital itself that Gandhi wrote on the 7th February his first letter after release. The letter was addressed to M. Mohammad Ali, the Congress President.
110. On this day Gandhi participated in the 'inauguration' of *The Hindustan Times*.
111. Remark of December 1924.
112. Madeleine Slade (1892–1982), who was given the name Mira by Gandhi. These words were the first spoken by him to her, as she bent to touch his feet, on arriving at Sabarmati Ashram.

Part Eleven: 1926–32

1. Bhagat Singh (1907–31), the most famous revolutionary of the Indian independence movement, popularly referred to as 'Shaheed' Bhagat Singh. Believed by many to have held Marxist beliefs and been described by the Communist Party of India (Marxist) as 'one of India's earliest Marxists', Bhagat Singh led the Hindustan Socialist Republican Association. Bhagat Singh was hanged for shooting a police officer who had beaten up the veteran Lala Lajpat Rai on 30 October 1928, who succumbed to his injuries on 17 November.
2. Premlila Thackersey (1894–1977).
3. The identity of the addressee, who was in Ceylon, is not known.
4. Gandhi had received from the addressee a letter dated 21 May 1926.
5. Swami Shraddhananda was stabbed to death by Abdul Rashid in Delhi on 23 December where the Swami was lying ill.
6. Reacting to the news of the murder of Swami Shraddhanandaji, Gandhi said the above at the All India Congress Committee.
7. Katharine Mayo (1867–1940) author of *Mother India* (New York, Blue Ribbon Books: 1927).
8. Lakshmi Rajagopalachari (1912–83) Rajaji's younger daughter to marry Devadas Gandhi in 1933.

9. Gandhi had addressed nine gatherings before this meeting on that day.
10. Devadas was to have been on this trip to Ceylon but was prevented at the last minute by illness. The Devadas–Lakshmi wedding took place more than five years later, in 1938. Surendra was a born ascetic who joined the Sabarmati Ashram and worked there as a tanner. A linguist and gifted writer in Hindi, he travelled extensively in the Himalaya. He was among a very small number that took a portion of Gandhi's ashes to be immersed at the lake Manasarovar in 1948. 'Surendraji' or 'Sadhu Surendra' as he came to be known lived in later years at Samanvaya Ashram, near Bodh Gaya.
11. In reply to Nehru's letter, dated 11-1-1928.
12. One of the princely States in Saurashtra.
13. Gandhi belonged to this sub-caste of Banias.
14. From Mahadev Desai's 'The Week', which reported this speech under the caption 'A Solemn Ceremony'.
15. Gandhi's illness at this time occasioned many rumours one of which had it that on 10 February 1928, he invited some persons to dine with him in order to share with them the foreknowledge that he was to die on 12 February. The 'date' was later modified to one in March. The date 17 March 1928 also acquired salience on account of Gandhi's having said on 18 March 1922, when he was sentenced to six years' imprisonment that he 'expected India to be free at the end of that period or, alternatively, to be dead by then'.
16. Sam Higginbottom, born in 1903, founded the Agriculture University in Allahabad.
17. After his return to India in 1914, Gandhi devoted much of his time to mobilise Indian public opinion in support of the Indians in South Africa. But he repeatedly stressed that the Indians should maintain friendly relations with the Africans and that if Indian rights conflicted with the interests of the African majority, they should not be pressed. Sarojini Naidu said during her visit to South Africa in 1924 that the struggles of the Indian and African people were for a common objective. She was applauded by Dr Abdulla Abdurrahman and Clemens Kadalie, the South African trade union leader.

The same message was carried by the Rev. C.F. Andrews, who made several visits to South Africa at the request of Gandhi and Rabindranath Tagore.

In 1928, after the Cape Town agreement between South Africa and India, Mr Habib Motan, the honorary secretary of the Government Indian School Committee in the Transvaal, protested against arrangements to send Indian students to the Fort Hare Native College as humiliating and degrading. He was supported by P.S. Aiyar, the publicist who always tried to be more 'radical' than Gandhi. Andrews replied in *The Modern Review* of Calcutta in March 1928: 'The poet, Rabindranath Tagore, gave me a definite message to the Indians in South Africa. He stated that if the Indian community could not win the respect and affection of the Africans (who had the true right to be in South Africa, as the children of the soil) then they had no place there. They were imperialist intruders. Mr Habib Motan's statement ... must shock every Indian nationalist who reads it.'

18. Dr Bidhan Chandra Roy (1882–1962), physician, politician and later Chief Minister of West Bengal, had requested Gandhi to deliver the Kamala lectures at the Calcutta University instituted by Asutosh Mookherjee. The earlier lecturers included Annie Besant, Srinivasa Sastri, and Sarojini Naidu.

19. Sir Asutosh Mookerjee (1864–1924). Well-known educationist and jurist; Judge, Calcutta High Court, and Vice-Chancellor, Calcutta University four terms; Member, Sadler Commission, etc.

20. The Gujarati original of this appeared in *Navajivan*, 30-9-1928.

21. The Gujarati original has 'ahimsa'.

22. Mira Behn writes in *The Spirit's Pilgrimage* (Coward-McCann, Inc., New York; 1960) pp. 98–9: ... One of the heifers in the Ashram cowsheds had fallen sick and become quite helpless. She lay on her side with all four legs stretched out, and yet she couldn't die. Bapu heard about it and went to see her. A veterinary doctor was called and he said she was past all hope of recovery. Bapu felt his Ahimsa was again on trial, and this time the sanctity of the cow was involved. The heifer was quite big, and it was impossible to lift her about as one could a human being so as to prevent bed sores. She refused nourishment, flies were tormenting her, and in every way her life was a torture. Bapu decided in his own mind that true Ahimsa required him to put the heifer out of her misery by having her killed in as painless a way as possible, but he did not wish to take the step without trying to convince the Ashramites of its correctness. Intense discussions took place, and most of the inmates accepted Bapu's reasoning. But there were one or two who most vehemently opposed it, and Ba was on their side as was Kashiben, Ba's bosom companion. So Bapu told them to go out and nurse the heifer, and if they found they could save her from suffering, all very well and good. Accordingly they went and sat down in the straw by the poor creature, whisked away the flies and tried to persuade her to take nourishment, but when they found that they could neither feed her nor easer her pain, they sorrowfully returned to Bapu and said they would no longer oppose him. Bapu knew that Seth Ambalal Sarabhai would be with him in this interpretation of non-violence, so he sent

him a message asking him to arrange for an injection whichi would be as quick and painless as possible in its effect. Promptly Seth Ambalal arrived, accompanied by his family doctor armed with a big syringe and necessary poison. Bapu led them to the cowshed, with only the dairyman and myself following. Everyone was silent. We entered the room where the heifer was lying, and the doctor prepared the syringe. Then Bapu stooped down and gently held for a moment one of the heifer's front legs, the syringe was applied, there was a spasm and the heifer was dead. No one spoke. Bapu took a cloth and spread it over the heifer's face, and then walked silently back to his room. ...

23. The words 'especially in Ahmedabad' do not occur in the Gujarati original.

24. Lala Lajpat Rai (1865–1928) led a procession in Lahore on 31 October 1928 to oppose the Simon Commission, a Parliamentary Committee so named after its head, which was boycotted by both the Congress and the Muslim League on the grounds that it had no Indian on it. The boycott included protest marches all over India which met with police repression in one of which, on 30 October 1928, Lalaji received direct blows to which he succumbed.

25. Prabhavati Narayan (1906–73) daughter of Babu Brajkishore Prasad and wife of Jayaprakash Narayan, she spent years in the care of Gandhi and Kasturba.

26. Jiddu Krishnamurti (1895–1986), initiated into a role of spiritual leadership by Dr Annie Besant, philosopher and thinker acclaimed internationally as the 'seer who walked alone', teaching a conditioned humanity that truth was a 'pathless land'.

27. Dated 22 November 1928, which read: 'I was so greatly looking forward to seeing you ... but most unfortunately I have had to cancel my whole tour on account of my having a bad cold ... I hope I may have the pleasure of meeting you soon.' In the event, Gandhi and Krishnamurti never met.

28. Niece of Hermann Kallenbach.

29. Explaining this, Jawaharlal Nehru has written: 'I think this letter was written soon after the incident at Lucknow when many of us demonstrated peacefully against the arrival of the Simon Commission there. We were severely beaten by the baton and lathi blows of the police'.

30. Padmaja Naidu (1900–75), younger daughter of Sarojini Naidu and Governor of West Bengal from 1956–67. This was in reply to her letter dated 16 November, which read: 'I have been very bad for the last fortnight'.

31. Sarojini Naidu, then on a tour of America.

32. Albert West.

33. John Haynes Holmes (1879–1964), founder and minister of The

Community Church of New York who, along with C.F. Andrews, was coordinating the publication of Gandhi's works in the West.

34. On 17-12-1928. Bhagat Singh, Rajguru, and Sukhdev were accused of killing Saunders in the Lahore conspiracy case and sentenced to death.

35. In his comment on the Nehru Report named after Motilal Nehru, the Chairman of the All-Parties Committee that prepared it, as a response to the British claim that India's diverse political groups and communities would not and could not agree on a Constitution. The Report offered Muslims three new Muslim majority provinces—Sind, North West Frontier Province and Baluchistan and, among other gestures, a 25 per cent quota in the Central Assembly.

36. From the session.

37. Rasik Harilal Gandhi (1912-29).

38. Manilal and Sushila did indeed spend their entire lives in South Africa, running *Indian Opinion*.

39. An African employee who had been at the Phoenix Press from its very start, had died. Prabhudas Gandhi's character-portrayal of this dedicated worker in *Jivan-nun Parodh* is worth studying.

40. Slave girls or maidservants.

41. Devadas Gandhi.

42. The original Gujarati letter to Devadas has 'maya', a far weightier word (than its English equivalent used in this translation here) suggesting 'delusion' and 'illusion' among other concepts, indicating the shadowy ephemerality of human perceptions.

43. A deputation of heads of Buddhist religious orders in Burma, presented Gandhi a long interrogatory. The two replies given here are collated from reports in *The Tribune* and accounts by Mahadev Desai and Pyarelal.

44. Only extracts are reproduced here.

45. The correspondent had requested Gandhi to substitute 'hajam' by 'Valand' because the former word had become a term of contempt for the barber.

46. Edward Frederick Lindley Wood, 1st Earl of Halifax, KG, OM, GCSI, GCMG, GCIE, PC (1881-1959), The Lord Irwin, Viceroy of India (1926-31).

47. At Sabarmati Ashram.

48. The District Magistrate accompanied by the Superintendent of Police and a party of 20 armed constables arrived at the camp at 12.45 a.m., when Gandhi was asleep.

49. Gandhi was escorted in a train to Borivli, a suburban station of Bombay, and from there taken by car to Yervada.

50. Jail Superintendent. The text of this was communicated by Doyle to the Home Department on 12 May.

51. Mira Behn in *Young India*, 22-5-1930, says that this was addressed to Devadas Gandhi.

52. Indira Nehru (1917–84).

53. Vijayalakshmi Pandit (1900–90).

54. Krishna Hutheesing (1907–67).

55. 'Gandiv' was the name of Arjuna's bow in the Mahabharata. A charkha developed in Surat was given the same name. Gandhi said of it 'It is essentially a poor man's wheel. The inventor is no mechanic. How it came to him, I do not know. But every part of it, in my opinion, shows solicitude for the starving. It costs Rs $1^1/_2$ but it can be made for only 8 annas, I am sure. It is the lightest wheel going in India. It requires the least attention. It occupies the smallest space of all the wheels I know. A little child can work at it'.

56. Upton Sinclair (1878–1968) Pulitzer Prize winning socialist novelist who contested unsuccessfully but heroically for the office of Governor of California.

57 & 58. Books by the author, published in 1925 and 1930, respectively.

59. Vanamala Parikh (1922–97); daughter of Narahari Parikh, later to marry Mahendra Valji Desai (1922–2002).

60. Lord Irwin.

61. Said by Gandhi to Lord Irwin when the Viceroy said he could not accept Gandhi's demand for an inquiry into police brutalities because that would demoralize the police. The Gandhi-Irwin Pact was signed on 4 March 1931.

62. Said by Gandhi to Viceroy Lord Irwin's secretary Emerson in response to the compliment 'You are a remarkably good draughtsman, Mr Gandhi', after Gandhi dictated in detail a summary of the discussions with the Viceroy.

63. In reply to his 'private' letter dated 6 March which read: 'I want to write you a personal note of my own. Very great thanks to you for all you have done, while we have been working together during these last difficult days. It has been a great privilege to me to be given this opportunity of meeting and knowing you; and I hope that, either before I leave India or in England, you will give me the pleasure of seeing you again. I do pray—as I believe—that history may say you and I were permitted to be instruments in doing something big for India and for humanity. Believe me, with again much thanks, and with deep understanding. ...'

64. With G.D. Birla in New Delhi on 18 February 1931.

65. Being Monday, a silence day. On the very day in his letter superscribed 'confidential' the Viceroy wrote: 'I have again thought very carefully over everything that you have said—and the last thing I should wish to do would be to make your task, especially at this juncture, more difficult.

But I am afraid, for the reasons I sought to explain fully to you in conversation, I cannot see my way to feel that it would be right to take the action you request ...'

66. The addressee had sought Gandhi's permission to use his photo as a trade mark for roofing tiles.

67. Bibi Amtussalam (1907–85). Born to a prominent Muslim family of Patiala, met Gandhi in 1930–1 and joined his Ashram 'circle', working for Hindu-Muslim unity. Well versed in her own religious scriptures, could also recite the Guru Granth Sahib. Possessed of a Joan of Arc-type spirit of surrender to her concept of God and right-doing.

68. With G.D. Birla in New Delhi on 18 February 1931.

69. Subhas Chandra Bose (1897–1945?); General Secretary of the Congress, 1927; President of the Congress, 1938 and 1939; resigned Presidentship and founded the All-India Forward Bloc; placed under house arrest but escaped to Germany in 1941; one of the organizers of Indian Independence League in South East Asia; organized and led the Indian National Army.

70. Vasudev Gogate, a student of Fergusson College, Poona, fired at Acting Governor Hotson when he was entering the Reading Room of the Library.

71. Rajagopalachari's elder daughter Namagiri (1906–95), who was critically ill.

72. Scheduled to be held from 8 September.

73. On seeing leather suitcases and a camp-bed brought on board by the party accompanying him to London for the Round Table Conference, held from 12 September to 5 December 1931.

74. James D Hunt writes in *Gandhi in London* (Promilla & Co., Publishers, New Delhi, 1978, pp. 212–13): Gandhi's residence in London was in a small room on the top floor in Kingsley Hall. Mira stayed at the Hall with him as cook, housekeeper, alarm clock, and general aide. The rest of the party was domiciled at 88. While admiring the work of Kingsley Hall, Gandhi still maintained his perspective on the status of the people of Bow. When asked for his impressions of the neighbourhood, his answer showed that his thoughts were, as always, with India:

I love the East End, particularly the little urchins in the streets. They give me such friendly greetings. I have seen a tremendous change in social conditions since I was in London forty years ago. The poverty in London is nothing to what it is in India. I go down the streets here and I see outside each house a bottle of milk, and inside the door there is a strip of carpet, perhaps a piano in the sitting room... It is perhaps not an exaggeration to say that the poor in London have as high a standard of living as the rich in India. (*CWMG* Vol. 48, pp. 25–6).

75. While driving with Gandhi to St James' Palace for the second day of the Conference.

76. Tea for the delegates to the Conference hosted by King George V and Queen Mary. In a letter to the Lord Chamberlain, Gandhi said he would be wearing his usual attire, not ceremonial clothes.

77. James D. Hunt in *Gandhi in London*, writes: Horace Alexander reports that Gandhi, Mahadev Desai, and Sarojini Naidu set off for the Palace from 88 Knightsbridge 'hoping for a pleasant social occasion which might at least bring a little sweetness into a painful situation', but that 'they returned deeply distressed', for the King had taken the opportunity to deliver Gandhi a severe political lecture on an occasion which should have been entirely non-political. Gandhi and Mahadev felt that the King had completely disregarded the proprieties. The King, acting on instructions from the India Office, concluded a gracious chat with a warning, 'Remember, Mr Gandhi, I won't have any attacks on my Empire'. What followed was variously reported. Wigram, the King's secretary, said that 'Gandhi spluttered some excuse', but Hoare heard a gracious reply, 'I must not be drawn into a political argument in Your Majesty's Palace after receiving Your Majesty's hospitality'. Alexander suggests that probably the King did not listen to the courteous answer. Hoare, however, thought to himself 'what exquisite worldly manners the unworldly possess'.

78. When asked if the King had given him any encouragement.

79. The second session of the Round Table Conference was held between 7 September and 1 December 1931. There were altogether 112 delegates—20 representing the British Government, 23 Indian States, and 69 British India. Gandhiji attended the second session as the sole representative of the Congress. Ramsay MacDonald, Prime Minister, was the Chairman of the Conference. The second session did not open with a meeting of the full Conference. The Federal Structure Committee reassembled on 7 September, and the Minorities Committee on 28 September, followed by a Plenary Session beginning on 28 November 1931. The other Committees of the Conference did not reassemble.

80. The interview took place at the house of Dr Katial in Canning Town. The report has been extracted from Mahadev Desai's *London Letter* and *My Autobiography* by Charlie Chaplin.

81. Sardar Ujjal Singh (1895–1983), Parliamentarian, nominated representative of the Sikhs at the Round Table Conferences, Governor of Punjab in 1965 and of Madras in 1966.

82. All the speakers that followed supported the adjournment motion. Dr Ambedkar, Sir Henry Gidney, and Rao Bahadur Pannirselvam, did not oppose the adjournment. But they said that since Gandhi recognized

only two minority communities, namely, the Muslims and the Sikhs, they could not be expected to participate in the committee's work.

83. The luncheon at Westminster Palace, marking Gandhi's 62nd birthday, was arranged by the Independent Labour Party, the Indian National Congress League, and The Gandhi Society. As many as 388 persons were present with Fenner Brockway in the chair. A charkha, was presented to the 'birthday boy'.

84. Maria Montessori (1870–1952) was an Italian educator, scientist, physician, philosopher, devout Catholic, feminist, and humanitarian. She was born in Chiaravalle (Ancona), Italy to Alessandro Montessori and Renilde Stoppani. Montessori was the first woman to graduate from the University of Rome's Medical School. She was a member of the University's Psychiatric Clinic, trying to educate the 'mentally retarded' and the 'uneducable' in Rome. She opened her first school, in a housing project in Rome, on 6 January 1907.

85. Editor of *The Spectator*. The account has been extracted from Wrench's report *An Evening with Mr Gandhi*. The interview took place at Wrench's residence between 8 and 11 p.m.

86. This was in response to Einstein's letter, dated 27 September, which read: 'You have shown by all that you have done that we can achieve the ideal even without resorting to violence. We can conquer those votaries of violence by the non-violent method. Your example will inspire and help humanity to put an end to a conflict based on violence with international help and co-operation guaranteeing peace to the world. With this expression of my devotion and admiration I hope to be able to meet you face to face'—*The Statesman*, 22-5-1965.

87. Presumably, V.A. Sundaram, Registrar of Benares Hindu University.

88. At a very influential gathering of Englishmen and Englishwomen, drawn from all parts of England and representing many institutions and many interests.

89. Extracted from Mahadev Desai's report: 'The week-end at Eton and Oxford: Among Future Empire-Builders'.

90. Extracted from Mahadev Desai's report: 'The week-end at Eton and Oxford: Among Future Empire-Builders'.

91. Extracted from Mahadev Desai's 'London Letter'.

92. The first question was asked by some students at Oxford, where he was on 24 October.

93. The question was put by Mrs Eustace Miles.

94. At the Majlis, Cambridge, 1 November 1931.

95. Although the word 'negro' is no longer used, it is retained here for reasons of fidelity to the original. The discussion took place at the London School Of Economics, London, 10 November 1931. According

to a Press report 'The theatre of the London School of Economics did not suffice to accommodate the members of the School's Students' Union who assembled to hear Mahatma Gandhi. The audience consisted mostly of English students and was perhaps the largest English audience Mahatma Gandhi had addressed in England'.

96. Gandhi left London on 5 December 1931.

97. A memorandum, submitted 'on behalf of the Mohammedans, the Depressed Classes, the Anglo-Indians, the Europeans, and a considerable section of Indian Christian groups', demanded *inter alia* that these communities 'shall have representation in all legislatures through separate electorates ... provided that, after a lapse of ten years, it will be open to Muslims in the Punjab and Bengal and any minority communities in any other provinces to accept joint electorates ... With regard to the Depressed Classes no change to join electorates ... shall be made until after 20 years ...' Special claims were advanced on behalf of Mussalmans, the Depressed Classes, the Anglo-Indians, and the Europeans. The document was signed by the Aga Khan, Dr Ambedkar, Rao Bahadur Pannirselvam, Sir Henry Gidney, and Sir Hubert Carr.

98. Mahadev Desai says in his 'London Letter', the questions were put 'by the son of a prominent public man'. On 25 November *The Hindustan Times* carried a brief report of an interview given to Randolph Churchill who was acting on behalf of the Hearst Press.

99. The session began on 30 November and after adjourning at 11.50 p.m., was resumed at 12.05 a.m.

100. Gandhiji had looked at his watch just as the interview commenced.

101. Mahadev Desai records in his Diary (1932), *Vol. 1, p. 82:* This evening (April 20, 1932) Bapu returned from his walk and I was wiping the dust off his feet when he said: 'The image of Jesus Christ which I saw in the Vatican at Rome is before my eyes at all times. The body was covered only by a small piece of cloth such as is worn by poor men in our villages. And what a wonderful look of compassion he had!'

102. Sistine Chapel. Gandhi examined the tall Crucifix from all sides, in order to take in the full import of the dying Christ.

103. Extracted from Mahadev Desai's 'Letter from Europe'.

104. According to an entry under this date in 'Diary, 1931'.

105, 106. British security officers specially permitted to escort Gandhi up to Rome. Gandhi presented them a wrist watch each while saying farewell.

107. This was dictated to Mahadev Desai on 3 January at 4 a.m. and signed the next day, 'a few moments after his actual arrest', according to a covering letter Mahadev Desai sent along with it.

108. Mira Behn writes in *The Spirit's Pilgrimage*: ... Now we knew Bapu's arrest must come, but the Government held its hand for four days,

and then on 4th January, when the excitement of expectation had died down a little, they came at 3 o'clock in the morning to take Bapu away to Yeravda Jail. Everyone in the house got up and gathered around Bapu. The English Commissioner of Police, handing him the warrant, said, 'It is my duty to arrest you.' It was Bapu's Silence Day; he intimated that he would like half an hour in which to get ready, which was granted. I hurriedly rolled up Bapu's bedding and fastened the other things which since 31st December I had packed up each night and kept in readiness for the expected arrest. Bapu scribbled down on a paper a message to the nation in which he said: *Infinite is God's mercy, never swerve from truth and non-violence, never turn your back, and sacrifice your lives and all to win Swaraj* [Self-rule]. Then we all sat around while Bapu's favourite hymn was sung, the police standing considerately at a little distance. After this Bapu rose, everyone bent down to touch his feet, and away he went surrounded by the police.

109. Gandhi was in the Yeravda Prison from 4 January 1932 to 8 May 1933.

110. Valji Govindji Desai (1892–1982). Born at Jetpur, Saurashtra. Graduated from Bombay University in English and Sanskrit. Met Gandhi in 1915, resigned from Gujarat College, Ahmedabad. In 1921 was Deputy Editor of *Young India*, used to write for *Navajivan* and *Harijan*. In 1925, Secretary of All India Cow Protection Committee 1930, participated the in Salt March, imprisoned with Gandhi. In 1934 joined Gandhi's Harijan Tour. In 1938 was Campaign Secretary in Haripura Congress. Translated some books of Gandhi into English. Dedicated and studious worker, voracious reader, maintained a library even in jail. He suggested the name 'Sevagram' for the Sevagram Ashram. (Source: *Freedom Fighters of Gujarat*, Pub. by Gujarat Vishwakosh Trust.)

111. Madan Gopal Bhandari (1893–1971), retired as Major General.

112. Indu N. Parekh was a student from the Ashram School.

113. Lakshmi, daughter of C. Rajagopalachari, to marry Devadas Gandhi the following year.

114. Letter to Narandas Gandhi.

115. Indu Parekh.

116. Letter to Manu Harilal Gandhi.

117. Manu Harilal Gandhi.

118. Baliben Vora, maternal aunt of Manu Harilal Gandhi.

119. Letter to Devadas Gandhi.

120. This letter to Verrier Elwin was in reply to one from the addressee saying that a Bishop had called him a traitor to Christ and had prohibited him from preaching in churches.

Verrier Elwin (1902–64) was an Oxford scholar who came out to India in 1927 as a missionary. He first joined Christian Service Society in Pune. The first time he visited the central India, current states of

Madhya Pradesh, Chattisgarh, and parts of eastern Maharashtrawas with another Indian from Pune Shamrao Hivale. Their studies are on the tribes are the first anthropological studies in the country. Over the years he was influenced by the philosophies of Mahatma Gandhi and Rabindranath Tagore. He regularly visited the Sabarmati Ashram and was a close friend of Mahadev Desai's. The Church however soon found objections to the ways of Elwin's when he began working and living with them. He married a woman from the Gond community. He came out with numerous works on various tribal groups in India, the best acclaimed being those on Maria and Baiga. After India attained independence in 1947 he was asked by the Jawaharlal Nehru to find solutions to the problems that emerged in the North Eastern States of India, then called NEFA currently the region has seven states adjunct to the state of Assam.

121. Maithilisaran Gupta (1886–1964); outstanding Hindi poet and nationalist, later a nominated Member of Parliament (Rajya Sabha). His most famous work was *Saket* a poetic account of life in Ayodhya during the years when Rama, Sita, and Lakshmana were in exile. Lakshmana's wife Urmila is the central figure in this work.

122. Harilal had written a letter to his father demanding that his daughter, Manu, should be taken away from the custody of his wife's sister, Balibehn Vohra, and be restored to him. He had also complained about Bali's assault on him and held his father responsible for it. Ramchandra Gandhi (1937–2007) in his Foreword to Tridip Suhrud's translation (Orient Longman, 2007) of C.B. Dalal's Gujarati classic *Harilal Gandhi: A Life* says:

> On one point (Harilal's being born to the teenage couple) Bapu seems to me to be theologically wrong. He thought that his own carnal nature as a youth was punished by God in the form of a bad son. Surely God must have more things to do than punish fathers with recalcitrant sons!

123. To Ramdas Gandhi.

124. Talking to Mahadev Desai about keeping a diary, Gandhi said this.

125. In reply to Phulchand who was in Visapur prison.

126. To someone who asked if Gandhi had met anybody who was never perturbed.

127. This was sent along with the 'Letter To Narandas Gandhi' on 19/23-5-1932.

128. In response to a query from a girl if he believed in marriage between followers of different faiths as he was in favour of inter-caste marriages.

129. Letter to Vidya R. Patel, daughter of Raojibhai Manibhai Patel (1866–1962). Raojibhai had joined the Phoenix Ashram and started

participating in public life with the support of Gandhi. Joined the training of soldiers for World War I. Participated in the Flag Satyagraha of Nagpur and was imprisoned for a year. Successfully fought against land revenue for Petlad Taluka Farmers Union. Joined Dandi March and was jailed for two years. Contributed to the establishment of Vitthal Kanya Vidyalaya at Nadiad. Participated in Individual Satyagraha in 1940. Participated in the Quit India movement and was imprisoned for two years.

130. To Bhau Panse, a co-worker of Vinoba Bhave and an Ashram inmate.

131. To D.V. Parachure Shastri (who came to the Ashram in 1939 and stayed there till his death on 5 September 1945). A patient of leprosy, he was at this time in the ward for leprosy patients in Yeravda Central Prison. He was a Sanskrit scholar, particularly of the Vedas, went to jail several times during the freedom struggle. It is not known when the leprosy manifested itself. Mira Behn one day found him sitting outside the Sevagram Ashram and took him to Gandhi. After some introspection Gandhi gave him a place in the Ashram, and personally nursed his wounds and massaged him everyday. Towards the end of his life he was entrusted to the care of the leprosy home (Maharogi Seva Mandal) run by Manoharji Divan in 1945, where he died.

132. To Jal A.D. Naoroji who had written about Cooper's invention of a new plough capable of increasing the yield of crops by 15 to 150 per cent.

133. Mahadev Desai recorded in his Diary this conversation between the two inmates, Gandhi and Sardar Vallabhbhai Patel.

134. To Mira Behn.

135. Gandhi had been asked if he 'allowed a venomous snake crawl over his body'.

136. This was in reply to a letter protesting against political prisoners being taken out of jail for work, chained, and fettered.

137. The diary of Mahadev Desai, Vol. I, p. 174 has: 'A wire from Devadas ... was received yesterday: "The maximum temperature was 102°, and has now gone below 100°. The climate of Gorakhpur is very bad ..." The Sardar suggested that Devadas has refered to the climate in the expectation that we should try to get him transferred from Gorakhpur. The Sardar suggested that he should certainly be transferred to some place with a better climate. Bapu said, "Yes, but we must apply for the transfer ourselves, if we want it, and I have no mind to do so. Harilal was in the worst prison in South Africa, but his transfer was arranged by him himself and not by me." The Sardar said, "The circumstances in India are different." Bapu yielded after all and wired to Hailey ...'

138. This is in a letter to Devadas, written after reading Rajagopalachari's views on Sinclair.

139. Letter to Prema Kantak.
140. Namagiri, daughter of C. Rajagopalachari.
141. S. Varadachari.
142. The change in the form of Gandhi's addressing of Saraladevi speaks for itself.
143. The addressee's son
144. The *Diary of Mahadev Desai*, Vol. I, p. 254, has: 'There was a heart-rending letter from Shirinbai, the sister of the missing airman. His 72-year-old mother was still alive; and his only brother had been in a London nursing home for 8 years. The sister had picked up a little Gujarati 30 years ago, but still she took great pains and wrote a good Gujarati letter and at the end of it requested permission to write to Bapu in English.'
145. Eldest son of Dr Pranjivan Mehta.
146. Dr Pranjivan Mehta passed away on 3rd August.
147. Sarojini Naidu's daughter.
148. Presumably Virendranath Chattopadhyay.
149. In the Arthur Road Prison, Bombay, where Sarojini Naidu was imprisoned along with Mira Behn and Kamaladevi Chattopadhyay.
150. One of the many self descriptions, drawn from her witticisms, adopted by Gandhi in his letters to Sarojini Naidu.
151. Letter to Ramdas Gandhi from the *Diary of Mahadev Desai*, Vol. I, pp. 279–80. Desai says: 'Today's letters were all from prisoners. One of these was from Ramdas who complained that Bapu who was very strict at a time in doing and imposing penance had now become too lenient and people took an undue advantage of this leniency ...'
152. The place under reference is the Sabarmati Ashram.
153. To Pyarelal.
154. The fast was begun on 20 September 1932, in protest against separate electorates for the depressed classes announced in the Communal Award of Prime Minister Ramsay MacDonald on 17 April 1932.
155. To the press correspondents who were allowed, after convention, to interview Gandhi in prison on the first day of the fast.
156. In his telegram, received on 26 September Jawaharlal Nehru said: 'First news your decision fast caused mental agony confusion but ultimately optimism triumphed regained peace mind. No sacrifice too great for suppressed downtrodden classes. Freedom must be judged by freedom of lowest but feel danger other issues obscuring only goal. Am unable judge from religious view-point. Danger your methods being exploited by others but how can I presume advise magician. Love.'
157. Indira Nehru (1917–84).
158. Vijayalakshmi Pandit.
159. Chandralekha (b. 1924) and Nayantara (b. 1927).

160. In an interview to Ellen Wilkinson and V.K. Krishna Menon of the India League first published in *The Daily Herald* of London.
161. The settlement was signed on 24 September.
162. Letter to Dr Suresh Chandra Banerji (1887–1961).

Part Twelve: 1933-6

1. Ex-Diwan of Morvi State.
2. The questions are reproduced from the addressee's letter dated 9 January 1933.
3. Father W.Q. Lash, British priest. Member, Christa Seva Sangha, Poona, 1932–4. Acharya, Christa Prema Seva Sangha, Poona, from 1934. Consecrated Lord Bishop of Bombay, 1947. Arrived in India in December 1932. Soon after, met Gandhi in Yeravda prison. Spent some time in Sabarmati Ashram. Worked at the ashram of Christa Seva Sangh in Poona. Consecrated Lord Bishop of Bombay, 1947, of Christa Seva Sangh, Poona (1933). Father (or Brother) Lash stayed for some time in Sabarmati Ashram in 1933 (when Gandhi was in jail).
4. Notably, the 'others' included C. Rajagopalachari, whose timely letter to Gandhi on the subject, has been alluded to in Rajmohan Gandhi's *Mohandas* (Penguin/Viking 2006).
5. To Verrier Elwin
6. 'Ala Pocha was a young doctor in Sevagram Ashram. Verrier confessed to Gandhi to a previous romance with Ala but denied any promise of marriage.' (Ramachandra Guha in *Savaging the Civilized—Verrier Elwin, His Tribals And India*, OUP, 1999)
7. Mary Gillett of the Christa Seva Sangh was a teacher trained in Roehampton. She first met Elwin in England in 1929, she came to Poona to join the CSS. Ramachandra Guha writes in *Savaging the Civilized—Verrier Elwin, His Tribals And India* (OUP, 1999): 'Mary was in love, but Verrier, at least in the beginning, resisted ... On the 25th of January 1933, two weeks after she had arrived on a visit, Mary joined the ashram as 'Brother Mary', to live with Shamrao and Verrier much as 'Mira Behn lives with Bapu and his brothers'—that is, in the purest platonic friendship. Another fortnight and Verrier and Mary had written to friends that they would be married after Easter in their mud chapel of St Francis, this to be followed by a honeymoon tour by bullock cart through the jungle villages fo the district. The marriage would unite them 'in love of Christ and of India, of ashram life and St Francis, of the life of poverty and of the poor. Our marriage therefore will mean little change in our way of life. We want to give our lives to India, to her poor and for their freedom.'

8. Letter to Kasturba.
9. In a letter to T. Titus.
10. Mahadev Desai states: 'Gandhiji addressed a few words to the bride and bridegroom. He took over five minute to gather sufficient strength to speak. The part addressed to Devadas was in Gujarati, and that addressed to the bride was in Hindi.'
11. To Manilal and Sushila Gandhi.
12. J.B. Irwin; the statement was made under section 3(2) of the Bombay Act XVI of 1932.
13. In a telegram to Home Secretary, Government of Bombay, on 30 July Gandhi conveyed his decision to march to Ras. In an appeal to the people of Gujarat, Gandhi announced his proposal to leave the Ashram on the march to Ras with 33 companions on 1 August. On 1 August, along with Kasturba and Mahadev Desai, he was arrested after prayers. Bidding farewell to Harijans who had gathered on the road on the way to Sabarmati Jail, he made this statement before District Magistrate, Ahmedabad and in a letter to Shri Advani, Superintendent, Ahmedabad Central Prison, asked for permission to do Harijan work. Ahmedadad observed hartal.
14. Gandhi, on his release at 9 a.m., was served with an order to remain within Poona city limits. He was, within an hour, re-arrested for disobeying the order and taken to Yeravda Jail for trial, which began at 3.15 p.m. before Hyam S. Israel, Additional District Magistrate, Poona.
15. Gandhi was released unconditionally on the eighth day of his fast, which began on 16 August.
16. From Anand Hingorani's obituary tribute to Gandhi in *Harijan*, 15 February 1948. Hingorani describes the conversation's setting in these words: *Within five days of his fast his condition grew so bad that he had to be removed to Sassoon Hospital, Poona, and two days later, when it was realized that further detention might prove fatal, the Government ordered his release unconditionally on 23 August 1933, and he was brought over to Parnakuti. I happened to be then in Poona in charge of the Harijan by Bapu's orders as the editor had gone on leave. Naturally I had the great good fortune to be with Bapu after his release for the entire period of his convalescence in Parnakuti. He had been sentenced to one year's imprisonment in consequence of his defiance of the Government's restraint order. This unexpected, premature release, therefore, raised a moral problem for him. He didn't quite know what to do till the termination of the period of his sentence. One evening I was all alone with Bapu. He was taking a stroll in the terrace garden of Parnakuti. He appeared to be immersed in deep thought then. The faint glow of the setting sun was still on the flowers and trees of the garden*

which had, as a result, taken on a new colour and charm. Suddenly he broke the silence ...

17. Letter to Padma, daughter of Sitla Sahay, a Congress worker from U.P. and Smt Sarojinidevi Sahay.

18. Literally, 'purificatory rite'. Here, re-conversion to Hinduism.

19. *Shubhgaman* 'auspicious departure', instead of *Shubhagaman*, 'welcome'.

20. The Gujaratis, Marwari, and Sindhi residents welcomed Gandhi at 9.30 a.m.

21. The meeting was held at the beach at 6 p.m. and was attended by 15,000 people.

22. The meeting was held in the morning at the Municipal Market. The audience numbered about 20,000.

23. The Bihar earthquake occurred on 15 January 1934.

24. About 25,000 people attended this meeting and various addresses and purses were presented to Gandhi. At the end of the meeting the addresses were auctioned.

25. A surprising question as it was common knowledge that the 32-year-old socialist leader was in Nasik prison at the time.

26. Pyarelal tells us that Gandhi delivered this speech at Sonepur station standing in the doorway of the train.

27. One of the 'lowest' castes in the old order, generally engaged in the work of handling the remains of the dead.

28. Speech at Dayaram Jethamal Sind College.

29. Letter to Kanti Harilal Gandhi.

30. Speech at a public meeting.

31. Nehru had been discharged on 12 August from prison on account of his wife's illness.

32. M.R. Masani met Gandhi on 24 May; the reference is perhaps to *What Marx Really Meant*. Jayaprakash Narayan had finished his jail term in Nasik in April 1934 and organized a convention which met in Patna under the Presidentship of Acharya Narendra Deva on 17 May 1934 to inaugurate the Congress Socialist Party and lead to an all-India conference. He was elected General Secretary.

33. Letter to Mathuradas Trikumji.

34. Sardar Patel.

35. To Ramdas Gandhi.

36. The talk took place at the close of one of the sessions of the All-India Village Industries Association held at Wardha on 14 and 15 December 1934.

37. To Prema Kantak. Gandhi used to prefix letters with the word 'unrevised' often, if he had signed them without going through them in a final revision.

38. To Dr James Henry Cousins who had requested Gandhi to recommend his name for the Nobel Prize for Literature.

39. A leading social worker of Cochin. The notes of the interview prepared by the interviewer were revised by Gandhi.

40. Goshi (1904–76), Perin (1888–1958), and Khurshed (1917–68), the 'Captain' sisters, were grand-daughters of Dadabhai Naoroji.

41. Kamala Nehru.

42. Feroze Gandhi (1912–60), husband of Indira Nehru Gandhi.

43. Dr Zakir Husain.

44. Jamia Millia Islamia.

45. Krishna Hutheesing (1907–67) younger sister of Jawaharlal Nehru.

46. Of the All India Village Industries Association.

47. Goshibehn Captain.

48. Agatha Harrison.

49. Dr Josiah Oldfield (1863–1953), editor of *The Vegetarian*, a journal of the London Vegetarian Society, who remained a steadfast friend throughout Gandhi's life.

50. Amala. Gandhi gave this name to Margarete Spiegel, a German follower of his. Margarete was taking training from Mira Behn at the Ashram for Harijan work and learning Hindi.

51. S. Satyamurti (1887–1943) had asked for blessings on his becoming President of the Tamil Nadu Provincial Congress Committee.

52. Agatha Harrison.

53. In her letter, the writer had appealed to Gandhi to keep faith in Jesus.

54. This is extracted from 'Weekly Letter' by Mahadev Desai, who had reported: 'A socialist holding a brief for machinery asked Gandhi if the village industries movement was not meant to oust all machinery.'

55. Gandhi was spinning at the time of the discussion.

56. Lilavati Asar, sister of Shri Laxmidas Asar who pioneered khadi work in Gujarat. Joined the Ashram and lived with Gandhi at Sabarmati and Wardha. She undertook to study for her matriculation at the late age of 37, cleared it, and thereafter went on to obtain a degree in Medicine.

57. To Amrit Kaur.

58. Keisho, a Japanese monk staying at Ashram had purchased Japanese cloth.

59. To Manilal and Sushila Gandhi.

60. To Delhi, where Devadas was laid up with typhoid.

61. Manu, Harilal Gandhi's daughter, was with Kasturba in Delhi at this time.

62 & 63. Similar telegrams were sent to the Governors of Bengal and the United Provinces. The Government of India, after having communication with the Secretary of State for India, released Jawaharlal Nehru unconditionally

18. The partition of Bengal, which took place in 1905, was annulled in December 1911.
19. Speech at Students Hall, Calcutta, 31.3.1915.
20. Vinoba Bhave (1895–1982) was present at the Benares meeting of 6 February 1916. He arrived at Sabarmati ashram on 7 June 1916. Chosen by Gandhi to inaugurate the Civil Disobedience Movement in 1940; initiator of the Bhoodan (Land Gift) Movement.
21. To Kallenbach.
22. 26 to 27 December 1916, presided over by Pandit Motilal Nehru. Gandhi first met Jawaharlal Nehru at this session.
23. Brajkishore Prasad, brother of Dr Rajendra Prasad and future father-in-law of Jayaprakash Narayan.
24. 9 April 1917.
25. To Kallenbach.
26. Florence A. Winterbottom, corresponding Secretary, Union of Ethical Societies, London.
27. Letter to Devadas Gandhi.
28. Reply to Albert West's letter from Phoenix mentioning that 'it was difficult to conduct the *Indian Opinion*. It could be maintained only if it was transferred to Durban and some practical, business-view was introduced in its working. That was his idea as well as of all others (in Phoenix).'
29. Jivanji Desai, an Ahmedabad-based barrister had offered on rent his large house at Kochrab for the ashram where the inmates would be required to observe eleven vows: non-violence, truth, non-stealing, chastity, non-possession, bread-labour, control of the palate, fearlessness, respect for all religions, swadeshi (India-made things), and the abolition of untouchability.
30. Rajmohan Gandhi writes in *Mohandas*: Gandhi was thinking of moving the ashram into a Dhed settlement when a young industrialist in his twenties, Ambalal Sarabhai, quietly drove up with a wad of currency, handed Rs 13,000 to Gandhi, and went away (A, pp. 356–7). He and Gandhi had met only once before, in the Sarabhai home, to discuss prospects of an ashram in Ahmedabad, but Sarabhai had been impressed by Gandhi's readiness to address caste inequalities, which young Sarabhai had always found offensive. By the summer of 1918, the ashram moved from the plague-affected Kochrab to an airy site on the banks of the Sabarmati. This shift coincided with a labour uprising in Sarabhai's mills. To quote from *Mohandas* again: Gandhi found that the workers' case was indeed strong. They had asked for a 35 per cent increase; the mill-owners had declared that 20 per cent was the

maximum they would accept. Gandhi asked the mill-owners to refer the dispute to arbitration. When they refused, Gandhi advised the workers to go on strike if they were willing to abide by his conditions: no violence, no molestation of blacklegs, no begging for alms, and no yielding. 'The leaders of the strike understood and accepted the conditions' and at a general meeting the workers pledged themselves to strike work and not resume it until arbitration or their wage demand was accepted. It was the first strike in Ahmedabad's history. The owners announced a lockout ... Daily, the strikers met under the shade of a babul tree near the the ashram to be advised by Gandhi and the England-educated Anasuya Behn Sarabhai, sister of Ambalal Sarabhai, the young industrialist who had quietly left money for Gandhi's ashram and was the city's leading mill-owner. From time to time Gandhi met Ambalal and other mill-owners and asked for justice for the workers, only to be told that the workers were 'like our children' and that in family matters arbitrators had no place. Though on occasion Ambalal would come to the ashram for a meal (with a chuckle Gandhi would have Anasuya Behn serve her brother), the young industrialist did not budge.

31. To Manilal.

32. This was in a leaflet, issued on the day Gandhi commenced his fast which resolved the dispute.

33. Anasuya Behn Sarabhai (1885–1972) sister of Sheth Ambalal Sarabhai, owner of the Mills.

34. Lord Chelmsford (1916–21).

35. 28 April 1918.

36. Shaukat Ali (1873–1938) and Mohammed Ali (1878–1931), founders of Khilafat movement. Shaukat Ali was elected President of the First Khilafat Conference in 1919 while in prison; Secretary and Chief Executive Officer of the Central Khilafat Committee; totally committed to the cause of freedom movement and imprisoned several times.

37. Meetings to encourage volunteer recruitment to the army for the war effort.

38. Gandhi went on a fast.

39. Harilal had at one stage expressed an interest in becoming his father's secretary, a project Gandhi had welcomed.

40. Sorabji Shapurji Adajania (1883–1918).

41. In reply to a letter from a civilian Englishman, Robert Henderson, which said: 'I am very sorry that when writing a short summary of the fine recruiting speech you made at Surat, I made a serious mistake. I am writing to you personally about the matter as I have great admiration for the splendid recruiting work you have been doing in the Kaira District (in which I spent a good many years) and elsewhere. I am, therefore, more sorry than I can say that, owing to a serious clerical error in the

on 2 September. He left Almora Jail for Allahabad on 3 September and from there for Germany on 4 September.

64. Rajmohan Gandhi (b. 1935).

65. Extracted from Mahadev Desai's 'Weekly Letter'.

66. This statement marks a noteworthy shift in Gandhi's approach to the caste system.

67. Margaret Sanger, the American pioneer of birth control met him on this day.

68. Nehru's autobiography

69. Vide letters to Prema Kantak, 6-5-1936 and 21-5-1936.

70. 17 to 21 January 1936.

71. This appeared under the title 'With Our Negro Guests' by Mahadev Desai. According to Mahadev Desai, 'the meeting was the first engagement of an important nature undertaken by Gandhi since the breakdown in his health'.

72. From C.B. Dalal's *Gandhi—1915-48: A Detailed Chronology*.

73. A professor of comparative religion and philosophy.

74. Pastor of Salem, USA. Before leaving, Mrs Thurman sang two famous 'Negro spirituals': 'Were you there, when they crucified my Lord?' and 'We are climbing Jacob's ladder.'

75. Jawaharlal Nehru, on return, met Gandhi at Harijan Colony, Kingsway Camp, Delhi, on 17 March 1936.

76. JP's adherence to Marx was then at its height, although he and the CSP had severed links with the Communist Party. The CSP's second conference held in Meerut in January 1936 described the CSP as 'an organized body of Marxist Socialists' and declared 'Marxism alone can guide the anti-imperialist forces on their ultimate destiny'.

77. Introducing the interviewer, Mahadev Desai writes in his 'Weekly Letter': 'Sir Chandrashekara Venkata Raman came up the hill one afternoon with Professor Rahm from Switzerland, a reputed biologist.'

78. Gandhi reached Nandi Hills on 10 May 1936.

79. Muslim Prayer.

80. The Associated Press announced the news of Dr Ansari's sudden death. Gandhi issued the Press message immediately thereafter. Dr M.A. Ansari had died on the train while going from Dehra Dun to Delhi on 10 May.

81. To Rajkumari Amrit Kaur.

82. Custom.

83. The source has 'bribery'.

84. Harilal announced on 29 June 1936 at Bombay's Jumma Masjid that he had converted to Islam and taken the name 'Abdulla'.

85. Harilal Gandhi, in his new persona as 'Abdullah Gandhi' visited Ernakulam around this time, to propagate Islam. He received a welcome

address at a public event organized by local Muslims when he declared 'I am no longer a (Hindu) baniya'. He came for the same purpose to Calicut on 16 September. On 17 September he was apprehended by the public in Madras for drunkenness. On 27 September, Kasturba dictated to Devadas, a letter for Harilal which was published as an 'open letter'. Gandhi seems to have mistakenly thought at first that the letter had more of Devadas than of Kasturba in it. He corrects himself in his letter of 10 October 1936.

86. Devadas Gandhi.

87. Harilal Gandhi made a statement on 10 November 1936 that he was seriously thinking of returning to Hinduism. Harilal did so on 12 November 1936. In a separate development on that day, the Maharaja of Travancore promulgated an enactment throwing open all temples within his jurisdiction to all Hindus thereby removing the bar on 'untouchables'.

88. John R. Mott (1865–1955) was born of 'pioneer stock' in Livingston Manor, New York. Mott enrolled at Upper Iowa University and later transferred to Cornell University in 1885. In the summer of 1886, Mott represented Cornell University's YMCA at the first international, inter-denominational student Christian conference ever held. As chairman of the executive committee of the Student Volunteer Movement for Foreign Missions he went on a two-year world tour, during which he organized national student movements in India and elsewhere. He died at his home in Orlando, Florida.

Part Thirteen: 1937–42

1. Louis Fischer (1896–1970), well known American journalist of the 1950s, contributor to *The God that Failed*. He met Mahatma Gandhi and wrote a biography of him, *The Life of Mahatma Gandhi,* on which the Oscar-winning film *Gandhi* drew significantly. Louis Fischer was born in Philadelphia on 29 February 1896. After studying at the Philadelphia School of Pedagogy (1914–16) he became a school teacher, joining the Jewish Legion, a military unit in Palestine. On his return to the United States Fischer worked for a news agency in New York. In 1922 Fischer went to Moscow and began working for *The Nation* publishing books including *Oil Imperialism: The International Struggle for Petroleum* (1926), *The Soviets in World Affairs* (1930) and an autobiography, *Men and Politics* (1941). Books by Fischer other than *The Life of Mahatma Gandhi* (1950) include *Stalin* (1952) and *Lenin* (1964).

2. Gandhi also visited Balaramapuram, Neyyatinkara, Trekkalai, Thiruvettar, Nagercoil, and Kanyakumari on the same day.

3. Ayyankali (1863–1914) was the pre-eminent leader of the 'untouchables' in Travancore, Kerala, heading successful movements for dalits to walk on public roads, dalit children to join schools, and dalit women to cover their breasts—which they used to be forbidden to do. Ayyankali was also nominated to the Sri Moolam Legislative Assembly of Travancore in 1910. V.K. Ramachandran in an article on the history of school education in Kerala for a centenary publication of the Bethune School, Kolkata, writes: *One of the first strike actions of agricultural labourers in Kerala (it has been suggested that it was the first) was organized by Ayyankali in 1914. Ayyankali attempted to gain admission for a Dalit girl in a government school in Ooroottambalam village in Neyyatinkara taluk near Thiruvananthapuram. The people of the upper castes of the area began a campaign of violence against the Pulayas for this act, and, after violent clashes, burned the school down. Ayyankali organized a strike of agricultural labourers, and work stopped in the fields of the upper castes. Government intervened, and after a magistrate's inquiry, the strike ended in success for the workers. In retrospect, this stirring and deeply significant historical event encapsulated the diverse components of Kerala's struggle for mass education, involving as it did elements of class struggle, the struggle against caste and gender discrimination and the assertion of the people's right to state-supported schooling.*

4. From the manuscript of Mahadev Desai's Diary.

5. Dr Crane was a clergyman from America, who had given up active service in the midst of World War I in disgust for its violence.

6. Dr Sampurnanand (1889–1969) educationist, journalist, Congress-Socialist, Minister for Education, UP (1938–39), later Chief Minister of UP and Governor of Rajasthan.

7. Acharya Narendra Deva (1889–1956) savant, socialist, educationist, Secretary of the Independence of India League; Member of the Congress Working Committee (1936–8); declined ministership in UP in 1936 and 1946; resigned from the Congress in 1948 and founded with others of his thinking the Praja Socialist Party.

8. Yusuf Jafar Meherally (1903–50) active in the socialist movement, demonstration against Simon Commission (1928), Civil Disobedience Movement (1930), Salt Satyagraha (1930), Congress Socialist Party (1935–6), and Quit India Movement.

9. Gandhi presided over this convocation of the Dakshina Bharat Hindi Prachar Sabha.

10. Gandhi was in Tithal, a seaside village for a week. 'We walk through

the sea water every morning and evening', he wrote to Rajkumari Amrit Kaur, 'It is a bracing walk. Kanu, the little one enjoys it the most'. (Kanu being Ramdas Gandhi's son, captured in a famous photograph, leading his grandfather who prods Kanu with his walking staff.) Hermann Kallenbach joined Gandhi in Tithal and later in Segaon.

11. Rajkumari's pet dog.

12. To Rajkumari Amrit Kaur.

13. The Congress Working Committee met in Segaon from 5 to 7 July, presided over by Jawaharlal Nehru in Gandhi's guiding presence. The historic decision for the Congress to accept office in the Provinces was taken at this session.

14. In his letter dated 16 July to G.D. Birla, Mahadev Desai explains: 'C.R. asked for Bapu's blessings to be wired to him and his colleagues when they were all sworn in as Ministers.' Rajagopalachari formed the Congress Ministry in Madras on 15 July 1937.

15. Congress Working Committee.

16. The Congress Working Committee meeting held at Wardha from 15 to 22 March had passed the following resolution: 'Apart from free provision to be made by the State for residence and conveyance, the salaries of Ministers, Speakers, and Advocates-General shall not exceed Rs 500 per month, as laid down in the Karachi Resolution on Fundamental Rights and Economic Programme.'

17. Jawaharlal Nehru used this phrase in his appeal to the country to celebrate 1st August as 'Ministry Day'.

18. By this time Premier of Madras.

19. For the meeting of the Congress Working Committee which was to be held at Wardha from 14 to 17 August.

20. William Benton (1900–73) was an American journalist who set up in partnership with Chester Bowles (later Ambassador to India) an advertising firm, Benton and Bowles. In 1949, Chester Bowles, than governor of Connecticut, appointed him to fill a vacant U.S. Senate seat. In the Senate Benton joined other Liberal Democrats in supporting Truman's Fair Deal. He became a member of the Banking and Currency Committee, the Rules Committee, the Select Committee an Small Business, and the Joint Committee on the Economic Report.

21. E.M.S. Namboodiripad (1909–98) then Joint Secretary of the All-India Congress Socialist Party and Organizing Secretary of the Kerala Provincial Congress Committee. Later, the first elected communist Chief Minister in India. EMS had drawn Gandhi's attention to the search carried out by the Congress Government's police for a proscribed book.

22. Dr S. Muthulakshmi Reddi (1886–1968), first girl student to be admitted to Maharaja's College, Pudukkottai State, first girl student

to join MBCM course in Madras Medical College, standing first; first woman legislator in India, nominated in 1926 to the Madras Legislative Council, being instrumental in the abolitioin of the 'Devadasi' system through Act No. 5 of 1927; started the Anti-Cancer Movement.

23. Literally, servants of God; women dedicated to temples.

24. To Syed Bashir Ahmed the addressee, editor of *Isha'at-e-Taleem*, who had enquired: 'Would you not agree with me that you want to realize truth by following the right path based on honesty, straight-forwardness, and ethical soundness? The Congress offers Ministries to Muslims who have been elected on the Muslim League ticket, provided they sign the Congress pledge. Do you want the Muslim members who have sworn their loyalty to the League before their election by God and the Holy Koran to break their sacred oaths?'

25. As President at the 25th session of the All-India Muslim League held from 15–18 October.

26. Foreword to Acharya Kripalani's *Lekho*.

27. Letter to Ramdas Gandhi.

28. Netaji Subhas Chandra Bose arrived at Karachi from London on 23-1-1938.

29. Bose was elected President of the Congress on 18 January 1938. M.N. Roy also returned to his home province, Bengal, after an interval of 25 years on 20 January 1938. Gandhi had talks with Bengal Minister Nalini Ranjan Ray and Dr B.C. Roy in Segaon on 24 January.

30. Subhas Bose visited Gandhi at Segaon on 2/3 February. Working Committee members met him 4/5 February.

31. To Amrit Kaur.

32. The Mahant of the Jagannath temple at Puri came to meet Gandhi on 29 March. Gandhi asked him to open the temple to Harijans; the Mahant refused. On 30 March, it so transpired that Kasturba along with some others including Durgaben Mahadev Desai visited the temple. Gandhi took them to task for this severely. He summarily rejected Mahadev Desai's 'explanation', leading to Desai wanting to be relieved of his duties as secretary ('I am not worthy'). Gandhi, of course, refused to let Desai go.

33. Gandhi was in the North West Frontier Province from 1 to 8 May visiting Naushera, Peshawar, Torkhan, Kulashabeg, Saudzai, Shabkadav, Utmanzai, Mardan. He saw, while at Peshawar, the Khyber Pass. He addressed public meetings all through.

34. C. Rajagopalachari, then Premier of Madras.

35. On his way back to Segaon from the NWFP, Gandhi broke journey in Bombay (12 to 20 May), staying at the Birlas' cottage in Juhu. He had discussions with Congress President Subhas Bose on the latter's parleys

with Jinnah, with Jawaharlal Nehru and with Jinnah himself (20 March) at his Malabar Hill residence.

36. To Amrit Kaur.

37. In a letter to Jamnalal Bajaj. Bajaj had a conversation with Sri Ramana Maharshi on 16 August 1938. 'JB: Is the desire for Swaraj right? Maharshi: Such desire no doubt begins with self-interest. Yet practical work for the goal gradually widens the outlook so that the individual becomes merged with the country. Such merging of the individuality is desirable and the related Karma is *nishkama* (unselfish).'

38. To Rajkumari Amrit Kaur.

39. Gandhi sent the Rajkumari to Travancore to study the situation as regards the people of the State vis-à-vis the administration of the Princely State. The State was being harsh on the Congress which it regarded as subversive. It had prevented Kamaladevi Chattopadhyay from addressing meetings in its territories. While deputing the Rajkumari to Travancore, Gandhi assured the Diwan Sir C.P. Ramaswami Aiyar that she would not address public meetings. In his letter Gandhi hopes she would take the chance to visit Cape Comorin.

40. Sri Ramana Maharshi. In *Letters to Rajkumari Amrit Kaur*, she says: 'But both Mahadev Desai and I refused to see him as we said our hearts were with Gandhi. Gandhi did not appreciate the argument.'

41. After the invasion of Austria in March 1938, Hitler turned his attention to the Sudetenland of Czechoslavakia. The Munich Agreement of 29 September sealed the fate of Czechoslavakia. Gandhi was in Delhi from 20 September to 4 October. On the 21st and 22nd he held discussions with Congress Working Committee members and other leaders about the possibility of India setting up a non-violent army in the wake of the drums of war sounded in Europe. On 1 October, the London-based Society of Friends proposed Gandhi's name for the Nobel Peace Prize. (He was nominated five times altogether, viz., 1937, 1938, 1939, 1947, and 1948 and shortlisted thrice viz., 1937, 1938, and 1948. There is reason to believe he would have won the prize in 1948 but the assassination intervened.)

42. The talk took place at Utmanzai where Gandhi spent 9 to 14 October at the Khan brothers' country-house before proceeding on a tour of Mardan and Naushera on 15 October.

43. In reply to his usual question to the Khudai Khidmatgars whether they would remain non-violent in all circumstances, one of them replied that they could put up with every kind of provocation except the abuse of their revered leaders.

44. To Prabhavati Narayan.

45. To N.R. Malkani (1890–1974).

46. Rev. Timothy Tingfang Lew, a member of the Legislative Yuan of China, was on the Chinese delegation to the Missionary Conference at Tambaram. He was brought by Muriel Lester, along with many other delegates. Gandhi described his visitors as 'a world in miniature'.

47. Headed by Dr Dwarkanath Kotnis.

48. This appeared in the source under the title 'I Rejoice In This Defeat' and was also published in *The Bombay Chronicle*, 1-2-1939, *The Hindu*, 31-1-1939, *The Hindustan Times*, 1-2-1939, and various other papers.

49. At Tripuri, Central Provinces.

50. The resolution, sponsored by Gobind Ballabh Pant in the Subjects Committee at the Tripuri Congress, read: '... The (All India Congress) Committee expresses its confidence in the work of the Working Committee which functioned during the last year and regrets that any aspersions should have been cast against any of its members. In view of the critical situation that may develop during the coming year and in view of the fact that Mahatma Gandhi alone can lead the Congress and the country to victory during such crisis, the Committee regards it as imperative that the Congress executive should command his implicit confidence and requests the President to nominate the Working Committee in accordance with the wishes of Gandhiji.'

51. To Rajkumari Amrit Kaur.

52. The song occurs in *Anandmath* by Bankim Chandra Chattopadhyay. In 1937, the Congress Working Committee meeting in Calcutta passed a resolution that 'Whenever and wherever *Vandemataram* is sung only the first two stanzas should be sung, with perfect freedom to the organizers to sing any other song of unobjectionable character in addition to, or in the place of, *Vandemataram*.'

53. To Amrit Kaur from the beachside residence of the Birlas.

54 Jawaharlal Nehru was Chairman of the National Planning Committee appointed by the Indian National Congress in 1938.

55. Jan Christian Smuts (1870–1950); South African soldier and statesman; Prime Minister, 1919–24 and 1939–48.

56. Gandhi reached Abbottabad on 7 July 1939. He stayed there (Raosaheb Parmanand's residence) until 26 July. Received there the welcome news that on 8 July 1939, the Minakshi Temple at Madurai was to be thrown open to Harijans. Jawaharlal Nehru left on a tour to Ceylon on 15 July. Three major developments during this period were: (i) Discussions with B. Shiva Rao sent by the Government to advise Gandhi against supporting proposed satyagraha by Indians in South Africa following which Gandhi urged the S.A. Indians to desist; (ii) Letter to Hitler, which the Government prevented from being sent—23 July; (iii) Discussions with Jayaprakash Narayan—8 July.

57. This appeared under the title 'A Dialogue with A Buddhist' by Mahadev Desai, who explains: '... an archaeologist ... Dr Fabri ... has been in India for many years. He was a pupil of Professor Sylvain Levi and came out as assistant to the famous archaeologist, Sir Aurel Stein. ... He is a Hungarian and had in the past corresponded with Gandhiji and even sympathetically fasted with him. He had come to Abbottabad specially to see Gandhiji. ...'

58. Gandhi left Abbottabad on 26 July 1939.

59. Here, Mahadev Desai explains: 'Dr Fabri got up to go with the parting wish that there may be many more years of helpful activity left for Gandhiji.'

60. South African Indians announced on 29 July suspension of satyagraha, following Gandhi's advice.

61. Letter from Chhaganlal Joshi described how people and cattle were starving.

62. Which, inter alia, said '... Should war by any chance break out it has been in my mind to invite you to come to see me at once. ... I hope that you will not misunderstand it if I sent you a telegram ... to come to see me.'

63. Of the Benares Hindu University, succeeding Pandit Madan Mohan Malaviya whose health had deteriorated.

64. Germany invaded Poland on 1 September and war was consequently declared by England and France on 3 September.

65. This appeared under the title 'The Simla Visit'. An A.P.I. report of the statement was also published in *The Hindu*, 5-9-1939, and *The Hindustan Times*, 6-9-1939, as released in the 'afternoon prior to his departure' from Simla.

66. Mahadev Desai explains: '... six friends came to Wardha on the 23rd of last month. These included a barrister and his wife, an American journalist, a European who was a railway official, and a gifted lady, daughter of a one-time army officer ...' The 'Oxford Group' was later known as Moral Re-Armament, now 'Initiatives For Change'.

67. Gandhi went to Delhi on 1 October and held discussions on 2 October at Birla House with Jawaharlal Nehru and Rajendra Prasad. Both these leaders met the Viceroy on 3 October. Gandhi met the Viceroy on 5 October. Chief Justice Sir Maurice Gwyer called on Gandhi on the same day. Gandhi left that evening for Segaon. Jawaharlal Nehru had discussions with him on 6 October, while the Congress Working Committee met at Segaon from 7 to 11 October. In the face of the Viceroy's inability to meet Congress' demands pertaining to the war, all Congress Premiers were asked to resign on 17 October 1939.

68. *Essays and Reflections on Mahatma Gandhi* (by Sarvepalli Radhakrishnan, presented to Gandhi on his seventieth birthday, in 1939).

69. Letter to Haribhau G. Pathak.
70. V.D. Savarkar with Chimanlal Setalvad, Cowasji Jehangir, V.M. Chandavarkar (Liberals), N.C. Kelkar, and Dr B.R. Ambedkar issued a statement from Bombay on 2 October, expressing the view that the Congress and the Muslim League did not represent the whole or even the bulk of India and that any constitutional or administrative arrangement arrived at between the Government and the Congress and the Muslim League could not be binding on the Indian people.
71. C. Rajagopalachari met Gandhi at Segaon on 7 December; H.N. Kunzru on 8 December.
72. Gopalrao Kulkarni, a teacher at the Ashram School.
73. This is the first time Gandhi used that description in a letter to M.A. Jinnah.
74. Gandhi left Segaon on 3 Febuary for Delhi to meet the Viceroy at his invitation. At the commencement of their talks on 4 February, Gandhi told Lord Linlithgow that he was not representing the Congress. He returned to Segaon on 7 February and left for Bengal on 16 February.
75. Welcoming Gandhi, Rabindranath Tagore said: 'I hope we shall be able to keep close to a reticent expression of love in welcoming you into our Ashram and never allow it to overflow into any extravagant display of phrases ... Let us for a while pass beyond the bounds of this turmoil and make our meeting today a simple meeting of hearts whose memory will remain when all the moral confusions of our distracted politics will be allayed and the eternal value of our endeavour will be revealed.'
76. C.F. Andrews.
77. While at Santiniketan, Gandhi saw an enactment of Tagore's 'Chandalika'.
78. Jayaprakash Narayan was arrested on 7 March.
79. The Indian National Congress met at its annual session at Ramgarh, Bihar under the presidentiship of Maulana Azad. Gandhi attended the session from 14 to 20 March. News reached Ramgarh of the assassination of the former Lt. Governor of Punjab Michael O'Dwyer by Mahanand Singh Azad (Sardar Uday Singh).
80. In his Presidential address at the Lahore session of the All-India Muslim League on 22 March.
81. C.F. Andrews died at 1.40 a.m. on 5 April 1940. This appeared in *Harijan* under 'Notes', sub-title 'A True Friend of the Poor'.
82. The report of the discussion by Amrit Kaur is date-lined 'Sevagram, 7 April 1940'.
83. The Working Committee met at Sevagram from 15 to 17 April 1940.
84. Herbert George Wells (1866–1946); English novelist, and historian; author of *The Time Machine, The War of the Worlds, The Shape of Things to Come, The Outline of History, The Invisible Man*, and various other works.

85. Wells had sought Gandhi's opinion on the 'Rights of Man' drawn up by him, a public discussion on which was going on in the British and Indian Press.

86. Published in *The Hindustan Times*.

87. Master Tara Singh, leader of the Akali Party. He had pointed out that Azad's statement that the Congress would accept the Pakistan scheme of the Muslim League if the same got the approval of the Muslims had caused much anxiety amongst the Congress-minded Sikhs, who did not like the idea of partition.

88. The report carrying the item is dated 21 May 1940.

89. After this discussion Gandhi withdrew his own draft on the Congress' attitude to the War and C. Rajagopalachari placed his draft before the Working Committee for its consideration.

90. The source has January, obviously a slip.

91. Ela Gandhi (b. 1940 in Phoenix to Sushila and Manilal Gandhi), subsequently a Member of the South African Parliament from the African National Congress, renowned human rights activist and actively involved in the restoration of Phoenix in the late 1990s, awarded the Padma Bhushan by the President of India in 2007.

92. The Gujarati original of this was published in *Harijanbandhu*, 3-8-1940. The English translation is reproduced from *Harijan*.

93. The Gujarati original of this appeared in *Harijanbandhu*, 10-8-1940. This English translation is reproduced from *Harijan*, where it appeared under the heading 'Question Box'.

94. The letter was carried by Mahadev Desai to the addressee in Calcutta. Vide also 'Telegram to A.K. Chanda', 28-9-1940.

95. The report said: 'Gandhiji was speaking at a meeting organized to celebrate his 72nd birthday. He distributed prizes to winners in spinning, carding, and weaving competitions.'

96. The Working Committee met from 11 to 13 at Sevagram. Gandhi had discussions with Vinoba Bhave at Paunar, a village 5 miles from Wardha, where Vinoba was based, on 13 October. Mahadev Desai went on Gandhi's behalf to Bengal from 4 to 8 October, met Tagore and Subhas Bose (in Calcutta Jail). On 10 October, Miss Mayo, author of 'Mother India' passed away in New York.

97. The source, however, has '1916'.

98. On 7 June 1916.

99. Mahadev Desai wired Jawaharlal Nehru saying Gandhi was contemplating a fast.

100. On 17 February 1941, Vinoba again offered satyagraha and was imprisoned and sentenced to six months' imprisonment. Gandhi visited Jabalpur on 27 February and viewed the marble rocks. He reached Allahabad on 28 February and, staying at Anand Bhavan,

called on the ailing leaders Pandit Madan Mohan Malaviya and Sir Tej Bahadur Sapru. On 1 March he met Mahadev Desai in Naini Jail, Allahabad.

101. On Tagore's eightieth birthday which fell on 14 April.

102. According to *The Hindu*, 15-4-1941, the addressee, in his reply, said: 'Thanks for your message. But, if four score is impertinence, five score will be intolerable.'

103. Rabindranath Tagore died in Calcutta on 7 August. Lord Willingdon, former Governor of Bombay and Madras and Viceroy of India died in London on 12 August.

104. Gandhi had agreed to attend the Silver Jubilee celebrations of the University.

105. Mahadev Desai's summary here makes no mention of Sardar Patel.

106. Generalissimo and Madame Chiang Kai-shek arrived in Delhi on 9 February and were the Viceroy's guests. Jawaharlal Nehru met them on the 10th and, with Maulana Azad, on the 11th and, again, by himself on the 12th. Gandhi wrote to the Generalissimo on the 11th morning, regretting the fact that he being 'in a village out of touch with the outside world', they would not be able to meet. Later that afternoon, Jamnalal Bajaj died of cerebral haemorrhage at Wardha. Gandhi rushed to his bedside but life was ebbing away as he arrived.

107. Breathing exercise.

108. Letter of felicitation to Uday Shankar (1900–77) and Amala Shankar on their wedding.

109. Extracted from Mahadev Desai's 'Two Australian Visitors'. Bertram Stevens was a member of the Eastern Group Conference and sometime Prime Minister of the Province of New South Wales in Australia.

110. Gandhi was in Delhi from 27 March to 4 April. He met Sir Stafford Cripps on the 27th and saw the proposals the Minister had brought. Describing them as 'a post-dated cheque', he advised Cripps to take the next flight back home. The last four words in the description ascribed to Gandhi 'a post-dated cheque on a crashing bank' were authored by the journalist, J.N. Sahni. Only the first four words were used by Gandhi. The Working Committee met from 28 March to 1 April. The idea of 'Quit India' began to germinate at this session and Cripps' proposals were rejected. Nehru and Azad met Cripps to inform him of the session.

111. Presumably, in Delhi.

112. Both the Indian National Congress and the Muslim League rejected the Cripps formula; the Congress because it did not concede independence immediately, left the control of defence of India with the British Government and indirectly envisaged the partition of India

by giving rights to the provinces to secede if they wished. The Muslim League opposed it because the fundamental proposals were not open to any modifications.

113. Sir Stafford Cripps left India on 12 April 1942.

114. Nehru was reported to have advised people in the event of a Japanese invasion, to resort to the scorched-earth policy.

115. Acharya Kripalani, then General Secretary of the Congress.

116. Gandhi was in Bombay from 10 to 13 May, staying at Birla House.

117. Those present at the interview which lasted for about 85 minutes, included Vallabhbhai Patel, Bhulabhai Desai, B.G. Kher, Morarji Desai, and other prominent Congressmen. The report of the interview, sent by Sharaf Athar Ali, a Communist worker, to P.C. Joshi, was intercepted. It is not possible to vouch for its authenticity, but the Government placed a high degree of reliance in it and the Viceroy cabled a summary of it to Amery on 27 May.

118. Someone had said it was the demand of the Muslim masses.

119. The reference is, obviously, to Africa.

120. Only extracts from Louis Fischer's book have been reproduced here.

121. There was such a report in March 1942.

122. Preston Grover of the Associated Press of America had especially come over from New Delhi for the interview.

123. Generalissimo Chiang Kai-shek.

124. C. Rajagopalachari was the victim of an irate crowd opposing his stand on the War. Tar was thrown on his face.

125. In the article 'For the Sikh Friends', 26-6-1942, Gandhi had said that he could not find the writing in which he was alleged to have said that Guru Gobind Singh was 'a misguided patriot'.

126. This was published in three Japanese newspapers—*Nichi Nichi*, *Yomiuri*, and *Miyako*.

127. The last issue of *Harijan* was finalized on this date.

128. Gandhi addressed the concourse in Hindi and then switched to English. This is a translation of his Hindi speech. Gandhi was in Bombay from 3 to 9 August, attending the Working Committee which met from 4 to 6 August. The Working Committee and AICC met again on 7th August. The Quit India Resolution was adapted at a public meeting at Gowalia Tank, on 8th August. Gandhi was taken, with Mahadev Desai, into custody on 9 August, early in the morning and taken to Poona, which had become his 'regular' prison-station. Except that this time, the precise lodgings were different. He was taken to the Poona palace of the Aga Khan. This was his eighth and last imprisonment in India. Kasturba was brought to the Aga Khan Palace Prison, where Gandhi was lodged.

Part Fourteen: 1942–8

1. Governor of Bengal from 1944–6, later Foreign Minister and Governor General of Australia.

2. The reference is to the Bengal Famine, 1943. In a Press Statement on 20 August 1943 broadcast on the Rangoon Radio the same day, Subhas Bose said: 'There is a serious famine prevailing in India, particularly in Bengal and Calcutta. On receipt of these reports from India, the Indian League of Independence in East Asia is extremely anxious about the welfare of the Indian people and is, therefore, trying to do everything in its power to take the necessary measures in order to help them. Today, I am in the happy position to announce that 100,000 tons of rice are waiting to be transported from Burma to relieve hunger in India. This rice is put at the disposal of the Indian people unconditionally. These 100,000 tons of rice are at present lying in a harbour in the vicinity of India. At the moment when the British Government expresses its willingness to accept this delivery, the name of the harbour as well as of the authorities, who will hand over the rice, will be named. At the same time the Japanese Government will be asked for a guarantee of a safe conduct for the ships calling for this quantity of rice.' (*Chalo Delhi—Writings and Speeches of Subhas Chandra Bose—1943–5*).

3. Extracted from Pyarelal's article 'The Santiniketan Pilgrimage'. The heads of the various departments had met Gandhi in the evening informally to place before him their difficulties.

4. Bibhutibhushan Gupta (1898–1970) had mentioned the complication arising from the admission of day scholars. Bibhutibhushan Gupta had come to Santiniketan in 1904 as a student in the *Brahmacharyasrama*. He passed the Matriculation examination in 1916 and graduated from Calcutta University in 1920. He came back to Santiniketan and taught Bengali in the School for six to seven years. In 1933, he did his M.A. from Calcutta University. Joined Lady Abala Bose's Narisiksha Samiti as its secretary and later was Headmaster of the Vidyasagar Bani Bhavana. In 1944, he came back to Santiniketan as a teacher in Bengali. From 1960 to 1962, he was the Adhyaksha of Patha Bhavana, Santiniketan. Bibhutibhushan was not a prolific writer, but earned a name in Bengali literature for his books, *Bidal Thakurji*, a unique collection of folk tales from West Bengal with a foreword by Rabindranath and *Kathbidalibhai*. Bibhutibhushan was associated with the editing of *Santiniketan Patrika* and worked as joint editor of *Budhvar* with Pramathanath Bisi.

5. Lila Roy (1900–70). An indomitable fighter, a dauntless leader with revolutionary zeal, strength of character, and élan. Her indomitable spirit evoked in others an aspiration to work towards the spread of female

education and the placement of women in rightful position. The first girl student from Dacca University, she got her M.A, degree in 1923, formed Deepali Sangha for the emancipation of women, gave a reception to Mahatma Gandhi and Tagore in 1925/26. The reception to Gandhi was attended by 3000 women. Tagore after this reception, remarked he had not seen such a big gathering of women in the whole of Asia. Detained twice 1931-7, and 1942-6, she was a member of the womens' sub-committee on the National Planning body formed by Subhas Chandra Bose. Founder editor of 'Jayasree', a Bengali monthly journal. Her service in Noakhali and Calcutta to the riot stricken distressed people was greatly appreciated by Gandhi.

6. Ujjwala Majumdar (1914-92). Her father, Suresh Chandra Majumdar, a zamindar of Kusumhati (Dhaka) was closely involved with revolutionary freedom fighters. By virtue of the milieu she was brought up in, Ujjala was much a part and parcel of the revolutionary team from a very early age. Involved in the attempt to assassinate Governor John Anderson on 8 May 1934 at Lebong Race Course, Darjeeling, and was convicted and received lifetime imprisonment. Released subsequently in 1939 from Dhaka Jail by the advocacy of Gandhi. Arrested in 1942 for taking part in Quit India Movement and released from jail in 1946. Involved with the formation of the Forward Bloc. Toured Noakhali to help the victims of riots in 1946. Joined Socialist Republican Party led by Sarat Chandra Bose, after Independence.

7. The Caseys' dachshund.

8. Horace Alexander (1889-1989) born in England, studied history at King's College, Cambridge, life-long member of the Religious Society of Friends, pacifist, crusader for Indian independence and ornithologist.

9. Abha Gandhi *nee* Chatterjee (1927-95), daughter of Amritlal Chatterjee and wife of Kanu, Gandhi's grand-nephew.

10. Dr Prafulla Chandra Ghosh (1891-1983); born in Dacca district; first Chief Minister of West Bengal; ardent Gandhian.

11. Syed Mohammed Usman (1901-75). Mayor of Calcutta (1945); Lawyer by profession; joined Non-cooperation movement in 1920 and suffered imprisonment; migrated to East Pakistan and settled in Karachi.

12. According to the source the Muslim friends hesitated but ultimately gave the required guarantee on their and Muslim League's behalf. They promised to dispatch wires to the local League leaders in Noakhali and undertook to send emissaries to help maintain peace in Noakhali.

13. Now renovated and renamed 'Gandhi Bhavan'.

14. Surendra Mohon Ghosh (1893-1976), Congress Member of Constituent Assembly, President, Bengal P C C 1939-50, M.P.

15. Tushar Kanti Ghosh (1898-1994)–Editor of *Amrita Bazar Patrika*.

16. Aruna Asaf Ali (1909–96). Married Asaf Ali, revolutionary and freedom fighter; active in the 1942 movement; Mayor of Delhi; received Lenin Peace Prize and Bharat Ratna (posthumous).

17. Hemchandra Naskar (1890–1960). A Congress leader; was Councillor, Alderman, Deputy Mayor and Mayor of Calcutta; Minister of West Bengal till his death.

18. Now known as 'Rajasthan Club', Mayo Road, Maidan, Kolkata 16.

19. Kamala Dasgupta (1907–2000). A revolutionary, daughter of Surendranath Dasgupta, well-known scholar; helped Bina Das, another revolutionary, with a revolver for shooting at Sir Stanley Jackson, Governor of Bengal, at Calcutta University Convocation on Saturday, 6 February 1932; imprisoned several times and later kept in home internment; greatly influenced by Gandhi's non-violence movement and travelled with him to Noakhali; did axtensive relief work in Calcutta, Noakhali, Comilla, and other riot affected areas in East Bengal.

20. A Scotsman, he was Principal of the Scottish Church College from 1944 to 1954.

21. Prayer meeting held on Narkeldanga Main Road.

22. Shivbalak Bisen, an associate of Satish Chandra Dasgupta, substituted for N.K. Bose as a Bangla language tutor to Gandhi and accompanied Gandhi in the March 1947 tour of Bihar.

23. Mahadev Desai collapsed and died within minutes on 15 August. He was cremated the same day. The authorities posted this telegram as a letter; vide 'Letter To Secretary, Home Department, Government of Bombay'.

24. Narayan, Mahadev Desai's son.

25. On 16 August Gandhi collected the *asthi* (ashes) and made a *tilak* on his forehead with the dust of the *asthi* clinging to his fingers.

26. The Aga Khan Palace, Poona, where Gandhiji was detained without any charge being framed against him, after his arrest in Bombay on 9 August 1942.

27. According to *The Transfer of Power*, Vol. III, pp. 439 and 458, the Viceroy cabled the text of this letter on 3 January to Amery, who in his reply dated 5 January ruled out any 'great haste for an immediate reply'. Linlithgow however, sent his reply, after consultations with Amery and the British Cabinet, on 13 January.

28. Additional Secretary to the Government of India in the Home Department.

29. The fast commenced on 10 February and lasted for 21 days, ending on 2 March.

30. Doctors found him in a cheerful mood when they visited him at 10 o'clock: 'His pulse and heart are in the same condition as yesterday. He continues to drink water mixed with sweet lime-juice, but he has

further reduced the quantity of lime-juice as he is now able to take water freely. His mental alertness is as bright as ever. He distinctly remembers his condition was grave on Saturday and Sunday last.'

31. 21 February; according to *The Transfer of Power*, Vol. III p. 719, 'a bulletin signed by Mr Gandhi's six doctors and published by the Bombay Government' read: 'After a restless day on 21st, Mr Gandhi entered a crisis at 4.30 p.m. He was seized with severe nausea and almost fainted, and pulse became nearly imperceptible. Later he was able to take water with sweet lime-juice. He rallied from the crisis and slept for about $5\frac{1}{2}$ hours during the night. ...'

32. The talk was recorded by Mira Behn under the following note: 'Bapuji to me on morning of 27 February 1943'. In this and other talks with Mira Behn, the text, as written down by Mira Behn, was corrected by Gandhi.

33. Mira Behn continues: 'Bapuji murmured something more which I could not catch. Something about liking to take complete silence and not troubling to answer or explain anything further—but that he must not turn down Rajaji and others like that—and something about gaining strength to fling himself against the whole world and dying in peace and joy.'

34. This remark was written after he had read through the text of the talk.

35. Madan Gopal Bhandari (1893–1971).

36. Gandhi broke his fast at 9.34 a.m. I.S.T. (and 8.34 a.m. according to time maintained at Aga Khan Palace) ... Besides the doctors only inmates of the detention camp were present. The inmates sang 'Vaishnava jana to' and two stanzas from *Gitanjali*. 'Lead Kindly Light' and passages from the Holy Koran were also recited. After prayers, those present observed a five minutes' silence. With folded hands Gandhi closed his eyes and seemed to be in meditation. Kasturba then handed him a glass containing six ounces of orange juice. He is reported to have taken twenty minutes to sip the juice.

37. Rajmohan Gandhi writes in *The Rajaji Story 1937–72*:

The fast commenced on February 10, 1943 and ended without mishap three weeks later. At one point it looked as if the ordeal might claim his life, and three of Linlithgow's councillors, Mody, Aney and Sircar, resigned when their proposal of release was not accepted. But the crisis passed. Some of Gandhi's family were allowed to visit him. So was C.R. For four days, from the 17th day of the fast, C.R. saw him daily. Their public duel a year earlier had not been without pain. Neither offered an apology but the joy of reunion was great. In the words of Bombay's Home Secretary at the time, H.V.R. Iengar, to who the Raj's intelligence agents reported, 'Their first meeting was most affectionate'.

C.R. obtained a complete disapproval from the Mahatma of sabotage and violence—and learnt that in a letter to the Viceroy soon after his arrest Gandhi had deplored the deeds of violence, while disclaiming responsibility for them.

The Mahatma and C.R. talked 'both seriously and lightly,' as the latter informed the press. Gandhi asked C.R. to enlighten him on passages in Francis Thompson's *Hound of Heaven*, which the latter did—and an earnest intelligence agent reported to the raj that the two were discussing dogs. Not one to waste his chance, C.R. referred to Jinnah's demands and claimed he had a formula. 'Describe it,' said the Mahatma. C.R. did. Gandhi, who had given given Quit India its opportunity, said he could agree to it. But C.R. did not want to take any risks. He wrote the formula out for the Mahatma, who read it and repeated his assent.

Thus was launched the much-discussed, much-reviled and prophetic Rajaji Formula. Entitled 'Basis for terms of settlement between the Indian National Congress and the All-India Muslim League to which Gandhiji and Mr Jinnah agree and which they will undertake respectively to get the Congress and the League to approve,' it said:

(i) Subject to the terms set out below, the League endorses the Indian demand for independence and will cooperate with the Congress in the formation of a provisional government while the war lasts.

(ii) At the end of the war, a commission will demarcate contiguous districts in the North-West and East of India, wherein the Muslim population is in absolute majority. In the areas thus demarcated, a plebiscite of all the inhabitants shall ultimately decide the issue of separation from Hindustan. If the majority decided in favour of forming a sovereign state separate from Hindustan, such decision shall be given effect to.

(iii) In the event of separation, mutual agreements shall be entered into for safeguarding defence, commerce and communications and for other essential purposes.

38. G.D. Birla explains: 'These are the recorded answers to questions put to Gandhiji while he was interned.'

39. From the reference to the fast which ended on 3 March.

40. According to *The Transfer of Power*, Vol. III, p. 982, on 24 April in his Presidential address to the annual session of the Muslim League at Delhi, Jinnah said: 'Nobody would welcome it more than myself, if Mr Gandhi is even now really willing to come to a settlement with the Muslim League on the basis of Pakistan ... If he has made up his mind, what is there to prevent Mr Gandhi from writing direct to me? ... I cannot believe that they will have the daring to stop such a letter if it is sent to me ...'

41. The Government did not forward this letter to Jinnah.

42. On 6 October, Jayaprakash Narayan was arrested in Lahore.

43. Linlithgow, in his reply dated 7 October said: 'I am indeed sorry that your feelings about any deeds or words of mine should be as you describe. But I must be allowed, as gently as I may, to make plain to you that I am quite unable to accept your interpretation of the events in question. As per the corrective virtues of time and reflection, evidently these are ubiquitous in their operation and wisely to be rejected by no man.'

44. When a nature-cure expert was permitted to examine Kasturba in prison, it was with the condition that no one else would be present in the room. The letter had the desired effect.

45. From 4 January onwards Kasturba's health deteriorated. On 18 January Gandhi was himself unwell and took the medicine 'sarpagandha'. Treating that as an item of food, he reduced one element of food out of the five he had restricted his diet to.

46. Also called 'Kanaiyo', younger son of Narandas Gandhi as distinct from Kanu, son of Ramdas Gandhi.

47. The reply dated 3 February 1944, read: (1) Government have agreed to Kanu Gandhi staying in for the purpose of helping in nursing Mrs Gandhi on condition that he agrees to be bound by the same regulations as other security prisoners in the detention camp. Government consider that with Kanu Gandhi staying in, the nursing assistance provided should be adequate and they cannot agree to any requests for further assistance. (2) Government have decided that no outside doctors should be allowed unless the Government medical officer considers that it is absolutely necessary for medical reasons ... (3) Interviews with near relatives have been sanctioned for Mrs Gandhi. While Government have no objection to your being present during those interviews, they consider that other inmates should not be present except to the extent demanded by the condition of Mrs Gandhi's health.

48. On 17 and 18 February Harilal Gandhi came to visit Kasturba. He came again on 22 February inebriated and had to be removed from her presence.

49. On 8 February, the Central Legislative Assembly rejected Lalchand Navalrai's resolution for releasing political prisoners. In his speech, Sir Reginald Maxwell, Home Member, had said that 'if Government were asked to release the Congress leaders, they must be assured that the results would be beneficial to India and to the war effort'. (The Indian Annual Register 1944, Vol. I)

50. On 7 February, the Assembly rejected A.C. Datta's adjournment motion to censure the Government on this order under Defence of India Rules passed on Sarojini Naidu on 26 January. Sir Reginald Maxwell who

defended the prohibitory order had, in his speech, argued that it was unfair to give freedom of speech to Mrs Naidu which was denied to her colleagues of the Congress Working Committee.

51 & 52. Kasturba Gandhi died, with her head on Gandhi's lap, at 7.35 p.m. Pyarelal explains that this was 'Gandhiji's reply taken down by the Inspector-General of Prisons in writing from dictation at 8.07 p.m. on 22 February 1944, in answer to his inquiry on behalf of the Government as to what Gandhiji's wishes in the matter were'. Harilal, Ramdas, and Devadas were present at the last moments, as also Prabhavati Narayan, Mira Behn, Sushila Nayar, Santok Chhaganlal Gandhi, and Manu Jaisukhlal Gandhi. Kasturba was draped in a sari made of cotton spun by Gandhi. The cremation took place on 23 February at 10.30 a.m. adjoining the side of the one on which Mahadev Desai's body was cremated. From the cooling embers, Kasturba's two glass bangles emerged intact.

53. On 15 August 1942, when Gandhi lit the pyre on the Aga Khan Palace grounds.

54. Messages of condolence came from the Viceroy and the Governor of Bombay on 23 February.

55. R.A. Butler, President of the Board of Education, had expressed British Government's regret at the death of Kasturba Gandhi.

56. Sir Girija Shankar Bajpai who was reported to have told the American public that 'at various times, the Government considered her (Kasturba's) release for health reasons but she wished to remain with her husband, and her wishes were respected. Furthermore, on the premises, she has the benefit of care from an eminent doctor living on the (same) premises'.

57. See 'Letter to Secretary, Home Department'.

58. To Lord Wavell.

59. This was in reply to a telegram dated 9 May from the addressee, leader of Khaksars, a militant Muslim organization, urging him to parley with the Quaid-e-Azam. He sent a similar telegram to the Quaid-e-Azam.

60. Gandhi detained at Matunga and was driven to Juhu where he stayed in a shack constructed by Jehangir Patel on the compound of Sheth Narottam Morarjee's residence.

61. Gandhi went into a fifteen-day vow of silence to give himself rest.

62. Pyarelal explains: 'Aruna Asaf Ali had been suffering from acute dysentery. It had been accentuated by the vicissitudes of her underground life.'

63. Puran Chandra Joshi, General Secretary of the Communist Party of India.

64. Gandhi held discussions during this period with Sir Homi Mody (11 June), M.R. Jayakar (14 June).

65. According to the report, the telegram was received by the ailing eminent scientist, on 12 June.

66. Acharya P.C. Ray (1861–1944), died on 16 June.

67. Gandhi reached Panchgani on 2 July, staying at 'Dilkhusha', the residence of Kanji Dwarkadas. He was there until 1 August. Sarvepalli Radhakrishnan met him on 5 July. On 6 July Subhas Bose addressed Gandhi through a radio broadcast seeking his blessings. In the source, the telegram is placed among the items of 1944; the date is inferred from the reference to 'Rajaji's offer' which was published on 10 July. Rajagopalachari joined Gandhi in Panchgani at Gandhi's suggestion.

68. Sir Ziauddin Ahmed, Member, Central Legislative Assembly, Vice Chancellor, Aligarh Muslim University.

69. The addressee had requested Gandhi to write an article on Jinnah for a series of biographies of all prominent Muslim leaders of India.

70. To Churchill.

71. The addressee's reply in English, of 24 July, inter alia, read: 'I shall be glad to receive you at my house in Bombay on my return which will probably be about the middle of August. ... I would like to say nothing more till we meet. I am very pleased to read in the Press that you are making very good progress, and I hope you will soon be all right.'

72. From *Cavalcade*, a British news magazine.

73. Undivided.

74. Of the Aligarh Muslim University, led by Ibadat Yar Khan and consisting of Mohammed Ashfaq, Amiruddin Alvi, and A.M. Safi.

75. Jinnah's sister.

76 & 77. To C. Rajagopalachari. The Gandhi–Jinnah meeting lasted three-and-a-quarter hours. Gandhi reported the talk to Rajagopalachari. Gandhi was in Bombay from 9 September to 23 September.

78. After Gandhi gave this report to Rajagopalachari the following conversation took place:

CR: Do you think he wants a settlement?

MKG: I am not certain. He thought he probably did.

CR: Then you will get it through.

MKG: Yes ... If the right word comes to me.

79. As reported by Gandhi to Rajagopalachari.

80. M.A. Jinnah.

81. Gandhi was in Bombay, staying at Birla House, from 9 to 24 September. For over a week before his departure for Bombay, Hindu hardliners picketed Gandhi's hut at Sevagram asking him to refrain from holding talks with the Quaid. On 8 September, the police took some of them into custody and recovered a sturdy dagger from one of the picketers.

82. The Quaid in his reply said: '... I may say that it is not a case of your being asked to put your signature as representing anybody till you clothe yourself with representative capacity and are vested with authority. We stand by, as I have already said, the basic and fundamental principles embodied in the Lahore Resolution of March 1940. I appeal to you once more to revise your policy and programme, as the future of this sub-continent and the welfare of the peoples of India demand that you should face realities.'

83. The letter has been placed among those for September 1944. Id fell on this date.

84. Fatima Jinnah.

85. This report is taken from Pyarelal's diary based on Gandhi's narrative to C. Rajagopalachari, giving 'the story of the final breakdown of the talks'.

86. The renowned Carnatic musician (1916–2004), recipient of the Sangita Kalanidhi (1968), the Magsaysay Award (1974), Bharat Ratna (1998).

87. The signature is in Tamil.

88. A Press conference of about 40 Indian and foreign journalists was held at Birla House; Sarojini Naidu, C. Rajagopalachari, Bhulabhai Desai, Nagindas Master, M.Y. Nurie, Dr M.D.D. Gilder, and S.K. Patil were among others present. Gandhi first read out his statement.

89. Of London, represented by Stuart Gelder.

90. *The Hindu*, 2-10-1944, however reports this interview under the date 30 September.

91. The report of this and another interview with N.G. Ranga on 28 November 1944, was released to the Press by Pyarelal with the following note: 'Soon after his release from prison Prof. Ranga saw Gandhiji at Sevagram. He had two interviews with him on 29th October 1944 and 28th November 1944. It was understood on both sides that the interviews were not for publication. As, however, parts of those interviews have already appeared in the Press, I am, under Gandhiji's instructions, releasing to the Press my full notes of the talks.' At the first interview Prof. Ranga presented Gandhi with a lengthy written questionnaire.

92. This was sent in connection with Jawaharlal Nehru's birthday on 14 November.

93. Originally written in Hindi, these 'thoughts' were translated and published under this title by Anand T. Hingorani, who explains in the Preface that after the death of his wife, Vidya, on 20 July 1943, during his eight-week stay in Sevagram from 30 September 1944, Gandhi would greet him 'every morning, after the prayer ... speak words of sympathy and solace, and ... write down something ... to meditate upon ... From

13 October 1944, onwards he wrote continuously for a fortnight, and then off and on...' Hingorani had requested Gandhi to write something for him daily, which Gandhi began to do from 20 November 1944. In June 1946, when Hingorani sought permission to publish the 'thoughts' in a book form, Gandhi remarked: 'What is there about them that you are so keen on publishing them? If, however, you wish to publish them, do so after my death. Such writings are generally never published during the lifetime of their authors. Who knows, I may not be able to live up to what I have written! But if I live up to it till the last breath of my life, then alone will it be worthwhile to publish these thoughts.' Gandhi, however, discontinued the practice by the end of 1946, as he put it, 'for the sake of my Noakhali mission, I renounced practically everything ... gave up the Ashram, all my companions and even writing for the *Harijan* ...'

94. Narsinhrav Bolanath Devetiya (1859–1937). A poet, critic, philologist, translator and one of the Nine Learned Men from (Sakshar Bhumi) Nadiad. Born at Ahmedabad, did his B.A. is Sanskrit from Elphinston College, Bombay. Gandhi requested him on 15 September 1915 to translate one of his favourite Hymns 'Lead Kindly Light ...' of Cardinal Newman (Gandhi had first heard it in South Africa from Rev. Joseph Doke's daughter Olive when assaulted by Mir Alam) when he came to meet him in the morning at Sabarmati Ashram. On 23 October 1915 he came with the translation as 'Premal Jyoti Taro Dakhvi ...' which used to be sung in the evening prayer of the Ashram on every Friday.

95. Ramdas Gandhi's son, Kanu.

96. An underground worker wanted by the police met Gandhi at Sevagram and left behind a note. On learning this, the police had asked for the note.

97. To Jaya, sister of Jaisukhlal Gandhi, father of Manuben Gandhi.

98. To Krishnachandra.

99. A corpse-like spreadeagled yogic posture for the relaxation of the mind and body.

100. Hermann Kallenbach died in Johannesburg on 25 March 1945.

101. Gope Gurbuxani had asked: 'How can a historian best serve the country and how can he write a progressive history of India?'

102. To G.D. Birla. Gandhi was in Bombay from 1 to 20 April.

103. K.R. Narayanan, then on the staff of the *Times of India*, was proceeding to London on a Tata scholarship to do a Masters at the London School of Economics. Gandhi's answers were in writing, it being a day of silence for him.

104. Narayanan, obtaining a First at LSE as an outstanding student of Harold Laski, returned to India and joined the Indian Foreign Service,

serving as Ambassador to Turkey, China, and the USA. He was later elected thrice to the Lok Sabha from Ottapalam, Kerala, becoming a Minister of State (1984–9), Vice President of India (1992–7) and then President of India (1997–2002).

105. President F.D. Roosevelt died on 2 April 1945.

106. Germany surrendered to the Allies on 7 May and Japan on 14 August.

107. To Purushottamdas Tandon (1882–1962); Tandon entered the legal profession in 1906 and joined the Bar of the Allahabad High Court in 1908 as a junior to Sir Tej Bahadur Sapru. Gave up his practice in 1921 on account of his involvement in public affairs; joined the Indian National Congress in 1899 while a student and represented Allahabad at the All India Congress Committee in 1906. Imprisoned in 1921 for active participation in the Non-cooperation Movement, he had earlier organized the Allahabad District Peasants' Committee to improve the working conditions of the agriculturists. His contribution was especially notable in the field of organizing Kisan Sabhas to secure the cooperation of the peasantry to the cause of India's Independence. He worked for long years as the Speaker of the Legislative Assembly of U.P. He was also elected to the Constituent Assembly in 1946, to the Lok Sabha in 1952 and to the Rajya Sabha in 1956. He retired from active public life after 1956 due to indifferent health though he continued to do constructive work for many years. He was intimately associated with many institutions like the Servants of the People Society, the Hindi Sahitya Sammelan, and the Rashtrabhasha Prachar Samiti. He devoted the major part of his energies to the propagation of Hindi. Tandon was fondly called 'Rajarshi' by Mahatma Gandhi. Conferred 'Bharat Ratna' in 1961.

108. Letter to Saraswati Gandhi, wife of Kantilal Gandhi and daughter-in-law of Harilal Gandhi.

109. Interview to Ralph Coniston of the *Colliers Weekly*.

110. From the contents it is obvious that this discussion took place before the San Francisco Conference which opened on 25 April 1945.

111. To Maganbhai P. Desai. During this period: (i) Japan left Rangoon on 23 April, the INA on 24 April; (ii) Mussolini was killed on 29 April; (iii) Hitler killed himself on 1 May; and (iv) Germany surrendered unconditionally on 7 May, bringing World War II to an end.

112. The reference is to the death of Sarojini Naidu's younger son Ranadheera.

113. Sarojini Naidu had given to Gandhi the epithet (among others) of 'Spinner of India's Destiny'.

114. To the Press.

115. Defence Member in the Viceroy's Executive Council from October 1943 and later Prime Minister of Pakistan. He was one of the three members

of the Indian delegation to the San Francisco Peace Conference; the other two being A. Ramaswami Mudaliar and V.T. Krishnamachari. Noon was answering questions in an interview to Indian journalists attending the Conference.

116. To Manu Jaisukhlal Gandhi.

117. Dr P. Subbaroyan (1889–1962), leading figure of Justice Party, Chief Minister of Madras (1926–30), Ambassador to Indonesia (1949), Governor of Maharashtra (1962).

118. Sumati S. Morarjee (1907–98), is regarded as the 'mother of Indian shipping'. Close associate of Gandhi, daughter-in-law of the founder of Scindia Steam Navigation, Narottam Morarjee, held important responsibilities in the Indian and world shipping scene.

119. Churchill resigned on 23 May and a new government took office.

120. In the event, neither name was given, the one endorsed by the newborn's maternal grandfather, Rajagopalachari, was selected: Gopalkrishna.

121. The addressee's father, Rajagopalachari. 'Anna' means elder brother in Tamil, but is used in certain Tamil communities to denote 'father'.

122. This was in reply to a request from Mohan Kumaramangalam on P.C. Joshi's behalf to publish the correspondence that had passed between Gandhi and P.C. Joshi.

123. Bharatan Kumarappa.

124. To Mohan Kumaramangalam.

125. Rajani Palme-Dutt, Marxist economist and outstanding theoretician, who successfully contested the Sparkbrook constituency of Birmingham against L.S. Amery, Secretary of State for India. The letter appeared in *The Bombay Chronicle*, 13-6-1945.

126. Purushottam Patel.

127. To Shanta.

128. Ganesh Shankar Vidyarthi (1890–1931) a fearless journalist. As editor of the Kanpur-based 'Pratap' opposed parochialism, sectarianism and sectionalism'. He was killed when he placed himself between two rioting mobs, one Hindu and the other Muslim at Kanpur, on 25 March 1931.

129. The article appeared under the date-line 'Panchgani, 12 June'.

130. Gandhi went to Poona on 19 June and visited the samadhis of Kasturba and Mahadev Desai at Aga Khan Palace. He was in Bombay from 20 to 22 June, attending the Working Committee meetings at which it was decided to attend the Simla Conference. He reached Simla on 24 June via Delhi when he called on Swami Shraddhananda's ailing grand-daughter Satyawati.

131. The Viceroy's reply, dated 29 June, inter alia, read: 'I have already given instructions to the Provincial governments not to execute the

sentences in any of these cases until the Privy Council has passed orders on the petition for special leave to appeal ... I will bear your letter in mind when I consider the whole question after the decision of the Privy Council is known'.

132. Rajkumari's pet dog which had died during Gandhi's stay at Simla.

133. During this period: (i) Gandhi resigned from the Hindi Sahitya Sammelan on 25 July on account of its inability to accept his position on Hindi/Urdu being protected from Sanskritization and Persianization and (ii) Labour Party came to power in Great Britain and C.R. Attlee became Prime Minister on 26 July.

134. Mahendra Chowdhury.

135. Sucheta Kripalani *nee* Mazumdar (1908–74); In-charge, Women's Department, A.I.C.C; member, Congress Working Committee, 1950–2; member, Lok Sabha, 1952–62; Chief Minister, U.P., October 1963 to March 1967.

136. Sucheta's husband, Acharya J.B. Kripalani, (1888–1982); General Secretary of the Indian National Congress, 1934–46; its President in 1946. One of the founders of the Congress Democratic Front and later of the Praja Socialist Party, Member of Parliament for several years.

137. During this period: (i) Pethick-Lawrence was appointed Secretary of State for India on 2 August; (ii) US bomb fell over Hiroshima on 6 August and over Nagasaki on 9 August; Japan surrendered on 10 August; (iii) Rajagopalachari was re-admitted to Congress on 12 August after nearly 3 years; (iv) Saraladevi Choudhurani passed away in Calcutta on 18 August; (v) Reports came in on 23 August that Subhas Chandra Bose had succumbed to injuries sustained in an aircrash, after being admitted to a Japanese hospital.

138. This was given during a talk with Labanya Kumar Chowdhary, an engineer from Sylhet, when he visited Sevagram.

139. Saraladevi Choudhurani.

140. This was in reply to Amiya Bose's telegram dated 26 August which read: 'Kindly advise us about uncle's *shraddha* ceremony and observance of period of mourning.'

141. Presumably about the reported death of Subhas Chandra Bose in an air crash.

142. Acharya Parachure Shastri.

143. 1897–1953; Son of Lakshmidas Gandhi; Gandhi's nephew.

144. During this period: (i) Proceedings against INA personalities—Captain Shah Nawaz Khan, Captain Lakshmi, Lt. G.S. Dhillon started in Delhi on 5 October. Jawaharlal Nehru donned a lawyer's robe for the first time in 22 years for their defence alongside Sir Tej Bahadur Sapru,

Bhulabhai Desai, Kailas Nath Katju, and others; (ii) Churchill signed a warning on 7 October: 'Do not give Soviet Russia the secret of the atom bomb'.

145. Vallabhbhai Patel's birthday on 31 October.

146. A historical novel by the addressee.

147. Of Gujarat.

148. To Narahari D. Parikh.

149. Manilal Gandhi's son, born in 1934, co-founder with his late wife Sunandi of the M.K. Gandhi Institute for Non-violence, USA.

150. Manilal Gandhi's daughter (see n. 91, Part Thirteen).

151. To Lilavati Asar.

152. On 8 December, Gandhi was shown an advance copy of the Governor's radio broadcast. In response to certain portions of it, Gandhi said poverty would be removed from India not by grandiose schemes but by a proper utilization of the surplus time of people. On 10 December, he called on Lord Wavell at the Government House, Calcutta, met Dr N.B. Khare on 12 December and on 14 December encountered a cobra at the Sodepur grounds while on a walk.

153. Rathindranath (1888–1961), Rabindranath Tagore's elder son.

154. Environmentalists worldwide would be surprised by this espousal of 'dams' by Gandhi. But we should bear in mind the following: (a) he does not speak of the size of dams and (b) he does not anticipate the problem of human displacement as a result of dams.

155. G.E.B. Abell, private secretary to the Viceroy.

156. Originally written in Gujarati, this appeared as 'from *Harijanbandhu*' published simultaneously with the source.

157. *Harijanbandhu* has 'twenty-five'.

158. At the Press Conference in Bombay on 24 February 1946.

159. The reference is to the 'mutiny' of naval personnel on board the H.M.I.S. *Talwar*, on 19 February.

160. Rajagopalachari in a letter dated 3 March had said: 'Your *nagari* is so illegible that I have only with great difficulty gathered what you wished to tell me ... It won't do to discard what we both know well and handle as medium and adopt deliberately a difficult medium except occasionally as a joke! I shall begin replying in Tamil, if you write to me in illegible Nagari!'

161. Replying to this letter of 11 March, Rajagopalachari, on 13 March, said: 'Regarding Hindustani I plead guilty and ask for mitigation. Old age (not youth) being the excuse. But don't argue further. Your very sweetness makes me feel so guilty.'

162 & 163. These words are in Tamil. However, the source has *ambudan*, a slip for *anbudan* which means 'with love'.

164. According to Pyarelal, Agatha Harrison had not quite approved of

Gandhi's suggestion to Rameshwardas Birla to replace the flower beds in the terrace garden in Birla House, Bombay, by vegetables.

165. The Congress Working Committee met in Bombay from 12 to 16 March. Gandhi attended the meeting. Prime Minister Attlee told the House of Commons on 15 March that Britain had indeed decided to relinquish India. 'If India elects for independence, she has a right to do so', adding: 'We are mindful of the rights of the minorities. On the other hand, we cannot allow a minority to place a veto on the advance of the majority'. Jinnah objected to this qualification in Attlee's observation.

166. Water.

167. With much love.

168. The reference is to the death of the Viceroy's son-in-law, Capt. Simon N. Astley, in an accident at Quetta.

169. Uruli had a large military camp. After Gandhi's arrival in Uruli, groups of Indian military would come up and talk to him. They did so during his morning walks. They also assembled at his evening prayer gatherings. Two batches saw him at his residence.

170. Gandhi reached Uruli-Kanchan on 22 March.

171. They shouted 'Jai Hind' and 'Netaji ki Jai', repeatedly.

172. Originally written in Hindi, this appeared as 'from *Harijan Sevak*' published simultaneously with the source.

173. Deep breathing exercise.

174. Originally written in Hindi, this appeared as 'from *Harijan Sevak*' published simultaneously with the source.

175. In March 1942.

176. An announcement emanated from Tokyo on 23 August 1945 to the effect that Netaji had died in a plane crash on 18 August 1945. Nevertheless, doubts on the authenticity of the report persisted. The issue was raised in Parliament. Prime Minister Nehru said on 3 December 1955 in Parliament that an official committee would be appointed to go into the matter and the Government of India appointed a three-member Inquiry Committee, by its Notification No. F-30(26)FEA/55 dated 5 April 1956, with Shri Shah Nawaz Khan, Parliamentary Secretary to the Ministry for Transport and Railways, as its Chairman and Shri Suresh Chandra Bose, elder brother of Netaji and Shri S.N. Maitra, ICS, Chief Commissioner, Andaman and Nicobar Islands, as its members. Two members of the Committee (Shri Shah Nawaz Khan and Shri S.N. Maitra) came to the conclusion that Netaji had died in the plane crash. Shri Suresh Chandra Bose, the other member, submitted a dissenting report. The majority report was accepted by the Government of India.

In response to a demand for a fresh inquiry into the matter, the

Government of India constituted another Inquiry Commission headed by Shri G.D. Khosla, Retired Chief Justice of Punjab High Court in 1970. That Commission also came to the conclusion that Netaji had succumbed to his injuries sustained in the plane crash at Taihoku. A Writ Petition was later filed before the High Court at Calcutta. A Division Bench of the High Court by its judgment dated 30 April 1998 directed the Union of India to launch a vigorous inquiry into the alleged disappearance/death of Netaji in accordance with law by appointing a Commission of Inquiry for the purpose of putting an end to the controversy.

The Government of India appointed a one-man Commission by its Notification No. SO 339(E) dated 14 May 1999 consisting of Mr Justice M.K. Mukherjee, a retired Judge of the Supreme Court of India to inquire into all the facts and circumstances related to the disappearance of Netaji Subhas Chandra Bose in 1945 and subsequent developments connected therewith including:

(a) whether Netaji Subhas Chandra Bose is dead or alive;
(b) if he is dead, whether he died in the plane crash, as alleged;
(c) whether the ashes in the Japanese temple are ashes of Netaji;
(d) whether he has died in any other manner at any other place and, if so, when and how;
(e) if he is alive, in respect of his whereabouts.

The response of the Commission to the terms of reference, in its Report, was as follows:

(a) Netaji Subhas Chandra Bose is dead;
(b) He did not die in the plane crash, as alleged;
(c) The ashes in the Japanese temple are not of Netaji;
(d) In absence of any clinching evidence a positive answer cannot be given; and
(e) Answer already given in (a) above.

The Commission also expressed the view—consequent upon its findings—that in undertaking the scrutiny of publications touching upon the question of death or otherwise of Netaji, the Central Government can proceed on the basis that he is dead but did not die in the plane crash, as alleged. The report of the Justice Mukherjee Commission is now a public document. Apart from it having been placed (along with the Action Taken Report) before both Houses of Parliament on 17.5.2006, it has been also put on the website of the Ministry of Home Affairs (*http://mha.nic.in*). The Government of India have not accepted the findings of the Justice Mukherjee Commission to the effect that Netaji did not die in the plane crash and that the ashes in the Renkoji Temple, Tokyo, are not of Netaji. The Action

Taken Report has been placed before both Houses of Parliament along with the report of JMCI on 17-5-2006.

Requests for access to more information from Government of India records continue to be made.

177. In *Harijan*, the speech appeared under the title 'Message of the I.N.A.' by Pyarelal. The opening paragraph is from *The Bombay Chronicle Weekly*. Gandhi met INA personnel on 4 April.

178. The *Harijan* report, which appeared under the title 'Heart Searching' by Pyarelal, has been collated with the version in *Mahatma Gandhi— The Last Phase*. Only excerpts are given here.

179. The last remark is believed to have startled the visitor.

180. This too was not expected by the visitor who had, like most people, regarded railways as one of the proudest achievement of British rule in India.

181. During this period, Gandhi met Lord Pethick-Lawrence on 14 April and once again, with Stafford Cripps on 18 April. He called on the ailing Pandit Madan Mohan Malaviya on 18 April, visited Dr M.A. Ansari's grave on 19 April.

182. Absentee landlordism.

183. Gandhi concluded the interview, pointing in a mute petition of mercy, as it were, to the heap of papers in front of him awaiting disposal.

184. The burden, material and moral, of militarization.

185. Against the Axis powers.

186. During his ten days' stay at Mussoorie some foreign correspondents managed to interview Gandhi during his morning walks.

187 & 188. Gandhi left Mussoorie on 9 June and reached Delhi on 10 June.

189. Lord Wavell. Gandhi visited the Viceroy on 11 June and held discussions with Lord Pethick-Lawrence on 12 June. He attended the Working Committee meetings on 13 June. He had further meetings with Lord Pethick-Lawrence on 16 June and, after a session with the Working Committee on 19 June, a meeting with Cripps on 20 June and with Pethick-Lawrence again on 27 June.

190. In his letter to Lord Wavell dated 8 June, the Quaid-e-Azam had claimed that the Viceroy had given him 'the assurance that there will be only twelve portfolios, five on behalf of the League, five Congress, one Sikh, and one Christian or Anglo-Indian'.

191. Fourteen persons were invited to join the national government: Six 'Congress Hindus'—Nehru, Patel, Prasad, Rajagopalachari, Mahtab, and Jagjivan Ram; Five 'League Muslims' including Jinnah; a Sikh (Baldev Singh), a Parsi (N.P. Engineer); and a Christian (John Mathai). The plan contained a Clause 8 which provided that the Viceroy could proceed with the formation of an Interim Government comprising

persons who accepted the 16 May plan, if the Congress or League or both found a coalition Government under the 16 June plan unacceptable. For Congress the composition was unacceptable as it typecast the Congress as a Hindu party and validated the League's claim to be the sole representative of the Muslim.

192. Pyarelal records (19 June 1946): Bapu gave a final notice to the Working Committee today that if they agreed to the non-inclusion of a nationalist Muslim and the inclusion of the name of N.P. Engineer, which the Viceroy had foisted upon them, he would have nothing to do with the whole business and leave Delhi ... Bapu told the Sardar on 21 June that negotiations for the inclusion of a nationalist Muslim in the Cabinet should be conducted not by the Maulana Saheb but someone else as the Maulana Saheb being himself a nationalist Muslim might feel it embarrassing to carry the insistence to its logical end.

Mahatma Gandhi—The Last Phase Vol. I, Book 1, p. 222 and 353

193. Gandhi drafted this on behalf of the Congress President.

194. Afterwards it was learnt that the overzealous official who had sent the telephone message, had acted without authority.

195. The meeting of the Working Committee was held in the afternoon. Gandhi asked Pyarelal to read out the note he had written for the Congress Working Committee.

196. It being Gandhi's silence day this written message was read out after the prayers.

197. This was sent to Rashtriya Vidyalaya, Panchmarhi, which was bringing out a Jayaprakash number of its handwritten journal.

198. Dr Ram Manohar Lohia.

199. Gandhi left Delhi on 29 June for Bombay and Poona. Boulders had been placed on the railway track between Neral and Karajat and a major derailment was averted by the engine driver's quick reflexes on 30 June.

200. On alighting from the train Gandhi personally thanked the engine driver, L.M. Pereira and the guard.

201 & 202. On the night of the accident while the repairs were being carried out for over two hours, unaware of the mishap Gandhi slept peacefully. He wrote this remark on his photograph taken while he was asleep.

203. Then Minister of Home and Revenue in the Government of Bombay, later Prime Minister of India.

204. Communal riots broke out in Ahmedabad on 1 July, resulting in the death among others of two satyagrahis—Vasantrao Hegishte and Rajabali Lakhani who tried to quell the riots.

205. Ashad Sud 2, on which day images of deities are taken out in a procession.

206. Policemen.

207. Wanda Dynowska.
208 & 209. Extracted from Pyarelal's 'After Four Years'. Louis Fischer met Gandhi twice on the 17th and then on the 18th. The report here reproduced covers the two interviews on the 17th.
210. Including Rajabali Lakhani and Vasantrao Hegishte.
211. A translation of this was also published in *Harijan*, 18-8-1946, under the title 'Is God a Person or Force?'
212. The reference is to the 'Great Calcutta Killings'.
213. Wavell's response was not helpful. He cabled Sudhir Ghosh in London to the following effect: 'Gandhi says Viceroy unnerved Bengal tragedy. Please tell friends he should be assisted by abler and legal mind. Otherwise repetition of tragedy a certainty.' Sudhir Ghosh conveyed Gandhi's feelings to Pethick-Lawrence and Attlee.
214. The Viceroy invited the President of the Congress to make proposals for an Interim Government and said that the Congress President had accepted the invitation.
215. On the 29th June, the Cabinet Mission left Delhi. Lord Wavell, the Viceroy, continued the effort which the Mission had initiated, and on the 24th August, went on to announce the formation of an Interim National Government, headed by the Viceroy, replacing the Viceroy's Executive Council. Pandit Nehru, the Congress President, was to be its Vice-President. The Muslim League declined to join the Government saying it had not been given the exclusive right to nominate the Muslim members in the Cabinet. The Interim Government comprising Congress Ministers alone took office on 2 September 1946, with Jawaharlal Nehru being sworn in as Vice President of the Council.
216. (Yusuf Dadoo) Indian leader; Chairman of the Passive Resistance Council of the Transvaal and Democratic Action Committee.
217. During this period: (i) Jawaharlal Nehru informed the Congress Subjects Committee that ever since the Muslim League had joined the Executive Council, things had deteriorated and the Congress members had twice contemplated resigning; (ii) Nehru and Jinnah flew to London on 1 December at the invitation of the British Government for talks, which failed. They returned on 8 December; (iii) Asaf Ali was named India's first Ambassador to the U.S.A. on 6 December; (iv) The Constituent Assembly began its deliberations on 9 December (without the Muslim League participating in it) and Dr Rajendra Prasad was elected its President on 11 December; (v) On Christmas Day, Gandhi received gifts from South Africa which included a shaving kit and— cigarettes! Keeping the kit for himself, he put the cigarettes aside for being given to Jawaharlal Nehru; (vi) Jawaharlal Nehru came on 28 December to Srirampur and gave Gandhi the present of a fountain

pen; and (vii) Gandhi was amused to learn that a beedi with the brand name of 'Mahatma' had been introduced in the Indian market.

218. To Acharya Kripalani. Rajmohan Gandhi says in *Mohandas* (pp. 576–7): Kripalani gently recalled the Gita's stress on conserving a society's values, equally gently asked whether Gandhi was not treating his female associates 'as means rather than as ends in themselves', but added that he knew that Gandhi had never exploited women. Continued Kripalani: 'I can only say that I have the fullest faith in you. No sinful man can go about his business the way you are doing ... I can never be disillusioned about you unless I find the marks of insanity and depravity in you. I do not find any such marks.'

219. Gandhi to Nehru, 6 February 1947.

220. President of the district Muslim League, Monghyr (Bihar).

221. To an Advocate from Aligarh who wanted him to come to Bihar.

222. To a barrister from Patna who wrote that it was 'very surprising indeed' that Gandhi was 'wasting' his time in Noakhali.

223. Responding to a reference by Shaheed Suhrawardy to Gandhi's 'inner voice'.

224. Maulvi Fazlul Huq, the ex-Premier of Bengal, in a speech, had wondered how the Muslims of Noakhali and Tipperah had tolerated Gandhi's presence so long. Rising to a peroration, he declared that if Gandhi had gone to his home-district of Barisal, he would have driven him and his goat into the Khal! He followed it up by a wire asking for an interview with Gandhi in order to have a 'heart-to-heart' talk with him! The meeting came off after several delays on the 27 February at Haimchar.

    The Maulvi Saheb began: Gandhi had not gone to Bihar; his place was in Bihar rather than in Noakhali; Noakhali Muslims, far from being aggressors, were the victims of police repression.

225. In the course of his prayer address at Abdullah Chak that evening.

226. Some members of the Muslim League Relief Committee at Phulwari Sharif met Gandhi on the 15 March and asked him several questions on behalf of the refugees.

227. At a joint gathering of Hindus, Muslims, and Sikhs, held in Gurudwara Har Mandir, the birth place of the Sikh Guru Govind Singh, in Patna City.

228. Telling Premier Sinha that the Bihar killings were 'like the Jallianwala massacre', Gandhi spoke with bluntness to Congress committees and the public. Gandhi said the above to Congress workers in Bir.

229. 'We are drifting everywhere,' Pandit Nehru wrote to Gandhi in the second week of February 1947, 'and sometimes I doubt if we are drifting in the right direction. We live in a state of perpetual crisis and have no real grip of the situation.'

The first act of Lord Mountbatten on arrival in India on the 22 March 1947, was to send two letters to Jinnah and Gandhi, inviting them to meet him. Gandhi left Patna for Delhi on the 30th March, travelling third-class. Lord Mountbatten had offered to send his personal plane to fetch him but he declined the offer. He similarly turned down the suggestion for a special train.

230. Pyarelal writes: At three in the afternoon 31 March 1947, he had his first meeting with the Viceroy. Very little politics was discussed. The Viceroy desired to know all about his early life, his education, his sojourn in England and subsequent struggles in South Africa and in India. On his part, Gandhiji was equally eager to meet the whole man in the Viceroy.

The Viceroy found the plan 'attractive' and suggested that Gandhiji should discuss it with Lord Ismay, his Chief of Staff, so that Ismay could cast it into proper shape.

... The plan was discussed in the Viceroy's staff meeting on the 5 April, and dubbed 'an old kite flown without disguise'. The consensus of opinion was that 'Mountbatten should not allow himself to be drawn into negotiation with the Mahatma, but should only listen to advice.'

The second meeting took place in the open on a terrace in the Viceregal garden. It was a typical spring morning, cool and fresh. The sun shone mildly through a soft, pearly haze. The flower-beds in the Moghul Garden were a blaze of colour.

The Mahatma's lunch was brought in the middle of the meeting by Manu and Brijkrishna Chandiwala.

Introductions over, the Viceroy remarked to Manu: 'You are a lucky girl. My daughter tells me she feels jealous of you on seeing your photographs with Mr Gandhi. I shall be sending her to attend your prayer meeting.'

While the one had his lunch and the other his tea, an A.D.C. photographed them together.

Pyarelal records that Gandhiji asked the Viceroy if Manu could, in the meantime, roam about the garden so that they could proceed with their talk uninterrupted.

'Certainly', replied the Viceroy. Then addressing Manu, he added: 'All this is yours; we are only trustees. We have come to make it over to you.'

231. To one of his companions as he came out of the pandal.

232. Khwaja Saheb Abdul Majid, a nationalist Muslim leader and a very old friend came to see him. He was most unhappy at the prospect of the division of India but tried to laugh away his grief. 'Bapuji is now going to drive us out of India in our old age', he remarked to

a member of Gandhi's party, affecting a laugh. 'When India is divided, I shall come to take asylum with you. You won't let the Hindus murder me, will you?', he added playfully. Gandhi, overheard the remark.

233. Gandhi returned from Patna to Delhi on 1 May. Pandit Nehru met him shortly thereafter. Gandhi expressed the view that the Congress must not 'engage in the game of diplomacy with the British to score an advantage over the League.' In no case, he said, should Congress barter India's unity for any concession. It should ask the British to play straight. In his prayer meeting he spoke of the sincerity of the Joint Appeal issued by him and Jinnah.

234. Reuter's special correspondent, on 5 May 1947.

235. In response to the same correspondent's further probing query: 'What sort of Indo-British relationship did he envisage after June 1948?

236. Commenting on Jinnah's statement in his prayer address on the 7 May.

237. Said when Gandhi was told that Badshah had observed: *Before long we shall become aliens in Hindustan. The end of our long fight for freedom will be to pass under the domination of Pakistan—away from Bapu, away from India, away from all of you. Who knows what the future holds for us?'*

   Gandhi left for Calcutta on 7 May. Badshah Khan saw him off at the railway station.

238. Pyarelal records that the Viceroy's reaction to Gandhi's letter was conveyed by a colleague a few days later: 'I came up here (Simla) and dined at Viceregal Lodge last night ... He said 'I am much touched and moved by your Bapu's letter. Though he gives me more headache than anyone else, I admire his instinct. I would love to be able to do what he says, but I can't always ... and what is more, the Congress members of the Interim Government do not see eye to eye with him.'

239. Bihar Ministers had come to meet Gandhiji at the Patna railway station. The whistle was about to be blown. They had not finished, however. The station master was in a fix. Hesitatingly he came and asked if the 'line clear' could be given. 'You do not go to any other passenger to take orders', answered Gandhiji disconcertingly. 'Why this exception then?' Pyarelal has recorded: Bowing respectfully, as he took leave, the station master ventured: "If there were even one individual in every department to observe discipline like you, it would change the whole face of administration."' The signal was given. The train bore Gandhiji Calcutta-wards.

240. Dr Bidhan Chandra Roy, who came on 14 May, noticed on Gandhi's face signs of extreme fatigue and exhaustion. He advised stopping all

interviews and the observance of two days' silence in the week instead of one.

241. Addressing his prayer gathering on the evening of 26 May.

242. On the 29 May, a co-worker said to Gandhi 'You and your ideals have been given the go by'. The above records that conversation.

243. At Prayer Meeting

244. Chakrayya, a talented young Andhra Dalit had been with the Sevagram Ashram in 1935 and did khadi work. He died on 28 May 1947 during an operation for a brain tumour in a hospital in Bombay. Gandhi had nursed high hopes for Chakrayya.

245. On 2 June, at Prayer Meeting.

246. In a conversation during his walk with Dr Rajendra Prasad.

247. To Rajkumari Amrit Kaur when she gave the news that all the three parties—the Congress, the Muslim League, and the Sikhs—had signed the Mountbatten plan. The League, she said, would not accept any other solution and the Congress had no other choice but to yield. Gandhi listened without comment and then with a deep sigh said the above.

248. To a group of foreign visitors.

249. Two Hindu Mahasabha youths accosted him during his morning walk and said 'You are no Mahatma. You are making the Hindus weak by preaching Ahimsa to them. You should not mislead them.' Affectionately putting his hands on the shoulders of the newcomers, Gandhi said the above to them.

250. S.K. Patil, President of the Bombay Congress Committee was reported to have said in a public speech that if any harm befell the Hindus in Pakistan, the Congress would 'after the 15 August' take reprisals in India. The above was in response to that.

251. In a letter to Asaf Ali, the Indian Ambassador to the United States, in the third week of July.

252. This was in the context of the discussion in the Congress over the design of the Flag of the Indian Union.

253. On Independence day—the 15 August—Lord Mountbatten declared that following the Government's negotiations with the Princes, 'nearly all' the States had signed 'Instruments of Accession' which left the constitutional independence of the States untouched except in respect of three subjects—defence, external affairs, and communications, which now belonged to the Union Government. The 'nearly all' meant, by exclusion, Hyderabad, Junagadh, and Kashmir. The above was written by Gandhi on 24 July to Sardar Patel.

254. In a report to Pandit Nehru, which he shared with Sardar Patel.

255. In a letter to the Sardar.

256. Said to the railway guard on his journey from Lahore to Patna. By-passing Delhi on his way back from Kashmir, he journeyed straight from Lahore to Patna, from where he would go to Noakhali via Calcutta. The Congress leadership did not dissuade him this time. Did they feel he would be out of place in the capital on Independence Day? Pyarelal has suggested that.

There were crowds at all the stops en route. It also began to rain heavily at night. The roof of Gandhi's carriage leaked, flooding the compartment. The guard suggested that he shift to another compartment.

257. To S.K. Patil, the Bombay Congress leader, who, according to press reports, had spoken of reprisals after 15 August by the Congress in India if Hindus were harmed in Pakistan.

258. 'Hydari Manzil'; an old abandoned Muslim house in an unsanitary locality in Calcutta, had hastily been cleaned up for Gandhi's occupation. It was a ramshackle building open on all sides. The windows had been smashed. There was only one latrine used indiscriminately by people, including the police on duty.

259. At a prayer meeting outside Hydari Manzil, Beliaghata, attended by 10,000 people. After the prayer, Gandhi returned to his room and resumed work. But outside the uproar continued though without any stone throwing. After a few minutes he got up went with Manu to the window and throwing open a shutter, began to address the crowd outside. He bemoaned the attack on Suhrawardy.

260. To members of the West Bengal Cabinet who came for his blessings on 15 August 1947. That night Gandhi drove round the city and witnessed the scenes of fraternization. Shaheed Suhrawardy was at the wheel. At a crowded street corner some people recognized them and hundreds of Muslims instantly surrounded the car. They shouted, 'Mahatma Gandhi Zindabad'.

261. At the prayer meeting on 16 August 1947.

262. Id fell on 18 August. Gandhi scribbled the above on a piece of paper.

263. In an article captioned 'Miracle or Accident?' in *Harijan*.

Wrote Lord Mountbatten to Gandhi: 'In the Punjab we have 55,000 soldiers and large scale rioting on our hands. In Bengal our forces consist of one man, and there is no rioting. As a serving officer, as well as an administrator, may I be allowed to pay my tribute to the One-Man Boundary Force, not forgetting his Second in Command, Mr Suhrawardy. You should have heard the enthusiastic applause which greeted the mention of your name in the Constituent Assembly on the 15 of August, when all of us were thinking so much of you.'

264. The signature is in the Devanagari and Bengali scripts.
265. At about 10 p.m., a heavily bandaged man was taken to Hydari Manzil at the head of a procession. There were conflicting versions of the scene and its origins. One was that the man had fallen out of a tram. Another that he had been asked to shout 'Pakistan Zindabad' and on his refusing to do so, was injured. Yet another version was that he had been stabbed in a Muslim locality. The Chief Minister, Dr Prafulla Ghosh, had the victim immediately examined. The doctor's report was that he bore no mark of stabbing.

    Gandhi, who had gone to bed, was woken up by the noise.
266. By the next afternoon, it was clear that violent communal conflagrations had broken out in several parts of the city. Gandhi used to have a drink of fruit juice in the afternoon. That day when it was brought to him, he waved it away.

    The poorer Muslim inhabitants of Beliaghata who, on the strength of Gandhi's previous entreaties, had returned to their homes, were in panic. One batch of them boarded an open truck to move to the nearest Muslim locality. As they passed by the side of a graveyard near Hydari Manzil, hand-grenades were hurled upon it from the roof of an adjoining building. Two Muslims were instantaneously killed.

    When Gandhi heard of this incident, he rushed to the site. The dead men must have been day-labourers. One of them was clad in a tattered *lungi*. A four anna piece, which he carried on his person, had rolled out of the fold of his lungi and lay near his lifeless frame. Gandhi stood transfixed at the sight. While returning to his residence he was asked if he was contemplating a fast.
267. To Vallabhbhai Patel.
268. To Vallabhbhai Patel.
269. A medical check up by the nature-cure doctor, Dinshaw Mehta, showed an average of 4 missing heart beats in 19 seconds, i.e., nearly every fourth beat—an indication of great strain.
270. On the third day of the fast, Gandhi was perceptibly weak. The voice had sunk to a whisper and the pulse was rapid. He had a feeling of giddiness on getting up and a 'buzz' in the ears. But by then the scene in the city began to change. People began to come and confess what they may not have confided to another. Hindus and Muslims combined now to save the life that was being offered as sacrifice for peace between the communities. 'Mixed' processions, comprising all communities, now went through the affected parts of the city to restore communal harmony.
271. Gandhi broke the fast seventy-three hours after it was commenced, at 9.15 p.m. on the 4 September. He did so by slowly sipping a glass of

diluted orange juice handed by Suhrawardy who bowed and wept. This was preceded by a short prayer, in which all present joined, followed by the singing of Tagore's song, 'When the heart is hard and parched up, Come upon me with a shower of mercy' and Ramdhun. Before the leaders had dispersed, Gandhi called Rajaji to his side and said, 'I am thinking of leaving for the Punjab tomorrow.'

272. September 7 was Gandhi's last day in Calcutta. At half-past-eight at night, some ladies came to bid him farewell by performing arti by waving lights fed with pure *ghee*. As they approached him bearing the salver on which the lights were placed, he stopped them.

273. Gandhi arrived in Delhi, on the morning of the 9 September 1947, from Calcutta. He was met by Sardar Patel at the railway station.

     Delhi was ghostly in its quiet. While driving into the city the Sardar gave him the news. Communal riots had broken out in the capital.

     Pandit Nehru's drove up within minutes of Gandhi reaching Birla House. A twenty-four hour curfew was in force in the city, he said. The military had been called, but the streets were littered with the dead.

274. In a statement to the Press.

275. From 10 September, Gandhi toured the riot-affected parts of the city and the refugee camps, beginning with Arab-ki Sarai, near Humayun's tomb, where Muslim Meos from Alwar and Bharatpur States were waiting to be taken to Pakistan.

     From Arab-ki Sarai he went to the Jamia Millia Islamia, at Okhla. A number of Muslim men and women from the surrounding villages had taken shelter there. For two days they had lived in great danger of death. But there was courage and faith of Dr Zakir Husain, the Vice-Chancellor of the Jamia.

     One of the Muslim refugee women held in her arms a two-month-old baby that had lost both its parents during the disturbances.

276. Replying to questions and answers at a rally in a sweepers' colony to which RSS leaders took Gandhi.

277. To the Communist leader, P.C. Joshi.

278. Gandhi had learnt with sorrow that Dr Ansari's daughter and her husband had been forced to leave their own house in Daryaganj, where he used to stay as the doctor's guest. They were now living in fear, in a hotel. Pyarelal records:

     'Is it not a shame,' he said at his prayer meeting in the evening, 'that the daughter of a pillar of the Congress and doyen of Hindu-Muslim unity should have to leave her home like that?'

279. Delhi experienced a thunderstorm on the night of the 14 September. Gandhi lay awake in bed worrying about the thousands of refugees—men, women, and children—in refugee camps that were in knee-deep

water. This was said in a written message to his evening prayer gathering the next day.

280. Addressing the Hindus and Sikhs at the same meeting.

281. To a Sikh refugee from the West Punjab who met Gandhi on the 19 September and wept as he narrated to him how his womenfolk had been dishonoured.

282. Pyarelal records that at the end of a particularly agonizing day, he was heard muttering in his sleep. On being asked about it, he said he had a dream that a crowd of Hindu youths had rushed into his room. One of them started abusing him and, it seemed, wanted to assault him.

283. On another occasion, Pyarelal says, when Gandhi's sleep was similarly disturbed, he explained that he had been dreaming that he was surrounded by a Muslim crowd and was trying to bring home to them their duty.

284. Towards the end of September, Gandhi suffered from a severe attack of influenza. On the 26 September, his temperature rose to 102. But he did not stop giving interviews. Spinning of course, continued.

In the small hours of the night he was awakened by a particularly severe spasm of coughing. 'It reminds me of Ba's (Kasturba's) last illness', he muttered.

Manu tried to quieten him. 'Bapu, you must not talk. Try to snatch some sleep.'

285. The second of October 1947, was Gandhi's birthday. It was the last to be observed in his lifetime. When he entered his room after his bath at half-past-eight a small party of intimate friends was already there. It included Pandit Nehru who brought a tray of *parijat* flowers, the Sardar, G.D. Birla—his host—and all the members of the Birla family in Delhi.

Then came members of the Diplomatic Corps, some of them with greetings from their respective Governments. Lady Mountbatten arrived with a sheaf of letters and telegrams addressed to him.

286. 2 October 1947

287. To Sardar Patel.

288. In response to a Harijan reader who had written against sheltering 'frozen Muslim snakes' which would bite on revival.

289. In reply to a question from Acharya Kripalani whether it would not be better to work for a planned exodus of non-Muslims from Sind instead of allowing them to be turned away to India as homeless destitutes, Gandhi replied that he was opposed to an exchange of populations. In fact, he felt that the place of Sind Congress leaders at that juncture was in Sind. They should go there, he said, and, if necessary, die there and by their example teach the non-Muslims to meet with courage, faith, and self-respect the crisis that fed them.

290. Gandhi on 8 November 1948 at the All-India Congress Committee.

291. As the General was later to put it, this was 'a rocket'! On his return to India he called on Gandhi in the first week of December, on the eve of taking over the command of the Eastern Army. This was their first meeting. It happened to be Gandhi's day of silence. Declining to take his seat on a chair that Gandhi had offered him, the General respectfully sat on the floor. 'I have come here to receive your blessings...' he said to Gandhi. Gandhi scribbled this on a piece of paper.

292. When the General returned from Kashmir on the afternoon of 30 January 1948, the Mahatma was crossing over to another world.

293. In an interview to Vincent Sheean, the American author who interviewed him.

294. Some refugees from Bannu, survivors of the massacre on the train at Gujarat railway station on the eve of Gandhi's fast, came to Birla House in the afternoon of the 29 January for an audience with him. One of them said to him: 'You have done enough harm. You have ruined us utterly. You ought now leave us alone to retire to the Himalayas.'

    The whole day on the 29 January was crammed with engagements. At the end of it, he told Abha. 'My head is reeling. And yet I must finish this', pointing to the draft of the Congress constitution, which he had undertaken to prepare for the Congress Working Committee, and then added: 'I am afraid I shall have today to keep late hours.' (Pyarelal)

295. He mused why Congressmen, who had toiled and sacrificed for freedom's sake and on whom now rested the burden of independence, were succumbing to the lure of office and power. And then in a tone of infinite sadness he repeated the well-known verse of Nazir, the celebrated Urdu poet of Allahabad:

    Short-lived is the splendour of Spring
    in the garden of the world,
    Watch the brave show while it lasts. (Pyarelal)

The Pencil's Stub

Part One (1869–85)

So, father, your son is now, in your eyes, no better than a common thief!

p. 3

* * *

At his feet, his son, Mohandas.

p. 17

Part Two (1887–91)

A man at Brindisi: Sir, there is a beautiful girl of fourteen, follow me, sir, I will take you there, the charge is not high, sir.
19 year old MKG: Go away.

p. 26

* * *

My name is Gandhi. You have of course never heard of it.

p. 29

* * *

It (the Effiel Tower) was the toy of the Exhibition. We are attracted by toys and the Tower was a good demonstration of the fact that we are all children attracted by trinkets.

p. 31

Part Three (1891–3)

The sahib said, 'you must go now' ... He called his peon and ordered him to show me the door. I was still hesitating when the peon came in, placed his hands on my shoulders and put me out of the room ... This shock changed the course of my life.

p. 37

Part Four (1893–7)

I am yet inexperienced and young and, therefore, quite liable to make mistakes. The responsibility undertaken is quite out of proportion to my ability ... (Yet) I am the only available person who can handle the question.

p. 55

Part Five (1898–1901)

Kastur: '... what right have you to my necklace?'
Mohandas: '... is the necklace given to you for your service or my service?'
Kastur: 'I have toiled and moiled for you day and night. Is that no service?

p. 75

Part Six (1901–2)

I went to the Kashi Vishvanath temple for darshan. ...

... I had no mind to give any dakshina. So I offered a pie. The panda in charge got angry and threw away the pie. He swore at me and said, 'This insult will take you straight to hell.'

This did not perturb me. 'Maharaj,' said I, 'whatever fate has in store for me, it does not behove one of your class to indulge in such language. You may take this pie if you like, or you will lose that too.'

'Go away,' he replied, 'I don't care for your pie.' And then followed a further volley of abuse.

I took up the pie and went my way, flattering myself that the Brahman had lost a pie and I had saved one ...

p. 83

Part Seven (1902–5)

... if one's heart is pure, calamity brings in its train men and measures to fight it.

p. 96

* * *

The life of the tiller and of the handicraftsman is the life worth living.

p. 97

Part Eight (1906–9)

... my mind is now quite clear, my aspirations are higher and I have no desire for worldly enjoyments of any type whatever.

p. 108

* * *

I pondered over brahmacharya and its implications and my convictions took deep root ... I could not live both after the flesh and the spirit.

p. 109

* * *

Millie Graham Polak: What did the man want—anything special?

MKG: Yes, he wanted to kill me.

MGP: To kill you? To kill you? How horrible! Is he mad?

MKG: No, he is not mad, only mistaken; and you saw, after I had talked to him, he handed over to me the knife he had intended to use on me.

MGP: He would have stabbed you in the dark. I ... .

MKG: Do not disturb yourself so much about it. He thought he wanted to kill me; but he really had not the courage to do so. If I were as bad as he thought I was, I should deserve to die. Now we will not worry any more about it. It is finished.

p. 116

* * *

Then my assailants struck me with an iron pipe and a stick, and they also kicked me. Thinking me dead, they stopped. I only remember having been beaten up.

p. 117

* * *

I want every Indian to do what Harilal has done. ...

p. 119

* * *

My enthusiasm is such that I may have to meet death in South Africa at the hands of my own countrymen ... In this struggle, a two-fold inner struggle is going on. One of them is to bring the Hindus and Muslims together.

p. 123

* * *

Only a pitch-black wall separated one of the greatest murderers in South Africa and me. We were both in isolation cells by design, for we were both considered dangerous to society. I had to suffer in that cell for nearly two months.

p. 125

* * *

Part Nine (1909–14)

The Indians for whom I speak are comparatively poor and inferior in numbers, but are resolute unto death ...

p. 138

* * *

As in India, no socks were needed in the Transvaal but we thought that the feet must be protected against thorns, stones, and the like. We therefore determined to learn to make sandals.

p. 142

* * *

The weak became strong on Tolstoy Farm and labour proved to be a tonic for all.

p. 142

* * *

Please remember you are to try to make cheese without rennet.

p. 146

* * *

I have I think often told you that no man may be called good before his death. Departure by a hair's breadth from the straight and narrow path may undo the whole of his past.

p. 149

* * *

Dear Mr Gokhale,

Will you forgive me for all my imperfections? I want to be a worthy pupil of yours. This is not mock humility, but Indian seriousness. I want to realize in myself the conception I have of an Eastern pupil. We may have many differences of opinion, but you shall still be my pattern in political life ...

p. 151

* * *

It is wonderful what the human system is capable of doing when it is put to it.

p. 152

* * *

Devadas ... said ... he was afraid of being hit by me, as if I am in the habit of hitting boys. And so I felt that by way of a lesson to him I would deposit a few slaps on my cheeks which I did ... and wept bitterly.

p. 155

* * *

- I have (during this period) often wanted to take out the knife from my pocket and put it through the stomach. Sometimes I have felt like striking my head against the wall opposite, and at other times I have thought of running away from the world.

p. 158

(During the Great March) the following conditions were read out to them (marchers):

... They must not retreat even in the face of death ...
... No trees or plants on the way should be harmed ...
... They should cheerfully bear the hardships in gaol ...

p. 160

* * *

How can I forget her? Valliamma R. Munuswami Mudaliar was a young girl of Johannesburg only sixteen years of age. She was confined to bed when I saw her. As she was a tall girl, her emaciated body was a terrible thing to behold.

'Valliamma, you do not repent of your having gone to jail?' I asked.

'Repent? I am even now ready to go to jail again if I am arrested', said Valliamma.

'But what if it results in your death?' I pursued.

'I do not mind it. Who would not love to die for one's motherland?' was the reply.

Within a few days after this conversation Valliamma was no more with us in the flesh, but she left us the heritage of an immortal name.

p. 161

* * *

What a snare, a delusion this wretched civilisation in the midst of which you and I are still living. ...

p. 165

* * *

I have a strain of cruelty in me.

p. 170

* * *

... it was a great wrench for me to leave South Africa, where I had passed twenty-one years of my life sharing to the full in the sweets and bitters of human experience, and where I had realized my vocation in life.

p. 172

Part Ten (1914–25)

I remember, and he will remember how he came to me in Johannesburg Gaol, and said: 'Will not this letter do?' 'No Mr Cartwright,' was my reply, 'not until this alteration is made.' 'But everything is achieved by compromise', he urged. 'There can be no compromise on principles', I answered. There never was any compromise on principles from 1906 to 1914.

p. 184

* * *

Indians are altogether too generous, they overlook faults and magnify virtues; this had led us to incarnating our heroes.

p. 184

* * *

It was quite clear to me that participation in war could never be consistent with ahimsa. But it is not always given to one to be equally clear about one's duty. A votary of truth is often obliged to grope in the dark ...

p. 185

* * *

I hesitated to accept the courteous offer. I knew that my wife had no right to avail herself of the second class bathroom, but I ultimately connived at the impropriety. This, I know, does not become a votary of truth. Not that my wife was eager to use the bathroom, but a husband's partiality for his wife got the better of his partiality for truth. The face of truth is hidden behind the golden veil of maya, says the Upanishad.

p. 189

* * *

I see around me on the surface nothing but hypocrisy, humbug, degradation, yet underneath it, I trace a divinity I missed there as elsewhere. This is my India.

p. 191

* * *

... whenever I hear of a great palace rising in any great city of India ... I become jealous at once and I say 'Oh, it is the money that has come from the agriculturists.'

p.192

* * *

I honour the anarchist for his love of the country; but I ask him: Is killing honourable?

p. 192

* * *

The measure of progress is the measure of resistance to temptations. The world may judge us by a single fall.

p. 193

* * *

... peace with cowardice is much worse than a battlefield with victory.

p. 202

* * *

... I see that my countrymen are refraining from acts of physical violence not because of love for their fellows but from cowardice, and peace with cowardice is much worse than a battlefield with victory. I would rather they died fighting than cringe with fear. ...

p. 201

* * *

I thought I could finish the wheel of rebirth in this incarnation. I know now that I can't and that I shall have to return to it.

p. 202

* * *

Death does not matter.

p. 204

* * *

The will to live proved stronger than the devotion to truth.

p. 206

* * *

... Strange as it may appear, I feel lonelier here than in South Africa ... I do not know the people here; nor they, me.

p. 210

* * *

My complaint is not against pomp and splendour. Those who have money and no high aim in life will no doubt have them. They must have occasions to use their wealth. But I wish to see in all these things some discrimination and thought, some restraint and art. ...

p. 219

* * *

Personally I do not mind Governmental fury as I mind mob fury. The latter is a sign of national distemper and therefore more difficult to deal with than the former which is confined to a small corporation.

p. 220

* * *

It is easier to oust a Government that has rendered itself unfit to govern than it is to cure unknown people in a mob of their madness.

p. 220

* * *

Whenever I am in Calcutta the thought of the goats being sacrificed haunts me and makes me uneasy ... I am qualifying myself for the service of these fellow creatures of mine who are slaughtered in the name of my faith. I may not finish the work in this incarnation. I shall be born again to finish that work or someone who has realized my agony will finish it. ...

p. 225

* * *

To a people famishing and idle, the only acceptable form in which God can dare appear is work and promise of food as wages.

p. 229

* * *

I am an *anekantavadi*. I can see many sides of a question.

p. 233

* * *

I cannot imagine anything as ugly as the intercourse of man and woman.

p. 233

Part Eleven (1926–32)

... I have remained absolutely free from the habit of masturbation. Even today I am not able to understand it.

p. 257

* * *

If Miss Mayo had confessed that she had gone to India merely to open out and examine the drains of India, there would perhaps be little to complain about her compilation. But she says in effect with a certain amount of triumph, 'The drains are India'. ...

p. 258

* * *

I am clear in my mind that there is no room for castes in the Hindu faith.

p. 265

* * *

I cannot exist without dietetic experiments if I am fixed up at any place for any length of time.

p. 265

* * *

There can be no living harmony between races and nations unless the main cause is removed, namely, exploitation of the weak by the strong. We must revise the interpretation of the so-called doctrine of 'the survival of the fittest'.

p. 266

* * *

Indians...cannot exist in South Africa for any length of time without the active sympathy and friendship of the Africans.

p. 267

* * *

The world knows so little of how much my so-called greatness depends upon the incessant toil and drudgery of silent, devoted, able, and pure workers, men as well as women.

p. 268

* * *

I have no false modesty about me. I am undoubtedly a politician in my own way, and I have a scheme for the country's freedom. But my time is not yet and may never come to me in this life.

p. 269

* * *

I am but an ordinary mortal susceptible to the same weakness, influences, and the rest as every other human being and that I possess no extraordinary powers.

p. 270

* * *

The Congress crown has ceased to be a crown of roses. The rose petals are year by year falling off and the thorns are becoming more and more prominent. Who should wear such a crown? ... My own feeling in the matter is that Pandit Jawaharlal should wear the crown. The future must be for the youth of the country.

p. 270

* * *

... supposing that in the case of an ailing friend I am unable to render any aid whatever and recovery is out of the question and the patient is lying in an unconscious state in the throes of fearful agony, then I would not see any himsa in putting an end to his suffering by death.

I have never entered into any business transaction about my writings.

p. 272

* * *

I have never tabooed all Western ideas, nor am I prepared to anathematize everything that comes from the West as inherently evil.

p. 272

* * *

... Generally speaking, I would say 'no divorce'. But if your temperaments are incompatible, you should live in voluntary separation.

p. 274

* * *

I have never entered into any business transactions about my writings.

p. 275

* * *

Jawaharlal ... has no secrets. If he finds any use for revolvers in his scheme for the freedom of the country, he will carry it himself and use it effectively when in his opinion the occasion has arrived.

p. 276

* * *

Unless the capitalists of India (devote) their talents not to amassing wealth for themselves but to the service of the masses in an altruistic spirit, they will end either by destroying themselves or being destroyed by them.

p. 276

* * *

He who is born dies, and he who dies is born again. Some do escape this cycle, but neither they nor the others need rejoice at birth or grieve over death.

p. 279

* * *

You read your Milton, your Browning, and your Whittier, all right. Is this what you have learnt from them to reduce your wives who should be the queens of your hearts and your homes into londis? Shame, shame on you!

p. 280

* * *

It is of course God's will that prevails and human intelligence follows the laws of *karma*. Man is however entitled to use his reason.

p. 281

* * *

I must admit that wherever I go I am sought out by fools, cranks, and faddists.

p. 283

* * *

I have always felt that riding in cars makes men proud. The chauffeurs who drive are vain and hot-tempered. One should beware of drivers with a hot temper.

p. 283

* * *

We can call this (spitting in public places) a national vice.

p. 284

* * *

Surely there is no necessary connection between honesty and khadi. Even rogues must cover themselves and therefore may wear khadi. I am sorry also to have to confess that not all the workers in the employ of the All India Spinners' Association have always been found to be honest ...

p. 285

* * *

From violence done to the foreign ruler, violence to our own people whom we may consider to be obstructing the country's progress is an easy and natural step.

p. 287

* * *

I hold that a murderer is just as much entitled to have his needs supplied as any other prisoner.

p. 294

* * *

Asanas and pranayama may be of some slight help in steadying the mind and making it single-purposed, provided that they are practised to that end. Otherwise they are no better than other methods of physical training.

p. 297

* * *

Q. Do you believe in immortality?
A. Yes, reincarnation and transmigration of souls are fundamentals of the Hindu religion.

p. 302

* * *

Execution is an irretrievable act. If you think there is the slightest chance of error of judgment, I would urge you to suspend for further review an act that is beyond recall.

p. 303

* * *

Bhagat Singh and his companions have been executed and have become martyrs ... And yet I must warn the youth of the country against following their example. We should not utilize our energy, our spirit of sacrifice, our labours, and our indomitable courage in the way they have utilized theirs. This country must not be liberated through bloodshed. ...

p. 303

* * *

If I go to England I shall ... appear not as the English would have me but as my representative character demands ... I can therefore appear neither in English costume nor in that of the polished Nehrus.

p. 307

* * *

MKG: How many children have you?
Ben Platten: Eight, sir, four sons and four daughters.
MKG: I have four sons so I can race with you half-way.

p. 311

* * *

I am sure that most people eat much too much.

p. 314

* * *

You must realize that we cannot afford to have doorkeepers at your (English officialdom in India) rate of wages, for you are no better than doorkeepers and a nation with an income of two pence a day per head cannot pay those wages.

p. 315

* * *

I have the highest regard for Dr Ambedkar ... But the separate electorates that he seeks will not give him social reform. He may himself mount to power and position, but nothing good will accrue to the untouchables ...

p. 316

* * *

Q. Do you say that you are completely fit for independence?
A. If we are not, we will try to be.

p. 316

* * *

Q. How far would you cut India off from the Empire?
A. From the Empire entirely; from the British nation not at all.

p. 316

* * *

Q. Do you ever suffer from nerves?
A. Ask Mrs Gandhi. ...

p. 317

* * *

Q. I thought you were the sworn enemy of all machines. How does
    it happen that you use a watch?
A. I must know what time it is ...

p. 320

* * *

... Please send me the larger size flask. It will be useful for keeping
hot water, saving the labour of warders early morning ...

p. 324

* * *

The Mahabharata is a poem and not history.

p. 325

* * *

I have no idea what I am going to say on any occasion but God gives
me the appropriate word. This is power indeed, but it should be
generated spontaneously.

p. 330

* * *

I certainly did not drink but Harilal has made up for that. I sought
my pleasure only with one woman. Harilal seeks his with many. It is
only a difference of degree, not of kind.

p. 336

* * *

Uncle Tom's Cabin is propaganda pure and simple, but its art is inimitable.

p. 337

* * *

It is the heart which matters; all else is false. ...

p. 338

* * *

... if we knew all the laws of God we should be able to account for the unaccountable.

p. 338

* * *

(Do not) behave towards his wife as I did towards Ba.

p. 340

* * *

Only one in millions meets the death for which he has prayed.

p. 343

* * *

What I want, what I am living for, and what I should delight in dying for, is the eradication of untouchability root and branch.

p. 343

* * *

...I am not too proud to make a confession of my blunder, whatever the cost of the confession, if I find myself in error. ...

p. 343

* * *

Ambedkar: But I have only one quarrel with you, that is, you work for the so-called national welfare and not for our interests alone. If you devoted yourself entirely to the welfare of the Depressed Classes, you would then become our hero.

Gandhi: Very sweet of you to say so.

p. 344

* * *

Untouchability is a soul-destroying sin. Caste is a social evil.

p. 347

Part Twelve (1933–6)

Do you keep any idol or any picture of Shri Rama or Shri Krishna when you offer prayers in the morning and at night?
MKG: No.

Do you believe that it is necessary to go to a temple for darshan of the image for attaining emancipation and for acquiring supreme love for God?
MKG: No.

p. 354

* * *

I had, not very many years ago, all but fallen, but the thought of Devadas, who was then living with me, of Mahadev, Mathuradas, and others who were at that time surrounding me and whom I believed to be themselves leaning on me, and the thought of my wife, kept me from going to perdition.

p. 355

* * *

I can live for some days at least without the daily bread, but I cannot live without Harijan service for one single minute.

p. 361

* * *

My dear Jawaharlal,

India cannot stand in isolation and unaffected by what is going on in other parts of the world. I can, therefore, go the whole length with you and say that 'we should range ourselves with the progressive forces of the world'. But I know that though there is such an agreement between you and me in the enunciation of ideals, there are temperamental differences between us. ...

p. 362

* * *

... one should never read what has been scored out by the writer of a letter. If one reads it by chance, one should not pay any attention to it.

p. 363

* * *

... if there was a map of untouchability made for the whole of India, Malabar would be marked as the blackest spot in all the land ...

p. 369

* * *

I want you to be 'superstitious' enough with me to believe that the earthquake is a divine chastisement for the great sin we have committed and are still committing against those whom we describe as untouchables, Panchamas, and whom I describe as Harijans.

p. 371

* * *

I am not affected by posers such as 'why punishment for an age-old sin' or 'why punishment to Bihar and not to the South' or 'why an earthquake and not some other form of punishment'. My answer is: I am not God.

p. 372

* * *

I do believe that super-physical consequences flow from physical events. How they do so, I do not know.

p. 372

* * *

I have felt that in cases of domestic illness or sorrow the government has acted in a becoming manner ... we ought to recognize this fact by not using the liberty thus obtained for any other purpose not inconsistent with that of the government.

p. 375

* * *

What is this about music and cinema? Do they wish to turn the Congress session into a Felix Circus or Barnum show? But, then, what can I say in this matter? I do love music, but everything is good in its place.

p. 376

* * *

I make no hobgoblin of consistency. If I am true to myself from moment to moment, I do not mind all the inconsistencies that may be flung in my face.

p. 379

* * *

Mary Chesley: Have you had any mystical experiences?

MKG: If, by mystical experiences, you mean visions, no. I should be a fraud if I claimed to have had such. But I am very sure of the voice which guides me.

p. 380

* * *

Mary Chesley: How do you understand what is God's guidance for you when it is a question of choosing between two good things?

MKG: I use my intellect on the subject and if I don't get any strong feeling as to which of the two I should choose, I just leave the matter, and before long I wake up one morning with the perfect assurance that it should be A rather than B.

p. 380

* * *

My ignorance is really appalling in the domain of literature ...

p. 381

* * *

Mrs C. Kuttan Nair: Will not the teaching of sex hygiene in schools in the most scientific and informal manner be really beneficial to our boys and girls?

MKG: Yes. And there should be no reason why one should not be able to talk freely on this matter.

p. 383

* * *

Mrs Nair: Are you in favour of sterilization as is being done in Germany under Hitler?

MKG: Sterilization is a sort of contraceptive and though I am against the use of contraceptives in the case of women, I do not mind voluntary sterilization in the case of man, since he is the aggressor.

p. 383

* * *

Anger is a kind of madness and when it subsides you will laugh at yourself ...

p. 385

* * *

I remember Josiah Oldfield well. He was of the greatest help to me when I went to London as a lad. He is a fellow crank.

p. 385

* * *

If one is to consider the degrees of cruelty, the pig seems to require the most cruelty before it can be killed. My purpose in writing this is to show that Harijans are the least offenders in this matter ... We must not take up any stick that comes our way to beat the poor Harijan with.

p. 386

* * *

I can't put my faith in vaids. Their remedies are like black magic.

p. 388

* * *

... the more intimate the blood-relationship, the stricter should our attitude be.

p. 389

* * *

When I was in Africa, I tried to use as many things as I could, made by African hands.

p. 391

* * *

Visitor: You would judge the Buddha?
MKG: I never said so. I simply said, if I had the good fortune to be face to face with one like him, I should not hesitate to ask him why he did not teach the gospel of work, in preference to one of contemplation.

p. 396

* * *

... My wife I made the orbit of all women, and in her I studied all women.

p. 396

* * *

Whilst I was asleep I suddenly felt as though I wanted to see a woman. Well, a man who had tried to rise superior to the instinct for nearly forty years was bound to be intensely pained when he had this frightful experience. I ultimately conquered the feeling, but I was face to face with the blackest moment of my life and if I had succumbed to it, it would have meant my absolute undoing.

p. 397

* * *

I am not aware of any of us having derived any benefit, mental, spiritual, or physical from sexual union. Momentary excitement and satisfaction there certainly was. But it was invariably followed by exhaustion.

p. 400

* * *

I had a discharge, but I was awake and the mind was under control. I understood the cause and from that time stopped taking rest as prescribed by the doctors. And my state now is better than it was, if such a state could be imagined.

p. 401

* * *

John R. Mott: What is the cause of your greatest concern, your heaviest burden?

MKG: My greatest worry is the ignorance and poverty of the masses of India, and the way in which they have been neglected by the classes, especially the neglect of the Harijans by the Hindus ...

p. 407

* * *

Women, as it is, are slaves. In the act of piercing their noses and ears, I have never seen anything but a symbol of their slavery. By tying a string to her ear-rings, a woman can be pulled like a bullock.

p. 408

Part Thirteen (1937–42)

... my non-violence is independent of the sanction of scriptures.

p. 419

* * *

I write not a line without deep conviction.

p. 421

* * *

I think it is not only a right, but a duty for any Congressman to openly criticize acts of Congress officials, no matter however highly placed they may be. The criticism has got to be courteous and well-informed.

p. 425

* * *

... Acharya Kripalani is quite correct in saying that there is no such thing as Gandhism.

p. 427

* * *

How can one eat one's fill without a sense of guilt in this poverty-stricken country?

p. 427

* * *

Dear Mr Jinnah,

... When in 1915 I returned from the self-imposed exile in South Africa, everybody spoke of you as one of the staunchest of nationalists and the hope of both Hindus and Mussalmans. Are you still the same Mr Jinnah? If you say you are, in spite of your speeches I shall accept your word.

p. 428

* * *

... I wish you to visit Ramana Maharshi as early as possible.

p. 430

* * *

The cry for the national home for the Jews does not make much appeal to me ... I have no doubt that they are going about it the wrong way. The Palestine of the Biblical conception is not a geographical tract. It is in their hearts. But if they must look to the Palestine of geography as their national home, it is wrong to enter it under the shadow of the British gun.

p. 433

* * *

I rarely read anything outside my beat.

p. 434

* * *

... It will be waste of good money to spend Rs 25,000 on erecting a clay or metallic statue of a man who is himself made of clay. ...

p. 437

* * *

There are certainly differences between Jawaharlal and me. But they are not significant. Without him I feel myself a cripple. He also feels more or less the same way. Our hearts are one.

p. 440

* * *

Jawaharlal ... thinks I am impossible for an organization. He is right there.

p. 440

* * *

As a lad, when I knew nothing of *Anandmath* or even Bankim, its immortal author, *Vandemataram* had gripped me, and when I first heard it sung, it had enthralled me. I associated the purest national spirit with it. It never occurred to me that it was a Hindu song or meant only for Hindus. Unfortunately now we have fallen on evil days. All that was pure gold before has become base metal today. In such times it is wisdom not to market pure gold and let it be sold as base metal. I would not risk a single quarrel over singing *Vandemataram*.

p. 440

* * *

Supposing I have a cancer, and it is only a question of time for me to pass away, I would even ask my doctor to give me a sleeping draught and thereby have the sleep that knows no waking ...

p. 442

* * *

C. Rajagopalachari knows me well and so he has wisely vetoed the proposal to declare my birthday a public holiday. ...

p. 444

* * *

I cling to an old superstition, if it may be so called. When in doubt on a matter involving no immorality either way, I toss and actually read in it divine guidance. I have no other scientific basis.

p. 446

* * *

All of us live in the jaws of death. As long as it does not swallow us we may go about dancing.

p. 446

* * *

I am proud of being a Hindu, but I have never gone to anybody as a Hindu to secure Hindu-Muslim unity ... whatever talks I had with Quaid-e-Azam or any other have been on behalf of the Congress which is not a Hindu organization. Can a Hindu organization have a Muslim divine as President, and can its Working Committee have four Muslim members out of 15?

p. 450

* * *

Q. Is it true that an Indian is a Hindu or a Muslim first and an Indian afterwards?

MKG: It is not true, generally speaking, though neither will sell his religion for his country.

p. 451

* * *

Who can dispute the fact that the grinding poverty of the masses is due to their having no land that they can call their own?

p. 451

* * *

My life is made up of compromises, but they have been compromises that have brought me nearer the goal. Pakistan cannot be worse than foreign domination.

p. 453

* * *

Q. Would you prefer Muslim rule to British rule?

MKG: The question is badly put ... Muslim rule is equivalent to Indian rule ... It makes no difference to me that some Muslims regard themselves as a separate nation. It is enough for me that I do not consider them as such. They are sons of the soil.

p. 453

* * *

Q. ... don't you agree that the test-tube technique of begetting babies is ideal since it altogether eliminates lust and carnality from procreation?

MKG: ... Your method, as far as I can see, can only result in multiplying idiots or monsters, not human beings, thrown into the sea of passions. ...

p. 454

* * *

Q. I am a believer in ahimsa as well as Pakistan. How can I use the ahimsa principle for the realization of my ideal?

MKG: It is not possible to attain an iniquitous end by non-violent means. For instance, you cannot commit theft non-violently.

p. 456

* * *

In this *Kali Yuga*, you get more fruit for less work.

p. 458

* * *

I am afraid our universities are the blotting-sheets of the West.

p. 463

* * *

Q. I want to ask just this: A man is strangling me. Meanwhile another man comes to strangle him. Should I not help the other fellow to strangle my strangler?

MKG: I am a non-violent person, and I say by all means struggle for your freedom but then stop. My self-esteem will not allow me to help in strangling my strangler. No, I cannot help the Japanese.

p. 472

* * *

Louis Fischer: What is your programme for the improvement of the lot of the peasantry?

MKG: The peasants would take the land. We would not have to tell them to take it. They would take it.

LF: Would the landlords be compensated?

MKG: No. That would be fiscally impossible. You see, our gratitude to our millionaire friends does not prevent us from saying such things.

p. 475

* * *

Louis Fischer: I would like to talk to you for a few moments about Subhas Chandra Bose, who has escaped to Axis territory.

MKG: I regard Bose as a patriot of patriots. He maybe misguided. I think he is misguided. I have often opposed Bose. Twice I kept him from becoming president of Congress. Finally he did become president, although my views often differed from his. But suppose he had gone to Russia or to America to ask aid for India. Would that have made it better?

LF: Yes, of course. It does make a difference to whom you go.

MKG: I do not want help from anybody to make India free. I want India to save herself.

p. 476

* * *

Louis Fischer: Well, how do you actually see your impending civil disobedience movement? What shape will it take?

MKG: In the villages, the peasants will stop paying taxes ... refusal to pay it will give the peasants the courage to think that they are capable of independent action. Their next step will be to seize the land.

LF: With violence.

MKG: There maybe fifteen days of chaos, but I think we could soon bring that under control

LF: You feel then that it must be confiscation without compensation?

MKG: Of course. It would be financially impossible for anybody to compensate the landlords ... I am a man possessed by an idea. If such a man cannot get an organization, he becomes an organization. ...

p. 477

* * *

Here is a mantra, a short one, that I give you. You may imprint it on your hearts and let every breath of yours give expression to it. The mantra is: 'Do or Die.' We shall either free India or die in the attempt; we shall not live to see the perpetuation of our slavery.

p. 486

Part Fourteen (1942–8)

I have called the Nazis and Fascists the scum of the earth.

p. 516

* * *

... It is no pleasure for me to be in this camp, where all my creature comforts are supplied without any effort on my part, when I know that millions outside are starving for want of food.

p. 519

* * *

Though for her sake I have welcomed her death as bringing freedom from living agony, I feel the loss more than I had thought I should. We were a couple outside the ordinary ...

p. 522

* * *

I myself feel firmly that Mr Jinnah does not block the way, but the British Government do not want a just settlement of the Indian claim for independence which is overdue, and they are using Mr Jinnah as a cloak for denying freedom to India ...

p. 526

* * *

The more I think about the two-nation theory the more alarming it appears to be ... I am unable to accept the proposition that the Muslims of India are a nation, distinct from the rest of the inhabitants of India ... Once the principle is admitted there would be no limit to claims for cutting up India into numerous divisions, which would spell India's ruin.

p. 534

* * *

I was wondering what I shall send you today. It should be fair on my part to let you and your sister share equally the crisp chapatis they make for me. Here is your share. Please regard it as a token of my love and do please help yourself to it.

p. 535

* * *

... I want to make it clear that I believe Mr Jinnah is sincere, but I think he is suffering from hallucination when he imagines that an unnatural division of India could bring either happiness or prosperity to the people concerned.

p. 538

* * *

N.G. Ranga: Are we right in thinking that you stand for the abolition of this process of exploitation of the producers of primary commodities and the agricultural masses of the world?
MKG: Root and branch.

p. 539

* * *

Jawaharlal is a jewel among men. Happy is the land that owns him.

p. 539

* * *

The *atman* has neither birth nor death.

p. 541

* * *

I don't want Hindi to die nor Urdu to be banished.

p. 542

* * *

I say, let Hindi and Urdu both prosper. I have to take work from both. Even today, Hindustani exists but we do not utilize it. This is the age of Hindi and Urdu. These are two streams from which the third will flow. Hence it will not do if the first two dry up.

p. 542

* * *

Life is only a short spell of moonlight. In the end all is dust.

p. 542

* * *

Sleep in *shavasana* as I do.

p. 543

* * *

He can serve by writing a true and original history of the people. If there is progress he will describe the progress; if he finds there is decline he will record that decline.

p. 544

* * *

K.R. Narayanan: How can a Harijan who goes abroad best serve his country and community from abroad?

MKG: He cannot serve the one without the other. Abroad you will say it is a domestic question which you are determined to solve for yourselves.

p. 545

* * *

The national language is = Hindi + Urdu.

p. 546

* * *

I know the European mind well enough to know that when it has to choose between abstract justice and self-interest, it will plump for the latter.

p. 547

* * *

I react to a situation intuitively. Logic comes afterwards, it does not precede the event.

p. 548

* * *

I hope to live for 125 years but there are many obstacles in the way. Even supposing I survived, it seems to me I shall only be an adviser.

p. 548

* * *

Why should a woman be given a different name when she goes to live with her husband and why not a man? This custom irks me very much.

p. 551

* * *

Ram Rajya ... can be religiously translated as Kingdom of God on Earth; politically translated, it is perfect democracy in which inequalities based on possession and non-possession, colour, race or creed, or sex vanish; in it, land and State belong to the people, justice is prompt, perfect, and cheap and, therefore, there is freedom of worship, speech, and the Press—all this because of the reign of the self-imposed law of moral restraint.

p. 555

* * *

Correspondent: What will be the composition of the interim government if you have your way?

MKG: (*laughing*) The interim government will consist of top men, irrespective of caste, creed, or colour. If I became the Viceroy of India, I would startle the world with my list and yet make it acceptable.

Of course, nobody will take the trouble of appointing me the Viceroy of India ...

p. 558

* * *

My window opens on the Himalayas ... Now the eyes are stuck on the scene, so is the mind.

p. 558

* * *

How useful it would be if the engineers in India were to apply their ability to the perfecting of village tools and machines. This must not be beneath their dignity.

p. 561

* * *

... can you make the whole of India forget it? Can you reverse the flow of water and make it go upward? After the British have left, will it be possible to wipe all the consequences of the British connection off history?

p. 563

* * *

The Ganapati festival, and such others, are entirely of a political character and have nothing to do with religion. We cannot, therefore, celebrate them ... man himself being, in a sense, an image, he will always remain an image-worshipper.

p. 564

* * *

What message can a labourer give to a labour union? I have not heard of anyone sending a message to himself.

p. 566

* * *

Q. Should Santiniketan allow itself to be drawn into political work?
A. I have no difficulty in saying that Santiniketan and Visva-Bharati ought not to be mixed up with politics ...

Q. In order to make Visva-Bharati really an international university, should we not try to increase the material resources of the university?

A. By material resources I suppose you mean finance. Let me then say that your question is addressed to a person who does not swear by material resources. 'Material resources' is after all a comparative term. For instance, I do not go without food and clothing. In my own way I have tried—more than perhaps any other man—to increase the level of material resources of the average man in India. But it is my firm conviction that Visva-Bharati will fail to attract the right type of talent and scholarship if it relies on the strength of the material resources or material attractions that it can offer. Its attraction must be moral or ethical, or else it will become just one out of the many educational institutions in India.

p. 567

* * *

Music in Santiniketan is charming, but has the professor there come to the conclusion that Bengali music is the last word in that direction?

p. 568

* * *

The hypnotism of the Indian National Army has cast its spell upon us. Netaji's name is one to conjure with. His patriotism is second to none. (I use the present tense intentionally.) His bravery shines through all his actions. He aimed high but failed. Who has not failed? Ours is to aim high and to aim well. It is not given to everyone to command success. My praise and admiration can go no further.

p. 569

* * *

There is a time for laughing and shouting and a time for observing silence and being serious ... But laughter becomes an offence against decorum, if it is out of season. Similarly shouting out of season is an exhibition of bad manners.

p. 570

* * *

I do not appreciate any underground activity.

p. 573

* * *

Agatha Harrison: Won't you ask people to grow flowers on a small piece of land? Colour and beauty are necessary to the soul as food is to the body.

MKG: No, I won't. Why can't you see the beauty of colour in vegetables? And then there is beauty in the speckless sky. But no, you want the colours of the rainbow which is a mere optical illusion.

p. 573

* * *

Zamindar: Where shall we stand when India is independent?

MKG: You will be as free as any scavenger ...

p. 581

* * *

India will have to decide whether attempting to become a military power she would be content to become, at least for some years, a fifth-rate power in the world without a message ...

p. 582

* * *

Valmiki is another word for *Bhangi*. Their living quarters in Simla are deplorable. No one bothers about them.

p. 583

* * *

An English friend: If all nations were armed with the atom bomb would not they refrain from using it as it would mean absolute destruction for all concerned.

MKG: They would not. The violent man's eyes would light up with the prospect of the much greater amount of destruction and death which he could now wreak.

p. 584

* * *

The blood of the villages is the cement with which the edifice of the cities is built.

p. 584

* * *

I have discovered honourable members of Assemblies using most expensive embossed note-paper even for private use. So far as I know, office stationery cannot be used for private purposes such as writing to friends or relatives or for letters from members of assemblies to Constituents outside matters of public business.

p. 586

* * *

If I were appointed dictator for a day in the place of the Viceroy, I would stop all newspapers ... With the exception of *Harijan* of course.

p. 589

* * *

Jayaprakash is an outstanding general in India's fight for freedom. Any country will be proud of such jewels among men. Like Jawahar and Subhas, he too is impatient to a degree, but this is a virtue considering the prevailing circumstances. I adore Jayaprakash.

p. 591

* * *

They (the Cabinet Mission) should not have dealt with him (Jinnah) in that legalistic manner. ... He is a great Indian and the recognized leader of a great organization.

p. 593

* * *

Louis Fischer: The growing anti-white feeling here is bad. In the Taj Mahal Hotel (Bombay) they have put up a notice 'South Africans not admitted'. I do not like it. Your non-violence should make you more generous.

MKG: That won't be non-violence. Today the white man rules in

India. So, if the Taj Mahal Hotel has the gumption to put up that notice, it is a feather in its cap.

p. 597

* * *

Q. Is God a person or a principle?
MKG: Nobody knows ... and nobody is likely ever to know.

p. 599

* * *

We are not in the midst of civil war. But we are nearing it.

p. 600

* * *

... We shall have full freedom only when our uncrowned king Pandit Jawaharlal Nehru and his colleagues in the Interim Government devote themselves to the service of the poor as people expect them to do.

p. 601

* * *

It is far better to magnify your mistake and proclaim it to the whole world than leave it to the world to point the accusing finger at you.

p. 609

* * *

I find myself in the midst of exaggeration and falsity. I am unable to discover the truth. There is a terrible mutual distrust.

p. 613

* * *

What shall I do? What shall I do?

p. 615

* * *

I don't want to die a failure. But I may be a failure.

p. 615

* * *

I have seen enough of ravages in Noakhali to make me weep my eyes out but I am not going to shed a tear for what has happened. We have a long way yet to go.

p. 615

* * *

Noakhali has become a laboratory, where a crucial test is being made; the remedy will apply to situations all the world over where disputes arise between communities and nationalities and a new technique is needed for peaceful adjustment.

p. 617

* * *

I don't want to return from Bengal defeated. I would rather die, if need be, at the hands of an assassin.

p. 617

* * *

Everything seems to be going awry. There is falsehood all around.

p. 618

* * *.

A surgeon who fights shy of performing an appendectomy, when a patient comes to him with a suppurating appendix, sends his patient to certain death. He has to be prompt and ruthless if he is to save the patient's life. I am a surgeon of that type.

p. 620

* * *

Jinnah had declared that in Pakistan the minorities would, if possible, have better treatment even than the Muslims, there would be no under-dog nor upper-dog; if the Muslim majority Provinces, where it was as good as Pakistan, became wholly independent of the British Power and realized that ideal set forth by Jinnah in practice, the whole of India would welcome such an order, no matter by what name it was called, and the whole of India would be Pakistan.

p. 621

* * *

If there are women who when assailed by miscreants cannot resist themselves without arms, they do not need to be *advised* to carry arms. They will do so.

p. 622

* * *

A.V. Thakkar: Why this experiment here?

MKG: You are mistaken, Bapa; it is not an experiment but an integral part of my *yajna*. One may forgo an experiment; one cannot forgo one's duty. Now if I regard a thing as a part of my yajna—a sacred duty—I may not give it up even if public opinion is wholly against me. I am engaged in achieving self-purification. The five cardinal observances are the five props of my spiritual striving. Brahmacharya is one of them ...

AVT: Your Ahimsa has not failed. Do not miss the wood for the trees ... Just think what would have been the fate of Noakhali if you had not come. The world does not think of brahmacharya as you do.

MKG: If I accept your contention then it would amount to this that I should give up what I hold to be right for me, for fear of displeasing the world ...

AVT: What if your example is copied?

MKG: If there is blind imitation or unscrupulous exploitation of my example, society will not and should not tolerate it. But if there is sincere, bona fide, honest endeavour, society should welcome it and it will be the better for it ...

p. 628

* * *

I find today darkness reigning over India and my eyes vainly turn from one direction to another to see light.

p. 632

* * *

Anger is a sort of madness. But it should be up to you and me to meet madness not with madness but with sanity.

p. 635

* * *

MKG: Who listens to me today?

Co-worker: ... The people are behind you.

MKG: Even they are not. I am being told to retire to the Himalayas. Everybody is eager to garland my photos and statues. Nobody really wants to follow my advice.

Co-worker: They may not today, but they will have to before long.

MKG: What is the good?

p. 642

* * *

The time is fast approaching when India will have to elect the first President of the Republic. I would have proposed the name of Chakrayya, had he been alive.

p. 642

* * *

Dare the British impose Pakistan on an India temporarily gone mad?

p. 642

* * *

Partition has come inspite of me. It has hurt me. But it is the way in which the partition has come that has hurt me more.

p. 644

* * *

If the women of Asia wake up, they will dazzle the world.

p. 649

* * *

I shall be alive in the grave and, what is more, speaking from it.

p. 649

* * *

Much water has flown under the bridge since August 1946. What the Muslims did then was utterly wrong. But what is the use of avenging the year 1946 on 1947?

p. 650

* * *

From tomorrow (15 August) we shall be delivered from the bondage of the British rule. But from midnight today, India will be partitioned too. While, therefore, tomorrow will be a day of rejoicing, it will be a day of sorrow as well.

p. 651

* * *

Is this to be called a miracle or an accident? By whatever name it may be described, it is quite clear that the credit that is being given to me from all sides is quite undeserved ... We have drunk the poison of mutual hatred and so this nectar of fraternization tastes all the sweeter and the sweetness should never wear out.

p. 653

* * *

Thousands have been killed! A few thousand girls have been kidnapped! Hindus cannot live in the Pakistan area, nor Muslims in the other portion. Add to this the information that the two wings of the army took sides and worked havoc! Can any of this be true?

p. 654

* * *

What madness is this? Why do not you attack me? I offer myself for attack.

p. 655

* * *

C. Rajagopalachari: Why not wait and watch a little?

MKG: The fast has to be now or never ...

CR: But supposing you die, the conflagration would be worse.

MKG: At least I won't be a living witness of it. I shall have done my duty. More is not given to a man to do.

CR: Why add sour lime juice to water if you are to put yourself entirely in God's hands?

MKG: You are right. I allowed it out of weakness. It jarred on me even as I wrote it. A satyagrahi must hope to survive his conditional fast only by the timely fulfilment of the terms of his fast.

p. 657

* * *

It is we who make the goondas and we alone can unmake them. Goondas never act on their own. By themselves they cannot function.

p. 661

* * *

India has to expiate for the massacre of the innocents.

p. 662

* * *

I would urge the Muslims of Delhi to shed all fear, trust God, and discover all the arms in their possession which the Hindus and Sikhs fear they have. Either the minority rely upon God and His creature man to do the right thing or rely upon their firearms to defend themselves against those whom, they feel, they must not trust.

p. 664

* * *

Those who seek justice must do justice, must have clean hands.

p. 664

* * *

The desire to live for 125 years has completely vanished as a result of this continued fratricide.

p. 666

* * *

Hindus and Muslims are not two nations. Muslims never shall be slaves of Hindus nor Hindus of Muslims. Hence you and I have to die in the attempt to make them live together as friends and brothers, which they are.

p. 666

* * *

... when someone commits a crime anywhere I feel I am the culprit.

p. 667

* * *

We should never make the mistake of thinking that we never make any mistakes.

p. 667

* * *

I fancy I know the art of living and dying non-violently. But I have yet to demonstrate it by one perfect act.

p. 667

* * *

When it is relevant, truth has to be uttered, however unpleasant it may be ... Misdeeds of the Hindus in the Union have to be proclaimed by Hindus from the housetop, if those of the Muslims in Pakistan are to be arrested or stopped.

p. 668

* * *

My sole hope and prayer is that Kashmir should become a beacon light to this benighted sub-continent.

p. 670

* * *

If the invaders, tribesmen, and others, would withdraw and leave the issue to the rebels in Poonch and the rest of Kashmir without any aid from outside, it would be time to ask the Indian troops to withdraw.

p. 671

* * *

As things are, we cannot hold our heads high in the world today and we have to confess that we have been obliged to copy Pakistan in its misdeeds and have thereby justified its ways ...

p. 671

* * *

The fool! Don't you see, there is a terrible and widespread conspiracy behind it?

p. 679

* * *

If I die of a lingering illness...it will be your duty to proclaim to the world, even at the risk of making people angry with you, that I was not the man of God that I claimed to be.

p. 681

* * *

I hate being late. I like to be at the prayer punctually at the stroke of five.

p. 683

The I's, I am's, Me's, Mine's and My's in Gandhi's Essential Writings

IMPRISONMENTS

(The periods listed include the days of arrest and of release.)

SOUTH AFRICA

10.1.1908 to 30.1.1908	Johannesburg
7.10.1908 to 25.10.1908	Volksrust
26.10.1908 to 5.11.1908	Johannesburg
6.11.1908 to 12.12.1908	Volksrust
25.2.1909 to 2.3.1909	Volksrust
3.3.1909 to 24.5.1909	Pretoria
6.11.1913 to 7.11.1913	Charlestown
9.11.1913 to 12.11.1913	Dundee
12.11.1913 to 17.11.1913	Volksrust
18.11.1913 to 17.12.1913	Bloemfontein

INDIA

9.4.1919 to 11.4.1919	Railway carriage
10.3.1922 to 20.3.1922	Sabarmati Jail
21.3.1922 to 11.1.1924	Yeravda Jail
12.1.1924 to 5.2.1924	Yeravda Jail (Sassoon Hospital)
5.5.1930 to 26.1.1931	Yeravda Jail
4.1.1932 to 8.5.1933	Yeravda Jail
1.8.1933	Sabarmati Jail
2.8.1933 to 4.8.1933	Yeravda Jail
4.8.1933 to 23.8.1933	Yeravda Jail
9.8.1942 to 6.5.1944	Aga Khan Palace Prison, Poona.

(C.B. Dalal's compilations in *Gandhijini Dinavari: 1869–1915* and *1915–48*)

FASTS

(Gandhi went on fasts several times, the durations ranging from 24 hours to 21 days. Sometimes he commenced fasts saying they could be 'unto death', unless certain conditions were fulfilled. The periods shown include the day on which the fast started, but not the day on which it ended. The list does not include the fasts in South Africa.)

Date/Duration	Venue	Reason
1915		
June 1	Ahmedabad	Following the detection of untruth among Ashram boys.
September 11	Ahmedabad	To counter 'protest fasts' of some Ashramites who objected to a Harijan being admitted to the Ashram.
September 12	Ahmedabad	After detecting an Ashramite smoking.
1916		
May or June 12 to 15	Ahmedabad	Because Manilal Gandhi had sent a sum of money to Harilal Gandhi.
1918		
March 15 to 17	Ahmedabad	For a rise in the wages of the mill-hands of Ahmedabad.
1919		
April 6	Bombay	First-day of the first Satyagraha in India. (Thereafter every year on this date).
April 13	Ahmedabad	Jallianwallah Bagh massacre at Amritsar. (Thereafter every year on this date).
April 13 to 15	Ahmedabad	Following disturbances at Bombay, Ahmedabad, and other places.

Date/Duration	Venue	Reason
1921		
November 19 to 21	Bombay	Following disturbances at Bombay in the wake of the visit of the Prince of Wales.
November 28	Ahmedabad	Following disturbances at Bombay. (Thereafter, every Monday all his life).
1922		
February 12 to 16	Bardoli	Massacre at Chauri Chaura.
1924		
September 17 to 30	Delhi	For Hindu–Muslim Unity.
October 1 to 7	Delhi	For Hindu–Muslim Unity.
1925		
November 24 to 30	Ahmedabad	After the detection of sexual aberrations in some boys and girls of the Ashram.
1928		
June 22 to 24	Ahmedabad	On account of a moral lapse by an Ashram inmate.
1932		
September 20 to 25	Yeravda Jail	In protest against the decision of the Prime Minister of Britain to set up separate electorates for the Harijans. (The decision was subsequently cancelled).
December 3	Yeravda Jail	In protest against Government not allowing a fellow-prisoner to do scavenging work.
1933		
May 8 to 28	Parnakuti, Poona	For self-purification.
August 16 to 22	Yeravda Jail	In protest against Government's decision not to grant all the facilities for Harijan work which he had availed previously.

Date/Duration	Venue	Reason
1934 August 7 to 13	Wardha	To atone for the injury caused to Pandit Lalnath in a confrontation between Sanatanists on the one side and the members of the public engaged in Harijan welfare on the other.
1939 March 3 to 6	Rajkot	In protest against a breach of promise by the Rajkot ruler.
1940 November 12 to 13	Sevagram	On account of a suspicion of theft by an Ashram inmate.
1941 April 25 to 27 (or May 5 to 7)	Sevagram	Presumably on account of communal riots in Bombay and Ahmedabad.
June 29	Sevagram	For communal unity.
1943 February 10 to March 2	Aga Khan Palace Prison	In protest against Government propaganda that the responsibility for disturbances after arrest of leaders (following the 'Quit India' resolution) lay with the Congress.
1944 November 30(?)	Sevagram	Fasted or thought of fasting.
1946 October 20 to October 23 or so	Delhi	Probably on account of an error by the person who prepared the fair copy of a letter written during negotiations with the Muslim League.
1947 August 15	Calcutta	To mark the bitter-sweet moment of freedom and Partition.

Date/Duration	Venue	Reason
September 1 to 3	Calcutta	To quell communal violence in the city.
October 11	Delhi	His birth date according to Vikrami Calendar. (Fasted instead of celebrating it).
1948		
January 13 to 17	Delhi	To quell communal violence.

(C.B. Dalal's compilation—Gandhi: 1915-1948—A Detailed Chronology*)*

BIBLIOGRAPHY

For Further Reading

Ambedkar, B.R., *Thoughts on Pakistan* (Bombay: Thacker, 1941).

Amrita Bazar Patrika, The, English newspaper of Calcutta which first appeared in 1868 as a Bengali Weekly; a daily since 1891, ceased furnishing in 1996.

Mahatma Gandhi's Ideas (London: Allen & Unwin, 1929).

_____ Andrews, C.F., *Mahatma Gandhi: His Own Story* (London: Allen & Unwin, 1931).

_____ *Mahatma Gandhi at Work* (London: Allen & Unwin, 1931).

_____ *Mahatma Gandhi His Life and Ideas* (New Delhi: Radha Publishers, 1996).

Aryanayakam, Asha Devi, *Gandhi the Teacher* (Bombay: Bharatiya Vidya Bhavan, 1966).

Ashe, Geoffrey, *Gandhi: A Study in Revolution* (Bombay: Asia, 1968).

Attenborough, Richard (ed.), *The Words of Gandhi* (USA: Newmarket Pub., 1982).

Avadhut, Swami Purushottam, *Mahatmajir Gathan-Karma Padhati* (Bangla–Calcutta: Gandhi Smarak Nidhi, 1372 Bangabda).

Bagal, Jogesh Chandra, *Nari Unnayan* (Bangla–Calcutta: Gandhi Satabarsiki Samiti, 1969).

Bagchi, Reeta, *Mahatma Gandhi and Dr B.R. Ambedkar on Islam and Indian Muslims* (Delhi: B.R. Publication, 1998).

Bandyopadhyay, Amritalal, *Satyagrahi Mahatma Gandhi* (Calcutta: Biswas Publishing House, 1376 Bangabda).

Bandyopadhyay, Anu, *Bahurupee Gandhi* (Calcutta: Rupa & Co., 1967).

Bandyopadhyay, Gitasree, *Constraints in Bengal Politics, 1921–41* (Calcutta: Sarat Book House, 1984).

Bandyopadhyay, Haridas, *Mahatma Gandhir Darshan* (Calcutta: Rabindra Library, 1968).

Bandyopadhyaya, Jayantanuja, *Social and Political Thought of Gandhi* (Ramrajatala, West Bengal: Manuscript India, 2000).

Bandyopadhyay, Jogesh Chandra, *Satyasraee Bapuji* (Bangla—Calcutta: Deb Sahitya Kutir, 1374 Bangabda).

Bandyopadhyay, Kanak, *Mahamanab Mahatma Gandhi: Gandhijir Jiban Vashya* (Bangla—Calcutta: Saraswati Book Depot, 1355 Bangabda).

Bandyopadhyay, Sailesh Kumar (ed.), *Gandhi Parikrama* (Bangla—Barrackpore: Supriyo Munsi, Secretary, Gandhi Sangrahalaya, 1999).

——— *Chhatrader Prati—Mohandas Karamchand Gandhi* (Bangla—Calcutta: Mitra Ghosh, 1958).

Banerjee, Debkumar, *Marx And His Legacy* (Calcutta: K.P. Bagchi, 1988).

Basu, Anath Nath, *Gandhiji* (Calcutta: Orient Book Co., 1942).

——— *Mohan Mala* (Bangla—Calcutta: Gandhi Smarak Nidhi, 1965).

Bose, Nirmal Kumar, *Studies in Gandhism* (Calcutta: Indian Associated Publishing Co. 1947).

——— *My Days with Gandhi* (Calcutta: Nishana, 1953).

——— *Gandhiji: The Man and his Mission* (Bombay: Bharatiya Vidya Bhavan, 1966).

——— *Gandhi in Indian Politics* (Bombay, New Delhi, Calcutta: Lalvani Publishing House, 1967).

——— *Lectures on Gandhism* (Ahmedabad: Navajivan, 1971).

Bhattacharya, Bhabani, *Mahatma Gandhi* (New Delhi: Arnold Heinemann, 1977).

Bhattacharya, Bijan Bihari, *Gandhijir Jiban Pravat*, (Bangla—Calcutta: Jigyansha, 1946).

Bhattacharya, Buddhadev, *Evolution of the Political Philosophy of Gandhi* (Calcutta: Calcutta Book House, 1969).

Bhattacharya, Sabyasachi (ed.), *The Mahatma and the Poet* (New Delhi: National Book Trust, 1997).

——— *Vande Mataram—The Biography of a Song* (New Delhi: Penguin, 2003).

Birla, G.D., *In the Shadow of the Mahatma: A Personal Memoir* (Bombay: Orient Longmans, 1953).

Biswas, C.C., *Bengal's Response to Gandhi* (Kolkata: Minerva, 2004).

Bose, Anima, *Dimensions of Peace and Non-Violence: The Gandhian Perspective* (New Delhi: Gian Publishers, 1987).

Bose, R.N., *Our Gandhian Heritage* (Calcutta: Tagore Research Institute, 1970).

Bose, Subhas, *The Indian Struggle: 1920–1942* (Reviewed Work; Bombay: Asia Publishing House, 1964).

Bose, Sisir K., and Sugata Bose, *Chalo Delhi: Writings and Speeches of*

Subhas Chandra Bose—1943–1945 (New Delhi: Permanent Black, 2007).

Brown, Judith M., *Gandhi: Prisoner of Hope* (Calcutta: Oxford University Press, 1990).

Campbell-Johnson, Alan, *Mission with Mountbatten* (London: Robert Hale, 1972).

Catlin, George, *In the Path of Mahatma Gandhi* (Macdonald & Co., 1948).

Chadha, Yogesh, *Gandhi: A Life* (New York: John Wiley & Sons, 1999).

Chandra, Bipan, *Communalism in Modern India* (New Delhi: Vikas, 1984).

Chakrabarti, Mohit, *Gandhian Aesthetics* (New Delhi: Atlantic Publishers, 1991).

_____ *Gandhian Mysticism* (New Delhi: Atlantic Publishers, 1991).

Chatterjee, Bimanesh, *Thousand Days with Rajaji* (New Delhi: Affiliated East-West Press Pvt Ltd, 1973).

Chatterjee, Dilip Kumar, *Gandhi and Constitution Making in India* (New Delhi, Associated Publishing House, 1943).

Chattopadhyay, Sachinandan, *Mahatma Gandhi* (Calcutta: Jingyasha, 1376 Bangabda).

Chaturvedi, Benarsidas and Marjorie Sykes, *Charles Freer Andrews* (London: George Allen & Unwin, 1949).

Choudhari, Manmohan, *Exploring Gandhi* (New Delhi: Gandhi Peace Foundation, 1989).

Chowdhury, Narayan, *Gandhiji* (Calcutta: Sovona Press Publication, 1970).

Chunder, Dr Pratap Chandra, *On Understanding Gandhiji* (Mumbai: Bharatiya Vidya Bhavan, 2003).

Dalal, Chandulal B. (ed.), *Gandhijini Dinavari (1915–1948)*, (Gujarati—Gandhinagar: Information Department, 1970).

_____ (comp.), *Gandhijini Dinavari (1869–1915)* (Gujarati—Ahmedabad: Sabarmati Ashram Trust, 1976).

Dalton, Dennis, article 'Gandhi During Partition: A Case Study in the Nature of Satyagraha' in *The Partition of India* by Philips & Wainwright, of the School of Oriental and African Studies (1970).

Dalton, Dennis (ed.), *Mahatma Gandhi: Selected Political Writings* (USA: Hackett Publishing, 1996)

Das, Amritananda, *Foundations of Gandhian Economics* (Calcutta: Allied Publishers, 1979).

Das, Krishna, *Seven Months with Mahatma Gandhi* (Ahmedabad: Navajivan, 1951).

Dasgupta, Sugata, *Philosophical Assumptions for Training in Non-Violence* (Ahmedabad: Gujarat Vidyapeeth, 1984).

Datta, Amlan, *Gandhi O Rabindranath* (Bangla—Calcutta: Ananda Publishers, 1393 Bangabda).

—— *The Gandhian Way* (Shillong: North-Eastern Hill University Pub., 1986).

—— *Assorted Essays* (Kolkata: Amiyo Puspo Prakashani, 2006).

Dear, John, *Mohandas Gandhi: Essential Writings* (Modern Spiritual Masters Series, Oxford India, 2002).

Debi, Maitryee (ed.), *Gandhi Darshan* (Bangla—Calcutta: Sampradaik Sampriti Parisad, 1970).

De, Amalendu, *Gandhi—Jinnah Correspondence and Communal Question* (Calcutta: 1999).

—— *Mahatma Gandhi and Islam* (Calcutta: Rabindra Bharati University, 2000).

Desai, Mahadev, *Gandhiji in Indian Villages* (Madras: S. Ganesan, 1927).

—— *The Diary of Mahadev Desai* (Ahmedabad: Navajivan Publishing House, 1953).

—— *Day-to-Day with Gandhi*, Vol. 1 to 8 (New Delhi: Sarva Seva Sangh Prakashan, Rajghat, 1972).

Desai, Narayan, *Bliss Was it to be Young-with Gandhi* (Bombay: Bhavan, 1988).

—— *Agnikundma Ugelun Gulab* (Gujarati—Ahmedabad: Navajivan, 1992).

—— *My Gandhi* (Ahmedabad: Navajivan, 1999).

Devanesen, Chandran, *The Making of the Mahatma* (New Delhi: Orient Longmans, 1969).

Dhar, Niranjan, *Aurobindo, Gandhi and Roy* (Calcutta: Minerva, 1986).

Dhupelia-Mesthrie, Uma, *Gandhi's Prisoner? The Life of Gandhi's Son Manilal* (New Delhi: Permanent Black, 2005).

Dutta, Amarendra Nath, *Netajir Path O Gandhijir Mat* (Bangla—Calcutta: Standard Book Co.)

Dutta, Manindra, *Gandhijir Agni Pariksha* (Bangla—Calcutta: Mitralaya).

Erikson, Erik H., *Gandhi's Truth* (New York: Norton, 1969).

Fischer, Louis, *A Week With Gandhi* (London: George Allen & Unwin, 1943).

—— *The Life of Mahatma Gandhi* (New York: Harper, 1950).

Fisher, Frederick B., *That Strange Little Brown Man—Gandhi* (New York: 1932).

Gandhi Centenary Volume; foreword by Indira Gandhi (Santiniketan: Visva-Barati, 1969).

Gandhi In Cartoons (Ahmedabad: Navajivan, 1970).

Gandhi, Arun, *Kasturba—A Life* (New Delhi: Penguin, 2000).

Gandhi, Kanu and Abha, *Bapu ke Sath* (Hindi—New Delhi: Publications Division, 1990).

Gandhi, M.K., *Satyagraha in South Africa* (translated by V.G. Desai; Ahmedabad: Navajivan, 1928).

____ *Collected Works of Mahatma Gandhi*, 100 vols. (New Delhi: Publications Division).

____ *My Experiments with Truth* (Ahmedabad: Navajivan, 1929).

Gandhi, Manu, *Bapu—My Mother* (Ahmedabad: Navajivan, 1949).

____ *Biharni Komi Aagmaan* (Gujarati—Ahmedabad: Navajivan, 1956).

____ *Ekla Chalo Re* (Hindi—Ahmedabad: Navajivan, 1957).

____ *The Miracle of Calcutta* (Ahmedabad: Navajivan, 1959).

____ *My Memorable Moments with Bapu* (Ahmedabad: Navajivan, 1960).

____ *Last Glimpses of Bapu* (Agra: Shiva Lal Agarwala, 1962).

____ *The Lonely Pilgrim* (Ahmedabad: Navajivan, 1964).

____ *Dillimaan Gandhiji*, 2 vols. (Ahmedabad: Navajivan, 1966).

____ *Bapu Ki Ye Baaten* (Hindi—Ahmedabad: Navajivan, 1969).

Gandhi, Rajmohan, *The Rajaji Story (1937–1972)* (Bombay: Bharatiya Vidya Bhavan, 1984).

____ *The Good Boatman* (New Delhi: Viking, 1995).

____ *Rajaji: A Life* (New Delhi: Penguin, 1997).

____ *Mohandas* (New Delhi: Penguin-Viking, 2006)

Gandhi, Tushar, *Let's Kill Gandhi!* (New Delhi: Rupa, 2007).

Gangopadhyay, Binoy Kumar, *Mrityunjai Gandhiji* (Bangla—Calcutta: Brindaban Dhar & Sons, 1354 Bangabda).

Ganguly, Debjani and John Docker, (eds) *Non-Violent Relationality: Rethinking Gandhi in the World* (Contributors—Leela Gandhi, Tridip Suhrud, Sandhya Shetty, Penny Edwards, Rhonda Williams, Sean Scalmer, Thomas Weber, Charles Di Salvo, Christine Mason, Michael Fox, Edward Curthoys, John Docker, Anjali Roy, Debjani Ganguly, and Ajay Skaria. Hyderabad: Orient Longman, *forthcoming*).

Ghosh, Mani, *Sramik Andolan O Gandhiji*, (Bangla—Calcutta: Gandhi Satabarshiki Samitee, 1971).

Ghosh, P. C., *Mahatma Gandhi* (Calcutta: Dasgupta & Co Pvt Ltd., 1963).

____ *Mahatma Gandhi: As I Saw Him* (Calcutta: S. Chand & Co., 1968).

Ghosh, Satyabrata, *Gandhibad* (Bangla—Calcutta: Narayan Distaff & Chemical Works, 1970).

Ghosh, Subodh, *Amrita Patha Jatri* (Bangla—Calcutta: Indian Associated Publishing, 1359 Bangabda).

Ghosh, Sudhir, *Gandhi's Emissary* (Calcutta: Rupa, 1967).

Gupta, Yogendra Nath, *Gandhijir Jibanyagna* (Bangla—Calcutta: Indian Publishing House, 1357 Bangabda).

Gopal, S., *Nehru*, 3 vols. (New Delhi: OUP, 1976, 1979, and 1984).

Gordon, Leonard A. *Brothers Against The Raj*, (New Delhi: Rupa 1990)

Goswami, K.P. (comp.), *Mahatma Gandhi: A Chronology* (New Delhi: Publications Division, Ministry of Information and Broadcasting, G.I., 1971).

Green, Martin, *Gandhi: Voice of a New Age Revolution* (New York: Continuum, 1993).

Gregg, Richard B. *Ahingsar Sakti* (Bangla—Calcutta: Messers Mandol & Sons, 1973).

Guha, Samar, *The Mahatma and the Netaji: Two Men of Destiny of India* (New Delhi: Sterling Publishers, 1986).

Guharaja, Sanjib Kanti, *Krantadarshi Mahatma* (Bangla—Calcutta: Abhoy Ashram, 1969).

Gupta, Ashoka, *Noakhalir Durjoger Diney* (Bangla—Kolkata: Dey's Publishing, 1999).

Gupta, Nagendranath, *Gandhi and Gandhism* (Bombay: Hind Kitabs, 1945).

Habib, Irfan, Bipan Chandra and others *Towards a Secular & Modern India: Gandhi Reconsidered* (New Delhi: Safdar Hashmi Memorial Trust, 2004).

Hardiman, David, *Gandhi in his time and ours* (Delhi: Permanent Black, 2003).

Harijan, English weekly edited by R. V. Shastri, published under the auspices of Harijan Sevak Sangh. First published from Poona on February 11, 1933, shifted to Madras on 27 October 1933; brought back to Poona on April 13, 1935; subsequently published from Ahmedabad.

Harijanbandhu, Gujarati weekly edited by Chandrashanker P. Shukla, first published on 12 March 1933 from Poona and then from Ahmedabad.

Hasan, Mushirul (ed.), *India's Partition* (New Delhi: OUP, 1993).

Hindu, The, English daily published from Madras; first appeared as a weekly in 1878, became a tri-weekly in 1883 and a daily since 1889.

Hunt, James D., *Gandhi in London* (New Delhi: Promilla & Co., Publishers, 1978).

Hutheesing, Krishna, *The Story of Gandhiji* (Bombay: Kutub Publishers, 1949).

Huttenback, Robert, *Gandhi in South Africa* (London: Cornell University, 1971).

Indian Opinion, Weekly founded by Gandhi in Durban and later shifted to Phoenix; had English and Gujarati and also initially Hindi and Tamil sections, (1903–61).

In Memory of Mahatma Gandhi (New Delhi: Gandhi Smarak Nidhi, 1976).

Iyer, Raghavan, *The Essential Writings of Mahatma Gandhi* (New Delhi: Oxford University Press, 1993).

Jack, Homer A. (ed.), *The Gandhi Reader: A Sourcebook of his Life and Writings* (Grove Publication, 1995).

—— (ed.), *The Wit and Wisdom of Gandhi* (Dover Publications, 2005).

Jha, D.C., *Mahatma Gandhi: The Congress and Partition of India* (New Delhi: India Research Press, 2004).

Juergensmeyer, Mark, *Gandhi's Way: A Handbook of Conflict Resolution* (USA: University of California Press, 2005).

Karim, Rejaul, *Sampradayik Samashya O Gandhiji* (Bangla—Kolkata: Prakasan Upasamiti, Paschimbanga Gandhi Satabarshiki Samiti, 1969).

Khaliquzzaman, Choudhary, *Pathway to Pakistan* (Lahore: Pakistan Longman, 1961).

Kripalani, J.B., *Gandhi: His Life and Thought* (New Delhi: Publications Division, 1970).

Kripalani, J.B., *My Times—An Autobiography* (New Delhi: Rupa, 2004).

Kripalani, Krishna, *Gandhi-Kathamrita* (Bangla—New Delhi: Sahitya Akademi, 1968).

Kulkarni, Sumitra, *Anmol Virasat*, 3 vols. (Hindi—Delhi: Prabhat Prakashan, 1988).

Kumar, Ravindra, *Champaran to Quit India Movement* (New Delhi: Mittal, 2002).

—— *Theory and Practice of Gandhian Non-Violence* (New Delhi: Mittal, 2002).

Kundu, Priya Ranjan (comp.), *Netaji vs Gandhiji* (Madhyamgram, West Bengal: the author 2000).

Lahiri, Prafulla Kumar, *In Search of Truth: a picture album depicting a few eventful landmarks from the life of Mahatma Gandhi* (picture and commentary by P.C. Lahiri, PICIEL, *Amrita Bazar Patrika*, Calcutta: A. Mukherjee & Co., 1947).

Lloyd, Rudolph, Susanne Hoeber, *Gandhi—The Traditional Roots of Charisma* (Chicago: University of Chicago, 1983).

Lohia, Rammanohar, *Guilty Men of India's Partition* (Allahabad: Kitabistan, 1960).

Mazumdar, Bharati, (comp.) *Gandhiji on Communal Harmony* (Mumbai: Mani Bhavan Gandhi Sangrahalaya, 2003).

Mitra, Gajendra Kumar, *Gandhi Jibani* (Bangla—Calcutta: Amar Sahitya Prakashan, 1376 Bangabda).

Mitra, Khagendra Nath, *Mahatma Gandhi—Jiban Katha* (Bangla—Calcutta: Barada Agency, 1338 Bangabda).

Mitra, Sudhir Kumar, *Amader Bapuji* (Bangla—Calcutta: Sree Guru Library, 1354 Bangabda).

Morton, Eleanor, *Women behind Mahatma Gandhi* (Calcutta: Jaico Publishing House, 1961).

Mukherjee, Hiren, *Gandhiji: A Study* (New Delhi: People's Pub. House, 1960).

Mukherjee, Rabindra Nath, *Gandhijir Arthanaitik Darshan* (Bangla— Calcutta: Gandhi Smarak Nidhi, 1372 Bangabda).

Mukherjee, Rudrangshu (ed.), *The Penguin Gandhi Reader* (USA: Penguin, 1995).

Mukherjee, Subrata, *Economic and Social Principles of Mahatma Gandhi* (New Delhi: Deep & Deep, 1998).

Munshi, Supriya, *Mahatma Gandhi In Murals and Text*, edited by Shyamalkanti Chakravarti; painting by Dhirendranath Brahma. Foreword by Dr Phularenu Guha (Barrackpore: Gandhi Memorial Museum, 2005).

Murray, Gertrude, *Gandhiji: The Story of his Life* (Calcutta: Orient Longmans, 1965).

Nanda, B.R., *Mahatma Gandhi (A Biography)* (London: Unwin Books, 1959).

⸻ *In Search of Gandhi—Essays and Reflections* (New Delhi: Oxford University Press, 2002).

Nandurkar, G.M. (ed.), *Sardar Patel Centenary Volumes*, 5 vols. (Ahmedabad: Sardar Patel Smarak Bhavan, 1974-8).

Navajivan, (Gujarati) (1919-31): Gujarati weekly (with occasional biweekly issues) edited by Gandhiji and published from Ahmedabad; first issued on September from Navajivan and Satya Gujarati Monthly (1915-19). Also issued in Hindi from August 19, 1921.

Nair, P. Thankappan, *Indian National Songs and Symbols* (Calcutta: Firma KLM Pvt Ltd, 1987).

Nayar, Sushila, *Mahatma Gandhi*, vols. 4 & 5 (Ahmedabad: Navajivan, 1989, 1994).

Pal, Jaladhar, *The Moral Philosophy of Gandhi* (New Delhi: Gyan Publishers, 1998).

Parikh, Nilam, *Gandiji's Lost Jewel: Harilal Gandhi* (New Delhi: National Gandhi Museum, 2001).

Payne, Robert, *The Life and Death of Mahatma Gandhi* (New York: Smithmark: 1969).

Polak, Millie Graham, *Mr Gandhi: The Man* (Bombay: Republished by Vora & Co., 1950).

Pramanik, Prahalad Kumar, *Mahatma Gandhi* (Calcutta: Orient Book Co., 1969).

Prasad, Rajendra, *Mahatma Gandhi and Bihar: Some Reminiscences* (Bombay: Hind Kitabs Ltd., 1949).

____ *Autobiography* (Bombay: Asia, 1957).

____ *At The Feet of Mahatma Gandhi* (Bombay: Asia Pub., 1961).

Prabhu, R.K. (ed.), *Truth Called Them Differently (Tagore-Gandhi Controversy)* (Ahmedabad: Navajivan Publishing House, 1961).

Prayer, Mario, *The Gandhians of Bengal. Nationalism, Social Reconstruction and Cultural Orientations 1920–1942* (Rome: *Dipartimento Di Studi Orientali, Università Studi di Roma 'La Sapienza'*, 2001).

Pyarelal, *The Epic Fast* (Ahmedabad: Navajivan, 1932).

____ *Mahatma Gandhi: The Last Phase*, 2 vols. (Ahmedabad: Navajivan 1956).

____ *Mahatma Gandhi: The Early Phase* (Ahmedabad: Navajivan, 1965).

____ *Mahatma Gandhi: Volume 2* (Bombay: Sevak, 1980).

____ *Mahatma Gandhi: Volume 3* (Ahmedabad: Navajivan, 1986).

Radhakrishnan, S., *Mahatma Gandhi 100 Years* (New Delhi: Gandhi Peace Foundation, 1968).

____ (ed.), *Mahatma Gandhi: Essays and Reflections on his Life and Work* (Republished in Mumbai: Jaico Pub. House, 2005).

Ramchandran, G., *Gandhi Upakhyan* (Bangla–Bombay: Hind Kitab, 1948).

Rao, U.S. Mohan, *Mahatma Gandhir Bani* (Bangla–New Delhi: Publications Division of the Government of India, 1971).

Rao, U.R., *Mahatma Gandhi the Man and His Mission* (Bombay: Asia Publishers, 1971).

Ray, Annada Shankar, *Gandhi,* (Bangla–Calcutta: M. C. Sarkar & Sons, 1376 Bangabda).

____ *Yes, I Saw Gandhi* (Bombay: Gandhi Peace Foundation and Bharatiya Vidya Bhavan, 1976).

Ray, Reba, *Gandhi To The Women* (Calcutta: Gandhi Sata Barshiki Samitee, 1971).

Ray, Sibnarayan (ed.) *Gandhi, Gandhism and Our Times: An International Symposium* (Kolkata: Renaissance Pub., 2003).

Ray, Sukumar, *Noakhalite Mahatma* (Bangla–Calcutta: Orient Book Co., 1969).

Reddy, E.S., and Gopalkrishna Gandhi (eds), *Gandhi and South Africa* (Ahmedabad: Navajivan, 1993).

Roy, Asit Kumar, *Mahatma Gandhi's Struggle: Against Imperialism, Capitalism and Communism* (Calcutta: World Press, 1994).

Roy, Benoy G., *Gandhian Ethics* (Ahmedabad: Navajivan Publishing House, 1958).

Roy Chaudhury, P.C., *Gandhi The Man* (Mysore: Geetha Book House, 1974).

Roy, Kshitis, *Gandhi and the eclipse of the Raj* (*India's final struggle to loosen the shackles of bondage from the British Imperial Rule*). (Barrackpore: Gandhi Smarak Sangrahalaya, 1994).

Roy, Kshitis and Mazumdar, Mohit Kumar, (comp.) *A Gandhi-Tagore chronicle* (Santiniketan: Rabindra-Bhavana, Visva-Bharati, 2001).

Roy, Samaren, *M. N. Roy and Mahatma Gandhi* (Calcutta: Minerva, 1987).

Saaedullah, Sayya, *Leninbadir Chokhe Gandhibad* (Bangla–Calcutta: Nabajatak Prakashan, 1971).

Sabanta, S. D., *Mahatma Gandhir Kahini* (Bangla–New Delhi: Publications Division, Government of India, 1966).

Saha, Panchanan, *Tagore and Gandhi: Confluence of Minds* (Kolkata: Barasat Barta, 2001).

Saha Ray, Rabidas, *Amader Bapuji* (Bangla–Calcutta: Deb Sahitya Kutir, 1375 Bangabda).

Sanyal, Hiteshranjan and Ghosh, Arun, (eds.), *Mohandas Karamchand Gandhi–Granthapunji*, (New Delhi: *Bharatiya Samajik Vijnan Anusandhan Parishad*, © ICSSR 1986).

Sen, Anath Gopal, *World Situation And Gandhian Economics* (Calcutta: The Book House, 1947).

Sen, Ela, *Gandhi (A Biographical Study)* (Calcutta: Susil Gupta, 1945).

Sen, Parvati Charan, *Kusta Seva* (Bangla–Kolkata: Prakasan Upasamiti, Paschimbanga Gandhi Satabarshiki Samiti, 1968).

Sen, Priyaranjan, *Gandhism* (Calcutta: A. Mukherjee & Co., 1957).

Sengupta, B., Chowdhury, R., (eds) *Mahatma Gandhi and India's Struggle for Swaraj* (Calcutta: Modern Book 1932).

Sengupta, Pramod Bandhu, *Gandhiji* (Calcutta: Banerjee Publishers, 1969).

Sheean, Vincent, *Lead, Kindly Light* (Bombay: Jaico Publishing House, 1949).

—— *Mahatma Gandhi (A Great Life in Brief)* (Publications Division, Government of India, 1968).

Shukla, Chandra Shanker (ed.), *Incidents of Gandhiji's Life* (Bombay: Vora & Co, 1949).

—— *Reminiscences of Gandhiji* (Bombay: Vora & Co, 1951).

Sinha, Brojo Kishore, *The Pilgrim of Noakhali* (Calcutta: the photographer 1948).

Som, Reba, *Gandhi, Bose, Nehru and the Making of the Modern Indian Mind* (New Delhi: Penguin, 2004).

Suhrud, Tridip, *Harilal Gandhi: A Life* (by Chandulal Bhagubhai Dalal; translated by Tridip Suhrud; Foreword by Ramchandra Gandhi) (Hyderabad: Gandhi Studies Series, Orient Longman, 2007)

Tagore, Rabindranath, *Mahatma Gandhi* (Visva-Bharati, 1963).

Tendulkar, D.G.; M. Chalapathi Rau; Mridula Sarabhai; Vithalbhai K. Jhaveri, (eds) *Gandhiji—His Life And Work* (Bombay: Keshav Bhikaji Dhawale, 1944)

Tendulkar, D.G., *Mahatma—Life of Mohandas Karamchand Gandhi*, 8 vols. (The Publications Division, Government of India, 1960).

Thomson, Mark, *Gandhi and His Ashrams* (Bombay: Popular Prakashan, 1993).

The Task of Peace-Making (Calcutta: Visva-Bharati, 1949).

Watson, Francis and Hallam Tennyson, *Talking of Gandhiji* (London: British Broadcasting Corporation, 1969).

Young India, Bombay from May to October 1919; Ahmedabad from October 1919 to 1931.

Zinkin, Taya, *The Story of Gandhi* (London: Methuen & Co., 1965).

Index of Persons

GENERAL INDEX

notes from which I prepared the summary, I made you say almost exactly the opposite of what you actually did say ... I can only say that I am sincerely sorry that I misreported you.'

42. 'Lokamanya' Bal Gangadhar Tilak (1856–1920), outstanding patriot, taught in a college at Poona and edited journals in English and Marathi (Kesari and Mahratta); Leader of the 'extremists' in the Congress, sentenced to long terms of imprisonment notably in Mandalay, writing works with the authority of scholarship on religion, philosophy, and history.

43. 7 September 1918.

44. Vallabhbhai Patel (1875–1950) organizer of the no-rent campaign in Bardoli (1920); President of the Indian National Congress in 1931, member of the Interim Government 1946–7; Deputy Prime Minister of India and Minister of Home Affairs, States, Information and Broadcasting.

45. Written after the death of Harilal's wife, Chanchal in October 1918.

46. Shankerlal Ghelabhai Banker (1889–1985) came in close contact with Gandhi during the Ahmedabad textile mill workers' strike; publisher of Young India; secretary, All-India Spinners' Association; was convicted with Gandhi in 1922; Secretary of the Home Rule League.

47. Manu (1917–94), later to be married to Kishorelal Mashruwala (1890–1952) younger daughter of Harilal. Not to be confused with Manu Jaisukhlal Gandhi (1927–69).

48 & 49. Harilal's sons, Rasik (1912–29) and Kanti (1911–83).

50. Rami (1908–55), elder daughter of Harilal.

51. The Rowlatt Bills were a body of enactments passed in March 1919, extending indefinitely measures enacted during the First World War to 'control public unrest and root out conspiracy'. Under this, the government could imprison without trial any person suspected of 'revolutionary activities'. The Rowlatt Act came into effect in March 1919. Mahatma Gandhi was among many Indian leaders, who opposed the Act saying it raised issues of self-respect. He gave a call for satyagraha on 6 April 1919, when business would remain suspended and people would fast as a sign of their protest. Rioting in the Punjab and other provinces overshadowed the hartal. Gandhi suspended the hartal. In the Punjab, where the protest movement was particularly strong, two outstanding leaders of the Congress Dr Satya Pal and Dr Saifuddin Kitchlew, were arrested on 10th April. A protest meeting was held in Amritsar four days later, culminating in the Amritsar Massacre of 1919.

52. Chakravarti Rajagopalachari (1878–1972) lawyer and early associate of Gandhi, Premier of Madras (1937–9), Minister in the Interim Government of India (1946–7), Governor of West Bengal (1947–8), Governor General of India (1948–50), Minister for Home (1950–1), Chief

Minister of Madras (1952–4); founder of the Swatantra Party opposing Nehru's socialist programmes; author of scholarly interpretations of the Ramayana and Mahabharata. His daughter Lakshmi (1912–83) married Gandhi's youngest son Devadas Gandhi (1900–57), in 1933.

53. 22 March 1919.

54. Gandhi addressed this as a letter to the secretaries of the Satyagraha Sabha, Bombay, and released it to the Press.

55. Madhavdas Kapadia, businessman brother of Kasturba.

56. Muhammad Ali Jinnah. This letter was written to Jinnah when he and his Parsi wife, Rattanbai were in London.

57. The Minto-Morley Reforms.

58. Kalinath Roy (1878–1945), Editor of *The Tribune* was tried for seditious writing by a Special Tribunal, denied legal help of his choice and sentenced two years' rigorous imprisonment.

59. Thomas Babington Macaulay (1800–59), British historian, essayist, poet, politician, Secretary of State.

60. The letter was evidently written on the Sunday preceding the Congress session.

61. Pandit Madan Mohan Malaviya (1861–1946); President of the Congress in 1909, 1918, and 1936, attended the second Round Table Conference in London, 1931; founded the Benares Hindu University.

62. A well-known solicitor from England invited to help in the collection of evidence by the Congress sub-Committee.

63. Command or order (Urdu).

64. The post-World War I Treaty of Sevres curtailed the temporal powers of the Caliph (Khalifa) who was Sultan of Turkey. This meant that he would cease to be Caliph of the Islamic world, a step that was received with indignation amongst Muslims everywhere and triggered the Khilafat Movement which Gandhi twinned with the mass non-violent non-cooperation movement, inaugurated in September 1920.

65. Saraladevi Choudhurani (1872–1945) was the daughter of Swarnakumari (Rabindranath Tagore's sister) and Janakinath Ghosal, a leading Bengal Congressman. Nationalist poet, singer, educationist, and orator, Saraladevi was a disciple of Vivekananda before meeting Gandhi in 1919. She was to play an important if brief role in Gandhi's circle in the early 1920. In the English translation of the original in Gujarati, her name is mis-spelt as 'Sarla'. For a fuller description of the equation between Saraladevi and Gandhi, see Rajmohan Gandhi's *Mohandas* (Penguin/Viking, 2006).

66. 'Bharati' was started by Saraladevi's under Jyotindranath Tagore in 1877.

67. This was in reply to the following letter dated Poona, 18 January 1920, from Lokamanya Tilak: I am sorry to see that in your article on 'Reforms